NEW TESTAMENT COMMENTARY

NEW TESTAMENT COMMENTARY

By

WILLIAM HENDRIKSEN

Exposition
of
The Pastoral Epistles

22255

BAKER BOOK HOUSE
GRAND RAPIDS 6, MICHIGAN
1957

COPYRIGHT 1957, BY WILLIAM HENDRIKSEN

Library of Congress Catalog Card Number: 54-924

All rights in this book are reserved. No part may be reproduced in any manner without permission in writing from the copyright holder, except brief quotations used in connection with reviews in a magazine or a newspaper.

PRINTED IN THE UNITED STATES OF AMERICA
BY AMERICAN BOOK-STRATFORD PRESS, NEW YORK

TABLE OF CONTENTS

	PAGE
LIST OF ABBREVIATIONS	vii

INTRODUCTION TO THE PASTORAL EPISTLES
Why Should We Study Them? 3
Who Wrote the Pastorals? 4
To Whom Were They Addressed? 33
What Is Their Historical Background and Purpose? . . . 39

COMMENTARY ON I TIMOTHY
Chapter 1 49
Chapter 2 91
Chapter 3 117
Chapter 4 145
Chapter 5 165
Chapter 6 191

COMMENTARY ON II TIMOTHY
Chapter 1 223
Chapter 2 245
Chapter 3 281
Chapter 4 307

COMMENTARY ON TITUS
Chapter 1 339
Chapter 2 361
Chapter 3 385

LIST OF ABBREVIATIONS

The letters in book-abbreviations are followed by periods. Those in periodical-abbreviations omit the periods and are written in italics. Thus one can see at a glance whether the abbreviation refers to a book or to a periodical.

A. Book Abbreviations

A.R.V.	American Standard Revised Version
A.V.	Authorized Version (King James)
Gram.N.T.	A. T. Robertson, *Grammar of the Greek New Testament in the Light of Historical Research*
I.S.B.E.	*International Standard Bible Encyclopedia*
L.N.T.	Thayer's *Greek-English Lexicon of the New Testament*
M.M.	*The Vocabulary of the Greek New Testament Illustrated from the Papyri and Other Non-Literary Sources,* by James Hope Moulton and George Milligan (edition, Grand Rapids, 1952)
N.N.	*Novum Testamentum Graece,* edited by D. Eberhard Nestle and D. Erwin Nestle (most recent edition)
N.T.C.	W. Hendriksen, *New Testament Commentary*
R.S.V.	Revised Standard Version
W.D.B.	*Westminster Dictionary of the Bible*
W.H.A.B.	*Westminster Historical Atlas to the Bible*

B. Periodical Abbreviations

EQ	*Evangelical Quarterly*
JBL	*Journal of Biblical Literature*
JThS	*Journal of Theological Studies*
GThT	*Gereformeerd Theologisch Tijdschrift*
WThJ	*Westminster Theological Journal*
ZNTW	*Zeitschrift für die Neutestamentliche Wissenschaft*

Please Note

In order to differentiate between the second person singular and the second person plural (without reverting to the archaic "thou" and "ye" except where it is proper to do so), we have indicated the former as follows: "you"; and the latter, as follows: "y o u."

Introduction to The Pastoral Epistles

I. Why Should We Study Them?

A thorough study of the Pastoral Epistles is necessary for the following reasons:

(1) Because they shed much needed light on the important problem of *church-administration*. Do these letters contain any directions regarding Public Worship which we do well to heed? What qualities must a man possess in order to be a good pastor? A worthy elder? A conscientious deacon? To what extent should women be employed in the work of the church? Upon whom does the primary responsibility rest of providing for the needy? How should a minister deal with aged men who are in need of pastoral counseling? With aged women? With young men? With young women?

(2) Because they stress *sound doctrine*. Is it true that it makes no difference *what* a person believes as long as he is *sincere* in what he believes? Is the Bible "the Word of God" as it lies there, or does it merely *become* the Word of God when it "touches" you? How must one deal with heretics? Is it possible to pay too much attention to their errors?

(3) Because they demand *consecrated living*. Is it possible for a person to be "doctrinally *sound*" but "corrupt in practice"? Must evil men be disciplined? How soon? With what purpose in mind?

(4) Because they answer the question, *"Are creeds of any value?"* Did the church in the transition-period believe in creedal formulations, pithy sayings, and other means of transmitting the truth of the gospel to enquirers and to the youth? Were there any hymns? Is the slogan, "No Creed But Christ" in harmony with the teaching of The Pastorals?

(5) Because they tell us about *the closing activities in the life of the great apostle Paul*. Does the book of Acts give a full account of all his journeys? Were there really two Roman imprisonments?

(6) Because they are *a valuable source for the understanding of the history of the church in the third quarter of the first century A. D.* (See M. C. Tenney, *The New Testament, A Survey*, p. 354).

(7) Because *in these epistles* as well as in the others *God speaks to us.*

II. Who Wrote the Pastorals?

The term "pastoral epistles," as a common title for I Timothy, II Timothy, and Titus, dates from the early part of the eighteenth century.[1] Now these letters do indeed furnish worth-while directions for pastors. Yet, the title is not exact. Timothy and Titus were not "pastors" in the usual, present-day sense of the term. They were not ministers of local congregations, but rather vicars apostolic, Paul's special envoys or deputies sent by him on specific missions. They were entrusted with concrete assignments according to the need of the hour. Their task was to perform their spiritual ministry here or there, carrying forward the work which had been started, and then reporting to the apostle their findings and accomplishments.

Marcion, in the middle of the second century, rejected these three letters. Tertullian states, "I am surprised, however, that when he (Marcion) accepted this letter (Philemon) which was written but to one man, he rejected the two epistles to Timothy and the one to Titus, which all treat of ecclesiastical discipline" (*Against Marcion* V. xxi). Now in a man like Marcion, who preached the strictest asceticism, denied the lawfulness of marriage, and issued rigid rules for fasting, such a rejection of the Pastorals, in which asceticism is condemned (I Tim. 4:3, 4; Tit. 1:14, 15), is altogether natural. A heretic does not like a writing which directly or indirectly condemns his or a somewhat similar heresy.

In the nineteenth century (1807 to be exact) F. Schleiermacher rejected the Pauline authorship of I Timothy. F. C. Baur in his work on the Pastoral Epistles (Stuttgart and Tübingen, 1835) defended the position that it is inconsistent to accept II Timothy and Titus but to reject I Timothy. All three must be considered in the class of pseudepigraphic literature. Many enthusiastic disciples — the Tübingen School — endorsed his view. Today this position is accepted by many, though some have adopted a somewhat more conservative view (see p. 17).

Can it be truthfully maintained that in this negative attitude the critics are as thoroughly objective as they claim to be? Is it just possible that the manner in which these three little gems deal with "some of the fondest shibboleths of the modern mind"[2] has something to do with the decisive way in which their Pauline authorship is denied? The Pastorals place particular emphasis on such matters as *the reality and importance of ecclesiastical offices* (I Tim. 3; Tit. 1), *the inspiration of the written word* (II Tim. 3:16), *the necessity of maintaining doctrinal soundness* (I Tim. 4:1-6;

---

[1] P. Anton called his work, *"Exegetische Abhandlung der Pastoralbriefe."* He first suggested the term in 1726.
[2] Cf. Edmund K. Simpson, "The Authenticity and Authorship of the Pastoral Epistles," *EQ* 12 (1940), 311.

INTRODUCTION

II Tim. 3:14; 4:3; Tit. 2:1), *the reality of the resurrection* (II Tim. 2:18), *and the divine requirement that faith shall make itself militantly manifest* (II Tim. 4:2, 7, 8).

Now, whether or not subjective bias has asserted itself, one conclusion becomes inescapably clear when the facts are examined: the critics have failed to prove their thesis that Paul cannot have written the Pastorals.

The arguments of the critics may be summarized as follows: [3]

---

[3] Anyone who reads the following literature — a selection from among hundreds of books and articles on this subject — will have both the arguments of the critics and the answers of those who cling to the traditional view with reference to the authorship of the Pastorals. We acknowledge indebtedness to all of the following:

Bouma, C., *I, II Timotheus en Titus* (in *Korte Verklaring der Heilige Schrift met Nieuwe Vertaling*), second edition, Kampen 1953, especially pp. 13-35.

Bouma, C., *De Brieven van den Apostel Paulus aan Timotheus en Titus* (in *Kommentaar op het Nieuwe Testament*), Amsterdam, 1942, especially pp. 17-60.

Brooks, A. E., "The Problem of the Pastoral Epistles," *JThS* 23 (1922).

Dibelius, M., *Die Pastoralbriefe*, second edition, Tübingen, 1931.

Easton, Burton Scott, *The Pastoral Epistles*, New York, 1947, especially pp. 29-35.

Goodspeed, E. J., *Paul*, Philadelphia, 1947, p. 238.

Greydanus, S., *Bizondere Canoniek*, Kampen, 1949, Vol. II, pp. 205-226.

Harrison, P. N., *The Problem of the Pastoral Epistles*, Oxford, 1921.

Hawkins, R. M., *The Recovery of the Historical Paul*, Nashville, Tenn., 1943, p. 13.

Holtzmann, H. J., *Die Pastorale Briefe*, Leipzig, 1880.

Knox, John, *Chapters in a Life of Paul*, New York and Nashville, 1946, p. 20.

Lock, W., *A Critical and Exegetical Commentary on the Pastoral Epistles* (in *International Critical Commentary*), New York, 1924, pp. xxv-xxxi.

Michaelis, W., "Pastoralbriefe und Wortstatistik," *ZNTW* 28 (1929), 69-76.

Michaelis, W., *Pastoralbriefe und Gefangenschaftbriefe. Zur Echtheitsfrage der Pastoralbriefe*, 1930.

Moffatt, J., *Introduction to the Literature of the New Testament*, New York, 3rd ed., 1918.

Nageli, Th., *Der Wortschatz des Apostels Paulus*, Göttingen, 1905, pp. 85-88.

Parry, John, *The Pastoral Epistles*, 1920.

Pherigo, Lindsey P., "Paul's Life After the Close of Acts," *JBL* 70 (December, 1951), 277-284.

Plummer, Alfred, *The Pastoral Epistles* (in *The Expositor's Bible*), reprint Grand Rapids, Mich., 1943, vol. 6, pp. 389-392.

Riddle, W. and Hutson, H. H., *New Testament Life and Literature*, Chicago, 1946, pp. 203-208.

Robertson, A. T., *Word Pictures in the New Testament*, New York and London, 1931, Vol. IV, pp. 555-558.

Schleiermacher, F., *Ueber den Sogenannten Brief von Paulus an den Timotheus*, 1807.

Schweitzer, A., *The Mysticism of Paul the Apostle*, New York, 1931, p. 42.

Scott, E. F., *The Literature of the New Testament*, 6th ed., New York, 1940, pp. 191-197.

Scott, E. F., *The Pastoral Epistles* (in *The Moffatt Commentary*), New York and London, no date.

Simpson, E. K., "The Authenticity and Authorship of the Pastoral Epistles," *EQ* 12 (October, 1940), 289-311.

Simpson, E. K., *The Pastoral Epistles*, London, 1954, pp. 1-23.

Torm, F., "Ueber die Sprache in den Pastoralbriefen," *ZNTW* 18 (1918), 225-243.

(1) *In vocabulary the three epistles are very similar to each other, but entirely different from the other ten epistles which are traditionally assigned to Paul, namely, Romans, I Corinthians, II Corinthians, Galatians, Ephesians, Philippians, Colossians, I Thessalonians, II Thessalonians, and Philemon.*[4]

The following points are emphasized under this general heading, some critics stressing one point, others another:

a. The great similarity in the vocabulary of the three Pastorals.

b. The contrast between the vocabulary of the Pastorals and that of the ten.

At times it would almost seem that a single glance at Harrison's well-known diagrams (in his book, *The Problem of the Pastoral Epistles,* Oxford, 1921) was enough to convince some that Paul could not have written I Timothy, II Timothy, and Titus. Is not the number of new words, *per page* (!) of Greek text, introduced by the author of these three letters, completely out of proportion to the much smaller number of new words per page used by Paul in his ten epistles? If the apostle wrote the latter, is it at all possible that he also wrote the former?

Besides, do not such expressions as the following clearly point away from Paul: "guard the deposit" (τὴν παραθήκην φύλαξον I Tim. 6:20; II Tim. 1:12, 14); "follow doctrine" (a form of παρακολουθέω with τῇ διδασκαλίᾳ, I Tim. 4:6; II Tim. 3:10); "profane chatter" (βέβηλοι κενοφωνίας, I Tim. 6:20; II Tim. 2:16); "man of God" (ἄνθρωπος θεοῦ, I Tim. 6:11; II Tim. 3:17)?

And, on the other hand, is it not true that many words that are used again and again in the ten are absent from the three: "to do wrong" (ἀδικέω), "blood" (αἷμα), "uncircumcision" (ἀκροβυστία), "works of the law" (ἔργα νόμου), etc.? Burton Scott Easton points out that the real Paul uses "Spirit" about 80 times; the author of the Pastorals only 3 times!

c. The presence of entirely new or greatly expanded word-families in the Pastorals.

Is it not true that the Pastorals present, either for the first time or with unparalleled ramification, not only many single words but even whole families of words? To give just one example: the family of compounds which center about the common idea of teaching or *didactics*:

Van Oosterzee, J. J., *The Pastoral Epistles* (in *Lange's Commentary on the Holy Scriptures*), reprint, Grand Rapids, Mich., no date, pp. 2-6.

White, N. J. D., *The First and Second Epistles to Timothy and the Epistle to Titus* (in *The Expositor's Greek Testament*), reprint, Grand Rapids, Mich., no date, Vol. 4, pp. 57-82.

Zahn, Th., *Einleitung in das Neue Testament*, 1897-1900, Vol. II, p. 85 ff.

[4] See, for example, E. F. Scott, *Literature of the New Testament,* New York, 1932, p. 193. Also the same author, *The Pastoral Epistles* (in The Moffatt Commentary), p. xxi.

INTRODUCTION

Occurring nowhere in the ten are the following:

διδακτικός	*apt at teaching,* I Tim. 3:2; II Tim. 2:24
νομοδιδάσκαλος	*a teacher of the law,* I Tim. 1:7
καλοδιδάσκαλος	*a teacher of that which is good,* Tit. 2:3
ἑτεροδιδασκαλεῖν	*to teach differently, to teach a different doctrine,* I Tim. 1:3; 6:3

Occurring also in two or three of the ten are:

διδάσκαλος	*a teacher,* I Tim. 2:7; II Tim. 1:11; 4:3
διδασκαλία	*teaching,* in the Pastorals occurring with great frequency, in both the active and the passive sense (*doctrine*)
διδαχή	*teaching,* II Tim. 4:2; *doctrine,* Titus 1:9

Occurring also in six of the ten are:

διδάσκω	*to teach,* I Tim. 2:12; 4:11; 6:2; II Tim. 2:2; Tit. 1:11.

d. The absence of Pauline word-families.

This is the obverse of the preceding.

e. The fact that several words found in I Timothy, II Timothy, and Titus, but not in the ten, occur in the vocabulary of the Apostolic Fathers, and the complementary fact that a large percentage of genuinely Pauline words which do not occur in the three have also dropped out of the vocabulary of the Apostolic Fathers. It is argued that for the Pastorals this points to a date early in the second century.

In this connection it is also usually pointed out that during the second century there was a revival of classical diction. It is maintained that this explains the presence of a considerable number of classical words in these letters.

f. The frequent use of Latin words and idioms.

It is said that this indicates that the author of the Pastorals cannot have been Paul but must have been someone living in or near Rome. Or, if this conclusion is not stated in so many words, the argument from Latinisms occurring in the Pastorals is at least enlisted in the cause of skepticism.

g. The totally different meaning which in the Pastorals is carried by words that are common to them and to the ten.

Examples: *faith,* in the Pastorals used objectively = what is believed, the true religion; but by Paul in the sense of subjective trust.

to take up, used in I Tim. 3:16 of Christ's ascension, but in Eph. 6:13, 16 of "taking up" spiritual weapons.

letter, used in an unfavorable sense by Paul, but *letters* used in favorable sense in II Tim. 3:15 = *the sacred writings.*

h. Finally, the fact that not only "the stones" differ from those used by Paul but also "the clamps and the mortar" (particles of transition and inference, which abound in the ten but are largely lacking in the Pastorals).

It is not difficult to show that the value of this argument and of its ramifications has been greatly over-estimated.

As to a., to a certain extent the very opposite is the truth. Of new words (*new* in the sense that they do not occur in the ten) only a very few are found in *all* three letters; only 9 out of a total of 306! Hence, *if dissimilarity in new vocabulary proves different authorship, something can be said for the proposition that a different author would have to be posited for each of the Pastorals!* Of new words I Timothy has 127, II Timothy has 81 others, and Titus has 45 others. *Together* I Timothy and II Timothy have only 17; I Timothy and Titus have only 20; II Timothy and Titus have only 7; all three together only 9. (Yet both vocabulary and style, taken as a whole, point rather to *unity* of authorship.)

As to b., fact is that slightly over one-fourth of the total vocabulary of Paul's epistle to the Romans is "new" in the sense that these words do not occur in the other nine epistles. The percentage of new words, in proportion to total vocabulary, in II Timothy (words not occurring in the ten) is hardly any higher than in Romans. The same holds for Titus. In I Timothy about one-third of the words are new. Surely, on the basis of these facts the thesis of the critics, namely, that Paul cannot have written the Pastorals, does not follow! [5]

In each epistle Paul uses the (Spirit-inspired) words which he needs in order to express his (Spirit-inspired) thoughts regarding the specific subject with which he deals. For this reason it is not surprising that certain words, found in the ten, are lacking in the three. As an example, let us take the first three words mentioned in Harrison's list on p. 31, taking them just as they come. The first is ἀδικέω: to do wrong, to commit unrighteousness. The second is αἷμα: blood. The third is ἀκροβυστία: uncircumcision. Now this entire subject of *righteousness,* obtained for the sinner by the *blood* of Christ and not by means of rites such as *circumcision,* belongs to such

---

[5] Proportion of new words to total vocabulary is given by Michaelis and Greydanus as follows:

Romans:	261:993	= 26.3%
II Timothy:	114:413	= 27.6%
Titus:	81:293	= 27.6%
I Timothy:	173:529	= 32.7%

See Michaelis, the article cited, p. 73; Greydanus, *op. cit.,* p. 210.

This harmonizes with the figures given by Harrison, *op. cit.,* p. 140. Bouma, *Kommentaar op het Nieuwe Testament,* p. 54, stresses the fact that of the 582 words that occur in the ten but not in the Pastorals, no less than 469 are found *in only one* letter; and that, accordingly, *these 469 are lacking in the other nine as well as in the Pastorals!*

INTRODUCTION

epistles as Romans, Galatians, and to some extent I Corinthians. Hence, it is in these epistles that we must look for such or similar words. But surely the apostle did not need to expound in detail to Timothy and Titus, his intimate friends and fellow-workers, the doctrine of justification by faith! Hence, it is altogether natural that these three words do not occur here, though the doctrine itself is not completely absent; see Titus 3:5-7. The same holds for the other words given by Harrison on pp. 31 and 32 of his book. The absence of not a single one of them from the Pastoral epistles is strange, though in one case it is more immediately apparent why a word should not be found than in another. Moreover, if the Pauline authorship of the Pastorals must be rejected because the word "Spirit" occurs only 3 times, must we not also reject the Pauline authorship of Colossians, II Thessalonians, and Philemon?

As to c. and d., this is a sword that cuts both ways, for one might also say that the very presence of entire word-families *here in the Pastorals just as in the ten,* points in the direction of identical authorship. That the basic word around which the word-family has developed is not the same in the different epistles is easily explained: in the letters to Timothy and to Titus, who were definitely in need of good counsel with respect to their own specific task of *imparting instruction,* the word-family which centers about the idea of *teaching* is certainly not at all surprising.

Besides, it can be shown that if the presence or absence of certain words and word-families is decisive in determining authorship, it will not be easy for the critics to defend the Pauline authorship of *all* the ten, for in Harrison's list of 41 words which occur in *five Pauline* epistles but not in the Pastorals (*op. cit.* p. 31), only *one* word out of the first 22 occurs in II Thessalonians! Some, of course, would be perfectly willing to drop II Thessalonians also!

As to e., our knowledge of actual vocabulary in use during the second half of the first century A. D., in comparison with the first half of the second century A. D., is far too scanty to be able to serve as a trustworthy criterion. How often has it not happened that words which were formerly considered "late" suddenly turned up in newly discovered writings of a much earlier date? The idea that the use of "classical" words indicates a second century A. D. author looks like begging the question. Why should it be accounted unreasonable to assume that Paul himself wrote the Pastorals, and that he derived his knowledge of "classical" vocabulary from his own reading or listening? Had he not been a student in his youth? Did Gamaliel's curriculum provide nothing in the line of ancient and contemporary literature? Is it not true that the Paul whom we have learned to know from the ten recognized epistles must have had a rather extensive knowledge (direct or indirect) of Greek authors, so that he was able to quote Menander (I Cor. 15:33) and Aratus (Acts 17:28)? Is it absurd to posit the possibility that during his lengthy first imprisonment (and according to some perhaps even during his second imprisonment, cf. II Tim. 4:13) the apostle added to this knowledge by now and then making excursions into extra-canonical literature? We know, at any rate, that some of the words not found elsewhere in the New Testament but used both by the author of the Pastorals and by writers of the second century A. D. were also used by the apostle's contemporaries. Who will dare to maintain that many other words may not also have been in common use as early as the first century A. D. or even earlier? [6]

The similarity in vocabulary which appears when the Pastorals are compared with *Christian* writings of the second century A. D. does not necessarily mean that whoever wrote I Timothy, II Timothy, and Titus flourished in the days of the Apostolic Fathers and Apologists. It could also mean that these second century Christian authors had read, studied, and to a certain extent copied or paraphrased Paul!

As to f., the frequent use of words and idioms derived from the Latin, this argument hangs by a slender thread! The critics are able to point to a total of no more than *two* Latin words in the three Pastorals, namely, μεμβράνα (Latin *membrana*), *parchment*, II Tim. 4:13; and (same passage) φελόνης (Latin *paenula*), which has been variously interpreted as *cloak, book-cover, brief-case*. But Latin words also occur in those epistles which even by the critics are ascribed to Paul: θριαμβεύω, to lead in triumph (cf. Latin *triumphus*), II Cor. 2:14; Col. 2:15; μάκελλον, meat-market (Latin *macellum*), I Cor. 10:25; and πραιτώριον, Praetorian Guard (Latin *praetorium*), Phil. 1:13. Besides, in his Gospel and Acts, Luke, who had been Paul's companion, and who, according to II Tim. 4:11, was again with him during the apostle's second imprisonment, uses almost half of a total of about thirty different Latin words that occur in the New Testament. If Paul's frequent companion can use Latin words, why cannot Paul do the same?

It is true that echoes of the Latin have also been heard in such expressions as:

δεσπότης	(*dominus*), I Tim. 6:1, 2; 2:21; Tit. 2:9, master, lord
δίλογος	(*bilinguis* in one of its meanings), I Tim. 3:8, double-tongued
ἑδραίωμα	(*firmamentum*), I Tim. 3:15, support, bulwark, foundation
εὐσέβεια	(*pietas*), I Tim. 2:2; 4:7, 8, piety, reverence, devotion, godly living, godliness, religion

---

[6] See W. Lock, *op. cit.* p. xxix, and especially E. K. Simpson, the *Pastoral Epistles*, pp. 16-18; 103, 104.

INTRODUCTION

ματαιολογία	*(vaniloquium)*, I Tim. 1:6, futile talk
οἱ ἡμέτεροι	*(nostri)*, Tit. 3:14, "our folk," our people
πρόσκλισις	*(inclinatio)*, I Tim. 5:21, inclination, partiality
πρόκριμα	*(praeiudicium)*, I Tim. 5:21, pre-judging, prejudice
σεμνότης	*(gravitas)*, I Tim. 2:2; 3:4; Tit. 2:7, dignity, respectability, gravity, seriousness
χάριν ἔχειν	*(gratiam habere)*, I Tim. 1:12, to acknowledge gratitude

But in connection with this, observe the following:

1. Words and phrases which remind one of parallels that are very common in Latin are also found in other New Testament writings.[7]

2. Even during the first century A. D. Greek and Latin had reached the stage of mutual loaning and back-and-forth translation.

3. What may look like a copied idiom may be simply the result of parallel development in cognate languages.

Besides, even though one should admit a considerable measure of influence from the Latin upon the Greek of the Pastorals, would this in any way prove that *Paul* could not have written them? Is it not entirely natural that a man who had at last reached the world's metropolis, where very recently he had spent not less than two years, a man, moreover, who was highly susceptible to environmental influences and eagerly desirous of becoming all things to all men, would now begin to make even fuller use of "Roman" diction and phraseology than he had done heretofore? On this point the argument of the critics would seem to break down completely!

With respect to g., these illustrations readily vanish upon closer examination. Thus, it is claimed that Paul uses the term *faith* in the subjective sense (reliance on God and on his promises), but that the author of the Pastorals uses it in the objective sense (creed, body of truth). But, to begin with the Pastorals, the expression "faith and love that are in Christ Jesus" (I Tim. 1:14) indicates the exercise of these virtues. "To continue in faith and love and holiness" (see I Tim. 2:15) also illustrates the subjective use. And when the author teaches that one obtains "salvation through faith in Christ Jesus," everyone immediately understands that he is speaking about the attitude and exercise of trust in the Redeemer (hence, again subjective sense). See also I Tim. 3:13; 6:11, 12 and II Tim. 1:13; 3:10; 4:7. — And as to the ten epistles, their author does not always use the term in the subjective sense. Thus, in Gal. 1:23 he speaks about "preaching the faith." In Gal. 6:10 he uses the expression, "those who are of the household of the faith." And Phil. 1:27: "striving for the faith of the gospel," furnishes another excellent example of the objective use. Moreover, it is

---

[7] See Gram. N.T., p. 109.

not at all surprising that in the Pastorals Paul, being a man who is about to depart from this life, should be concerned about the preservation of "the truth," and should, accordingly, frequently employ the term "faith" in this objective sense (I Tim. 1:19; 3:9; 4:1; 5:8; 6:10; II Tim. 3:8; Titus 1:13).

As to the other examples that are supposed to prove that when the author of the three uses a Pauline word it frequently attains an altogether different meaning, thus proving that the apostle cannot have written the three, it is not at all clear why one and the same author would not be able to use the verb "to take up" both with respect to the "taking up" of spiritual weapons and the "being taken up" of Jesus into heaven. Similarly, the fact that the expression "the letter," singular, is used in one sense, but the term "letters," plural, in a different sense, is not so strange. Many languages contain idioms of this character: for example, to take in fresh *air*, singular, is very necessary, but to give oneself *airs*, plural, is not advisable. And is it not true that in those epistles which even by the critics are assigned to Paul the terms "flesh" and "law" are used in more than one sense, just as the author of the Fourth Gospel uses the term "world" in several senses?

Finally, anent h., in *expository or argumentative discourses* — think especially of Romans, I and II Corinthians, Galatians — we can naturally expect a much wider use of *particles of transition and inference* than in a *manual of warnings* and *directives* for "pastors." In the latter we look for and find the imperative mood.

In brief, here is *Paul,* "the aged" (thus self-styled already in Philemon 9), writing a letter. Does a man of advancing years use the vocabulary of a younger person? In spite of vigorous denials, is it not possible that age and the experience of imprisonment, whether in the recent past or at the very moment of writing, might have something to do with vocabulary and/or grammar?

The author of the Pastorals is writing to *intimate fellow-workers,* his own *deputies.* Today when a minister of a large congregation gives advice to his "assistant" with whom he is on good terms, does he employ the Sunday pulpit-oratory style?

In writing to his assistants the author advises them how the church should be organized, what kind of elders should be appointed, what should be done about heretics, etc. Do *subjects* of this nature require the vocabulary which one would use in expounding to the congregation the doctrine of "justification by faith" (Romans) or of "the unity of all believers in Christ" (Ephesians)? N. J. D. White, *op. cit.,* pp. 63, 65, 66, accounts for some of the new words that occur in the Pastorals by showing that their presence is quite natural in letters which condemn heresies. He places such terms under the heading "Polemical phraseology in reference to false teaching." An example is "profane chatter."

INTRODUCTION

In conclusion, we would like to ask the critics, At the beginning of his writing-career was the apostle handed a list of words with the requirement that, no matter what the circumstances might be, either of himself or of the readers, and no matter what might be the purpose of any epistle or the subject on which he would write, he must invariably use *these* words, and *only* these words, and, in addition, must distribute them in equal proportion over all his letters, like the spots on a polka-dot dress? In actual, physical compass the literary heritage which Paul has left us is not at all imposing: a mere 138 small pages of print in N.N. (for the *ten* epistles). Do we have any right to assume that what is written on these 138 pages (reduced to 67 larger pages in the English Bible that lies on my desk) comprises Paul's *total* vocabulary and syntax, so that any deviation (either in words or in grammar) which one encounters in the Pastorals proves that the latter must be ascribed to another author? Has any person the right to apply to Paul's writings a criterion which would do away with much of Milton, Shelley, and Carlyle, if it were applied to *their* writings?

The argument based on vocabulary and grammar leads nowhere. Even the staunchest defender of the authenticity of the Pastorals will readily grant that there is a remarkable difference in vocabulary, when these three are compared to the ten, just as there is considerable variation when each of the three is compared with either or both of the others. It is entirely possible that the explanations which have been given — such as, Paul's age and imprisonment (past or present), the character of the readers, the subjects covered, the purpose — do not fully account for these differences. Other factors may also have been operative, for example, the rapid advance and development of the church as a new entity, growing, changing, vigorous, and of necessity developing a new phraseology. Such expressions as "guard the deposit," "follow doctrine," and "man of God" are by White considered to belong to this category. Here, we may assume, Paul is using phraseology which he hears round about him. It has also been suggested that Paul's "secretary" or "secretaries" may have influenced the final product to some extent. On this point see footnote 193.

The point to note, however, is this: *the burden of proof rests entirely on the negative critic!* It is not the conservative believer who claims that vocabulary and grammar *prove* Paul to have been the author, but *it is the critic who now loudly proclaims that vocabulary and grammar indicate that Paul could not have been the author. The literary critics of the early centuries, who were well aware of grammar and style peculiarities, and therefore called in question the Pauline authorship of Hebrews, never had any such difficulty with the Pastorals!* The modern critic has failed completely to prove with respect to even a single word of the total Pastoral vocabulary, that Paul could not have written it! I have worked this out in detail in connection with the vocabulary of the second chapter of Titus. See footnote 193.

(2) *The style of the Pastorals betrays their forged origin.*

Some, in speaking about "style," use this term in a sense which approaches "vocabulary," "diction." This has already been discussed. Others, however, give a broader connotation to the term, and under this heading discuss *what* the author of the Pastorals says and especially *how* he says it, *the general character* of his thoughts and particularly *the manner* in which he expresses them. We shall here take the term in this broader sense.

On *one* matter the critics are agreed, namely, on the proposition that the style of the Pastorals points away from Paul. But as soon as the question is raised, "Why is this true?" the answers divide and become contradictory, some asserting that the style itself is altogether un-Pauline, others that it reminds one at so many points of Paul that a forger, a conscious imitator, must have been at work. He must have had a copy of Paul's genuine epistles in front of him. From these he copied phrase upon phrase, acting as if he were Paul!

From this confusion in the camp of the critics there is only one safe retreat, namely, a candid examination of the actual facts. *These point to Paul as the author.* Observe the following:

We find in these short letters the same kind of a person as is revealed in the ten. It is the character of *Paul* which is here reflected, just as, for example, in I Thessalonians and II Thessalonians. See N.T.C. on I and II Thessalonians, p. 22. The author of the Pastorals is deeply interested in those whom he addresses, namely, in Timothy and Titus, displaying warm affection for them (I Tim. 1:2; 5:23; 6:11, 12; II Tim. 1:2, 5, 6, 7; 2:1, 2, 15, 16; 4:1, 2, 15; Tit. 1:4). He shares their experiences and is fond of commending whatever is good in them (II Tim. 1:8; 3:10-15; 4:5-8; Tit. 1:4). He ascribes to the sovereign grace of God whatever good there is in himself or in those addressed (I Tim. 1:12-17; 4:14; II Tim. 1:6, 7, 13, 14; 2:1). He shows wonderful tact in counseling (I Tim. 1:18; 4:6, 11-16; 5:1; 6:11-16; II Tim. 1:2-7; Tit. 1:4; 2:7). He takes up, one by one, matters of special concern to Timothy and Titus (evident to anyone who reads these three short letters from beginning to end). He is anxious to see them (II Tim. 1:4; 4:9, 11; Tit. 3:12).

He is, moreover, fond of the figure of speech called *litotes,* that is, affirmation by negation of the opposite. This may be viewed as a kind of *understatement* or *miosis.* Thus, instead of saying that he is "proud" of preaching Christ, he states that he is *"not* ashamed" of the One whom he has believed (II Tim. 1:12; cf. 1:8, 16). Similarly he affirms that the Word of God is "not chained" (II Tim. 2:9) and that God is the One who does *"not* lie" (Tit. 1:2). This reminds strongly of Paul, the man who declared that he was a citizen "of *no* mean city" (Acts 21:39); that he had *"not* been

INTRODUCTION

disobedient" to the heavenly vision (Acts 26:19); that he was *"not* ashamed of the gospel" (Rom. 1:16); that his entering in among the Thessalonians was *"not* emptyhanded" (I Thess. 2:1); that his appeal did *"not* spring from delusion" (I Thess. 2:3); that he does *not* want the readers to be in ignorance (I Thess. 4:13); and that they "must *not* become weary in welldoing" (II Thess. 3:13).

He is fond of enumerations. Thus, he groups virtues or vices, listing them in series (I Tim. 3:1-12; 6:4, 5; II Tim. 3:2-5; 3:10, 11; Tit. 3:3). This is exactly what Paul does in the other epistles (see Rom. 1:29-32; II Cor. 12:20; Gal. 5:19-23).

He is not averse to introducing here and there a "play upon words." Thus he admonishes the *rich* to fix their hope on him who gives *richly* (I Tim. 6:17). He contrasts "lovers of pleasure" with "lovers of God" (II Tim. 3:4). He informs us that one of the purposes of the inspired writings is "that the man of God may be *complete* (or *equipped*), furnished *completely* (or *thoroughly equipped*) for every good work" (II Tim. 3:17, a passage where the R.S.V., by its translation, misses the evidently intentional play upon words). And he admonishes Timothy that in preaching the Word he must "be on hand in season, out of season."

Here again one thinks inevitably of Paul and his fondness for the same stylistic characteristic. It is Paul who, cognizant of the fact that the name *Jew* (cf. Judah) indicates "let him (that is, *God*) be praised," writes, "But he is a *Jew* . . . whose *praise* is not of men but of God" (Rom. 2:29). It is also Paul who makes use of the fact that the name of a fugitive slave, namely, Onesimus, means *useful, beneficial, profitable:* "I appeal to you in the interest of my child . . . Onesimus, who once was *unprofitable* (or *useless*) to you, but now is profitable (or *useful*) to you and to me."

Again, Paul likes "compendious compounds" (E. K. Simpson). He often chooses terms that are composed of several words (often one or more prepositions plus a verb). Thus, it is he who says that the Holy Spirit *helps* us in our weakness. Now this word *help* originally meant *"he lays hold of* (λαμβάνεται) *along with* (σύν) a person, either *facing* that person or else *taking his turn,* so that he carries the burden *instead of* (ἀντί) that person. The entire verb is συναντιλαμβάνεται.[8]

Here also the Pastorals resemble the ten, witness such compounds as καταστρηνιάσωσιν (they grow wanton, I Tim. 5:11), διαπαρατριβαί (mutual altercations or incessant friction, I Tim. 6:5), εὐμετάδοτοι (ready to share with others, generous, I Tim. 6:18), θεόπνευστος (God-breathed, II Tim. 3:16), and αὐτοκατάκριτος (self-condemned, Tit. 3:11).

Paul's love for phrases "in apposition" — see, for example, Rom. 12:1, "to

---

[8] I have discussed this verb in my doctoral dissertation, "The Meaning of the Preposition ἀντί in the New Testament," pp. 83, 84.

present yourselves as a living sacrifice ... (which is) y o u r service according to reason (or *reasonable worship*)" — is well-known and can be illustrated by several passages from the ten epistles. Similar instances of apposition occur throughout the Pastorals. See, for example, I Tim. 1:17; 3:15, 16; 4:10, 14; 6:14, 15; II Tim. 1:2; 2:1; Tit. 1:1, 10; 2:14.

The sudden breaking in of doxologies, which feature one has met in studying the ten (see Rom. 9:5; 11:36; 16:27; Eph. 1:3 ff.; 3:20) appears once more in the Pastorals (I Tim. 1:17; 6:15, 16; II Tim. 4:18; and cf. other instances of elevated style — "near-doxologies" — in I Tim. 3:16; Tit. 2:13, 14).

The expression of personal unworthiness (Eph. 3:8; I Cor. 15:9) recurs in I Tim. 1:13; the "if not ... then how" phraseology (I Cor. 14:6, 7, 9) is found also in I Tim. 3:5; moreover, who but the Paul whom we have learned to know from the ten could have penned that intensely personal and exuberant line, "I have fought the noble fight, I have finished the course, I have kept the faith," etc. (II Tim. 4:7, 8)?

A glance at those phrases in the Pastorals which Harrison has underscored (to indicate that they are also found in the ten) adds to the accumulation of evidence *in favor* of Pauline authorship, though it was not Harrison's intention to bolster that conclusion.

The argument according to which Paul cannot have written the Pastorals because the style of *certain passages* in the ten is not characteristic of I Timothy, II Timothy, and Titus proves either *nothing* or *too much*. Is there *any* author of note who *always*, under *all* circumstances, at *every* period of his life, and *no matter to whom or on what subject* he writes, employs *the same unvaried* style?

We admit, of course, that there is a striking contrast between the lengthy and involved sentence-structure of such passages as Eph. 1:3-14; Phil. 2:5-8, on the one hand, and many short and pithy admonitions of the Pastorals, on the other. But is this comparison fair? Lengthy sentences are not entirely wanting in the Pastorals (see I Tim. 1:5-7; 1:8-11; 1:18-20; 2:5-7; etc.). Brief statements abound in the ten.

Neither is it fair to contrast the exuberant tone of certain paragraphs in the ten with the much calmer and more matter-of-fact manner of expression which characterizes much of the material of the Pastorals. One should not compare I Tim. 2:8-15 with the vigorous climax of Romans 8 but with the somewhat similar paragraph: I Cor. 11:1-16. Neither should one place Tit. 3:9-14 next to I Cor. 13 but next to I Thess. 5:12-22. If variation in style proves different authorship, then the author of I Cor. 13 cannot have written the letter to Philemon, and the author of Romans 8 cannot even have written Romans 13!

Moreover, is it not entirely natural that the man who was well along

INTRODUCTION

in years when he wrote the Pastorals should *now*, as the race was drawing to a close, employ a more reserved style? Are we surprised that rather often in the Pastorals we notice that the rugged fervor and fiery vigor of earlier years has disappeared?

When the Pastorals are compared with those sections in the ten which form the basis for legitimate comparison, it becomes evident — as has been indicated by numerous examples — that their style is characteristically Pauline. In fact, so signally Pauline is the style of these three short letters that several critics are willing to make a concession. They grant that here and there one encounters genuinely Pauline material; for example, the personal notes found in II Tim. 4:6-22. In that paragraph Timothy is urged to come before winter and to take along the prisoner's "cloak" and books, especially the parchments. Demas is represented as a renegade, Luke as true-blue. There is a brief sketch of the "first defence." And personal greetings are extended to several individuals. — A somewhat similar passage is Tit. 3:12.

Now though some critics (especially some of the earlier ones) have been bold enough to consider also these personal notes to be the work of a clever falsifier, who tried to lend color and verisimilitude to his crafty literary product, and who invented unreal — but seemingly real — situations in order to attain this end, meanwhile breathing the air of profoundest regard for the truth, this solution has not found general acceptance.

It is objectionable from many an angle. It is hardly probable that a forger would have used so many personal names. Moreover, he would have been hard-pressed to make his personal notes sound so real and life-like. He surely would not have spoken in such an uncomplimentary tone about Demas (II Tim. 4:10), who by Paul elsewhere is never pictured as a deserter, a man who had fallen in love with the world (contrast Col. 4:14; Philemon 24).

But is the alternative which other negative critics propose any better? That alternative would make of the author of the Pastorals a second century dove-tailer who took certain genuine Pauline passages, fitted them into his own composition, and thus created the impression that Paul was the author of the whole.

But this theory does not explain how it is that the transitions from genuine to forged material are so unobtrusive. As has been remarked, one would expect the seams to show! And besides, is it not strange that of the earlier correspondence between the great apostle and his associates only a few genuine personal notes have remained? In brief, the theory is vulnerable from several aspects, and today is rejected by many of the negative critics themselves. Albert Schweitzer who, as one could have expected, denies the Pauline authorship of the Pastorals, remarks that the repeated attempts to discover in them "short notes written by Paul" is "in vain." [9]

Now, the true alternative to the "scissors and paste" or "jigsaw-puzzle" theory of the critics is not total denial of Pauline authorship but, in conformity with the data which have been presented, acceptance of Pauline authorship for the *entire* contents. The argument from style, when all the facts are examined, points in only *one* direction, namely, to Paul as the author of the Pastorals.

3. *The theology is not that of Paul. The cross is no longer in the center. There is undue stress on good works.*

One stands amazed that this argument is still being repeated. Any reader of the English Bible who carefully studies the Pastorals from beginning to end, and who is acquainted with Paul's doctrine as unfolded in the other ten epistles can easily answer the critics on this point.

It is true, of course, that here in the Pastorals there is no *detailed exposition* of the doctrine of salvation through faith in Jesus Christ apart from the works of the law. Nevertheless, that doctrine is clearly stated in more than one passage, and is assumed throughout.

The truth is that the doctrine which is taught and presupposed in the Pastorals is clearly the same as that which is held before us in the ten:

The redeemed have been chosen from eternity. They are called *the elect* (II Tim. 2:10; cf. Eph. 1:4; I Thess. 1:4).

Their salvation is due to the grace of God in Christ, and not to human works (I Tim. 1:14; II Tim. 1:9; Tit. 3:5; cf. Gal. 2:16; Rom. 3:21-24).

Christ is God (Tit. 2:13; cf. Rom. 9:5; Phil. 2:6; Col. 2:9).

He is the Mediator between God and man, himself man, our Lord Jesus Christ (I Tim. 2:5; cf. Rom. 9:5; I Cor. 8:4, 6).

His purpose in coming into the world and assuming the human nature was to save sinners, of whom Paul considers himself chief (I Tim. 1:15; cf. II Cor. 8:9; I Cor. 15:9; Eph. 3:8).

Men are saved through faith in this divine and human Mediator Jesus Christ (II Tim. 1:12; cf. Rom. 1:17; Eph. 2:8).

This faith implies mystic union with Christ: dying with him, living with him; enduring with him, reigning with him (II Tim. 2:11, 12; cf. Rom. 6:8; 8:17).

Good works are necessary (I Tim. 2:10; 6:11, 18; II Tim. 2:22; 3:17), and are to be viewed as the fruit of God's grace (hence, also the fruit of faith) operating in the believer (Tit. 2:11-14; 3:4-8; cf. Gal. 5:22-24; Eph. 2:10).

The glory of God is the chief purpose of man (I Tim. 6:16; II Tim. 4:18; cf. Rom. 11:36; 16:27).

---

[9] A. Schweitzer, *The Mysticism of Paul the Apostle* (translated into English by William Montgomery), New York, 1931, p. 42.

INTRODUCTION

Where, in all this, is there contrast in doctrine, a contrast supposedly so marked and definite that the author of the ten cannot have been the author of the three? When, even in recent literature, such a thoroughly unwarranted position is still being defended, and *no evidence of any kind is furnished,* one is led to ask, "Is the higher criticism scholarly?"

Most appropriately God, in his providence, has seen to it that in Paul's *final* three epistles *the fruit* (good works) of faith is emphasized, the *nature* of faith and its *necessity* over against law-works having been fully set forth in the letters which preceded. The tree is first; then comes the fruit.

4. *The Pastorals controvert second century gnosticism, especially Marcionism. Now Marcion was expelled from the Roman church in the year 144 A. D. Hence, the Pastorals must have been written about this time, that is, not earlier than the second quarter of the second century. This shows that Paul cannot have been the author.*

To lend support to the view that whoever wrote the Pastorals is here combating the views of second century gnostics the following points are usually emphasized:

(a) The "genealogies" (I Tim. 1:4; Tit. 3:9) are the second century gnostic "aeons" which emanate from the bosom of God.

(b) The "fables" or "myths" (Tit. 1:14) represent second century gnostic speculations.

(c) The ascetic practices against which the author issues a warning when he condemns the views of those who forbid marriage and who enjoin abstinence from foods (I Tim. 4:3) point to Marcion who practiced the strictest asceticism, revolting from marriage, meat, and wine.

(d) The denial of a physical resurrection (II Tim. 2:18) was a feature of second century gnostic dualism.

(e) The affirmation that *all* Scripture is inspired and useful (II Tim. 3:16), and that there is only *one* God (I Tim. 2:5) cannot fail to remind one of Marcion, who rejected all the books of the Old Testament and drew a sharp *antithesis* between the merely *just* Jehovah of the Old Testament and the *gracious* God of the (i.e., of *Marcion's* mutilated edition of the) New Testament.

(f) The "very title of Marcion's book" ("Antitheses") in I Tim. 6:20, clinches the argument! Surely one who mentions the title of the work of an author who flourished in the *second* century cannot have been Paul, who died in the *first* century!

It is, indeed, very strange that by some this six-point argument, which has been so often and so ably refuted, is still being repeated, either as a whole or in part, as if it contained at least a considerable element of value. The answer is clear and simple:

With respect to (a): The "genealogies," in the light of the entire context, are clearly *Jewish* in character. One is immediately reminded of those which are found in the book of Genesis (cf. also Chronicles). Embellishing speculations with reference to Old Testament names and stories abound in the *Book of Jubilees*. The Jews were past masters in the art of *eisegesis* (introducing one's own thoughts and sentiments into a passage; opposed to *exegesis:* bringing out the author's own meaning). Now Marcion himself fails to discuss *aeons*. One must not confuse his teaching with that of Valentinus. But *nowhere* in gnostic literature is the term "genealogy" used as a synonym for "aeon."

With respect to (b): The "fables" or "myths" are definitely called *Jewish* (Tit. 1:14). Hence, it simply is not fair to equate them with the vagaries of second century gnosticism.

With respect to (c): The critics seem to forget that the apostle Paul warned against similar ascetic tendencies in Col. 2:16-23. Must we conclude, then, that Colossians also belongs to the second century?

Besides, we may readily grant that I Tim. 4:3 warns against ascetic gnosticism, such as that of Marcion. But that does not prove that the author was Marcion's contemporary. There is nothing here that disproves the fact that a first century author, namely, Paul, was able, under the guidance of the Holy Spirit, to predict a second century development of an error which, in its incipient form, was present already in his own day.

With respect to (d): Denial of a physical resurrection is "as old as the hills." It manifested itself in different forms. Sometimes the idea that the body will rise again was frankly and directly rejected. At other times the rejection was by implication, just as in our own day: a spiritual meaning was assigned to the term *resurrection*. This was done, for example, by the heretics described in II Tim. 2:18. In any event, in view of Paul's lengthy argument in I Cor. 15 against those who said, "There is no resurrection of the dead," it is evident that the statement, "The resurrection is past already" (II Tim. 2:18) does not prove what the critics are trying to prove. It does not prove that Paul cannot have written the Pastorals!

With respect to (e): The passages to which reference is made should be read in the light of their own specific contexts. Then it becomes clear that when the author is speaking of *one* God, he is not contrasting a New Testament God with an Old Testament "demiurge." Neither is he placing the Old Testament in antithetical relationship to the New when he uses the expression "all Scripture." He is contrasting the wrong with the right use of Scripture. If proper use is made of Scripture so that one abides in its clear teaching, the conclusion will prove inescapable that *"all* Scripture is inspired of God and profitable."

Finally, with respect to (f): If this has any value, it would amount to the syllogism:

INTRODUCTION

Major Premise: The author of the Pastorals makes use of the term "antitheses."

Minor Premise: Marcion, a second century heretic, also makes use of the term "antitheses," using it as the title of a book which he wrote.

Conclusion: Therefore, the author of the Pastorals must have been acquainted with Marcion's book.

Similarly, one might say:

Major Premise: The author of the book of Genesis writes about Paradise, the river, the tree of life, the serpent.

Minor Premise: The apostle John, a late first century A. D. author, employs these same terms in his book of Revelation.

Conclusion: Hence, the author of the book of Genesis must have read the book of Revelation!

Now anyone who reads I Tim. 6:20 with an unbiased mind and in the light of the entire epistle will easily reach the conclusion that in speaking of "antitheses" what the author has in mind is not Marcion's contrast between Christianity and Judaism but *the conflicting opinions* of those who speculated in Jewish genealogies! Surely, *a merely verbal coincidence* between a word used by one author and a title used by another cannot do duty as a convincing argument with respect to authorship.

In addition to what has been said in answer to the argument of the critics, note the following:

It is being increasingly recognized today that gnosticism did not arise full-blown in the second century but had its origin much farther back in history. Besides, it is not an organically unified system but a speculative religious syncretism or accretion, to which not only Platonic philosophy but also Oriental mysticism, Cabbalistic Judaism, and Christianity contributed. Hence, though it is certainly true that the heresy condemned in the Pastorals *had certain traits in common with* second century gnosticism, this by no means identifies the two.

The error against which the Pastorals warn is both *present* (I Tim. 1:3-7, 19; 4:7; 6:4, 5, 9, 10, 17; II Tim. 2:16-18; Tit. 1:10-16; 3:9) and *future* (I Tim. 4:1-3; II Tim. 3:1-9) — taken together it spans the entire new dispensation until Christ's return — ; both chiefly *doctrinal* (I Tim. 4) and chiefly *moral* (II Tim. 3); both *within* and *without* the gate.

One fact, however, is very evident, namely, that *in the main,* the error which is here condemned has reference to *the Old Testament law and its interpretation* (see I Tim. 1:7; cf. 6:4, 5; II Tim. 4:4; Tit. 1:14; 3:9). Here lies the emphasis. And it was exactly this law with which second century gnosticism would have nothing to do! Hence, there is nothing here which compels one to hunt for a second century author. On the contrary, everything points to the first century and to Paul's day and age.

For the reasons indicated it is not surprising that even among the critics the more careful authors no longer mention "the argument based upon the heresy that is here condemned." It seems that they would like to forget that it was ever seriously used against the Pauline authorship of the Pastorals.

(5) *The Pastorals reveal a marked advance in ecclesiastical organization, far beyond the time of Paul. In his day there was as yet no official ministry. When the Pastorals were written, on the other hand, there was a rather complex organization, with salaried officials whose qualifications had become standardized.*

One critic calls this "the chief argument" proving that Paul cannot have written the Pastorals. Some try to "strengthen" it by affirming that *the beginning* of pyramidal organization is evident from the fact that while the Pastorals recognize only *one* "bishop" (I Tim. 3:1, 2; Tit. 1:7), they speak of *many* "presbyters" or "elders" (Tit. 1:5) who are evidently serving under him.

Other critics, however, scrupulously avoid making reference to the argument in any form. Apparently also in this case they would like to forget that anyone ever brought it up. And, indeed, among the many poor arguments that have been presented in defence of the thesis that Paul cannot have written the Pastorals this is one of the poorest. The *facts* are as follows:

(a) The entire conception according to which ecclesiastical *office* (divine commission with implied authority over life and doctrine) was a late development is erroneous. It simply is incorrect to say that at first there was nothing else than spontaneous leadership based only on spiritual endowment, and that at a later time this made way for elective office. See N.T.C. on the Gospel of John, Vol. II, pp. 461, 462. It is true, of course, that the extraordinary offices were gradually replaced by the ordinary. The Pastorals are Paul's *last* writings. It is not surprising, therefore, that the "ordinary" office of "overseer" or "elder" comes into prominence here.

(b) The notion that in Paul's day there was as yet no official ministry is in conflict with the facts mentioned by Scripture. Jerusalem had its *deacons* (men who "served tables") long before Paul went on his missionary journeys (Acts 6:1-6). From very early times the church also had its *elders* (Acts 11:30), an office which in a way was a natural outgrowth of the institution of elders in ancient Israel. Already on his first missionary journey Paul "appointed for them elders in every church" (Acts. 14:23). It has been indicated that in one of the earliest letters written by Paul there is definite mention of "those who labor among y o u and are over y o u in the Lord and admonish y o u" (see N.T.C. on I Thess. 5:12, 13). On the return from his third missionary journey Paul "calls to him the elders of the church" (of Ephesus or of Ephesus and surroundings). He characterizes them as "overseers" over God's flock, even the church "which the Lord pur-

INTRODUCTION

chased with his own blood" (Acts 20:17, 28). In a prison-epistle both "overseers and deacons" are mentioned (Phil. 1:1).

Now on the basis of all this it surely should cause no surprise that in the epistles which the apostle wrote just before his death the office of "overseers" or "elders" is recognized as well-known. It is also very natural that Paul, about to depart from this earthly realm, should specify certain qualifications and regulations for office, so that the church might be guarded against the ravages of error, both doctrinal and moral.

(c) In the Pastorals the term "elder" (or "presbyter") and "overseer" (or "bishop") are clearly synonymous, as is proved by Tit. 1:5-7 (cf. I Tim. 3:1-7; Phil. 1:1; I Peter 5:1, 2). See on that passage.

(d) The episcopate, a system of ecclesiastical government in which the bishop rules over the presbyters, seems to have arisen during the obscure transition period: the end of the first and the beginning of the second century. It emerges step by step and becomes evident first of all in the epistles of Ignatius of Antioch (who was sent to his martyrdom about the year 110 A. D.), where it appears as congregational (not diocesan) episcopacy.[10] Now this very fact indicates that *the Pastorals, in which the "overseer" or "bishop" is simply another name for the "elder" or "presbyter," point back to the first century and away from the second.*

(6) *Since Paul was not released from his one and only Roman imprisonment but was put to death at the end of it, and since the book of Acts, which tells the story of his life from the time when he persecuted the church until the end of his imprisonment, leaves no room for the journeys that are implied in the Pastorals, therefore Paul cannot have written these letters.*

J. Moffatt boldly declares that as a matter of fact Paul *was not released from his imprisonment.*[11] This view has been advocated both before and especially after him by many others.

Now if that be correct, then the critics have won the argument, for it is indeed true that the Pastoral Epistles imply a number of journeys which cannot be fitted into the itineraries of Paul that are recorded in the book of Acts, and, in fact, for which no room can be found in the life-span of the apostle as covered in Acts. The following will make this clear:

As to I Timothy, the author reminds Timothy of the fact that the latter had been instructed to stay behind *in Ephesus* while the author was headed *north-westward from Ephesus toward Macedonia* (I Tim. 1:3). He also informs him (Timothy) that he (the author) hopes to come to him *shortly* (I Tim. 3:14).

---

[10] For a summary of the entire argument regarding the rise of the episcopate see P. Schaff, *History of the Christian Church*, New York, 1924, Vol. II, pp. 132-148.
[11] See his *Introduction to the Literature of the New Testament*, third edition, 1918, p. 417.

NEW TESTAMENT COMMENTARY

Now according to Acts, on his first missionary journey Paul never crossed over into Europe (toward Macedonia) at all. On his second journey: on the outward-bound trip the Holy Spirit prevented him from speaking the word in Asia (Acts 16:6); hence, he was not in Ephesus; and on the homeward-bound trip he went from Corinth in an *easterly* direction to Ephesus, then toward the *south-east,* by way of Cesarea to Antioch (Acts 18:18-23). On the third journey, outward-bound, Paul did, indeed, perform a mighty task in Ephesus (Acts 19). He continued there for a long time (three years, Acts 20:31) and he also afterward crossed over into Macedonia (Acts 20:1). But this time *Timothy was not left behind in Ephesus,* but was sent to Macedonia and Corinth (Acts 19:21, 22; I Cor. 4:17; 16:10), and soon is back with Paul in Macedonia (II Cor. 1:1). With Paul he then goes to Corinth, returns with him to Macedonia, awaits him at Troas, and is probably with him in Jerusalem (Rom. 16:21; Acts 20:3-5; I Cor. 16:3). Finally, on the trip to Rome, Ephesus was left far to the north. Arrived in Rome, the two-year imprisonment followed. And with the recording of that event the book of Acts closes. It is clear that nowhere in this account in Acts is there any room for the journey presupposed in I Timothy.

With respect to Titus the situation is similar. According to this Pastoral Epistle the writer has left Titus in Crete to complete the organization of churches on that island (Tit. 1:5). He now instructs his fellow-worker to meet him at Nicopolis (in Epirus on the east coast of the Ionian Sea), where he expects to spend the winter (Tit. 3:12).

But according to Acts, on none of his three missionary journeys did Paul get anywhere near Crete. And on the journey to Rome, though he and Luke did sail "under the lee of Crete," and did reach Fair Havens, the apostle is pictured as *a prisoner,* who is not carrying on any evangelistic work on the island and who has nothing whatever to say about the place where he expects to spend the winter or where he desires to meet Titus (see Acts 27:7-15).

And finally, II Timothy pictures a prisoner (in Rome, cf. II Tim. 1:17), considered "a malefactor" (II Tim. 2:9), on the eve of his execution. The prospect, *humanly* speaking (but see II Tim. 4:7, 8!), is very gloomy. Only after diligent search does Onesiphorus succeed in finding Paul (II Tim. 1:16, 17). Release is nowhere in sight. Nearly everyone has left him. Luke alone is with him (II Tim. 1:15; 4:10, 11). The time of departure from the earthly scene has (or has just about) arrived (II Tim. 4:6, 18).

In sharp contrast with this, the description of the *Roman* imprisonment which is recorded *in Acts and in Paul's prison-epistles (previous* imprisonments certainly do not enter into the picture in this connection) closes hopefully (see also p. 26). The apostle is living in his own hired dwelling, and expects to be released shortly (Acts 28:30; Phil. 1:25, 26; 2:24; Philemon 22).

INTRODUCTION

The conclusion is inescapable: if *Paul* wrote the Pastorals, he must have been released from that Roman imprisonment which is recorded in the book of Acts. He must have made further journeys, and he must have been imprisoned once more.

For a long time critics (intimidated by the prestige of Moffatt?) either denied the historicity of such a release or at least remained agnostic with respect to the subject. Of late, however, there seems to be the beginning of a return to the conservative position. In a recent issue of the *Journal of Biblical Literature* L. P. Pherigo argues strongly in favor of the position that Paul was actually released from the imprisonment recorded in Acts and that he labored a few years longer.[12]

Now, it should be evident to anyone who is willing to examine the evidence, that the arguments against the position that Paul was released are very weak. For example, the contention that had he been released, the author of Acts would have said so — as if Acts were Paul's biography! — , is met by the counter-argument, "Had he *not* been released, Luke *certainly* would have thus indicated, for the favorable note on which his account ends has caused the readers to expect Paul's release" (Acts 28:30, 31). — And the conclusion that Paul never returned to Ephesus, hence, cannot have written I Tim. 1:3, an inference which is drawn from the apostle's statement to the Ephesian elders, namely, "I know that y o u all, among whom I went about preaching the kingdom, will see my face no more" (Acts 20:25, cf. verse 38), is not warranted. In that passage from Acts the apostle did not say, "I know that I will never return to Ephesus," but predicted that making the rounds of Asia Minor, confirming all the churches, going from place to place preaching the gospel of the kingdom and thus seeing believers everywhere he went, would never be resumed by him personally. Paul did not even say, "I know that *none* of y o u, elders here at Ephesus, will ever see my face again," but he said, "I know that *y o u all among whom I went about preaching the kingdom* will see my face no more." The apostle was addressing the elders *as representatives of the churches of Asia Minor*. An occasional brief visit to Ephesus is not excluded. What *is* excluded is anything comparable to three years of day-by-day Kingdom-activity in the Ephesus-region (see *the context*, Acts 20:31).[13]

The arguments in favor of the traditional (and, as we see it, *correct*) position that Paul was, indeed, released from his first Roman imprisonment, made some more journeys, on one of which he wrote I Timothy

---

[12] L. Pherigo, "Paul's Life After the Close of Acts," *JBL* LXX (December, 1951), 277-284. See also the doctoral dissertation of N. G. Veldhoen, "Het Proces van den Apostel Paulus," Leiden, 1924. And see *GThT*, Vol. 55, No. 2, 3 (1955), pp. 60, 61.
[13] Thus also F. W. Grosheide in his comments on this passage in *Korte Verklaring*. For a different solution of the problem regarding Acts 20:25 see R. C. H. Lenski, *Interpretation of the Acts*, pp. 843, 844.

and Titus, was imprisoned for the second time, during which final imprisonment he wrote II Timothy, and was then executed, are as follows:

a. The book of Acts leads the reader to expect Paul's release, and *may* even imply this release.

Luke constantly emphasizes the relative fairness, at times even the friendliness and helpfulness, of the Roman authorities. Rescued by the military tribune out of the hands of the murderous mob at Jerusalem, Paul is permitted to make his defence, first before the people, then before the Jewish council (Acts 21:31-23:9). By the tribune he is rescued once more, this time out of the hands of quarreling Pharisees and Sadducees (Acts 23:10); and even a third time, now from a band of more than forty oath-bound Jews. He is brought to Cesarea. Claudius Lysias writes a letter in his favor (Acts 23:12-35), addressing it to the governor Felix. The latter also permits Paul to make his defence, but desiring to do the Jews a favor, leaves him in prison. When Festus succeeds Felix, the apostle appeals to Cesar. Festus tells King Agrippa that Paul had done nothing worthy of death, and permits him to make his defence before the king. On board a ship on his way to Rome, the apostle is treated kindly by the Roman centurion, Julius (Acts 27:3), who also subsequently saves his life (Acts 27:43). After the storm and the shipwreck, having first been hospitably entertained by the chief of the island of Malta (Acts 28:7), and having afterward covered the final leg of the journey, he arrives at Rome, where he is permitted to stay by himself with a soldier to guard him (Acts 28:16). Though he is a prisoner awaiting trial, he is allowed considerable personal liberty as well as opportunity to preach the gospel (Acts 28:30, 31). — Surely, the notion that he was then *condemned and executed* is completely out of harmony with the entire preceding account. In fact, it has even been suggested (see the article by Pherigo above referred to) that the expression, "And he lived two whole years" in his own hired dwelling (or "at his own expense") *may* have a *legal* meaning, namely, he waited *the full two years* (the limit established by law?) during which the accusers had the opportunity to press their charge. No one appearing (does Acts 28:21 hint in this direction?), the trial ended by default, and Paul was released, the legal requirement of two years having come to an end. — Whether or not this interpretation is correct has not been established. The *main point* is: the closing chapters of Acts point toward release, not toward execution.

b. Paul's prison-epistles show that he expected to be released (Phil. 1:25-27; 2:24; Philemon 22).

c. The very fact that the Pastoral Epistles, which presuppose journeys that require such a release and re-imprisonment, survived and were accepted by the early church as authentic and inspired, would seem to point in the direction of a strong and early tradition to this effect.

INTRODUCTION

d. Even long before the Roman imprisonment recorded in Acts, the apostle had cherished the desire to go to Spain (Rom. 15:24, 28).

e. That he actually was released, went to Spain, was afterward reimprisoned, and having borne witness before the authorities, was executed, is certainly the most natural interpretation of the much-disputed passage of Clement of Rome, who, writing about the last decade of the first century A. D., *from Rome,* the *hub* of the empire, to the Corinthians, admonishing them to put an end to their striving engendered by jealousy, says:

"Paul . . . having taught righteousness to the whole world, *and having gone to the limits of the West,* and having given testimony before the rulers, thus passed from the world and was taken up into the Holy Place, having become the outstanding model of endurance" (First Epistle of Clement to the Corinthians V. vii).

The expression *"the limits of the West,"* especially when used by someone who is writing *from Rome, the heart and center of the empire,* most naturally refers to the extreme western part of Europe.[14]

Similarly, the Muratorian fragment mentions Paul's journey to Spain.[15] And the great church-historian Eusebius states significantly:

"Luke also, who handed down the Acts of the apostles in writing, brought his narrative to a close by the statement that Paul spent two whole years in Rome in freedom, and preached the word of God without hindrance. Tradition has it that the apostle, having defended himself, was again sent upon the ministry of preaching, and coming a second time to the same city, suffered martyrdom under Nero. While he was being held in prison, he composed the second epistle to Timothy, at the same time signifying that his first defence had taken place and that his martyrdom was at hand" (*Ecclesiastical History* II. xxii. 1, 2). Later tradition also accepts a second Roman imprisonment (Chrysostom, Jerome, Theodore of Mopsuestia, etc.).

It has become clear, accordingly, that the so-called "historical" argument against the possibility that Paul could have written the Pastorals has no more substance than have any of the others. Better reasons will have to be found if the weight of tradition is to be counterbalanced.

---

[14] Thus Herodotus, in the 5th century B. C., described the Celts as the *Western* nation. Theodoret, in the 5th century A. D., speaks of the people of Spain, Gaul, and Britain as "those who dwell in the bounds of the West." Strabo's usage is similar. See the article by Pherigo, above referred to; also Lightfoot, *St. Clement of Rome,* London, 1869, pp. 49, 50. See also E. G. Kraeling, *Rand McNally Bible Atlas,* New York, Chicago, San Francisco, 1956, p. 462.

[15] The Latin is corrupt: lucas obtime theofile comprindit (for: Lucas optimo Theophilo comprehendit) quia sub praesentia eius singula gerebantur sicuti et semote (semota) passione petri (Petri) evidenter declarat sed et profectione pauli (Pauli) ab urbe ad spania (Spaniam) proficiscenti (proficiscentis); that is, "Luke relates them for the most excellent Theophilus because in his presence the individual events transpired, as he clearly declares by omitting the passion of Peter as well as the departure of Paul when the latter proceeded from the city to Spain." "The city" is Rome, of course.

Enough has been said to indicate the inadequacy of the arguments of the critics. On the supposition that the Pastorals were the last of Paul's epistles, written after his first Roman imprisonment, with a purpose quite different from that of the other ten letters, the main problem has been solved, at least to a considerable extent.

According to the information furnished by the Epistles themselves the author was:

(1) A man by the name of "Paul, an apostle of Christ Jesus" (I Tim. 1:1; II Tim. 1:1), or "Paul, a servant of God and an apostle of Jesus Christ" (Tit. 1:1). Thus we see that these three letters are self-attested, in contrast with Hebrews which does not mention the name of its author. In this respect the three are like the ten.

(2) Not only does the writer *name* himself; he also *describes* himself. This description agrees with that which is found in Acts and in the ten *with respect to Paul:*

a. The "Paul" of both used to be a blasphemer and persecutor (I Tim. 1:12-17; cf. Acts 8:3; 9:1, 2; 22:4, 5; 26:9-11; I Cor. 15:9).

b. Converted, he was divinely appointed to be a preacher and apostle (I Tim. 1:1, 11; 2:7; II Tim. 1:1, 11; Tit. 1:1; cf. Acts 9:15; 22:14, 15; 26:16-18; II Cor. 12:12; Gal. 1:1; 2:7).

c. In the defence of the truth he suffered much, for example, on his journey through Antioch, Iconium, and Lystra (II Tim. 1:12, 13; 3:10, 11; cf. Acts 14; II Cor. 11; I Thess. 1:6; 2:2).

(3) This man writes three letters which, with minor variations, are similar *in structure* to the ten Pauline epistles. For the nature of Paul's letter-plan, see N.T.C. on I and II Thess., p. 20. As an example let us take II Timothy. Here we find:

a. The mention of the writer's name and office (1:1)
b. The designation of the one to whom the letter is addressed (1:2a), with brief description of that person
c. The opening salutation (1:2b)
d. The thanksgiving, blending into the body of the letter (1:3 ff)
e. The concluding salutation, in the present instance rather detailed (4:19-21)
f. The benediction.

Even in such a minor detail as e: the presence or absence of words of greeting at the end of the letter, *these three letters* exactly resemble the variation which is found among *the ten*. Thus I Timothy has a closing benediction (6:21b: "Grace be with y o u") but no greetings. This reminds one of Galatians (6:18). In II Timothy those who wish to be remembered are mentioned one by one, and there are several names (4:19-21). This re-

INTRODUCTION

sembles what is found at the close of Romans (chapter 16) and of I Corinthians (16:19-21). In Titus, the closing salutation is very general (3:15: "All who are with me send greetings to you"). With this, one should compare II Corinthians (13:13).

(4) These three letters point to the same relation between the writer and the addressed (Timothy and Titus) that we know from letters commonly ascribed to Paul and (in the case of Timothy) from Acts.

It was a relationship of one who is in authority writing to one who recognizes this authority, of spiritual "father" to spiritual "son," of friend to friend (implying both affection and confidence).

In this connection, for Paul's relation to *Timothy* one should compare I Tim. 1:2; II Tim. 1:2 with I Cor. 4:17; 16:10; Phil. 2:19-23; Col. 1:1; I Thess. 3:2; and Philemon 1; and for his relation to *Titus* one should compare Tit. 1:4 with II Cor. 2:13; 7:6, 13; and 8:17, 23.

(5) These three letters mention by name certain individuals whom, from other sources, we have learned to recognize as companions and co-laborers of *Paul*. See on II Tim. 4 and on Tit. 3.

(6) They reveal an author whose warm interest in the churches which he had established, whose style, and whose theology point clearly to Paul, as has been shown (see pp. 14-19).

The testimony of the early church is in harmony with the conclusion which has been derived from the three epistles themselves.

Thus Eusebius, having made a thorough investigation of the literature at his command, states: "But clearly evident and plain are the fourteen (letters) of Paul; yet it is not right to ignore that some dispute the (letter) to the Hebrews" (*Ecclesiastical History* III. iii. 4, 5). Obviously Eusebius, writing at the beginning of the fourth century, knew that the entire orthodox church accepted the Pastorals as having been written by Paul. We have already observed that he makes specific mention of II Timothy as having been composed by the great apostle "while he was being held in prison," having come for the second time to the same city (*Ecclesiastical History* II. xxii. 1, 2; and cf. III. ii). The negative attitude of a few heretics (Basilides and Marcion) with respect to all three, and of Tatian and some like-minded persons with respect to I Timothy and II Timothy, was probably due to the fact that the teaching of these men was out of harmony with the contents of the Pastorals. That, at least, is the explanation given by Tertullian, Clement, and Jerome. Surely the opinion of a few heretics must not be placed above the considered judgment of the entire church!

From Eusebius we can go back to Origen (fl. 210-250), who quotes ever so many passages from the Pastorals (for example, in his work *Against Celsus:* I Tim. 2:1, 2; 3:15, 16; 4:1-5, 10, 17, 18; 6:20; II Tim. 1:3, 10; 2:5; 3:6-8; 4:7, 11, 15, 20, 21; Tit. 1:9, 10, 12; 3:6, 10, 11), and ascribes them to

Paul: "Moreover, Paul, who himself also subsequently became an apostle of Jesus, says in his epistle to Timothy: This is a faithful saying, that Jesus Christ came into the world sinners to save, of whom I am chief" (quoting I Tim. 3:15, *Against Celsus* I. lxiii).

From Origen we can go back still farther, to his teacher, Clement of Alexandria (fl. 190-200). The latter quotes the passage with reference to the "knowledge falsely so called" (I Tim. 6:20, 21), ascribing this passage to "the apostle" (*Stromata* II. xi). He also quotes the prediction that "in later times some will fall away from the faith" (I Tim. 4:1, 3), referring it to "the blessed Paul" (*Stromata* III. vi). A look at the Textual Index of Clement's works (for example, in *The Ante-Nicene Fathers*, reprint 1951, Grand Rapids, Mich., Vol. II) and an actual reading of these passages in the original or even in a good translation suffices to prove that in the works of this early Father there are numerous references to — and actual quotations from — the Pastorals, regarded as having been written by the apostle Paul.

About the same time Tertullian (fl. 193-216), in the short compass of a few lines, quotes several passages from I and II Timothy (I Tim. 6:20; II Tim. 1:14; I Tim. 1:18; 6:13; II Tim. 2:2, in *Prescription Against Heretics* XXV), definitely declaring that "Paul addressed this expression to Timothy." We have already seen that he frowns upon Marcion's rejection of the Pastorals (*Against Marcion* V. xxi).

Earlier by a few years, but still for a long time a contemporary of Clement of Alexandria and of Tertullian, was Ireneus. He opens his work *Against Heresies* (about 182-188) with a quotation from I Tim. 1:4 (the passage about the "endless genealogies" which fail to edify), which he definitely ascribes to *the apostle* (see the Preface to the aforementioned work by Ireneus). In the same work he quotes or alludes to several other passages, for example, I Tim. 1:9 (IV. xvi. 3); 2:5 (V. xvii. 1); 3:15 (III. i. 1); 4:2 (II. xxi. 2), and not only from the first but also from the second epistle to Timothy (II Tim. 2:23; cf. *Against Heresies*, IV. Preface, 3), and from Titus (Tit. 3:10; cf. *Ag. Her.*, I. xvi. 3). Note especially that in the last passage Ireneus states that it is *Paul* who commands us to avoid men who give heed to fables.

Now when Ireneus ascribes the Pastorals to "the apostle" namely to "Paul," his word should carry considerable weight. He had traveled widely, was intimately acquainted with almost the entire church of his day, and had been a pupil of a pupil (Polycarp) of one of the apostles (John).

The Muratorian Fragment (about 180-200), a survey of New Testament books, states that "the blessed Paul . . . writes . . . out of affection and love one to Philemon, and one to Titus, and two to Timothy . . . held sacred in the honorable esteem of the church universal in the regulation of ecclesiastical discipline."

INTRODUCTION

Among the orthodox writers who flourished at one time or another during the period 90-180 we find that toward the close of that era Theophilus of Antioch refers to "the water and laver of regeneration" (*To Autolycus* II. xvi), which may be regarded as a collation of Eph. 5:26 and Tit. 3:5. He definitely quotes I Tim. 2:2: "that we may lead a tranquil and quiet life" (Same work, III. xiv).

Athenagoras — sometimes called "the Christian philosopher from the Athenian Agora" (cf. his name *Athen — agoras*) —, was an Athenian who has been pictured as having one day sauntered into the market-place where the Christians were being mocked, and then, moved by curiosity, having begun to read the Scriptures in order to refute them. It is claimed that in the process of this Scripture-study he was converted. He, a contemporary of Theophilus, describes God as "light inapproachable" (*A Plea For the Christians* XVI). This certainly reminds one of I Tim. 1:16.

Writing some time between 155 and 161, Justin Martyr also showed that he was acquainted with the Pastorals. It is true that not all the seeming resemblances between certain passages in his writings and the Pastorals have evidential value. Thus, for example, the expression "this very Christ ... the Judge of all the living and the dead" (*Dialogue with Trypho* CXVIII), while reminding one of II Tim. 4:1 ("Christ Jesus who shall judge the living and the dead"), from which, indeed, it *may* have been derived, was probably a "faithful saying" which had gained currency at a very early stage of Christian belief (see also Acts 10:42; I Peter 4:5; cf. Matt. 25:31-46; John 5:25-29; II Cor. 5:10), so that no argument can be based upon it to prove that Justin knew the Pastorals. However, his reference to "the kindness of God and his love toward man" — note God's *philanthropy!* — is almost certainly derived from Tit. 3:4 ("But when the kindness of God ... and his love toward man appeared").

Also when we come to Polycarp (probably writing some time between 100 and 135), we feel that we are on firm ground. The fact that he knew the Pastorals and quoted from them would seem to be indisputable. Let the reader judge for himself:

POLYCARP (*To the Philippians*)	THE PASTORALS
"But the beginning of all evils is the love of money" (IV).	"For a root of all the evils is the love of money" (I Tim. 6:10).
"Knowing therefore that we brought nothing into the world and that we can take nothing out of it, let us arm ourselves with the armor of righteousness" (IV).	"For nothing did we bring into the world ... neither are we able to carry anything out of it" (I Tim. 6:7).

POLYCARP *(To the Philippians)*	THE PASTORALS
"Likewise must the deacons be . . . not doubletongued, not lovers of money, temperate in all things . . ." (V).	"Deacons similarly must be . . . not doubletongued, not addicted to much wine, not greedy of shameful gain" (I Tim. 3:8).
"We shall also reign with him, if, indeed, we have faith" (V).	"If we endure, we shall also reign with him" (II Tim. 2:12).
"For they did not fall in love with the present world" (IX).	"For Demas has deserted me because he fell in love with the present world" (II Tim. 4:10).
"May the Lord grant them true repentance" (XI Lat.).	". . . in the hope that possibly God may grant them conversion" (II Tim. 2:15).
"Pray also for the rulers and for potentates and for princes . . ." (XII Lat.).	"First of all, then, I urge that supplications, prayers, intercessions, thanksgivings be made in behalf of all men, in behalf of kings and all who are in high positions" (I Tim. 2:1, 2).

Here, clearly, one writer is using the words of another, varying the language somewhat as the need requires. It is surely most natural to conclude that when one writer states "Demas . . . fell in love with the present world," and the other refers to persons who *"did not* fall in love with the present world," it is the latter writer who is borrowing from the former, and not vice versa. Moreover, if *the pupil*, Ireneus, ascribed the Pastorals to Paul, as has been shown, is it not probable that the *teacher*, Polycarp, did the same?

Ignatius (not later than 110), in urging Polycarp to be pleasing to him for whom he is soldiering *(To Polycarp* VI), immediately reminds one of II Tim. 2:4. (Other assumed resemblances are less convincing.)

Because of their debatable character we pass by a few possible allusions to the Pastorals in the *Epistle of Barnabas,* and we come, last of all, to Clement of Rome (90-100). The clearest resemblances are the following:

CLEMENT OF ROME *(To the Corinthians)*	THE PASTORALS
"Y o u were . . . ready for every good work" (11).	"Remind them to be ready for every good work" (Tit. 3:1).

INTRODUCTION

CLEMENT OF ROME *(To the Corinthians)*	THE PASTORALS
". . . those who with a pure conscience serve his excellent name" (XLV)	"I acknowledge gratitude to God whom I, like my forefathers serve with a pure conscience" (II Tim. 1:3).

Summing up the entire argument regarding authorship we may now safely state the following:

(1) The arguments of the negative critics have been examined in detail and have been found wanting; that is, these critics have failed to prove that Paul could not have written the Pastorals.

(2) According to the evidence of the epistles themselves the author was no one else than the apostle Paul.

(3) Within the orthodox church there is a uniform tradition ascribing the Pastorals to the apostle Paul. This tradition can be traced back from Eusebius at the beginning of the fourth century to Ireneus and the Muratorian Fragment at the close of the second. Moreover, the Pastorals are included not only in *this* list (the Muratorian) but in *all* the ancient lists of Pauline epistles, and also in *all* the manuscripts and versions that have come down to us.

(4) Even in the period A. D. 90-180 we find clear evidence that I and II Timothy and Titus were already in existence, were held in high esteem as the very word of God, and were being frequently quoted and paraphrased. It is true that these early witnesses do not mention Paul by name as the author. Not mentioning authors of New Testament books by name is rather characteristic of them. They and their readers were living so close to the time of the apostles that this was not considered necessary.

The very fact that already in the days of these earliest witnesses — Theophilus of Antioch, Athenagoras, Justin Martyr, Polycarp, Ignatius, and Clement of Rome — the Pastorals have attained this high fame and wide circulation shows that their date of origin must go back to a period that is still earlier by several years. Hence, all the historical evidence points to Paul as the one who during the period 63-67 A. D. was in a real sense the responsible author of these three little gems of inspired truth.

III. To Whom Were They Addressed?

It is natural to turn from the sender to the addressees: Timothy and Titus.

A most remarkable person was Timothy or Timotheus, meaning: honoring or worshiping *god,* originally a heathen name of very common occurrence,[16] adopted by devout Jews and by Christians, with changed reference, namely, to *their God*. His character was a blend of *amiability* and *faithfulness in spite of natural timidity*. Paul loved Timothy and admired his outstanding personality-traits.

As to Timothy's *amiability*, it is concerning him that the apostle wrote these touching words: "Now I hope in the Lord Jesus to send Timothy to y o u soon, so that I also may be cheered when I get to know about y o u r condition. Indeed, I have no one of similar disposition, who will be genuinely interested in y o u r welfare. For they all look after their own affairs, not those of Jesus Christ. But y o u know his proved worth, how as a child (serves) with (his) father, so he served with me in the gospel" (Phil. 2:19-22). Indeed, Timothy was the apostle's "beloved child" (II Tim. 1:2).

As to his unswerving *faithfulness* and unwavering readiness for the sake of the gospel to sacrifice whatever may have looked like his own immediate interests, this is evident not only from the passage just quoted but also from the fact that none of Paul's companions is mentioned as often and is with him as constantly as is Timothy. In the very last chapter from prison the great apostle writes: "Do your utmost to come to me soon . . . do your utmost to come before winter" (II Tim. 4:9, 21). Paul knew that he could depend on Timothy, just as he knew that he could depend on Luke (II Tim. 4:11).

This dependability is also evident from the fact that in spite of his *youth* — he was Paul's junior by several years (cf. I Tim. 4:12; II Tim. 2:22) —, his natural *reserve* and *timidity* (I Cor. 16:10; II Tim. 1:7), and his *"frequent ailments"* (I Tim. 5:23), he was willing to leave his home to accompany the apostle on dangerous missionary journeys, to be sent on difficult and even perilous errands, and to remain to the very end a worthy servant of Jesus Christ (Rom. 16:21; see also on I Thess. 3:2).

Timothy is first mentioned in Acts 16:1, from which passage it may probably be inferred that he was an inhabitant of Lystra (cf. Acts 20:4). He was the offspring of a "mixed marriage": a Greek pagan father and a devout Jewish mother, Eunice (Acts 16:1; II Tim. 1:5). From the days of his childhood he had been instructed in the sacred writings of the Old Testament (II Tim. 3:15). In all probability Paul, on his first missionary journey (about 47 A. D.), had been the means of Timothy's conversion, so that from that day on he could be referred to as Paul's (spiritual) "child" (I Cor. 4:17; I Tim. 1:2; II Tim. 1:2). Hence, it is not strange to read that he was acquainted with the persecutions and sufferings which the missionaries had experienced on this *first* journey (II Tim. 3:11), that is, *before* Timothy himself had joined Paul in active work. Though Paul was Timothy's spiritual father, it is not at all improbable that grandmother

---

[16] Cf. A. Sizoo, *Uit De Wereld van het Nieuwe Testament*, p. 190.

INTRODUCTION

Lois and mother Eunice, whose conversion to the Christian faith preceded that of Timothy (II Tim. 1:5), co-operated very effectively to bring about this happy event.

When Paul and Silas, on the second journey, came to Derbe and Lystra, Timothy responded favorably to the request of the apostle to join the group in missionary labors. This must have occurred about the year 51. From Acts 16:2 we learn that he was "well spoken of" by the people of his own community. Because it was well-known that Timothy's father was a Greek, so that the young man's influence among the Jews would be reduced to almost zero unless something were done to bring out clearly his own devotion to the sacred writings of the covenant people, he was, accordingly, circumcised (Acts 16:3). In all probability another important event also took place at this time: by the elders of the local church (which had been established and organized on the first journey) Timothy was now ordained for his new task, Paul himself taking part in this solemn "laying on of hands" (Acts 14:23; and see on I Tim. 1:18; 4:14; II Tim. 1:6).

Along with the other missionaries Timothy subsequently crossed over into Europe, Luke having by this time joined the company. We have already stated our reasons for believing that though Luke stayed behind at Philippi (contrast "we" in Acts 16:11, 13 with "they" in Acts 17:1), Timothy went along with Paul and Silas to (or at least soon joined them at) Thessalonica (see N.T.C. on I and II Thessalonians, p. 5). He also helped the others in the next place to which they came, namely, Berea, where he and Silas were left behind in order to give spiritual support to the infant church, while Paul himself, escorted by some of his friends, made his way to the coast and finally reached Athens (Acts 17:10-15). Acting upon the request of Paul, Timothy left Berea and found the apostle while the latter was still in Athens (I Thess. 3:1, 2). He was sent back to Thessalonica for the purpose of strengthening and encouraging the brothers there (see N.T.C. on I Thess. 3:1, 2). After Paul had left Athens and had begun his labors in Corinth, both Silas and Timothy "came down from Macedonia" to rejoin the apostle (Acts 18:1, 5; see on I Thess. 3:6).

At Corinth Timothy carried on his missionary labors with Paul and Silas. Hence (and because he was well-known in Thessalonica) his name is associated with theirs in the addresses of the two epistles to the Thessalonians, sent from Corinth (see on I Thess. 1:1; II Thess. 1:1).

On the third missionary journey (53/54-57/58 A. D.) Timothy is with the apostle during the latter's lengthy ministry at Ephesus. From here he is sent to Macedonia and to Corinth (Acts 19:21, 22; I Cor. 4:17; 16:10). As Timothy went by the land route – i.e., to Corinth by way of Macedonia – Paul expected that his fellow-worker would arrive in Corinth after I Corinthians had reached its destination.

When Paul arrives in Macedonia, Timothy has rejoined him, as is evident from the fact that his name is associated with that of the apostle in the letter which was now sent to Corinth (II Cor. 1:1). It is also clear that the assistant and partner accompanied the apostle to Corinth (Rom. 16:21), and that together with others he is with Paul on his return to Macedonia (Acts 20:3, 4), and is waiting for him at Troas (Acts 20:5). He was probably also with Paul in Jerusalem (I Cor. 16:3).

For a little while we lose sight of Timothy, but during Paul's first imprisonment at Rome the two are in close contact with each other again, as is evident from Phil. 1:1; Col. 1:1; Philemon 1:1. When the apostle expects to be released in the very near future (Phil. 2:24), he tells the Philippians that he hopes to send Timothy to them soon (Phil. 2:19).

Again there is a gap in the information that has come down to us. The next time we hear of Timothy he is at Ephesus, where Paul has joined him. The apostle, on leaving, asks Timothy to remain at this place (I Tim. 1:3). While there Timothy one day receives the letter which we now call I Timothy.

Many months pass, during which nothing is heard with reference to Timothy. Then another letter arrives, in which Paul, writing from Rome as a prisoner facing death, urges his friend to do his best to come to him before winter (II Tim. 4:9, 21). Whether the two ever actually saw each other's face again is not recorded. (The enigmatical statement regarding Timothy in Heb. 13:23 cannot be discussed here.) That Timothy *tried* to see the apostle may be taken for granted. It is in line with his entire character. Though he is hesitant and reserved, yet his love for Paul and even more for the Lord Jesus Christ and for his cause always win out in the end. He may *shrink* for a moment (cf. I Cor. 16:10), he never *refuses*. His is a character to be admired. In his becoming diffidence the dynamic aggressiveness of Paul finds its true counterpart. It is not surprising that Paul and Timothy are friends!

Timothy and Titus have in common unwavering loyalty to the cause of the Gospel, willingness to be sent on difficult missions, high regard for their friend and superior, Paul. Yet, in one respect the two differ. Titus is more of a leader; Timothy is a follower. Titus is the type of man who is able not only to take orders but also to go ahead of his own accord (II Cor. 8:16, 17). Timothy needs a little prodding (II Tim. 1:6), though here the emphasis must fall on "a little" and not on "prodding." Titus is resourceful, a man of initiative in a good cause. One finds in him something of the aggressiveness of Paul. Timothy is co-operative, a man who shows this spirit even when such co-operation requires him to do things which run counter to his natural shyness. That is the way these two characters are exhibited in the Art Gallery of Holy Writ.

INTRODUCTION

Now as to Titus, nowhere in the book of Acts does his name appear, but elsewhere in the New Testament it is found thirteen times: twice in Galatians (2:1; 2:3), once in II Tim. (5:10), once in Titus (1:4), and no less than nine times in II Corinthians (2:13; 7:6; 7:13; 7:14; 8:6; 8:16; 8:23; 12:18; and again 12:18). Yet the first *implied* reference to Titus is found in the book of Acts, though there his name is not mentioned. By comparing Acts 15:2 ("some of the others") with Gal. 2:1, 3 ("taking Titus along with me ... even Titus who was with me") we learn that when, after the first missionary journey, Paul and Barnabas were sent to Jerusalem in order to help the church in reaching a conclusion regarding the question whether Christians from among the Gentiles should be circumcised, they were accompanied by "some of the others," among whom was "Titus." In all probability Titus was one of the apostle's converts, being called his "genuine child in a common faith" (Titus 1:4). Some are of the opinion that Syrian Antioch was his home and that he had been converted during the signally blessed gospel-campaign conducted at that place by Paul and Barnabas (Acts 11:19-26; cf. Acts 14:26; 15:2; Gal. 2:1, 3), but this is no more than a plausible conjecture.

Titus, then, becomes a person of great importance for the progress of the Christian faith. He is taken along to "the apostles and elders" at Jerusalem as *a test case*, a definite challenge to the Judaizers. Titus is a Greek (Gal. 2:3), *both* of his parents being Gentiles (contrast Timothy whose mother was a Jewess). Naturally the Judaistic party at Jerusalem demands that he be circumcised. But Paul does not yield even for a moment (Gal. 2:5), and the matter in dispute is decided in favor of the free admission of Gentiles into the church, solely on the basis of faith in Christ, without being required to keep the Jewish law (Acts 15:13-29). The significance of this victory for Christian liberty and for the progress of Christianity can hardly be over-estimated.

Nothing further is heard about Titus until Paul's third missionary journey is reached (probable date 53/54 — 57/58). During this journey Paul's faithful helper is sent to Corinth on more than one occasion, though commentators differ with respect to the question whether he was sent two or three times.[17] Probably the simplest reconstruction of his journeys is also the best. I shall assume that on this third missionary journey Titus made only two trips to Corinth, one *from Ephesus* (was he then the bearer of I Corinthians?), and one *from Macedonia*, when he carried II Corinthians to its destination.

Returning now to that first trip (Ephesus to Corinth), it was Titus who was charged with the difficult and delicate task of solving "the Corinthian

---

[17] This is not the proper place to discuss the question in detail. It involves exegesis of such passages as II Cor. 2:4; 8:6, 10.

Situation" (party-strife, fornication, etc.; see I Cor. 1:11; 5:6; 16:17). True, his arrival in Corinth seems to have been followed almost immediately by that of Timothy, but nothing at all is reported with reference to the latter's accomplishments in that city. The Corinthians were told, however, to see to it that when Timothy arrived, he would be with them "without fear" (I Cor. 16:10). As to Titus, the apostle had expected that he would meet this returning emissary at Troas. When Paul did not find him there, his mind had no rest. So he departed from Troas and crossed over into Europe (Macedonia, II Cor. 2:13). Here his spirit was refreshed and his heart filled with joy when he not only met Titus but heard from his lips a report which, *on the whole,* was favorable (II Cor. 7:6, 13, 14).

The mission which Titus had been called to perform had been successful to a considerable extent. It seems that at Corinth he had acted on the principle that the best way to overcome evil is "with good." So, while there he had made a beginning of setting in motion again the work of collecting funds for the needy saints at Jerusalem. This important work, which had been started several months earlier (II Cor. 8:10), had been lagging of late. Titus in his own dynamic manner had given fresh impetus to it.

As already indicated, the report which Titus brought was *not altogether* favorable. Paul's enemies had not taken kindly to the rebuke which they had received. They assailed Paul's apostleship, and charged that he was fickle because he had changed his traveling-plans (II Cor. 1:15-24); that he displayed a boastful courage which veiled an inner cowardice; and that even when he preached the gospel without remuneration his motives were not pure. Accordingly, from Macedonia (Philippi?) Paul now writes II Corinthians, which is delivered by (the same man who brought I Corinthians to its destination? namely) Titus. He was the proper man to deal with a difficult situation. At the same time he would be enabled to complete the work of collecting for the Jerusalem poor. This time Titus is accompanied by two others, one of whom was a noted preacher (II Cor. 8:16-24). Titus, true to his character, was eager to go on his mission (II Cor. 8:16, 17). In *him* one discovers no hesitancy.

There follows a long interval (perhaps from about 56 to about 63 A. D.) during which we hear nothing of Titus. The next time his name is mentioned, he is in charge of a church (or churches) in Crete. Paul, having been set at liberty from his first Roman imprisonment and being now on an eastward journey, has left him there in order to carry out the mandate described in Titus 1:5 (see on that passage). We shall meet Titus again (see points 2, 5, 6, and 10, pp. 39, 40).

A comparison between I Tim. 4:12 ("Let no one despise your youth") and Titus 2:15 ("Exhort and reprove with all authority. Let no one despise thee") would seem to indicate that Titus was older than Timothy. He loved the Corinthians. He loved his Lord. He loved the work of the

INTRODUCTION

Lord, and gave ample evidence of this in the spontaneous manner in which he shouldered his task at Corinth. He breathed the spirit of Paul, and followed closely in his steps (II Cor. 12:18). He was original, tactful, courageous, loyal, a close and trusted friend of the great apostle, the latter's true representative in the cause of Christ.

IV. What Is Their Historical Background and Purpose?

It has been established (see pp. 23-27) that all the historical evidence points in the direction of Paul's release from his first Roman imprisonment. Where did he go immediately after his release? We simply do not know with any degree of certainty. The Pastorals, to be sure, imply a number of journeys, but these are merely "links" which can be joined together in ever so many different ways. Did Paul go *at once* to Spain? Did he go from Rome to Philippi, and from there to Ephesus, as is held by some, or vice versa (Rome — Ephesus — Philippi), as is held by others? Just *when* did he travel to Spain? Did Timothy ask Paul for permission to leave Ephesus, which permission was refused? If so, where was the apostle when this request came? Was he somewhere on his way back from Spain to Macedonia, as some have supposed? Or — and this to me seems preferable — should we drop the entire idea of *a request* coming from Timothy, and should we perhaps place *Paul at Ephesus with Timothy,* when the younger man was urged to remain at his post, while the apostle goes on his way to Europe? Similar questions can easily be added. Among the many possible combinations the following scheme is perhaps as good as any. It has the advantage of suggesting a natural line of travel. See a good Bible-map of the Roman world as it was in Paul's day (I suggest W.H.A.B., Plate XV); also the excellent map in the December, 1956, issue of *The National Geographic Magazine,* the map which bears the title "Lands of the Bible Today." *I emphasize, however, that certainty is entirely lacking:*

1. Immediately after his release Paul sends Timothy to Philippi with this good news (Phil. 2:19-23). The date 63 A. D. cannot be off very far. After July 19-24 of the year 64 A. D. (the burning of Rome) release would have been very improbable.

2. Paul himself starts on his journey toward Asia Minor, and on the way to that destination leaves Titus on the island of Crete to bring to completion the organization of the church (or churches) which had been established there (cf. Acts 2:11; Titus 1:5).

3. The apostle arrives at Ephesus, travels on until he reaches Colosse just as he had intended (Philem. 22), and returns to Ephesus.

4. Here he is joined by Timothy who brings news from the congregation at Philippi (see 1 above). On leaving, Paul asks Timothy to remain at Ephesus, which was in need of his ministry (I Tim. 1:3, 4).

5. Paul himself goes to Macedonia, just as he had planned (Phil. 2:24; I Tim. 1:3). He hopes to return to Ephesus shortly, but rather *expects* that his absence may be prolonged (I Tim. 3:14, 15). From Macedonia (Philippi?) he writes two epistles which resemble each other very closely: I Timothy and Titus. In his letter to Titus he requests that beloved brother to meet him at Nicopolis (Tit. 3:12).

6. Accordingly, the apostle journeys to Nicopolis (in Epirus), located on the east coast of the Ionian Sea. Here he spends the winter (Tit. 3:12) and is joined by Titus.

7. Paul journeys to Spain (Rom. 15:24); according to some "taking Titus with him," but of this there is no hint anywhere. The mere possibility that, if Paul went to Spain at this time, Titus went along must be granted. As to Titus, there is nothing definite until we reach II Tim. 4:10 (see Number 10).

8. Having returned from Spain, Paul proceeds to Asia Minor (see 5 above), and leaves Trophimus sick at Miletus, south of Ephesus (II Tim. 4:20). Did the apostle also meet Timothy again, and did the tearful separation (II Tim. 1:4) take place at this time or very shortly afterward?

9. At Troas he visits Carpus, at whose home he leaves his cloak (II Tim. 4:13). By way of Corinth, where Erastus remained (II Tim. 4:20) he goes to Rome. He is rearrested. (Where the arrest occurred — Troas, Corinth, Rome, or elsewhere — is not known.) Cruel Nero is reigning. This is the monster who had murdered his step-brother, *his own mother,* his wife (Octavia), his tutor (Seneca), and many others. When Rome was burned in the year 64, the people accused Nero of having set the city on fire. He sought to turn attention away from himself and placed the blame on the Christians. Frightful was the carnival of blood which followed.

10. Accordingly, Paul, having returned from Spain, no longer enjoyed a measure of political protection. His second Roman imprisonment is severe and brief (II Tim. 1:16, 17; 2:9). Luke only is with him. Demas has forsaken him, having fallen in love with "the present world," and has departed for Thessalonica. Crescens has gone either to Galatia or to Gallia (Gaul), Titus to Dalmatia (see on II Tim. 4:10, 11). Urging Timothy to come to him quickly, he asks him to take Mark with him. These details are found in II Timothy, the letter which was written when death was already staring the apostle in the face (II Tim. 4:6-11). He is condemned to death and beheaded on the Ostian Way, about three miles outside of the capital. Whether Timothy and Mark reached Rome before the apostle's death we do not know.

INTRODUCTION

Let us now return to 4 and 5 above. At Ephesus the Judaists were spreading their strange doctrines, placing great stress upon such things as endless genealogies, profane and old wives' fables, and posing as teachers of the law (I Tim. 1:4, 7; 4:7). According to many interpreters — and they may be right — these errorists also assumed that matter was evil or at least the seat of evil, and therefore recognized only a spiritual resurrection (II Tim. 2:18). Soon they would also prohibit marriage and the use of certain foods (I Tim. 4:3). We have already shown that the errors condemned were partly present, partly future, partly present and future (see above, p. 21).

In addition, to advocating false doctrine and ethics, these sinister teachers (and perhaps others with them) seem to have made it necessary for Paul to lay down some very "plain rules" regarding proper conduct at *public worship* (see especially chapter 2). The ladies also stood in need of special instruction with respect to this point.

The situation was really serious. This becomes evident when two additional facts are borne in mind: a. from such passages as I Tim. 1:6, 20; 3:3, 6; 5:17-25 it may probably be assumed that prominent church-members — including some with a "superiority-complex" ("puffed up" persons) — were among the errorists; and b. Timothy himself, as we have seen, was by nature of the very opposite disposition. He seems to have been a man with an "inferiority-complex." For *such* a man to cope with *such* a situation was, indeed, difficult.

Hence, about the year 63 Paul, having recently departed from Ephesus, where he had left Timothy, and being now in Macedonia (I Tim. 1:3), tells Timothy *how to administer the affairs of the church*. Specifically, he writes in order:

(1) To bolster the spirit of Timothy, reminding him of the "gift" which he had received (see on I Tim. 4:14), of his "good confession" (see on 6:12), and of "the deposit" which had been entrusted to him (see on 6:20).

(2) To impart guidance in the critical conflict against soul-destroying errors that were being spread in the church at Ephesus, and to exhort Timothy to continue in the "sound doctrine" (1:3-11; 1:18-20; ch. 4; ch. 6). Such guidance would be all the more necessary if the apostle's absence should be prolonged (see on I Tim. 3:14, 15). In connection with this battle against the spread of error, stress is laid on the importance of *proper organization:* choosing the right kind of leaders (especially elders and deacons), and of admonishing them if they go astray (ch. 3; ch. 5).

(3) To give directions for proper conduct during *public worship* (see on ch. 2).

Returning once more to point 5, we note that Paul, now in Macedonia (Philippi?), also writes to Titus, whom he had left at Crete and whom he wishes to meet at Nicopolis. The reputation of the Cretans was none too good. The need of thorough-going *sanctification* in congregational, individual, family, and public life had to be stressed here even more than elsewhere. The elders who are to be appointed must be "blameless" (1:5, 6). The mouths of unruly individuals, vain talkers and deceivers, must be stopped (1:10). People (especially church-members!) must be taught to abstain from worldly lusts and to live moderately and righteously and godly in the present world, in the expectation of the Redeemer's glorious appearing (2:11-14). In public life they should be obedient to the authorities and should deport themselves properly toward all (3:1, 2). Impenitent troublemakers should be disciplined (3:10). On the other hand, sincere gospel-workers (such as Zenas and Apollos), whose itinerary would include Crete, and who probably carried with them Paul's letter addressed to Titus, must receive every assistance (3:13).

Accordingly, the letter to Titus was written with this threefold purpose in mind:

(1) To urge Titus to come to Paul at Nicopolis, as soon as a substitute has taken over the work in Crete (3:12).

(2) To speed on their way Zenas the law-expert and Apollos the eloquent evangelist (3:13).

(3) To give directions for the promotion of the spirit of *sanctification* in congregational, individual, family, and social relationships.

Of these three purpose-items the last covers by far the most territory.

When we leave I Timothy and Titus and turn to II Timothy, we immediately notice that the entire atmosphere has changed. When the apostle wrote I Timothy and Titus, he was a free man, able to make traveling-plans. When he writes II Timothy, he is a prisoner, facing death. Crete (Tit. 1:5), Ephesus (I Tim. 1:3), Macedonia (I Tim. 1:3; cf. Phil. 2:24), and Nicopolis (Tit. 3:12) are the places mentioned by name in I Timothy and Titus (taken together), and they form an easily traceable route on the map. Though no one knows whether the apostle actually journeyed to these places *in that order*, every one will have to admit that such a line of travel is natural. Miletus (II Tim. 4:20), Troas (II Tim. 4:13), Corinth (II Tim. 4:20; cf. Rom. 16:23), are the places which Paul visited on the journey(s) presupposed in II Timothy, until he reached Rome and final imprisonment (cf. II Tim. 1:8; 4:6). Here also, *if* the order in which we have arranged these "stations" is correct, the route is logical. It is therefore natural to assume that the journey to Spain intervened between these two courses of travel, that is, between the route presupposed in I Timothy and Titus, on the one hand, and the route that is probably indicated in II Timothy, on the other.[18]

For the reason given it is probably incorrect to say that Tit. 3:12 and II

---

[18] See also R. C. H. Lenski, *op. cit.*, pp. 473-480.

INTRODUCTION

Tim. 4:21 refer to the same "winter," and then to date Titus accordingly, bringing it as close as possible to II Timothy. It must be borne in mind that the apostle had made definite plans as to the place where he, as a *free man,* would spend "the winter" referred to in Tit. 3:12 (namely, at Nicopolis). No such plans were possible with respect to the place where Paul, *the prisoner,* would spend "the winter" indicated in II Tim. 4:21. These two winters are not the same! When II Timothy is written, the entire picture has changed. See the situation as described under point 10 above (p. 40). *This* is the winter of A. D. 65 or 66 or 67. It is Paul's *last* winter on earth. The great apostle, writing from his prison in the world's metropolis, and being in doubt whether his assistant will be able to reach Rome before his death, admonishes Timothy that, whatever happens, he must keep clinging to *the sound doctrine* and must defend it unceasingly against every adversary.

Though II Timothy does not state where *Timothy* was when it was written, yet there are several passages which point to Ephesus. Thus Paul says that Timothy knows that "all who are in Asia" had turned away from the apostle (1:15). If the one addressed was laboring in Ephesus, which was in "Asia," it is understandable that he would know about this situation. Similarly, Paul writes that Timothy "knows better" than the apostle, or "knows very well," how many services Onesiphorus had rendered, and takes for granted that Timothy "at Ephesus" (1:18), is able to convey Paul's greetings to the family of this "profit-bringer" (4:19). There is another reference to Ephesus in 4:12: "But Tychicus I am sending to Ephesus." Moreover, if Timothy is living in Ephesus, it will not be too difficult for him to "bring with him the cloak" which Paul had "left *at Troas* with Carpus" (4:13). And we would not be at all surprised to find Priscilla (or Prisca) and Aquila (4:19) back again in Ephesus (though the place is not mentioned), where they had been living previously (Acts 18:18, 19, 24, 26; cf. I Cor. 16:19). It is true that subsequent to their first stay in Ephesus they had returned to Rome (Rom. 16:3), but with a persecution of Christians raging fiercely in Rome it is not strange that they had again left the capital. Once before, and for a somewhat similar reason, they had departed from Italy (Acts 18:2).

One additional item in the circumstantial evidence linking Timothy with Ephesus when this letter was written is the nature of the heresy which is here condemned (see on II Tim. 2:14-18). To a certain extent it resembles that which was exposed in I Timothy (addressed to Timothy while he was *at Ephesus,* I Tim. 1:3).

We may suppose, then, that Timothy has not yet left *Ephesus, where error and persecution of believers are raging* (1:8; 2:3, 12, 14-18, 23; 3:8, 12).

Accordingly, Paul's purpose in writing II Timothy may be summarized as follows:

(1) To urge Timothy to come to Rome as soon as possible in view of the apostle's impending departure from this life (4:9, 21; cf. 4:6-8).

(2) To admonish him to keep clinging to the *sound doctrine,* defending it against all error, and enduring hardship as a good soldier.

This second item is characteristic of the entire letter.

Commentary on I Timothy

Outline of I Timothy

Theme: *The Apostle Paul, Writing to Timothy, Gives Directions For the Administration of the Church*

Chapter I

The Apostle Paul

A. Salutes Timothy.
B. Repeats his order that Timothy remain at Ephesus to combat the error of those who refuse to see *their sinful condition* in the light of God's holy law, and who pretend to be law-experts.
C. By contrast, thanks God for having made him, *"chief of sinners,"* a minister of the gospel.

Chapter II

Directions with respect to Public Worship

A. Prayers must be made "in behalf of all men."
B. In connection with public worship both the men and the women must behave properly:
   1. The men, in every place of public worship, must lift up holy hands;
   2. The women, in getting ready "to go to church," must dress becomingly, and at the place of public worship must show that they understand and have accepted their divinely ordained position.

Chapter III

Directions with respect to the Institution of the Offices

A. Incentive for becoming an overseer: the glorious character of the work. Directions regarding the necessary qualifications of overseers.
B. Directions regarding the necessary qualifications of deacons and of women who assist them.
   Incentive for faithful performance of the task of deacons and of deacons' assistants.
C. The reasons for conveying these instructions in written form.

Chapter IV
Directions with respect to
Apostasy

A. Description of this apostasy and proof of its dangerous character.
B. How Timothy should deal with it.

Chapters V and VI
Directions with respect to
Certain Definite Groups and Individuals

Chapter V
- A. Old(er) men, young(er) men, old(er) women, young(er) women
- B. Widows in distress
- C. Widows engaged in spiritual work
- D. Elders and prospective elders

Chapter VI
- E. Slaves
- F. Novelty-teachers who aspire to fame and riches
- G. Timothy himself ("Keep the commission")
- H. People who are rich in terms of this present age
- I. Timothy himself ("Guard the deposit")

Outline of Chapter 1

Theme: *The Apostle Paul, Writing to Timothy, Gives Directions For the Administration of the Church*

The Apostle Paul

1:1, 2	A.	Salutes Timothy
1:3-11; 18-20	B.	Repeats his order that Timothy remain at Ephesus to combat the error of those who refuse to see *their sinful condition* in the light of God's holy law, and who pretend to be law-experts;
1:12-17	C.	By contrast, thanks God for having made him — *"chief of sinners"* — a minister of the gospel.

CHAPTER I

I TIMOTHY   1:1

1 1 Paul, an apostle of Christ Jesus by order of God our Savior and Christ Jesus our Hope, 2 to Timothy (my) genuine child in faith; grace, mercy, peace from God the Father and Christ Jesus our Lord.

1:1, 2

1. As was customary, the sender mentions his own name first; then the name of the person addressed. Hence, **Paul** . . . **to Timothy**. In a world held together politically by Rome and culturally by Greece it was natural that the writer should use his Greek-Roman name *Paul* instead of his Jewish name *Saul*. (For further details on the meaning and use of these names see N.T.C. on I Thess. 1:1.)

Perhaps in order to make it easier for Timothy to carry out the instructions which Paul is about to give him, and also in order to add weight to the words of encouragement contained in this letter, the writer adds to his name the words **an apostle of Christ Jesus.**

Timothy needs to know that this letter is not just a substitute for a friendly, confidential chat, a tête-a-tête; even though its tone is naturally very cordial, for a friend is indeed writing to a friend. The letter, however, rises above the purely human level. The writer is a friend, to be sure, but also an apostle of Christ Jesus.

Now in the broadest sense an *apostle* (ἀπόστολος a term derived from a verb which means *to send, to send away on a commission, to dispatch*: ἀποστέλλω) is any*thing* which is sent or by which something is sent, or any*one* who is sent or by whom a message is sent. Thus, in classical Greek the term could refer to a naval expedition, and "an apostolic boat" was a cargo-vessel. In later Judaism "apostles" were envoys sent out by the Jerusalem patriarchate to collect tribute from the Jews of the Dispersion. In the New Testament the term takes on a distinctly religious sense. In its widest meaning it refers to any gospel-messenger, anyone who is sent on a spiritual mission, anyone who in that capacity represents his Sender and brings the message of salvation. Thus used, Barnabas, Epaphroditus, Apollos, Silvanus, and Timothy are all called "apostles" (Acts 14:14; I Cor. 4:6, 9; Phil. 2:25; I Thess. 2:6, cf. 1:1; and see also I Cor. 15:7). They represent God's cause, though in doing so they may also represent certain definite churches whose "apostles" they are called (cf. II Cor. 8:23). Thus Paul and Barnabas represent the church of Antioch (Acts 13:1, 2), and Epaphroditus is Philippi's "apostle" (Phil. 2:25). Under this broader connotation some would include also Andronicus, Junius (Rom. 16:7), and James, the Lord's brother (Gal. 1:19), but the exact meaning of the passages in which, together with the term "apostles," these men are mentioned is disputed.

But in determining the meaning of the term "apostle" here in I Tim. 1:1 it will be far better to study those passages in which it is used in its more usual sense. Occurring ten times in the Gospels, almost thirty times in Acts, more than thirty times in the Pauline epistles (including the five occurrences in the Pastorals), and eight times in the rest of the New Testament, it generally (but note important exception in Heb. 3:1 and the exceptions already indicated) refers to the Twelve and Paul.

In that fullest, deepest sense a man is an apostle *for life* and *wherever he goes*. He is clothed with *the authority of* the One who sent him, and that authority concerns both *doctrine and life*. The idea, found in much present-day religious literature, according to which an apostle has no real office, no authority, lacks scriptural support. Anyone can see this for himself by studying such passages as Matt. 16:19; 18:18; 28:18, 19 (note the connection!); John 20:23; I Cor. 5:3-5; II Cor. 10:8; I Thess. 2:6.

Paul, then, was an apostle in the richest sense of the term. His apostleship was the same as that of the Twelve. Hence, we speak of "the Twelve and Paul." Paul even stresses the fact that the risen Savior had appeared to *him* just as truly as he had appeared to Cephas (I Cor. 15:5, 8). That same Savior had assigned to him a task so broad and universal that his entire life was henceforth to be occupied with it (Acts 26:16-18).

Yet Paul was definitely *not* one of the Twelve. The idea that the disciples had made a mistake when they had chosen Matthias to take the place of Judas, and that the Holy Spirit later designated Paul as the real substitute, hardly merits consideration (see Acts 1:24). *But if he was not one of the Twelve yet was invested with the same office, what was the relation between him and the Twelve?* The answer is probably suggested by Acts 1:8 and Gal. 2:7-9. On the basis of these passages this answer can be formulated thus: The Twelve, by recognizing Paul as having been specially called to minister to the Gentiles, were in effect carrying out through him their calling to the Gentiles.

The characteristics of full apostleship — the apostleship of the Twelve and Paul — were as follows:

In the first place, the apostles have been chosen, called, and sent forth by Christ himself. They have received their commission directly from him (John 6:70; 13:18; 15:16, 19; Gal. 1:6).

Secondly, they are qualified for their tasks by Jesus, and have been ear-

and-eye witnesses of his words and deeds; specifically, they are the witnesses of his resurrection (Acts 1:8, 22; I Cor. 9:1; 15:8; Gal. 1:12; Eph. 3:2-8; I John 1:1-3).

Thirdly, they have been endowed in a special measure with the Holy Spirit, and it is this Holy Spirit who leads them into all the truth (Matt. 10:20; John 14:26; 15:26; 16:7-14; 20:22; I Cor. 2:10-13; 7:40; I Thess. 4:8).

Fourthly, God blesses their work, confirming its value by means of signs and miracles, and giving them much fruit upon their labors (Matt. 10:1, 8; Acts 2:43; 3:2; 5:12-16; Rom. 15:18, 19; II Cor. 12:12; I Cor. 9:2; Gal. 2:8).

Fifthly, their office is not restricted to a local church, neither does it extend over a short period of time; on the contrary, it is for the entire church and for life (Acts 26:16-18; II Tim. 4:7, 8).

Now Paul is here called an apostle *of Christ Jesus*.[19] He belongs to Christ, is sent and commissioned by him, and has accordingly received his authority from him. It is, in the final analysis, Christ himself who binds and makes loose. It is he who is operating in Paul. Paul's message is Christ's message. Paul's authority is Christ's delegated authority.

The personal name *Jesus,* meaning either "he will certainly save" (cf. Matt. 1:21), or "Jehovah is salvation," is preceded by the official designation *Christ* (Anointed), showing that this Person to whom Paul owes his apostleship was *ordained* and *qualified* by God to carry out the task of providing salvation for his people, a salvation which Paul, as apostle, takes joy in

---

[19] The question is asked, "Why Christ Jesus" instead of "Jesus Christ"? It is probably correct to say that no special significance attaches to the exact order in which these two names occur. It would seem that in the New Testament there are about 127 instances in which the order is "Jesus Christ," and about 91 cases in which it is "Christ Jesus." In Paul's epistles the order "Christ Jesus," though not so prominent at first, gradually takes over, so that in the end the order "Jesus Christ" becomes the exception and "Christ Jesus" the rule. In the earlier epistles (Galatians, I Thessalonians, II Thessalonians; I Corinthians, II Corinthians, and Romans) the figures are (or are approximately): 32 instances of "Christ Jesus" to 54 instances of "Jesus Christ." In the epistles of the first Roman imprisonment — Ephesians, Colossians, Philemon, and Philippians — they are: 31 "Christ Jesus" to 13 "Jesus Christ." In the last-written epistles, the Pastorals: 25 "Christ Jesus" to only 5 "Jesus Christ." To account for this phenomenon it has been suggested that at first the Aramaic "Jesus, the Christ" was rendered into the Greek rather literally, supplying the order in which the proper name Jesus is followed by the appelative Christ, indicating his office. After a while the term Christ began to be felt increasingly as a second proper name next to Jesus. Being now on a par with the name Jesus, the flexible character of the Greek language made it possible to reverse the order; hence, "Christ Jesus" or "Jesus Christ," with no difference in meaning. See on the entire subject S. Vernon McCasland, "Christ Jesus," *JBL* 65 (December, 1946), 377-383. We would add that to the early church the designation "Christ" was never a "mere" name, meaningless as so often among us. Whenever it was pronounced, his followers thought of him as the Anointed. One might compare the name "Christ Jesus" to the somewhat similar one "President Eisenhower." In both cases the designation of office is followed by the personal name.

proclaiming. (Further details on the meaning of "Jesus" and "Christ" are found in N.T.C. on I Thess. 1:1.)

No usurper was Paul. Had he not been appointed to be an apostle, he would never have been one. But he had been *appointed,* and this appointment had come not from men but directly from God. It is for this reason that he calls himself an apostle of Christ Jesus **by order of God our Savior and Christ Jesus our Hope.** It was God in Christ who had separated him from his mother's womb and through his grace had called him (Gal. 1:15); had chosen him in order that he might make known God's name before the Gentiles and kings and children of Israel (Acts 9:15); and had sent him to distant nations (Acts 22:21).

Paul says, "*God* our Savior" here, also in I Tim. 2:3; 4:10; Titus 1:3; 2:10; 3:4; but elsewhere he uses "Savior" with reference to "Christ" (Eph. 5:23; Phil. 3:20; II Tim. 1:10; Titus 1:4; 2:13; 3:6). Yet the expression "*God* our Savior" in the Pastorals but nowhere in the earlier epistles does not mean that Paul cannot have written the Pastorals. In fact, that line of reasoning, were it valid, would mean that an unknown author wrote I Timothy (here the Savior is *God*); that Paul wrote II Timothy (here the Savior is *Christ*); and would leave Titus a question-mark (here the Savior is both *God* and *Christ*).

The fact that here in the Pastorals the name Savior is frequently applied to God is, after all, not at all surprising, for even in his earlier epistles Paul frequently ascribes the work of *saving* man to "God"; for example, "It was *God's* good-pleasure through the foolishness of the preaching *to save* those who believe" (I Cor. 1:21); "but God . . . made us alive together with Christ . . . for by grace have y o u been *saved* through faith; and that not of yourselves, it is *the gift of God*" (Eph. 2:4, 5, 8); "y o u r *salvation,* and that *from God*" (Phil. 1:28). To "God" he also ascribes the distinct acts in the program of salvation. It is God who spared not his Son but delivered him up for us all. It is God who sets forth his Son as a propitiation for our sins. It is he who commends his love toward us. It is God who blesses us with every spiritual blessing in the heavenly places in Christ. Foreknowledge, foreordination, calling, justification, glorification are all ascribed to *him.* It is *he* who chose us. It is *he* who causes the gospel to be proclaimed. It is *he* who bestows his grace upon us. Faith is *his* gift (Rom. 1:16; 3:24-26; 4:17; 5:8, 15; 8:3, 4, 11, 28-30, 31-33; 9:10, 11; 15:5, 13; I Cor. 1:9, 26-31; 15:57; II Cor. 2:14; 4:7; 5:5, 8, 19, 20, 21; 9:15; Gal. 1:15; 3:26; 4:4-7; Eph. 1:3-5; 2:4, 5; Phil. 2:13; 3:9; Col. 3:3). In view of all this we can almost say that it would have been strange if somewhere in his epistles the apostle would not have called *God* "our Savior." [20] Calling God "our Savior" is

---

[20] See the more detailed discussion of the concept Soter (Savior, Deliverer, Preserver) in connection with I Tim. 4:10.

entirely proper. And since for Paul God ever saves *through Christ,* verse 1 is also a fitting prelude to verse 15: "Christ Jesus came into the world sinners to save."

Amid circumstances which to man might seem *hopeless* Christ Jesus is pictured as "our Hope," that is, the very foundation for our earnest yearning, our confident expectation, and our patient waiting for the manifestation of salvation in all its fulness (cf. 1:16; 6:14-16, 19). It is he who made this hope possible and actual. It is he who revitalizes it from day to day. The Source as well as the Object of this hope is he (cf. Acts 28:20; Col. 1:27).

2. To Timothy (my) genuine child in faith.

Apostolic authority and tender love are beautifully blended, for the apostle of Christ Jesus calls the addressee "Timothy (my) genuine child in faith." Though some commentators write at great length in order to prove that the omission of the possessive *my* in the original indicates that Paul was thinking of Timothy not as *his* child but as *God's* child, the effort must be considered futile. The omission of the possessive in such a case is not at all unusual; and II Tim. 2:1, where it does occur, surely indicates that here in I Tim. 1:2 and elsewhere (see verse 18; also II Tim. 1:2) it is implied. Timothy was Paul's *child* (Greek τέκνον from τίκτω to beget, bring forth), because it was to the apostle as a means in God's hand, that he owed his spiritual life (cf. I Cor. 4:15; Gal. 4:19). The great change in Timothy's life had taken place on Paul's first missionary journey, as has been explained on p. 34. If we are careful to stress the fact that Paul was Timothy's father in a secondary sense only, the apostle functioning as God's instrument, so that God himself remains the *real* Father, we shall have no difficulty with other passages of Scripture, such as "And call no one on earth y o u r Father: for One is y o u r heavenly Father" (Matt. 23:9; and cf. John 1:13; I John 3:9). It is exactly as Calvin has pointed out: though God — he *alone!* — is the Father of all believers because he has regenerated them by his Word and Spirit and because no one but himself bestows faith, yet his ministers have a subordinate right to this title.[21]

The designation "child" was a very happy one, for it combined two ideas: "I have begotten you," and "you are very dear to me." Timothy was,

---

[21] Sed qui conveniet hoc cum sententia Christi: Nolite vobis patrem vocare in terra (Matt. 23:9)? . . . Respondeo, Paulum ita sibi usurpare nomen patris, ut Deo nullam honoris sui particulam abroget aut minuat. . . . Unicus in fide pater omnium est Deus, quia omnes verbo suo et spiritus sui virtute regenerat: quia solus est qui fidem confert. Sed quibus ad eam rem dignatur uti ministris, eos in honoris sui communicationem etiam admittit, nihil tamen sibi derogando. Erat ergo Deus spiritualis Timothei pater: et quidem solus, proprie loquendo. Sed Paulus, qui minister fuerat Dei in gignendo Timotheo, quasi subalterno iure titulum sibi vindicat (John Calvin).

moreover, a *genuine* child, not a bastard son, not a merely nominal believer. Timothy was no Demas! See on II Tim. 4:10. Not, of course, in the physical sense but *with respect to,* or *in the sphere of,*[22] *faith* the apostle had begotten Timothy. It is probably best to take *faith* here in the subjective sense, a true knowledge of God and of his promises and a hearty confidence in him and in his only-begotten Son. This corresponds with such phrases as "... if they continue in faith and love" (I Tim. 2:15); "in love, in faith, in purity" (I Tim. 4:12); "Hold the pattern of sound words which thou hast heard from me in faith and love which is in Christ Jesus" (II Tim. 1:13).

Upon his genuine child in the sphere of faith the apostle now pronounces **grace, mercy, peace from God the Father and Christ Jesus our Lord.** *Grace* is God's unmerited favor in operation in the heart of his child, and *peace* is that child's consciousness of having been reconciled with God through Christ. *Grace* is the fountain, and *peace* is the stream which issues from this fountain (cf. Rom. 5:1). This grace and this peace have their origin in God the Father, and have been merited for the believer by Christ Jesus, their Lord. (All this has been treated much more fully in N.T.C. on I Thess. 1:1. Hence, both for the nature of the salutation and for the meaning of the concepts "grace" and "peace" and of the divine names I refer to what is given there.)

In one important respect this salutation differs from others. Nowhere except in his letters to Timothy does Paul in his salutations use the *three* substantives: grace, mercy, and peace. This triad is, however, also employed by John in one of his salutations (II John 3; cf. Jude 2: "mercy, peace, and love").

When the question is asked, Why did Paul insert *"mercy"* between "grace" and "peace" the probable answer is:

a. The term "mercy" is very fitting in this context, in which Paul has just shown his *affectionate interest* in Timothy, calling him "(my) genuine child." The very essence of "mercy" is *warm affection* which includes but must not be restricted to *tender compassion.*

b. Timothy was in a difficult situation. He faced problems which were all the more trying for a man of his disposition. Hence, God's *tender love toward those in need* was definitely required.

All this will become even clearer when the concept "mercy" is given further study. Paul uses this word ten times: five times outside the Pas-

---

[22] The phrase "in faith" in the sense of "in the sphere of faith" is not un-Pauline, and does not prove that Paul cannot have written the Pastorals. It occurs *with* the article in I Cor. 16:13 and II Cor. 13:5; *without* the article in Gal. 2:20. It *is* true that it is found with greater frequency in the Pastorals (I Tim. 1:2, 4; 2:7, 15; 3:13; 4:12; II Tim. 1:13; Titus 1:13; 3:15; and in connection with I Tim. 2:15 cf. Acts 14:22).

torals (Rom. 9:23; 11:31; 15:9; Gal. 6:16; and Eph. 2:4), and five times in the Pastorals (I Tim. 1:2; II Tim. 1:2, 16, 18; Titus 3:5).

The usual way of distinguishing between *grace* and *mercy* is to say that grace pardons while mercy commiserates; grace is God's love toward the guilty, mercy his love toward the wretched or pitiable; grace concerns the state, mercy the condition. To a considerable extent this distinction is correct. The term "mercy" frequently occurs in a context of extending help to those in misery. It is the word that is used in the parable of The Good Samaritan (Luke 10:37; cf. 10:33). There it describes what that noble character did for the man who had fallen among robbers, had been stripped and wounded and was left lying by the road-side half dead. Similarly the Lord says in Is. 54:7, "With great mercies will I gather thee," where "mercies" (LXX ἔλεος) translates the Hebrew raḥamîm: tender feeling, motherly kindness, compassion, pity (here plural). So also when from among the mass of mankind viewed as fallen and in a condition of misery God chooses some, these are called "vessels of mercy" (Rom. 9:23; cf. 11:31).

Nevertheless, the word employed in the original (ἔλεος) is often somewhat broader in scope. It indicates not only the actual outpouring of *pity* upon those *in distress* but also the underlying lovingkindness of which God's creatures, particularly his people, are the objects, regardless of whether in the given context they are viewed as being "in deep misery" or more generally "in need of help." In the latter case the person concerned is usually viewed as God's child, dependent in all things on the heavenly Father, who cherishes toward him a feeling of *tender affection* and is *ever ready to help* him. Timothy, upon whom mercy "drops as a gentle rain from heaven," furnishes an excellent example of the use of the term in this somewhat broader sense.[23] The salutation, accordingly, assures him not only of pardoning grace, operating as a spiritual dynamic in his life, but also of the closely related divine *lovingkindness* in his present difficulties and in every situation of life. When this *grace* and this *mercy* or *kindness*

---

[23] In the Old Testament, which forms the basis of Paul's use of terms, this broader connotation is illustrated in such passages as the following, in each of which the Septuagint has ἔλεος as a translation for the Hebrew ḥeṣedh:
"Jehovah showed *kindness* to him (Joseph)" (Gen. 39:21).
". . . showing *lovingkindness* to thousands of them that love me" (Ex. 20:6; cf. Deut. 5:10).
"But my *lovingkindness* shall not depart from him (David)" (II Sam. 7:15).
". . . who keeps *covenant and lovingkindness*" (Neh. 1:5 = LXX II Esdras 11:5).
(Note close connection between God's convenant and his lovingkindness!)
See further various passages in the Psalms, such as those which in our English versions are found in Ps. 5:7; 36:5, 7, etc.
The term God's "mercy," accordingly, may be translated either *kindness, lovingkindness* (cf. German Herzensgüte, Huld; Dutch "goedertierenheid") or *compassion, pity* (cf. German Barmherzigkeit; Dutch "barmhartigheid"). It all depends upon the specific context in which the word is used. The two meanings, moreover, blend into each other as do the colors of the rainbow.

are present, *peace* naturally follows. That which was broken and severed by sin is made whole and bound up by grace. The resulting sense of *wholeness, tranquility,* and *assurance* is *peace*. (By some the Greek word for *peace* — εἰρήνη — is traced to a verb which means *to bind* or *join;* cf. Latin *sero;* English *series*.)

3 As I urged you when I was on my way to Macedonia, do stay on at Ephesus,[24] in order that you may charge certain individuals not to teach differently, 4 nor to devote themselves to endless myths and genealogies which foster disputes rather than faith-centered stewardship required by God; 5 whereas the purpose of the charge is love (which springs) from a pure heart and a conscience good and a faith without hypocrisy; 6 from which objectives certain individuals, having wandered away, have turned aside to futile talk, 7 yearning to be law-teachers, although they understand neither the words which they are speaking nor the themes on which they are harping with such confidence. 8 Now we know that excellent is the law if one makes a lawful use of it, 9 bearing this in mind, that not for a righteous man is law enacted, but for lawless and insubordinate, for impious and sinful, for unholy and profane men, for murderers of fathers and murderers of mothers, for those who kill their fellows, 10 for immoral men, sodomites, kidnapers, liars, false swearers, and for whatever else is contrary to the sound doctrine, 11 (which is) in harmony with the glorious gospel of the blessed God, (the gospel) with which I have been entrusted.

1:3-11

3. As I urged you when I was on my way to Macedonia, do stay on at Ephesus.

Writing, then, to his trusted friend, Paul gives immediate expression to what he considers the most pressing necessity, namely, that Timothy by all means stay on duty at Ephesus in order to continue the battle for the truth. It is hardly necessary to point out that the apostle was not interested in Timothy's mere *staying* in Ephesus, but in his remaining there *in order to* straighten out what was wrong.

It should be noted that Paul urges Timothy *to stay on* at Ephesus. This is the stronger way of expressing it (stronger than *to stay*) and probably also implies that the two had been together at Ephesus.[25]

[24] Or: "I urge you now, as I did when I was traveling to Macedonia, to stay on at Ephesus, in order" etc. Cf. the Swedish: "Jag bjuder dig, nu sasom när jag for astad till Macedonien, att stanna kvar i Efesus, och där . . ." (Bibeln eller Den Heliga Skrift, Konungen 1917, edition Stockholm, 1946).

[25] Although the construction of the sentence is not easy, the most natural explanations yield the same resultant meaning. Whether we read the sentence as an anacoluthon, "As I urged you when I was on my way to Macedonia to stay on at Ephesus, in order," etc., with "so do I now" (or "so do") understood; or whether *the infinitive* "to stay on" be immediately interpreted as *an imperative;* or, finally, whether *the very act of writing* be itself considered a substitute for the "omitted"

"Timothy," says Paul, "you must stay on in Ephesus," and with this purpose: **in order that you may charge certain individuals not to teach differently.**

"Certain individuals," says Paul. Does he purposely omit their names from a desire *to spare them?* The fact that he definitely mentions names in verse 20 but not here in verse 3, has led to the opinion that these "certain individuals" of verse 3 do not include men as far advanced in error as were Hymenaeus and Alexander. And it is, indeed, true that the apostle was a very tactful person, and may have expressed himself thus indefinitely for the reason given by these interpreters. (One might compare II Thess. 3:11, 15, where the "busybodies" with respect to whom Paul expresses the wish that they be treated as "brothers" are referred to in a similar indefinite manner; see N.T.C. on that passage.) Nevertheless, the argument in favor of excluding Hymenaeus and Alexander is hardly conclusive. *By reading on and on* — an exegetical rule to which reference is made repeatedly in the present set of commentaries — one rather arrives at the conclusion that the expression "certain individuals" here in verse 3 is broad enough and strong enough to include even the men mentioned in verse 20. For, it should be noted that what is said in verses 6 and 7 about these "certain individuals" of verse 3 is by no means mild: "yearning to be law-teachers, although they understand neither the words which they are speaking nor the themes on which they are harping with so much confidence." Moreover, in verse 19 the apostle is *still* (or *again*) speaking about "certain individuals." He continues, "of whom are Hymenaeus and Alexander" (verse 20). It is natural to believe that the "certain individuals" of verse 3 and the "certain individuals" of verse 19 are the same people, and that of this group Hymenaeus and Alexander are the worst representatives, the ring-leaders. On this supposition, the indefinite reference (both in verse 4 and in verse 19) is probably due to one or more of the following reasons:

a. The group includes not only some who must be named but also several who need not be named as yet, the milder cases.

b. Timothy, living right among these people in Ephesus, is naturally better able than is Paul (in Macedonia) to tell who belongs to the group and who does not.

c. The group is not large; hence, "certain individuals" or simply "some," not "many."

d. Those who belong to the group are not as important as they think they are. They are not "big shots" but merely "certain individuals." This explanation tallies with what the apostle says about them in verse 7.

---

words, there is no substantial difference in sense: Paul, alarmed by the encroachment and influence of dangerous doctrines, once more impresses upon Timothy the idea that this surely is not the time for him to leave Ephesus!

Now though these "certain individuals" yearn to be *"law*-teachers" (verse 7), in reality they are nothing but *novelty*-teachers. They are teaching *differently*, that is, they are teaching "something different" or translated somewhat freely, "different doctrine." (cf. I Tim. 6:3; also Ignatius, *To Polycarp* III.) One is immediately reminded of Paul's stern message to the Galatians:

"I am astonished that so quickly y o u are changing over from the One who called y o u in the grace of Christ, to *a different* — which is not an *other* — gospel" (Gal. 1:6, 7).

Some people are ever anxious to welcome whatever is *new* or *different*. Like the Athenians of old "they devote their leisure-time to nothing else than telling or hearing something new" (Acts 17:21). They like to pit their strength against whatever is by them considered to be fuddy-duddy. One finds this tendency at times on the college or seminary campus, where some immature minds, having hardly begun a systematic study of the old and established, loudly acclaim the new about which they know nothing. Quite generally what they consider "new" is old heresy in a new dress. To strike the proper balance between being on the alert for any new discovery by which knowledge is really advanced, and being eager to preserve all that is good in the old, requires much grace. The errorists at Ephesus lacked this sense of careful scrutiny and cautious reflection.

For such people, then, Paul has a *message* which Timothy is urged to *pass along* to them (note the verb παραγγέλλω). He must *charge* or *command* them to desist.

4. Not only must they desist from wrong *teaching* but also from wrong *thinking*, for the former is the result of the latter. The individuals in question were occupying their minds with a dangerous fad. Hence Paul continues: **Nor to devote themselves to endless myths and genealogies.** That was the trouble! These would-be law-doctors were engaged in the business of *turning* (their minds) *to* (from προσέχω with νοῦν implied) "myths and genealogies."

The expression "myths and genealogies" is *one*. It must not be divided, as if Paul were thinking, on the one hand, of myths, and on the other, of genealogies. The apostle refers undoubtedly to man-made supplements to the law of God (see verse 7), mere myths or fables (II Tim. 4:4), old wives' tales (I Tim. 4:7) that were definitely Jewish in character (Titus 1:14). Measured by the standard of *truth*, what these errorists taught deserved the name *myths*. As to *material contents* these myths concern *genealogical narratives* that were largely *fictitious*.

We feel at once that here we have been introduced into the realm of typically *Jewish* lore. It is a known fact that from early times the rabbis would "spin their yarns" — and *endless* yarns they were! — on the basis of what they considered some "hint" supplied by the Old Testament. They would take a name from a list of pedigrees (for example, From Genesis, I Chronicles, Ezra, Nehemiah), and expand it into a nice story. Such interminable embroideries on the inspired record were part of the regular bill of fare in the synagogue, and were subsequently deposited in written form in that portion of *The Talmud* which is known as *Haggadah*.

The Book of Jubilees (also called *The Little Genesis*) offers another striking example of what Paul had in mind. It is a kind of *haggadic* commentary on the canonical Genesis; that is, it is an exposition interspersed with an abundant supply of illustrative anecdotes. The book was probably written toward the close of the second or at the beginning of the first century B. C. It covers the entire era from the creation until the entrance into Canaan. This long stretch is divided into fifty jubilee-periods of forty-nine (7×7) years each. In fact, the entire chronology is based on the number 7, and heavenly authority is claimed for this arrangement. Thus not only does the week have 7 days, the month 4×7 days, but even the year has $52 \times 7 = 364$ days, the year-week has 7 years, and the jubilee has $7 \times 7 = 49$ years. The separate events regarding the patriarchs, etc., are pin-pointed in accordance with this scheme. The sacred narrative of our canonical book of Genesis is embellished, at times almost beyond recognition. Thus, we now learn that the sabbath was observed already by the arch-angels, that the angels also practised circumcision, that Jacob never tricked anybody, etc.

In every age there are people who love to indulge in such strange mixtures of truth and error. They even treat these adulterations as being the all-important thing. They carry on lengthy debates about dates and definitions. Instead of brushing aside all such syncretistic rubbish, they discover fine distinctions and engage in hairsplitting disputes. They pile myth upon myth, fable upon fable, and *the end* is never in sight. Thus the law of God is made void by human tradition (cf. Matt. 15:6), and the picture drawn in the sacred original becomes grossly distorted.

In our own day the same error occurs, and in many different forms. Instead of studying the infallible Word, some resort to all kinds of millennial fancies, or prefer to see on a screen an unscriptural embellishment of the story of Joseph, with special emphasis, of course, on that famous incident in connection with Potiphar's wife; or an equally unscriptural supplement to the story of Samson, with exaggerated stress, naturally, on his Delilah.

Now there is, indeed, a legitimate place for the exercise of the gift of the imagination. There is room for dramatization, yes even for fables and fairy-tales. Grown-ups as well as children can enjoy Hans Andersen's "Fir Tree" and can take its lesson to heart. But one who begins to mix sacred history with fiction and this for the purpose of theatrical effect, gross enjoyment, intoxicating thrill, or the satisfaction of vain curiosity, tampers with the very essence and purpose of the inspired record. God's law was not given in order that those who arrogate to themselves the name "law-teachers" might "shine" in the eyes of the public, or in order that the public itself might be "entertained" with endless myths and fictitious genealogical histories **which foster disputes rather than faith-centered stewardship required by God** (literally, "the stewardship of God, the one in faith").

It has been correctly observed that a person's teaching should be judged by its fruits. Whatever fails to promote stewardship should be rejected, even though it have no other fault. And everything which arouses nothing but disputes deserves double condemnation.[26]

The true objective of every leader and gospel-teacher, the aim and goal of all his striving, should be "faith-centered stewardship required by God." This stewardship [27] is *the care* which the Lord has ordained with respect to the house or household of God, the wise *administration and distribution* of the gospel-mysteries unto the edification of the church. The term *stewardship* is undoubtedly used here in the same sense as in I Cor. 9:17: "I have a stewardship entrusted to me." See also Titus 1:7, where the overseer is called God's steward; and I Cor. 4:1, 2 where the apostle refers to himself and his associates as "stewards of the mysteries of God," and states that the chief qualification of a steward is that he be faithful.

The New Testament passages in which the term *stewardship* occurs are Luke 16:2-4; I Cor. 9:17; Eph. 1:10; 3:2, 9; Col. 1:25 and I Tim. 1:4 (the passage now under discussion). The term seems to refer to the office with which the steward has been entrusted and/or to the active administration of affairs by the one who holds that office. A "steward" (οἰκονόμος) is literally the manager of a household or of an estate (Luke 12:42; 16:1, 3, 8; I Cor. 4:2; Gal. 4:2). The figurative meaning usually shines through, however. In the highest sense of the term, the steward is an administrator of spiritual treasures (I Cor. 4:1; Titus 1:7).[28]

5. Now such a divinely ordained stewardship, a stewardship that originates in God and is, accordingly, required by him, centers in the active

---

[26] Says John Calvin similarly, *op. cit.* p. 252: Aestimat a fructu doctrinam. Quaecunque enim non aedificat, repudianda est, etiamsi nihil aliud habeat vitii: quaecunque vero ad concertiones solum excitandas valet, duplici damnanda est.

[27] The best reading has οἰκονομίαν (stewardship), not οἰκοδομήν (building up, edifying).

[28] Uses of the term that require special comment are the following:
a. In Rom. 16:23 the οἰκονόμος is a *treasurer,* which meaning of the term finds abundant support in extra-canonical Koine literature (see M.M., p. 443).
b. In I Peter 4:10 the metaphorical meaning is broadened and applied to believers generally.
c. In Eph. 1:10 and related passages the meaning of the term is disputed. The sense "dispensation" when that term is defined as "*a period of time* during which a particular divine arrangement of things is operative" is debatable.

exercise of *faith,* whose fruits it seeks to multiply. Hence, its goal is *love* rather than a vain show of speculative *learning.* So Paul continues: **whereas the purpose of the charge is love.** Timothy had been urged to deliver a *charge* to the church at Ephesus, *to pass along a message* which had special reference to "certain individuals" (see on verse 3). This charge, we may be sure, was not strictly limited to negative injunctions, such as, "*Do not* teach that which differs from the sound gospel, and *do not* waste y o u r time on genealogical fables and fancies." The negative naturally implied the positive: "*Do* bear witness to the sound gospel, and *do* exercise living faith in the Lord Jesus Christ, a faith which operates by means of love." Thus viewed, this charge is in reality the sum and substance of *all* Christian admonition, specifically of all admonitory preaching. *Love* is the fulfilment of the law (*both* tables, Mark 12:30, 31) as well as the essence of the gospel. Hence, what is stated in the present passage is in exact harmony with that other great saying of Paul, "For in Christ Jesus neither circumcision nor uncircumcision has any validity, but faith working through love" (Gal. 5:6). Note also the emphasis on love in such other passages in I Timothy as 1:14; 2:15; 4:12; 6:11.

This love may be described as a personal delight in God, a grateful outgoing of the entire personality to him, a deep yearning for the prosperity of his redeemed, and an earnest desire for the temporal and eternal welfare of his creatures. Far better, however, is Paul's own description of its meaning in I Cor. 13.

Now not everything that is called love *is* really love. Hence, the apostle specifies that he is thinking of love which springs **from a pure heart, and a conscience good, and a faith without hypocrisy.**

When a sinner is drawn to Christ, *the heart* is first of all regenerated. The result is that the man's *conscience* begins to plague him in such a manner that, having come under conviction, he is happy to embrace the Redeemer by means of a conscious, living *faith.* Hence, the sequence *heart, conscience, faith* is entirely natural. Moreover, it is clearly evident why the apostle states that these three — and in that order — *give rise to love.* When the God *of love* (love is his very name, I John 4:8) implants his own new life in man's *heart,* the latter naturally becomes a *loving* heart. A *conscience* cleared of guilt and made obedient to God's law will begin to approve only such thoughts, words, and deeds, past or contemplated, which are in harmony with the one, summarizing aim of that law, namely, *love.* And genuine *faith,* which embraces Christ and all his benefits, will result in genuine *love* for the Benefactor and for all those who are embraced in his love. — Hence, Paul speaks of "love *from* (or "out of") a pure heart, and a conscience good, and a faith without hypocrisy."

The heart is the fulcrum of feeling and faith as well as the mainspring of words and actions (Rom. 10:10; cf. Matt. 12:34; 15:19; 22:37; and see

1:5   **I TIMOTHY**

N.T.C. on John 14:1). It is the core and center of man's being, man's inmost self. "Out of it are the issues of life" (Prov. 4:23). "Man looks on the outward appearance, but Jehovah looks on the heart" (I Sam. 16:7). Now the purpose of the gospel-charge is love out of a *pure* heart. The heart is *pure* when it experiences the cleansing work of the Holy Spirit (Ps. 51:10, 11). When this happens, fervent love begins to rise to the surface (I Peter 1:22).

Conscience is man's moral intuition, his moral self in the act of passing judgment upon his own state, emotions, and thoughts, also upon his own words and actions whether these be viewed as past, present, or future.[29] It is both positive and negative. It both approves and condemns (Rom. 2:14, 15).

The word used in the original and in (closely or remotely) related languages has the same meaning when analyzed etymologically. It means *knowledge along with, joint-knowledge,* or *co-knowledge:* Greek συνείδησις, Latin *con-scientia,* English (from Latin) *con-science,* Swedish *sam-vete,* Danish *Sam-vittighed.* But how must this *co-knowledge* be interpreted? Some say, "It is man's knowledge along with God's knowledge, man's own inner voice in the act of repeating God's voice, his own judgment endorsing God's judgment, his own spirit bearing witness with God's spirit." Others reason somewhat as follows, "It is man's *moral* self echoing his *cognitive* self."

This difference of opinion is not very important, just so it is borne in mind that whatever be the true story of the manner in which *the term* originated, its *meaning,* according to Scripture, is by no means obscure. The fact that "con-science is the response of man's moral consciousness to the divine revelation concerning himself, his attitudes, and his activities" cannot be doubted (see Rom. 2:14, 15).

It is *in the believer* that conscience attains its highest goal. For the regenerated individual *God's will,* as expressed in his Word, becomes "the Lord of conscience, its Guide and Director" (I Peter 2:19). The "conscience *good*" of which the apostle speaks here in I Tim. 1:5 is more than merely a *"clear* conscience." Rather, it is the conscience which:

a. is guided by God's special revelation as its norm;

b. pronounces judgments that are accepted, and issues directives that are obeyed;

c. produces "godly sorrow which works repentance unto salvation" (II Cor. 7:10), a salvation by means of which "the love of God is spread abroad

---

[29] Though *the term conscience* does not occur in the Old Testament, *the idea* certainly is found there (Gen. 3:7, 10; 39:9; I Sam. 24:17; 26:21; II Sam. 24:10; Job 42:5, 6; Is. 6:5; Dan. 9:19). In the New Testament the word occurs twice in Acts (23:1; 24:16); five times in Hebrews (9:9; 9:14; 10:2; 10:22; 13:18); three times in I Peter (2:19; 3:16; 3:21); and at least twenty times in Paul's writings. In the Pastorals it is found in I Tim. 1:5, 19; 3:9; 4:2; II Tim. 1:3; Titus 1:15).

in our hearts through the Holy Spirit" (Rom. 5:5). And God's love evokes the response of love.

The positive aspect of a really "good" conscience is *faith,* for a good conscience not only abhors the wrong but embraces the right. *Such* faith is true and genuine. It is not mere play-acting, "a vile conceit in pompous words expressed," a mere *mask,* like the one which an actor puts on and *under* which he hides his real self. Was Paul contrasting living faith with the "faith"(?) of the ring-leaders among the errorists? However that may be, the *faith* which he has in mind is "a *true* knowledge of God and of his promises revealed to us in the gospel, and a *hearty* confidence that all my sins are forgiven me for Christ's sake" (Compendium to the Heidelberg Catechism, answer 19). Such faith results in love.

The substance, accordingly, of verse 5 is this: the essence of the charge given to you, Timothy, which you by public preaching and private admonition must convey to the Ephesians is, "Pray and strive daily to obtain a pure heart, a conscience good, and a faith without hypocrisy, in order that these three, working together in organic co-operation, may produce that most precious of all jewels, *love.*"

6. Now whenever this chief aim of all preaching and of the entire work of the Christian ministry is lost sight of, sad results follow, as the apostle points out when he continues: **from which objectives certain individuals, having wandered away, have turned aside to futile talk.**

These "certain individuals" are the people to whom reference was made in verse 3 (see on that passage). They are said to have *wandered away* or *deviated* (see also on I Tim. 6:21 and on II Tim. 2:18) from their proper objectives: the pure heart, the conscience good, and the faith without hypocrisy. Naturally, they also missed the true *destination,* the final goal, namely *love.* They are like marksmen who miss their target, like travelers who never reach their destination because they have taken the wrong turn and have failed to look for the familiar signs along the road. The path which these people have taken is not even a detour. It is more like a dead-end street beyond which lies a swamp, in their case the swamp of "futile talk," useless reasoning, argumentation that gets nowhere (cf. Titus 1:10), dry as dust disputation, a wrangling about fanciful tales anent pedigrees! Yes, their vaunted learning has finally landed them in the no-man's land of ceremonious subtleties, in the dreary marsh of ridiculous hair-splitting. And the owner of that quagmire is . . . Satan, who heads the welcoming-committee (I Tim. 5:15).

7. And why have these men *turned aside* to futile talk? Because they want to shine! Says Paul: **yearning to be law-teachers.** Now in itself the desire to be a teacher of the Old Testament, particularly the law of Moses, is not bad. But the trouble with these men is that they desire to reach this goal

1:7 I TIMOTHY

although they understand neither the words (or things) which they are speaking nor the themes (or subjects) on which they are harping with such confidence (or on which they lay so much stress).

With relish these would-be law-doctors flourished their highfaluting words, their ponderous phrases. But all this was pure bombast, rant and cant. Whenever they would hear a jaw-breaker, they would be sure to commit it to memory and to use it in spinning their tedious tales; but they themselves did not know the meaning of the latest addition to their vocabulary. Worse even, they failed to understand the very subjects on which they lectured with such cock-sureness (cf. Titus 3:8).

8. However, lest anyone should think that Paul under-estimates daily teaching and study of the law, he adds: **Now we know that excellent is the law if one makes a lawful use of it.** The best comment on this is Rom. 7:7, 12, "What then shall we say? 'The law is sin?' Of course not! In fact, sin I would not have recognized except through the law; for instance, covetousness I would not have known had not the law said, 'You shall not covet.' . . . Accordingly, the law (is) holy, and the commandment (is) holy and just and good."

"We *know*," says Paul. In other words, he wishes to impress upon Timothy — and through him upon the Ephesians, particularly upon those who were promoting erroneous doctrines — that the proposition, "Constant law-study is an excellent thing," is not new. "This proposition," says the apostle as it were, "is a widely recognized principle, something we all know very well." Read Ps. 19; Ps. 119; Matt. 5:17, 18.

Of course, Paul does not mean that "any and all" use of the law is admirable. No, only then is the law of great practical value "if one makes a lawful use of it." Thus one might also say that preaching is an excellent thing, but surely not *all* preaching. It is an excellent thing on the supposition that one knows how to preach!

When the law is buried under a load of "traditions" which nullify its very purpose (Matt. 15:3, 6; Mark 17:9; then Matt. 5:43) or when it is used as a "take-off" point for spell-binders about ancestors, it loses its power. Just as in the public games only that man received the wreath of victory who played according to the rules (cf. II Tim. 2:5), so also only that person can expect to receive a blessing from the law who uses it as it should be used. Hence, Paul continues:

9a. bearing this in mind, that not for a righteous man is law enacted.
That was the very point which these false teachers in Ephesus were forgetting. The reason why they wasted their time on all kinds of fanciful tales regarding ancestors was that they had never learned to know themselves as *sinners* before God. They were "puffed up," arrogant, boastful, haughty, self-righteous (see on verse 7 above; also on I Tim. 6:4, 20; II

Tim. 3:2; and cf. Titus 1:10; 3:5). That was their big sin, as Paul points out repeatedly. They lacked humility, the consciousness of guilt.

These people could study God's holy law with its basic precepts and injunctions, and could remain very calm under it all, as if it did not touch them. They would simply read on (or go back) until they came to some proper name or perhaps some ceremonial detail. *Then* of a sudden they would become enthused! *Now* they could shine with their stories and spiritualizations.

Instead, they should have been *crushed* by the law, as was, for instance, Paul (see below, on verse 15, and see also Rom. 7, especially the closing verses). But *these* people considered themselves to be *good* by nature, not bad. They were "righteous" in their own eyes, just like the Pharisees, with reference to whom Jesus said, "I came not to call the righteous but sinners" (Matt. 9:13; and cf. Luke 15:7 and 18:9). In fact, it is very well possible that the apostle had that Matt. 9:13 *saying* of the Savior in mind when he wrote as he did. (The actual date when the Gospels were written has nothing to do with this, of course.) This possible conclusion is strengthened somewhat by what he says in verse 15 of the present chapter:

"Reliable is the saying, and entitled to full acceptance, that Christ Jesus came into the world *sinners* to save, foremost of whom am I." Cf. also Titus 3:5.

Now it stands to reason that for "a righteous" man *law — any* law, to be sure (that is, any law touching morals), but here with special reference to the Mosaic law — has not been enacted. If I am so good that I just naturally keep the law, then I do not need the law (whether it be a traffic law or the law of the ten commandments). One of the main purposes of the Mosaic law was to bring *sinners* to the point where they would feel utterly crushed under the load of their sins. But granted, for the sake of argument, that these Ephesian would-be leaders and those who cluster around them, are what, according to Paul's description, they consider themselves to be; granted that they are in themselves good and righteous, then surely *law* is wasted on them.[30] How can it be *a bridle* (Mark 10:20; Ps. 19:13)

---

[30] The idea that Paul here teaches that "the justified Christian" has "nothing to do with the law" is burdened by the following objections:

a. It is totally foreign to the context, in which the apostle (barring the salutation which pertains to the entire letter) as yet has said nothing about justified Christians.

b. Here in verse 9 he is speaking entirely in general about "a (notice *a*, not *the*) righteous person; and he is saying that for such *a* righteous person *law* is not laid down.

c. A word is often explained by its antonyms. Here "a righteous person" stands over against persons who are "lawless, insubordinate, impious, sinful, unholy, profane, murderers of fathers, murderers of mothers," etc., all of which terms have to do with sins in the moral-spiritual realm, sins of attitude and conduct, sins against the moral law of the Ten Commandments. Hence, it certainly seems very probable that we are here in the moral, not in the forensic realm.

1:9a   **I TIMOTHY**

for those who feel that they need no restraint? How can it be a *dirt-revealing mirror* (source of the knowledge of sin, Rom. 3:20; then Gal. 3:24) for those who think that they show no filthy specks that must be washed away? How can it be *a guide* (Ps. 119:105; 19:7, 8; cf. Rom. 7:22) to point out avenues of gratitude for deliverance from sin, for those who in their pride and arrogance (of which Paul speaks again and again) are convinced that they have not lost the way?

9b, 10. No, not for these people is law enacted, **but for lawless and insubordinate, for impious and sinful, for unholy and profane men, for murderers of fathers and murderers of mothers, for those who kill their fellows, for immoral men, sodomites, kidnapers, liars, false swearers, and for whatever else is contrary to the sound doctrine.**

It would seem that the apostle, in referring to people for whom law (here with particular reference to the divine moral law) was laid down, first describes them in general — as being lawless and insubordinate, impious and sinful — and then descends to particulars, more or less following the order of the ten commandments.

The Ephesian errorists should have asked themselves, "Does not this description fit us?" Paul admitted that it applied to himself. The teachers of false doctrine in the Ephesus region admitted *nothing*. That was the difference!

The first descriptive term which he uses is *lawless*. Lawless persons (pl. of ἄνομος) are not here persons who are ignorant of the law but those who live as if there were no law (see N.T.C. on II Thess. 2:3). They "live themselves out," doing as they please. They thus live apart from the law and contrary to its basic demand. Was Paul thinking at all of himself (as included in this group) and his own former life? (Cf. Rom. 7:9.) In order that the proper exegesis may be given to this portion, one must bear in mind that in the immediate sequel the apostle refers repeatedly to himself and his own sinful life (verses 13, 15, 16). A text, after all, should be interpreted in the light of its context. Otherwise our interpretation lacks unity. — Now, lawless persons are, of course, also *insubordinate*. They refuse *to range themselves under* (note the word: pl. of ἀνυπότακτος) the rule of the God who laid down the law. In practical, every-day life, this means that such people are, *negatively* speaking, *impious*, irreverent, ungodly (pl. of ἀσεβής), a word which in Pauline usage applies even to the elect as long as (or to the extent in which) they are still living in harmony with the principle of unbelief. There are, accordingly "ungodly," though by God's sovereign grace they are (or sometime during their life are going to be) justified (Rom. 4:5; 5:6). Paul would certainly place himself among them. *Positively* speaking, such people are by nature *sinners* (pl. of ἁμαρτωλός), those who have missed the mark or goal of their existence, namely, the conscious glorification of God. Paul very definitely and explicitly tells us that he includes himself, note verse 15 (which must already have been in the mind of the writer when he wrote verse 9): ". . . Christ Jesus came into the world *sinners* to save, *foremost of whom am I*."

The law, then, was laid down for lawless and insubordinate, for ungodly and sinful persons, in order that it might shake them to the very depths of their being, might frighten them out of whatever self-complacency remained in them. *It was enacted to make the disturbed even more disturbed so that they would cry out in self-despair, "Wretched man that I am, who shall deliver me?"* (Rom. 7:24, and cf. Rom. 3:20).

The apostle now gives a summary of the law of the Ten Commandments. That summary shows clearly that there is no room for *anyone (least of all for the Ephesian errorist)* to sit at ease in Zion, to be filled with a sense of security, so that with perfect composure he can now begin to use the law as a kind of crossword puzzle or as raw material for the fabrication of interesting stories about ancestors.

First, accordingly, the apostle states that law has been enacted ἀνοσίοις καὶ βεβήλοις

"for unholy and profane men."

The term *unholy* (ἀνόσιος), in the New Testament occurring only here and in II Tim. 3:2, and linked here in verse 9 with *profane,* is very suitable in a context which describes those who are careless of their duties *toward God.* In his *Gorgias* (507 B) Plato represents Socrates as saying, "And again, when one is doing what is fitting with respect to *men,* he does things that are *just* (δίκαια); (when he does what is fitting) with respect to *the gods,* (he does things that are) *holy* (ὅσια).[31] Similarly, in II Macc. 7:34 Antiochus Epiphanes, who tried his utmost to destroy the religion of Jehovah, is called an "unholy man."

What is stated negatively in the adjective "unholy" is expressed positively in the adjective *profane* (βέβηλος from βαίνω, to walk, step, tread). That which is "profane" *can be trodden.* It is, as our English word implies, "in front of the temple," that is, "*outside* the temple" (*pro* = before or in front of; *fane* = temple, sanctuary). A *profane person* is one who does not refrain or hesitate *to trample* on that which is holy. The adjective is used with respect to *things* in I Tim. 4:7; 6:20; II Tim. 2:16 (see on these passages) and with respect to *persons* in our present passage and

---

[31] I do not mean that the adjectives ὅσιος and ἀνόσιος are restricted so that *in every* instance they refer to man's attitude with respect to his duties under the first table of the law. Trench is correct when he points out that Scripture recognizes no such arbitrary division between the first and second tables. What I *do* mean is that in the present passage the very use of the word *unholy* in immediate connection with *profane* seems to point in the direction of the classical distinction. For the rest see R. C. Trench, *op. cit.* lxxxviii; also M.M., 45, 460.

in Heb. 12:16. The latter passage mentions the typically *profane* person, namely, Esau, who for a single meal sold his birthright with its Messianic implications.

It is therefore altogether natural to suppose that when Paul mentions *unholy and profane* persons, he is thinking of those who ridicule the very idea that there is only one true God, and of those who deny that this God is the Spirit of infinite perfection, that his name, or the name of Christ, should be reverenced, and that his day should be observed. Those who are unholy and profane flout the four commandments of the first table of the law. Let no one say that Paul excluded himself (see verse 13, also Acts 26:11), or any other *sinner*.

Secondly, this law has been laid down
"for murderers of fathers and murderers of mothers."
The sin here indicated is a flagrant violation of the next commandment of the Decalogue, "Honor your father and your mother, that your days may be long in the land which the Lord your God gives you" (Ex. 20:12). Moreover, the law specifically stated, "And he who strikes his father or his mother shall surely be put to death" (Ex. 21:15). Now if even the *striking* of one's father or one's mother incurred the death-penalty, how much more the *smiting* (striking with a destructive blow, murdering)! Yet the greater sin, in each instance, includes the lesser. *Any* failure to honor one's parents is here condemned. *No sinner escapes.*

Thirdly, this law was intended
"for those who kill their fellows."
Literally, the original has here "for men-slayers." However, in English this term is rather ambiguous, and could be taken to refer exclusively to those who kill *unintentionally* though unlawfully (those guilty of "manslaughter"). The original, however, refers to any one who wrongfully takes the life of another. It has reference to *any and all homicides*.

The commandment violated is the sixth, "You shall not kill" (Ex. 20:13). See Christ's interpretation, Matt. 5:21-26. How it must have hurt Paul to write this. It brought back to his mind memories of the past, *Paul's own past* (Acts 9:1, 4, 5; 22:4, 7; 26:10).

Fourthly, this law was established
"for immoral persons, sodomites."
This clearly refers to those who transgress the seventh commandment, "You shall not commit adultery" (Ex. 20:14).

Note that here also (just as in the phrases "for impious and sinful," "for unholy and profane") the negative description (immoral) precedes the positive (sodomites). The violation indicated is, first, very inclusive "fornication" or immorality; secondly, very flagrant, "sodomy." With respect to the first term (fornication), it is not true that this is always strictly confined to illicit sexual intercourse between *unmarried* persons. As is true with respect to our own word *fornication*, so also with respect to the Greek word, the sense, though restricted at first, gradually acquires a more inclusive meaning, so that in the present passage it is simply *sexual immorality* in whatever form it may occur. That it may even include *adultery* (illicit sexual intercourse between persons at least one of whom is married) is clear from Matt. 5:32; 19:9. In Eph. 5:5 the fornicator or immoral person is mentioned in one breath with the impure or unclean. Cf. also Heb. 13:4. According to Matt. 5:27, 28 every unclean thought is a form of "adultery." *What sinner is not guilty?* A most gruesome instance of immorality is described by Paul in I Cor. 5:1. The heathen world was full of such vices, but the case mentioned in Corinthians is described as one "not found even among pagans."

Immediately after "immoral persons" Paul mentions "sodomites." The word employed in the original is composed of two parts: *male* and *bed* (particularly, marriage-bed). The reference is, therefore, *directly* to *male* homosexuals, in other words to sodomites (cf. Gen. 19:5), "abusers of themselves with men" (Rom. 1:27; I Cor. 6:9); *indirectly*, the reference is to *all* homosexuals, male and female.

Fifthly, the law was instituted

"for kidnapers."

In the New Testament the word (ἀνδραποδιστής) occurs only here. Its origin is rather uncertain, though in view of its component elements some derive it from the verbal idea "to catch a man by the foot." But whatever be its origin, it clearly refers primarily to "slave-dealers" (the word ἀνδράποδον means slave) and then, by extension, to *all* "men-stealers" or "kidnapers." The apostle has in mind a gross violation of the eighth commandment, "You shall not steal" (Ex. 20:15; on stealing *men* see Ex. 21:16; Deut. 24:7). Certainly also those who enter into the homes of Christians, dragging out those who are of "The Way," whether they be men or women, are included, in spite of the fact they may carry with them letters from the high-priest (cf. Acts 9:1, 2)! Yes, men-stealers of every hue or color are meant. Paul is included, and by a legitimate extension of the idea so is every one who has ever infringed on the rights or liberties of his fellowmen. *What sinner goes free?*

Sixthly, this law was made

"for liars, false swearers."

The apostle certainly has in mind the ninth commandment, "You shall not bear false witness against your neighbor" (Ex. 20:16). As Paul sees it, however, not only are *the Cretans* liars (Titus 1:12) but by nature *every man* is a liar (Rom. 3:4). The liar, according to the scriptural usage of the term, is not only the person who actually tells an untruth, but also he whose actions and attitudes are out of harmony with his confession (I John

2:4; 4:20). The arch-liar of all is the devil (see N.T.C. on John 8:44, 55). His most ardent disciple, antichrist, naturally is also a liar (I John 2:22; and see N.T.C. on II Thess. 2:9, 10).

"False swearers" are those who are guilty of *solemnly* ("by my name," Lev. 19:2) asserting that which is false, with the intention of hurting their neighbor; or those who, while making a solemn vow, do not intend to keep it. This is a most shocking form of the sin against the ninth commandment, just like kidnaping is a most shameful manifestation of the sin against the eighth, and sodomy a gross example of sin against the seventh commandment. Of course, as in the case of the preceding violations against the moral law, so here: *the sin mentioned includes the sins which lead to it and all kindred sins.* The selfish design of the Pharisees to restrict the meaning of the evil so that only those would be accounted guilty of perjury who failed to keep *that promise in connection with which the name of God had been literally taken upon the lips,* was exposed by the Lord (Matt. 5:33-37).

If we bear in mind that the sin of swearing falsely was sometimes committed with a view to obtaining possession of the neighbor's property, it becomes clear that the theory is not too far-fetched that in making mention of this particular violation of the moral law Paul is thinking not only of sin against the ninth but also of sin against the tenth commandment, "You shall not covet your neighbor's house . . . or anything that is your neighbor's (Ex. 20:17). *False swearing* often (perhaps we can even say *always*) has as its root *covetousness*.

Having now given both a general and a more detailed description of those people for whom the law was intended, the apostle adds "and for whatever else is contrary to the sound doctrine." *No sinner and no sin can escape,* least of all the errorists at Ephesus, *as God saw them!* The only one for whom the law was not laid down was the *righteous* person, the errorist *as he sees himself!* See on 1:9a. For the rest, the law condemns each and all, causing its sentence of condemnation to be felt! It is *laid down* (κεῖται) for whatever is *laid against* (ἀντίκειται) the sound doctrine. This *doctrine* touches both theory and practice. Hence, *every* sin is a sin against sound doctrine. And this doctrine is called *sound*[32] (ὑγιαινούσῃ, whence we have our word "hygienic") because it promotes spiritual health. See also II Tim. 4:3; Titus 1:9; 2:1; then Titus 1:13; lastly I Tim. 6:3; II Tim. 1:13. This is not surprising, for this teaching is:

---

[32] The idea that Paul cannot have written the Pastorals because the word "sound" is used here, and that this word must mean "in harmony with reason," must be rejected. "Soundness" is not a purely intellectual concept; and the metaphorical use of the word was surely known to Paul, for example, from the LXX rendering of Prov. 13:13, second line. Cf. footnote 193.

11. in harmony with the glorious gospel of the blessed God.
The sound doctrine demands that man *must* keep God's law. It also declares that by nature he *cannot* keep it. Hence, it reveals his utterly lost, his thoroughly *sinful* condition. This, of course, exactly matches (is "according to" or "in harmony with") *the gospel,* for the latter's central thrust is, "Christ Jesus came into the world *sinners* to save" (verse 15). What a *glorious* gospel! [33] It is glorious because it displays the radiance of the divine attributes. (See N.T.C. on John 1:14.) It declares the righteousness, grace, love, etc., of "the blessed God." With respect to this divine blessedness a great theologian wrote as follows:

"Now *blessedness* when ascribed to God comprises three elements: In the first place it expresses the fact that God is absolute perfection, for blessedness is the property of every being that is perfect or complete: that has life, and is free from disturbance, whether inwardly or outwardly. . . . Because of the fact that God is absolute perfection, the sum-total of all virtues, the highest essence, the supreme of goodness and truth, in other words, because he is absolute life, the fountain of all life, he is the God of absolute blessedness. . . . Secondly, the word *blessedness* when applied to God implies that this absolute perfection is the object of God's knowledge and love . . . God knows himself with a knowledge that is absolute, and he loves himself with a love that is absolute. Hence, the word *blessedness* when applied to God implies thirdly that God delights in himself in an absolute sense, that he rests in himself, that he is perfectly self-sufficient. His life is not a continual development, a mere striving and becoming, as is taught by pantheism, but an uninterrupted rest, an eternal peace" (H. Bavinck, *The Doctrine of God,* my translation, Grand Rapids, Mich., 1951, p. 248).

The word employed in the original to express this blessedness is μακάριος. It is the same word which occurs in The Beatitudes, for example, *"Blessed are the poor in spirit"* (Matt. 5:3), elsewhere in the Gospels (see N.T.C. on John 13:17), in James, I Peter, and Revelation. Paul uses it in Rom. 4:7, 8 (quotations from Ps. 32); 14:22; I Cor. 7:40; our present passage; also I Tim. 6:15; and Titus 2:13.[34]

---

[33] In agreement with the A.V., Berkeley Version, Goodspeed, Moffatt, R.S.V., Weymouth, Williams, etc., we construe the genitive "of the glory" as adjectival. (II Cor. 4:4 proves nothing to the contrary.) It is not true that when δόξης is preceded by the article it cannot be adjectival. Cf. "steward of the unrighteousness" in Luke 16:8. Moreover, in biblical Greek the adjectival genitive is of frequent occurrence, due, no doubt, to the Semitic background.
There is no need of searching for a remote connection for the phrase under discussion. It is the immediately preceding "sound doctrine" which is "according to" or "in harmony with" the glorious gospel of the blessed God.

[34] A close synonym of μακάριος is εὐλογητός. The former is the equivalent of the Hebrew *'ashrey,* which as a construct plural may be rendered, "O the blessedness of . . . !" It occurs, for example, with reference to men who have communion with God, are the recipients of God's special benefits, particularly, of the blessing of for-

1:11 **I TIMOTHY**

In mentioning "the glorious gospel of the blessed God" the apostle naturally thinks of his own relation to it. Hence, he continues **(the gospel) with which I have been entrusted.** Paul was deeply conscious of this "trust." He refers to it again and again (I Cor. 9:17; Gal. 2:7; and see N.T.C. on I Thess. 2:4). It is for that very reason that he calls himself "an apostle of Christ Jesus" (see above, on verse 1). It is for that same reason that he is able to commit a "charge" to Timothy (see on verse 3). Now Timothy himself was fully conscious of this sacred trust with which Paul had been entrusted. Others, however — think of the teachers of strange doctrine at Ephesus — need a reminder!

Yet, it is not primarily the desire to remind others of his authority that prompts the apostle to write about this trust. Rather, he mentions it here in order to make a transition to a paragraph (verses 12-17) in which he is going to express his gratitude to God, who made *him,* the chief of sinners, a minister of the gospel! According to the context, therefore, the true sense of the closing clause of verse 11 is this, "the glorious gospel of the blessed God, (the gospel) with which I, *thoroughly unworthy of such a great privilege,* have been entrusted."

---

12 I acknowledge my gratitude [35] to him who gave me strength, Christ Jesus our Lord, that [36] he considered *me* trustworthy and appointed *me* for himself [37] to (this) ministry, 13 though previously I was a blasphemer and a persecutor and a wanton aggressor. But I was accorded mercy because I acted ignorantly in unbelief. 14 And it superabounded (namely) the grace of our Lord, with faith and love (which center) in Christ Jesus. 15 Reliable (is) the saying, and worthy of full acceptance, that Christ Jesus came into the world sinners to save, foremost of whom am I. 16 But for this reason I was accorded mercy, in order that in me as foremost Jesus Christ might exhibit all his longsuffering as a sketch for those who would come to rest their faith on him with a view to life everlasting. 17 So to the King of the ages, the imperishable, invisible, only God (be) honor and glory forever and ever! [38] Amen.

---

giveness (Ps. 32:1; cf. Rom. 4:8). The latter translates the Hebrew *baruk,* and means "to be praised," or "worthy of praise" (Mark 14:61; Luke 1:68; Rom. 1:25; 9:5; II Cor. 1:3; 11:31; Eph. 1:3; I Peter 1:3).
[35] Or simply, "I thank him," etc. But χάριν ἔχω is perhaps a trifle stronger than εὐχαριστέω. It seems to mean, "I both feel and express my gratitude." See also p. 11; and cf. Luke 17:9; Heb. 12:28.
[36] Or "because." Whether ὅτι is taken as declarative or as causal makes very little difference here.
[37] The original has θέμενος, nominative, sing., masc., second aor. participle, *middle,* from τίθημι; hence, "having appointed me for himself," but in such cases — the action expressed by the participle being simultaneous with the action expressed by the finite verb — the meaning can be conveyed by using two finite verbs connected with "and."
[38] Literally "for the ages of (the) ages."

1:12-17

12. I acknowledge my gratitude to him who gave me strength, Christ Jesus our Lord, that he considered *me* trustworthy and appointed *me* for himself to (this) ministry.

The personal reference in the last clause of verse 11 is now expanded. Beautifully the apostle combines two ideas: a. I, though entirely unworthy, have been commissioned to proclaim the gospel of God's grace; and b. that grace and mercy was most gloriously displayed in my own conversion.

In this short paragraph (verses 12-17) we find not the usual stiff, stereotyped, and formal "thanksgiving to the gods or to a particular deity" which in ancient letters ordinarily follows the opening address. Instead, here we meet an outburst of gratitude, sincere and warm. Issuing from a heart that is filled with intense emotion, it rises to a higher and higher pitch until it ends in a sublime doxology (verse 17). What we actually see here is Paul as a radiant example of what God's law, lawfully used, can accomplish in the life of a former persecutor. Let the false teachers at Ephesus take note of this, so that they may no longer look upon the law as a toy, or as a tool for the aggrandizement of their own ego.

Deeply conscious is the apostle of his own inability to give adequate expression to his feeling of fervent gratitude. And this thankfulness is rendered not "to the gods," but "to Christ Jesus our Lord" (cf. verse 2).

Paul acknowledges his gratitude to Christ for three closely related benefits: a. for having imparted strength to him (he calls Christ his Enabler or Qualifier), b. for having judged him to be trustworthy or reliable, and c. for having "appointed" — this combines *destination* and *duty* (cf. N.T.C. on I Thess. 5:9) — him to the "ministry" (of the apostleship), a service rendered to the Lord in the spirit of love and personal devotion (for that is the meaning of the word διακονία; see Eph. 4:12; Col. 4:17; Heb. 1:14; also N.T.C. on I Thess. 3:2. For the technical sense see on I Tim. 3:10). Of course, these *three* ideas blend into *one*. It may be paraphrased as follows, "I thank him, Christ Jesus our Lord, my Strength-Imparter (cf. II Cor. 12:9; Phil. 4:13; II Tim. 4:17), who in his sovereign mercy considered me trustworthy — looking not at what I was in myself but at what his grace was doing within me (cf. I Cor. 4:7; Eph. 2:8) — , and accordingly for his own purpose appointed me to the ministry of the apostolic office." The *enabling*, the *favorable judging*, and the *appointing* were simultaneous. They all occurred when Paul was converted on the way to Damascus. See his *own* vivid account in Acts 9:15, 16; 22:1-21; 26:16-18; cf. Acts 13:1-4; and see N.T.C. on I Thess. 2:4.

13. He did this for such a one as I, though previously I was a blasphemer and a persecutor and a wanton aggressor.

That exactly was the astounding fact, namely, that on *such* a sinner *such* mercy had been bestowed.

"I know not why God's wondrous grace to me he hath made known,
Nor why, unworthy, Christ in love, redeemed me for his own."

Such mercy! for, note well: this very great sinner was not only *saved*, but was even deemed worthy to be entrusted with the ministry of the apostleship! All this happened though previous to his conversion the apostle had belonged to the very category of terrible sinners whom he has just described (see on verses 9b, 10 above): unholy and profane persons, etc. Yes, with reference to the first table of the law the apostle had been a *blasphemer* (Acts 26:11), ridiculing the name of Christ; and with reference to the second he had been a *persecutor* (see N.T.C. on I Thess. 3:12; II Thess. 1:4; cf. Acts 9:1, 4, 5; 22:4, 7; 26:10; Gal. 1:13). Moreover, in persecuting the church of God "beyond measure" he had persecuted Christ himself. "Saul, Saul, why do you persecute *me?*" Jesus had asked him. (Hence, in reality, here as always, man sins against *both* tables at once!) So violent and outrageous had been his attack upon believers – his very breath had been a threat of murder (Acts 9:1) – that he had been nothing less than "a wanton aggressor," one who committed outrage upon outrage against those who were of "The Way." We must never forget that the man who after his conversion (at Philippi) was "shamefully treated" had himself previous to his conversion "shamefully treated" the followers of Christ.

Thus this retrospect of sins reaches its sad climax: "blasphemer, persecutor, wanton aggressor." It was thus that grace had found this sinner. Surely, had this grace not been *sovereign, unconditional,* it would never have found *him!* **But I was accorded mercy because I acted ignorantly in unbelief.** Though his past conduct had been frightful, it had not amounted to the sin against the Holy Spirit, the wilful sin against better knowledge (Heb. 10:26). For such a sin there is no pardon (Matt. 12:31, 32; Heb. 6:4-6; I John 5:16; cf. Num. 15:30), nor does the one who lives in it have any desire for pardon. But *Paul's* case was different. During his campaign of aggression the apostle, in his state of "unbelief" with respect to the truth in Christ, had actually thought that he was offering service to God (see N.T.C. on John 16:2). He had been thoroughly convinced that he "ought to do many things contrary to the name of Jesus of Nazareth" (Acts 26:9). So, for *him* there was forgiveness, just as for the same reason there was forgiveness for the men of Israel who had killed the Prince of life (Acts 3:17; cf. also Luke 23:34). Yes, *mercy* – divine pity (see above, on verse 2) – had been accorded to this former member of a group of legalists – the Pharisees! – who were always bragging about "showing mercy" ("donating alms") to others. (Note that in the original the noun "alms" in

Matt. 6:2-4 and the verb "was accorded mercy" here in I Tim. 1:13 are derived from the same root.)

14. This *mercy,* as always, was united with *grace.* Grace abounding, yes super-abounding! Says Paul, **And it super-abounded (namely) the grace of our Lord, with faith and love in Christ Jesus.**

The transition from verse 13 to verse 14 is that from abounding sin to super-abounding grace. Here in verse 14 the emphasis is on the great change which by this grace was brought about in the life of the apostle. Note the position of the verb at the head of the sentence, for the sake of emphasis: "And it super-abounded, (namely) the grace of our Lord." *Grace,* here as in 1:2, is God's unmerited favor bestowed on the elect, producing consecrated lives (see N.T.C. on I Thess. 1:1). The verb *super-abounded* clearly points to *Paul* as the author of the Pastorals, for nowhere in the New Testament do we find such constant emphasis on the "super" character of redemption in Christ. It is Paul who declares:

"Where sin abounded, grace *super*-overflowed (overflowed all the more, Rom. 5:20)."

"Faith *super*-increases (is growing beyond measure, II Thess. 1:3)." So does love.

"I *super*-overflow (overflow abundantly) with joy (I am overjoyed, II Cor. 7:4)."

"We are praying *super-abundantly* (with intense earnestness, I Thess. 3:10)."

"The peace of God *sur* (-super)-passes all understanding (Phil. 4:7)."

"Esteem them (the leaders) *super*-abundantly (very highly) in love (I Thess. 5:13)."

"In order that I might not *super*-exalt myself (uplift myself to an excessive degree), there was given me a thorn in the flesh" (II Cor. 12:7).

It is clear that this "super" vocabulary is characteristic of Paul.

The phrase "with faith and love" indicates the effect of grace in Paul's heart and life. Grace *kindles* faith and love, floods the soul with these divine gifts. The apostle is fond of this combination (see N.T.C. on I Thess. 1:3 and 5:8). With him grace is ever *the root,* faith and love are *the trunk,* and good works are *the fruit* of the tree of salvation. That holds for the Pastorals as well as for the other epistles (Rom. 4:16; 11:6; Gal. 5:22-24; Eph. 2:4-10; II Thess. 2:13; Titus 2:11-14; 3:4-8). For the concepts "faith" and "love" see N.T.C. on I Thess. 5:8. This faith and this love are "in Christ Jesus," that is, they are centered in him. Paul possesses these graces because of his mystic union with Christ, the Savior.

15. Moreover, what holds for Paul holds for all saved sinners. Hence, there is first the statement of a truth applicable to *all* sinners whom Christ came to save. This is followed immediately by a clause of *personal* appro-

priation. **Reliable (is) the saying, and worthy of full acceptance, that Christ Jesus came into the world sinners to save, foremost of whom am I.**

Paul's saying with respect to the glorious purpose of Christ's first coming, this is the theme of the marvelous declaration which may be regarded as the very core of the gospel, its sum and substance. (It is comparable to John 3:16, on which see N.T.C.).

The *saying* is viewed from three aspects: 1. its reliability, 2. its contents, and 3. its personal appropriation.

1. *Its reliability*

Simple and great, like a granite rock, stands the word *reliable,* at the head of the sentence, without any connecting particle. It indicates that the proposition which it introduces has sustained the very crucial, fiery test of experience. It is not a mere *formula* but a considered *judgment.* It has been passed from mouth to mouth, as such sayings have the habit of doing, and, having embedded itself in the heart of the Christian community, where all the fears, hopes, struggles, and joys of these early Christians played around it, has survived gloriously. It has, in fact, become a sparkling epigram, a pithy, current commonplace, demanding and receiving the immediate, spontaneous, and enthusiastic assent and endorsement of all believers who hear it. The saying is the testimony of Christian experience, and is now also the utterance of the Holy Spirit.

The Pastorals contain five of these *reliable sayings:* I Tim. 1:15; 3:1; 4:8, 9; II Tim. 2:11-13; Titus 3:4-8. Although the clause, "Reliable is the saying," occurs only in these five passages of the Pastorals, and exactly in that form nowhere in the other ten epistles, this does not give anyone the right to conclude that Paul cannot have written the Pastorals. Surely no reason can be shown why the one who wrote, "Reliable (is) God," (I Cor. 1:9) and "Reliable (is) the One who calls y o u," (I Thess. 5:24) could not have written the grammatically exactly similar statement, "Reliable (is) the saying."

The famous saying, having been subjected to the flames of persecution and ridicule of Satan, had emerged from this crucible more sparkling and glorious than ever. Though not even four decades had elapsed since the death of the Savior, it had become even at this early date an unshakable conviction, "worthy of full acceptance," that is, entitled to wholehearted and universal *personal appropriation* with no reservations of any kind (or as we say colloquially "with no strings attached").

2. *Its contents*

The saying is, "That Christ Jesus came into the world sinners to save." Something should be said, first, about the *form* of this statement; then, about its *meaning.*

As to *the form,* it is asserted by several commentators that the saying is distinctly Johannine, since only John speaks of the Savior as "coming into the world." Some, even among those who regard *Paul* as the author of the Pastorals, proceed farther, and do not hesitate to connect this Johannine character of the language with the fact that the destination of I Timothy and II Timothy was *Ephesus* (where Timothy was carrying on his work as Paul's special envoy), *the very headquarters of John!* Accordingly, it is maintained that Timothy and the membership of the Ephesian church (on the assumption that the epistle was also read to the church), having become used to John's style, through his labors in their city, would appreciate such phraseology more than would believers who lived elsewhere.

However, this representation is open to the following objections:

a. The name "Christ Jesus" is Pauline rather than Johannine (it is never found in John's writings, often in Paul's).

b. It would seem altogether probable that the apostle John did not reach Ephesus until *after* Paul's death, hence also *after* the date of composition of I Timothy. The fact that Peter had received his "inheritance" in the heavens, and Paul his "crown" may have induced John to take charge of the orphan churches of Asia Minor. When we surmise that John reached Ephesus in the year 67 or 68, we cannot be far amiss (see also N.T.C. on John, vol. I, p. 29). But Paul wrote I Timothy in the year 63 or 64!

c. To a considerable extent the phraseology is, indeed, Johannine, but only in this sense that John has *preserved* and *transmitted* it. He did not *coin* it! It was *Jesus himself* who, according to the Fourth Gospel, again and again referred to himself as having "come into the world" (John 3:19; 9:39; 12:46; 16:28; 18:37). His earliest disciples learned it from him and copied it. Hence, it is not surprising that "the disciple whom Jesus loved" began to use it (John 1:11); and so did others, for example, Martha (John 11:27). Accordingly, here in I Tim. 1:15 Paul is simply making use of the Savior's own way of speaking about himself, and is employing language which, having been adopted from his lips by the earliest disciples, had been spread far and wide. It is only natural — in view, for example, of the close contact between Jerusalem and Ephesus, and of the "scattering" of the disciples due to persecution — that the saying had also reached Ephesus. And in this connection it is not at all improbable that the great apostle John, *before leaving Palestine,* had contributed his share toward perpetuating it.

As to the *meaning* of the expression, the combination "Christ Jesus" has already been explained (see N.T.C. on I Thess. 1:1, and footnote 19 in the present Commentary). The fact that this divinely anointed Savior "came into the world" indicates *not merely a change of location,* a "descent" from one place to another (from heaven to earth), but *a change of state and of moral and spiritual environment.* Hence, it implies the supreme *sacrifice,* the climax of condescending grace. From the infinite sweep of eternal delight in the very presence of his Father, Christ was willing to descend deeper and deeper into the realm of sin and misery. (The "coming into the world" includes incarnation, suffering, death.) In the original the word *sinners* immediately follows the word *world;* hence, not as most versions have it, ". . . came into the world to save sinners," but ". . . came into *the world sinners* to save." The juxtaposition of *world* and *sinners* shows that *world* is an *ethical* concept. For the meaning of *world* see also N.T.C. on John 1:10, 11, including footnote 26. The Lord of glory, so pure and holy that before his presence even the most consecrated men fall down as though dead (Rev. 1:17; cf. Is. 6:1-5), voluntarily entered the sphere to which he does not seem to belong, namely, the sphere in which the curse reigns. The reason for his entrance into this realm of sin is given in the words "sinners to save." This shows that the paradoxical *coming* was, after all, fully justified and gloriously motivated.

It took a former Pharisee to pour full and terrible meaning into that word *sinners.* As Pharisees saw it, even to eat with *sinners* was scandalous (Mark 2:16; Luke 5:30; 15:1, 2). With *a sinner* a prophet was not supposed to have any dealings (Luke 7:39). When the Pharisees wanted to heap insults upon Jesus, they would call him "a glutton, a drinker, *a friend of* (tax-collectors and) *sinners*" (Luke 7:34). They divided mankind into two groups: "the righteous," which was tantamount to saying, "ourselves," and "sinners," that is, "everybody else," "the riffraff," "the scum," "the people of the soil," "those who do not know the law." The Holy Spirit through Paul takes this opprobrious epithet "sinners," and applies it to *all* persons who are brought under conviction through the proper use of God's law. For them, for them *alone,* Christ Jesus came (Matt. 9:13; Luke 15:7; 19:10):

> "Come, ye sinners, poor and needy,
>   Weak and wounded, sick and sore;
> Jesus ready stands to save y o u,
>   Full of pity, love, and power;
> He is able, He is able,
>   He is willing, doubt no more;
> He is able, He is able,
>   He is willing, doubt no more.
>
> "Come, ye weary, heavy-laden,
>   Bruised and mangled by the fall;
> If y o u tarry till y o u're better,
>   Y o u will never come at all;
> Not the righteous, not the righteous,
>   Sinners Jesus came to call.
> Not the righteous, not the righteous,
>   Sinners Jesus came to call."
>
>   (Joseph Hart)

If those in Ephesus who were using the law *un*lawfully were ever going to be saved, they would have to experience a fundamental change. These "righteous" persons would have to become "sinners" before God. Thus it is seen that verse 15 stands in close connection with *everything* that precedes (not only with verses 12-14 but also with verses 3-11).

It was *to save* sinners that Christ Jesus came into the world. He did not come to help them save themselves, nor to induce them to save themselves, nor even to enable them to save themselves. He came *to save* them!

In Paul's writings the expression *to save* means:

NEGATIVELY	POSITIVELY
to rescue men from sin's:	to bring men into the state of:
a. guilt (Eph. 1:7; Col. 1:14)	a. righteousness (Rom. 3:21-26; 5:1)
b. slavery (Rom. 7:24, 25; Gal. 5:1)	b. freedom (Gal. 5:1; II Cor. 3:17)
and	and
c. punishment:	c. blessedness:
(1) alienation from God (Eph. 2:12)	(1) fellowship with God (Eph. 2:13)
(2) the wrath of God (Eph. 2:3)	(2) the love of God "shed abroad" in the heart (Rom. 5:5)
(3) everlasting death (Eph. 2:5, 6)	(3) everlasting life (Eph. 2:1, 5; Col. 3:1-4).

Note that over against each evil stands a corresponding blessing. To be saved, then, means to be emancipated from the greatest evil, and to be placed in possession of the greatest good. The state of salvation is opposed to the state of "perishing" or being "lost." Cf. Luke 19:10; John 3:16.

3. *Its personal appropriation*

". . . Christ Jesus came into the world *sinners to save, foremost of whom am I.*" This final clause (beginning with the word "foremost") has caused a wider variety of interpretation than almost any other in Paul's writings. The difficulty is this: it does not seem right that one who himself declares that before his conversion to the Christian faith he had lived according to the strictest sect of his religion as a Pharisee (Acts 26:5), should now call himself "chief of sinners." For various interpretations which I reject, and the reasons why I reject them, see the footnote.[39]

---

[39] The apostle means:
1. "I *belong to that group* of persons which consists of *foremost sinners.*" In Acts 28:17 the word "foremost" is used as a plural. Hence, what the apostle means is, "I am *one of the greatest* of sinners" (not necessarily *the greatest*). Moreover, he does not use the definite article. Hence, he does not really say, "I am *the* chief of sinners."

Objection: The presence or absence of the article makes very little difference, as is shown by the fact that the New Testament contains several passages in which "foremost" (or "first"), though without the article, has the absolute meaning: Matt.

Complete objectivity in exegesis demands that we state that the immediate context would seem to leave room for only *one* explanation, and that this explanation is the very one which the ordinary student of Scripture in reading his Bible, in quiet meditation, and also in song, generally gives to it. When the apostle, his heart troubled by the vivid recollection of the gruesome deeds of the past, gives written expression to the deeply rooted conviction and the poignant sorrow of his inner soul, and states, "Christ Jesus came into the world sinners to save, foremost of whom am I," he must have meant, "Of all sinners whom Christ Jesus came into the world to save, I am the greatest."

In fact, he not only states but *emphasizes* that no one else than he himself is "the chief of sinners." In the original he reserves for the first personal pronoun singular a place at the very end of the clause. I can see

---

10:2; John 8:7; 20:4; Eph. 6:2; I John 4:19. — In the present case the immediately following context (verse 16) also shows that the apostle describes himself as the *one* person who leads the procession.

2. "I am the chief of sinners, that is, the greatest sinner." But this is simply a figure of speech: *hyperbole*, as is, for example, the statement in II Kings 17:10, according to which the children of Israel set up idolatrous pillars "on every high hill and under every green tree."

Objection: verse 16 clearly shows that the apostle consistently carries through the idea contained in "foremost." Hence, this is no rhetorical exaggeration.

3. "*Historically* I am sinner No. 1. In course of time others will follow."

Objection: Even though there is perhaps *a small element* of truth in this explanation (see verse 16), it certainly does not account for the intensity of feeling which is expressed in the famous clause, and which causes it to end in a doxology! What Paul says is clearly nothing less than an instance of self-reproach and praise of God's infinite, incomprehensible mercy!

4. "I am *the most important sinner*, since as an apostle I have labored more abundantly than all the others" (cf. I Cor. 15:10).

Objection: This interpretation is foreign to the context, in which Paul, far from commending himself, describes himself as a former blasphemer, persecutor, and wanton aggressor (verse 13).

5. "I am the worst sinner." This is clearly what the apostle meant. It shows what a humble man he was, and how his past sins troubled him. However, though psychologically such self-reproach is understandable and to a certain extent justifiable, it is not necessary for us to agree with Paul's estimate of himself. He was actually a far better man than he thought he was.

Objection: This view under-estimates the seriousness of Paul's life as a persecutor, and fails to do full justice to Scripture's infallibility.

6. "Of *all* men, past, present, and future, I am the worst." The statement must be taken in its most absolute sense.

Objection: Then the apostle would be saying that he considers himself even worse than Judas and also even worse than "the man of lawlessness." The context does not point in this direction, and we cannot believe that the man who wrote II Thess. 2 would render such a verdict concerning himself.

7. "I am the worst of men." This self-abasement is morbid. Paul cannot have written these words. They sound insincere and point to another author.

Objection: The fact is that this self-reproach or self-condemnation is so characteristic of *Paul* (see what he says about himself in I Cor. 15:8, 9; Eph. 3:8) that others have exclaimed, "No one except Paul could have written it."

no good reason for radically changing this word-order. The translation should be, "of whom foremost am *I*," or "foremost of whom am *I*." Paul fixes the attention upon himself as a clear illustration of the depth of human *sin,* in order that in verse 16 he may return to that wonderful theme on which he has just dwelt (see verses 12-14), namely, the exaltation of the power of divine *grace, mercy* and *longsuffering.*

This interpretation of the disputed clause not only suits the context but is also in line with what Paul says about himself elsewhere:

"For I am the least of the apostles, not fit to be called an apostle, because I persecuted the church of God" (I Cor. 15:9).

"To me, the very least of all saints, was this grace given, to preach to the Gentiles the unsearchable riches of Christ" (Eph. 3:8).

In both these cases, just as here in I Tim. 1:15, the apostle is making a comparison between himself and other people whom Christ came to save (whether they were destined to become apostles or believers not clothed with any special office), and he makes the humble confession that he is *the least* of all saints, *the foremost* (or "chief") of sinners whom Christ came to save.

Taken in that sense and as a description of what *Paul* felt, the words of the familiar hymn are entirely correct:

> "Chief of sinners though I be,
> Jesus shed his blood for me;
> Died that I might live on high;
> Lives that I may never die."
>
> (William McComb)

That the apostle, who certainly knew his own past, was able in all sincerity to describe himself as being "of sinners foremost" is less difficult to grasp if the following facts are borne in mind:

When, years before this, Paul for the first time heard the good tidings of salvation in Christ, he disbelieved. This disbelief he shared with many. Had his attitude to the Christian faith remained on this level, namely, one of unbelief, he would probably never have called himself, "of sinners *foremost."* However, he became *a persecutor,* and not only "a" persecutor but *the most bitter persecutor of all!* His entire soul was wrapped up in the work of annihilating the church. He breathed threats and slaughter (Acts 9:1). Ruthlessly he bound and imprisoned both men and women. He did not confine his efforts to Jerusalem but was bent on uprooting the new religion wherever it was found, even if this would necessitate a trip all the way to Damascus. He was busy persecuting God's people "unto death," as he himself subsequently declared (Acts 22:4, 5). Had his plan succeeded, the church would have been smothered in its very birth; God's eternal decree would have been annulled; and Satan would have triumphed.

Indeed, so very great was his sin that, had it not been done in ignorance (see on verse 13), it would have been unpardonable.[40] Accordingly, when the apostle now says, ". . . sinners to save, foremost of whom am I," we must not begin to attenuate the meaning of "foremost." We should permit this glorious confession to stand within its own context, without either adding to it or subtracting anything from it.

Paul writes *"am I,"* not *"was I."* This indicates that even now, years after his conversion, he deeply regrets his past. Besides, even a fully pardoned sinner is a sinner.

16. The *purpose* of God's marvelous grace is now stated: *proximate* purpose, verse 16; *ultimate* purpose, verse 17. **But for this reason I was accorded mercy, in order that in me as foremost Jesus Christ might exhibit all his longsuffering.** Chief of sinners, *nevertheless* the recipient of infinite mercy! That accounts for the "but." In fact, the magnitude of the sin made it necessary for mercy, if it was to be shown at all, to superabound. That is the very point which the apostle makes here in verse 16. For the expression "I was accorded mercy" see on verse 13. The purpose clause, "in order that in me as foremost," in connection with what follows, indicates that the apostle considers himself not only the chief of sinners but *also* — and in a certain sense *for that very reason* — the most glorious illustration of Christ's longsuffering. Here in verse 16 two ideas blend into one: Paul is "foremost" as an example of what Christ's longsuffering can accomplish. He is at the same time "foremost" as the head of a procession of persons to whom that longsuffering is shown. *Longsuffering* indicates the divine patience with respect to persons, by virtue of which wrath is withheld, the sinner is spared, and mercy is shown (for further details see N.T.C. on I Thess. 5:14). In the case of Paul this longsuffering had been exhibited *in full measure* (note "all his longsuffering," or as one might say, "the whole of it"), forgiving his frightful crimes, appointing him to the apostleship, and giving him strength for each day. This longsuffering had been thus exhibited **as a sketch for those who would come to rest their faith on him with a view to life everlasting.** In his gallery of grace the Artist-Savior had, as it were, drawn and put on exhibition *a sketch* (ὑποτύπωσις, acc. — ιν, used only here and in II Tim. 1:13), just like a master will first draw a rough pencil-sketch before attempting his final work. This sketch revealed Paul, as an illustration, pattern or model, of the type of work sovereign grace was going to perform in the lives of all those who through its efficacy *would come to* (cf. Acts 13:48: "had been ordained to") *rest their faith* (note durative present infinitive πιστεύειν) *on* (note ἐπί) Christ, the solid rock or the precious cornerstone (Matt. 7:24, 25; Is. 28:16;

---

[40] See J. Van Andel, *Paulus' Brieven aan Timotheus,* Leiden, 1904, p. 28.

cf. Rom. 9:33; 10:11; I Peter 2:6), with a view to *life everlasting,* a life that is opposed to "corruption" (Gal. 6:8) and "death" (Rom. 6:22). Death is *wages;* life everlasting is *a free gift* (Rom. 6:22, 23). It manifests itself in fellowship with God in Christ (John 17:3), partaking of the love of God (John 5:42), of his peace (John 16:33), and of his joy (John 17:13). It is also actually what its name indicates ever-lasting, never-ending life.

17.   "And from my smitten heart with tears,
        Two wonders I confess:
        The wonders of his glorious love
        And my own worthlessness."
                    (Elizabeth C. Clephane)

The contemplation of these "two wonders" which Paul has been discussing leads naturally to a doxology, which is all the more exuberant because in the present case the attention is riveted on Christ's incomprehensible longsuffering exhibited not only to *one* sinner but to an entire procession of sinners whom Christ came to save: Paul "the foremost" and those who followed him. Through Christ, accordingly, God displays his glorious attributes *in every* age, for he is "the King of the ages." This accounts for the form in which this doxology is cast: **So to the King of the ages, the imperishable, invisible, only God (be) honor and glory forever and ever! Amen.**

Man proposes; God disposes. Man — for instance Paul before his conversion — may try *to destroy* the church; God will *establish* it. And for that purpose he will use the very man who tried to destroy it! Hence, though man is a mere *creature* of time, God is *the King* of the ages, over-ruling evil for good; directing to its predetermined goal whatever happens throughout each era of the world's history. His "dominion endures throughout *all* generations" (Ps. 145:13).

This implies that he is the eternal God, and as such "imperishable"[41] (the best reading). *His* arms never become tired (Deut. 32:27). *He* never grows weary (Is. 40:28). Decay and death are not applicable to *him* (Ps. 103:15-17). *He* never changes (Mal. 3:6). On the contrary, *he* is the inexhaustible reservoir of strength, ever new, for his people (Is. 40:29-31). For the doctrine of God's *imperishability* see also Rom. 1:23; and cf. the synonym *immortality* (see on I Tim. 6:16).

When one thinks of God as the *im*perishable, the mind inevitably turns

---

[41] Although it is true that the idea of God's "imperishability" is also found in the works of Greek and later Jewish philosophers, to speak of Paul's "borrowing" or "deriving" the idea from them is highly precarious, and this for two reasons: a. the doctrine of God's imperishability is taught and presupposed throughout the Old Testament; b. the philosophical idea and the scriptural idea are not identical (see on I Tim. 6:16).

to those objects that are perishable, for example, grass, the flowers of the field (Ps. 103:15-17), man's body, birds, quadrupeds, creeping creatures (Rom. 1:23). These are all visible. God, being imperishable, is also *invisible*, "whom no one has seen or can see" (I Tim. 6:16). It is only in his Image (Col. 1:15, 16) that man "sees Him who is invisible," and then only *by faith* (Heb. 11:27), and in a finite manner. Never shall we be able to "find out the Almighty unto perfection" (Job 11:7, 8). Paul surely was not able to comprehend the grace of God which had been shown to him. Here all reasoning stops. There is room only for doxologies!

Such a God, finally, is the "only" God; not merely in the coldly abstract sense that numerically there is but *one* God, but in the warm, scriptural sense, namely, that this *one* God is "unique, incomparable, glorious, lovable" (Deut. 6:4, 5; Is. 40:12-31; Rom. 16:27; I Cor. 8:4, 5).

Out of the wellsprings of Paul's spontaneity issues the exclamation — it is a veritable outburst coming from a heart that has experienced what it means to have *such* a God as one's own God — that "for the ages of (the) ages," that is, "forever and ever," *honor and glory* (praise and adoration) be rendered to the God who in his being and attributes is so wonderful. The doxology ends with the word of solemn assent and emphatic confirmation, "Amen" (see N.T.C. on John 1:51).

---

18 This charge I commit to you, my child Timothy, in agreement with the previous prophetic utterances concerning you, in order that with their aid you may war the good warfare, 19 holding on to faith and a good conscience, (the kind of conscience) which some have discarded and have suffered shipwreck with reference to their faith; 20 among whom are Hymenaeus and Alexander, whom I have handed over to Satan, in order that they might be disciplined not to blaspheme.

1:18-20

18. This charge I commit to you. The charge referred to has been clearly set forth in the entire preceding section, especially in verses 3-11. It is the "mandate" or "instruction" (see N.T.C. on I Thess. 4:2) that Timothy stay on at Ephesus in order that he may teach certain individuals not to make misuse of the law but to use it lawfully, unto conversion to Christ, *the sinners'* Savior.

Paul *commits* or *entrusts* (cf. Luke 12:48; 23:46) this charge to one whom he calls **my child Timothy**. This expression of endearment is not strange if the following three facts are borne in mind: a. under God, Timothy owed his conversion to Paul, who was therefore his spiritual father; b. the disciple was the apostle's junior by several years; c. he was amiable, dependable, and co-operative even to the extent of performing tasks that ran counter to his natural disposition.

I TIMOTHY 1:18

The charge was not new, arbitrary or unfair, but entirely **in agreement with the previous prophetic utterances concerning you.** The construction of this compound phrase is difficult, and has led to widely different interpretations.[42]

The previous prophetic utterances include *at least* the following:

a. The Spirit-guided recommendations whereby on the *second* missionary journey, about the year 51, Paul's attention had *once more* been turned to Timothy (Acts 16:1-3). — It should be borne in mind that previously Paul and Barnabas had themselves been "separated" by the church, with the co-operation of certain *prophets* (Acts 13:1-3). Timothy's *conversion* to the Christian faith seems to have occurred on the *first* missionary journey.

b. The inspired words which had been spoken in connection with Timothy's ordination (see especially on I Tim. 4:14. Cf. I Tim. 6:12; II Tim. 2:2; Acts 14:23).

These previous prophetic utterances had probably been of the following nature. They singled out Timothy for special service in God's kingdom, summarized his duties, predicted his suffering, and strengthened him with the promise of divine help in all his trials. At least, such were the prophetic utterances in connection with *Paul's own* call to duty (Acts 9:15, 16; 22:14, 15, 21; 26:16-18). We may assume that in Timothy's case words of somewhat similar character had been spoken.

"My child Timothy, I wish to remind you of these prophetic utterances," says Paul as it were, **in order that with their aid you may war the good (or noble or excellent) warfare.** Timothy is viewed as a high-ranking officer, who has received his "orders," and is "warring his warfare" (see I Cor. 9:7; II Cor. 4:4; 19:3) against evil, particularly against the Satan-inspired perversion of doctrine described in verses 3-12 (cf. I Tim. 6:12; II Tim. 4:7; Eph. 6:10-20). In this warfare reflection on former prophecies can be very encouraging (see N.T.C. on John 16:1, 4). They remind one of the fact that nothing happens contrary to the eternal decree of God, that one is engaged

---

[42] The original has κατὰ τὰς προαγούσας ἐπὶ σὲ προφητείας. In the New Testament the verb προάγω means *to lead* (or *to bring*) *out* or *forth* (Acts 12:6; 16:30; 17:5; 25:26); or *to precede* (Matt. 2:9; 14:22; 21:9; 21:31; 26:32; 28:7; Mark 19:32; 14:28; 16:7). In all the instances mentioned so far the verbal form has an immediately following pronoun-object. However, at times either the object is not mentioned, though implied, or the verbal form may even become entirely intransitive (Mark 6:45; 11:9; Luke 18:39; I Tim. 5:24). The intransitive connotation would seem to be especially present in such cases as II John 9 ("whoever *goes ahead*") and Heb. 7:18 (in which case the participle has the force of an adjective: "a foregoing commandment" = "a *former* commandment"). In the passage under study (I Tim. 1:18) no pronoun-object is expressed, and probably none is implied. We seem to have an intransitive use similar to that in Heb. 7:18. Hence, we translate, "the preceding prophetic utterances with respect to you," or "the previous prophetic utterances concerning you." The fact that ἐπί with acc. may mean "concerning" is clear from Mark 9:12.

1:18   **I TIMOTHY**

in a battle which is not merely his own but the Lord's, and that courage and faithfulness will certainly be rewarded.

19. The manner in which this warfare must be carried on is now set forth: **holding on to faith and a good conscience.**

Timothy is admonished *to hold* faith, that is, *to hold on* to it. In warring his warfare against errors and errorists he must keep clinging to *the truth* of the gospel. The fact that the word *faith* here in verse 19 means *truth* is clear from II Tim. 2:17, 19. By living and teaching in accordance with this truth, remaining firm and stedfast in the midst of all opposition, Timothy will be obeying the voice of *conscience.* For the meaning of "a good conscience" see on verse 5. Paul continues: **(the kind of conscience) which certain individuals have discarded and have suffered shipwreck with reference to their faith.**

A Christian must be both a good soldier and a good sailor. Now a good sailor does not *thrust away* or *discard* the rudder of the ship. The good conscience — one that obeys the dictates of the Word as applied to the heart by the Holy Spirit — is the rudder, guiding the believer's vessel into the safe harbor of everlasting rest. But "certain individuals" (the Ephesian heretics; see on verse 3) have discarded that rudder.[43] The inevitable result was that with reference to their *faith* — the truth which they had confessed with their lips; the name of Christ which they had named (see on II Tim. 2:17-19) — they *suffered shipwreck.* If even literal shipwreck is agonizing, as Paul had experienced (Acts 27:39-44; II Cor. 11:25), how much more to be feared is *religious* shipwreck!

20. The ringleaders among the shipwrecked are now mentioned: **Among whom are Hymenaeus and Alexander.** The name of the first is derived from Hymen, the god of marriage. This Hymenaeus is also mentioned in II Tim. 2:17. Associated with him was Alexander, which means "defender of men." Then as now it was a very common name. Hence, there is no good reason to identify the Alexander to whom Paul refers here in I Tim. 1:20 with the one mentioned in Acts 19:33, 34, who on the occasion of the Ephesian riot tried to turn the anger of the mob away from the Jews; nor with the one mentioned in II Tim. 4:14, 15, who was a metal-worker *in*

---

[43] Paul does not definitely say that he regards conscience to be *the rudder.* In the abstract he may have been thinking of conscience as the ship's furniture, tackle, or cargo. In that case the verb which we have translated "discarded" may be rendered "thrown overboard" (cf. Acts 27:18, 19, 38). He may even have been thinking of the ship's anchor. However, if, as seems probable, his reference to shipwreck as a result of "pushing away" conscience implies that he is thinking of conscience under the symbolism of some object pertaining to the ship, what figure would be more logical than that of a *rudder?* Cf. Rom. 2:14, 15, in which passage conscience is represented as a law which one obeys (for example, just like a ship obeys its rudder). — Also, a ship without a rudder may readily suffer shipwreck.

Rome. The Hymenaeus and Alexander to whom Paul refers here in I Tim. 1:20 were leaders among the Ephesian *heretics*. They were self-righteous persons who yearned to be law-teachers, although they understood neither the words which they were speaking nor the themes on which they were harping with such confidence (see on verse 7). As has been indicated (see on verse 4), they specialized in myths and fanciful stories about family-trees. See also on II Tim. 2:17.

So far did these heretical teachers advance in error that they even railed at the true presentation of the gospel. Hence, Paul declares **whom I have handed over to Satan in order that they may be disciplined not to blaspheme.** The expression "handed over to Satan," which also occurs in I Cor. 5:5, is somewhat obscure. That it refers to expulsion from the church ("excommunication") — a sentence to be carried out by the congregation under the direction of its elders — seems certain (cf. I Cor. 5:2, 7). Did it imply even more than this, for example, *bodily* suffering or disease? Though this is denied by some,[44] the evidence, nevertheless, seems to favor the idea. Let anyone study Job 2:6, 7; I Cor. 5:5; 11:30; Rev. 2:22; then also Acts 5:1-11; 13:11. This extraordinary gift, namely, to commit a person to Satan's power, in order that he might suffer anguish not only in soul but also in body, may strike us as unbelievable, but is it, after all, so strange that added to the charismatic gift of bodily *healing* was the power to inflict bodily *suffering*? If we deny the latter, should we not also deny the former?

However, even when this extreme measure was resorted to, its purpose was *remedial*. Not damnation but reclamation was the object, "in order that they may be *disciplined* (cf. II Tim. 2:25) not to blaspheme." Here speaks the same loving heart as in II Thess. 3:14, 15 (see N.T.C. on that passage) and in II Cor. 2:5-11. The apostle is earnestly desirous that the discipline — the divine pedagogy — imposed may have a salutary effect on Hymenaeus and Alexander. He is hoping and praying that by means of this dire affliction these false teachers may come to see themselves as grievous sinners and may be brought to genuine repentance, so that they will no longer rail at the truth and thereby revile its Author.

Synthesis of Chapter 1

See the Outline at the beginning of the chapter.

Paul salutes Timothy. In this salutation the apostle shows that he belongs to Christ Jesus who has entrusted him with the task of preaching the gospel. His authority is equal to that of the Twelve. Beautifully blending apostolic authority and tender love, Paul calls Timothy his genuine child in the sphere of faith, and pronounces upon him grace, mercy, and

---

[44] For example, by Lenski, *op. cit.*, p. 534.

peace, springing from the twofold source, "God the Father and Christ Jesus our Lord."

He charges Timothy to stay on at Ephesus in order to combat the errors of novelty-teachers, who instead of being crushed by God's moral law, here summarized, use that law as a take-off point for fictitious narratives about ancestors. The apostle calls their argumentations "futile talk," and accuses them of selfish ambition. He indicates the essence of the charge which Timothy must deliver to the churches of Ephesus and vicinity, namely, "love which springs from a pure heart, a conscience good, and a faith without hypocrisy."

Paul thanks God who has made him — *"chief of sinners"* — a minister of the glorious gospel of salvation full and free.

In this connection he introduces the first of five "reliable sayings." Taken together, the five comprise a summary of doctrine (from Theology to Eschatology) as confessed by the early church.

The Five Reliable Sayings

"Reliable (is) the saying, and worthy of full acceptance, that Christ Jesus came into the world sinners to save." Paul adds the words of personal appropriation, "foremost of whom am I" (I Tim. 1:15).

"Reliable is the saying, If anyone aspires to the office of overseer, he desires a noble work" (I Tim. 3:1).

"(For) while physical training is of *some* benefit, godly living is of benefit *in every way*. Reliable is that saying and worthy of full acceptance" (I Tim. 4:8, 9).

"Reliable is the saying:
 (For) if we died with (him), we shall also live with (him);
   if we endure, we shall also reign with (him);
   if we shall deny (him), he on his part will also deny us;
   if we are faithless, he on his part remains faithful" (II Tim. 2:11-13).

"(But) when the kindness of God our Savior and his love toward man appeared, he saved us, not by virtue of works which we ourselves had performed in (a state of) righteousness, but according to his mercy, through the washing of regeneration and renewing by the Holy Spirit, which he poured out upon us richly through Jesus Christ our Savior, in order that, having been justified by his grace, we might become heirs-in-hope of life everlasting. Reliable (is) this saying" (Titus 3:4-8a).

Outline of Chapter 2

Theme: *The Apostle Paul, Writing to Timothy, Gives Directions For the Administration of the Church*

*Directions with respect to
Public Worship*

2:1-7   A. When the congregation gathers for worship prayers must be made "in behalf of all men."

2:8-15 B. Both the men and the women must behave properly:
      1. The men, in every place of public worship, must lift up holy hands;
      2. The women, in getting ready "to go to church," must dress becomingly, and at the place of worship must show that they understand and have accepted their divinely ordained position.

CHAPTER II

I TIMOTHY   **2:1**

2 1 First of all, then, I urge that supplications, prayers, intercessions, thanksgivings be made in behalf of all men, 2 in behalf of kings and all who are in high positions, that we may lead a tranquil and calm life in all godliness and gravity. 3 This is excellent and acceptable in the sight of God our Savior, 4 who desires all men to be saved and to come to the acknowledgment of the truth. 5 For (there is) but *one* God and (there is) but *one* Mediator between God and men, the man Christ Jesus, 6 who gave himself as a ransom for all, the testimony (to be borne) in due season; 7 for which purpose I was appointed a herald and apostle — I am telling the truth, I am not lying — a teacher of Gentiles in (the realm of) faith and truth.

2:1-7

A new subject begins here: Directions for Public Worship:

1. First of all, then, I urge that supplications, prayers, intercessions, thanksgivings be made in behalf of all men.

Paul has something to "urge" upon Timothy. He is, as it were, "calling him aside" in order to exhort him with respect to a matter of utmost significance (note "first of all"). It concerns the relation of the church to the state. If churches are to flourish spiritually, public worship is highly desirable, to say the least; but such public worship cannot be conducted to the best advantage (calmly, without disturbance; see on verse 2b) unless the church does its duty with respect to the state. Besides, the church is a light shining in the darkness. It must seek to win others for Christ and his kingdom. Is it possible that Paul, on his visit to Ephesus, had noticed that prayer for rulers was being neglected?

So the apostle urges his representative to see to it that wherever in the Ephesian territory God's people may gather for public worship, kings and all that are in high positions be remembered in prayer, in fact that supplications, prayers, intercessions, thanksgivings be made in behalf of *all* men.

The four synonyms that are used here do not amount to meaningless repetitions.

The first word, *supplications,* means petitions for the fulfilment of certain definite needs which are keenly felt. Fully aware of his complete dependence on God, one asks that *this* particular illness may be removed, or that *these* disturbing tidings may be over-ruled for good, etc. Supplications, then, are humble requests which one makes in the light of this or that concrete situation in which God, he alone, can furnish the help that is needed.

The next word, *prayers,* is more general in meaning. As often used, it covers *every* form of reverent address directed to the Deity. Whether we "take hold on God" by means of confession, intercession, supplication, adoration, or thanksgiving, we can in each instance speak of being engaged in *prayer.* Both the Greek and the English word have that general meaning. However, in view of the fact that the word is here used as one of a list of four synonyms, and since it is clear that each of the other three stresses a particular aspect of prayer-life, the conclusion seems warranted that its meaning in this particular passage (and probably also in I Tim. 5:5 and Phil. 4:6) must be somewhat restricted. I venture the thought that it here refers to requests for the fulfilment of needs that are *always* present (in contrast with *supplications* in *specific* situations): the need for more wisdom, greater consecration, progress in the administration of justice, etc. Even when thus interpreted, the meaning is still very broad.

The noun *intercessions* occurs only here and in I Tim. 4:5. I have hesitated a long time before adopting as my own (for the *present* passage) the translation of the A.V., A.R.V., R.S.V., and many others. It is perhaps impossible to find *one* word in the English language which will be the full equivalent of the original. I might begin by stressing the fact that it is by no means true that the noun (used in the original: ἔντευξις) in and by itself (that is, apart from the context) necessarily conveys the thought which we *today* generally associate with the word *intercession:* "a pleading in the interest of others." In the only other New Testament passage in which it is used (I Tim. 4:5) it does *not necessarily* have that meaning. And the related *verb* (ἐντυγχάνω) can be used in connections in which (together with a preposition) it indicates a pleading *against* rather than a pleading *in behalf of* (Rom. 11:2; and cf. Acts 25:24).

The basic idea contained in both verb and noun is rather that of "falling in with," "meeting with in order to converse freely," hence, "freedom of access." A person (or *Person*) finds himself in the very audience-chamber of God the Father. The privilege of having a sacred interview with him is *his own,* whether *by nature,* as in the case of Christ or of the Holy Spirit, or *by grace,* as in the case of a believer.

But though this is the basic idea of the word, the particular context in which it is used changes the meaning slightly. Thus it is indeed true that the *verbal* form in the New Testament passages not yet referred to indicates a confident interview which is "in the interest of others." Hence, it takes on the meaning of *intercession.* According to Rom. 8:27 the Holy Spirit, having come to our assistance, *intercedes* for us. Christ, upon his heavenly throne, remembers us similarly (Rom. 8:34). In fact, he *evermore lives to intercede for us* (Heb. 7:25). In our present passage (I Tim. 2:1) this meaning — namely, pleading in the interest of others, and doing this without "holding back" in any way — fits exactly, as is shown by what immediately follows: "in behalf of all men, in behalf of kings and all who are in high positions."

The final word, *thanksgivings* (that is, completing the circle, so that the blessings that come from God return to him again in the form of *expressed gratitude*) is clear enough. Nevertheless, it must be borne in mind that not only supplications, prayers, and intercessions but also thanksgivings must be made *in behalf of all men,* including kings, etc.

Indeed, such invocations must be made "in behalf of" or "for" (see N.T.C. on John 10:11, for the meaning of the preposition) *all men*. Several expositors feel certain that this means every member of the whole human race; every man, woman, and child, without any exception whatever. And it must be readily admitted that *taken by itself* the expression *all men* is capable of this interpretation. Nevertheless, every calm and unbiased interpreter also admits that *in certain contexts* this simply cannot be the meaning.

Does Titus 2:11 really teach that the saving grace of God has appeared to every member of the human race without any exception? Of course not! It matters little whether one interprets "the appearance of the saving grace" as referring to the bestowal of salvation itself, or to the fact that the gospel of saving grace has been preached to every person on earth. In either case it is impossible to make "all men" mean "every individual on the globe without exception."

Again, does Rom. 5:18 really teach that "every member of the human race" is "justified"?

Does I Cor. 15:22 really intend to tell us that "every member of the human race" is "made alive in Christ"?

But if that be true, then it follows that Christ did not only *die* for every member of the human race, but that he also actually *saved* every one without any exception whatever. Most conservatives would hesitate to go that far.

Moreover, if, wherever it occurs, the expression "all men" or its equivalent has this absolutely universalistic connotation, then would not the following be true:

(a) Every member of the human race regarded John the Baptist as a prophet (Mark 11:32).

(b) Every member of the human race wondered whether John was, perhaps, the Christ (Luke 3:15).

(c) Every member of the human race marveled about the Gadarene demoniac (Mark 5:20).

(d) Every member of the human race was searching for Jesus (Mark 1:37).

(e) It was reported to the Baptist that all members of the human race were flocking to Jesus (John 3:26).

And so one could easily continue. Even today, how often do we not use the expression "all men" or "everybody" without referring to every member of the human race? When we say, "If everybody is ready, the meeting can begin," we do not refer to everybody on earth!

Thus also in the present passage (I Tim. 2:1), it is *the context* that must decide. In this case the context is clear. Paul definitely mentions *groups* or *classes* of men: kings (verse 2), those in high position (verse 2), the Gentiles (verse 7). He is thinking of rulers and (by implication) subjects, of Gentiles and (again by implication) Jews, and he is urging Timothy to see to it that in public worship not a single group be omitted. In other words, the expression "all men" as here used means "all men without distinction of race, nationality, or social position," not "all men individually, one by one."

Besides, how would it even be possible, except in a very vague and global manner (the very opposite of *Paul's* constant emphasis!), to remember in prayer *every person on earth?*

2. In explanation of the expression "in behalf of all men" the apostle continues: **in behalf of kings and all who are in high position.**

How necessary, this admonition! Even today! The apostle is probably thinking, first of all, of sovereign rulers of states, as they succeed one another in the course of history; and of all other functionaries subject to them. He must have had in mind the then-reigning emperor Nero, and further: the proconsuls (Acts 19:38), Asiarchs (Acts 19:31), the town-clerk (a rather influential position, Acts 19:35), etc.

However, had the emperor been Augustus or Tiberias or Caligula or Claudius, had he been Vespasian or Titus or Domitian; had those who ruled under them been *kings* properly so called, as for instance Herod the Great, tetrarchs such as Herod Antipas, ethnarchs such as Archelaus—even emperors, tetrarchs, and ethnarchs were sometimes called *kings* (John 19:15; Matt. 14:9; Matt. 2:22) —; had they been procurators such as Pontius Pilate, or had they been invested with any other political office, the charge, "Pray for them," would have been exactly the same. It is a commandment which holds for every age and for every region. President Eisenhower, Queen Elizabeth, Queen Juliana, etc., etc., the Holy Spirit via Paul bids us to remember them all before the throne of grace. The present precept is as general as is the closely related one found in Rom. 13:1.

And the purpose is hinted in the words which follow: **that we may lead a tranquil and calm life in all godliness and gravity.** The rare adjectives *tranquil* and *calm* (the former occurring only here; the latter only here and in I Peter 3:4) differ but slightly in meaning. The first seems to refer to a life which is free from *outward* disturbance; the second, to a life which is free from *inner* perturbation. Paul exhorts the Thessalonians to be ambitious about "living calmly" (see N.T.C. on I Thess. 4:11).

Of course, this merely "hints" at the real purpose of praying for the rulers. Paul certainly does not mean to encourage a life of ease. His aims are never selfish. Rather, the idea is this: freedom from disturbances, such as wars and persecutions, will facilitate the spread of the gospel of salvation in Christ to the glory of God. One must read the present passage in the light of the immediately following context (verses 3 and 4), of other passages from the Pastorals (I Tim. 1:15; 4:16), and of passages from Paul's other epistles (I Cor. 9:22; 10:31).

Included in the purpose of Paul's prayer is also this, that believers, leading a life of tranquility and calm, may do nothing to create unnecessary disturbance, and may conduct themselves "in all godliness and gravity," that is, "in all *piety* and *respectability* or *dignity*," striving to be blameless in their conduct or attitude both *toward God* and *toward men*. See also pp. 10, 11 on these two words. For the first see on I Tim. 3:16; for the second, I Tim. 3:4, 8, 11.

3, 4. How such prayers are viewed by God is now stated: **This is excellent (or beautiful, admirable) and acceptable in the sight of God our Savior, who desires all men to be saved and to come to the acknowledgment of the truth.**

To *the eye* of God such praying is excellent or admirable. To *his heart* it is acceptable, most welcome. This stands to reason, for his name is "God, our Savior" (see on I Tim. 1:1). Though *men* may at times feel inclined to skip prayer for kings and those who are in authority, especially when the co-operation from the side of princes is not what it should be, in God's sight the matter looks differently. He does not see things as we see them (I Sam. 16:7). In more ways than one, conditions of tranquility and calm promote the spread of the gospel of salvation. And it is he "who desires all men to be saved." The expression "all men" here in verse 4 must have the same meaning as in verse 1; see the discussion there. In a sense, salvation is universal, that is, it is not limited to any *one* group. Churches must not begin to think that prayers must be made for subjects, not for rulers; for Jews, not for Gentiles. No, it is the intention of God our Savior that "all men without distinction of rank, race, or nationality" be saved.[45] What

---

[45] On the question, "Did Christ die for each individual human being, including Judas and the antichrist, actually atoning for the guilt and paying the debt of each and everyone?" see N.T.C. on John, Vol. II, p. 111, and the excellent discussions in the following works:

L. Berkhof, *Vicarious Atonement Through Christ*, Grand Rapids, Mich., pp. 151-178.

this "being saved" implies has been shown in connection with I Tim. 1:15.

Now in the process of *being saved* (taken as a whole) men are not passive. On the contrary, they become active. It is God's will that they come to the acknowledgment of *the truth,* that is, of the way of salvation which is revealed in the Word. Such *acknowledgment* is more than intellectual *knowledge* (γνῶσις). It is joyful *recognition* (ἐπίγνωσις), deep, spiritual *discernment.* See its use in Phil. 1:9; Col. 1:9; 2:2; 3:10. Thus we can also understand the expression "repentance unto the acknowledgment of the truth" (II Tim. 2:25). It is possible for a person to learn a good many things in a merely intellectual fashion, and yet never really come to a *recognition* or *appropriation* of the truth (II Tim. 3:7). There is a "knowing" which is different from a "knowing fully" (see the related verb in I Cor. 13:12). The purpose of prayer for all men, without distinction of rank,

---

L. Boettner, *The Reformed Doctrine of Salvation,* Grand Rapids, 1932, pp. 150-161.

A source-document for the Arminian position is "the remonstrance" or "Five Arminian Articles" (A. D. 1610). P. Schaff, in *Creeds of Christendom,* New York, fifth edition 1919, Vol. III, pp. 545-549, gives the original Dutch text, a Latin, and an English translation, in parallel columns. Here we read, ". . . Jesus Christ, the Savior of the world, died for all men and for every man, so that he has obtained for them all, by his death on the cross, redemption and the forgiveness of sins; yet . . . no one actually enjoys the forgiveness of sins except the believer." On the whole, in this historic document the Arminians express themselves with restraint. (For other literature on this question, presenting either side — or both sides — , see the bibliographies in R. L. Dabney, *Systematic and Polemic Theology,* Richmond, 1927, p. 579; H. Bavinck, *Gereformeerde Dogmatiek,* Kampen, third edition, 1918, Vol. III, pp. 519-521; and the works listed at the end of the article "Arminius and Arminianism," in *The New Schaff-Herzog Encyclopaedia of Religious Knowledge,* Vol. 1, pp. 296, 297. Also *The Writings of Arminius* (3 vols.).

The dispute between the followers of Arminius and those of Gomarus was brought to a head at the Synod of Dort. Here the position of those who favored the limited Atonement won the day. See "The Canons of the Synod of Dort, held A. D. 1618, 1619," in P. Schaff, *Creeds of Christendom,* Vol. III, pp. 550-597. The second head of doctrine declares that the design of the Atonement is limited to the elect, but that the promise of the gospel should be published to all nations, and that the sacrifice of Christ is *sufficient* for everyone without exception. Among the various works in which the proceedings of the Synod of Dort are discussed I have found L. H. Wagenaar, *Van Strijd En Overwinning* to be especially informative. In their *conduct* both sides seem to have gone too far at times. Extreme "Remonstrants" (they preferred this name to "Arminians") branded the decisions of the Synod as "the devil's triumph." They grossly misrepresented the Calvinistic position, just as some of their followers are doing even today. And on the other hand, one finds it hard to defend the manner in which the Synod's strictly Calvinistic president dismissed the Arminian opponents. Brusquely gesturing for them to leave, the on the whole highly respected Rev. Johannes Bogerman reminded them that they had begun with lies and ended with lies. Then, in a voice of thunder, he shouted, "Y o u are dismissed. Get going."

The Arminian position on this and related doctrinal points gained many adherents, especially during the eighteenth century. It is said to have leavened religious thinking in America. A strong advocate of the unrestricted atonement view is Lenski in his commentaries.

I TIMOTHY 2:5

race, and nationality, is that they may be saved, and may come to "full knowledge," a knowledge in which not only the mind but also the heart partakes. The purpose of such praying corresponds with God's own sovereign desire.

5. The position, "God desires *all* men — men from *every* rank and station, tribe and nation — to be saved" is true, **For (there is but) *one* God, and (there is but) *one* Mediator between God and men, the man Christ Jesus.**

There is not one God for this nation, one for another; one God for slaves and one for free men; one God for rulers, one for subjects. Paul is his own best interpreter: "For in one Spirit were we all baptized into one body, whether Jews or Greeks, whether bond or free; and were all made to drink of one Spirit" (I Cor. 12:13). Again, "or is God the God of Jews only? Is he not the God of Gentiles also? Yes, of Gentiles also: if it be true (and it certainly is true) that God is *one* . . ." (Rom. 3:29). That the apostle is actually thinking of the distinction "ruler . . . subject" follows from the immediately *preceding* context (I Tim. 2:2a). That he has in mind the distinction "Jew . . . Gentile" is apparent from the immediately *following* context (I Tim. 2:7b).[46]

Not only the realm of creation but also that of redemption is united under *one* Head. Hence, not only is there only *one* God; there is also only "*one* Mediator *of* (here in the sense of *between*) God and men." The present is the only passage in which Paul speaks of *Christ* as "Mediator." However, in Gal. 3:19, the apostle also uses the term, with probable reference to Moses, who as mediator transmitted God's law to the people. In Gal. 3:20 he speaks in general about "a mediator." It is the author of the epistle to the Hebrews who discusses at some length the position of Christ, our heavenly Highpriest, as Mediator (Heb. 8:6; 9:15; 12:24), "the Mediator of a new covenant." By derivation the word simply indicates someone who stands "in the middle." The purpose for which he takes this in-between position must be derived, in each single case, from the context, or from parallel passages. In the present case it is not open to legitimate doubt that the apostle takes his *point of departure* in the fact that Christ is the One who has voluntarily taken his stand between the offended God and the

---

[46] It is not at all necessary here to regard *one* as subject and *God* as predicate, so that we should have to translate "For *one* is God; *one* also is Mediator," etc. Dr. C. Bouma in his comment on this passage is entirely correct when he points out that Paul's argument is not here directed (except by implication) against polytheism, but rather against one of the practical consequences of polytheism, namely, that each nation has its own God who is concerned especially with that nation. No, there is *one* God who cares for all his people gathered from all over the world!
What we have here, accordingly, is simply an instance of abbreviated expression. The words, "There is but" are easily supplied. The very context requires them. On "abbreviated expression" see N.T.C. on John 5:31.

offending sinner, in order to take upon himself the wrath of God which the sinner has deserved, thereby delivering the latter. This is clear because the entire context speaks of *salvation* (verse 4), and of Christ as a *ransom* (see on verse 6). A striking explanation is found in Gal. 3:13, "Christ redeemed us from the curse of the law, having become a curse *for* (or *over*) us." In that passage the Savior is pictured as standing *over* us, that is, *between* us and the curse of the law, so that the curse falls on him, and we are saved.[47] However, it is clear that in the present passage (I Tim. 2:5) the concept *Mediator* is even slightly broader. Not only does Christ in this capacity restore sinners to the right legal relationship to God, but he also brings them to *"the knowledge of the truth"* (verse 4); and causes *the testimony* of this glorious truth to be borne to them (verse 6). Hence, *he both establishes peace and reveals it to men,* persuading them to accept the good news. He stands revealed as Mediator in this *twofold* sense.[48]

Note the manner in which the identity of this Mediator is revealed: *"one* Mediator between God and *men, the man* Christ Jesus." To think of *men* in this connection means to think of *man,* the man Jesus Christ. Hence *men* and *man* are juxtaposed. Had salvation been intended only for one particular group — say, only for the Jews — the apostle would have written, *"the Jew* Christ Jesus." Since it was intended for both Jew and Gentile, that is, for men in general, without distinction of race or nationality, he writes *"the man* Christ Jesus." (By no means is this a denial of Christ's *deity.* That he is the object of faith and worship is clear from I Tim. 3:16. The word *man* here in I Tim. 2:5 is not contrasted with *God* but with *Jew* or *Gentile.*)

6. Prayer must be made in behalf of all men (verses 1 and 2) because:
a. salvation was intended for all, regardless of rank, station, race, or nationality (verses 3 and 4);
b. there is but one God and one Mediator for all (verse 5), not one for each group; and now:
c. there is but one ransom for all: **who gave himself a ransom for all.**

That is the basic element in Christ's position as Mediator, which Paul has just mentioned. By his suffering and death Christ paid the penalty which God's law demanded, thereby rendering satisfaction. He gave himself as "a substitute-ransom" (ἀντίλυτρον). See on Titus 2:14, for a list of

---

[47] See A. T. Robertson, *The Minister and His Greek New Testament,* New York, 1923, p. 39.
[48] Excellent with respect to this twofold Mediatorship are the words of L. Berkhof, *Systematic Theology,* Grand Rapids, Mich., fourth edition, 1949, pp. 282, 283. — It is immediately clear that the meaning "arbiter" (or "arbitrator") in legal disputes, a sense which the word often has in the papyri, is much too superficial to suit the context *here.* Christ not only *"talks* peace" but *establishes* it: lays the foundation for it by his active and passive obedience; *then* persuades men to accept it. On the sense in the papyri see M.M., p. 399.

pertinent passages. Christ's vicarious death, his sacrifice of himself *in the place of* others, is taught here as clearly as words can possibly convey it.⁴⁹

By adding the preposition "for" or "in behalf of" (on which see N.T.C. on John, Vol. II, p. 110) to the preposition "in exchange for" Paul conveys the twofold idea that Christ's *substitutionary* death was *to the advantage of* all. It merited not deliverance from wrath only, but salvation full and free (see on I Tim. 1:15) for *all men,* regardless of rank, station, race, or nationality.

The second element in Christ's position as Mediator is now indicated: **the testimony (to be borne)** *in due* **season.** Christ's death as a ransom, to satisfy God's justice, *must be proclaimed.* It was the intention of God that when "the appropriate seasons" or "favorable opportunities" arrived, the fact that God desires *all men* to be saved and to come to the acknowledgment of the truth, should be made known. Whatever is contained in verses 4-6 must be published. The "due season" (see footnotes 102 and 105) comprises the entire *new* dispensation. It is a "due season" or an *"appropriate season"* because it corresponds with God's eternal plan with respect to it. Moreover, at its beginning the ransom was brought, and this *for all;* and the Holy Spirit was poured out, again *upon all flesh.* (See also N.T.C. on John 7:6 and on I Thess. 5:1.) Hence, the proper moment for the publication of *the testimony* (especially by those whose eyes have seen and whose ears have heard; see N.T.C. on John 1:7, 8) had arrived. Not during the old dispensation but only during the new can the mystery be fully revealed that *all men,* Gentiles as well as Jews, are now on an equal footing; that is, that the Gentiles have become "fellow-heirs and fellow-members of the body and fellow-partakers of the promise in Christ Jesus through the gospel" (Eph. 3:6; cf. Eph. 2:11-22).

7. Now it was exactly for this purpose, namely, to bear testimony to *all men,* that Paul had been appointed "a teacher *of the Gentiles"* (with all the emphasis on this last phrase). Hence, he continues: **for which purpose I**

---

⁴⁹ From my doctoral thesis, *The Meaning of the Preposition ἀντί in the New Testament,* unpublished doctoral dissertation submitted to the Graduate School of Princeton Seminary, 1948, pp. 74, 75, I quote the following:

"That the prefix ἀντί (in ἀντίλυτρον) has here the substitutionary sense is clear. It means *in exchange for.* This conclusion is based on the following considerations:

"(1) The concept *substitution* is in harmony with the idea that is immediately suggested by the base-word to which ἀντί is prefixed. A λύτρον is a ransom; that is, it is the amount paid for the release of a person from captivity or slavery. Cf. I Peter 1:18, 19, which shows that the blood of Christ was understood to be the price.

"(2) The term ἀντίλυτρον in I Tim. 2:6 seems to be based on the expression λύτρον ἀντὶ πολλῶν (ransom for many) in Matt. 20:28; Mark 10:45. Moreover, if the independent preposition ἀντί in these Synoptic passages has the substitutionary sense, it is certainly probable that when the preposition is used in composition with the noun it has the same meaning."

was appointed a herald and apostle — I am telling the truth, I am not lying — a teacher of Gentiles in (the realm of) faith and truth.

Once it is seen that the expression "all men" in verses 1 and 3 indicates "all men regardless of social, national, and racial distinctions" and not "one by one every member of the entire human race, past, present, and future, including Judas and the antichrist," the logic of the entire paragraph becomes clear. *All men,* in the sense explained, must be remembered in prayer and thanksgiving (verse 1), rulers as well as subjects (verse 2), because God desires that all men be saved and come to acknowledge the truth (verses 3 and 4). There is not *one* God for this group, *another* for that group; there is not *one* Mediator for this nation, *another* for that nation, but only *one* God for all men, and only *one* Mediator for all men, the *man* Christ Jesus (verse 5), who gave himself as a ransom not just for this *one* particular group or nation but *for all,* to which good news testimony was to be borne when the favorable opportunity arrived (verse 6). Hence, I, Paul, was appointed to be a teacher *of Gentiles,* in order that not only Jews but also Gentiles — hence, *all men on an equal footing* — might come to accept the truth by a living faith (verse 7).

In order that God's plan for the salvation of men from every tribe and nation (not only from the Jews but also from the Gentiles) might be carried out, Paul had been divinely *appointed*. He was no usurper, no claimer of authority which was not his by right. He had not *forced* his way to the front, but had been *called* to office by no one less than God himself. Moreover, he was God's chosen vessel "to bear (Christ's) name before the Gentiles and kings and the children of Israel" (not *only* before the children of Israel, but also — yes *especially* — before the Gentiles and kings). He was to be a witness to "all men." He was sent to the Gentiles to open their eyes, that they might receive remission of sins and an inheritance among them that are sanctified by faith in Christ. All this is plainly stated in Acts 9:15; 22:15, 21; 26:17, 18.

It is very clear that Paul did not view the church as an exclusive, esoteric group with carefully guarded "secrets" that must be "concealed" from the public. What a difference between his inspired teaching and the "order" which we find in *The Manual Of Discipline* which was discovered recently in a cave near the Dead Sea. According to that Manual "the counsel of the law" must be "concealed" from "the men of error." If a question is asked about the belief of a member of the community, he must refuse to answer. See Millar Burrows, *The Dead Sea Scrolls,* New York, 1956, pp. 333, 377, and 383. Paul, on the contrary, had been appointed to proclaim the truth publicly.

At times this matter of having been divinely appointed had been called in question by the enemies (Gal. 1:1, 12). It is only natural to surmise that also at Ephesus the teachers of false doctrine would begin to raise questions with reference to it, *especially* with reference to the apostle's appointment to proclaim *to the Gentiles* the gospel of abundant grace. It is for this reason that he injects the words, "I am telling the truth, I am not lying" (cf. Rom. 9:1; II Cor. 11:31; Gal. 1:20).

Now this matter about which Paul is telling the truth and not lying is that he had been divinely appointed as a herald and apostle, a teacher of the Gentiles in the realm of faith and truth.

In the ancient world a "herald" was the person who by order of a superior made a loud, public announcement. Thus, in public games it was his function to announce the name and country of each competitor, and also the name, country, and father of the victor. According to Dan. 3:4, 5 the herald cried aloud, "To y o u it is commanded . . . that whenever y o u hear the sound of . . . all kinds of music, y o u fall down and worship the image which Nebuchadnezzar the king has set up , . ." It has been claimed that the gospel gave this title "of a subordinate official in connection with public and other gatherings" a "strange dignity and world-wide importance." [50] But it is probable that the dignity and importance which attached itself to the term preceded the era of the New Testament. Certainly it was the voice of *the herald* which, as predicted long before the beginning of the new dispensation, cried out, "Prepare in the wilderness the way of Jehovah; make ready in the desert a highway for our God" (Is. 40:6-9, and see N.T.C. on John 1:23). Just as in Isaiah's prophecy Jehovah promised to visit with new tokens of his grace those who are pictured as having returned from the Babylonian captivity, and employs a herald to announce the coming of the King of kings and to command the people to make straight the Lord's highway that leads into their hearts, so Paul is God's *herald* (only other New Testament occurrences: II Tim. 1:11; II Peter 2:5) and ambassador, proclaiming to the nations, "We beseech y o u, on behalf of Christ, be reconciled to God" (II Cor. 5:20). That is the very heart of "preaching," that is, of "heralding." Rebels — for sin is rebellion — who had deserved a message of *woe* receive good tidings of *weal.* The picture is beautiful. It is not the rebellious city which sends out an ambassador to sue for peaceterms, but the offended King of kings who sends his own herald to proclaim peace through a ransom, and that ransom: the blood of his own dear Son!

Paul had been appointed to be not only a herald but also an apostle, representing Christ, fully clothed with delegated authority over doctrine and conduct, an authority continuing for life and extending over the entire church, wherever it existed on earth. It was in this broad capacity as apostle that Paul was a herald. For the meaning of the term *apostle,* especially as applied to Paul, see on I Tim. 1:1.

Having been appointed to be a herald and apostle, Paul was "a teacher

---

[50] M.M., p. 343.

2:7   **I TIMOTHY**

of the Gentiles in (the realm of) faith and truth," that is, he and his message were used by God as means to bring to the minds and hearts of the Gentiles living faith in the truth of the gospel.

---

8 I will then that in every place the men offer prayer, lifting up holy hands without wrath and evil deliberation.

9 Similarly, that women adorn themselves in adorning attire with modesty and good sense, not in braids and gold or pearls or expensive clothing, 10 but — as is proper for women who profess to be God-fearing — (that they adorn themselves) by means of good works. 11 Let a woman learn in silence with complete submissiveness. 12 But to teach I do not permit a woman, nor to exercise authority over a man, but to remain silent. 13 For Adam was formed first, then Eve. 14 And it was not Adam who was deceived, but it was the woman who was indeed deceived and fell into transgression. 15 She will, however, be saved by way of her [51] child-bearing, if they continue in faith and love and sanctification along with good sense.

2:8-15

Having made clear that prayers must be offered for all men, the apostle proceeds to indicate who should offer these prayers and in what spirit they should be offered. This naturally concerns the conduct of *men* in public worship (verse 8). By a natural transition he then gives directions with respect to the proper behavior of *women* in public worship (verses 9-15).

8. I will then that in every place the men offer prayer.

Paul, exercising his full authority as an apostle of Jesus Christ, continues to give directions. The translation of the A.V. "I will" fits the context and suits the word that is used in the original. The word *then* (either loosely inferential or continuative; cf. N.T.C. on John, Vol. II, p. 386, footnote 246) connects this paragraph with the preceding. Prayers must be offered in behalf of all people (verses 1-7); hence, let these prayers be offered; not, however, by *the women* but by *the men* (verse 8). It is clear that the verb *offer prayer* or simply *pray* must here be taken in the broadest sense, including every form of invocation mentioned in 2:1 (see on that passage).

Such prayers must be offered "in every place" of public worship. Often a large room in the house of one of the members would be used for that purpose. There were probably several places of worship in Ephesus and surroundings. In order and manner of worship the customs prevailing in the synagogue were followed as far as possible. The idea that the *men* should lead in prayer cannot have surprised those who were used to the synagogue, except in so far as Paul's emphasis on the equality of the sexes "in Christ" (Gal. 3:28) may have caused some to wonder whether this

---

[51] Literally "by way of the."

spiritual emancipation of women might not imply a change in their position in public worship. Moreover, it must be borne in mind that many of the converts had been gathered from the *Gentile* world. And the church was still very young, with new centers of worship being established right along. Moreover, the possibility that false teachers had been spreading erroneous ideas with respect to the respective roles of *men* and *women* "in church" must not be entirely dismissed. However this may have been, Paul knew, at any rate, that instruction was necessary with respect to this point. He emphasizes that the Christian faith does not call for a complete break with the past. The *presence* of women in the religious assembly is, of course, assumed. Paul's point is that these women should pray as Hannah did, "She spoke *in her heart;* only her lips moved, but her voice was not heard" (I Sam. 1:13).

As for *the men,* they should offer prayer, **lifting up holy hands without wrath and evil deliberation.** Posture in prayer is never a matter of indifference. The slouching position of the body while one is supposed to be praying is an abomination to the Lord. On the other hand, it is also true that Scripture nowhere prescribes one, and only one, correct posture during prayer. Different positions of arms, hands, and of the body as a whole, are indicated. All of these are permissible as long as they symbolize different aspects of the worshipper's reverent attitude, and as long as they truly interpret the sentiments of the heart. Note the following *Prayer Postures:*

(1) *Standing:* Gen. 18:22; I Sam. 1:26; Matt. 6:5; Mark 11:25; Luke 18:11; Luke 18:13. (Note the contrast between the last two passages. It makes a difference even *how* and *where* one stands.)

(2) *Hands Spread Out or/and Lifted Heavenward:* Ex. 9:29; Ex. 17:11, 12; I Kings 8:22; Neh. 8:6; Psalm 63:4; Psalm 134:2; Psalm 141:2; Is. 1:15; Lam. 2:19; Lam. 3:41; Hab. 3:10; Luke 24:50; I Tim. 2:8; James 4:8. (Compare the "Orantes" of the Catacombs. And see A. Deissmann, *Light From the Ancient East,* translated by L. R. M. Strachan, fourth edition, New York 1922, pp. 415, 416.)

(3) *Bowing the Head:* Gen. 24:48 (cf. verse 13); Ex. 12:27; II Chron. 29:30; Luke 24:5.

(4) *The Lifting Heavenward of the Eyes:* Psalm 25:15; Psalm 121:1; Psalm 123:1, 2; Psalm 141:8; Psalm 145:15; John 11:41; John 17:1; cf. Dan. 9:3; Acts 8:55.

(5) *Kneeling:* II Chron. 6:13; Psalm 95:6; Is. 45:23; Dan. 6:10; Matt. 17:14; Mark 1:40; Luke 22:41; Acts 7:60; Acts 9:40; Acts 20:36; Acts 21:5; Eph. 3:14.

(6) *Falling Down with the Face Upon the Ground:* Gen. 17:3; Gen. 24:26; Num. 14:5, 13; Num. 16:4, 22, 45; Num. 22:13, 34; Deut. 9:18, 25, 26; Jos. 5:14; Judg. 13:20; Neh. 8:6; Ezek. 1:28; Ezek. 3:23; Ezek. 9:8;

Ezek. 11:13; Ezek. 43:3; Ezek. 44:4; Dan. 8:17; Matt. 26:39; Mark 7:25; Mark 14:35; Luke 5:12; Luke 17:16; Rev. 1:17; Rev. 11:16.

(7) *Other Postures:* I Kings 18:42 (bowing, with face between the knees); Luke 18:13 (standing from afar, striking the breast).

As is clear from this final reference, the indicated postures and positions of members of the body may occur in various combinations. In Luke 18:13 (1) and (7) are combined. I Kings 8:22 (Solomon) combines (1) and (2). Neh. 8:6 combines (1) and (3). John 11:41 (see verse 38) links (1) with (4). In addition to being combined with (1), number (2) may also be combined with (5), "Solomon arose from the altar of Jehovah, from kneeling on his knees, with his hands spread forth toward heaven" (I Kings 8:54; cf. Ezra 9:5). Moreover, the *bow* (3) was often so deep that the person would fall prostrate upon the ground (6). See, for example, Num. 22:31. In fact, a favorite method of prostration among Orientals has always been falling upon the knees (5), then gradually inclining the body, bowing the head until it touches the ground (3), which may become (6). And even in most cases where Scripture does not definitely indicate this, it may be gathered from the context that the man who spread out or lifted up his hands was *standing*. That is the case also in our present passage (I Tim. 2:8).

Now all these postures were appropriate. The standing position (1) indicates reverence. The lifting up or spreading out of the hands (2) — arms outstretched, with palms upward — is a fit symbol of utter dependence on God and of humble expectancy. Bowing the head (3) is the outward expression of the spirit of submission. The lifting heavenward of the eyes (4) indicates that one believes that his help comes from Jehovah, from him alone. Kneeling (5) pictures humility and adoration. Falling down with face toward the ground (6) is the visible manifestation of awe in the divine presence. Striking the breast (7) beautifully harmonizes with the feeling of utter unworthiness.

The present custom of closing the eyes while folding the hands is of disputed origin. Though unrecorded in Scripture and unknown to the early church, the custom may be considered a good one if properly interpreted. It helps the worshipper to shut out harmful distractions and to enter the sphere where "none but God is near." It is, at any rate, far better than some postures of the body that prevail among moderns when prayer is being offered.

What is stressed, however, throughout Scripture and also in the passage now under study, is not the posture of the body or the position of the hands but *the inner attitude of the soul*. The hands that are lifted up must be *holy*, that is, they must be hands unpolluted by previous crimes. A man who has just committed a murder or an act of adultery or a theft must not think that without pardon and restitution, when this "making good" is possible, his hands can now be lifted up in a prayer that is pleasing to God. See Psalm 24:3, 4; cf. Matt. 5:23, 24.

Moreover, this lifting up of hands must be done "without wrath and evil deliberation." *Wrath* (cf. N.T.C. on John 3:36), that is, *settled indignation* against a brother, the attitude of the unmerciful debtor of the parable (Matt. 18:21-35), makes prayer unacceptable (see also, in this connection, Matt. 6:14, 15; Eph. 4:31, 32; Col. 3:8; Jas. 1:19, 20). And so does *evil deliberation* of any kind whatever. The word used in the original is related to our English word *dialogue*. The soul of man is so constituted that it can carry on a dialogue with itself. Thus a man can debate within himself whether he shall do *this* to his neighbor or *that, balancing* one thought against another (our word *deliberate* — from Latin *de* and *libra* — literally means *to thoroughly weigh, libra* being *a balance*).[52] Although the word used in the original does not in itself brand the *dialoguing* as being *evil* (see Luke 2:35, in which passage the deliberations referred to are not necessarily evil), yet it is worthy of note (cf. Gen. 6:5; 8:21) that in almost every passage in which it is used the deliberation referred to is clearly of a sinful nature (Matt. 15:19; Mark 7:21; Luke 5:22; 6:8; 9:46, 47; Rom. 1:21; 14:1; I Cor. 3:20; Phil. 2:14. In Luke 2:35 it indicates *doubting, questioning*). Here in I Tim. 2:8 the use of the word in conjunction with *wrath* makes this meaning certain.

The sum and substance, therefore, of the present admonition is that in public worship *the men,* not the women, should stand with uplifted hands and offer prayer aloud. The elders naturally would take the lead (I Tim. 5:17). These hands, however, must be holy, and the prayer must be offered in the proper spirit. If the heart of a person is filled with wrath or malice against his brother, so that he is planning evil against him, prayer will not be acceptable.

9. Similarly, that women adorn themselves in adorning attire with modesty and good sense.

The word *similarly* shows that Paul is continuing his remarks about conduct in connection with *public worship*. Just as *the men* must make the necessary preparations, so that with prepared hearts and without previous disposition to evil they "come to church," able to lift up holy hands, so also *the women* must give evidence of the same spirit of holiness, and must show this while they are still at home, getting ready to attend the service.

They should, accordingly, "adorn themselves in adorning attire." Thus

---

[52] In Demosthenes (Athenian orator of the fourth century B. C.) and in other writers the word διαλογισμός indicates a *balancing of accounts;* cf. the etymological meaning of our *de-liberation*. It is easy to see that out of this literal meaning grew the figurative: mental balancing, calculation, consideration, etc. The suffix — μός is an action-ending; hence, primary sense, deliberat*ing;* then, deliberat*ion.*

2:9   **I TIMOTHY**

the sentence will have to be rendered if the alliteration of the original is to be preserved. We readily grant that alliteration cannot always be reproduced without changing the sense of the original. In the present instance, however, we believe that the alliteration of the original should be retained in the translation. Moreover, the argument employed by several commentators, to the effect that the adjective used in the original must here mean *virtuous* or *honorable*, because in non-literary sources it is used in that sense (see M.M., p. 356), ignores the fact that it has that meaning when it describes the *character* of a person (just as in I Tim. 3:2). Such references are of little value when the adjective modifies a noun which indicates not character but "dress." Surely in the latter case the more literal sense "adorning" immediately suggests itself. Women, then, must adorn themselves in *adorning* — that is, *becoming* — *attire* (καταστολή, literally "something let down").

It is clear, therefore, that the apostle does not condemn the desire on the part of girls and women — a desire created in their souls by their Maker — to adorn themselves, to be "in good taste." But if a woman's robe is to be truly such, it will be expressive of modesty and good sense. Hence, Paul writes, "in adorning attire with modesty and good sense." *Modesty* (αἰδώς) indicates *a sense of shame*, a shrinking from trespassing the boundaries of propriety; hence, *proper reserve*. The next word, which we have rendered *good sense*, means literally *soundness of mind* (σωφροσύνη). In getting dressed for church women must practise *sanity*. They must dress in *sensible* attire. They must not try to show off, to be "all the rage," wearing flashy apparel so as to make others jealous of them. They should *adorn* themselves, to be sure. They do not have to balk at fashion, unless a particular fashion happens to be immoral or indecent. They must not look decidedly old-fashioned, awkward, or queer. It must ever be borne in mind that a proud heart is sometimes concealed behind a mask of pretended modesty. That too is sin. Extremes must be carefully avoided. That is what "good sense" implies. The robe must be expressive of inner modesty and of a sane outlook on life, the outlook of the Christian. Applied to our own day and age this means that Pope's well-known lines should be pondered. They contain food for thought:

> "Be not the first by whom the new is tried,
> Nor yet the last to lay the old aside." [53]

Now to adorn oneself in adorning attire with modesty and good sense will mean that a woman does **not** adorn herself **in braids and gold or pearls or expensive clothing.**

---

[53] On this entire subject see W. A. Maier, *For Better Not For Worse*, St. Louis, Mo., 1935, pp. 205-219. This excellent book should be in every church-library and in every home that can afford it.

Paul has been criticized severely for these words, as if he did not want the members of the fair sex to look their loveliest. It has been remarked, "Think of it, he is even opposed to hair-braids! What is wrong with them?" Such criticism is, however, entirely unjustified. The very combination of the word "braids" with "and gold or pearls or expensive clothing" should have sufficed to inform the reader that the apostle is thinking of the sin of extravagance in outward adornment. As to these "braids," the sense is not that under any and all circumstances women throughout all future generations are here forbidden to wear their hair braided. Not at all. The following points must be borne in mind:

a. In view of the context (see verse 10) Paul means this: the Christian woman must understand that her real adornment is not coiffure or jewelry or splendid attire but something else, which the apostle is about to mention, namely, the doing of good works which are the fruits of character transformed by the Holy Spirit.

b. But what about these *braids* which were popular in the world of Paul's day? No expense was spared to make them dazzling. They actually sparkled. The braids were fastened by jewelled tortoise-shell combs, or by pins of ivory or silver. Or the pins were of bronze with jewelled heads, the more varied and expensive the better. The pin-heads often consisted of miniature images (an animal, a human hand, an idol, the female figure, etc.).[54] *Braids,* in those days, often represented *fortunes.* They were articles of luxury! The Christian woman is warned not to indulge in such extravagance.

Similarly, a woman who is a believer must not try to make herself conspicuous by a vain display of ornaments of *gold.* Also, she will not yearn for *pearls,* obtained (at that time) from the Persian Gulf or from the Indian Ocean. These were often fabulously priced and thus way beyond the purchasing power of the average church-member. In order to obtain a pearl of great value a merchant might have to sell all his possessions (Matt. 13:46). Yet someone who was living in Paul's day said, "I have seen Lollia Paulina [wife of emperor Caligula] covered with emeralds and pearls gleaming all over her head, hair, ears, neck, and fingers, to the value of over a million dollars."

A woman of faith will not (at least *should not*) crave *costly garments,* for example a most expensive and showy robe. The robe or mantle worn by the lady resembled a man's toga. However, it was often the product of finer

---

[54] See the picture and description in T. G. Tucker, *Life in the Roman World of Nero and St. Paul.* New York, 1922, p. 311. Also, *The Good News, The New Testament Of Our Lord and Savior Jesus Christ, With Over 500 Illustrations and Maps,* published by The American Bible Society, 1955; the illustration in connection with the text of I Timothy, p. G 19. Finally, *Everyday Life In Ancient Times,* published by The National Geographic Society, Washington, D.C., pp. 244, 245.

workmanship, and was characterized by richer ornamentation, and greater color-variation.[55]

Vain display on the part of women was and is offensive to what is best in Oriental taste. What is more important, it also offends the Creator. In a woman who professes to be a believer such pursuit of the cult of beauty and personal adornment is doubly unbecoming. It offends the Creator *and* the Redeemer. See also Is. 3:16-24 and I Peter 3:3, 4. Though always wrong, it is most reprehensible in a woman who is getting ready to attend church; for showy clothes ill befit broken and contrite hearts, the kind of hearts which God welcomes at the service of the Word and sacraments.

10. "I will then that . . . the women adorn themselves . . . not in braids and gold or pearls or expensive clothing, **but — as is proper for women who profess to be God-fearing — by means of good works.**

For women genuine adornment is attained by means of the performance of *good works* (cf. I Tim. 6:11, 18; II Tim. 2:22; 3:17). Divine grace brings into existence the tree of faith on which these good works grow as so many fruits. That is the apostle's doctrine both here in the Pastorals (Titus 2:11-14; 3:4-8) and elsewhere (Gal. 5:22-24; Eph. 2:10). Now for women to adorn themselves by means of good works is the *proper* thing to do, inasmuch as they *profess* to be *God-fearing*. Literally Paul says, "who profess *God-fearingness*." The verb rendered *profess* has the root-meaning *to convey a message loudly, clearly;* hence, *to proclaim*. Such a proclamation may be in the form of *a promise* or of *a profession;* generally the former (Mark 4:11; Acts 7:5; Rom. 4:21; Gal. 3:19; Titus 1:2; Heb. 6:13; 10:23; 11:11; 12:26; James 1:12; 2:5; I John 2:25), but here and in I Tim. 6:21 the latter. The noun *God-fearingness* (see LXX: Gen. 20:11) occurs nowhere else in the New Testament; but see the adjective in John 9:31.

The entire idea reminds us at once of I Peter 3:3, 4: "whose adorning let it not be the outward adorning of braiding the hair and of wearing jewels of gold, or of wearing robes, but . . . the hidden man of the heart with the imperishable jewel of a meek and quiet spirit which in the sight of God is very precious."

11, 12. Next, the apostle gives a few directions with respect to the relation of women to *gathering* and *imparting knowledge (learning* and *teaching),* again with special reference to public worship. He writes,

Let a woman learn in silence with complete submissiveness. But to teach I do not permit a woman, nor to exercise authority over a man, but to remain silent.

Though these words and their parallel in I Cor. 14:33-35 may sound a

---

[55] On the entire subject see A. Sizoo, *De Antieke Wereld En Het Nieuwe Testament,* Kampen, 1948, II. 62-64; T. G. Tucker, *op. cit.,* pp. 289-313.

trifle unfriendly, in reality they are the very opposite. In fact, they are expressive of a feeling of tender sympathy and basic understanding. They mean: let a woman not enter a sphere of activity for which by dint of her very creation she is not suited. Let not a bird try to dwell under water. Let not a fish try to live on land. Let not a woman yearn to exercise authority over a man by lecturing him in public worship. For the sake both of herself and of the spiritual welfare of the church such unholy tampering with divine authority is forbidden.

In the service of the Word on the day of the Lord a woman should *learn, not teach*. She should *be silent, remain calm* (see N.T.C. on I Thess. 4:11 and on II Thess. 3:12). She should *not cause her voice to be heard*. Moreover, this learning in silence should not be with a rebellious attitude of heart but "with complete *submissiveness*" (cf. II Cor. 9:13; Gal. 2:5; I Tim. 3:4). She should cheerfully *range herself under* God's law for her life. Her full spiritual equality with men as a sharer in all the blessings of salvation (Gal. 3:28: "there can be no male and female") does not imply any basic change in her nature *as woman* or in the corresponding task which she *as a woman* is called upon to perform. Let a woman remain a woman! Anything else Paul *cannot permit*. *Paul* cannot permit it because *God's holy law* does not permit it (I Cor. 14:34). That holy law is his will as expressed in the Pentateuch, particularly in the story of woman's creation and of her fall (see especially Gen. 2:18-25; 3:16). Hence, *to teach*, that is, to preach in an official manner, and thus by means of the proclamation of the Word in public worship to *exercise authority* over a man, *to dominate him,* is wrong for a woman. She must not assume the role of a master.

13, 14. As already indicated, these directives regarding the woman's role in connection with public worship are based not on temporary or contemporary conditions or circumstances but on two facts that have meaning for all time, namely, the fact of *creation* and the fact of *the entrance of sin*. Accordingly, Paul writes: **For Adam was formed first, then Eve. And it was not Adam who was deceived, but it was the woman who was indeed deceived and fell into transgression.**

In *forming* or *moulding* (cf. Rom. 9:20) the human pair, God first made Adam; afterward Eve. Not only that, but he made Eve *for the sake of* Adam, to be his helper (Gen. 2:18-25), and his glory (I Cor. 11:7-9). Neither is complete without the other (I Cor. 11:11). But in his sovereign wisdom God made the human pair in such a manner that it is natural for *him* to lead, for *her* to follow; for *him* to be aggressive, for *her* to be receptive; for *him* to invent, for *her* to use the tools which he invents. The tendency *to follow* was embedded in Eve's very soul as she came forth from the hand of her Creator. Hence, it would not be right to reverse this order in con-

2:13, 14   I TIMOTHY

nection with public worship. Why should a woman be encouraged to do things that are contrary to her nature? Her very body, far from *preceding* that of Adam in the order of creation, *was taken out of* Adam's body. Her very name — *Ish-sha* — *was derived from* his name — *Ish* (Gen. 2:23). It is when the woman recognizes this basic distinction and acts accordingly that she can be a blessing to the man, can exert a gracious yet very powerful and beneficent influence upon him, and can promote her own happiness, unto God's glory. Longfellow was right when he said:

> "As unto the bow the cord is,
> So unto the man is woman;
> Though she bends him she obeys him,
> Useless each without the other!"
>   (Hiawatha)

Added to this fact of *creation* is that of the entrance of *sin*. Eve's fall occurred when she ignored her divinely ordained position. Instead of *following* she chose *to lead*. Instead of remaining submissive to God, she wanted to be *"like* God." *She* — not Adam — *was indeed* (or *was completely*) *deceived or deluded*.[56]

Eve "was indeed deceived," but Adam "was not deceived." Of course, this cannot be taken absolutely. It must mean something on this order: Adam was not deceived in the manner in which Eve was deceived. See Gen. 3:4-6. *She* listened directly to Satan; *he* did not. *She* sinned before *he* did. *She* was the leader. *He* was the follower. She led when she should have followed; that is, she led in the way of sin, when she should have followed in the path of righteousness.

And so she fell *into transgression*, into the fatal *stepping aside* from the path of obedience. And now that which before was an unmixed blessing — namely, that Eve, by virtue of her creation, constantly followed Adam — is an unmixed blessing no longer; for now she who, by her sinful example, chose *to rule* him who at that moment was still her *sinless* husband, *must obey* the creature of her own designing, namely, her *sinful* husband. Hence, let none of her daughters follow her in reversing the divinely established order. Let none assume the role that was not intended for her. Let not the daughter of Eve teach, rule, lead, when the congregation gathers for worship. Let her learn, not teach; obey, not rule; follow, not lead.

---

[56] Though it is true that Paul uses the verbs ἀπατάω and ἐξαπατάω to express the same basic idea (see N.T.C. on II Thess. 2:3a), yet when, as here in I Tim. 2:14, he uses the strengthened and the unstrengthened form side by side, it is reasonable to assume that he intends to convey a difference in meaning. Hence, *was not deceived* ... *was indeed deceived* (or: *was completely deceived*).

I TIMOTHY   2:15

15. She will, however, be saved by way of her child-bearing.
Not by way of preaching to *adults* (see on verse 12) but by way of bearing *children* does a woman attain to real happiness, to *salvation,* with stress on its positive aspect (see on I Tim. 1:15). The path that leads to salvation is ever that of obedience to God's ordinances. It is his will that the woman should influence mankind "from the bottom up" (that is, by way of *the child*), not "from the top down" (that is, not by way of *the man*). She must choose to do that for which by God's creation-ordinance she is naturally equipped, both physically and spiritually. She must reach her goal *by way of* (διά) *her child-bearing.*

Again, not by way of *exercising dominion* over men but by way of *submission* does a woman reach the state of true freedom and blessedness (see on verses 11 and 12). Now the curse which was pronounced upon Eve included two elements: a. *submission* to her (now sinful) husband, and b. painful *child-bearing* (mentioned in reverse order in Gen. 3:16). It is therefore not at all surprising that Paul, thoroughly at home in The Law and writing by inspiration, immediately mentions *child-bearing* after having mentioned *submission.* He sees what Adam also saw. Paul, however, sees it more clearly. Adam already perceived that by God's grace *the curse* of child-bearing (think of its *painful* character) was changed into *a blessing* (Gen. 3:20). Because of the prospect of child-bearing Adam's wife was named *Eve,* that is "Life" (the mother of all *living*). Paul takes up this thought and develops it. Child-bearing will mean *salvation* for the Christian mother, for what Christian mother does not experience inner delight, joy, blessing, and glory in seeing the image of her Savior reflected in little ones who belong to him? In *bearing children* (here *the noun: child-bearing; the verb* is used in I Tim. 5:14) the Christian mother by faith in God's covenant promise (Gen. 17:7; Acts 2:38, 39) looks forward to all the joys of Christian motherhood unto the glory of God. This to her is *salvation.*[57]

When Paul says *she* (in the clause "She . . . will be saved by her child-bearing"), he is thinking of "the woman" of verse 14. This referred first of all to Eve, but then also to any Christian mother taken as a representative of *the entire class* to which she belongs. Hence, it is not strange that

---

[57] I reject the following explanations:
(1) "She will be saved by means of The Childbirth" (that is, the Birth of Christ).
(2) "She will come safely through child-birth."
Objection: both of these ideas are foreign to the present context. In addition, Number (2) assigns a meaning to the verb which in the present context is not warranted. See the verb in 1:15 and 2:4.
(3) "By means of bearing children she will be rescued from everlasting damnation and will merit everlasting glory."
Objection: this idea of making child-bearing a meritorious act strikes at the very heart of Paul's theology as expressed both in the Pastorals and elsewhere (see pp. 18, 19). Besides, the immediately following words (". . . if they continue in faith," etc., suffice to rule it out).

the apostle now shifts from the singular to the plural (from "she" to "they") as he continues: **if they continue in faith and love and sanctification along with good sense.** Not child-bearing as such procures salvation. The love of God shed abroad in the heart, the peace which passes all understanding, the delight which is experienced when one submits to God's ordinances, the joys of truly *Christian* motherhood, all these are experienced only if women "continue in faith," etc. Faith comes first. It is the product of God's sovereign grace. To be truly blessed, women must *continue* in it. The matter of salvation is regarded here from the side not of God but of the human individual. It is true, indeed, that once a woman (or a man, but the present passage deals with women) is truly saved, she remains saved forever; yet, God does not keep a woman on the way of salvation without exertion, diligence, and watchfulness on her part. The strength thus to persevere in the faith is ever from God, from him alone (see also N.T.C. on John, Vol. II, p. 299).

The nouns used in the present passage have all been explained. For *faith* and *love* see on I Tim. 1:5. For *sanctification* (the daily dying unto sin and being renewed unto holiness; here perhaps with special emphasis on active opposition to all immorality or uncleanness in thought and act, sins so often associated with the married state) see N.T.C. on I Thess. 4:3-8. And for *good sense* see on I Tim. 2:9. The complete thought is therefore as follows: if the women members of the church will abide in faith and love and sanctification, meanwhile exercising proper self-control and reserve, they will find their joy and salvation in bearing children to God's glory, yes, in all the duties and delights of Christian motherhood.

Synthesis of Chapter 2

See the Outline at the beginning of the chapter.

When the congregation assembles for public worship, *all* must be remembered in prayer, that is, rulers as well as subjects, for:

a. salvation is intended "for all," regardless of rank, station, race, or nation;

b. there is but one God and one Mediator, not one God and one Mediator for *this* group, and one for *that* group;

c. there is but *one* ransom;

d. hence Paul had been appointed to be a teacher *of Gentiles,* in order that not only Jews but also Gentiles might come to accept the gospel by a living faith.

At public worship *the men* — not the women — should stand with uplifted hands, offering prayer aloud. For such praying there should be adequate preparation, so that the heart may not be filled with malice against a brother or with predisposition to evil.

The women, too, must prepare themselves adequately when they are about to go to church. They must avoid all extravagance in outward adornment, bearing in mind that their true adornment is the doing of good works. In the place of public worship women should realize that their duty is to learn, not to teach; to obey, not to rule; to follow, not to lead. If they abide in faith and love and sanctification, meanwhile exercising proper self-control and reserve, they will find their joy and salvation in the delights of Christian motherhood. (To be sure, Priscilla — as well as Aquila — taught Apollos, but *not from the pulpit.* Read Acts 18:26.)

This teaching regarding the place which women should occupy when the congregation gathers for worship is based not on any temporary condition but on Adam's priority in creation and Eve's priority in transgression.

In this connection it should be pointed out that though the apostle definitely ascribes to women a *different* position than to men, he does not regard their role in church-affairs to be in any way less important than that filled by men.

The Dignity of Women in the Pauline Epistles

(1) He mentions with favor the following, to many of whom he sends greetings: Phoebe, Prisca, "Mary," Tryphena and Tryphosa, Persis, Julia, the sister of Nereus, Apphia, Lois and Eunice (see Romans 16; Phil. 4; II Tim. 1; Philemon).

(2) He employs women in the service of the gospel (Rom. 16:1-3; Phil. 4:3); specifically, the older widows (I Tim. 5:9, 10), deacons' assistants (I Tim. 3:11), women who are able to support others (I Tim. 5:16). Cf. what the book of Acts says with reference to Lydia (16:14, 40), Dorcas (9:36), Mary, the mother of John (12:2), and the daughters of Philip (21:8, 9).

What a difference between the status of women in the early church, on the one hand, and in the Qumran sect, described in the Dead Sea Scrolls, on the other. In the church women were given an honorable status. In the Qumran sect women played hardly any part. See Millar Burrows, *op. cit.,* pp. 233, 244 and 333.

(3) He emphasizes that "in Christ" there is neither male nor female (Gal. 3:28). In relation to him there is perfect equality.

(4) He recommends marriage, even for widows, and he praises the joys of *Christian* wifehood and motherhood (I Cor. 7:39; I Tim. 5:14; then I Tim. 2:15; 4:3). There are circumstances, however, under which Paul considers it better "not to marry" (I Cor. 7:26, 27).

(5) Anyone who maintains that Paul holds women in low esteem should read the following passages. If they are honestly interpreted, one will have to admit that in many ways no man is ever able to bestow upon a woman the full honor which according to Paul's teaching should be bestowed upon her:

"For the unbelieving husband is sanctified through his wife, and the unbelieving wife is sanctified through her husband" (I Cor. 7:14).

"The wife does not have power over her own body, but the husband has; and similarly, the husband has no power over his own body, but the wife has" (I Cor. 7:4).

"The woman is man's glory" (I Cor. 11:7).

"In the Lord neither is woman without (the) man, nor is man without (the) woman" (I Cor. 11:11).

"Husbands, love y o u r wives, even as Christ also loved the church, and gave himself up for it; that he might sanctify it . . . Even so ought husbands also to love their own wives as their own bodies. . . . Let each one of y o u love his wife as he loves himself; and let the wife see to it that she respects her husband" (Eph. 5:25-33).

Paul's practical attitude to women kingdom-workers is expressed in this beautiful, concise order:

"HELP THESE WOMEN" (Phil. 4:3).

Outline of Chapter 3

Theme: *The Apostle Paul, Writing to Timothy, Gives Directions For the Administration of the Church*

Directions with respect to the Institution of the Offices

3:1-7   A. Incentive for becoming an overseer; the glorious character of the work.
Directions regarding the necessary qualifications of overseers.

3:8-13   B. Directions regarding the necessary qualifications of deacons and of women who assist them.
Incentive for faithful performance of the task of deacons and of women who assist them: their glorious reward.

3:14-16   C. The reasons for conveying these instructions in written form:
1. Though I hope to see you soon, I fear that I may be delayed.
2. Yet, the matter permits of no delay, for it concerns God's house, the church, which is great because of its exalted Head, Jesus Christ. Hymn in adoration of the Christ.

CHAPTER III

I TIMOTHY 3:1

3 1 Reliable is the saying, "If anyone aspires to the office of overseer, he desires a noble work." 2 The overseer therefore [58] must be above reproach, one wife's husband, temperate, self-controlled, virtuous, hospitable, qualified to teach; 3 not (one who lingers) beside (his) wine, not given to blows, but genial, not contentious, not fond of money, 4 managing well his own household, with true dignity keeping his children in submission 5 (for if a person does not know how to manage his own household, how will he take upon himself the care of God's church?), 6 not a recent convert, in order that he may not become befogged by conceit and fall into the condemnation of the devil. 7 He must also have a favorable testimony from outsiders, lest he fall into reproach and a snare of the devil.[59]

Public worship generally precedes the institution of the offices. Hence, it is not surprising that Paul, having discussed the former, now proceeds to give directions regarding the latter. In the present chapter he shows that elders, deacons, and women who render auxiliary service must be spiritually and morally qualified in order to perform their tasks in the church of Jesus Christ, the One "who was made manifest in the flesh . . . taken up in glory."

3:1-7

1. Accordingly, the apostle begins by writing: **Reliable** [60] **is the saying, If anyone aspires to the office of overseer, he desires a noble work.**

---

[58] Something can be said in favor of the rendering "however" (for οὖν). But the more usual meaning of the Greek particle (inferential "therefore") makes excellent sense: *"in view of the fact that* the overseership is such a noble work, the man who fills this office must be above reproach. The continuative meaning ("now," "then") is also possible. See further N.T.C. on John, Vol. II, p. 386, footnote 246.
[59] With respect to possible parallels (to such a list of requirements) in secular literature see on Titus 2:1.
[60] The reading "popular" or "human" (ἀνθρώπινος) is the saying, is weakly attested; see N.N. It may possibly be ascribed to a scribe's hesitancy to prefix the profound introductory clause, *"Reliable* is the saying" to a statement which fails to give expression to a paramount essential of the Christian faith.
Possibly for the same reason some would construe this clause with the preceding paragraph (thus, for example, Lock and A. T. Robertson). But it is hard to see how anything in the immediately preceding paragraph (which deals with the behavior of women, their proper attire with a view to church-attendance, etc.) could have become "a watchword of Christian wisdom." The saying, moreover, harmonizes beautifully with the entire paragraph which follows.

117

This is the second of five "reliable sayings" or trustworthy current proverbs, wisdom maxims. For their general character see on I Tim. 1:15.

It is sometimes maintained that the present saying is not only devoid of great significance or value but is even harmful, encouraging sinful aspiration to office! But this opinion results from the fact that the saying is read in the light of later conditions. Some interpreters reason as follows, "It is decidedly wrong for anyone *to stretch out his hand* (note the verb ὀρέγω) in order to lay hold on the holy office. Such sinful ambition deserves *to be condemned.* The office should seek the man, not the man the office. Hence, it is very strange that Paul seems to have a word of praise for such sinful striving." But over against this the following two points deserve emphasis:

a. Although it is true that praise for the man who aspires *is implied* in the saying, it is not definitely *expressed*. The apostle simply says, *"If anyone aspires."* It is *the office* rather than the striving that is definitely described as being *excellent* or *noble* ("a noble work").

b. Though it is nevertheless true that praise for the aspirant *is implied*, it must be borne in mind that *in the early history of the church willingness to serve as an overseer meant sacrifice*. Again and again persecution would rage, from the side of the Jews, of the Gentiles, or, as often, of both. False teachers did their utmost to undermine the true foundation. Truly, in *such* a time and amid *such* circumstances an *incentive to overseership and a word of implied praise* for the man who indicated a willingness to serve in this high office were not at all out of place. And the office itself was surely "a noble work." It still is, but it was never more so than in the early decades!

When Paul speaks about the office of *overseer* (ἐπισκοπή, — ῆς), he has in mind the divinely authorized task of the *elders,* as has been (and will be) indicated (see also on Titus 1:5-7). These overseers or elders constituted a presbytery or board of presbyters or elders. With respect to age and dignity its members were called *presbyters* or *elders,* just as in Israel. With respect to the nature of their task they were called *overseers* or *superintendents.*

The manner in which, on the whole, these men conducted themselves in the sacred office, and their willingness to suffer innumerable hardships for the cause of Christ, justified the current saying, "If anyone aspires to the office of overseer, he desires a noble task." Let no one look down upon the overseer! Let no one despise him because he does not have *all* the special gifts. He is eager to give of his time and energies, and is even willing to sacrifice his physical ease and safety for the noble work of "feeding the church of the Lord which he purchased with his own blood" (Acts 20:28). May the glorious character of the work be *an incentive* to all who are considering overseership, so that they may eagerly desire it!

But just because the work is so noble and the task so grand certain qualifications are stipulated. In order that these qualifications may be seen as the apostle groups them, the following verses are here printed together according to what appears to be their intended and natural classification:

2-7.
2. The overseer therefore must be
    above reproach
    one wife's husband
    temperate
    self-controlled
    virtuous
        hospitable
        qualified to teach
3. not (one who lingers) beside (his) wine
    not given to blows
        but genial
    not contentious
    not fond of money
    4. managing well his own household, with true dignity
        keeping his children in submission; 5. (for if a person
        does not know how to manage his own household, how will
        he take care of God's church?)
6. not a recent convert, in order that he may not become beclouded by conceit and fall into the condemnation of the devil.
7. He must also have a favorable testimony from outsiders, lest he fall into reproach and a snare of the devil.

It is immediately clear that according to Paul's inspired teaching the prospective overseer must have a favorable testimony from two groups: (a) *insiders,* that is, church-members, and (b) *outsiders,* that is, those who are outside the church.

As was to be expected, the emphasis falls on the first, the reputation which the man has among church-members. The various items which belong to this first classification are divided into two sets of seven items each. However, the very first item — "above reproach" — may be considered a kind of caption or heading for all the items in both sets of this *first* classification. The *second* classification is summarized somewhat similarly, but without a list of detailed requirements.

Beginning with the first category, as far as his standing or reputation *with the members of the church* is concerned, the overseer must accordingly be *without* (or "above") *reproach.*

Note that the first set of seven characteristics is *positive* (except for the caption itself: *without* — or *above* — reproach or *un*-assailable). The second set is largely *negative.* Five times we read *not* (of these five, three have μή;

two have ἀ -privative). Thus, in all there are eight (6 plus 2) requirements expressed positively, six (1 plus 5) expressed negatively.

It must not escape our attention that the very first and the very last of the eight *positive* requirements describe the qualified person's relation to *his family*. That relationship is again emphasized in connection with the deacons. Paul (and the Holy Spirit speaking through Paul) must have regarded this family-relationship as being of great importance.

In the first set of seven requirements the subdivision is as follows: under the caption "above reproach" we find first a set of four requirements having to do with the man's attitude to *Christian morality in general:* he must be maritally pure, temperate, sensible, virtuous. Then, two requirements describing the man's attitude toward (and influence upon) people who stand in some definite relation to *the church*. How does he treat guests from other churches, etc.? Is he hospitable? What influence for good does he exert on those who require guidance or instruction? Is he qualified to teach?

In the second set of seven requirements we see the man in his *daily life*, rubbing elbows with his *fellow-men* at work and everywhere. The item "not (one who lingers) beside (his) wine" easily merges with the next one, namely, "not given to blows," for drunkenness often leads to blows. Over against this stands the positive requirement *genial*. Paralleling it is "not contentious." The contentious person is generally selfish, hence "fond of money." The question, accordingly, is this, "Can the candidate under review be trusted with the church's *funds?*" (Note how here, just as at the close of the first set of seven requirements, the attention is focused once more on the man's relation to *the church*.) Also, can he take care of its *affairs?* How does he manage his own family? That ought to show whether he can take upon himself the care over the affairs of the church! And finally, can it be reasonably expected that he will command the respect of its *members*, the experienced as well as those recently converted? But in that case he himself must be a man of some experience in Christian living. He must not be *a novice*.

We see, therefore, that the items in the list are not just thrown together in haphazard fashion. They follow each other logically and are neatly arranged.

A few remarks will now be made with reference to each of the fifteen (7 plus 7 plus 1) requirements. The *first set of seven* is as follows: The overseer must be:

1. *"Above reproach"* in the estimation of fellow church members

See also I Tim. 5:7 and 6:14. The word used in the original literally means "not to be laid hold of," hence *irreprehensible* or *unassailable*. Enemies may bring all manner of accusations, but these charges are proved to be empty whenever fair methods of investigation are applied. With

I TIMOTHY 3:2-7

the church and in accordance with the rules of justice, this man not only *has* a good reputation but *deserves* it.

Example of a man who was "above reproach":

Simeon

"And there was a man in Jerusalem, whose name was Simeon; and this man was righteous and devout, looking for the consolation of Israel, and the Holy Spirit was upon him" (Luke 2:25). Cf. Job 1:8.

The particulars with respect to which he is "above reproach" follow:

2. In *marital relationship* "one wife's husband"

See also I Tim. 5:9 ("one husband's wife"). This cannot mean that an overseer or elder must be a married man. Rather, *it is assumed* that he is married — as was generally the case —, and it is stipulated that in this marital relationship he must be an example to others of faithfulness to his one and only marriage-partner. Infidelity in this relationship is a sin against which Scripture warns repeatedly. That this sin and those related to it (sexual immorality in any form) were of frequent occurrence among the Jews and certainly among the Gentiles, is clear from ever so many passages (among many others: Ex. 20:14; Lev. 18:20; 20:10; Deut. 5:18; 22:23; II Sam. 12; Is. 51; Prov. 2:17; Prov. chapter 7; Jer. 23:10, 14; 29:23; Hos. 1:2; 2:2; 3:1; Matt. 5:28; John 8:3; Rom. 1:27; 7:3; I Cor. 5:1, 9; 6:9-11; 7:2; Gal. 5:19. See also N.T.C. on I Thess. 4:3-8). And let us not forget what Paul says in this very epistle (see on I Tim. 1:10).

Accordingly, the meaning of our present passage (I Tim. 3:2) is simply this, that an overseer or elder must be a man of unquestioned morality, one who is entirely true and faithful to his one and only wife; one who, being married, does not in pagan fashion enter into an immoral relationship with another woman.

In view of this, the attempt on the part of some to change the meaning of the original — making it say what it does not say — is inexcusable. In harmony with the views of *some* Church Fathers (for example, Tertullian and Chrysostom), and in disagreement with the explanations favored by others (for example, Jerome and Origen), these translators and commentators are of the opinion that Paul is here referring to men who, having been widowers, remarried. The translation (?) then becomes, "An overseer must be a man *who was married only once.*" [61] One can *understand* how men who reject or soft-pedal Scripture's infallibility — who, accordingly no longer feel obliged to accept as most certainly true the words, *"Paul . . . to Timothy"* (I Tim. 1:1, 2) — can also take the next step, and, assuming that the Pastorals reflect conditions which prevailed *after* Paul's departure from this earth, at a time when by many celibacy and the virgin-state began to be exalted above marriage, can read their private reconstruction of the

---

[61] Thus, or in similar fashion, Parry, Goodspeed, Moffatt, R.S.V., etc.

formation of these letters into the text, so that they think of the author of the Pastorals as a man who considered marriage and certainly *remarriage* to be sinful or nearly so. One *cannot excuse* an attempt to make a text say what it does not actually say in the original. The original simply says, "He must be . . . one wife's husband" (δεῖ — μιᾶς γυναικὸς ἄνδρα).[62]

The real author of the Pastorals, namely, Paul, did not oppose remarriage after the death of the marriage-partner (see especially I Tim. 5:14; then 4:3; cf. Rom. 7:2, 3; I Cor. 7:9), though *under certain specified conditions* he considered continuation in the unmarried state to be wiser than marriage (I Cor. 7:26, 38). Paul, we may be sure, was in entire agreement with the author of Hebrews, who said, "Let marriage be held in honor among all." (Heb. 13:4).

Example of a man who gives every evidence of having been true to his one and only wife, and of the beautiful harmony between the two, also in religious matters:

Aquila

"But when Priscilla and Aquila heard him (Apollos), they took him unto them, and expounded to him the way of God more accurately" (Acts 18:26).

3. In *mode of living (tastes and habits)*, "temperate"

See also I Tim. 3:11; Titus 2:2. For the related verb see N.T.C. on I Thess. 5:6, 8 and see on II Tim. 4:5. Other possible translations of the adjective would be *sober* (not, however, in the sense of *somber* or *sad*), *circumspect*. Such a person lives deeply. His pleasures are not primarily those of the senses, like the pleasures of a drunkard for instance, but those of the soul. He is filled with spiritual and moral earnestness. He is not given to excess (in the use of wine, etc.), but moderate, well-balanced, calm, careful, steady, and sane. This pertains to his physical, moral, and mental tastes and habits.

Example of such a well-balanced, sober, careful, temperate person:

Luke

". . . having investigated them all carefully from the beginning" (Luke 1:3). Even those who cannot be counted among the company of believers are at times not altogether devoid of this virtue; note the town-clerk at Ephesus, who subdued the tempers of the crowd (Acts 19:35).

---

[62] It is correctly rendered by the following (among others): Syriac (published by British and Foreign Bible Society, London, 1950, 1. 142); Latin (Theodori Bezae, "unius uxoris virum"); English (A.V., A.R.V., Weymouth, Lenski, Berkeley; the same idea, Williams: "must have only one wife"; Riverside: "true to one woman"); Dutch (Statenvertaling: "eener vrouwe man"; Nieuwe Vertaling: "de man van een vrouw"); Frisian; South African; French (Version D'Ostervald); German (Luther and subsequent versions); Swedish authorized in 1917, edition Stockholm 1946).

4. In *manner of judging and of acting on these judgments,* "self-controlled"

See also Titus 1:8; 2:2, 5; and see on I Tim. 2:9, 15 for the related noun. The *self-controlled* or *sensible* man is the man *of sound mind.* He is *discreet,* sane; hence, not swayed by sudden impulses over which he exercises no mastery, nor is he at all ready to accept the nonsense which was being disseminated by the errorists at Ephesus (see on I Tim. 1:3, 4, 6, 7). The sensible person is always ready and willing to learn.

Example of such a sane individual:

Apollos

Though he was a gifted orator, mighty in the Scriptures and instructed in the way of the Lord, still he was willing to be taught by Priscilla and Aquila, in order to learn the way of God more accurately (Acts 18:26, quoted above, under 2).

5. In *morals in general,* "virtuous"

See also I Tim. 2:9. The overseer must be a man "of inner moral excellency and of outward *orderly* behavior." It is an epithet of honor. See M.M., p. 356. The adjective naturally has a slightly different shade of meaning when applied to *character* than when applied to *clothes* or *outward appearance* (as in I Tim. 2:9). The root-meaning of the related noun is *order.* See N.T.C. on John, Vol. I, p. 79, footnote 26.

Example of a virtuous person, a person of moral strength:

Ruth

"All . . . know that thou art a virtuous woman" (a woman of worth, LXX: cf. strength, Ruth 3:11).

Further: Job (Job 1:8); Zechariah and Elizabeth (Luke 1:5, 6); Simeon (Luke 2:25); Anna (Luke 2:37).

6. In hospitality, "hospitable"

See also Titus 1:8; then Rom. 12:13; Heb. 13:2; I Peter 4:9. A hospitable person is literally a *friend of strangers* (φιλόξενος). He "communicates to their necessities." We can well imagine how deeply appreciated was such hospitality in a day when organized *social* welfare on any large scale was virtually non-existent; when widows and orphans were dependent on the kindness of relatives and friends; when persecutions with their imprisonments raged fiercely; when poverty and hunger were far more in evidence than they are today in the countries of the West; when messages from one section of Christendom to another had to be delivered by personal messenger, necessitating a great deal of travel; and when lodging with unbelievers was less than desirable. Hence, if hospitality was a requirement for *every* Christian according to his ability and opportunity to furnish it, it was all the more a requirement for the overseer.

Example:

Onesiphorus

"Onesiphorus . . . often refreshed me, and was not ashamed of my chain" (II Tim. 1:16). See also Gen. 18:1-8; I Kings 17:8-16; I Kings 18:13; II Kings 4:8; Heb. 13:2.

7. In teaching-ability, "qualified to teach"

See also I Tim. 5:17; II Tim. 2:2; 2:24; 3:14; then I Cor. 12:29. Every overseer or elder should possess this gift to some extent. No one, moreover, will be *able to teach* (διδακτικός) unless he himself is *taught* (διδακτός). Having been instructed by "faithful witnesses" one imparts this instruction to others, who in turn must teach still others.

But though all the overseers must have this ability in a certain degree, so that they can counsel those who seek their advice, some have received *greater* or *different* talents than others. Hence, even in Paul's day the work of the elders was divided, so that, while all took part in ruling the church, some were entrusted with the responsibility of laboring in the word and in teaching (I Tim. 5:17). Accordingly the distinction arose between those overseers who today are generally called "ministers" and those who are simply called "elders."

Example:

Ezra and his helpers

"He (Ezra) was a ready scribe in the law of Moses . . . Ezra the priest, the scribe, and the Levites who taught the people, said to all the people, This day is holy to Jehovah y o u r God" (Ezra 7:6; Neh. 8:9). See also Acts 6:10.

And now *the second set of seven requirements*. The overseer must also be *above reproach* in the following respects. He must be:

(1) "not (one who lingers) beside (his) wine"

See also I Tim. 3:8; Titus 1:7, and see on I Tim. 5:23. (The original has acc. of πάροινος.) With respect to drinking wine Scripture avoids extremes. The same inspired author who advises Timothy to use a little wine for the sake of his stomach and frequent illnesses (I Tim. 5:23), also clearly declares that one who fails to practise moderation has no right to a place in the presbytery. A wine-bibber, tippler, or drunkard cannot be a worthy overseer.

Example of those who were guilty of the sin here condemned:

Some Communicants at Corinth

"one is hungry and another is drunk" (I Cor. 11:21). Cf. I Sam. 25:36: Nabal. See also Gen. 9:20-27.

(2) "not given to blows"

See also Titus 1:7. Literally Paul says, "not a striker." He is thinking of a man who is ever ready with his fists, a bellicose person, a spitfire or fire-eater. Think of the backwoodsmen of former days who literally wore a chip on their shoulder as a challenge to fight anyone who would dare to knock it off, whence our expression, "He carries a chip on his shoulder."

Between the immoderate use of wine and the eagerness to engage someone in combat there is but a small step. Hence, these two follow each other here in the list of negatively expressed requirements for overseership. Seneca said, "Wine kindles wrath" (Vinum incendit iram). And the same close relationship is indicated in Prov. 23:29, 30. Hence, examples are:

The men against whom the author of Proverbs issues his warning

"Who has woe? Who has sorrow? Who has contentions? Who has wounds without cause? Who has redness of eyes?

"Those who tarry long over the wine,

"Those who go to try the mixed wine" (Prov. 23:29, 30). See also Gen. 4:23: Lamech; Gen. 49:5, 6: Simeon and Levi.

(3) "genial"

See also Titus 3:2; then Phil. 4:5; James 3:17; I Peter 2:18. The person here indicated is the very opposite of the spitfire. Though he never compromises with respect to the truth of the gospel, he is willing to yield when it comes to his own rights, in the spirit of I Cor. 6:7, "Why not rather suffer wrong?" The rendering "yielding" or "ceding" — which also corresponds with the root-idea of the word used in the original — expresses the meaning in part. However, it may be doubted whether any single word or expression in the English tongue is the complete equivalent of the original. The qualities of yieldedness, fairness, sweet reasonableness, gentleness, helpfulness, and generosity are combined in this *conciliatory, considerate, genial,* better than *debonair,* individual.

One who, but for what is recorded in Acts 15:39, approaches this ideal is

Barnabas

"And Joseph, who by the apostles was surnamed Barnabas (which being interpreted means *son of encouragement*) a Levite, a man of Cyprus by race, in possession of a field, sold it, and brought the money, and laid it at the apostle's feet. . . . But Barnabas took him (Paul), and brought him to the apostles. . . . He was a good man, and full of the Holy Spirit and of faith" (Acts 4:36, 37; 9:27; 11:24). Other examples: Abraham as pictured in Gen. 13:8, 9; Isaac (Gen. 22; 26:12-22); Joseph (Gen. 50:15-21); Moses (Num. 12:3); Jonathan (I Sam. 18:1); Timothy!

(4) "not contentious"

See also Titus 3:2. Note how "genial" is interposed between "not given to blows" and "not contentious," the reason being that it is contrasted with both. The requirement "not contentious," literally "averse to fighting," probes even deeper than "not given to blows." A person might not be eager to come to blows, but being disputateous, as were no doubt the errorists at Ephesus (see I Tim. 1:4), he would still be lacking one of those characteristics which are needed by an overseer.

In addition to the false teachers at Ephesus, who certainly were contentious persons, think also of:

The Corinthian Quarrelers

"Each one of y o u says, I am of Paul; and I of Apollos; and I of Cephas; and I of Christ" (I Cor. 1:12).

(5) "not fond of money"

See also I Tim. 3:8 and Titus 1:8. Not only must the overseer be a man who is far removed from the Judas-like attitude (John 12:6) of trying to enrich himself by dishonest means (the sin indicated in I Tim. 3:8 and in Titus 1:8), but he must also be far removed from making the acquisition of earthly treasure his chief goal in life even though the means employed should be honest. Paul must have been thinking first of all of some men in Ephesus where Timothy was carrying on his ministry (I Tim. 6:9, 10). In addition one can think of:

The Rich Fool

"Thou fool, this night is thy soul required of thee; and the things which thou hast prepared, whose shall they be?" (Luke 12:20). And think of the Rich Man in the parable of The Rich Man and Lazarus (Luke 16:19-31).

(6) "managing well his own household"

See also I Tim. 3:12; 5:17; then Rom. 12:8; I Thess. 5:12. The overseer, it being assumed that he is a married man with children, must be gifted with the ability to oversee, to preside, to manage. Paul reasons from the less to the greater, in this twofold sense:

a. If a man cannot even preside over or *manage,* how will he be able to *take upon himself* (that is, upon his heart) *the care of* anything? The latter activity indicates a watchful regard that is even more solicitous and incessant than the former.

b. If a man cannot discharge his responsibility with respect to *his own* family, how will he do this with respect to *God's* family, that is, the church (the local congregation), the family which has God as its Father?

Now this ability to manage or govern well his own family becomes evident when the father keeps his *offspring in submission* (see on I Tim. 2:11).

The so-called "progressive" idea of permitting the child to do as he pleases finds no support in Scripture. But though authority must be exercised, this must be done "with true dignity," that is, it must be done in such a manner that the father's *firmness* makes it *advisable* for a child to obey, that his *wisdom* makes it *natural* for a child to obey, and that his *love* makes it *a pleasure* for a child to obey.

Imagine how ideal must have been that early family-life which in later years blossomed forth into the relationship pictured in Acts 21:9:

Philip the evangelist

"And he had four virgin daughters who prophesied." And see the beautiful family-life portrayed in Ps. 128:3. Cf. Gen. 18:19; Is. 78:3, 4; 105:8-10; Luke 2:51; Acts 2:39; 16:14, 15; 16:33.

(7) "not a recent convert"

A member of the congregation may, however, possess all the characteristics mentioned in the preceding, and still not be qualified to serve as an overseer. He may be *a beginner,* one who was converted only recently, whether old or young. He lacks the maturity and prestige that is required in an overseer. He is *a novice.* Literally the apostle says, "not *a neophyte* (acc. of νεόφυτος, *newly planted;* hence, *young plant:* Job 14:9; Ps. 128:3; 144:12; Is. 5:7). The church is God's *field* (I Cor. 3:9). The believers are his *plants* (I Cor. 3:6). By a slight change of metaphor Paul also says that they have become "one-plant-with-Christ" (Rom. 6:5). Cf. N.T.C. on John 15:1-8.

The choosing of a neophyte might have disastrous results for himself; hence, also for the church. So, a novice must not be elected, "in order that he may not become beclouded (or: blinded) by conceit." The verb means literally "wrapped up in smoke," the smoke of arrogance in this case. See I Tim. 6:4; II Tim. 3:4. The result would be: "and fall into *the condemnation* (κρίμα) of the devil." This undoubtedly means "the condemnation pronounced upon the devil."[63] Cf. II Tim. 2:26. We read

---

[63] The idea that διαβόλου when in verse 6 it is used in the expression "condemnation of the devil" must be a subjective genitive because this same word when in verse 7 it occurs in the phrase "snare of the devil" is a subjective genitive, impresses me as being superficial. In determining the nature of these genitives, one question is paramount. It is this: What is the scriptural usage? Is it more scriptural to represent the devil as pronouncing a sentence of condemnation, or to represent him as being condemned? Of course, the latter! See the following passages: Gen. 3:15; Is. 14:12 (by implication); Zech. 3:2; Matt. 4:10; 12:29; Luke 10:18; John 12:31; Rom. 16:20; Eph. 6:11; James 4:7; II Peter 2:4; Jude 6; Rev. 12:7-9; 20:10. Hence, "the condemnation of the devil" means "the condemnation pronounced (and executed) upon the devil" (objective genitive).

Similarly, is it the more usual scriptural representation to speak of the devil as striving to lure others into his snares, or is he more generally described as becom-

about this sentence of condemnation in II Peter 2:4 (and see footnote 63). Pride ever leads to the fall. In order to prevent this from happening, the church must not choose a beginner to be an overseer.

In harmony with this rule, on his first missionary journey Paul did not appoint elders in every church until he revisited the churches (Acts 14:23). Also note that Timothy himself, upon his conversion, was not immediately ordained. Having been led to Christ on Paul's first missionary journey, he was not ordained until later (on the second journey at the earliest). The rule, "Whenever possible no neophytes shall be chosen to overseership in the church," was also adhered to in the case of

Joseph called Barsabbas and Matthias:

"Of the men who have accompanied us all the time that the Lord Jesus went in and went out among us . . . one must be chosen to become with us a witness of the resurrection" (Acts 1:21, 22). In fact, Paul himself, after his conversion in 33/34 A. D., spent three years in Arabia before doing effective work at Tarsus and Antioch, and was not commissioned to go on his first missionary journey until ten years after his conversion! See my *Bible Survey,* Grand Rapids, Mich., fourth printing 1953, pp. 189-195.

Having finished the list of requirements that pertain to the estimation in which the brother is held by his fellow church-members, the apostle proceeds now to the opinion of outsiders (those who do not belong to the church) with respect to him:

(1) Above reproach in the estimation of outsiders

"He must also have a favorable testimony from outsiders." Even with them the prospective overseer, and also the overseer who is already in office, must have a good reputation. The necessity of adding this requirement follows from the fact that often such "outsiders" know more about the man in question than do the members of the church. It frequently happens, for example, that most or all of those associated with him in his daily occupation are unbelievers. Their judgment is of some importance. Besides, the church seeks to exert a powerful influence for good upon the world, leading sinners to Christ. An overseer's bad reputation with the world will not be of any help in achieving this purpose.

Now it is a fact that frequently the world's adverse opinion of the Christian is motivated by hatred of the Christ (Rom. 15:3; Heb. 13:12, 13). But

---

ing himself ensnared? Of course the former. It is the devil who, also in the Pastorals, is depicted as setting snares. II Tim. 2:26 settles this point. Cf. I Tim. 6:9. Hence, "the snare of the devil" means "the snare which he sets" (subjective genitive).

it is not *this* light esteem that Paul has in mind. What he means is that in order to be an effective overseer a brother must be known even to worldly people with whom he is (or has been) in contact as *a man of character,* a man against whom it is not possible to level any *just* charges of *moral* turpitude. It must be possible to say with reference to him, "He conducts himself properly with respect to outsiders" (see N.T.C. on I Thess. 4:12. Cf. Col. 4:5).

A person who does not have this favorable testimony and who is nevertheless chosen to be an overseer in the church may easily "fall into reproach." But here for once "the reproach of the world" is not to the church-member's credit. It is not now an honor, as it is in the other passages where the same word "reproach" is used (Rom. 15:3; Heb. 10:33; 11:26; 13:13). We can imagine how, on the morning after this undeserving person's election to office, the men who work with him will greet him with the mocking exclamation, "What do we hear now? Have they actually made *you* an elder . . . *you?*" And *the devil* will rejoice.[64]

Moreover, such a person may easily become very bold, thinking, "If I can get away with this conduct of mine, and still be elected overseer, I can get away with anything." Thus he will fall into the devil's *snare,* that is, into the devil's *trap,* hence, into his *power.* See especially II Tim. 2:26; then also I Tim. 6:9; finally, Luke 21:35; Rom. 11:9; and for a synonym N.T.C. on John 6:61.

To have a good reputation even with those who are outside the church, is, under the most favorable circumstances, to be considered a blessing.

Example:

Cornelius

"well spoken of by the entire Jewish nation" (Acts 10:22).

---

8 Deacons similarly (must be) dignified, not double-tongued, not addicted to much wine, not greedy of shameful gain, 9 keeping hold of the mystery of our faith with a pure conscience. 10 And let these also first be tested; then let them render service, if they are blameless.

11 Women similarly (must be) dignified, no slanderers, temperate, reliable in all matters.

12 Let a deacon be one wife's husband, managing well his children and his

---

[64] This is true whether or not the word "reproach" as well as "snare" be construed as modified by "of the devil." Either is grammatically possible, arguments to the contrary (as in Lenski, *op. cit.,* p. 591) notwithstanding. The non-repetition of the preposition (εἰς) argues in favor of linking "of the devil" with both nouns, but does not absolutely settle the question. Materially, however, there is little if any difference in meaning. When the world reproaches, the devil, too, reproaches. When Lenski says that the devil is the last one to reproach a Christian for his faults, is he not forgetting Zech. 3:1-3?

own household. 13 For those who have served well acquire for themselves a noble standing and great confidence in the faith (which centers) in Christ Jesus.

3:8-12

8-12. Note how the qualifications of women who render auxiliary service are wedged in between the requirements for deacons.

Though the New Testament contains but few specific references to *deacons* (besides our present passage also Phil. 1:1, and of course Acts 6:1-6,[65] where however the term "deacon" does not occur), this does not mean that the work of the deacon was considered to be of inferior value. It was and is a glorious task. It is based upon Christ's loving concern for his people. So close to his heart is this tender solicitude that he regards what is done to the least of his brothers as if it had been done to himself (Matt. 25:31-46).

From Acts 6 we learn that deacons were chosen because the elders did not have the time and energy to take upon themselves the care of the poor and needy in addition to performing all their other work: governing the church, preaching the Word, administering the sacraments, leading the congregation in prayer, etc. The deacons, accordingly, were chosen in order to "serve tables." Their special task is to gather the offerings which God's people in gratitude make to their Lord, to distribute these gifts in the proper spirit to all who are in need, to prevent poverty wherever it is possible to do this, and by means of their prayers and words of Scripture-based comfort, to encourage the distressed.

Now in order to carry out so worthy a task, they, as well as the elders, must be men full of faith and of the Holy Spirit (Acts 6:5).

Accordingly, deacons similarly (must be):

(1) **Dignified**

See also Titus 2:2; cf. Phil. 4:8. For the noun see on I Tim. 2:2; Titus 2:7. This refers not only to their necessary decorum or propriety of manner and conduct but also to the fact that in their inner thoughts and attitudes they must be men of Spirit-wrought gravity and respectability. Such a serious-minded man was

Stephen

"a man full of faith and of the Holy Spirit" (Acts 6:5).

Moreover, when such a man administers cheer, he means what he says. Hence,

---

[65] Other references, such as Rom. 12:7; 16:1; I Cor. 12:28; and I Peter 4:11, would seem to be of a more general nature. They do not — or in some cases, do not exclusively — refer to the office and work of the deacon.

(2) **Not double-tongued** [66]

He does not say one thing to one person and something different to another. He does not "talk out of both sides of his mouth." He does not *say* one thing and *know* another, like:

Gehazi (II Kings 5:19-27) or *Sanballet and Geshem* (Neh. 6:2) or *Ananias and Sapphira*

"And she said, Yes, for so much" (Acts 5:8).

(3) **Not addicted to much wine**

Cf. "not (one who lingers) beside (his) wine" in verse 3. The qualified deacon is moderate in his use of wine if he drinks any. He is no

Nabal

"He was very drunk" (I Sam. 25:36).

(4) **Not greedy of shameful gain**

Cf. Titus 1:7; I Peter 5:2; also "not fond of money" in verse 3. However, here in verse 8 the emphasis is slightly different. A man who is fond of money is not necessarily an embezzler. But it is the embezzler or pilferer and the man who joins a good cause for the sake of material advantage whom Paul has in mind here in verse 8. It is the man with the mercenary spirit who goes all out in his search for riches, anxious to add to his possessions regardless of the method, whether fair or foul. Think of

Judas

"Now this he said, not because he was concerned about the poor, but because he was a thief and as he had the money-box he used to take what was put in it" (John 12:6). And cf. Simon the Sorcerer (Acts 8:9-24).

(5) **Keeping hold of the mystery of our faith with a pure conscience**

A good deacon, accordingly, is attentive to duty for Christ's sake. He is conscientious. Were he undignified, double-tongued, addicted to much wine, and greedy of shameful gain, he would not be the kind of man who with *a conscience* purified by the Holy Spirit (see on I Tim. 1:5) "keeps clinging to the mystery of *our* (literally, "of *the*") faith." It is hard to believe that the expression "the mystery of our faith" here in I Tim. 3:9 means something different than "the mystery of our religion" in verse 16. Hence, see on that verse. *For Christ's sake* the qualified deacon watches himself scrupulously, doing all in his power to remain in the closest possible

---

[66] Here one might have expected a form of δίγλωσσος, as in the apocryphal book Eccles. 5:9, where "the man who winnows with every wind" is so characterized (cf. Prov. 11:13 in the LXX). The word which Paul actually employs (acc. masc. pl. of δίλογος), and which elsewhere occurs with a different sense ("one who repeats," see M.M., p. 163), reminds one of the Latin *bilinguis* in one of its meanings. Does this mean that the author of the Pastorals borrows from the Latin? See pp. 10, 11.

union with *him*, that is, with the most sublime of all divinely disclosed mysteries, namely, "God revealed in the flesh" for the salvation, on equal terms, of Jew and Gentile.

The trait here described finds a beautiful illustration in

Joseph

who, *for God's sake,* remained on the straight path.

"How then can I do this great wickedness, and sin against God?" (Gen. 39:9).

(6) **And let these also first be tested; then let them render service, being blameless**

Cf. I Tim. 3:6. What holds for the overseers holds also for the deacons. No neophytes must be chosen. Only *tested* men should *serve* (see on verse 13) in this capacity. This does not mean that a prospective deacon must first serve a trial-period, but rather that by means of a consecrated life he must furnish a testimonial of character. He must be able to sustain the test of having the eyes of the whole church (plus the outsiders!) focused upon him. If he succeeds, he is then *blameless* (literally, "not to be called to account," a close synonym of "above reproach" or "irreprehensible" in verse 2).

This method of selecting deacons is surely far removed from the one which is suggested at times, namely, "May-be if we make him a deacon, he'll stop his criticizing. Let's place him on the nomination for deacons. If elected, we can perhaps make something of him."

The Seven Men of Good Report

who became the first deacons of the early church furnish an excellent example of the manner in which deacons should be chosen.

"Therefore, brothers, look around for seven men from among y o u of good reputation, full of the Spirit and of wisdom" (Acts 6:3).

The section with respect to deacons is interrupted by a passage stating the requirements in the case of *women*. That these women are not "the wives of the deacons" nor "all the adult female members of the church" is clear from the syntax: "The overseer therefore *must be* . . . Deacons similarly (must be) . . . Women similarly (must be) . . ." One and the same verb coordinates the three: the overseer, deacons, women. Hence, these women are here viewed as rendering special service in the church, as do the elders and the deacons. They are a group by themselves, not just the wives of the deacons nor *all* the women who belong to the church.

On the other hand, the fact that no special and separate paragraph is used in describing their necessary qualifications, but that these are simply wedged in between the stipulated requirements for deacons, with equal clarity indicates that these women are not to be regarded as constituting a third office in the church, the office of "deaconesses," on a par with and endowed with authority equal to that of deacons.

It is true that from early times, in justification of "the-office-of-deaconess-theory," an appeal has been made to such passages as the one now under consideration (I Tim. 3:11); I Tim. 5:9; and Rom. 16:1. But as to I Tim. 5:9, see on that passage. As to Rom. 16:1, no adequate reason has been given to prove that there the term used in the original does not have its far more usual meaning *servant* (correctly thus rendered in A.V. and in the text of the A.R.V.) or *assistant,* one who *ministers lovingly* (see N.T.C. on John, Vol. I, pp. 116, 119); in this case, to the cause of the gospel.

Nothing can erase the fact that according to Scripture, and particularly also according to Paul's epistles, women perform very important ministries in the church. It is also true that the extent and value of the service which they are able to render has not always been fully recognized or appreciated. See on I Tim. 5:9. But it is contrary to the spirit of Paul's remarks concerning women and their place in the church (see on I Tim. 2:11, 12; and cf. I Cor. 11:1-16; 14:34, 35), and contrary also to the significance of the manner in which the apostle here in I Tim. 3:11 *parenthesizes* the requirements for women-helpers, to regard their task as a third office, to be co-ordinated with that of the overseers and with that of the deacons.

The simplest explanation of the manner in which Paul, not yet finished with the requirements for the office of deacon, interjects a few remarks about women, is that he regards these women as the *deacons' assistants* in helping the poor and needy, etc. These are *women who render auxiliary service,* performing ministries for which women are better adapted. Here again we refer to our explanation of I Tim. 5:9. A few simple words indicate their necessary qualifications. Says Paul: **Women similarly (must be) dignified, no slanderers, temperate, reliable in all matters.**

For *truly respectable* or "dignified" see on verses 4 and 8. For *temperate* or *sober* see on verse 2. Also the requirement of thorough-going "reliability" or *trustworthiness* holds for the women as well as for elders and deacons (implied for the latter two groups in verses 6 and 10). Hence, these three virtues do not need to be discussed again.

It is also easily understood why Paul would emphasize that women who do the rounds of the church in performing loving ministries must not be gossipers. "No scandal-mongers please!" he says as it were. Those who *slander* imitate the evil one, whose very name is *diabolos,* that is, slanderer.

Lengthy is the list of truly respectable, temperate, trustworthy women who are mentioned in Scripture. Among them are, in greater or lesser degree, the two Deborah's (Gen. 35:8; Judg. 4:4); Jochebed (Heb. 11:23), Naomi and Ruth (Ruth 1:15-18), Hannah (I Sam. 1:15, 16; 1:22-2:10),

3:8-12   I TIMOTHY

Ichabod's mother (I Sam. 4:21), Abigail (contrasted with her *intemperate* husband, I Sam. 25:3, 25, 36), the widow at Zarephath (I Kings 17), the Shunammite woman (II Kings 4:8), Huldah (II Kings 22:14), Queen Esther (the book of Esther), Elizabeth (Luke 1:5, 6), Mary the mother of Jesus (Luke 1:46-55; 2:19; Acts 1:14), Anna (Luke 2:36, 37), Mary and Martha (Luke 10:38-42; John, ch. 11; 12:1-8), the women who followed Jesus and ministered to him, such as Jesus' aunt Salome, Mary the wife of Clopas, Mary Magdalene, Johanna, (Luke 23:55; 24:1, 10; John 19:25), Dorcas (Acts 9:36-43), Lydia (Acts 16:14, 15, 40), Priscilla (Acts 18:26), Phoebe (Rom. 16:1), Tryphosa and Tryphaena (Rom. 16:12), and last but not least Lois and Eunice (II Tim. 1:5). In spite of weaknesses which Scripture does not conceal, the names of Sarah (Gen. 12:5, and note her name in the list of heroes of faith Heb. 11:11, 12), Rebecca (Gen. 24) and Rachel (Gen. 29) — also Leah (Gen. 29:35) — should be added to the list. How sharp was the contrast between *these* women and some females of Timothy's acquaintance (II Tim. 3:6, 7)!

Opposed to the lengthy list of *noble* women, Scripture mentions such *evil slanderers* as Potiphar's wife (Gen. 39:7-33) and Jezebel (I Kings 21:5-10).

What Paul means, accordingly, is this, "Timothy, see to it that the deacons' assistants be carefully selected. They should be Ruths and Lydias, not 'silly women,' nor the kind that remind one of Jezebel!"

The enumeration of qualifications for deacons is now continued and concluded:

(7) **Let a deacon be one wife's husband, managing well his children and his own household.** See on I Tim. 3:2, 4.

13. The apostle proceeds to show how he knows that deacons *must* be all this. He is deeply convinced of it, and this not only because of direct divine revelation but also because of the manifest special reward by means of which it pleases God to crown the deacons' efforts. The sense of the words which immediately follow is, "I know this is true, **For those who have served well acquire for themselves a noble standing and great confidence in the faith (which centers) in Christ Jesus.**"

This is at the same time *an incentive* for deacons so that they may labor faithfully. It is not unscriptural to speak of such incentives. *It is* unscriptural not to recognize them (Matt. 19:29; II Tim. 4:7, 8; Heb. 12:2; Rev. 2:7, 10, 17, 26-29; 3:5, 6, 12, 13, 21, 22; etc.). Looking forward to a reward is not at all sinful, provided one plans to use this reward for the glory of God and for even greater service (if possible) in his kingdom.

It is entirely right and natural to regard the reward which is here promised as pertaining to *the deacons and their helpers*. The apostle has been speaking about *them,* and about no one else, in verses 8-12. The connection, moreover, is very close, being introduced by the word, "for." It will hardly do, therefore, to say that Paul is still thinking about *the overseers,* introduced in verse 1, and that he includes these in the reward here promised. To be sure, to these overseers also an incentive has been given, namely, the incentive based on the glorious character of their task (see verse 1). We may even go farther and admit that the blessing described in verse 13 will actually be enjoyed by elders as well as by deacons and their assistants. And we must probably accept as correct the position that the first verb used in the original here in verse 13 (cf. verse 10) should not be rendered *"have served* (well) *as deacons"* but simply *"have served* (well)." [67]

But though all this be freely granted, it still remains true that in the present passage the apostle is in all probability speaking about the persons mentioned in the immediately preceding context (verses 8-12). In verse 1 the incentive for the elders was indicated: their *task* is glorious. Verse 13 now adds the incentive for the deacons: their *reward* is rich. Let no one, permitting himself to be misled by the fact that it is the deacons' task *to serve* and not (like the elders) *to rule,* begin to think lightly of them and of their office. Let it be remembered that those deacons who have served well acquire for themselves a noble *standing.* The church will think highly of them because they have performed their tasks in a worthy manner. (Incidentally, the word rendered *standing* has the primary meaning *a step,* say of a staircase. Since such a staircase with its steps could be used to measure the sun's shadow, see II Kings 20:9-11 in the LXX, the meaning *degree* — cf. the "degrees" on a sun-dial — is not strange. Hence, in some such way the figurative meaning *degree, rank, standing* is easily reached.)

Moreover, the very consciousness of the fact that with the help of God he has done his best, so that he is not vexed by pangs of conscience, will give the deacon great *confidence.* He will not hold back, but will *tell all* (παρρησία is derived from πᾶς, *all,* and ῥῆσις *telling, speech*). This confidence has reference to *the faith* (subjective sense here) which centers in Christ Jesus. It is concerning *him* that the deacon will freely and gladly testify.

---

14 These things I am writing to you though I am hoping to come to you shortly, 15 but (I am writing them) in order that if I should be delayed, you may know how you should conduct yourself in God's house, which is the church of the living God, (the) pillar and foundation of the truth. 16 And confessedly great is the mystery of (our) devotion,

---

[67] Nowhere else in the New Testament does διακονέω mean *serve as deacon.* It means *to serve, to minister, to care for one's needs* (Matt. 20:28; Mark 10:45; Luke 10:40; 22:26, 27; John 12:2; II Tim. 1:18; I Peter 4:11; etc.) or *to supply by ministering*: (I Peter 1:12; 4:10). The mere fact that Paul has just been speaking about deacons would seem to be hardly sufficient to ascribe to the verb a technical sense which it has nowhere else in Scripture.

> Who was manifested in the flesh,
> Vindicated by the Spirit,
> Seen by angels,
> Heralded among (the) nations,
> Believed in by the world,
> Taken up in glory.

3:14-16

14. Paul now states the reasons for conveying these instructions (2:1-3:13) *in writing*. They are:

(1) Though I hope to see you soon, I fear that I may be delayed.

(2) Yet, the matter permits no delay, for it concerns *God's* house.

These things I am writing to you though I am hoping to come to you shortly. Did he mean, "I hope to come to you even before wintering at Nicopolis"? See p. 40.

15. But (I am writing them) in order that if I should be delayed, you may know how you should conduct yourself in God's house.[68]

Timothy must know how to supervise worship and the election of officers. Moreover, he must bear in mind that he has been entrusted not with a private business but with *God's house!* "House" is correct here, not "household" as in verses 4, 5, 12. Believers are God's *house* or *sanctuary* (I Cor. 3:16; 6:19; II Cor. 6:16) because *God dwells in them.* Hence, Paul continues: **which is** [69] **the church of the living God** (*not the temple of dead idols!* Cf. N.T.C. on I Thess. 1:9, 10), **the pillar and foundation of the truth.** Having been called "God's *house,*" we now note that the church is next compared to a pillar and foundation. As *the* [70] *pillar* supports *the roof,* even better (note the climax!) as *the foundation supports the entire superstructure,* so the church supports the glorious *truth* of the gospel. Cf. II Tim. 2:19; then Matt. 16:18. It supports the truth by:

---

[68] Condition of third class (stating the purpose after ἵνα). Protasis has ἐάν with first person sing. present active subjunctive of βραδύνω (cf. II Peter 3:9; and see the related adjective *slow* in Luke 24:25). Apodosis has second person sing. perfect active subjunctive of οἶδα.

Literally, "... how it is necessary in God's house *to conduct oneself* (ἀναστρέφεσθαι present middle infinitive of ἀναστρέφω, *to turn up and down, to conduct oneself, to behave*). This may mean either "how it is necessary *for anyone* to conduct himself," or "how it is necessary *for you* to conduct yourself." Note context: "I am writing *to you* ... I am hoping to come *to you* ... in order that *you* may know." Hence, "how it is necessary *for you* to conduct yourself" seems to be natural here.

[69] ἥτις (attracted to the gender of ἐκκλησία) ἐστιν "because it is," or "it being."

[70] The omission of the article does not make the nouns "pillar" and "foundation" indefinite, but stresses their qualitative force: the church is nothing less than the truth's *pillar;* better still, it is the truth's very *foundation.*

H earing and *H* eeding it (Matt. 13:9)
H andling it rightly (II Tim. 2:15)
H iding it in the heart (Ps. 119:11), and
H olding it forth as the Word of Life (Phil. 2:16).

Or, if one prefers, by

D igesting it (Rev. 10:9). That takes study and meditation.
D efending it (Phil. 1:16)
D isseminating it (Matt. 28:18-20)
D emonstrating its power in consecrated living (Col. 3:12-17).

The heart of this gospel and of our whole devotion is *Christ*. Hence, Paul continues:

16. And confessedly great is the mystery of our devotion.
Great is the church because great is its exalted Head, Jesus Christ. That the expression "the mystery of our devotion" refers to *Christ* is clear from the fact that whatever follows in verse 16 refers to him. It is he who is great, and this *confessedly*, that is, thus acknowledged by the church in its daily witness, its preaching, and, as here, its hymns.

"The mystery of our devotion" is "the mystery of our faith" (verse 9), meaning that it pertains to our faith, to our devotion. By faith we embrace him. By means of our devotion we glorify him. The word used in the original (εὐσέβεια, — ας) occurs here in a sense slightly different from *piety* or *godliness* when this is viewed as a *quality* or *condition* of the soul. It is here used in a more active sense. It is *piety in action* ("operative piety," M.M., p. 265), *godly living* (as in 4:7) the conscientious *devotion* of our lives to God in Christ, the fear of God, (cf. the German "Gottesfurcht," and the Dutch "godsvrucht").

Christ is called *the mystery* of our devotion, not only because had he not been revealed to us, we would not have known him (a "mystery" being "a revealed secret"), but also because he transcends our comprehension (Eph. 3:18, 19). The more we know him, the better will we be able to discern the mysterious, unfathomable character of his love and of all his attributes.

It is exactly this *immeasurable greatness of the Christ* which forms the subject of the hymn from which Paul now quotes six lines. That theme was a familiar one in the early church, as is shown by passages such as the following: Acts 2:22-36; 4:11, 12; 10:38-43; 13:26-41; Rom. 8:31-39; I Cor. 1:30; 15:1-20, 56, 57; Eph. 1:20-23; Phil. 2:5-11; Col. 1:12-20; II Thess. 1:7, 8; 2:8; Titus 2:13; Heb. 1:1-4; 7:23-8:2; 9:24-28; 10:5-25; 12:1-3; Rev. 5:6-14; 12:10-12; 19:6-8.

Depending on an antecedent such as *Logos* (Word) or *Christ(os)*, or Theos

3:16   **I TIMOTHY**

(God) [71] the hymn continues: "who" or "he who" (ὅς) was made manifest in the flesh, etc.

The Six Lines in their Chiastic Arrangement

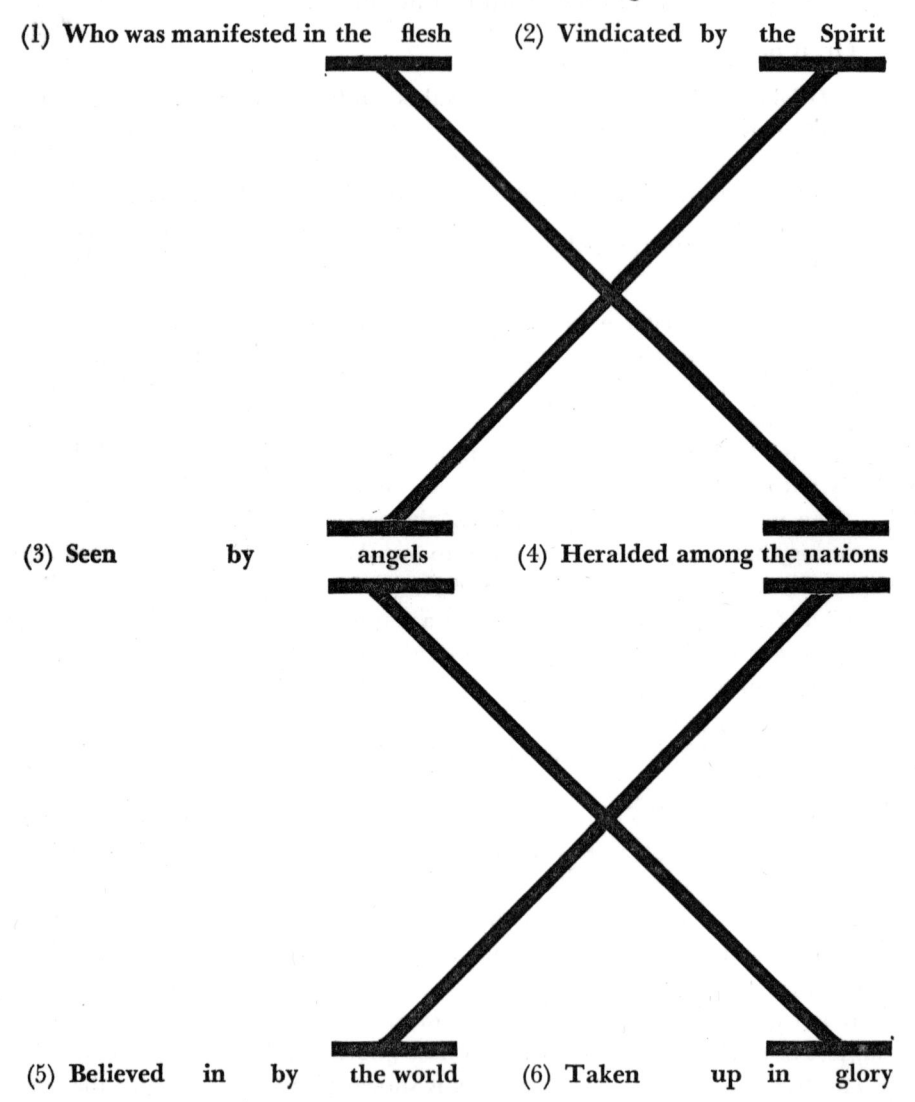

(1) **Who was manifested in the flesh**   (2) **Vindicated by the Spirit**

(3) **Seen by angels**   (4) **Heralded among the nations**

(5) **Believed in by the world**   (6) **Taken up in glory**

---

[71] Nevertheless, the reading θεός here in I Tim. 3:16 is regarded by many as weakly attested. It is defended by E. F. Hills, *The King James Version Defended*, Des Moines, Iowa, 1956, pp. 59, 60. The Western reading ὅ instead of ὅς is probably the result of a scribal attempt to make the relative agree with the gender of μυστήριον. But the relative agrees with whatever was its antecedent *in the hymn from which* the quotation was made!

I TIMOTHY   **3:16**

The movement of thought is:

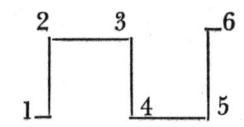

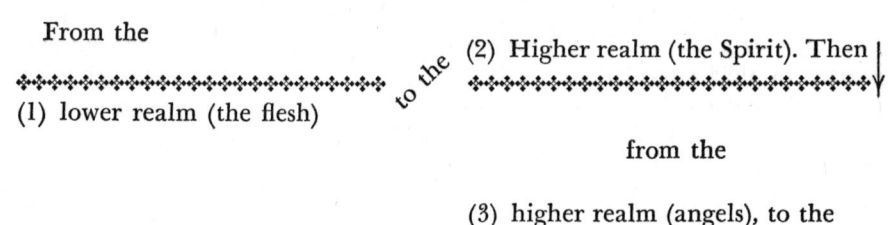

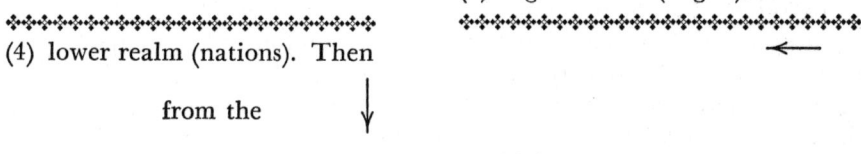

From the (1) lower realm (the flesh) *to the* (2) Higher realm (the Spirit). Then from the (3) higher realm (angels), to the (4) lower realm (nations). Then from the (5) lower realm (the world) *to the* (6) higher realm (glory)

By drawing connecting-lines between the words which indicate realities that belong to the same realm, *flesh, nations,* and *world* are linked; and so are *Spirit, angels,* and *glory.* See these lines on p. 138. Thus the X — which is the twenty-second letter of the Greek alphabet and is called *chi* — is drawn twice. We may say, therefore, that the six lines are arranged *chi*-astically.

The six lines of this *Hymn in Adoration of the Christ* begin with a line about *Christ's lowly birth* and end with a reference to *his glorious ascension.* It is clear that if in such a humiliation-to-exaltation hymn the chiastic thought-movement is to be maintained, there must be not less than six lines.

The contrasts are clearly drawn:

Weak flesh (line 1) contrasted with *strength-imparting Spirit* (line 2)
Heavenly angels (line 3) over against *earthly nations* (line 4)
The world below (line 5) over against *glory above* (line 6).

Yet, the beauty of it is this, that though the hymn pictures these regional contrasts, the thought is throughout that of *glory* and *adoration.* To be sure, the word *flesh* in line 1 indicates Christ's *humiliation;* but the expression "manifested in the flesh" ("veiled in flesh the Godhead see") points to his exalted, glorious nature. His glory is also indicated by the expressions "vindicated by the Spirit," "seen (with adoration) by angels," "heralded (joyfully) among the nations," "believed in (unto salvation) by the world," and "taken up (for exaltation) in glory." Hence what we have in these six lines is not antithetic parallelism (in the sense in which that term is usually employed), but *chiastic, cumulative parallelism.*

The Six Lines Considered Separately:

(1) "Who was manifested in the flesh." [72]

Into the human nature, weakened by the curse, came Christ, the Son of God. He was sent forth by God (Gal. 4:4); hence, Virgin-born. The fact that One so glorious in his pre-existence was willing to adopt the human nature in that curse-laden, weakened condition, was a manifestation of infinite, condescending love. Cf. John 1:1-14; II Cor. 8:9; Phil. 2:5-11. Hence, this voluntary self-concealment was at the same time a self-revelation. From the very beginning of his coming into the *flesh* self-concealment and self-disclosure walked side by side in connection with this "Mystery of our devotion." For the meaning of "flesh" see N.T.C. on John 1:14; and for the meaning of "was manifested" see N.T.C. on John 21:1, footnote 294.

(2) "Vindicated by the Spirit."

Not everyone saw his glory. "He was despised, and rejected of men" (Is. 55:3). By his enemies his claims were denied, and he himself was cast out (Heb. 13:12). But by the Spirit he was vindicated: his own perfect righteousness and the validity of his claims were fully established.

The A.V. and the R.S.V. are entirely correct in spelling Spirit with a capital letter, as referring to the Holy Spirit. The combination "flesh" and "Spirit" has scriptural warrant. Note: "And the Word became *flesh,* and dwelt among us as in a tent. And we beheld his glory, a glory as of the only begotten from the Father, full of grace and truth . . . And John testified, saying, I beheld *the Spirit* like a dove descending from heaven, and he remained on him" (John 1:14, 32; cf. 3:34). Having been thus anointed by the Holy Spirit (Ps. 2:2; 45:7; Matt. 3:16; Mark 1:10; Luke 3:22; Acts 4:27; 10:38), he was able, while in the "flesh" (the weakened human nature), to perform miracles, to cast out demons, etc. (Matt. 12:28). By means of every deed of power his *justice* was established, for surely the Holy Spirit would not have given this power to a sinner (John 9:31). But it was especially by means of *his resurrection from the dead* that the Spirit *fully* vindicated the claim of Jesus that he was the Son of God (Rom. 1:4).

(3) "Seen by angels."

The greatness of Christ *in his resurrection* stands out in the early preaching of the apostles. That resurrection was his complete vindication. It was also in connection with that resurrection that he was "seen by angels" (Matt. 28:2-7; Mark 16:5-8; Luke 24:4-7; John 20:12, 13). To be sure, angels had

---

[72] The six verbs are all third person singular passive *aorists*. The use of this tense indicates that each of the six indicated actions is viewed as a single whole, regardless of the time-element involved. Thus, though the statement, "He was manifested in the flesh," indicates not only Christ's *birth* but the entire period of earthly sojourn, from birth to burial, yet this entire manifestation in the flesh is viewed as *one fact.* The same holds with respect to the other five verbs.

shown an interest in his birth (Luke 2:9-14), and in his triumph over Satan when the latter tempted him in the desert (Matt. 4:11). Angels, moreover, addressed the disciples after his ascension (Acts 1:10, 11). Angels welcomed him back to heaven (Rev. 12:12). They were and are intensely interested in the whole program of redemption (I Peter 1:12). But although none of these great events need be excluded from the meaning of the line "seen by angels," the reference to Christ's glorious *resurrection*, a redemptive fact which stood out in the consciousness of the early church, is clear as daylight.[73] While the eyes of *men* — and *women* too! — were beclouded by the mist of "little faith" and, in a sense, lack of faith (Mark 16:11, 13, 14; Luke 24:10, 11; John 20:8, 9, 15, 24, 25), *angels* saw him clearly. They knew him as their glorious Lord.

(4) "Heralded among the nations."

It was *the resurrected Christ* who, *before his ascension*, issued The Great Commission, "Go, therefore, and make disciples of all the nations" (see Matt. 28:18-20: The Great Claim, The Great Commission, The Great Presence). And so the One who was not esteemed, the Despised One (Is. 53:3), began to be universally *heralded* or *proclaimed* (see on II Tim. 4:2) as The Savior of the World. Though this happened on and after Pentecost, **the** "great commission" was issued before the ascension!

(5) "Believed in by the world."

This, of course, was the direct result of the pre-ascension mandate. Men from every tribe and nation begin to worship him as their Lord and Savior, as had been predicted (Ps. 72:8-11, 17; 87; cf. Gen. 12:3; Am. 9:11, 12; Mic. 4:12).

(6) "Taken up in glory."

Having been manifested in the flesh, vindicated by the Spirit, seen by angels, and having issued the order which resulted in the proclamation of his name among the nations and the outgathering of a spiritual harvest from the world, he "was taken up." This is the same verb as is used in Mark 16:19 and in Acts 1:2. Luke 24:51 has "he parted from them," and Acts 1:9, "he was lifted up." While the echo of men's voices, "Crucify, crucify," had scarcely died, heaven opened wide its portals, and, upon receiving back its victorious King, resounded with the echoes of the jubilant anthem, sung by ten thousand times ten thousands and thousands of thousands, "Worthy is the Lamb." Truly, he was taken up *in glory*.

How great is the church which has such an exalted Head! Let Timothy bear this in mind as he goes about his task of supervision.

---

[73] Hence, I cannot agree here with interpreters who see little if any reference to the *resurrection*-activities of the angels; e.g., C. Bouma, *Kommentaar op het Nieuwe Testament* (Timotheus en Titus), pp. 149, 150. When Lenski says, in explanation of this line, "Angels saw him risen indeed," he is certainly right, *op. cit.*, p. 614.

Synthesis of Chapter 3

See the Outline at the beginning of the chapter.

We have here a list of requirements for office; also a statement regarding the glorious character of such work and its crowning reward. The qualifications of overseers and deacons (and in the latter connection, of deacons' female assistants) are stated. The emphasis falls on such qualities as reliability, dignity, temperance, helpfulness, proper relationship to one's family, and to some extent, Christian experience.

The lists reveal two facts:

On the one hand, the requirements for office are high enough so that persons with outstanding moral defects are excluded from office and in fact from any position of considerable responsibility in the church.

Yet, on the other hand, these requirements are low enough so that almost any member in good standing and of deserved reputation can qualify. Sinlessness, material riches, exceptional cultural attainment, these are not required.

Accordingly, a group of converts which displays a manifest lack of such qualities as are here mentioned is not yet ready to be organized into a congregation.

In stating his reasons for transmitting these lists *in written form,* Paul quotes from a beautiful early Hymn in adoration of the Christ, confessing the latter's glory from his incarnation to his coronation. Here we have proof of the fact that there was at least *a beginning* of hymnody during this early period. On the subject of psalm-singing and hymn-singing in the days of the apostle see also Acts 16:25; I Cor. 14:26; Eph. 5:19; and Col. 3:16. And do not forget the Old Testament Psalter, with its many cries for rescue, songs commemorating deliverance, and anthems of praise.

Outline of Chapter 4

Theme: *The Apostle Paul, Writing to Timothy, Gives Directions For the Administration of the Church*

*Directions with respect to
Apostasy*

4:1-5   A. Description of this apostasy and proof of its sinister nature.

4:6-16   B. How Timothy should deal with it:
1. By nourishing himself on the words of faith, and training himself for godly living;
2. By shunning profane and old-womanish myths;
3. By continuing stedfastly in positive exhortation and teaching, based upon the Word.

CHAPTER IV

| I TIMOTHY | 4:1 |

4 1 But the Spirit expressly says that in later seasons some will depart from the faith by giving heed to seducing spirits and doctrines of demons, 2 (embodied) in (the) insincere utterance of those who speak lies, whose own conscience is seared, 3 forbidding (people) to marry, and (enjoining them) to abstain from foods which God created in order that those who believe and acknowledge the truth may partake of them with thanksgiving. 4 For, every creature of God is good, and nothing is fit to be thrown away if it is received with thanksgiving; 5 for it is consecrated by the word of God and prayer.

Though the church be ever so glorious, reflecting the radiance of its precious Lord and Savior (I Tim. 3:15, 16), apostasy is just around the corner, for not all who belong outwardly to the church belong to it inwardly.

The present chapter deals with this apostasy.

4:1-5

1. But the Spirit expressly says that in later seasons some will depart from the faith.

"The Spirit says," that is, "is now saying." To whom was the Spirit speaking? Acts 20:29, 30 leads me to think that the apostle meant "to myself" (perhaps also to others). The Spirit, then, is saying that "in later seasons" — eras of this new dispensation, eras definitely marked out in God's foreknowledge — some will *depart* or *apostatize* from *the faith* (objective sense), the body of redemptive truth, the Christian religion.

The Spirit was saying this *expressly* ("in stated terms"). There was neither doubt nor vagueness about it. A half dozen years ago Paul, addressing the elders of the churches located in the very region where Timothy was now laboring, had spoken as follows: "I know that after my departure grievous wolves will enter in among y o u, not sparing the flock; and from among y o u r own selves men will arise, speaking perverse things, to draw away the disciples after them." A few years after that speech recorded in Acts 20, the apostle, writing to the Colossians from his first Roman imprisonment, had warned them against accepting the error that faith in Christ's atoning work has to be supplemented by ascetic beliefs and prac-

4:1   **I TIMOTHY**

tices (Col. 2). And now, writing to Timothy from Macedonia, he is distinctly informed by the Holy Spirit that the error, *already present* in its incipient form, *will grow and develop* in the manner indicated in verse 3.

Men will depart from the faith by **giving heed to seducing spirits and doctrines of demons**. As the context indicates (and see also I John 4:6 where "the spirit of seduction" is contrasted with "the Spirit of truth"), these *spirits* are not men but *demons*. Like *planets* that seem *to wander* back and forth among the constellations, these spirits wander; moreover, they *cause men to wander*. They *seduce, lead astray*. By giving heed to them one is giving heed to *doctrines of demons* (cf. II Cor. 4:4; Rev. 13:11, 14).

2. These doctrines are **(embodied) in (the) insincere utterance** (literally, *in hypocrisy*) **of those who speak lies**. As Satan made use of a serpent to deceive Eve, and this by means of *an insincere utterance* (Gen. 3:1-5: he was hiding his real objective; for while he pretended to raise Eve to a higher level of glory, so that she would be "like God," his real aim was to dethrone God and enthrone himself), so these seducing spirits or demons make use of *men who speak lies,* and who talk piously and learnedly in order to cover up their own arrogance or immorality.

These hypocrites are described as the men **whose own conscience is seared** (literally, *"who are cauterized as to their own conscience"*). By constantly arguing with conscience, stifling its warnings, and muffling its bell, they at last have reached the point where conscience no longer bothers them. *Grieving* the Holy Spirit has led to *resisting* him, and *resisting* him to *quenching* him. Then, through their own rebellion and obstinacy, their conscience will have been rendered (and thus will be permanently) *seared*. It will have been made callous. A good example is Balaam (Num. 22:12, 19, 21, 22, 32; 25:1-3; II Peter 2:15; Rev. 2:14).

3. Their teaching is — or will be — as bad as their character: **forbidding (people) to marry, and (enjoining them) to abstain from foods**.

Principles bear fruit. The false teachers who are here described, probably accept as one of their starting principles the thesis: Anything physical or sensuous is contaminating. It is not difficult to see how such a principle would in course of time cause the errorists to frown on *marriage*. *Foods,* too, would be condemned, though, of course, not absolutely. Fasting would be praised.

An early fulfilment of the prophecy came in the second century. It is not difficult to understand how Jewish ritualistic scruples, *already* in evidence in near-by Colosse as well as elsewhere (see Col. 2 and cf. Rom. 14), would ally itself with dualistic heathen philosophy. They had in common *Asceticism,* the renunciation of the comforts of life with a view to attaining happiness and perfection.

The second century syncretistic cult (see p. 20) in which the prophecy was partly fulfilled, was *Gnosticism,* which elevated *gnosis,* that is, *knowledge,* to a position of prominence above *pistis,* that is, *faith.* According to this system, the good God — the God of the new dispensation — could not have created the world, for the world is matter, and matter is the seat of evil. It was the Jehovah of the Old Testament, the Demiurge, who created the world, the human body, matter. These are our enemies. They must be conquered. Hence, all Gnostics favored "the abuse of the flesh." But this abuse of the flesh can express itself in two diametrically opposite imperatives: a. "Shun it"; b. "Overcome it by indulging in it." The first was advocated by *Ascetic Gnostics,* such as Marcion, Saturninus, and Tatian (see Tertullian, *Against Marcion,* I. xxix; Irenaeus, *Against Heresies,* I. xxviii); the second by *Antinomian* or *Licentious Gnostics,* such as the Nicolaitans. The apostle Paul, here in I Tim. 4, predicts and warns against the former. The apostle John (I John 3:4-10; Rev. 2:15, 20, 24), the apostle Peter (II Peter 2:12-19), and Jude (verses 4, 8, 11, and 19) combat the latter. But the two are never far apart. Paul in reality combats *both* varieties, for we have not only his statements here in I Tim. 4 but also that in II Tim. 3:1-9. (For the Cerinthian application of the basic thesis of Gnosticism see N.T.C. on John, Vol. I, pp. 33, 83, 84.)

But this is only *one* fulfilment. Others follow; for though in its ancient forms Gnosticism has passed away, its spirit has been in evidence again and again throughout the centuries. Also in our own day, whenever the Old Testament is frowned upon, whenever human reason is exalted above Christian faith, whenever the thesis: "Sin is real and is in its essence rebellion against God" is rejected, or whenever man's ability to save himself is proclaimed (which is a denial of Christ as the only and perfect Savior), the ghost of Gnosticism stalks again.

Gnosticism despises God's ordinances, for example, the marriage-ordinance (Gen. 2:24) and the ordinance concerning food (Gen. 1:29, 30; and especially Gen. 9:3). These errorists, whose coming Paul in a measure *describes* but even more *predicts,* order men to abstain from foods **which God created in order that those who believe and acknowledge the truth may partake of them with thanksgiving** (literally, *which God created for participation with thanksgiving by those who believe and who acknowledge the truth*).

These words pertain to *foods,* not to *marriage.* Of course, by implication they apply to both, but *directly* only to foods. The apostle has expressed his favorable view of *marriage and the family* in such passages as I Tim. 2:15; 3:2, 4, 12. With respect to foods, then, note that God — the only true God, who is the same in both dispensations — has created them. Hence, they cannot be bad or contaminating. And he has created them with a definite purpose, namely, "for participation with thanksgiving" (I Cor. 10:31), so that the circle may again be completed, and what came from God may, in the form of thanksgiving, be returned to him. But the *natural* man is not able to pour out his heart in thanksgiving unto God. Hence, Paul adds, "by those who believe and acknowledge the truth." Such joyful acceptance of the truth leads not to asceticism but to partaking with thanksgiving. This thought receives further emphasis as Paul continues:

4. For every creature of God is excellent, and nothing is fit to be thrown away if it is received with thanksgiving. This sentence confirms the preceding passage. Foods that were created for consumption with accompanying thanksgiving are excellent. In fact, *every* creature of God is excellent: "And God saw everything that he had made, and behold, it was very good" (Gen. 1:31). Nothing is fit to be thrown away, as if it were evil or the seat of evil. Of late, science is beginning to discover that what used to be regarded as of no direct value to man may prove to be a source of great blessing; may, in fact, help to solve the food-problem of future generations; think, for example, of "plant-food from the ocean."

Every creature of God is excellent:

(a) For the very reason that God *created* it
  and
(b) Because he also *consecrated* it.

Hence, Paul continues:

5. For it is consecrated by the word of God and prayer. By means of God's *blessing* upon it and by means of our *confident prayer*, it has been *consecrated* (cf. II Tim. 2:21), that is, set apart for holy use, lifted into the spiritual realm. For the Christian, eating and drinking are no secular activities (I Cor. 10:31). While, before partaking of food, *he* utters his petition and thanksgiving, *God* at the same time pronounces his word of blessing (cf. Deut. 8:3). He remembers his gracious covenant (Ps. 11:5).

---

6 By submitting these matters to the brothers you will be an excellent minister of Christ Jesus, nourished on the words of the faith and of the excellent doctrine which you have been following. 7 But profane and old-womanish myths shun. Train yourself for godly living. 8 For, while physical training is of *some* benefit, this godly living is of benefit *in every way*, as it holds promise of life both for the present and for the future. 9 Reliable is that saying and worthy of full acceptance. 10 For to this end we toil and strive, because we have set our hope on the living God, who is the Savior of all men, especially of those who believe.

11 Command these things and teach (them). 12 Let no one despise your **youth**, but become the believers' model in speech, in conduct, in love, in faith, in **purity**. 13 Until I come, attend to the (public) reading (of Scripture), to the exhorting and to the teaching. 14 Do not grow careless about the gift that is in you, which was granted to you through prophetic utterance with the laying on of the hands of the presbytery. 15 Let these things be your constant care; in these things be (absorbed), so that your progress may be evident to everyone. 16 Look to your-

self and to the teaching, persevere in them, for by doing this you will save both yourself and those who hear you.

4:6-16

6. By submitting these matters to the brothers you will be an excellent minister of Christ Jesus.

Timothy must warn against coming danger. He must point out what will be the outcome of certain errors which in their initial form were manifesting themselves even now but which as to their further development belonged to the future. He must make plain to the leaders and to the people of Ephesus and surroundings what the Spirit has distinctly revealed as to the nature of the approaching falsehood and as to the way in which it should be combated. Hence, the expression "these matters" refers to the things touched upon in verses 1-5. Timothy must *submit* these things to the brothers, that is, he must *place* a firm foundation *under* their feet (note the verb ὑποτίθημι only here and in Rom. 16:5).

The apostle writes that these things must be submitted to "the brothers" (cf. 5:1; 6:2; II Tim. 4:21). Paul is fond of this term (see N.T.C. on I Thess. 1:4). Though he is never afraid to assert his *authority* as an apostle of Jesus Christ, nevertheless, he places the emphasis on *love*. Believers in the Ephesus-community are *brothers,* members of Paul's (and of God's!) spiritual family. *Paul* loves them. *God* loves them.

Now, by submitting these things to the brothers, Timothy will prove himself to be "an excellent *minister* of Christ Jesus." For "minister" the original uses the term "diakonos," from which we have derived the word "deacon." In I Tim. 3:8, 12 its meaning is "deacon." But in I Tim. 1:12 the closely related "diakonia" does not mean *deaconate* but *ministry,* and it is probable that the related verb, wherever it is used in the New Testament (see on I Tim. 3:13), does not mean "to function as deacon" but "to minister," or "to supply by ministering." "An excellent minister" is one who, in loving devotion to his task, to his people, and above all to his God, warns against departures from the truth and shows how to deal with error. Such a man truly represents (and belongs to) Christ Jesus. "Doing your duty, you, Timothy," says Paul, will fit this description, being **nourished on the words of the faith and of the excellent doctrine which you have been following.**

"The words" are the ones which embody "the faith" and "the excellent teaching" of the church, true Christian doctrine. The apostle may be thinking of certain summaries of doctrine which (perhaps in the form of current "reliable sayings" and other fixed formulations of truths) could be considered good spiritual nourishment. Timothy had been and is still following this excellent doctrine or teaching. If he is to remain a highly qualified minister

4:6   **I TIMOTHY**

of Jesus Christ, he must be *constantly nourished* by (or "on") this kind of food. A minister who neglects to study his Bible and the doctrine based upon it *atrophies* his powers by disuse.

7a. Timothy must be nourished. Of course he must use the *proper* victuals. He must not feed on trash. So Paul continues: **But profane and old-womanish myths shun.** Note that the apostle definitely continues to tell Timothy what the latter should do in order to be and remain an excellent minister. The expressions: "being nourished on the words of the faith," "shun profane and old-womanish myths," "train yourself in godly living," belong together. Doing the one and shunning the other is, of course, a contrast. Hence, the translation "but" (for δέ) here at the beginning of verse 7 fits excellently.[74]

The profane and old-womanish myths which the apostle tells Timothy to shun are the "endless myths and genealogies" mentioned in I Tim. 1:4. In contrast with the heresy against which Paul warned Timothy in the section which has just been discussed (I Tim. 4:1-5), a heresy which had reference largely, though not exclusively, to *the future,* these inane Jewish anecdotes, by means of which errorists were trying to embellish the law, pertained to *the present.* Timothy should refuse to be bothered with them (cf. II Tim. 2:23). He should "beg off." These myths are *profane,* fit to be trodden under foot (see on I Tim. 1:9). They are nothing but drivel, and belong to the category of silly superstitions which *old women* sometimes try to palm off on their neighbors or on their grandchildren.

7b, 8. In continuing his advice with respect to Timothy's spiritual advancement and the means which he should use to that end, Paul says: **Train yourself for godly living. For while physical training is of** *some* **benefit, this godly living is of benefit** *in every way.*

The figure which underlies the passage is, of course, that of the Greek *gymnasium* (or its popular imitation), comprising grounds for running, wrestling, etc. It was a place where *stripped* youths by means of physical training would try to promote the grace and vigor of their bodies. Timothy, then, is told *to gymnasticize.* But, in keeping with the immediately preceding context, which pictured him as being nourished on the words of

---

[74] I agree here with A.V., A.R.V., and in fact with very many versions and commentators. I cannot follow the reasoning of Lenski on p. 629 of his Commentary. Verse 6 and verse 7 mark a clear contrast. Verse 6 implies: "Continue to be nourished on the words of the faith." Verse 8 states, "But profane and old-womanish myths shun." Paul is not merely telling Timothy how to deal with those myths, but he is also, and at the same time, advising his young colleague what to do for his own spiritual and professional advancement in order to become an even more useful minister of Jesus Christ. That interpretation harmonizes beautifully with what follows directly in verse 8, with respect to training for godly living versus physical training.

faith and as shunning profane myths in order that thus he may be (and may continue to be) "an excellent minister of Christ Jesus," he is told to train himself with a view to *godliness* or *godly living*. The *exercise* which he is urged to take is to be of a *spiritual* character.

What Paul had in mind, accordingly, must have included *one or more* of the following comparisons:

(a) Just as a youth in the gymnasium exerts himself to the utmost, so you, too, by God's grace and power, must spare no efforts to attain your goal.

(b) Just as that youth discards every handicap or burden in order that he may train the more freely, so you, too, should divest yourself of everything that could encumber your spiritual progress.

(c) Just as that youth has his eye on a goal — perhaps that of showing superior skill on the discus range, that of winning the wrestling match or boxing-bout in the palestra, that of being the first one to reach the post which marked the winning-point on the running track, at least that of improving his physique — so you should be constantly aiming at your spiritual objective, namely, that of complete self-dedication to God in Christ.

It is not at all surprising that the apostle, with this figure of the gymnasium or its less pretentious substitutes in mind, now draws a comparison between the value of *physical training* (literally "bodily gymnastics") and *training for godly living*. He states that the former is *of some benefit*. It is useful for something. The latter, however, is of benefit *in every way*. It is useful for all things. He is by no means belittling the value of physical exercise. He is saying two things: a. that the boon which bodily training bestows, however great it may be, is definitely inferior to the reward which the godly life promises. The former at best bestows health, vigor, beauty of physical form. These things are wonderful and to be appreciated. But the latter bestows life everlasting! b. that the sphere in which bodily training is of benefit is far more restricted than that in which godly living confers its reward. The former concerns the here and now. The latter concerns the here and now but also reaches far beyond it.

That this is, indeed, what he means is clearly shown by what follows in verse 8, after the words, "this godly living is of benefit in every way," namely, **as it holds promise of life both for the present and for the future.**

The essence and contents of the promise is *life,* fellowship with God in Christ, the love of God shed abroad in the heart, the peace of God which passes all understanding. (See also N.T.C. on John, Vol. 1, pp. 71-73, 141.) Complete devotion, godliness, or godly living, itself the fruit of God's grace, results in the increasing *possession and enjoyment* of this reward, according to the teaching of Scripture throughout (Deut. 4:29; 28:1-3, 9, 10; I Sam. 15:22; Ps. 1:1-3; 24:3-6; 103:17, 18; I John 1:6, 7; I John 2:24, 25; Rev. 2:10, 17; 3:5, 12, 21).

God has promised this, and he always fulfils his promise. And this *life* which God bestows, and which surpasses all other blessings in value, is both for the present and for the future, for the age that *now* is and for *the coming* age. It can never cease.

The explanation of I Tim. 4:7b, 8 which I have given departs in some points from that which is favored by others. See the footnote.[75]

9. Over against the widely proclaimed value of *physical* training, the church confessed its faith in the infinitely superior value of *spiritual* training. Hence, with reference to the significant declaration which we have just studied — namely, "While physical training is of *some* benefit . . . godly living is of benefit *in every way*, as it holds promise of life both for the present and for the future" — believers were constantly saying, **Reliable is that saying and worthy of full acceptance** (see on I Tim. 1:15, where exactly the same formula occurs).

10. That Paul and also Timothy are indeed deeply convinced of the reliability of the declaration regarding the gift of life, now and in the future, to be enjoyed by all those who live godly lives, follows from what the apostle now states: **For to this end we toil and strive, because we have set our hope on the living God.**

It is true that we are deeply convinced of the truth expressed in the faithful saying, *for* otherwise we missionaries (I, Paul, and you, Timothy) would

---

[75] The divergent explanations are legion. I shall mention only two of the main differences between my own explanation and that of others. They are:

(1) Some interpret the expression "bodily gymnastics" as referring to ascetic practises, whether they be those referred to in verse 3, or those pertaining to "Christian asceticism" (keeping the appetites in control).
Objections:
a. Here in verses 7b, 8 the apostle is no longer thinking of the heresy which to a large extent is still future (verses 1-5), but of the heresy of the present (see verse 7a), and even that is not his main thought. The point which he stresses is what Timothy must do in order to grow in spiritual and professional efficiency as a minister of Christ Jesus. This emphasis naturally suggests the figure of the athlete, for he, too, is trying to improve his skill.
b. The very term *gymnastics* brings to the mind physical training rather than fasting. To call abstention from food "bodily gymnastics" seems rather inappropriate.
c. Paul frequently borrows metaphors from the sphere of athletics (Rom. 9:16; I Cor. 9:24-27; Gal. 2:2; 5:7; Phil. 2:16; II Thess. 3:1).
d. He definitely derives illustrations from that sphere *in the Pastorals* (I Tim. 6:12; II Tim. 2:5; 4:7, 8). It is therefore entirely reasonable to conclude that he is doing the same here in I Tim. 4:7b, 8.

(2) Some translate the final clause of verse 8 as if it read: "having promise for the present life and for the one to come" (or something similar).
Objection:
That is obviously not what the apostle writes. He does not use the dative "for the life" but the genitive of quality "of the life." Life in its fullest, most blessed meaning, is ever the content of the promise (John 3:16; I John 2:24, 25). And that holds both for the age that now is and for the one which is to come.

not be toiling and striving so hard. That seems to be the connection between verses 7b, 8, 9, on the one hand, and 10, on the other.

The end or purpose for which Paul and Timothy are toiling and striving is, of course, this, that men from all over the world, be they Jews or Gentiles, shall hear the blessed gospel of salvation, and better still, shall accept it and obtain everlasting life. It is this *life,* that is, *salvation,* that God has promised (verse 8).

These missionaries *labor* or *toil.* They exert themselves to the utmost in the work of bringing the gospel, applying it to concrete situations, warning, admonishing, helping, and encouraging, generally amid great difficulties. Paul uses this word *labor* or *toil* with reference to manual labor (I Cor. 4:12; Eph. 4:28; II Tim. 2:6; cf. the noun in I Thess. 1:3; 2:9; II Thess. 3:8) and also in connection with religious work (Rom. 16:12 twice; I Cor. 5:10; Gal. 4:11; Phil. 2:16; 16:16; I Thess. 5:12; I Tim. 5:17; and in our present passage).

They *strive,* that is, in the spiritual arena they struggle against the forces of darkness, in order that they may bring men out of the darkness into the light. They suffer *agonies.* Cf. I Tim. 6:12; II Tim. 4:7; then Col. 1:29; 4:12. See N.T.C. on I Thess. 2:2.

They gladly carry on this difficult task because they have their hope set not on idols, which can neither make nor keep promises, for they are *dead,* but on the *living* God (see N.T.C. on I Thess. 1:9, 10), **who is the Savior of all men, especially of those who believe.**

This clause has given rise to a variety of interpretations. Here one should tread very carefully. Some explanations, as I see it, are wrong even on the surface:

(1) God is the Savior of all men in the sense that ultimately he *actually* saves *every human being* who has ever lived on the earth.

Objection: This is contrary to all biblical teaching. Not all men are saved in that full, spiritual sense. Moreover, if this were true, why would Paul have added, *"especially* of those who believe"? That last phrase would make no sense.

(2) He *actually* bestows salvation — in the full, evangelical sense of the term — on *all kinds of people.* He gives to them all everlasting life.

Objection: This explanation, too, is impossible in view of the final phrase, *"especially* of those who believe."

(3) He *wants* all men to be saved (see I Tim. 2:3), but in the case of some his will is "frustrated" by obstinate unbelief. (Lenski's explanation is along this line; *op. cit.,* p. 639.)

Objection: The present passage, however, does not say that he *wants* to save, but that he *actually* saves; he is *actually* the Savior (in some sense) of all men. Also, *"frustration"* — in the absolute, ultimate sense — of the divine will is impossible. Otherwise God would not be God!

4:10   **I TIMOTHY**

(4) He *is able* to save all men; but though all *can* be saved, only the believers are *actually* saved. (See N. J. D. White, *The Expositor's Greek Testament* on this passage.)

Objection: That is not what the text says. It says, "He *is* the Savior of all men."

The true explanation is found, it would seem to me, by making a thorough study of the term *Savior* in a passage of this kind. The final phrase "especially of those who believe" clearly indicates that the term is here given a twofold application. Of *all* men God is the Savior, but of *some* men, namely, believers, he is the Savior in a deeper, more glorious sense than he is of others. This clearly implies that when he is called the Savior of all men, this cannot mean that he imparts to all everlasting life, as he does to believers. The term *Savior*, then, must have a meaning which *we today* generally do not immediately attach to it. And that is exactly the cause of our difficulty. One must study this term in the light not only of the New Testament but also of the Old Testament and of Archaeology.[76]

Now in the LXX version of the Old Testament the word *Soter* which is used here in I Tim. 4:10, and which is usually rendered *Savior*, is at times employed in a sense far below that which we generally ascribe to it. So, for example, the judge Othniel is called a *Soter* or "savior" or "deliverer" because he *delivered* the children of Israel from the hands of Cushan-rishathaim, king of Mesopotamia (Judg. 3:9). See also II Kings 13:5: "And Jehovah gave Israel a savior (deliverer), so that they were delivered from the hands of the Syrians." In a sense all the judges of Israel were "saviors," (deliverers), just as we read in Neh. 9:27, "Thou gavest them saviors (deliverers) who saved (that is, *delivered*) them out of the hand of their adversaries." Cf. also a somewhat similar use of the word in Obadiah verse 21, "And saviors (deliverers) shall come up on mount Zion to judge the mount of Esau, and the kingdom shall be Jehovah's."

It is not strange that especially Jehovah would be called Savior, for it was he who again and again rescued or delivered his people (Deut. 32:15; Ps. 25:5). He "did great things in Egypt . . . terrible things by the Red Sea," being, accordingly, "God, their Savior" (Ps. 106:21).

Having delivered Israel from the oppression of Pharaoh, he had been the Savior of that entire multitude that went out of Egypt. Yet, "with

---

[76] See the following:

Deissmann, A., *op. cit.*, p. 363, and see his Index; I.S.B.E. on "Saviour"; M.M., pp. 621, 622; Ramsay, W., *The Bearing of Recent Discovery on the Trustworthiness of the New Testament,* reprint Grand Rapids, Mich., 1953, pp. 172-198; Taylor, F. J., on "Saviour" in *A Theological Word Book Of The Bible* (edited by Alan Richardson), New York, 1952; W.D.B., on "Saviour"; Wendland, "Soter," *ZNTW,* Number 5 (1904), p. 335 ff.

most of them God was not well pleased" (I Cor. 10:5). *In a sense,* therefore, he was the Savior or Soter of all, but *especially* of those who believed. With the latter, with them alone, he was "well pleased." All leave Egypt; not all enter "Canaan."

It is especially in certain beautiful passages of Isaiah that the word Soter is given a rich, spiritual content: Jehovah is Israel's Savior, and this not only because he delivers his people from oppression but also because *collectively* he *loves* them. Yet, even in these exalted passages the meaning which we today generally attach to the word has not been reached. The passages cannot be interpreted to mean that he gave everlasting life to all the individuals in the group. Note Is. 63:8-10:

"For he said, Surely they are my people, children who will not deal falsely: so he was their Savior. In all their affliction he was afflicted, and the angel of his presence saved them: in his love and in his pity he redeemed them; and he bare them, and he carried them all the days of old. But they rebelled and grieved his Holy Spirit: therefore he was turned to be their enemy, and he himself fought against them. . . ." Cf. Is. 43:3, 11; 45:15, 21; 49:26; 60:16. Cf. Jer. 14:8; Hos. 13:4. (In the last reference note especially the context: "besides me there is no Savior" preceded by "Jehovah thy God from the land of Egypt," and followed by, "I knew thee in the wilderness.") According to the Old Testament, then, God is *Soter* not only of those who enter his everlasting kingdom but in a sense also of others, indeed, of all those whom he delivers from temporary disaster.

Besides, the Old Testament teaches everywhere that God's kind providence extends to all men, in a sense even to plants and animals: Ps. 36:6; 104:27, 28; 145:9, 16, 17; Jonah 4:10, 11. He provides his creatures with food, keeps them alive, is deeply interested in them, often delivers them from disease, ills, hurt, famine, war, poverty, and peril in any form. He is, accordingly, their *Soter* (Preserver, Deliverer, and in *that* sense Savior).

In the New Testament this teaching is continued, as was to be expected. In his love, kindness, and mercy the heavenly Father "makes his sun to rise on the evil and on the good, and sends rain on the just and the unjust" . . . "is kind toward the unthankful and evil" (Matt. 5:45; Luke 6:35). The wickedness of evil men consists partly in this that they have not given thanks for this goodness of God (Rom. 1:21). It is he who "gives to all life and breath and all things" (Acts 17:25). It is he "in whom we live and move and have our being" (Acts 17:28). He preserves, delivers, and in that sense *saves,* and *that* "saving" activity is by no means confined to the elect! On the Voyage Dangerous (to Rome) God "saved" not only Paul but all those who were with him (Acts 27:22, 31, 44). There was no loss of life.

Moreover, God also causes his gospel of salvation to be earnestly proclaimed to *all men,* that is, to men from every race and nation. Truly, the kindness of God extends to all. There is no one who does not in one way

4:10 I TIMOTHY

or another come within the reach of his benevolence,[77] and even the circle of those to whom the message of salvation is proclaimed is wider than the circle of those who accept it by a true faith.

This is really all that is needed in clarification of our present passage, I Tim. 4:10. What the apostle teaches amounts, accordingly, to this, "We have our hope set on the living God, and in this hope we shall not be disappointed, for not only is he a kind God, hence the *Soter* (Preserver, Deliverer) of all men, showering blessings upon them, but he is in a very special sense the *Soter* (Savior) of those who by faith embrace him and his promise, for to them he imparts salvation, everlasting life in all its fulness (as explained in connection with I Tim. 1:15; see on that passage).

It is *this living God* who in Jesus Christ is the Savior! In classical and in Koine Greek the term *Soter* was used as a designation of various gods (Zeus, Apollo, Hermes, Ascelepius), Roman emperors, and leading officials, inasmuch as these were viewed as delivering men from this or that calamity, supplying this or that physical need, or bestowing general health or "well-being." But according to Paul, back of every real deliverance stands God, the living One. The most glorious "well-being" of all (for the soul but in the end also for the body), and that everlasting, is promised and given by him to all who believe. For them, *for them alone,* God is the *Soter* in the sense in which the term is also used in I Tim. 1:1; 2:3; Titus 1:3; 2:10; 3:4. Them he rescues from the greatest evil, and upon them he bestows the greatest good. It is in that full, evangelical sense that the term is applied to God also in Jude 25 (and, according to some, also in Luke 1:47).

Though as a title for God Paul did not use the term until he wrote the Pastorals, the *idea* that God is the *Soter* is certainly present in his earlier writings, as has been shown (see on I Tim. 1:1). It is probable that the closer Paul and believers in general came into contact with the Roman world and with the epithet *Soter* as applied to its gods and leaders, the more they began to make use of that same term *Soter* as a designation for the true and living God, basing *the contents* of this conviction not on anything which the world round about them offered but upon special revelation as given in the Old Testament and in the teaching of the Lord.

11. Command these things and teach (them).

Timothy is told *to command* (or: to keep on commanding) *and teach* (or: to keep on teaching; both verbs are present imperatives) these things. He must *command* such things as, "Profane and old-womanish myths shun,"

---

[77] Says Calvin, *op. cit.,* on this passage: Intelligit Dei beneficentiam ad omnes homines pervenire. Quod si nemo est mortalium, qui non sentiat Dei erga se bonitatem eiusque sit particeps, quanto magis eam experientur pii qui in eum sperant? Somewhat similar is the explanation given by Chrysostom, Bengel, Barnes, Lock, J. Van Dyk, C. Bouma, J. Van Andel (see Bibliography for titles).

"Train yourself (and yourselves) for godly living" (verse 7). Orders such as these apply not only to Timothy himself but to all the presbyters, yes, and even to all Christians. It is probable that the expression "these things" in connection with "command" refers also to *implied* commands, such as, "Never reject what God has intended for use, but partake of it with thanksgiving" (verses 3, 4), "Nurture yourself (yourselves) on the words of faith and sound doctrine" (verse 6), "Rely on the living God and on his promise to all who live the godly life and who accept him by genuine faith" (verses 8, 9).

Timothy must *teach* such things as, "Apostasy is coming, in the form of asceticism" (verses 1-3), *"That* error is an insult to God and to his work of creation" (verses 4, 5), "An excellent minister is one who is nourished on sound doctrine which he transmits to others" (verse 6), "The benefit which accrues from godly living transcends that which results from physical training (verses 8-10).

12. Let no one despise your youth.

It may be assumed that about the year 51, when Timothy joined Paul who was on his *second* missionary journey, the former had reached the age of 22-27 years of age. It is hardly probable that the apostle would have permitted a man even younger than that to join him in such a difficult task. Besides, we know that Timothy must have reached a degree of maturity even during Paul's *first* missionary journey, for it was then that he had "confessed his faith." If this calculation be correct, then Timothy is *now* — i.e., about the year 63 — somewhere between 34 and 39 years of age. According to Ireneus, the first stage of life embraces thirty years and extends onward until forty years (*Against Heresies,* II. xxii). Hence, Timothy was still "a young man." Besides, he must have been considered *very young for the position* which he occupied: apostolic representative and as such chief over all the *presbyters* in the churches of Ephesus and surroundings. These *presbyters* (as the very name implies), in ancient Israel, in the later synagogue, and also in the early church — which in many ways copied the synagogue — were generally *old* or at least *elderly* men. And here is Timothy, a much younger man and moreover a person of natural reserve and timidity, wielding authority over those who were his seniors by perhaps 10-40 years! Hence, the command, "Let no one *look down* upon you" — the Greek idiom says, "Let no one *think down* upon you" — was called for. Timothy must not permit anyone to despise him because of his youth. He must see to it that he is respected because of his office. But he must attain this end not by "acting big" or bragging about his credentials, but by conducting himself as a man of sage counsel and consecrated, practical wisdom. Respect for *the man* will mean respect for his *office!* Hence, Paul continues, **But become the believers' model in speech, in conduct, in love,**

in faith, in purity. In an altogether natural and organic manner he must win the respect of all the believers. Note that Paul does not really say that Timothy should become a model *for* the believers, that is, for them to follow (see N.T.C. on I Thess. 1:7; II Thess. 3:9), but that ever increasingly he should become a model *of* what the believers are; and this in five respects:

a. *in speech,* that is, in personal conversation (for *preaching* see the next verse).

b. *in conduct,* that is, in customs, habits, ways of dealing with people, etc.

c. *in love,* that is, in deep personal attachment to his brothers and in genuine concern for his neighbors (including even his enemies), always seeking to promote the welfare of all.

d. *in faith,* that is, in the exercise of that gift of God which is the root from which love springs (note: *love* here probably indicates the horizontal relationship; *faith,* the vertical).

e. *in purity* (see also I Tim. 5:2), that is, in complete conformity, both in thought and act, with God's moral law.

13. Reaffirming the directive of verse 11 Paul continues, **Until I come, attend to the (public) reading (of Scripture), to the exhorting and to the teaching.**

"Until I come" is the correct translation, and harmonizes with 3:14 ("hoping to come to you shortly"). The idea is, "If and when I return, I will give you new instructions." Perhaps Paul had in mind some other mission on which Timothy could then be sent.

During the apostle's absence, then, his representative is given instructions anent his duty with respect to public worship in the entire district. He must see to it that in all the churches of Ephesus and surroundings three elements receive due prominence, namely,

a. *the public reading of Scripture* (just as in the synagogue, Luke 4:16; Acts 13:15; II Cor. 3:14; but now not only the reading of law and prophets, but in addition portions of the growing New Testament, Col. 4:16; I Thess. 5:27; Rev. 1:3).

b. *exhorting.* This includes warning (for example, against error in doctrine and morals), advice, and encouragement. See further the discussion of the word in N.T.C. on Thessalonians, p. 62, and on John, Vol. II, p. 276.

c. *teaching.* It *does* make a difference *what* one believes! The *attitude* of heart is not everything. There are certain *facts* with respect to doctrine and morals which must be taught, and which one must accept and embrace, so that one's life is founded upon them. See, for example, John 3:16, and all the teaching in the present epistle.

This is not a complete summary of the essentials which comprise public worship. For instance, *prayer* is not mentioned. But it did not need to be mentioned, for Paul had dwelt on this in detail in chapter 2. So much is clear: if there be no pulpit-reading, exhorting, and teaching, *divine worship* is a misnomer. In the early church, when very few individuals owned private copies of the sacred writings, and all such material had to be copied by hand, one can imagine how important was the *public reading* of Scripture. But even today the careful selection, and clear and interpretive reading of an appropriate portion of Holy Writ is "the most important part of public worship." [78] And even today if the choir takes so much time that little is left for exhorting and teaching, something is wrong. Timothy, then, must *continue to devote his attention* to these important matters.

Is there not another hint here that has value for today as well as for the times of Paul and Timothy, namely, that a minister should strive to effect a proper balance between the reading of Scripture, exhorting, and teaching? Some never exhort. Others never teach. And the reading of Scripture is prone to be regarded merely as a necessary preface to what the preacher himself is going to say!

14. Timothy had been specially gifted for his task. Hence, Paul continues, **Do not grow careless about the gift that is in you.** That gift of discernment between the true and the false, and consequently of being able to exhort, teach, and guide, Timothy must employ to the best advantage. He must make use of it when he himself administers the Word and he must also exercise it when he tells others how to preach. He must *never grow careless* about it or neglect it. It is a precious *charisma*, that is, a special gift of God's grace bestowed upon him by the Holy Spirit. Hence, Paul continues: **which was granted to you through prophetic utterance with the laying on of the hands of the presbytery.** In all probability this refers to what had happened at Lystra on Paul's second missionary journey. It was then that Timothy by the operation of the Holy Spirit had been amply endowed with this gift. Of this and of the character of his task he had been made aware *through* (διά) *prophetic utterance* of inspired bystanders. Moreover, all this was *in association with* (or *accompanied by:* μετά) the imposition of the hands of *the presbytery* (used elsewhere to indicate the Sanhedrin — Luke 22:66; Acts 22:5 —, but here for *the college of elders* or, in that sense, *the consistory of the church*). Paul's own hands had also rested upon him (II Tim. 1:6). This imposition of hands symbolizes *the transfer* of a gift from the Giver to the recipient. In the present instance it signifies that gracious act of the Holy Spirit whereby he confers

---

[78] See A. W. Blackwood, *The Fine Art Of Public Worship,* Nashville, 1939, chapter VII, "The Public Reading of the Scriptures," pp. 128-141; note especially the excellent suggestions on pp. 140, 141.

his special favor upon Timothy, enabling him to carry out the duties of his important office as apostolic representative (cf. also Acts 6:6; 8:17; 13:3, 4).

15. Let these things be your constant care. Over against "*Do not grow careless,*" Paul places, "Let these things be your constant care" (cf. verses 14 and 15). By the expression "these things" he is thinking of the entire contents of chapter 4 (that defection is on the way, against which Timothy must warn others; that even now there are those who would substitute profane myths for the true gospel; that Timothy must be nourished on the words of the faith, and must train himself for godly living; that he must so conduct himself that no one will despise his youth; that he must not neglect but must exercise and cultivate his special gift; etc.). **In these things be (absorbed).** "Be *in* them," says the apostle, as if to say, "Be *in* them with your whole heart, with all your soul; be completely wrapped up in them." The contemplated result will be **so that your progress may be evident to everyone.** We accept the usual interpretation of these words to be the correct and natural one, namely, that if Timothy will devote himself completely to his task, as indicated, *all* (especially those in the church, but to some extent even outsiders who come into close contact with believers) will take note of his spiritual and professional advancement, to the glory of God. Cf. Phil. 1:12, 25. The closing words of the chapter are:

16. Look to yourself and to the teaching, persevere in them.

Holy living and sound teaching must go together if Timothy (or, for that matter, any apostolic representative, any minister, any elder, etc.) is to be a blessing. Hence, Paul admonishes Timothy to continue *to focus* (*his mind,* understood) *on himself,* that is, on his own duties, his own gift, his own privilege to go to the depths of God's promise; particularly also upon *the* teaching (his own and that of others in the Ephesus district). He must *stay on* or *persevere* in them, that is, in holy living and in vigilance with respect to teaching. The promise is: **"for by doing this you will save both yourself and those who hear you."** To be sure, a man is saved by grace, through faith; not by works (Titus 3:3; cf. Eph. 2:6-8); yet, since holy living and sound teaching are a fruit of faith, Paul is able to say that "by doing this" Timothy will save himself and his hearers. It is *along the path of* holy living and diligence in teaching and in watching over the life and teaching of others, that *salvation* (both present and future; see on I Tim. 1:15) is obtained. Besides, God promises a special reward to his faithful ministers, yes, to *all* his faithful witnesses (Dan. 12:3; Matt. 13:43; James 5:20); and threatens with severe punishment the unfaithful ones (Ezek. 33:7, 8).

Synthesis of Chapter 4

See the Outline at the beginning of the chapter.

Though the Christ be ever so exalted (see the close of Chapter III), and the church ever so glorious, apostasy is just around the corner. The instigators are the seducing spirits who invade the hearts of deceivers. These deceivers will forbid people to marry, and will order them to abstain from certain foods, as if salvation could be attained by practices such as these, practices, moreover, which detract from Christ as the one and only Savior. As to the foods in question, these are excellent because God created them and because he in answer to our prayers consecrates them.

Timothy, in combating such developing errors, which will grow worse and worse, must make himself strong. Hence, he must use *positive* weapons. He should not concentrate his attention and energy on *myths*. Rather, he should nourish himself on the words of faith, and continue stedfastly in the public reading of Scripture, exhortation and teaching.

Yes, let Timothy train himself for godly living. Positive living and positive teaching are the best means of spiritual self-development and also the best weapons against error. As to this training for godly living, it confers a blessing far greater than physical training can ever confer. It brings everlasting life, which is a boon for the present and for the future. If Paul and his helpers had not been thoroughly convinced of this, they would not have labored so hard. But they have placed their complete confidence in a God who will not disappoint them, for he is the God of love. He preserves not only man and beast but especially his people. Let Timothy then attend faithfully to his ministerial duties. Let him conduct himself in such a manner that no one will look down upon him, thinking, "He is still so young." By using to the full the gift which he received when he was ordained, and by being absorbed in such things as the public reading of Scripture, exhortation, and teaching, he will save both himself and those who hear him.

Note especially the words:

"While physical training is of *some* benefit, godly living is of benefit *in every way*."

The Greeks worshiped at the shrine of beauty and physical culture. Long before the days of Paul they had already established their Olympian, Isthmian, and Pythian games. In Paul's time contests of this character were held in many of the Roman provinces.

Now in this comparison between the value of bodily training and the value of training in godly living, one important item must not be overlooked. Physical exercise, especially with a view to partaking in the public contests, was closely connected with *pagan religion*. In fact, in the popular mind, the two were almost inseparable. The Olympian games were held in honor of Zeus; the Isthmian games in honor of Poseidon; and the Pythian in honor of Apollo. *Roman* athletic contests were preceded by processions in which the statues of the gods were carried on beautiful chariots. *Their* most important contests were held in honor of such gods as Jupiter, Apollo, Diana, etc. And even in connection with the execution of criminals in the amphitheater the stories with reference to the pagan deities were often made vivid to the public and re-enacted in the manner in which the death-sentence was carried out. On this whole subject see *Everyday Life in Ancient Times,* published by the National Geographic Magazine, pp. 209, 227; also Erich Sauer, *In the Arena of Faith,* Grand Rapids, 1955, pp. 30-68.

In view of all this, is it any wonder that Paul says, "Physical training is of *some* benefit." It benefited the body, to be sure. Before it could even contribute in its own small way to the welfare of the soul, it would have to be placed in an entirely different context.

Outline of Chapter 5

Theme: *The Apostle Paul, Writing to Timothy, Gives Directions For the Administration of the Church*

Directions with respect to Certain Definite Groups and Individuals

5:1, 2	A.	Older men, younger men, older women, younger women
5:3-8	B.	Widows in distress
5:9-16	C.	Widows engaged in spiritual work
5:17-25	D.	Elders and prospective elders

CHAPTER V

I TIMOTHY 5:1

5 1 An old(er) man do not treat harshly, but admonish him as you would a father; young(er) men as brothers; 2 old(er) women as mothers, young(er) women as sisters, in all purity.

Up to this point Paul has imparted counsel with respect to matters most of which touched the entire Christian community which had its center in Ephesus. He has stated the reason why Timothy had been left in Ephesus (chapter 1), has given directions for the conduct of both men and women in connection with public worship (chapter 2), has stipulated the qualifications of elders and deacons (chapter 3), and has pointed out the path which Timothy (and the presbyters under his supervision) must tread in order to cope with apostasy and to grow in efficiency as minister(s) of Christ (chapter 4).

To a large extent — but with important personal digressions — all this was quite general. Now the apostle begins to direct his attention more especially to *individuals* and *groups* within the Christian community. See the Outline.

It must be borne in mind, however, that this is a genuine letter, and that the divisions are never rigid. Thoughts continually overlap. Ideas once stated return in slightly altered form. The Outline covers the contents and marks the divisions *in general*.

5:1, 2

1. An old(er) man do not treat harshly, but admonish him as you would a father.

In the course of his pastoral work Timothy will at times have to correct the faults of certain church-members. These individuals can be distinguished as to age and sex: old(er) man, young(er) men; old(er) women, young(er) women. The comparative idea (*older* instead of *old; younger* instead of *young*) has almost vanished.

None of these must be treated harshly, least of all the senior members of the congregation. See Lev. 19:32; Prov. 20:29; Lam. 5:12b. The verb used in the original literally means *to strike at;* then *to treat harshly*. The word which we have rendered "old(er) man" is πρεσβύτερος. Elsewhere in

The Pastorals (I Tim. 5:17, 19; Titus 1:5) it means *an elder* or *presbyter*. Here it is used in its primary sense of a man of advanced age (cf. Acts 2:17), as the context clearly shows.

Instead of dealing harshly with those who need correction, Timothy must *admonish*. The verb used in the original means *to call aside*. This calling aside may be for the purpose of encouraging, comforting, exhorting, entreating, appealing to, or admonishing. It is obviously the latter thought which is predominant in the present passage.

Now it should be emphasized that also here Paul maintains beautiful balance. On the one hand, he does not want Timothy to spare the older people, permitting them to "get away" with their sins. On the other hand, he desires that they be treated with due respect. Timothy must admonish an old man as if the latter were *his own father*. How considerately, with what tact, what gentleness and moderation, would he deal with one who stood so close to him! Let him then treat this erring one with the same humility, love and tenderness. For, after all, the Christian community *is* a family, the most glorious family of all (Matt. 12:49, 50); and it *does* indeed consist of fathers, mothers, brothers, and sisters . . . *in the Lord!* Hence, old(er) men must be treated as fathers, that is, with respect; **young(er) men as brothers,** that is, in the spirit of equality, an equality of persons, which does not exclude the exercise of authority on the part of him who administers the admonition.

2. **Old(er) women as mothers.**

Female members of the congregation must not be excluded from the sphere of private pastoral counseling with respect to sin. Though this task may at times prove to be delicate, it must not be shunned. But when Timothy admonishes the old(er) women, he must deal with them as a good and loving adult son deals with his erring mother! To correct one's own mother surely requires deep humility, genuine searching of heart, wrestling at the throne of grace, wisdom! It is in that spirit that Timothy must proceed when he feels duty-bound to admonish old(er) women who have erred.

Young(er) women as sisters, in all purity.

Young(er) women, too, are the objects of pastoral care. They should be admonished *as sisters;* hence, *in all purity*. When one seeks to help *his sister* to overcome a certain blemish of character, *impurity* (at least in the more popular sense of the word) is completely absent. Let Timothy treat the young ladies and the young married ladies who are under his spiritual care in that same fashion, just as if they were his own sisters, for they really are . . . *in the Lord!* In agreement with Calvin, we believe that the phrase "in all purity" belongs to the immediately preceding clause: "admonish . . . young(er) women as sisters." Now it is certainly true that here

I TIMOTHY 5:3

as well as in 4:12 the phrase "in all purity" means "in complete conformity in thought and word with God's moral law," and is not to be restricted to *sexual* purity. Nevertheless it would be incorrect to say that the idea of sexual purity is excluded from it. That the command was altogether in place as a word not only for Timothy but for all "ministers" in every age is clear to anyone who will take the trouble to read the sad accounts which describe what happens when it is not heeded.[79]

It is true, of course, that the direction which Paul gives in these two verses is not for Timothy *only* but also for his assistants in the various churches of Ephesus and vicinity. On the other hand, the very language employed clearly indicates that it is wrong to regard Timothy as a "superintendent" without any pastoral duties of his own. Even his superior, Paul, *was a real pastor,* deeply concerned about every member (Acts 20:20; and see N.T.C. on I Thess. 2:7-11). Then why not Timothy?

---

3 As widows, honor those (who are) really (what is implied in the name) *widows.* 4 But if a widow has children or grandchildren, let these first learn their religious duty to their own family and make a real return to their parents; for this is acceptable in the sight of God. 5 Now the real widow, the one who was left all alone, has set her hope on God, and continues in her supplications and her prayers by night and by day; 6 but the one who is giving herself up to luxury, though living, is dead.

7 These things, too, you must command, in order that they may be above reproach. 8 Now if any one does not provide for his own, and especially for the members of his own family, he has denied the faith and is worse than an unbeliever.

5:3-8

3. As widows, honor those (who are) really (what is implied in the name) widows.

Distressed widows are discussed in verses 3-8; *those employed by the church* in verses 9-16.

If older women must be treated as *mothers,* as Paul has just stated (see verse 2), and if mothers must be honored (Ex. 20:12; Deut. 5:16; Eph. 6:2), it follows that distressed widows must also be honored.

Such widows (described in verse 5), must be *honored,* that is, treated with high regard, with great consideration, and this implies that those who are in need must receive material support. See also on I Tim. 5:17.

Strikingly beautiful is what Scripture teaches with respect to widows:

(1) God is "a father of the fatherless, and a judge of the widows" (Ps. 68:5).

---

[79] See for example, C. Chiniquy, *Fifty Years In The Church Of Rome,* pp. 580-602; also his work *The Priest, The Woman, and The Confessional.*

They are under his special care and protection (Ex. 22:23; Deut. 10:18; Prov. 15:25; Ps. 146:9).

(2) By means of the tithe and "the forgotten sheaf" he provides for them (Deut. 14:29; 24:19-21; 26:12, 13). At the feasts which he has instituted, they too should rejoice (Deut. 16:11, 14).

(3) He blesses those who help and honor them (Is. 1:17, 18; Jer. 7:6; 22:3, 4).

(4) He rebukes and punishes those who hurt them (Ex. 22:22; Deut. 24:17; 27:19; Zech. 7:10; Job 24:3, 21; 31:16; Ps. 94:6; Mal. 3:5).

(5) They are the objects of Christ's tender compassion, as is clear from the Gospels, especially from the Gospel according to Luke (Mark 12:42, 43; Luke 7:11-17; 18:3, 5; 20:47; 21:2, 3).

(6) In the early church they were not forgotten. It was the neglect of certain widows which led to the appointment of the first deacons, so that in the future widows might receive better care (Acts 6:1-6). And according to James, one of the manifestations of a religion that is pure and undefiled is this: "to visit the fatherless and widows in their affliction" (James 1:27).

Timothy, then, certainly knows what Paul means when he says, "Honor ... those who are really (what is implied in the name) widows."

There is here a play upon words, for in the original the word *widow* means the one *bereaved, deprived* (of her husband; hence, often without means of support). Hence, what the apostle is saying amounts to this, "As *deprived* ones, honor those (who are) really *deprived*" (or "As *destitute*, honor those who are really *destitute*"). If certain etymologists are correct (not all agree), then we could have a similar play of words in English, for the word "widow" = Latin *vidua,* is by them linked with such words as *void* and *devoid.* Hence, one might say, "As *viduae* (widows), honor those who are really de*void* (of means of support)."

Gainful employment for widows was scarce. Besides, some widows were too old to provide for themselves. Hence, those who had no other means of support must be provided for by the church.

4. There are, however, widows who do not fall within this category. Hence, Paul continues, **But if a widow has children or grandchildren, let these** [80] **first learn their religious duty to their own family and make a real return to their parents; for this is acceptable in the sight of God.**

The church must not be unnecessarily burdened. Yet, that is not the main reason for the present command. It is rather this: Children and

---

[80] The idea that the expression "Let *these* first learn" refers to *the widows* and not to the children — an idea favored even by Calvin — must be considered erroneous. Note the order of the words in the sentence, the use of the plural verb (the singular is weakly attested), the natural and entirely scriptural idea that children shall honor their parents, that in doing this they are "making a return," etc.

grandchildren should honor their progenitors! That is their first religious (cf. Acts 17:23) duty toward those who brought them up. They should strive to make a *real return* (acc. pl. of ἀμοιβή, plural of intensity) for all the care that was so lovingly bestowed upon them. Note, "Let these first *learn*" this lesson. By nature children are often disinclined to provide for their needy parents. According to a Dutch proverb it frequently seems easier for *one* poor father to bring up *ten* children than for *ten* rich children to provide for *one* poor father. But even if it means self-denial, this lesson must be *learned*. It is certainly implied in the fifth commandment. Moreover, it should be done with gladness, in the spirit of love, as a token of appreciation for that which the children have themselves received from their parents. Joseph's genuine concern for the welfare of his father should serve as a lesson for all time: "I am Joseph; is my father still alive?" (Gen. 45:3). Note with what tenderness and whole-hearted devotion he provided for *his father* (Gen. 45:9-13; 46:28-34; 47:7, 27-31; 50:1-14). And read also the words of the crucified Christ with respect to *his mother* (see N.T.C. on John 19:26, 27). Surely, when children honor their parents and grandparents, such conduct is acceptable in the sight of God! His *promise* is bound to be fulfilled.

5. The apostle now returns to the discussion of *the real widow* (see verse 3), the one who does not have children and/or grandchildren who can support her. Says he, **Now the real widow, the one who was left all alone, has set her hope on God.**

The real widow, then, has nowhere else to go! Her refuge is the living God, for on earth she is no one's dependent. She was left *all alone,* and abides in that condition. There is no child or grandchild or anyone else whose duty it would be to support her. On God she has permanently fixed her hope (third per. sing. perfect indic.). Her expectation is of him (Ps. 123:1, 2).

This hope is real and vital. Hence, Paul adds: **and continues in her supplications and in her prayers by night and by day.**[81] The terms *"supplications and prayers"* have been explained before (see on I Tim. 2:1). In the present instance the original has the article with each noun: *"the* supplications . . . *the* prayers." In other words, they are *her* very own, the outpourings of her own soul. Moreover, she prays not only by day, at set times and whenever the need arises, but also by night: every night, and perhaps especially, when, vexed with anxiety, she cannot sleep, during nightly vigils, etc. The emphasis rests on the fact that, with her, praying is not a "now and then" affair; she *continues* in her supplications and in her pray-

---

[81] "Night and day" (instead of "day and night") is the order also in I Thess. 2:9; 3:10; II Thess. 3:8; II Tim. 1:3; cf. Jer. 14:17; contrast 16:13.

ers. Part of every night and part of every day is spent in supplication and prayer. She reminds one of the widow Anna (Luke 2:36, 37).

This is a truly beautiful description of "the real widow." The apostle does not repeat that such a widow should be "honored" by the church. Timothy will, of course, link verses 3 and 5. The obvious does not have to be repeated.

6. Our admiration and high regard for "the real widow" grows when we compare her with her "opposite" as now described by Paul: **but the one who is giving herself up to luxury, though living, is dead.** This widow is living luxuriously, perhaps even riotously (cf. James 5:5), like the daughters of Sodom (Ezek. 16:49). She is gay, frivolous, dissolute, pleasure-mad, "a merry widow." Whatever interest in religious matters she may have displayed at one time is now completely gone. Like the seed that fell among the thorns and was choked by them (Matt. 13:7, 22), so also in this woman's case, the word of God, to which at one time she listened outwardly, was choked by her delight in riches and pleasures. She reminds us of Kipling's Widow at Windsor with "ships on the foam and millions at home." Though *physically alive,* she *has actually died* and *is therefore now dead to all higher interests.* Of course, she never was a real Christian, but she used to pay her respects to *religion.* She went to church, and seemed to listen to the reading of the Word. Her lips used to move in prayer, and she was even emotionally stirred at times. Today, however, all *that* belongs definitely to the past. She is dressed in her gayest attire, and her purpose is "to have fun" and, perhaps, "to make a good catch." It is not necessary for Paul to add, "Do not honor such widows."

7. These things, too, you must command, in order that they may be above reproach.

Timothy is to urge obedience not only to the things referred to in I Tim. 4:11 ("Command these things and teach them") but also to the things which Paul has just now been saying. Surely, the most natural view is that the expression "these things" refers to the entire paragraph (verses 3-6). Timothy must see to it that the church honors really dependent and deserving widows (verses 3 and 5); that children and grandchildren do their duty to their parents (verse 4); and that everyone knows how to distinguish between the widow who should be honored and the widow who should not be honored (implied in verses 5 and 6).

If all the interested persons obey these commands, they will be above reproach both from the side of the world and from the side of the church.

8. Now if anyone does not provide for his own, and especially for the members of his own family, he has denied the faith and is worse than an unbeliever.

What has been stated positively in verse 4 is now stated negatively, more inclusively, and with greater force. The sin here censured is present in every community and in every age. Hence, the rule "Bear one another's burdens, and so fulfil the law of Christ" (Gal. 6:2) has validity for all time, particularly with reference to those whom one should consider "his own." Does this expression "his own" as here used mean "his own close relatives," for example, a widowed mother or grandmother, an aged and infirm father or grandfather, a physically or mentally ill cousin, an uncle or aunt on the verge of collapse? Are *friends* included or only *relatives?* No doubt, indefiniteness is here a virtue. Each case must be judged on its own merits, according to the need which exists and the ability to render assistance. But John 13:34; 15:12; Gal. 6:2 are always applicable.

However, within this rather indefinite (not sharply delimited) circle of dear ones there is a smaller one which is far more definite: "and especially for the members of his own family." Here the immediate family is meant, that is, immediate in the sense indicated in verse 4.

The apostle, then, has a word of rebuke for the person who neglects his duty toward "his own," and especially for him who fails to support the members of his immediate family. Such a neglectful individual *"has denied the faith."* (Same verb with same meaning in II Tim. 2:12; but see also on Titus 2:12.) He has denied it not by means of *words* necessarily but (what is often far worse) by means of his *sinful negligence.* Lack of positive action, the sin of omission, gives the lie to his profession of *faith* (subjective sense). Though he professes to be a Christian, he lacks the most precious of all the fruits that grow on the tree of a truly Christian life and conduct. He lacks *love.* Where this good *fruit* is absent, there cannot be a good *tree.*

Such a person is said to be "worse than an unbeliever." This is true for the following reasons:

(1) Most "unbelievers" (in the sense of "outsiders") have never heard about *the specific precept* found in John 13:34; 15:12; Gal. 6:2. But he who has been instructed in the Christian religion has heard this command again and again.

(2) Most "unbelievers" are complete strangers to *Christ's glorious example* of love for his own (including the love for his mother). But the church-member has become acquainted with the story of his infinite love.

(3) "Unbelievers," in general, know nothing about the promise of an *enabling power,* namely, the power of the Holy Spirit operating in the believer's heart. But he who professes to be a Christian has witnessed the evidences of this power in the lives of others.

(4) Yet, in spite of this threefold lack, "unbelievers" do often show some affection toward those who belong to their family-circle, in wider or more restricted sense. Frequently they do actually provide for their widowed mothers and grandmothers, and pagan reverence for ancestors is a well-

known religious phenomenon. Hence, the person who wishes to be viewed as a Christian but who, in spite of the clearer light and the many privileges which he has received, does not perform his religious duty with respect to those whom God has placed within the sphere of his special responsibility, is, indeed, "worse than an infidel."

---

9 A widow, in order to be placed on the list of widows, must not be less than sixty years of age; (she must have been) one husband's wife, 10 well-attested for noble deeds. (She can be placed on the list) if she has reared children, if she has practised hospitality, if she has washed the feet of saints, if she has assisted the afflicted, if she has been devoted to every kind of good work.
11 But younger widows you must refuse (to place on the list); for often when, contrary to (their pledged devotion to) Christ, they grow restless with desire, they want to get married (again); 12 incurring guilt because they have repudiated their former pledge. 13 At the same time they also learn to be idle, gadding about from house to house, and not only idle but also gossipy and meddlesome, saying things which they should not (say).
14 So I would have young widows marry (again), bear children, manage a home, and give the adversary no occasion whatever for slandering. 15 For even now some have turned aside after Satan. 16 But if any believing woman has widows, let her assist them, and let the church not be burdened, so that it may assist those who are really (what is implied in the name) widows.

5:9-16

9. A widow, in order to be placed on the list of widows, must not be less than sixty years of age.

The subject of verses 9-16 differs in one important respect from that treated in verses 3-8. *There* the theme was "Widows and *their Need.*" *Here* Paul discusses "Widows and *their Work.*" *That* section dealt with widows in general; *this* one has to do with "widows that are placed on a list" or "catalogued."

With respect to the question, "Who are these widows?" there are, in the main, four views:

(1) They are the deaconesses (Schleiermacher).
Objections:
a. Note the age: not under sixty (verse 9).
b. "Deaconesses" (rather, "deacons' assistants," "women who minister") have been discussed previously (see on 3:11).

(2) They are those widows who are entitled to material support from the church (Chrysostom, Calvin, N. J. D. White in *The Expositor's Greek Testament,* Dibelius, and many others). The theories vary. Some think of *all* the widows of 60 and above, who possess the qualities that are mentioned. Others believe that only such widows are meant who were willing to *work* for the church. They think of a contract, "We, older widows, promise to

render service to the church." — "We, the church-authorities, promise to provide for y o u when the need arises."

Objections:

a. Would the church refuse to support widows *under* sixty, *with small children?*

b. Does not verse 10 indicate that the widows of which this section speaks were comparatively well-to-do?

c. Is it not true that the question, "Which widows should receive aid from the church, and which should not?" has already been discussed (verses 4, and by implication, 5, 7, and 8)? Why would another set of restrictions be added now, and those "of so very exclusive a nature" (Ellicott); see verse 10?

(3) The question must be left unanswered (Lenski).

Objection:

Though I share Lenski's objections to the second view, I do not agree with his argumentation against view Number (4).

(4) These are the widows who possessed the necessary qualifications for the performance of certain spiritual and charitable functions in the church (C. J. Ellicott, A. T. Robertson, E. F. Scott, C. Bouma, and many others).

I believe that this is the correct view. Reasons:

a. The qualifications for inclusion in the list point in the direction of *work* to be done, just as did the list of qualifications for "women-helpers" in 3:11, and the lists for elders and for deacons in 3:1-10, 12.

b. Let it be granted that most widows over sixty might be considered too old to take care of orphans — Lenski's objection, *op. cit.*, p. 669 — the answer to this (aside from the fact that *some* women at that age are still *not* too old, and, in fact, insist on performing work of that kind!) is simple: *verse 10 does not state that they must take care of orphans but that they must have reared children!* Surely, widows who have successfully brought up children are the very ones who can impart good advice to younger women. They can train them "to love their husbands and to love their children" (Titus 2:4), and can give them all kinds of valuable hints!

c. There is sufficient evidence to show that in the early church such a body of *widows, with definite functions* actually existed. Thus Tertullian (possibly about the year 204), referring definitely to I Tim. 3:9 ("sixty years"), states that the task of these women was, "that their experienced training in all the affections may have rendered them capable of readily assisting all others with counsel and comfort" (*On The Veiling Of Virgins,* IX).

In the early church such a widow was called "the intercessor of the church," "the keeper of the door," and "the altar of God."

Their duties seem to have been: giving good counsel to the younger women, praying and fasting, visiting the sick, preparing women for baptism, taking them to communion, and giving guidance and direction to widows and orphans who were supported by the church (see article "Woman" in I.S.B.E., IV. 5, Vol. V, p. 3103).

d. If even today, as any minister who has served large churches knows, older women are at times consulted and sent on missions in which *they* excel, and which may be too delicate for others to perform, it is readily understandable that *in Bible-lands* (and particularly *at that time,* but to a degree even today), with their social and psychological barriers between men and women (see N.T.C. on John 4:27) there would be much work which these widows were able to perform with greater effectiveness than anyone else (especially work *among women*). And there would be plenty of somewhat similar work left for the younger *married* women. The reasons why *the younger widows* — those less than sixty years of age — were to be excluded from the performance of much of this work is stated by Paul in verses 11-15.

As a second requirement Paul states: **(she must have been) one husband's wife** (see on I Tim. 3:2, 12). Of course, this cannot mean, "She must not have been a widow who subsequently remarried, and who then lost also her second husband," for had Paul meant that, he would have been contradicting himself. Such a widow would have done the very thing which the apostle wanted young widows to do — he wanted them to remarry (verse 14) — , and it surely would have been unjust afterward to bar them from The Widow's List! The expression "one husband's wife" must simply mean that while married she had been faithful to her one husband. Other qualifications follow:

10. well-attested for noble deeds. Anyone who performs church-work must have a good reputation (see on I Tim. 3:2, 7, 10; cf. Acts 6:3; 16:2; Heb. 11:2).

There follow five "if" or "whether" clauses. We have here another instance of *abbreviated discourse* (which we have discussed in N.T.C. on John 5:31, Vol. I, p. 206). One can fill in the implied words in either of two ways, with very little difference in resultant meaning:

Either:

One should enquire whether she has reared children, *whether* she has practised hospitality, etc.

Or:

She can be placed on the list if she has reared children, *if* she has practised hospitality, etc.

In either case the meaning is: she should not be placed on the list unless her record shows that she has been diligent in these matters.

The items themselves are readily understandable. Surely a woman who is to perform the work which has been indicated (see on verse 9) must have the qualifications that are implied in the five clauses:

a. **(She can be placed on the list) if she has reared children.** She must be experienced in this line if she is to give counsel and direction to others.

b. **if she has practised hospitality.** See on I Tim. 3:2. This grace was practised beautifully by the widow of Zarephath who "sustained" Elijah (I Kings 17:9), by the Shunammite woman ("a great woman") who lodged Elisha (II Kings 4:8-11), and by Lydia (Acts 16:40).

c. **if she has washed the feet of saints.** Perhaps meaning literally, that this service was rendered by her or under her supervision; surely figuratively: that she has rendered humble service to traveling preachers. See Gen. 18:6; I Sam. 25:41. On the entire matter of footwashing see N.T.C. on John, Vol. II, pp. 219-241, especially p. 236 and the footnote there.

d. **if she has assisted the afflicted.** The early Christians were persecuted, oppressed. Cf. John 16:33; I Thess. 1:6; II Thess. 1:4. They needed relief, help (same verb in verse 16). Burdens must be shared (Gal. 6:2).

e. **if she has been devoted to every kind of good work.** This may be viewed as a re-iteration of "well-attested for noble deeds" at the beginning of the verse. However, it is possible that the thought is somewhat strengthened here: not only must this widow *have a reputation for noble deeds;* she must actually *have been diligently devoted to (she must have followed) every kind* of *good work!* Reputation is a fine thing, but sometimes it is undeserved. To be placed on the list, it must have been deserved!

11, 12. The apostle now proceeds to give two reasons why younger widows should be excluded from the list. The first reason is stated in verses 11 and 12: **But younger widows you must refuse (to place on the list); for often when, contrary to (their pledged devotion to) Christ, they grow restless with desire, they want to get married (again).**

For much of the work which Paul has in mind (see on verse 9) older women would be required, women with experience, who had the time and the opportunity, *old widows* therefore. But the possibility existed that also younger widows might *apply.* However, the importance of the work required whole-hearted devotion. If the interests are divided, so that the widow's mind, even during the performance of her spiritual functions, is pre-occupied with the idea of finding a suitable husband, her efficiency will suffer. This is *often* the case (note the indefinite ὅταν). This is one of the reasons why the application of *younger* widows (those under sixty) should be rejected.

Of course, Paul finds no fault whatever with the idea that younger widows should wish to marry again. In fact, he *wants* them to do just that (see verse 14). But he definitely finds fault with young widows *who have pledged themselves to an important spiritual ministry* and who then, nevertheless, break their pledge by marrying again! The apostle says, "contrary to . . . Christ." That he means "contrary to their pledged devotion to Christ" (that is, to the work of Christ which they have pledged to perform) is clear from verse 12.

Such young widows, as Paul must have noticed again and again, tend to *grow restless with desire.* Because their minds are occupied with other matters (for example, with respect to the next husband), they become bored with their church-duties, and begin to rebel against them. The verb καταστρηνιάω is used only in this one passage. It seems to mean "to exercise one's youthful vigor against" (see M.M., p. 593). The uncompounded verb is also found in Rev. 18:7, 9, where Babylon and the kings of the earth are said to have "waxed wanton" with wealth and pleasure. The upsurge of feeling which is indicated here in I Tim. 5:11 is not necessarily evil. It is natural for a young widow to cherish the desire to remarry. She is young, throbbing with life, longing for a husband. Let her then get married again if the opportunity presents itself, but as long as she is a young widow let her not be placed on the list of widows who perform special services in the church. Paul was a very practical man!

He continues: **incurring guilt because they have repudiated their former pledge.** The idea of several commentators that these young widows have rejected their *faith* in Jesus Christ, that they wish to marry *pagans,* and that they consequently suffer the judgment of "everlasting damnation" is surely foreign to the entire context. The apostle is writing about Christian young widows, who love the Lord sufficiently that they have applied for a position of special service in his kingdom! That they might subsequently become pre-occupied with the idea of remarriage is, after all, quite natural. Only, in that case they would be *repudiating* (as in Luke 10:16) their former (πρώτην) *pledge* (πίστιν) to the church, namely, to continue in the work of the Lord. This would involve them in *a judgment,* that is, in *guilt* (κρίμα). Paul wishes to spare them, and to promote the spiritual and charitable work of the church. Hence, he advises that such young widows be not placed on the list, but that they marry again (verse 14).

13. The second reason why such young widows should not be placed on the list is now stated: **At the same time they also learn to be idle, gadding about from house to house, and not only idle but also gossipy and meddlesome, saying things which they should not (say).**

Of course, Paul does not mean that *all* young widows are like that. He does mean that this is likely to happen, and surely the church cannot afford to "take a chance."

Writing, then, about a certain type of young widows, the apostle's description becomes very vivid.

First, he says, they "learn to be" (μανθάνουσιν; the Greek idiom does not require εἶναι) idle: they get into habits of idleness. This idleness is brought about by their "gadding about from house to house" (literally, "making the circuit of the houses"; cf. Acts 19:13; 28:13). Now this business of "going from house to house" was in all likelihood included in their work (see on verse 9), the purpose being to render assistance and impart counsel. But these *young* widows would tend "to make *everything*" of this *one* phase of their task, and a person can easily guess why: they were the sociable type. They enjoyed boon companionship. They liked to be entertained at (what in our day would be called) a "tea-party." And so they made a purely *social affair* of their assignment! They would become not only *idle* but *chatty* and *meddlesome*. (Note the play upon words: ἀργαί περίεργοι. One might translate: "not busy workers but busybodies" as were some people in Thessalonica; see N.T.C. on II Thess. 3:11.) The description is so very vivid that one cannot help thinking that young widows had been tried out for this kind of work, and that this was what had happened. Of course, the result was that thus they might easily be doing more harm than good. In the midst of their vivacious chatter they would often "say things which they should not (say)," *creating* problems for the church instead of *solving* any!

14, 15. What, then, should young widows do? The answer is: **So I would have young widows marry (again), bear children, manage a home.**

Paul does not favor asceticism. He does not want young widows to remain unmarried. This surely indicates that the apostle does not regard celibacy as a higher form of Christianity. There is a wide gulf between Paul and Tertullian. The latter came to regard second marriage as "successive polygamy." In the early church (second century and afterward) there were many who took a somewhat similar view, though they did not always advance so many and such lengthy arguments in favor of absolute monogamy as did Tertullian.

Paul wants these young widows to be entirely happy, and to fulfil their natural calling. Hence, not only does he desire that when a good opportunity presents itself they get married again (always "in the Lord," of course, I Cor. 7:39), but also that they *bear children* (the verb occurs only here, but for the related noun see I Tim. 2:15). Moreover, he wants them to assume their divinely ordained role in the rearing of these children. He wants them to "manage a home" or "rule a household" (this verb, too, occurs nowhere else in the New Testament; but see M.M., p. 441).

It is clearly evident that Paul is seeking to promote the welfare not only of the church but also of these young widows. He does not want them to do what is unbecoming. Let them accept the offer of marriage if they can conscientiously do so. Let them not waste their time in idle gossip. Let them adorn their confession with a life to God's honor. Hence, he adds:

and give the adversary no occasion whatever for slandering (or: favorable to slandering). Paul is thinking of a human adversary, whether he be a Jew or a Gentile. Such a person would always be ready to rail or revile (cf. I Peter 3:9). Thus not only would the reputation of the widow suffer, but God's name would be dishonored. With sadness of heart the apostle adds: **For even now some have turned aside after Satan.** He is still thinking about *young widows*. The meaning is, "It is necessary that I emphasize this, namely, that the adversary must not receive any occasion for slandering, *for* I know of concrete cases where this has already taken place." These widows had *turned aside* from the right path (see on I Tim. 1:6), and were now following *Satan* instead of obeying Christ's command, "Follow *me*" (John 21:19).

16. Is there, then, no work in the kingdom for a young widow with means and with the desire to help the good cause? O yes there is! In addition to what she is able to do in a strictly personal way (for example, pray for the church and for all those in need, make a *personal* visit to those in need, etc.), there is another way in which she can help the church. And not only *she* but *any believing woman* (πιστή is the best reading here; see N.N.) who has the means can do the thing which Paul expresses in these words: **But if any believing woman has widows, let her assist them.**

Here, let us say, is a lady like Lydia, who has a spacious home. She has a servant, a friend, or a relative, who happens to be a widow. Perhaps she can provide a home for that widow, or even for more than one widow. Or else she can help the widow financially or by providing work. Let her then do her Christian duty so that God may be glorified, so that this gracious lady may herself experience in her heart the peace which results from divine approval of deeds well done, and so that the needy one may be relieved. Paul, however, gives expression not to these objectives but to another. Says he: **And let the church not be burdened, so that it may assist those who are really (what is implied in the name) widows.**

Here the apostle returns to the thought expressed in verses 3 and 4. Needy widows are *first of all* the responsibility of those who are nearest to them; for example, children, grandchildren, women of means who stand in a relation of closeness to them. Let them then do their duty. Not only is this morally the right thing to do, but there is also a very practical consideration. The church has its hands full as it is. It does not count many rich people among its members (Mark 10:25; cf. I Cor. 1:26). Hence, it should not be *burdened* (weighed down with too heavy a load; for the verb see also II Cor. 1:8; 5:4; then Matt. 26:43; Luke 9:32; 21:34). Without this extra burden it will be able to assist "those who are really (what is implied in the name) *widows*." This last clause has already been explained (see on verse 3). These are the widows who are completely destitute, having no one to support them. If everyone does his part, it will be so much easier for the church to care for *these* widows. Truly, a lesson also for today!

---

17 Let the elders who rule well be counted worthy of double honor, especially those who labor in preaching and teaching. 18 For the Scripture says, "A threshing ox you shall not muzzle," and "Worthy of his pay (is) the worker." 19 Never entertain an accusation against an elder unless (it is) supported by two or three witnesses. 20 Those who do wrong you must rebuke in the presence of all, so that also the others may be filled with fear.

21 I charge (you) in the sight of God and of Christ Jesus and of the elect angels that you observe these instructions (or: these things) without prejudice, doing nothing from partiality. 22 Do not lay hands (of ordination) upon anyone hastily, neither be a partaker in the sins of others: keep yourself pure. 23 No longer drink water (only), but use a little wine for the sake of your stomach and your frequent ailments.

24 The sins of some men are clearly evident, proceeding ahead of them to judgment, but the sins of others follow after (them). 25 Similarly, the noble deeds (are) clearly evident, and even those that are otherwise cannot remain hidden.

5:17-25

17. Let the elders who rule well be counted worthy of double honor, especially those who labor in preaching and teaching.

Honor due to widows suggests honor due to elders. Moreover, just as the word *widow* was used first in a general sense (verse 3), but later (verse 9) in the sense of those whose names had been entered upon a list and who performed certain functions in the church, so also the word *presbyter* occurs first in the general sense of *old man* (5:1), but now as a synonym of *overseer,* the latter term indicating the character of the man's work, the former his age and the dignity which pertains to him because of his age and office.

It is clear that by the terms *overseer* and *elder* the same person is indicated, for in both cases we are told that these men *rule* and *teach* (cf. I Tim. 3:2, 5 with 5:17). That an overseer would be called a *presbyter* or *elder* is not strange, for in ancient Israel, in the synagogue, and also in the early church, the *older* men were clothed with this office. Very fittingly the term *overseer* is used when the emphasis is on their *work* (I Tim. 3:1), the term *elder* when the emphasis is on the *honor* that is their due (the present passage, I Tim. 5:17).

It is worthy of note that Timothy is here instructed to see to it that "the excellently ruling elders" (thus literally) are honored by the congregation. The apostle must have been aware of the fact that in many cases church-members are apt to forget this. They are prone to believe that the overseers are living on Easy Street, "especially those who labor in preaching and teaching," or that if any honor is to be bestowed it should be by means of the funeral-sermon! Is it surprising that so many ministers suffer nervous breakdowns? And that among them there are several who were doing their work conscientiously?

The words "especially those who labor in preaching (literally *in word*) and teaching" show that already in Paul's days a distinction began to be made between those whom today we call "ministers" and those whom we still call "elders." *All* rule, and to a certain extent *all* teach, but *some* (in addition to ruling) *labor* in *preaching* (expounding the Word to the assembled congregation), and *teaching* (imparting instruction to the youth, to enquirers, and to all who stand in need of it). They specialize in it, working hard at it. It requires much of their time and effort: preaching, teaching, and preparing for it.

Now all the excellently ruling elders must receive "double honor." But what is meant by this expression? Interpretations vary:

(1) honor and honorarium. They should receive both honor and material reward (Chrysostom, C. Bouma).

(2) ample pay, better remuneration, twice the salary they get (along this line, but with individual variations, Moffatt, White in *Expositor's Greek Testament*, Williams).

(3) twice as much "honor" as widows, or twice as great a portion of the firstfruits as widows (*Constitutions of the Holy Apostles* II. xxviii; in that same direction Calvin, Lock).

(4) honor as brothers and honor as rulers; or honor on account of age and honor on account of office (Tertullian, Bengel).

(5) honor as elders, extra honor as those who rule excellently (Lenski).

I believe that this last interpretation is the correct one, and I endorse the statement of Lenski that the context itself explains "twofold honor." Nevertheless, this double honor must not be so interpreted as if any idea of remuneration is completely excluded from it, and as if in connection with verse 18 the thought conveyed is simply this: Excellently ruling elders should receive their due, namely, double honor; just like the threshing ox receives its due, namely, wisps of grain; and just like the laborer receives his due, namely, wages (see Lenski on verse 18). In this way every notion of financial remuneration would be completely excluded from the "double honor" due to the elders who serve well and are in need of it. But that can hardly be correct, for also in the case of the widows the *honor* due them was immediately linked with that of material support (verses 3 and 4), and the analogies which Paul uses in verse 18 certainly point in the same direction as far as the elders are concerned. The true explanation, therefore, would seem to be this:

An elder deserves to be honored; particularly if his labor excels in quality. This honor is due especially to those who labor in preaching and teaching. And this implies, of course, that wherever it is necessary (and it would be necessary especially in the case of the "minister") the work should also be rewarded in a material way. A man who spends all his time and effort in kingdom-work (a "minister") certainly deserves "a good salary." *Not* that the word "honor" in and by itself has here the meaning *honorarium*.[82] It means *honor*. But it would be evidence of *lack* of honor if the church should demand of a man who devotes himself entirely to spiritual work that he do this gratis.

The explanation which I have given does not imply that *every* elder, or even *every* excellently ruling elder receive a salary. *All* who rule well deserve double honor, and in the case of those who devote themselves entirely to church-work this implies the right of remuneration. (And it implies more than that; see verses 19, 20, 22.)

18. For the Scripture says,
> A threshing ox you shall not muzzle
> and
> Worthy of his pay (is) the worker.

The two sayings are clearly co-ordinate. If the first is "scripture," so is the second. Thus a word spoken by Jesus is here placed on a par with a saying from the Old Testament canon.

The first saying is quoted from Deut. 25:4. Paul makes a similar use of it in I Cor. 9:8-12. The picture is that of a threshing-floor: a circular piece of level ground, exposed to the wind. Sometimes it is a flat rock on top of a hill. The sheaves of grain have been unbound and lie on this floor, arranged in circles. Oxen are driven over them, so that by the trampling of their hoofs the ripe grain may be shaken out of the ears (Hos. 10:11; Mic. 4:13). Or, for the same purpose the oxen may be harnessed to a rough sledge on which the driver stands or sits, as he guides the oxen around and around (Judg. 8:7; Is. 28:27; 41:15). This sledge or drag is a kind of sled consisting of two heavy boards, fastened side by side, and curved upward in front. To the bottom of it sharp pieces of stone are attached, to loosen the kernels of grain.[83]

Now cruel pagans would at times muzzle such threshing oxen, but Je-

---

[82] In the New Testament the word τιμή *never means wages or pay or salary*. Rather, it has the meaning *price* (Matt. 27:6, 9; Acts 5:2, 3; 7:16; I Cor. 6:20; 7:23; pl. Acts 4:34; 19:19), and *esteem, honor* (Rom. 12:10; 13:7; I Cor. 12:23, etc.). This corresponds with the connotation of the word in the papyri (M.M., p. 635). In classical Greek the word has a variety of meanings: worth, value, price; compensation, satisfaction, recompense; penalty; worship, dignity; lordship, office; reward, present, offering; esteem, honor.

[83] See W.D.B., pp. 604, 605, the picture and the article. Excellent pictures of the threshing dredge or drag and of threshing with oxen are found in I.S.B.E., art. "Agriculture"; see also art. "Threshing-floor." Also Thomson, *The Land and The Book*, Vol. II, p. 314; M.S. and J. L. Miller, *Encyclopaedia of Bible Life*, the article on p. 19, and the fine illustration opposite p. 15 and p. 22.

hovah had distinctly forbidden Israel to do this. The purpose of this injunction was that men might see the kindness of God; particularly, that they might discern this basic principle, namely, that *to every worker* (be that worker an ox, a common laborer, or a minister of the gospel) God has given the right to partake of the fruits of his work. (The context in Deuteronomy deals with *men,* not with animals. Cf. I Cor. 9:9, 10.) In the present instance this would mean that "those who proclaim the gospel should make their living by the gospel" (I Cor. 9:14).

The second saying, "Worthy of his pay is the worker" is found in this precise form in Luke 10:7. (In Matthew 10:10 the saying occurs in a slightly different form: "Worthy of his *food* is the worker.") Paul and Luke were friends, and were often together. Luke had been with Paul during the latter's first Roman imprisonment (Col. 4:14; Philemon 24). It is not impossible that Luke's Gospel had just been brought to completion. Hence, if that be true, the apostle was able to quote from it. Or else he may here be quoting from a collection of sayings which presumably was used as a source of Luke's Gospel.[84]

By combining the two quotations, and viewing them in the light of preceding context, we notice that Paul is emphasizing that the respect of which excellently ruling elders are worthy implies that those among them who devote themselves entirely to gospel-work have a right to wages, and that these wages should not be withheld.

19. Now this "honor" which is the elder's due should express itself also in another way: **Never entertain an accusation against an elder unless (it is) supported by two or three witnesses.**

An accusation against an elder must be *upon* — that is, must be based *upon* the oral testimony of — two or three witnesses. Note that though of old *any* Israelite was safeguarded against *indictment and sentencing* unless two or three reliable witnesses testified against him (cf. Deut. 17:6; cf. Num. 35:30; and see N.T.C. on John 5:31; 8:14), here (I Tim. 5:19) *presbyters* are safeguarded even against *having to answer a charge* (cf. Ex. 23:1 in LXX), unless it be at once supported by two or three witnesses. Lacking such support, the accusation must not even be *taken up* or *entertained.* The reputation of the elder must not be unnecessarily damaged, and his work must not suffer unnecessary interruption.

20. Nevertheless, at times a charge against an elder will have sufficient support to be *entertained,* and will afterward even be *sustained* by the facts. What then? Says Paul: **Those who do wrong you must rebuke in the presence of all, so that also the others may be filled with fear** (literally: *may have fear*).

---

[84] On the subject of probable dates when the New Testament books were written, and on the Synoptic Problem see my *Bible Survey,* p. 325, 383-394.

Elders who walk in sinful ways must not be spared. In fact, their sin must be punished even more severely than that of others. The law made the same distinction (Lev. 4:22, 27). Timothy must not only *bring their sin home to their conscience*,[85] but in *their* case he must do this *not privately* or in the presence of just a few (Matt. 18:15-17), *but publicly,* that is, in the presence of the entire consistory, so that the remaining elders may also become filled with godly fear of wrong-doing (cf. Gen. 39:9; Ps. 19:13).

21. Now in the matters discussed in verses 19 and 20, and, in fact, in any matter touching the discipline of church-leaders, one is easily influenced by purely subjective considerations. But this can spell ruin for the church and for all those concerned. Timothy, as apostolic delegate in the churches of Ephesus and vicinity, must not allow this to happen to him. Even today biased judges, ecclesiastical "machines," so-called "investigating-committees" manned by job-hunters, "buddy-ism," and the like can easily destroy a denomination. Corruption generally begins "at the summit." Church History furnishes many examples. The man in the pew does not know what happened "while he slept." When he wakes up — if he ever does! — it is generally too late.

Hence, absolute impartiality and unimpeachable honesty in all such matters are essential. It is for that reason that the charge which the apostle now lays on Timothy is so very grave. *Everything* is at stake! The church of the twentieth century may well take to heart these solemn words: **I charge (you) in the sight of God and of Christ Jesus and of the elect angels that you observe these instructions without prejudice, doing nothing from partiality.**

That the verb used in the original cannot *here* mean "I Solemnly *testify*" (as, for example, in I Thess. 4:6) but "I charge," that is, "I solemnly *admonish,*" or "I solemnly *order*" or even *"adjure,"* is clear from the clause which it introduces: "that you observe these instructions." Paul emphasizes that it is under the very eye and with the full approval of God that these directives (verses 19 and 20) have been issued. This is the very God who through Christ Jesus *will one day judge all men.* And these are the angels who will be associated with Christ in the final judgment. Hence, the apostle is, as it were, putting Timothy *under oath* to comply with the mandate which he has received (in the spirit of Gen. 24:3, 9). One who breaks the oath *will be judged.* That, in giving this charge, Paul is actually thinking of *the final judgment* is clear from a comparison with the similar language of II Tim. 4:1. Note the particulars that are mentioned here in I Tim. 5:21:

The Judge is *God* (Gen. 18:25; Heb. 12:23). The addressed must be

---

[85] For detailed discussion of the verb here used see N.T.C. on John, Vol. II, pp. 324-326.

deeply conscious of the fact that Paul in issuing and Timothy in dealing with this charge are acting in the sight of God, the Judge!

Yet, God judges not directly but through *Christ Jesus*. It is upon the Mediator that the honor of judging was conferred as a reward for the atonement which he rendered (Matt. 25:31-46; John 5:22, 23, 27; Acts 19:42; 17:31; II Cor. 5:10; Phil. 2:10, 11; II Tim. 4:1; Rev. 14:14-16).

Associated with Christ in this work of judging will be *the angels,* as is taught everywhere in Holy Writ (Dan. 7:10; Matt. 13:27, 41, 42; 16:27; 24:31-33; 25:31; II Thess. 1:7; Heb. 12:22; Rev. 14:15, 17-20). They will gather the redeemed and will drive the wicked before the judgment-seat.

These are God's *elect* angels, in distinction from the angels "who did not keep their own position" (Satan and his demons; cf. Jude 6). In his sovereign, inscrutable decree, which transcends all human understanding, God from all eternity decided that to *these* angels (here called *elect*) would be given the grace of perseverance, so that they would remain standing. Being *elect,* they are of course also *beloved.* (For the doctrine of election *of men,* as taught by Paul, see N.T.C. on I Thess. 1:4.) [86]

It is not strange that the apostle mentions also these *angels.* He wants Timothy *to obey* the all-important charge concerning the discipline of elders; that is, he wants him to resemble the angels *in obedience.* Besides, these angels are spectators of Timothy's actions and will accompany Christ at the final judgment when everything that was hidden will be revealed, and oath-breaking will be punished. According to Paul, and in harmony with all the rest of Scripture,

ANGELS ARE:

A ttendants of Christ (II Thess. 1:7), their exalted Head (Eph. 1:21, 22; Col. 2:10)

B ringers of good tidings concerning our salvation, having seen the Lord not only in his birth but also in his resurrection and post-resurrection glory (see on I Tim. 3:16; cf. Luke 2:14; 24:4; Acts 1:11)

C horisters of heaven (I Cor. 13:1; cf. Luke 15:10; Rev. 5:11, 12)

D efenders of God's children (II Thess. 1:7-10; cf. Ps. 91:11; Dan. 6:22;

---

[86] From the analogy of the election *of the angels* it has been argued that also in the case *of men* election must be conceived of as supralapsarian, so that, in listing under each other the elements which pertain to the decree, God's decision to reveal his mercy in the salvation of some men, and his justice in the perdition of others, would have to be placed *above* (supra) his decision to permit *the fall* (lapsus). However, the legitimacy of this reasoning from analogy is not granted by all. Most theologians would probably agree that, as far as predestination has to do with *men,* both supralapsarianism and infralapsarianism are one-sided. For this entire subject see L. Berkhof, *Systematic Theology,* pp. 118-125 (note the literature on p. 125); also my translation of H. Bavinck, *The Doctrine of God,* pp. 382-394.

10:10, 13, 20; Matt. 18:10; Acts 5:19; Rev. 12:7), though the latter outrank them and will judge them (I Cor. 6:3; cf. Heb. 1:14)

E xamples in obedience (I Cor. 11:10; cf. Matt. 6:10)

F riends of the redeemed, constantly watching them, deeply interested in their salvation, and rendering service to them in every way, also in executing the judgment of God upon the enemy (Gal. 3:19; I Cor. 4:9; II Thess. 1:7; cf. Matt. 13:41; 25:31, 32; Luke 16:22; I Peter 1:12; Heb. 1:14; Rev. 20:1-3).

Accordingly, since Timothy's actions are scrutinized by God, by Christ Jesus (both *divine,* note the *one* article in the original) and by the angels (*creatures,* note repetition of the article), and this with a view to the final judgment, let him observe (stand guard over) the given instructions "without prejudice," that is, uninfluenced by any sinful subjective considerations, guided only by the objective standard of the truth as revealed by God, and "doing nothing from partiality (or favoritism)," *leaning* neither *toward* this nor toward that side, neither toward the accuser nor toward the accused, until all the important facts in each concrete case have been fully established.

22. Much trouble can be avoided if in the matter of ordaining men to office Timothy will exercise the necessary precaution. Hence, Paul continues: **Do not lay hands (of ordination) upon anyone hastily, neither be a partaker in the sins of others: keep yourself pure.**

The symbolical indication of the impartation of gifts which one will need in discharging the duties of his office has been mentioned before (see on I Tim. 4:14), and will be mentioned again (II Tim. 1:6). This work must not be done "in a hurry." The qualifications of the men who are being considered must be fully examined before they can be nominated for office. This is in harmony with what the apostle has been saying in I Tim. 3:2, 7, 10. Ordination without preceding thorough investigation would render Timothy co-responsible for the wrongs which such elders might subsequently commit. This, in turn, would add to the difficulty of disciplining them. Timothy must strive to "keep himself *pure*" (in full conformity with God's moral law) with respect to this and all other matters. (For the related noun, *purity,* see on I Tim. 4:12; 5:2.)

23. The precept, "Keep yourself pure" was of a personal nature. This leads to another remark which is also personal: **No longer drink water (only), but use a little wine for the sake of your stomach and your frequent ailments.**

Timothy was a conscientious person. He did not want to be accused of being the kind of individual who "lingers beside his wine" (see on I Tim. 3:3). Hence, he had formed the habit of drinking nothing but water. However, in the Orient the water is often far from "safe." Those who have been there — including, for example, those who were there while serving in the armed forces — know this. If one insists on drinking nothing but unboiled water, attacks of dysentery may result. In fact, something worse might happen! Consequently, for the sake of helping Timothy to overcome his stomach-troubles and related ailments, which seem to have been coming to him "thick and fast," Paul advises him to stop being purely a water-drinker. Timothy must use some *wine*, not *much* wine, but *some* wine. That will do him good physically.[87] Paul is here speaking of wine as a *medicine,* not as a *beverage,* as Wuest correctly observes.

24, 25. Returning now to the subject of necessary caution before ordaining men to office (see verse 22), Paul says:

The sins of some men are clearly evident, proceeding ahead of them to judgment, but the sins of others follow after (them).

Similarly, the noble deeds (are) clearly evident, and even those that are otherwise [88] **cannot remain hidden.**

Of the many explanations the most reasonable would seem to be this one:

In verse 24 Paul is speaking about sins, namely, the sins of men who are unfit for office. In verse 25 he is speaking about noble deeds (or excellent works), namely, the noble deeds of men who are fit for office.

By implication he divides the first main group — the sins of men unfit for office — into two subdivisions:

a. the clearly evident sins of some men;

b. the not clearly evident sins of other men (this is implied rather than expressed).

---

[87] Note that with respect to the use of wine Paul avoids extremes. On the one hand he warns against the man who "lingers beside his wine" or is "given to much wine" (I Tim. 3:3, 8). On the other hand, he believes that in Timothy's case the use of some wine for the purpose of promoting health, and that caution in the use of water (probably because of the danger of pollution) is advisable.

Many have given their views on the subject of the sinister effects of social winedrinking and drinking of other alcoholic beverages. Very recently there appeared an article, "Negative or Positive" in *The Foundation Issue* of July, 1955, published by The Michigan Temperance Foundation, with headquarters in Lansing, Mich.; also another article, "Hereditary Consequences of Alcoholism," in *Christian Economics* of September 6, 1955. Similar literature is being distributed regularly, no doubt with many wholesome effects.

On the other side, the value of wine as food and medicine is discussed by Dr. Salvatore in his recently published book *Wine As Food And Medicine,* Blakiston Co. This was summarized and reviewed in the magazine *Newsweek,* the issue of July 19, 1954.

In the present day and age a vigorous campaign against *every* form of intemperance is certainly in order. Paul's word must be interpreted in the light of conditions prevailing in the Orient and in the light of *Timothy's* physical condition.

[88] ἔχω *plus adverb* means here *to be in a certain condition.* For this idiom see also Matt. 4:24; Mark 5:23; 16:18; John 4:52; Acts 7:1; 15:36; 21:13; 24:25; and II Cor. 12:14.

Expressly he divides the second main group — the noble deeds of men fit for office — into two similar subdivisions:
a. the clearly evident noble deeds of some men;
b. the not clearly evident noble deeds of other men.

With respect, then, to the first group Paul says that the sins of some men are so *clearly evident* (πρόδηλοι, see also Heb. 7:14), so conspicuous or obvious, that in their case thorough examination in order to reach a *decision* or *judgment* (see N.T.C. on John, Vol. I, pp. 142, 143) is hardly even necessary. The sins precede the man! This does not merely mean that the man in question has a bad reputation (for that, after all, might be based on slander), but that he *is bad:* his evil-doing is out in the open. It is there, for all to see. The very idea of nominating such men for office is preposterous.

In the case of other men the situation is different. *Their* sins *follow* them (literally *follow after* them, or *follow them up*). When their case is considered in order that a decision may be reached, they are found, after *thorough examination,* to be unfit for office. *Before* their case comes up, Timothy and perhaps several presbyters consider these men to be possible candidates for office. *After* thorough examination and the rendering of a judgment, things take on an altogether different aspect. The sins of these men have now been uncovered, so that, the judgment having been rendered, there is no longer any doubt about their unfitness for office.

The situation with respect to men who are spiritually fit for office is similar in this respect, namely, that also in their case Timothy, as a rule, need not be afraid that hidden qualities will remain hidden. In general, the noble deeds (or excellent works) which adorn the lives of these men will be clearly evident. And even in such exceptional cases in which they are not at once evident, they cannot remain hidden. Proper questioning and investigation will bring them to the surface.

For the encouragement of Timothy, who, as has been shown (see p. 34), was rather timid, Paul is trying to establish this point: if he will but exercise due caution, and will not be hasty in ordaining men to office (see verse 22), he will have good elders in the churches of Ephesus and vicinity; the rule being that even in the case of such men whose unfitness or fitness for office is not immediately clear, careful examination will lead to valid conclusions. And, in any case, Timothy will then not become involved in the sins of other men.

Synthesis of Chapter 5

See the Outline at the beginning of this chapter, which may be paraphrased as follows:

As to *those members who are in need of pastoral counseling or correction,* you (Timothy) should deal with them as their age and sex requires:

Admonish an old(er) man as you would a father, young(er) men as brothers, old(er) women as mothers, young(er) women as sisters in all purity.

As to *widows and their distress,* those who are really destitute should be honored and assisted in every way. They should receive both moral and physical support. The Object of their constant hope and prayer will by means of the church provide for them.

However, there are also widows who have children or grandchildren that can support them. These should discharge that debt which they owe to those who brought them up. God is pleased with this. If they neglect their duty, they are worse than infidels. It is the widow who has no means of support who should be assisted *by the church.*

There are some widows, however, who are living luxuriously. These, though physically alive, are spiritually dead. It is not even necessary to add that such widows do not deserve to be honored by the church. Constantly stress these regulations regarding the duty of the church and of children and grandchildren toward widows.

Now as to *widows and their work,* in order to qualify for such work as giving good counsel to younger women, preparing them for baptism, taking them to communion, giving guidance to orphans, etc. (this is a *conjecture* as to the nature of their work), such widows must not be less than sixty years of age, must have been faithful wives, wise mothers, good hosts, kind benefactresses; in fact, must have given proof of fitness for such a position.

For this type of work you must *not* engage *young* widows, for experience has shown that in many cases these become restless and break the work-pledge which they have made to the church, thereby incurring guilt. Also, they often place social affairs above kingdom-affairs, so that when they make the rounds of the various homes, ostensibly to help and to guide, they actually do nothing but gossip and meddle in other people's affairs. Thus they do more harm than good, and scandals will arise. Now these should be prevented by all means. Hence, instead of being engaged for such kingdom-work, let young widows fulfil their natural desire. When a good opportunity presents itself, let them marry again. Let them have a family and manage it properly. This is honorable, and will remove suspicion and slander. It is necessary that I add this, for I know of certain widows who have turned aside from the honorable course in order to follow *Satan.*

Nevertheless, this does not mean that for young widows there is no opportunity to perform kingdom-work. There is work for everyone, also for every woman. For example, if there be any believing woman of means, who stands in some relation of responsibility toward widows in distress, let her assist them, so that the church may not be burdened but may be better able to help those widows who are not being supported by anyone.

As to *elders and prospective elders,* note the following:

An elder should be honored for the sake of his office; and he should receive *double* honor if he does his work well. This holds with special emphasis with respect to "ministers," men who labor in preaching and teaching. Respect them highly and provide generously for them, for the Scripture says:

"A threshing ox you shall not muzzle" (Deut. 25:4)
and
"Worthy of his pay is the worker" (Luke 10:7).

As to an accusation against an elder, it should not even be entertained unless it is supported by two or three witnesses. But if the wrong has been definitely established, the man who committed it must be reproved in the presence of the entire consistory, so that the remaining elders may become filled with godly fear of wrong-doing. Now in connection with all such matters I charge you in the sight of God and of Christ Jesus and of the elect angels that you observe these instructions without prejudice. You must never allow yourself to be influenced by subjective considerations. Do not be in a hurry to ordain a man. Then you will not be co-responsible for the wrongs which he may afterward commit. Keep yourself pure. (Incidentally, take care of your body also. No longer drink water only, but use a little wine for the sake of your stomach and your frequent ailments.)

In connection with men who are being considered for office, you need not be unduly concerned *if you exercise due caution.* In the case of men who are *unfit,* their *sins,* which render them unfit, are often evident even before an investigation into their character is begun; and if they are not evident *before,* they will become evident *upon* investigation. And in the case of men who are *fit,* their *noble deeds,* which show that they are qualified, are generally clearly evident even prior to investigation; and if not before, then afterward.

Outline of Chapter 6

Theme: *The Apostle Paul, Writing to Timothy, Gives Directions For the Administration of the Church*

*Directions with respect to
Certain Definite Groups and Individuals (continued)*

6:1, 2	E.	Slaves
6:3-10	F.	Novelty-teachers who aspire to fame and riches
6:11-16	G.	Timothy himself ("Keep the commission!")
6:17-19	H.	People who are rich in terms of this present age
6:20, 21	I.	Timothy himself ("Guard the deposit!")

CHAPTER VI

I TIMOTHY   6:1

6 1 Let as many as are under (the) yoke, namely, slaves, regard their own [89] masters as worthy of all honor, in order that the name of God and the doctrine be not reviled. 2 And those who have believing masters, let them not, because these (masters) are brothers, look down upon them, but let them serve all the better because *believers* are the latter and *beloved ones,* who reciprocate this kind service. These things teach and urge.

Continuing his admonitions with respect to groups within the Christian community, Paul says:

6:1, 2

1. Let as many as are under (the) yoke, namely slaves, regard their own masters as worthy of all honor.

It is clear that in *this* passage the word used in the original (δοῦλοι) means *slaves,* not *servants.* It frequently has the latter meaning, and even in the present passage the apostle is trying his level best to change the *slave* into a beloved *servant.* (See further N.T.C. on John, Vol. II, p. 306, footnote 184.) In our passage, then, he starts out by talking about real *slaves,* as is clear from the fact that he defines the concept by saying, "as many as are under (the) yoke." The power of a master over his slave was almost absolute, like that over his *yoke*-animals.

The Roman world was full of slaves. It has been estimated that in Rome itself at one time about a third of the inhabitants belonged to this social class! They had become slaves: a. as prisoners of war, or b. as condemned men, or c. through debt, or d. through kidnaping (which evil reportedly is still continuing in certain parts of the world) or, e. as those who had been sold into slavery by their parents. Besides, many *were born* into slavery. Often slaves had their own slaves.

Among all these slaves there were some who had attained to a degree — sometimes a *high* degree — of culture. Not only the barber, the butler, and the cook but even the family-physician might be "under the yoke."

Roman law did not forbid the master to treat his slaves harshly. They could be condemned to hard labor, chained, severely lashed, branded upon the forehead (for instance, if they were considered thieves or runaways),

---

[89] Or simply "their," for ἴδιος (here ἰδίους) has lost some of its force.

or even crucified. Public opinion, however, often asserted itself as a kind of restraint upon intolerable unfairness and cruelty. Besides, in several recorded instances Romans treated their subordinates with eminent fairness, providing liberally for them, and even becoming their friends (cf., for example, the friendship of Pliny for his "slave" Zosimus). Manumission was not uncommon. A slave might be permitted to buy his freedom with a sum of money which he had been able gradually to accumulate through the liberality of the master or as a result of "extra" services, and which by this slave was then, amid ceremonies occurring on the day of emancipation, given to the god, from whom, as it were, he received his freedom and to whom he felt himself thereafter forever indebted. Often slaves were set free by the master's last will.

With the entrance of the Christian religion into the fabric of Roman society, difficult problems arose. It is not surprising, therefore, that Paul deals with various phases of slavery in passages such as the one now under consideration and also in Eph. 6:5-9; Col. 3:22-4:1; Titus 2:9; and in the letter to Philemon.

His way toward a solution commends itself by reason of its evident wisdom. It avoids extremes which would have resulted in much harm both to the slave and to his master, and would have reflected dishonor upon the cause of the Christian religion. *He advocated neither outright revolt by the slaves nor the continuation of the status quo.* Instead of recommending either of these he aimed by the law of indirection to destroy *the very essence* of slavery, with all its attendant evils. This method, though for a while maintaining "slavery" in outward form, was, nevertheless, the surest and most commendable way of working toward the final goal of complete abolition of this gruesome, inhuman institution. It aimed to destroy slavery without waging a war to do so! "Let the slave honor his master, and let the master be kind to his slave. Let both bear in mind that with God there is no respect of persons." That was the principle. Thus the ill-will, dishonesty, and laziness of many slaves would be replaced by willing service, integrity, and industry. Thus also the cruelty and brutality of many masters would melt into kindness and love. The grace of Christ, working *from within outward* — which is ever the way of the kingdom of God! — would become a penetrating leaven, tending to transform the whole lump.

Let then those who are under the yoke regard their *masters* (plural of "despot," cf. II Tim. 2:21; Titus 2:9, a word which even more than *kurios* stresses the *authority* which the slave-owner wielded over his slave) [90]

---

[90] See on these synonyms R. C. Trench, *Synonyms Of The New Testament*, par. xxviii. Because of the stress which this word "despot" places on unrestricted authority it is also used with respect to God (Luke 2:29; Acts 4:24; Rev. 6:10) and Christ (II Peter 2:1; Jude 4).

as worthy of all *honor* (see footnote 82). Whenever it is at all possible thus to respect the master, let the slave do so, **in order that the name of God and the doctrine be not reviled** (literally, *be not blasphemed;* for the related noun, *blasphemy,* see on I Tim. 6:4). God's redemptive revelation in Christ, in other words God's *name,* and also his *instruction,* the teaching of the gospel, would become contemptible in the eyes of the masters if the slaves treated them with disdain and the spirit of rebellion. And nothing is more important than God's *name* and his *doctrine!* These must not be exposed to ridicule or abuse (cf. Is. 52:5; Rom. 2:24).

2. A peculiar problem presented itself with respect to believing slaves who had *believing* masters. Says Paul: **And those who have believing masters, let them not, because these (masters) are brothers, look down upon them, but let them serve all the better because believers are the latter and beloved ones, who reciprocate this kind service.**

A Christian slave who had a Christian master might be inclined to say in his heart, "If my master is really a Christian, how can he keep me *as his slave?* His religion must not amount to very much. Besides, how can I be *equal* to my master *in church* (Gal. 3:28), and yet *inferior* to him *at home?*" Such an attitude would lead to trouble all around. So the apostle recommends the very opposite attitude: if the slave is in an exceptionally privileged position, having a believing master, let him render exceptional service! Christian masters are *brothers* in Christ. They are *believers, beloved, loved* both by their fellow-believers and by God (see N.T.C. on I Thess. 2:8). And not only for *this* reason should slaves serve such masters all the better, but also because the latter are gentle and considerate. Christian employers are the ones who "reciprocate [91] this *kind service*" (literally, *the good deed*). They are *taking upon themselves* (λαμβανόμενοι) the responsibility of giving *a return* (ἀντί; hence the entire participle is ἀντιλαμβανόμενοι) for the ready and enthusiastic co-operation of their slaves. But shall we still say *slaves;* have not the *slaves* become *servants* now?

These things teach and urge (Or: *keep teaching and urging*).

---

[91] In the New Testament this verb occurs three times (in the middle voice). In Luke 1:54 and Acts 20:35 it means *to help* (probably: to take hold of by oneself *in turn;* but see A. T. Robertson, *Gram. N.T.* for a different explanation). Very closely related to this is the meaning which may be ascribed to the verb here in I Tim. 6:2: *to re-ciprocate.* Thus, justice is done to the idea contained in the prefix ἀντί.

Interpretations which I cannot accept are:

(1) *to be devoted to, exert oneself in.* This wanders too far away from the idea contained in the prefix.

(2) *to benefit by.* The translation proposed is, "because those who benefit by their service are believers and beloved." But this changes a predicate into a subject. The clause "who reciprocate this kind of service" is clearly in the predicate, in apposition with "believers" and "beloved," which words are in the predicate position.

What Paul has been saying with reference to slaves (in verses 1 and 2) must be dinned into the ears of the people. Timothy must *teach* these things. However, not only upon *the minds* of the people and of their presbyters must he make an impression but also upon their *wills*. He must *urge* as well as *teach* these things. In *this* connection the present imperatives for both verbs probably point in the direction of the necessity of constant repetition: *keep on teaching* and *keep on urging*. The second verb has the basic meaning: to call to one's side. See also I Tim. 1:3; 2:1; 5:1; II Tim. 4:2; Titus 1:9; 2:6; 2:15. Derived meanings are: to appeal to or to entreat, to admonish, to exhort, to urge, to encourage or to comfort. Here the meaning *urge* best fits the context.

What is especially important in this connection is that, wholly contrary to certain present-day trends, the apostle is definitely *not* of the opinion that all propositions touching religion and ethics are necessarily subjective and relative, and that the only justifiable method of arriving at some measure of truth is that of *asking questions, such as,* "Brother Brown, what do you think of this?" and "Brother Smith, what is your opinion about that?" *Paul has accepted certain definite propositions which he considers to be the truth of God! He wants these to be taught! And he requests that Timothy urge their acceptance and application to life!* See also 4:11 and 5:7.

---

3 If anyone teaches differently and does not come over to the sound words of our Lord Jesus Christ and to the doctrine that harmonizes with godliness, 4 he is blinded with conceit, knowing nothing, but possessed with a morbid craving for controversies and word-battles, (the sources) out of which proceed envy, wrangling, revilings, base suspicions, 5 and mutual altercations between men depraved in mind and deprived of the truth, who imagine that the (practice of) godliness is gain.

6 And it *is* a great gain, namely, the (practice of) godliness *with soul-sufficiency*.[92] 7 For nothing did we bring into the world, (just as it is evident) that neither are we able to carry anything out of it. 8 But having nourishment and shelter, we shall regard these as sufficient.[93]

9 But those who are eager to be rich fall into temptation and a snare and numerous senseless and hurtful cravings, such as plunge the members of the human race into ruin and destruction. 10 For, a root of all the evils is the love of money, and some people, reaching out after it, have wandered away from the faith, and have pierced themselves with numerous pangs.

6:3-10

3-5. If anyone teaches differently and does not come over to the sound words of our Lord Jesus Christ and to the doctrine that harmonizes with godliness, he is blinded with conceit.

---

[92] Or: "with contentment." See also footnote 94.
[93] Or: "with these we shall be content."

From the sound and intensely practical doctrine of Paul — samples of which have just been given — to the unfruitful disputations of false teachers, was, indeed, a far cry. The very contrast causes Paul to return to the subject of chapter 1 (see especially in that chapter verses 3-7, 19, 20). Note the similarity between the two paragraphs:

Chapter 1:	Chapter 6:
certain individuals (verse 3)	anyone (verse 3)
teaching differently (verse 3)	teaching differently (verse 3)
disputes (verse 4)	controversies (verse 4)
sound doctrine (verse 10)	sound words (verse 3)

Novelty-teachers and hair-splitters! The apostle was fully acquainted with them. He emphasizes that any peddler of ponderous platitudes about the law of Moses, any specialist in specious speculations about ancestors, is "blinded with conceit." Such a person is "full of smoke," besmoked, befogged, beclouded (see on I Tim. 3:6). Two ideas are combined here: moral-spiritual *denseness* and *conceit*. The first is the result of the second. This description is true with respect to every dissenter who "does not *come over to* the sound words of our Lord Jesus Christ." The verb used in the original (προσέρχεται which is favored by textual evidence both internal and external) has here a meaning not far removed from its primary sense: *come to, approach*. Here it seems to mean *come over to*, that is, *join, fall in with*. This is a little stronger than *consent to* or *agree with*. A *mere* listener may mentally *agree with* the words of a speaker. An *enthusiastic* listener will *come over to* or *join* the speaker. He will not only *agree*, but he will *express* that agreement. He will "chime in." He will eagerly come to the same fountain and will drink the same water. He will take to heart and will begin to proclaim "the sound words of our Lord Jesus Christ," the pure and perfect "unimpaired," "uninfected," and in that sense "healthy," "sound" *truths* which issued from Christ's mouth and were exemplified in his life and death. Viewed as a whole, these "words" constitute "the doctrine that harmonizes with godliness." This doctrine is the expression of the inner attitude of "complete devotion to God," that is, of *godliness* (for this noun see on I Tim. 2:2; 3:16; 4:7, 8; 6:5, 6, 11; II Tim. 3:5; Titus 1:1. Cf. the verb, I Tim. 5:4; and the adverb, II Tim. 3:12; Titus 2:12).

Now the person who, in his blind conceit and obstinate dissent refuses to come over to such doctrine which tallies with godliness, is prevented from knowing anything. Living in a mental, moral, and spiritual world of his own making, he is now completely out of touch with reality. Hence, Paul continues: **knowing nothing, but possessed with a morbid craving for controversies and word-battles, (the sources) out of which proceed envy, wrangling, revilings, base suspicions, and mutual altercations between men depraved in mind and deprived of the truth.**

6:3-5   I TIMOTHY

When a person rejects *sound* or *healthy* words, *sickness* results. This sickness reveals itself in a "morbid craving for controversies and word-battles" (see on I Tim. 1:4). The man stricken with such a disease will make mountains out of molehills. Somewhat after the fashion illustrated in The Talmud, he will get "all excited" about questions like this one, "Is it permissible on the Sabbath to throw away the pits of dates?" One person might answer, "The pits of dates to which some of the meat adheres may be thrown away. Other pits must not be thrown away." Another person would disagree and express his contrary opinion in no uncertain terms. Again, the question might be asked, "If it be permissible to throw them away, *where* and *how* should they be thrown?" And the answer might be, "They should be thrown outside." To which another might reply, "No, indeed, they should be thrown under the bed." Or, he might say, "The person confronted on the Sabbath with the problem of what to do with datepits should turn his face toward the back of the bed and throw out the pits with his tongue."

At times a mere *name* of some ancestor might start a controversy. The name might be changed into several anagrams, one anagram suggesting this, the other that. Or, the name might cause one to recall a story which had been transmitted by oral tradition. But *one* story would contradict *another* story, and this, too, might lead to a heated argument.

Thus, broken cisterns which hold no water would be substituted for the living fountain of God's Word.[94]

Some people seem to take delight in such quibbling, such, *word-battles*. Hence, Paul sets forth its bitter fruits:

a. *envy*. One disputant, smarting under defeat, begins to waste away. He is filled with malignant ill will, with poisonous spite against the victor.

b. *wrangling*. This results from envy. The person who was worsted in the argument is unwilling to admit defeat. Bitter discord follows. One man is constantly contradicting the other. If we were to speak in the language of mythology, we might say that Eris, the goddess of strife, who was considered to be closely related to Ares, the god of war, has a field-day.

---

[94] One might compare the largely futile controversies in Reformed circles — only yesterday! — between extreme Infralapsarians and extreme Supralapsarians. Or, the still continuing "hot" debates about the age of the earth.

Now in discussions of this nauseating character the two opponents sometimes *mean* the same thing, but *express* it differently. To use a present-day illustration, one man may assert, "Obtaining salvation is *conditioned* on faith." Another insists with equal firmness, "Scripture recognizes *no conditions*." Yet, if only the first disputant would be ready to admit that God supplies what he demands, so that the exercise of faith is ever the result of the divine gift; and if only the second disputant would be willing to grant that (at least in the case of those who have arrived at years of discretion) the exercise of faith is *indispensable* unto salvation, and that it is *man* — not God — who believes, it would soon become clear that the dispute was *a battle of words*.

I TIMOTHY 6:3-5

c. *revilings*. The Greek word used is *blasphemies*. But in Greek this word has a somewhat broader meaning than in English. While in our language it refers to abusive language with respect to God or things religious, that is, to *defiant irreverence* (see on verse 1 above), in the original it refers to insults directed either against God or against man. In the present instance the latter is clearly meant: scornful and insolent language directed against a human opponent, slander, defamation.

d. *base suspicions*. "All looks yellow to the jaundiced eye" (Pope). The mind of the envious individual is haunted by mistrust and foreboding. He begins to suspect his opponent's every action, word, and even gesture. He imagines that there is "an occult reason" behind every move of the person whom he considers his adversary. This disease, moreover, is contagious.

e. *mutual altercations* or *incessant frictions*. When the "mad" novelty-dispenser meets his opponent again, to discuss other "religious" matters, he either glares and glowers, or else he smoulders within but puts on an act by the seeming imperviousness of his demeanor. Underneath, however, he "boils." He is vengefully nettled, convulsively agitated, thirsting for "blood." The two men *"rub* each other the wrong way" (note root-idea in the original). Their "religious" discussions frequently assume the nature of *diatribes,* in the unfavorable sense of that term (in the original "dia-para-tribes"). Such disputations are full of scurrilous abuse, stinging insult, and heated invective, or else of covert insinuation, malicious innuendo, and thinly veiled disdain.

Such conduct and its bitter fruits mark the men who are "depraved in mind and deprived of the truth." It is God himself who endowed man with intelligence, so that he is able to reflect on the higher things of life. Yet, with respect to this precious gift, namely, the intelligence, the errorists at Ephesus and vicinity have corrupted themselves, so that they have now entered the *abiding* state of being "depraved in mind." The depraved mind opposes the truth and welcomes the lie, until at last those who possess such a mind become completely and permanently separated from *the truth:* God's objective revelation as revealed in his Word. Envy, wrangling, revilings, base suspicions, and mutual altercations lead to mental, moral, and spiritual *sterility*. Those who practise such things are so completely occupied with themselves and their own interests that in their hearts there is neither time nor room for God and his revealed truth. This selfishness is clear also from the fact that the apostle describes them as being men **who imagine that the (practice of) godliness is gain.** For the sake of *becoming rich* (not merely for the sake of gaining a livelihood) they outwardly practise "godliness." They make a show of their "religion" (see on I Tim. 3:16). In the meantime they charge exorbitant fees for the "instruction"(?) which they impart. (For Paul's attitude with respect to the question of receiving remuneration for evangelistic labor see N.T.C. on I and II Thessalonians, pp. 66, 67.)

6, 7. The *truly* godly person is not interested in becoming rich. He possesses *inner resources* which furnish riches far beyond that which earth can offer. Hence, with respect to this genuine godly life Paul continues: **And it** *is* **great gain, namely, the (practice of) godliness** *with soul-sufficiency*. This is the life of true devotion to God. It is "of benefit in every way," (see on I Tim. 4:8). Such Christian living springs from the source of — and is accompanied by — *soul-sufficiency*.[95]

The truly pious individual has peace with God, spiritual joy, assurance of salvation, the conviction that "to them that love God all things work together for good, even to them that are called according to his purpose" (Rom. 8:28). Hence, he feels no need of "ample (earthly!) goods stored up for many years," which can never satisfy *the soul* (Luke 12:19, 20). He is *content* with what he has. Cf. Phil. 4:10-13. **For,** earthly possessions do not pertain to the "self," which is clear from the fact that **nothing did we bring into the world, (just as it is evident) that** [96] **neither are we able to carry anything out of it.**

---

[95] The word used in the original might be more literally translated "self-sufficiency" were it not for the fact that in English this word is ambiguous, as it may be used either in a favorable sense (inherent and adequate capacity for this or that activity) or in an unfavorable sense (self-satisfaction or extreme self-confidence). Used in the unfavorable sense, the antonym of the English word would be *humility*. In the favorable sense, its antonym is *spiritual impotence* or *soul-poverty*. It is in the favorable sense that the word is employed in the New Testament. By an easy transition this admirable *soul-sufficiency* begins to include the element of *contentment*. New Testament occurrences: only here and in II Cor. 9:8.

[96] Literally, the original reads, "For, nothing did we bring into the world, ὅτι neither are we able to carry anything out of it." The question is, Just what must we do with the particle ὅτι? Proposed solutions:

(1) The particle is superfluous (E. F. Scott).
Objection: This is an easy way out. Scott does not explain how that superfluous word crept in, nor how it is that even the earliest attempts to "correct" the text *retained* the particle.

(2) The particle should be taken in the causal sense: "Because we are not able to carry anything out of the world, we did not bring anything into it" (Along this line Belser, Weiss, Lenski).
Objection: This fits neither the present thought-connection nor the evident source of the saying in the Old Testament.

(3) The particle is recitative or has the meaning "for the proverb says." This is mentioned by Lock as one of several possibilities.
Objection: In that case we would have expected it at the beginning (and not in the middle) of the paraphrase from the Old Testament.

(4) ὅτι οὐδε should be οὐδ' ὅτι: "not to speak of being able to carry anything out." (This is favored by Parry; cf. also Lock.)
Objection: This, too, is not in keeping with the evident Old Testament source of the saying. Besides, it has the textual evidence against it. The textual evidence, both external and internal, favors not only the retention of ὅτι but also its position before οὐδε, exactly as the text of N.N. has it.

(5) The two clauses of the compound sentence are loosely co-ordinated, so that ὅτι must here be construed as meaning something like "just as." This is the solution proposed by Dibelius and Bouma.

The apostle is clearly thinking of Job's famous saying, "Naked came I out of my mother's womb, and naked shall I return" (Job 1:21; cf. Eccl. 5:14, 15).

8. Hence, we shall not strive after earthly riches. **But having nourishment and shelter, we shall regard these as sufficient** (or: *with these we shall be content*).

For "nourishment and shelter" the original has the plural (cf. "victuals and coverings"). Our word "nourishment" is sufficiently comprehensive to include all the articles of food that are necessary to support physical life, just as our word "shelter" indicates whatever is necessary for the outward protection of the body. The rendering "food and *clothing*" is less exact. The original ("shelter" or "coverings") in all probability, includes *the dwelling* in which a man resides as well as *the garment* which he wears. The Lord does not demand of us that, having clothing, we do not even look for a tent or a house in which to live. The desire to meet *the needs* of the body is not criticized. It is the yearning for *material riches,* as if these could satisfy the soul, that is here condemned, as is evident also from that which follows, namely,

9. **But those who are eager to be rich fall into temptation and a snare and numerous senseless and hurtful cravings.**

Paul does not condemn "desire" as such. He is not a Stoic but a Christian. What he condemns is the desire *to be rich*. Such people fall into *temptation*. (The word in the original means either *trial* or *temptation*. Classic example illustrating first the one and then the other meaning is James 1:2, 12. In the present instance the meaning *temptation* is clear from the context.) As a *snare* (see on I Tim. 3:7) keeps an animal imprisoned, so the ungovernable passion for wealth fastens its clutching tentacles about "those who pant after the dust of the earth" (Am. 2:7). Cf. Ps. 39:6; Prov. 28:20; Matt. 6:19-21, 24-26; 19:24; James 5:1-6.

Moreover, Sin never walks alone. The desire to become rich causes the man who, in today's terminology, is "an incarnation of fat dividends" to fall into numerous cravings. One kind of craving easily leads to another.

Comment: This solution is not open to the objections advanced against the others. It may be the correct one. It is either this or (6), with little difference in resultant meaning.

(6) We have here another instance of abbreviated expression. Note elliptical use of ὅτι in John 6:46 (see N.T.C. on John, Vol. I, pp. 54, 206). Fully rendered, the thought might be reproduced as follows: "For, nothing did we bring into the world, *just as it is evident* that neither are we able to carry anything out of it" (the words in italics being implied). While later texts wrongly inserted the word *evident* or *true,* as if the original contained such a word, they probably correctly discerned the thought which the apostle (who often abbreviates!) intended to convey. See also A.V., based on Textus Receptus.

6:9   **I TIMOTHY**

The person who craves riches generally also yearns for honor, popularity, power, ease, the satisfaction of the desires of the flesh, etc. All spring from the same root, selfishness, which, being the worst possible method of *really* satisfying the "self," is both senseless and hurtful (cf. Matt. 20:26-28; see N.T.C. on John 12:25, 26).

In the original the sentence is conspicuous by virtue of its beautiful alliteration. The constantly recurring letter p (π) strikes the eye and then the ear, and probably serves to fix the saying more firmly in the mind, as if we were to say:

"Those who desire to be opulent precipitate themselves into evil promptings and perilous pitfalls and into numerous precarious passions."

These cravings, passions, or lusts of which the apostle speaks are described **as such as plunge the members of the human race into ruin and destruction.**

Instead of the *gain* which they were seeking (see verse 5), the men whose hearts are set on riches experience only *loss*. In the original the words *ruin* and *destruction* are both derived from a verb whose secondary meaning is *to lose*.

Note the progressive and climactic character of the movement which is portrayed here. First, these men are described as *desiring* the wrong thing, namely, material wealth. Soon they lose their footing and *fall* into temptation and a snare and numerous senseless and hurtful cravings. Finally, these cravings *plunge* them into ruin and destruction. Wretched men! They have guided their vessel to the very brink of the cataract, which, in its turn, plunges them into the awesome depths. For examples see the next verse.

10. The situation as described is correct, **For a root of all the evils is the love of money.**[97]

The apostle does not say that the love of money is *the* (one and only) root of all existing evils, but that it is *a* root. Though it is true that a word does not always have to be preceded by the article *the* to be definite, it surely is not wise to apply the exception when this would bring Paul's words into conflict with the facts of daily experience and with other passages of Scripture. There are other roots or sources of evil besides the love of money, for example, "bitterness" (Heb. 12:15; cf. also James 1:15). But avarice is, indeed, *a* root "of all the evils," or "of all kinds of evil." It caused the man with very many flocks and herds (in Nathan's parable) to steal the poor man's one little ewe lamb, the rich young ruler to turn away from Christ, the rich fool (of Christ's parable) to deceive himself into think-

---

[97] The inspired saying reminds one of others, for example: "The love of money is *the metropolis of every evil* (or: of all the evils)," which has been ascribed to Bion and to Democritus; and "Expel *avarice, the mother of all wickedness,* who, always thirsty for more, opens wide her jaws of gold" (Claudianus). That Paul was "undoubtedly quoting" a current secular proverb cannot be proved.

ing that all was well, the rich man (of another parable told by the Lord) to neglect poor Lazarus, Judas to betray his master and commit suicide, Ananias and Sapphira to tell lies, and the rich oppressors of James' epistle (cf. Amos 2:6, 7) to exploit those who worked for them. None of these escaped punishment. The desire for riches, moreover, has been the cause of innumerable frauds, dollar-sign marriages, divorces, perjuries, robberies, poisonings, murders, and wars. And in the heart of man this sinful craving has led to "numerous pangs" (see below).

In the present connection Paul is thinking especially of church-members, as is also clear from what follows: **and some people, reaching out after it,[98] have wandered away from the faith, and have pierced themselves with numerous pangs.**

People who thus *reach out after* (or "aspire after," see on I Tim. 3:1) money are like the *planets*. They have *wandered* away from, literally "*planeted* away from" (ἀπεπλανήθησαν) the faith. The word *planet* means *wanderer*, for that is exactly what a planet is. Not in the sense that the earth or the other planets are "thrown out of their appointed orbits." Their orbits have been fixed, so that it is possible by means of six or seven "elements of a planetary orbit" to predict exactly where in the sky each planet will be. But in relation to the "fixed" stars, the planets, revolving around the sun, seem to wander about. This accounts for their name.

Now it is from *the faith,* the truth as confessed by the church (for this objective sense of the term *faith* see p. 11), that these people have wandered away. They have gone astray in inner attitude, in outward conduct, and even in the profession of the lips, that is, in the things which they are now teaching. But in so doing they have pierced themselves (as a man pierces himself with a spear) with *numerous pangs*. Among these pangs are unrest, boredom, dissatisfaction, gloom, envy. — In the pocket of a rich man who had just committed suicide was found $30,000 and a letter which read in part: "I have discovered during my life that piles of money do not bring happiness. I am taking my life because I can no longer stand the solitude and boredom. When I was an ordinary workman in New York, I was happy. Now that I possess millions I am infinitely sad and prefer death" (Quoted by W. A. Maier, *For Better Not For Worse*, p. 223).

---

[98] Literally, "*which* (ἧς) some reaching out after," etc. Cf. A.V. and A.R.V. The question is, To what does ἧς refer? Some interpreters (C. Bouma, R. C. H. Lenski) answer that it refers to φιλαργυρία. Bouma explains this as follows: consciously these avaricious people reach out after *money,* but unconsciously they reach out after *the love of money.* — But relative pronouns (especially in Koine Greek) are flexible. The rules which govern them are not at all rigid. Hence, the more natural explanation is to be preferred. Though grammatically ἧς agrees with φιλαργυρία yet in actual meaning it refers to ἀργύριον, which concept by the mind has been abstracted from φιλαργυρία. Thus also N. J. D. White (*The Expositor's Greek Testament*, Vol. IV, p. 144).

6:11   **I TIMOTHY**

11 But you, O man of God, flee away from these things, and run after righteousness, godliness, faith, love, endurance, gentleness. 12 Fight the noble fight of the faith; take hold of that everlasting life to which you were called when you confessed the beautiful confession [99] in the presence of many witnesses. 13 In the presence of God who endues all things with life, and of Christ Jesus who while testifying before Pontius Pilate made the beautiful confession,[100] 14 I charge you to keep the commission [101] without spot and above reproach until the appearing of our Lord Jesus Christ, 15 which in due season [102] he will display, (even he) the blessed and only Sovereign, the King of kings and Lord of lords, 16 the only One possessing immortality, dwelling in light unapproachable, whom no human being has (ever) seen or is able to see; to whom (be) honor and strength eternal. Amen.

6:11-16

11. Over against the vices which Paul has just condemned (see verses 3-10) stand the virtues which Timothy is urged to cultivate: **But you, O man of God, flee away from these things, and run after righteousness, faith, love, endurance, gentleness.**

Timothy is urged to *flee away from* such things as wickedness, gold-hunger, error, envy, wrangling, reviling; and to *run after, pursue* or *eagerly seek after* (see N.T.C. on I Thess. 5:15; cf. Rom. 12:13; I Cor. 14:1; Phil. 3:12) their opposites, namely, righteousness, godliness, faith, love, endurance, gentleness. This befits him as a "man of God." In the old dispensation this was a designation of the person who by God had been entrusted with a high office (Moses, Deut. 33:1; Ps. 90:1; David, II Chron. 8:14; Elijah, II Kings 1:9; the prophets, I Sam. 2:27). In the new dispensation, now that *every* believer is viewed as a partaker of the anointing of the Holy One, and therefore as a prophet, priest, and king (I John 2:20; cf. I Peter 2:9), the description is used with respect to any and every believer, as is clear from II Tim. 3:17. And surely, if *every* Christian is a "man of God," Timothy, having been placed in a position of great responsibility, is this in a special sense. Now a "man of God" is God's peculiar possession, his special ambassador. He is, accordingly, the very opposite of the man whose owner is Mammon, whose commands he obeys.

Timothy, then, as a "man of God," must *"run after" righteousness*,[103] the state of heart and mind which is in harmony with God's law, and will lead

---

[99] Literally, "to which you were called and confessed the beautiful (or *excellent* or *noble*) confession."
[100] Literally, "who witnessed (or *attested*) before Pontius Pilate the beautiful confession."
[101] Or, "the precept," "the mandate." See N.T.C. on John, Vol. II, pp. 252, 253.
[102] Or, "in its (or his) own season." See also footnote 105.
[103] I have tried thus to reproduce both the sense of the original and the alliteration: *r*un after *r*ighteousness represents δίωκε δικαιοσύνην. Thus also in II Tim. 2:22.

to godliness, the godly life, truly pious conduct. "Faith, love, and *endurance*" belong together [104] (Titus 2:2; cf. II Tim. 3:10 then I Thess. 1:3) just like "faith, love, and *hope*" (Col. 1:4, 5; cf. "faith, hope, and love," I Cor. 13:13), for *endurance* is the fruit of *hope* (I Thess. 1:3). It is the grace *to bear up under* adversities; for example, persecution. It amounts to *stedfastness* no matter what may be the cost, in the full assurance of future victory. (For a word-study of *endurance* and its synonyms see N.T.C. on I Thess. 1:3; 5:14 — footnote 108 — ; II Thess. 1:4; 3:5). As to *faith,* this concept is here used in the subjective sense, active reliance on God and his promises. And *love,* with Paul, is broad as the ocean, having as its object God in Christ, believers, and in a sense "everyone" (I Tim. 1:5, 14; 2:15; 4:12; II Tim. 1:7, 13; 2:22; 3:10; Titus 2:2; cf. I Thess. 3:12). When these virtues are present, *gentleness* of spirit will certainly result. The word thus translated is found only here in the Greek Bible. Comparison with II Tim. 3:10 indicates that it is akin in meaning to *longsuffering* (patience with respect to persons).

12. Comparing the Christian life with a contest, the apostle continues his admonition in these words: **Fight the noble fight of the faith.** The sense is that Timothy must *continue to* fight this noble fight, just as he must *continue to* flee away from the vices of his opponents and to pursue the opposite virtues. It is true that literally the words in the original are: "*Contend* (in) the noble *contest* of the faith," and that the word *contest* (ἀγών, a. *gathering*, especially for games or contests; b. the *contest* itself; c. the *agony*, anguish or anxiety that is connected with it; and d. agony, anguish, anxiety, concern or *solicitude,* in general) may refer to *any* kind of contest or conflict, whether physical — for example, a *race* (Heb. 12:1) — or spiritual (Phil. 1:30; Col. 2:1; and see N.T.C. on I Thess. 2:2). It is also true, however, that when *Paul* (in distinction from the author of the epistle to the Hebrews) is comparing the Christian life with a *race,* he makes this very clear by using such words as *running, race, stadium* (I Cor. 9:24; II Tim. 4:7). It is safe to conclude that when he compares the Christian life with any *contest* (using either the noun or the verb or both) except a *race,* the underlying figure is that of a *boxing-bout* or *wrestling-match* or something similar (see especially I Cor. 9:24-27). Therefore, the rendering, "Fight the good fight of the faith" (A.R.V., R.S.V., cf. A.V.) is not really wrong but approaches very nearly what the apostle had in mind. The passage, I Tim. 6:12, reminds one of the slightly different figure. "War the good (or *noble* or *excellent*) warfare" (I Tim. 1:18). (For Paul's use of metaphors borrowed from the sphere of athletics see on I Tim. 4:7b, 8.)

---

[104] Hence, I cannot agree here with Meinertz, Wohlenberg, and Lenski who divide the six into three groups of two each.

In distinction from the *word-battles* of the opponents (see on I Tim. 6:4), Timothy must carry on the *noble* fight that springs from and is inspired by his *faith* (probably the same sense as in the preceding verse).

Paul continues: **take hold of that everlasting life to which you were called when you confessed the beautiful confession in the presence of many witnesses.**

By putting up a successful fight, one is already *getting a firm grip on* (note the aorist tense now, in distinction from the present in the clause which precedes) *everlasting life*. This life pertains to the *future* age, to be sure, to the realm of glory, but in principle becomes the possession of the believer even here and now. It is actually *ever-lasting*, never-ending, life. Yet, though whenever the life so qualified pertains to man the *quantitative* idea is not excluded, the emphasis is on the *qualitative*: this is the life which manifests itself in fellowship with God, in partaking of his holiness, love, peace, and joy. (See N.T.C. on John 3:16.)

The idea that this everlasting life is here pictured as being *wholly* future — a kind of reward which one does not receive in any degree until the conflict is over —, hardly does justice to the flavor of the imperative, and would also seem to be in conflict with the words which immediately follow: "to which you were called when you confessed the beautiful confession in the presence of many witnesses." Note: *to which,* that is, this calling makes one a possessor of everlasting life. When, on Paul's first missionary journey, Timothy was "called" (both externally and internally), he had in connection with his baptism professed his faith publicly. While even today such a confession is "beautiful," or "noble" (καλή), it must have seemed more so at a time when practically the entire world was opposed to the gospel of Christ.

The admonition, "Fight the noble fight of the faith; take hold of that everlasting life to which you were called," does not imply that Timothy was remiss or lax in carrying out his religious duties. Every believer needs this admonition every day. A *timid* nature like Timothy, confronted with determined and subtle opponents, is especially in need of it. Let Timothy then remember the "many witnesses" who have heard his confession!

13 and 14. With impressive solemnity, which reminds one of I Tim. 5:21, the apostle continues: **In the presence of God who endues all things with life, and of Christ Jesus who while testifying before Pontius Pilate made the beautiful confession, I charge you to keep the commission without spot and above reproach until the appearing of our Lord Jesus Christ.**

Paul says, "I charge," or "I command," that is, "I pass along an authoritative message" (see on I Tim. 1:3; 4:11; 5:7). He presents two reasons why Timothy should do as he has just been told:

(1) Let him not fear for his life, for the charge is given and received under the very eyes of that God who is the Bestower and Preserver of life, the "life-generating" God. Cf. Luke 17:33; Acts 7:19.

(2) Let him remember what *Christ Jesus* (see on I Tim. 1:1; especially footnote 19) did when *he* was testifying before an enemy of the truth. Before Pontius Pilate he stood firm, and, bearing witness before him by *word* and *deed* (Matt. 17:1, 2, 11-31; Mark 15:1-20; Luke 23:1-7, 13-25; John 18:28-19:16), thus made the beautiful confession, thereby proving himself to be "the faithful witness" (Rev. 1:5; 3:14).

Hence, let Timothy *keep* — that is, stand guard over, protect, and preserve — his commission. That *commission, precept,* or *mandate,* comprises *all* that he has been ordered to do with respect to the ministry of the gospel and the government of the church. Cf. I Tim. 6:20; then Matt. 28:20. He must, moreover, take care that his attitude and conduct is such that this commission remains "without spot" (see James 1:27; II Peter 3:14; cf. Eph. 5:27) and "above reproach" (see on I Tim. 3:2; literally, "not to be laid hold of," hence, "irreprehensible," "unassailable").

A similar command comes to all those upon whom similar responsibility has been conferred. Every one must keep his commission untainted and unsullied until the very day of his death, or, if the consummation of the ages should occur before that time — Paul never sets dates; see N.T.C. on I Thess. 5:1, 2 — , then "until the appearing of our Lord Jesus Christ." This *appearing* or *manifestation* is literally Christ's *epiphany,* the first gleam of *the dawn,* namely, that dawn to which the believer looks forward with eager anticipation, *the rising* (never more to set!) of "the sun of righteousness with healing in its wings." Cf. Mal. 1:11; 4:2; Is. 60:1-3; Luke 1:78, 79; Rev. 1:7; and for the word *epiphany* itself see N.T.C. on II Thess. 2:8; and cf. II Tim. 1:10; 4:1, 8; Titus 2:13.

15, 16. With reference to this *appearing* Paul continues: **which in due season he will display, (even he)**

	Old Testament Parallels
a. the blessed and only Sovereign	Deut. 6:4; Ps. 41:13; Is. 40:12-31; Dan. 4:35
b. the King of kings and	Ezek. 26:7; Dan. 2:37; Ezra 7:12
c. Lord of lords	Deut. 10:17; Ps. 136:3
d. the only One possessing immortality	Ps. 36:9; Is. 40:28; Dan. 4:34
e. dwelling in light unapproachable	Ex. 24:17; 34:35; Ps. 104:2

    f. whom no human being has
       (ever) seen or is able to see   Ex. 33:20; Deut. 4:12; Is. 6:5
    g. to whom (be) honor and
       strength eternal.   Amen.   Neh. 8:6; Ps. 41:13; 72:19; 89:52

To the two reasons which have been given, indicating why Timothy should "keep the commission without spot and above reproach" a third is now added, but only by implication, namely, that he will receive his reward when Jesus returns in glory. However, the idea of reward for Timothy is pushed into the background by the rapturous contemplation and consequent exaltation of the majestic attributes of the One who, *in due season* (or: "in its — or *his* — own season"),[105] the season designated by the Father from eternity (Acts 1:7; 3:20, 21; cf. Gal. 4:4), will exhibit that great event to which, in a sense, the entire universe looks forward (cf. Rom. 8:19): the *epiphany* or visible shining forth of Jesus Christ upon clouds of glory. Just as, in Paul's thinking, it is *God* (I Cor. 6:14; Eph. 1:20), or more particularly, *God the Father* (Rom. 6:4; Gal. 1:1; cf. I Peter 1:3) who *raises* the Son (though it is also true that Christ arose through his own power, John 10:18), so it is *God* who displays the Son's *epiphany*. He *displays it as proof* (for the verb in this sense see John 2:18) to the world, for this is the public vindication of the Son and of his people.

The doxology in praise of God is one of the finest in Scripture. For its origin one must not look to pagan philosophy. Though some of its phrases have parallels in extra-canonical Jewish literature,[106] it should certainly be

---

[105] The original has the plural "seasons," here as well as in I Tim. 2:6; Titus 1:3. However, this is probably an idiomatic plural, to be rendered as a singular. Cf. for this use Jer. 5:26 (27:26 LXX); see also pl. of χρόνος as used in Luke 20:9; 23:8).
[106] S.BK. III, 656. Commentators have made the following guesses with respect to the origin of this doxology:
1. It was an element in a eucharistic prayer which Paul was wont to utter.
2. It was a Christian adaptation of a synagogue doxology.
3. It was taken from an early Christian hymn.
4. Part of it (especially b. and c.) was derived from pagan sources; particularly from the formulae of the imperial cult.

To begin with the last, the usurpation of divine titles by earthly rulers may have been *one* of several reasons why early Christians spoke of *their* Lord as (the only) King of kings and Lord of lords. See A. Deissmann, *op. cit.*, pp. 362-366. Also E. Stauffer, *Christ and the Caesars* (translated by K. and R. Gregor Smith), Philadelphia, 1955; esp. pp. 95, 150, 240. Over against idols and emperors who *are called* gods, he is the one and only *real* God. I Cor. 8:5, 6 points in that direction. Yet, the title as such was not derived from paganism. The Old Testament was the real source.

As to the suggestions made in 1, 2, and 3, these, even if true, do not point to the *original written* source, which must have been the Old Testament. Between that ultimate source and the mind of Paul there may have been many avenues, both direct and indirect. It should, however, be clear that what we have here in I Tim. 6:15, 16 is not mere copy-work but a spontaneous outburst of praise!

regarded as a spontaneous outburst coming from the heart of a devout believer in Jesus Christ, an apostle who, while he is writing or dictating, is thoroughly conscious of the loving presence of his Lord and who in his youth had made a thorough study of the Old Testament, so that its phraseology was embedded in his soul. The parallels from the Old Testament have already been indicated (see the incomplete list of references above, next to the quoted passage). It is possible to duplicate the sense — and in most cases the very words — of the doxology without departing from the text of the Old Testament. Thus, quoting throughout from the Old Testament, one might paraphrase the doxology as follows:

"the blessed and incomparable One, who does according to his will in the army of heaven and among the inhabitants of the earth, the King of kings and Lord of lords, with whom alone is the fountain of life, who covers himself with light as with a garment, whom no human being shall (ever) be able to see, whose glorious name be blessed forever, Amen and Amen."

It was to be expected that just as the contemplation of the *first* coming of Christ led to a doxology (I Tim. 1:17), so also the meditation upon the *second* coming (here in I Tim. 6:15, 16) would lead to a *similar* and *expanded* doxology.

The present doxology consists of seven terms descriptive of Deity. In the original, as in our translation, a., b., and c. are nouns; d. and e. are participial modifiers; and f. and g. are relative clauses.

As to thought-content, every element in this doxology stresses the transcendence or incomparable greatness of God. He is *Sovereign* (a word applied to human rulers in Luke 1:52; Acts 8:27; and to God in II Macc. 3:24; 12:15; 15:4, 23; but see Dan. 4:35). As Sovereign he is altogether *blessed*. See on I Tim. 1:11. He is, moreover, the *only* Sovereign (cf. Jude 25); hence, absolutely incomparable in his right to do as he pleases, for example, to choose the appropriate season for Christ's epiphany (note preceding context). Thus, "the blessed God" (of I Tim. 1:11) and "the only God" (of I Tim. 1:17) are here combined. Whatever titles *men* may bear, either rightfully or by usurpation, he — *he alone!* — is the real King of kings and Lord of lords. Literally, the original has, "the King of those kinging and the Lord of those lording" (Rev. 17:14; 19:16, used both times with reference to *Christ*, have the simpler form). The lengthened (participial) form probably adds freshness and vigor to the meaning.

Having set forth God's relation to the universe and particularly to all earthly rulers, Paul in the last four terms (d., e., f., and g.) dwells on the divine essence itself, the majestic *being* of God.

He alone possesses *immortality*. This must not be confused with "endless existence." To be sure, that, too, is implied, but the concept *immortality* is far more exalted. It means that God is life's never-failing Fountain. On the concept *life* as applied to God see N.T.C. on John 1:4. This immortality is the opposite of *death,* as is clear from the derivation of the word both in English and in Greek. *Athanasia* is deathlessness. It is fulness of life, *imperishable* (cf. I Tim. 1:17) blessedness, the inalienable enjoyment of all the divine attributes. The only human beings who, *as far as it is possible for creatures to do so,* share this immortality, and thereby become "partakers of the divine nature" (II Peter 1:4), are *believers,* though also unbelievers *exist* endlessly. It is *through the gospel* that immortality or imperishability was brought to light (II Tim. 1:10). For the believer immortality is therefore a redemptive concept. It is *everlasting salvation.* For God it is *eternal blessedness.* But while the believer *has received* immortality, as one receives a drink of water from a fountain, God *has* it. It belongs to his very being. He *is* himself the Fountain.

The idea of life, implied in immortality, naturally leads to that of *light.* "In him was life, and that life was the light of men" (John 1:4). Now, this light is like the sun. We need it to see by, yet we cannot look into it, for it is too intensely brilliant. In that sense, God, too, dwells in light *unapproachable.* The metaphor is even stronger than that employed in Ps. 104:2 ("He covers himself with light as with a garment"). Like a dwelling conceals its occupants, and hides them even more when it is *unapproachable,* so God's very essence, by virtue of what it is, conceals him. Hence, the term *light* as here used re-emphasizes his incomparable greatness. "Verily, thou art a God that hidest thyself, O God of Israel, the Savior" (Is. 45:15). "Behold, God is great."

This greatness of God has as its corollary, ". . . and we know him not" (Job 36:26). Similarly, here in I Tim. 6:16 the line, "dwelling in light unapproachable," already implies and is immediately followed by, "whom no human being has (ever) seen or is able to see." Cf. I Tim. 1:17, in connection with which the sense in which God is *invisible* has been explained. See also N.T.C. on John 1:18; and cf. I John 4:12.

The devout contemplation of this majestic Being, who has wonderful blessings in store for his children, leads to the climax, "to whom be honor and strength eternal. Amen." Truly, such a God is worthy of all *honor:* reverence, esteem, adoration (see footnote 82 above). He is also worthy of eternal *strength,* that is, power manifested in action, to the discomfiture of his enemies and to the salvation of his people. Paul's expressed wish is that God may receive this honor and may manifest this eternal strength. This wish is very deep-seated, for the apostle loves God very, very much. Hence, as in I Tim. 1:17, he seals the wish with the solemn word of affirmation or confirmation: Amen (cf. Num. 5:22; Neh. 8:6; Ps. 41:13; 72:10; 89:52; and see N.T.C. on John 1:51).

I TIMOTHY 6:17

17 As for those (who are) rich in terms of this present age, charge them not to be high-minded, nor to set their hope on (the) uncertainty of riches, but on God, who richly provides us with everything for (our) enjoyment. 18 (Charge them) to do what is good, to be rich in noble deeds, to be quick to give, ready to share, 19 (thus) storing up a treasure for themselves, (which will form) an excellent foundation for the (age) to come, so that they may take hold of the real life.

6:17-19

17. Truly, believers are rich in terms of the age to come, that age which will be ushered in by Christ's glorious epiphany! What a contrast between them and those who are rich *only* in terms of this *present* age. Let wealthy church-members beware lest the word "only" should apply to them! Paul does not *say* that their wealth is limited to this earthly sphere, but he *warns* them. Says he:

As for those (who are) rich in terms of this present age, charge them not to be high-minded, nor to have their hope set on (the) uncertainty of riches, but on God, who richly provides us with everything for (our) enjoyment.

Not those who are eager to become rich, as in verse 9, are here addressed, but those who are actually rich. By immediately adding, "in terms of this present age" (an expression used only here and in II Tim. 4:10; Titus 2:12), the apostle is already beginning to fix the mind of the reader and hearer upon the transitory character of earthly wealth. He means, "this present era which will soon be past." Timothy, then, must tell these people: (a) what should *not* be their attitude (verse 17a); and (b) what should be their attitude (verses 17b, 18, 19).

As to a., they must not be *high-minded* but humble (Eph. 4:2; Col. 3:12); and they must not *have their hope set* [107] on the uncertainty of riches, that is, on their riches, which, as a matter of fact, are very uncertain. Rich church-members, then, must be neither snobbish nor smug.

As to b., they should have their hope fixed on *God* (this is the best reading; better than, "on the living God"). This God is ever true to his promise. He is the God of love. He *richly* provides. Note play on words: "As for those (who are) *rich,* charge them . . . not to have their hope set on . . . *riches,* but on God, who *richly* provides." Not only is God rich (Ps. 50:10-12), so that with him *wishing* and *having* are one and the same, but he ever gives *"according to* his riches" (Eph. 1:7; cf. Titus 3:6), not only *"of* his riches." For God's munificence, by virtue of which he provides us with

---

[107] Note ἠλπικέναι, perfect active infinitive of ἐλπίζω, emphasizing that this action of hoping, having begun in the past, has continued until by this time it has become a fixed state. Rich church-members, accordingly, are warned not to get to the point where they will have rested the weight of their confidence on earthly treasures.

all things necessary both for body and soul, for time and eternity, see also Acts 14:17; James 1:17; and innumerable passages in the Psalter, such as 37:25; 68:19; 81:19b; and see Psalms 103, 104, 107, 111, 116, 145, etc. Moreover, all these things are given to us in order that we may not only "partake of" them (I Tim. 4:3), but may also *enjoy* them. When *we* sing, God sings along with us (Zeph. 3:17).

18. What should be the attitude of the rich is continued, with this difference: in verse 17b their proper attitude *toward God* has been pointed out; now in verse 18 their correct relation toward *other people*, particularly toward other believers is set forth. Says Paul: **(Charge them) to do what is good, to be rich in noble deeds, to be quick to give, ready to share.**

A rich church-member should strive to be rich in noble deeds, in "beautiful works," as was Mary of Bethany. He should be *quick to give,* being ever *ready to share* what he has with others who belong to the *fellowship* or *community* of believers in Christ. He should do this in the spirit of Acts 2:42-44; 4:34-37.

19. The result of following this proper procedure will be: **(thus) storing up a treasure for themselves, (which will form) an excellent foundation for the (age) to come, so that they may take hold of the real life.**

By practising the grace of sharing, a person is storing up a treasure for himself. *Gifts are investments.* By giving materially one enriches himself spiritually, and assures himself of future reward. "Sell whatever you have, and give to the poor, and you will have treasure in heaven" (Mark 10:21). That "treasure" in heaven consists of the following:

a. a good conscience (cf. I Tim. 1:5),

b. an enthusiastic reception by those who have been benefited (Luke 16:9),

c. in general, the entrance into all the joys and glories of heaven.

This treasure will be an excellent *foundation* [108] upon which to build when, in the age to come (particularly in the great Judgment Day), the believer's works are taken into account. His having been with Jesus in heaven is a *solid basis* for confidence in that great day. The believer himself will not have to give a review of his good works. In fact, if they were

---

[108] To say that the word used in the original means both *foundation* and *fund* affords little help in this connection, may even be confusing. It cannot very well have both meanings at the same time in the same passage. Paul's thought is, after all, simple and clear. Good works (the fruit of faith; hence, of grace) performed here below are rewarded with treasure above. And the consciousness of having enjoyed this heavenly treasure will be a firm foundation for the expectation of everything good on the Day of Judgment. — The apostle may have been thinking of Christ's utterances in the Sermon on the Mount, for there, too, the two ideas — *treasure* and *good foundation* — are found side by side (Matt. 6:19, 20; 7:24, 25).

really *good* works, he will not even be able to do so. Christ will do it for him (Matt. 25:34-40). With respect to both body and soul the believer, having listened to the words of approval which issue from the lips of Christ, will then enter into the fullest enjoyment of that life which alone is life indeed. Paul's teaching here in I Tim. 6:19 is in exact accord with Christ's in Matt. 25:34-40, 46b. Salvation, to be sure, is entirely *by grace through faith* (Eph. 2:8; Titus 3:5), but the reward is *according to works* (Dan. 12:3; II Cor. 5:10; Rev. 20:12).

---

20 O Timothy, what has been entrusted to you guard,[109] turning away from the profane empty-chatter and contradictions of what is falsely styled "Knowledge," 21 for by professing it [110] certain individuals have wandered away with respect to the faith.
Grace [111] (be) with y o u.

6:20, 21

20. O Timothy, what has been entrusted to you guard.
Having reached the end of the letter, Paul addresses his friend and fellow-worker with solemn earnestness: "O Timothy." [112] Timothy, then, is admonished to guard *the trust* or *deposit;* that is, he must faithfully watch over *that which has been committed to his care.* It is as if God had made a "deposit" in Timothy's bank. The word employed in the original is related to a verb meaning "to place by the side," hence, "to deposit," "to commit to (someone)." See M.M. for illustrations of the meaning "deposit," "pledge," "security."

Moreover, the object which has been thus given into his charge for protection is *the gospel,* as is clear from II Tim. 1:11. It is *God's redemptive truth* entrusted to him by the Holy Spirit (see II Tim. 1:14). But here the term "gospel" must be taken in its widest sense, as embracing "all (sacred) scripture" (II Tim. 3:16). This *includes,* of course, what the apostle is writing in the present letter: all the orders given to Timothy and all the teaching which this epistle contains. The point, then, is that this gospel belongs not to Timothy but *to God.* Cf. Rom. 3:2 (the Jews had been entrusted with "the oracles *of God*"). *He* has made it possible through the sending

---

[109] Literally, "the entrusted (thing) guard." One might also say, "Guard the deposit."
[110] Literally, "which certain individuals professing."
[111] Literally, "The grace."
[112] "O" with vocatives is not very common in Greek. The addition of the interjection strengthens the vocative. Other instances in Paul: I Tim. 6:11; then Rom. 2:1, 3; 9:20; 11:33; Gal. 3:1. It is also Paul who uses it in Acts 13:10; 27:21; Luke, in Acts 1:1; Gallio, in Acts 18:14. Jesus used it a few times: Matt. 15:28; 17:17 (cf. Mark 9:19; Luke 9:41); Luke 24:25.

of *his* Son. *He* has revealed it. *To God* Timothy will have to give an account as to what he has done with it. Ministers are God's "stewards" (Titus 1:7). The "talents" which they employ in performing their tasks are not their own, but *God's* property (Matt. 25:14-30). They must be used to the best advantage in the promotion of *his* cause and the progress of *his* Kingdom.

This implies that Timothy must continue to proclaim the pure gospel, and like a dauntless, vigilant *sentinel* (note Greek verb) must rush to the defence whenever its precious truths are attacked or misrepresented, as was the case in the Ephesus region. It is with this in mind that Paul continues: **turning away from the profane empty-chatter and contradictions of what is falsely styled** *Knowledge*.

Timothy must avoid one mistake. He must not waste any time on *the inanities* of those false teachers who "understand neither the words which they are speaking nor the themes on which they are harping with such confidence" (I Tim. 1:7). Such *profane* (unholy, unclean, II Tim. 2:16; Lev. 10:10) "empty-jabberings" he must simply *shun* (I Tim. 4:7). He must *turn away* from them in disgust. Why should he concern himself with "endless myths and genealogies" (I Tim. 1:4), with "idle talk" (I Tim. 1:6)? Why should he meddle with the "contradictions" or "word-battles" in which those men engage each other who are "depraved in mind and deprived of the truth" (I Tim. 6:5)? To be sure, these false teachers rave about their systems of "Knowledge." But their vapid mouthings are "Knowledge *falsely so called*." It should be *avoided* like the pestilence. Paul's inspired advice, by means of which, having reached the end of the letter, he returns to the theme which he had mentioned at the beginning, should be taken to heart by the church in every age. Also *today* far too much attention is being paid to the "empty jabberings" of men who, in the final analysis, reject God's infallible revelation! Paul's command addressed to Timothy is ever up-to-date. And the apostle John is in thorough agreement with him (II John 10). One *guards* the truth by *turning away from* all insipid ranting.

21. Against this pseudonymous "Knowledge," there follows a word of warning which emphasizes the necessity of heeding the admonition expressed in verse 20: **for, by professing it certain individuals have wandered away with respect to the faith.** Here are those "certain individuals" again. We have already seen that the manner in which they are here pictured is in perfect harmony with their description in I Tim. 1:3, 4, 6, 7, 19, 20. The "profane empty jabberers" of our present passage are the "futile talkers" of I Tim. 1:6. Even the same verb is used in both places to describe them. They are said to *have wandered away* (I Tim. 1:6; 6:21).

Now these "certain individuals," in *professing* (see on I Tim. 2:10), that is, proclaiming and making propaganda for, their vaunted "Knowledge," have wandered away from *the faith,* that is, from *the truth* (cf. I Tim. 6:10, 12; II Tim. 2:18). But this does not mean that they had all broken with "the church." There were *then,* as there are *now,* individuals *in* the church who have forsaken the truth. They prefer not to leave the church, but to drag it along with them into ruin.

Nowhere in Paul's letters is there a shorter benediction: **Grace (be) with y o u.** But though brief, it is rich in meaning, for *grace* is the greatest blessing of all. It is God's favor in Christ toward the undeserving, transforming their hearts and lives and leading them to glory. The apostle, who in his opening salutation had spoken of *grace,* as the first element in the series "grace, mercy, peace," now closes the letter by pronouncing *this* grace (note the article; hence really "the grace") upon . . . well, upon whom? The reader who is unacquainted with the original is almost sure to reason that the words "Grace be with you," of the A.R.V., mean, "Grace be with *you, Timothy.*" The R.S.V. has not improved matters any. And the A.V. is based upon an inferior reading; hence has "with thee." This shows how necessary it is in our translation to distinguish carefully between "you" (singular) and "y o u" (spaced letters, plural), for surprisingly, *it is the plural* that is used here! Though the epistle is addressed to just *one* person, Timothy, the latter would certainly see to it that its contents reached others. God's grace, accordingly, is pronounced upon *the entire Christian community.*

Synthesis of Chapter 6

See the Outline at the beginning of this chapter, which may be paraphrased as follows:

Let as many as are under the yoke, namely, slaves, regard their own masters as worthy of all honor. Otherwise the blame will be placed on the gospel, and the name and doctrine of God will be evil spoken of. Those slaves who happen to be in the exceptionally privileged position of having believing masters should render exceptional service. The fact that their masters are brothers is no reason for these slaves to look down upon them. Let them rather bear in mind that these beloved ones will reciprocate the kindness of their slaves.

Keep on teaching and urging these things.

If anyone is a teacher of novelties — hair-splitting so-called "deductions" from the law of Moses, fanciful stories about ancestors — and does not chime in with the sound words of our Lord Jesus Christ, the doctrine that promotes true piety, such a man is blinded with conceit. Though he may boast about his superior "Knowledge," in reality he does not know a thing. A morbid craving for controversies and word-battles has taken possession of him; and these, in turn, breed envy, wrangling, revilings, base suspicions, and mutual altercations between men depraved in mind and deprived of the truth. These men imagine that the real aim of being religious is to make a profit.

Now genuine religion, which exists when the soul is no longer empty but filled with grace and contentment, is actually profit-bearing. Material possessions, however, can never impart true riches to the soul, as is evident from the fact that no matter how rich a person may become in earthly goods, he will leave this world as devoid of them as he entered it. Hence, when we, believers, have nourishment and shelter, we shall regard these as sufficient.

But those who are eager to be rich fall into temptation and a snare and into numerous cravings. These cravings are senseless and hurtful because they defeat their very purpose. Instead of making men really rich and happy they make them poor and wretched, for they plunge men into ruin and destruction. For, a root of all the evils is the love of money; and some people, reaching out after it, have wandered away from the faith, and have pierced themselves with numerous pangs: unrest, worry, boredom, dissatisfaction, gloom, envy.

But you, O man of God, continue to flee away from such things as gold-hunger, envy, wrangling; and run after righteousness — the state of mind and heart which is in harmony with God's law —, godliness, faith, love, endurance, gentleness. Fight the noble fight of the faith. Get a firm grip on that everlasting life to which you were called when on the occasion of your baptism you confessed the beautiful confession in the presence of those many witnesses who heard it. Do not be afraid to lose your life. Remember that your mandate is given and received in the presence of a God who is the Bestower and Preserver of life, and of a Christ Jesus who while testifying before that enemy of the truth, Pontius Pilate, made the beautiful confession. Therefore you also must courageously cling to your commission with respect to preaching and discipline; yes, you must stand guard over it so that it remains unsullied and completely free from every possibility of justified criticism. Keep it then until the day when our Lord Jesus Christ shines forth brilliantly, the day of his appearing. God himself will display that great event. He, moreover, is the blessed and only Sovereign, the King of kings and Lord of lords, the only One possessing *immortality* — *not* just *endless existence* but *real life* possessed *eternally* —, dwelling in light unapproachable, whom no human being has (ever) seen or is able to see; to whom (be) honor and strength eternal. Amen.

As for those who are rich in material possessions, charge them not to be uppish nor to have their hope fixed on the uncertainty of riches but on God, who richly provides us with everything for our enjoyment. Charge them to do what is good, to be rich in noble deeds, to be quick to give, ready to share. Remember: gifts are investments. Hence, these givers are really storing up a treasure for themselves. They will not have only a good conscience but also, when soul and body separate, an enthusiastic reception in the glories of heaven. What a solid foundation this will be for the age to come, particularly for the day of the final judgment. With respect to both body and soul they will then begin to enter upon the fullest enjoyment of that life which alone is life indeed and which will never end.

O Timothy, guard as a most precious deposit the gospel which has been entrusted to you. Turn away meanwhile from the profane empty-chatter and contradictions of what is falsely styled "Knowledge," those endless myths and genealogies, those word-battles about the law. Remember that by making propaganda for it certain individuals have wandered away from the path of God's redemptive truth. The grace of God be with you, and not only with you but with the entire Christian community in whose midst you dwell.

Commentary on II Timothy

Outline of II Timothy

Theme: *The Apostle Paul Tells Timothy What To Do in the Interest of Sound Doctrine*

No brief outline can do full justice to the rich, varied, and overlapping contents of a letter which is as personal as is II Timothy. The dominant note, however, is clear: "Timothy, do not be ashamed, but by God's grace exert yourself to the utmost, being willing to endure your share of hardship in preserving and promoting sound doctrine."

There are no sharp divisions. Rather, the emphasis gradually shifts from one point to another. When a new point is made, the old one is not entirely relinquished. The thoughts overlap like shingles on a roof. For example, a key-passage in chapter 1 is, "Do not be ashamed" (verses 8, 12, 16). The idea recurs, however, in chapter 2 (verse 15). Similarly, a key-passage in chapter 2 is, "Suffer hardship along with us" (verse 3; cf. verse 9). But this has been anticipated in chapter 1 (verse 8).

I have called "Do not be ashamed" *a* key-passage. It can hardly be called *the* key-passage, at least not in the sense that Paul's main idea in the first chapter would be *negative*. "Do not be ashamed" is, of course, an example of the figure of speech called *litotes:* "strong affirmation by means of negation." Hence, the predominant idea of chapter 1 is "Be very courageous. Whatever happens, *hold on* to the precious doctrine of the church."

Similarly, in chapter 2 the predominant idea is not simply that Timothy must be willing to suffer hardship along with Paul and others, but that he must be willing to do this *in connection with* all the work pertaining to the gospel-ministry, one phase of which is emphasized in this chapter, namely, that of *teaching:* imparting proper instruction in the Word over against heresy.

In chapter 3 the admonition to *abide in* the true doctrine obtains its justified emphasis from the observation, "Grievous times will come."

And in chapter 4 the exhortation, *"Preach* (literally, "Herald") the word," is introduced very solemnly, as an authoritative charge, "I charge you."

In view of all this the main line of thought running through II Timothy can be briefly indicated in the following manner (note the overlapping):

AS REGARDS SOUND DOCTRINE:
HOLD ON TO IT	Chapter 1
TEACH IT	Chapter 2
ABIDE IN IT	Chapter 3
PREACH IT	Chapter 4

Main Divisions with Key-Passages

Chapter 1: HOLD ON TO IT
"Stir into full flame that gift of God" (verse 6)
"Do not be ashamed" (verse 8; cf. verses 12, 16)
"Hold on to . . . the sound words" (verse 13)
"That precious deposit guard" (verse 14)

Chapter 2: TEACH IT
"The things which you have heard . . . entrust to faithful men . . . able to teach others also" (verse 2)
"Suffer hardship along with (us)" (verse 3; cf. verse 9)
"The Lord will give you understanding in all things" (verse 14)
"A servant of the Lord must be . . . qualified to teach" (verse 24)

Chapter 3: ABIDE IN IT
"Grievous seasons will come" (verse 1)
"But you have followed my teaching, conduct, purpose" (verse 10)
"Continue in the things which you have learned" (verse 14)

Chapter 4: PREACH IT
"I charge you" (verse 1)
"Preach (or "Herald") the word" (verse 2)
"Do the work of an evangelist; your duties as a minister discharge to the full" (verse 5).

Outline with Divisions and Subdivisions

Chapter 1:   HOLD ON TO IT   "Do not be ashamed."
          A. As did Lois and Eunice.
          B. As I do, never ashamed of the gospel.
          C. As did Onesiphorus, not ashamed of my chain.

Chapter 2:   TEACH IT   "Suffer hardship along with (us)."
          A. It brings great reward; is glorious in contents.
          B. Vain disputes, on the contrary, serve no useful purpose.

Chapter 3:   ABIDE IN IT   "Grievous times will come."
          A. Knowing that enemies will arise, who have its form, not its power.
          B. Knowing that it is based on the sacred writings, as you learned from trustworthy persons.

Chapter 4:   PREACH IT   "I charge you."
          A. In season, out of season, for apostasy is coming. Remain faithful, in view of the fact that I am about to set sail.
          B. Items of personal information, requests, greetings.

Outline of Chapter 1

Theme: *The Apostle Paul Tells Timothy What To Do in the Interest of Sound Doctrine*

Hold On To It   "Do not be ashamed"

1:1-7   (Hold on) as did Lois and Eunice. Verses 1 and 2 contain the address and salutation.

1:8-14   As I do, never ashamed of the gospel.

1:15-18   As did Onesiphorus, not ashamed of my chain. Contrast "all that are in Asia," who deserted me.

CHAPTER I

II TIMOTHY 1:1, 2

1 Paul, an apostle of Christ Jesus through the will of God in harmony with the promise of life (which centers) in Christ Jesus, 2 to Timothy (my) beloved child; grace, mercy, peace from God the Father and Christ Jesus our Lord.

3 I acknowledge gratitude to God, whom I, like my forefathers, serve with a pure conscience, just as I cherish that constant recollection of you in my supplication by night and by day; 4 longing to see you, as I revive in my memory your tears, in order that (seeing you again) I may be filled with joy; 5 having received a reminder of your unfeigned faith, the kind (of faith) which first dwelt in your grandmother Lois and in your mother Eunice, and, I am convinced, also in you. 6 For this reason I remind you to stir into a living flame that gift of God which is within you through the laying on of my hands. 7 For God gave us not a Spirit of timidity but of power and love and self-discipline.

1:1-7

1, 2. **Paul, an apostle of Christ Jesus through the will of God in harmony with the promise of life (which centers) in Christ Jesus, 2 to Timothy (my) beloved child; grace, mercy, peace from God the Father and Christ Jesus our Lord.**

The opening phrases of the two letters addressed to Timothy resemble each other rather closely, as anyone can see for himself. In the columns below, the words that differ are printed in italics:

I Tim. 1:1, 2	II Tim. 1:1, 2
Paul, an apostle of Christ Jesus *by order* of God *our Savior* and Christ Jesus *our Hope*, to Timothy (my) *genuine* child *in faith;* grace, mercy, peace from God the Father and Christ Jesus our Lord.	Paul, an apostle of Christ Jesus *through the will* of God *in harmony with the promise of life* (which centers) *in* Christ Jesus, to Timothy (my) *beloved* child; grace, mercy, peace from God the Father and Christ Jesus our Lord.

Hence, for a more detailed discussion of the material that is common to the two passages I refer to the explanation of I Tim. 1:1, 2.

Briefly, then, the meaning of II Tim. 1:1, 2 is as follows:

Paul introduces himself as the official representative of Christ Jesus. He

1:1, 2 **II TIMOTHY**

has a right to say "of Jesus Christ," for by the latter he has been set apart for his high office. To *him* he belongs, and in *his* service he functions. Moreover, not self-appointed is Paul but invested with his authoritative commission "through the will of God" (cf. "by order of God," I Tim. 1:1). Though he is but a prisoner, his word has divine sanction! Cf. Eph. 1:1; Col. 1:1, also written from prison.

Now this apostleship by the will of God was "in harmony with (or "in accordance with") the promise of life," that is, it was a result of that promise, in the sense that had there been no such *promise* there could have been no *divinely willed apostle* to proclaim the promise. This promise and assurance is the one already implied in Gen. 3:15 and definitely stated in Ps. 16:11; 138:7, 9; John 3:16; 6:35, 48-59; 14:6. It was the promise "of life," that is, the promise which has *everlasting life* as its contents. It is very fitting that Paul, the prisoner who faces *death,* should rivet the attention on the promise of indestructible *life!* This is, indeed the life which *is* or *centers* (implied) "in Christ Jesus," for apart from *his* atonement and intercession no one would ever be in possession of that *life,* that *salvation* (see N.T.C. on John 3:16).

Paul is addressing his letter "to Timothy (my) beloved child." Cf. II Tim. 2:1; 3:14. As, in a secondary sense, a child owes his natural life to his earthly father, so Timothy owed his spiritual life to Paul (see p. 34). Moreover, as a child serves (with) his father, so Timothy served (with) Paul in the gospel. See Phil. 2:19-22, which passage also indicates why the apostle calls Timothy his *beloved* or *dear* (cf. I Tim. 1:2, "genuine") child. Moreover, the term of endearment is natural on the lips of one who, facing death, in his mind and heart reviews his entire past association with the precious young friend and helper whose life had been mingled with his own in so many ways.

Upon this "beloved child" Paul pronounces *grace* (unmerited pardoning and transforming favor), *mercy* (warm and tender affection shown to the one who is in a difficult situation), and that blessing which flows forth from grace and mercy just as a stream issues from a fountain, namely, the blessing of *peace* (the consciousness of having been reconciled to God through the accomplished mediatorial work of Christ).

These gifts are regarded as having as their source "God the Father and Christ Jesus our Lord." The Father bestows them. The Son has earned them.

3-5. When Paul adds to the words of introduction an expression of sincere and humble thanksgiving to God, he is following a custom (see N.T.C. on I and II Thessalonians, p. 45). With respect to the letters written by Paul the statistics are as follows:

"I (or *we*) thank God"	"I acknowledge gratitude"	"Blessed be . . ."	Absence of introductory thanksgiving or doxology
Rom. 1:8	I Tim. 1:12 ("to Christ Jesus")	II Cor. 1:3	Galatians
I Cor. 1:4		Eph. 1:3	Titus
Phil. 1:3	II Tim. 1:3 ("to God")		
Col. 1:3			
I Thess. 1:2			
II Thess. 1:3 ("We are obliged to give thanks")			
Philem. 4			

But though, as has been shown, the apostle was used to adding words of thanksgiving or praise, with him this was never *merely* a custom. Rather, we should view the situation as follows: Sitting in his gloomy dungeon and facing death, Paul, far from complaining, as many people in similar circumstances would have done, meditates on blessings past and present, and sincerely desires to express his gratitude. This is the background of the words:

I acknowledge gratitude to God, whom I, like my forefathers, serve with a pure conscience, just as I cherish that constant recollection of you in my supplication by night and by day; longing to see you,
    a. as I revive in my memory your tears,
        b. in order that (on seeing you again) I may be filled with joy;
    c. having received a reminder of your unfeigned faith, the kind (of faith) which first dwelt in your grandmother Lois and in your mother Eunice, and, I am convinced, also in you.

Paul states that he *acknowledges gratitude to God*. Though he will soon die the death of a criminal, he is not afraid to speak of *serving*[113] God, for in proclaiming the gospel he has done what his *conscience, purified* by the Holy Spirit, had told him to do. (For the meaning of *conscience* see on I Tim. 1:5; and for *pure conscience* see on I Tim. 3:9.) In this respect he was like his *forefathers* or *ancestors* (cf. I Tim. 5:4, but in that passage the word is used with reference to *still living* progenitors). They, too, served the same God, and they, too, did it with a pure conscience. The thought is the same as that which is expressed in Acts 24:14, 15:

"But this I confess to thee, that after the Way which they call a sect, so

---

[113] The original uses the verb λατρεύω here, not λειτουργέω. The latter always has an *official* connotation; the former embraces a wider area, and may denote either official or unofficial service or worship. See R. C. Trench, *op. cit.*, XXXV.

serve I the God of *our fathers*, believing all things which are according to the law and which are written in the prophets; having hope (which is directed) toward God . . . that there shall be a resurrection both of the just and the unjust."

The "forefathers" of our present passage are, in all likelihood, the "fathers" of the passage in Acts. The *service* rendered is the same in both instances.

What Paul stresses, therefore, is that he has not introduced a *new* religion. *Essentially* what he now believes is what Abraham, Isaac, Jacob, Moses, Isaiah, and all the pious ancestors also believed. There is continuity between the old and the new dispensation. The forefathers believed in the resurrection; so does Paul. They looked forward to the coming Messiah; Paul proclaims the same Messiah, who had actually made his appearance. It is *Rome* that has changed its attitude. It is *the government* which, after the burning of its capital in the year 64, has begun to persecute Christians. Paul's conscience is *pure*. *The prisoner* enjoys peace of heart and mind!

Literally Paul writes, "whom I *from* my forefathers serve." He means, "whom I serve with a faith *derived from* my forefathers," that is, with a faith which had its roots in their religion, and is therefore similar to theirs. Hence, the translation, "whom I, like my forefathers, serve," is justified.

By adding, "just as I cherish that constant recollection of you in my prayers by night and by day," Paul is saying that whenever he thinks of Timothy he views him as a man who *likewise* serves the true God with a pure conscience. It is in his *supplications by night and by day* (see on I Tim. 5:5) that the apostle cherishes this ever-recurring recollection of Timothy. These supplications are *accompanied by* (and probably to a certain extent even *caused by*) ardent *longing*: "longing to see you."

For this deep yearning there are two expressed motivations: one comes from within, the other from without. The motivation *from within* is stated in the words, "as I *revive in my memory* (or: recall to mind) [114] your tears."

---

[114] The present passage, verses 3-5, contains *three* different expressions that have to do with *the memory*. Adding verse 6, there are *four*. They should, however, be carefully distinguished, which is not always done (see the various versions and commentaries). Note the following:

a. "I have or cherish the (constant) recollection (of you)" or "I hold (you) in (constant) memory." Thus we would render ἔχω τὴν περὶ σοῦ μνείαν. This corresponds to the Latin: *(continuam tui) memoriam teno*. See N.T.C. on I Thess. 3:6, same idiom. This should not be confused with, "I make mention (of you)." That is the proper translation of μνείαν ὑμῶν ποιοῦμαι; Latin: mentionem facio. See N.T.C. on I Thess. 1:2; also see Rom. 1:9; Eph. 1:16; Philem. 4.

b. "reviving in my memory," or "recalling to mind." The original has μεμνημένος, nom. sing. masc. part. perf. "reflexive," from μιμνήσκω. In the New Testament this verb never occurs in the active voice, always middle or passive. Hence, μιμνήσκομαι; and perfect with present significance: μέμνημι; whence the participle used here. It may be freely translated, "as I revive in my memory," or, "as I recall to mind." Cf. the same middle or reflexive idea in the Dutch: "als ik mij (uw tranen) herin-

II TIMOTHY 1:3-5

It is entirely probable that when Paul and Timothy had parted *for the last time,* the latter had shed tears. Paul himself, no doubt, had done the same thing, but he does not now refer to his own tears but to those of Timothy. This parting was not the one referred to in I Tim. 1:3, but a much later one which in all probability took place after the apostle's return from Spain. See p. 40, not item 4 but item 8. By means of his tears the younger man had shown how wholehearted and genuine was his devotion to Paul, how warm and tender his affection, and how deep and poignant his sorrow at the thought of separation, especially under the circumstances then obtaining. Remember: it was a time of religious persecution; in fact, Paul was about to be captured. The memory of Timothy's loving tears motivated Paul's longing to see him again. The apostle was eager to have his friend come and visit him in his dungeon at Rome.

The motivation *from without* is somewhat obscure. All Paul says is, "having received a reminder of your *unfeigned* (literally: *unhypocritical*) *faith.*" Just how this reminder from without had reached Paul we do not know. Some interpreters are of the opinion that in Rome something had just now happened which had reminded the apostle of Timothy's early faith. Others believe that Paul had received a letter from Timothy. Still others suggest that someone who knew "all about" the younger man's childhood days and subsequent conversion had visited the apostle in prison, and that this friend had recited from memory incidents long past in the life of absent Timothy. Whatever may have been the precise nature of the reminder from without, one fact is certain: as a result of both motivations, the one from within and the other from without, Paul's soul is filled with longing *to see* Timothy.[115]

Paul is convinced that Timothy is no fair-weather believer, but that the faith of this "beloved child" is "the kind" (ἥτις) which first dwelt in his grandmother Lois and in his mother Eunice.

The apostle does not say that Timothy's grandmother and mother had "served God with a pure conscience," but that *faith* had *first* taken up its place of residence in *their* hearts; *afterward* in the heart of *Timothy*. What does he mean here by *faith?* Was it nothing more than "Old Testament Israelitish faith," or was it faith in Jesus Christ, as the fulfilment of the

---

ner." Similarly, the German has the idiom: ". . . wenn *ich mich* recht erinnere" (if my memory serves me right).
  c. "having received a reminder." Thus should be rendered ὑπόμνησιν λαβὼν (τῆς ἐν σοὶ ἀνυποκρίτου πίστεως).
  d. "I remind you." The original has ἀναμιμνήσκω.
[115] See the passage (verses 3-5) as printed on p. 225. As I construe it, a. and c. modify "longing to see you," but b. modifies only the last part of that expression, namely, "to see you." *Seeing* Timothy again, will fill the cup of Paul's joy. For a different view as to the grammatical construction of b. see C. Bouma, *op. cit.,* p. 243.

Old Testament promises? I believe that the latter view has probability on its side:

(1) Acts 16:1 clearly teaches that as soon as Timothy's mother is introduced, at the beginning of the second missionary journey, she is called "a *believing* Jewish woman." That adjective ("believing") is the one which, in a slightly modified sense ("faithful"), is used in the same chapter with respect to *Lydia* (Acts 16:15). That was *after* Lydia's baptism. *Before* that conversion to the Christian faith she was called, "one who worshiped God" (Acts 16:14).

(2) The same chapter also teaches that after the jailer had obeyed the missionaries' exhortation, he is spoken of as a *believer*. (Acts 16:31, 34.)

(3) In Paul's terminology "believers" are those of the old dispensation who trusted in the Christ-centered promises — for example, Abraham — , and those of the new dispensation who accept Christ as the fulfilment of these promises (Rom. 4:12; Gal. 3:9). As far as the new dispensation is concerned, "believers" are *Christians* (II Cor. 6:15). According to Luke, Jews converted to the Christian faith are "believers from among those circumcised" (Acts 10:45).

It would seem, therefore, that, at a date not later than Paul's first missionary journey, grandmother Lois (living, perhaps, with her daughter?) and mother Eunice had been converted, so that they saw in Christ the fulfilment of the promises, and placed their trust in him; and that these two women, in turn, had co-operated with Paul in that glorious work of grace which resulted in Timothy's conversion.

6, 7. On the basis, then, of this faith which dwells in Timothy's heart, just as it had previously established its home within the hearts of Lois and Eunice, Paul is able to continue: **For this reason I remind you to stir into a living flame that gift of God which is within you through the laying on of my hands.**

Paul knew that the fire of Timothy's *charisma* (the gift of God's grace which enabled the younger man to become the apostle's chosen representative) was burning low. Once before, in the earlier letter, the apostle had written, "Do not grow careless about the gift that is within you, which was granted to you by prophetic utterance with the laying on of the hands of the presbytery" (I Tim. 4:14; see on that passage). The repetition, in slightly altered form, of this exhortation is really not surprising. We should bear in mind the following:

a. Timothy was handicapped by frequent physical ailments (I Tim. 5:23).

b. He was naturally timid ("Now if Timothy comes, see to it that he is with you without fear," I Cor. 16:10).

c. He was, in a sense, "a young man" (I Tim. 4:12; cf. II Tim. 2:22).

II TIMOTHY 1:6, 7

d. The Ephesian errorists who opposed him were very determined (I Tim. 1:3-7, 19, 20; 4:6, 7; 6:3-10; II Tim. 2:14-19, 23).

e. Believers were being persecuted by the State. Think of Paul (I Tim. 4:6).

Of course, we do not know whether *all* or only some of these factors contributed to the expressed result, namely, that the flame of Timothy's ministerial office needed attention, nor do we know to what extent each contributed. The main idea, however, is clear. So Paul, having carefully selected the most gentle verb, *reminds* Timothy to "stir (up) into a living flame" the divine gift of ordination. The flame had not gone out, but it was burning slowly and had to be agitated to white heat. The times were serious. Paul was about to depart from the scene of history. Timothy must carry on where Paul was about to leave off. The gift of the Spirit must not be quenched (cf. I Thess. 5:19). Timothy loves Paul. Let Timothy remember, then, that at the time of his ordination *Paul's* hands, too, had rested upon him as a symbol of the impartation of the Spirit's gift!

The ministry is, indeed, the gift of the Holy Spirit, and this is the Spirit *of power* (Acts 1:8; 6:5, 8). Accordingly, Paul continues, **For God gave us not a Spirit of timidity but of power and love and self-discipline.**

In this passage some (in agreement with A.V., A.R.V., R.S.V.) spell Spirit with a small letter ("spirit"), while others capitalize. The former sometimes argue that the descriptive genitive (". . . of power and love and self-discipline") rules out any reference to the Holy Spirit.[116] But the use of such a genitive does not in itself settle the question, for a similar modifier is also used in passages which undoubtedly refer to the Holy Spirit. Thus, Jesus, in speaking about the coming Helper or Comforter, calls him "the Spirit *of truth*" (John 14:17; 15:26; 16:13). There are other similar phrases in which many interpreters find a reference to the Holy Spirit (Is. 11:2; Zech. 12:10; Rom. 8:2; Eph. 1:17; Heb. 10:29). Moreover, the idiom, "not the Spirit of . . . but (the Spirit) of . . ." is used by Paul in other passages which, in the light of their specific contexts, seem to refer to the Holy Spirit, though not every interpreter is ready to grant this (Rom. 8:15; I Cor. 2:12). And besides, do not *charisma* (verse 6) and *pneuma* (verse 7), in the sense of Holy Spirit, go hand in hand?

The gist of Paul's argument, then, would seem to be as follows:

"My dear child, Timothy, fight that tendency of yours toward fearfulness. The Holy Spirit, given to you and me and every believer, is not the Spirit of timidity but of power and love and self-discipline. Avail yourself of that limitless, never-failing *power* (δύναμις cf. our "dynamite"), and you will proclaim God's *truth;* of that intelligent, purposeful *love* (ἀγάπη see N.T.C. on John, Vol. II, pp. 494-501), and you will comfort God's *children,* even to

---

[116] Cf. Lenski, *op. cit.,* p. 755.

the extent of visiting me in my Roman prison; and of that ever-necessary *self-discipline* or *self-control* (σωφρονισμός, note the suffix; hence, *sound-mindedness in action,* a word used only here in the New Testament, see footnote 193), and you will wage God's *battle* against cowardice, taking yourself in hand."

If a person *fears* Satan's persecuting power more than he *trusts* God's ability and ever-readiness to help, he has lost his *mental balance.* Surely, Timothy has not reached that point! Let him then *hold on* to the truth. Let him *cling* to it by *giving it away* . . . as did Lois and Eunice!

---

8 Do not be ashamed, therefore, of the testimony concerning our Lord nor of me his prisoner, but in fellowship with (me) suffer hardship for the gospel, according to (the) power of God, 9 who saved us and called us with a holy calling, not according to *our* works but according to his own purpose and grace, which was given to us in Christ Jesus before times everlasting, 10 but has now been manifested through the appearing of our Savior Christ Jesus, who, on the one hand, utterly defeated death,[117] and, on the other hand, brought to light life and incorruptibility through the gospel, 11 for which I was appointed herald and apostle and teacher.

12 For this reason I am also suffering these things, but I am not ashamed, for I know him in whom I have placed my trust, and I am convinced that he is able to guard with a view to that day that which I have entrusted to him.

13 As a pattern of sound words hold on to those which you have heard *from me,* (and do this) in (the spirit of) faith and love (which center) in Christ Jesus. 14 That precious thing which was entrusted to you guard through the Holy Spirit who dwells within us.

1:8-14

Timothy should think of Lois and Eunice . . . *and of Paul.* The latter thought is stressed in this section (verses 8-14) in which the apostle refers to himself specifically no less than ten times: his willingness to suffer hardship for the gospel, his divine appointment, his trust in God, his stand on doctrine, and his method of proclaiming the message ("in faith and love"). Paul has supplied the "outline," or "rough sketch." Timothy should fill in the details. But in doing this he should be absolutely faithful to the "pattern." He should *hold on* to that which he has received from Paul. Similarly, a minister today should be up-to-date in his preaching. In his *application* he should figure with present-day conditions. But *the truth* which he applies should be the "old-fashioned" doctrine of Scripture, not some "liberal" substitute!

The rather lengthy section may be divided into three paragraphs (verses 8-11; verse 12; verses 13, 14). In the first paragraph the mention of *the*

---

[117] Literally, "the death," that well-known death, in its most comprehensive sense, which is the result of sin.

gospel, for which Paul suffers hardship and for which Timothy should be willing to suffer hardship along with him, leads the apostle to introduce his "beautiful digression" with reference to the work of redemption: *its character, motivation,* and *results.* Here we meet with an interesting style-characteristic, namely, *duadiplosis,* by which is meant that the clauses are joined to one another like overlapping shingles,[118] somewhat as follows:

After saying that Timothy should suffer hardship for the gospel according
    to the power of
GOD, Paul continues:
WHO saved us
        and
      called us with A HOLY CALLING
                NOT (A CALLING) according to our works
                            but
                                according to HIS GRACE
WHICH was given to us in Christ Jesus before times everlasting
        but
      has now been manifested through the appearing
                of OUR SAVIOR CHRIST JESUS
                        WHO on the one hand defeated death
                                and
                              on the other hand brought to light
                              life and incorruptibility through
                              THE GOSPEL
                                FOR WHICH I was appointed. etc.

8. Timothy has no legitimate excuse. The gift of God is within him (verse 7). So Paul continues: **Do not be ashamed, therefore, of the testimony concerning our Lord nor of me his prisoner.** The *testimony "concerning our Lord"* (objective genitive; cf. I Tim. 2:6) is, of course, the gospel, as the very parallelism of the compound clause indicates. "Do not be ashamed of *the testimony* concerning our Lord," is explained by, "But, in fellowship with (me) suffer hardship for *the gospel.*" And cf. Rom. 1:16. In the gospel we find the testimony concerning the works and words of the Lord (John 15:26, 27). Not to be ashamed of the gospel means to be proud of it.

---

[118] Another striking but slightly different type of example is found in the Epistle of James, especially 1:3-6. See my *Bible Survey,* Grand Rapids, Mich., third edition 1953, pp. 329 and 332. The difference is that James carries on the thought by means of the repetition of a word; Paul mostly by means of modifying participles, which can be rendered into English by relative clauses.

1:8   **II TIMOTHY**

Since *Paul* is so intimately associated with the gospel, it does not surprise us to read, "Do not be ashamed of the testimony concerning our Lord *nor of me his prisoner.*" Not *Nero's* prisoner is Paul, though it may seem that way, but "our Lord's." The apostle *always* emphasizes that thought in connection with the idea of being a prisoner (Eph. 3:1; 4:1; Philem. 1, 9). Now, the expression, "his prisoner" does not only mean that it was for the defence of "our Lord's" gospel that Paul had been imprisoned, but also that whatever pertained to his incarceration was entirely safe in the hands of the Sovereign Disposer of destinies.

So, Paul continues: **But in fellowship with (me) suffer hardship for the gospel, according to (the) power of God.** Timothy must be willing *to bear ill treatment* (cf. II Tim. 2:3) *along with* Paul. He must be willing to take his share of persecution; and this not in his own power, which would be impossible, but "according to (the) power of God." That power is infinite. It will enable a person to endure even unto death. It is the power of *that* God:

9. who saved us and called us with a holy calling. The result of the operation of the divine power within all believers (including Paul and Timothy) is characterized here according to a. its nature ("who saved us"), and b. its purpose ("and called us with a holy calling"). What is meant by *saving* us has been explained in detail in connection with I Tim. 1:15; see on that passage. Briefly, God has delivered us from the greatest of all evils and he has placed us in possession of the greatest of all blessings. But in saving us he made us the recipients of *the effective gospel call* (see N.T.C. on I and II Thess., p. 162, footnote 116), which is always "*a holy* calling," for not only does it reveal God's holiness but it is also distinctly a call unto holiness of life, unto a holy task, and unto a condition of everlasting sinlessness and virtue (Eph. 4:1; Phil. 3:14; II Thess. 1:11).

Now as to its *juridical basis* and glorious *motive,* this calling (and, in general, this act of saving us) was **not according to our works but according to his own purpose and grace.** This is the thought which occurs over and over again in Paul's epistles, especially in Romans and Galatians (Rom. 1:17; 3:20-24, 28; 10:5, 9, 13; 11:6; Gal. 2:16; 3:6, 8, 9-14; 6:14, 15; Eph. 2:9; Titus 3:5). Salvation is not based on our accomplishments but on God's sovereign *purpose* (Rom. 8:28; 9:11; Eph. 1:11), his wise (not arbitrary), fixed, and definite plan; and therefore on his *grace* or sovereign favor. And if it be by *grace,* it cannot be by *works.* This is clear from two considerations: a. grace, by virtue of its very nature, is something that is *given* to us, *cannot be earned by* us (though it is, indeed, merited *for* us); and b. grace *precedes* our works, for ideally we were already its objects before time began. Hence, Paul continues: **which was given to us in Christ Jesus before times everlasting** (literally, "before times of ages"). Time,

232

"like an ever-rolling stream," flows *on and on and on*. But *before* it even began we were already included in the gracious purpose of God.[119]

10. This grace which was *given* to us, that is, *designated* for us (cf. Eph. 1:11) "before times everlasting," has *now* been clearly revealed. Hence, Paul continues: **but has now been manifested through the appearing of our Savior Christ Jesus.**

That grace of God which was hidden from before the foundation of the world and was only dimly discerned in the old dispensation "has now been revealed or manifested." The verb *manifested* is of frequent occurrence in the Gospel according to John (see N.T.C., Vol. II, p. 476, especially footnote 294). Paul also uses it several times (Rom. 1:19; I Cor. 4:5; II Cor. 2:14; 11:6; Col. 4:4; Titus 1:3). It was through the *epiphany* or *appearing* (employed everywhere else to designate the Second Coming – II Thess. 2:8; I Tim. 6:14; II Tim. 4:1, 8; Titus 2:13 –, but here to indicate the First Coming), that is, through the *"rising* of the Sun of righteousness with healing in its wings" (Mal. 4:2; cf. Luke 1:78, 79; cf. Titus 2:11), that God's grace toward his people has become manifested. Note the Lord's title: "our Savior Christ Jesus." Cf. Titus 2:13. When one thinks of *grace,* he naturally also thinks of *our Savior,* divinely *anointed by God* (hence, called *Christ,* Anointed One) for the specific task of *saving* (think of the name *Jesus:* "he will certainly save") his people from their sins (Matt. 1:21). By means of that *entire* First Coming of his (from conception to coronation) the grace of God had been revealed. — What Christ did for sinners, in need of grace, is beautifully summarized in the words: **who, on the one hand, utterly defeated death, and, on the other hand, brought to light life and incorruptibility through the gospel.**

In connection with his first coming he *utterly defeated, put out of commission, rendered ineffective* (see N.T.C. on II Thess. 2:8) death. As a result of Christ's Atonement, for the believer *eternal death* no longer exists. *Spiritual death* is vanquished more and more in this life and completely at the moment when the soul departs from its physical enclosure. And *physical death* has been robbed of its curse and has been turned into gain (John 11:26; then Phil. 3:7-14; then I Cor. 15:26, 42-44, 54-57). *That* he did *on the one hand; and on the other hand* he *brought to light* (see N.T.C. on John 1:9) life and incorruptibility. He brought it to light by exhibiting it in his own glorious resurrection; most of all, he brought it to light by means of *his promise;* hence, through *the gospel.* The two concepts "life and incorruptibility" probably constitute a hendiadys; hence, *incorruptible* (or imperishable) *life.*

---

[119] Hence, I cannot agree here with C. Bouma, who, in commenting on this verse (*op. cit.,* p. 255), expresses the view that the expression πρὸ χρόνων αἰωνίων means "immediately after the fall in Paradise." Rom. 16:25 and Titus 1:2, properly interpreted, do not militate against my interpretation. See on Titus 1:2.

1:10   **II TIMOTHY**

This is the *immortality* (cf. I Tim. 1:17) which in the gospel is promised to believers. It transcends by far mere endless existence or even endless conscious existence. The gospel of our Savior Christ Jesus is far better than anything Plato ever excogitated!

It is clear, of course, that though even here and now the believer receives this great blessing *in principle,* and in heaven *in further development,* he does not *fully* receive it until the day of Christ's re-appearance. Until that day arrives, the bodies of all believers will still be subject to the laws of decay and death. *Incorruptible life, imperishable salvation,* in the full sense, belongs to the new heaven and earth. It is an inheritance stored away for us.

11. Reflecting on *the good news* which proclaims this wonderful blessing and which invites men to receive it by faith, Paul continues: **for which I was appointed herald and apostle and teacher.** This is the same thought as expressed in I Tim. 2:7; see on that passage (also on II Tim. 4:2). As a *herald* Paul must announce and loudly proclaim that gospel. As an *apostle* he must say and do nothing except that which he has been commanded to say and to do. And as a *teacher* he must impart carefully instruction in the things pertaining to salvation and the glory of God, and he must admonish unto faith and obedience. For this threefold gospel-task Paul has been *divinely appointed* or *commissioned.*

12. Thus the trend of thought has returned to that of verse 8: Paul's faithfulness to the gospel, as an example for Timothy. Accordingly, the second paragraph of the present section is very personal in character. Says the apostle: **For this reason I am also suffering these things.**

Because of the fulfilment of my assignment as an apostle of Jesus Christ I suffer here in this terrible Roman prison — a dismal underground dungeon with a hole in the ceiling for light and air —, with the prospect of execution as a criminal! **But I am not ashamed.** Though Paul has been subjected to ignominy, he has not disgraced himself. Along **with others,** such as Joseph, Jeremiah, Daniel, John the Baptist, and Peter, he has joined the ranks of prisoners for the best cause. After all, the place of dishonor may be the place of highest honor. Was not Jesus crucified between **two** malefactors? and cf. I Peter 4:16!

The reason why Paul is not ashamed is stated in these memorable words: **For I know him in whom I have placed my trust, and am convinced that he is able to guard with a view to that day that which I have entrusted to him.**

Paul has once for all placed his trust in the sovereign God (see verses 8, 9 above). One might also translate with the A.V., "for I know whom I have believed," i.e., I know God who revealed himself in his precious Son, "our

Savior Christ Jesus" (verse 10). The apostle has become abidingly convinced of God's infinite power, tender love, and absolute faithfulness.

Literally translated, the apostle says, "... and I am convinced that he is able to guard *my deposit* (τὴν παραθήκην μου) with a view to (or unto: εἰς) that day." This leads to the question on which commentators are hopelessly divided: Just what is meant by *my deposit?* Is it "that deposit which he has entrusted to me," or is it "that deposit which I have entrusted to him"?[120] Or, putting it differently, Is it *the gospel* or is it *myself and my complete salvation?*

As I see it, the latter view deserves the preference, for the following reasons:

(1) Clearly, *not Paul but God* (in Christ) *guards* this deposit ("*he* is able to guard"). Hence, the view that it is the deposit which Paul has entrusted to God has probability on its side. In verse 14 (see on that verse) and also in I Tim. 6:20 it is not God but Timothy who must do the guarding. Hence, in *that* case it is the deposit which God has entrusted to (Paul and to) Timothy.

Now if verse 12 has to do with the deposit which Paul has entrusted to God, then the view that the reference is to *my soul* or *my spirit* or *myself and my complete salvation* has logic on its side. Here some commentators favor *my soul;* others, *my salvation.* But the difference is not very important: "myself and my complete salvation" includes both.

(2) The immediate context favors this interpretation. Paul has just written, "I know whom I have believed," meaning, in the light of the clause which follows: "I know that this God in whom I have placed my confidence is dependable, and will certainly keep in perfect safety that which I have entrusted to him for safe-keeping and protection."

(3) The words of verse 10 also support this view. The apostle has just referred to "life and incorruptibility." But, as was noted in the explanation of verse 10, the believer does not *fully* receive this blessing until the day of Christ's glorious Return. Hence, the idea of verse 12 is that this truly immortal life possessed even now *in principle,* and deposited with God for safe-keeping, will be returned to Paul *more gloriously than ever* on "that day," the day of the great consummation (cf. verse 18 below; also II Tim. 4:8; then II Thess. 1:10).

(4) The idea of a treasure that is guarded by God is also found elsewhere; sometimes in a slightly different sense (I Peter 1:4).

---

[120] In favor of the former translation are, among others, the following: A.R.V. margin, R.S.V. text, Dutch (new version); Chrysostom, Gealy (in *Interpreter's Bible*), Koole, Lenski, Phillips, Scott, Van Dyk, Wuest. In favor of the latter are, among others, A.V., A.R.V. text, R.S.V. margin, Goodspeed, Verkuyl (Berkeley Version), Weymouth, Williams, Dutch (old version); and further: Barnes, Bouma, Calvin, Lock, Robertson, Simpson, Van Andel, Van Oosterzee (in Lange's Commentary), White (in *Expositor's Greek Testament*).

1:12　　　　　　　　　　　　**II TIMOTHY**

(5) Cf. the words of our Lord as he died on the cross (Luke 23:46; cf. Ps. 31:5; I Peter 4:19). Christ's spirit, having been *committed* to the Father, is on the third day re-united with the body, now gloriously resurrected.

The arguments of those who defend the opposite view are answered in footnote.[121]

13. Paul has been speaking about himself and his faithful Lord who is going to reward him in the Day of days. Let Timothy, then, copy Paul. Let him fill out the details of the sketch which Paul has outlined. So, in the third brief paragraph (verses 13, 14) of this section (verses 8-14) the author turns once more to the matter of Timothy's duty. Says Paul: **As a pattern of sound words hold on to those which you have heard** *from me,* **(and do this) in (the spirit of) faith and love (which center) in Christ Jesus.**[122]

As an artist has his *sketch* (see on I Tim. 1:16), so Timothy also had his model to go by. This sketch, model, or pattern consisted of the words which he had heard from Paul. Let him hold on to these, ever using them as his example, never departing from them. This is important, for Paul's teaching consisted of *sound* words. Note the emphasis on Paul's teaching (over against that of the Ephesian errorists): literally, "which *from me* you have heard." And it is exactly the necessity of remaining *sound* and of

---

[121] These arguments are as follows:
(1) If *deposit* means *the gospel* in I Tim. 6:20 and in II Tim. 1:14, why not here in II Tim. 1:12?
Answer: Because the "setting" of the word is entirely different. In the other passages *Timothy* is the guard; here in II Tim. 1:12 *God* is the guard. — Besides, a word does not always have the same reference. For example, the apostle has just used the word *appearing* (verse 10) with reference to Christ's *First* Coming, whereas everywhere else he uses it with reference to the *Second* Coming!
(2) The addition of "my" to the word "deposit" does not suffice to change the reference.
Answer: We agree. "My deposit" might conceivably mean either: a. "that which I have deposited," or b. "that which has been deposited with me." But that is neither here nor there. The argument either way should not be based on the word "my."
(3) The reference to "myself and my complete salvation" does not fit the words which follow, namely, "with a view to that day."
Answer: It fits beautifully, as we have shown in the text.

[122] The construction of the sentence is as follows: Subject: *you* (understood). Predicate: *hold on to* or *ever have.* Modifying phrase: *in* (the spirit of) *faith and love.* Hence, "ever have . . . in faith and love." Modifier of "in faith and love": (which center) *in Christ Jesus.* Direct object of the main verb: *those (words) which you have heard from me.* Predicate object in apposition with this direct object: *as a pattern of sound words.* Literal translation: "As a pattern of sound words ever have those which from me you have heard, in faith and love." Here ὧν may be construed as having been "attracted to the case of its antecedent" (so Lenski and many others), but this is not necessarily true. There is no hard and fast rule about the case of the object of ἀκούω, as Robertson has shown. See his *Word Pictures,* Vol. III on Acts 9:7, p. 118.

transmitting *sound* doctrine that is stressed throughout the epistle and, to a certain extent, in all the Pastorals (cf. I Tim. 1:10; 6:3; II Tim. 4:3; Titus 1:9, 13; 2:1, 2, 8). The slogan, so popular today, "It does not matter *what* you believe, just so you are serious in whatever you believe," is flatly contradicted in the Pastorals! Nevertheless, *the spirit* in which one clings to the truth and passes it along to others does matter. Hence, the apostle adds, "(Do this) in faith and love (which center) in Christ Jesus." Faith in God and his redemptive revelation, love toward him and the brotherhood is the spirit in which Timothy must hold on to the true doctrine. That these center "in Christ Jesus" is self-evident. Apart from his merits, his Spirit, and his example, there can be no faith and love.

14. Parallel with the thought just expressed is that contained in verse 14: That precious (or: excellent) thing which was entrusted to you guard through the Holy Spirit who dwells within us.

The "precious deposit" is, of course, *the gospel,* taken in its widest sense (see on I Tim. 6:20). It consists of "the sound words" which Timothy has heard from Paul (see the preceding verse). It is *precious* or *excellent* because it belongs to God and results in his glory through the salvation of those who accept it by sovereign grace (see verses 8-10 above). Again (as in I Tim. 6:20) Timothy is urged once for all to guard this deposit. He must defend it against every attack and never allow it to be changed or modified in the slightest degree.

But since the enemy is strong and Timothy is weak, Paul very wisely adds the thought that this guarding cannot be done except "through the Holy Spirit who dwells within us," that is, within Paul, Timothy, all believers (Rom. 8:11).

Timothy, then, should hold on to the pure gospel, the sound doctrine, as Paul has always done.

---

15 You are aware of this, that **all those in Asia turned away from me,** among whom are Phygelus and Hermogenes. 16 May the Lord grant mercy to the household of Onesiphorus, for he often refreshed me and was not ashamed of my chain. 17 On the contrary, when he was in Rome he diligently searched for me and found me. 18 May the Lord grant him to find mercy from the Lord in that day! And what services he rendered in Ephesus you know better (than I).

1:15-18

15. Timothy should imitate Lois and Eunice. He should also copy the example of Paul. There is one more pattern he should follow, namely, that of Onesiphorus. In every respect this wonderful man was true to the meaning of his name. He was, indeed, a "profit-bringer," a messenger of courage and cheer. The beauty of his character and the nobility of his

1:15 **II TIMOTHY**

actions stand out clearly upon the dark background of the sorry behavior of "all those in Asia."

In view of the fact that Timothy was right now living in the Roman province of Asia, Paul was able to say: **You are aware of this, that all those in Asia turned away from me, among whom are Phygelus and Hermogenes.** It is probable that several leading Christians in the province of which Ephesus was the capital had been asked by Paul to come to Rome in order to appear on the witness-stand in his favor. However, with the possible exception of the one to be mentioned in verses 16-18, no one had complied with the request. In all likelihood fear had held them back. That was true also with respect to two among their number, namely, Phygelus and Hermogenes, known to Timothy but not to us, there being no further reference to them in Scripture. Are these two singled out for special mention because *their* failure to function as "friends in need who are friends indeed" was especially surprising?

16. It would seem, however, that there was *one* significant exception. It must be admitted, however, that it is not even certain that he was one of those to whom Paul *had appealed.* Certain is the fact that he came, whether by request or entirely of his own accord. With warmth and enthusiasm Paul exclaims: **May the Lord grant mercy to the household of Onesiphorus, for he often refreshed me and was not ashamed of my chain.** Onesiphorus had shown mercy to Paul in his dungeon at Rome. Accordingly, may the Lord (Jesus Christ) grant mercy in return! This is in accordance with the rule laid down in Matt. 5:7. But why "to *the household* of Onesiphorus" (both here and in II Tim. 4:19), instead of simply "to Onesiphorus"? Here one can only guess. Some of the possibilities are as follows:

(1) Onesiphorus, having appeared in defence of a prisoner accused of a capital crime and having shown great interest in his case, was himself arrested and imprisoned. Hence, Paul's heart, filled with sympathy for the hero's *family,* utters the wish that the Lord may show mercy to these dear ones.

(2) Paul knows that the departure of Onesiphorus — from Ephesus to Rome — had caused worry to those whom he had left behind, but that they had nevertheless readily consented. Hence, not only Onesiphorus but also his household deserved to be specially mentioned by Paul. Besides, in circumstances that were "trying" for all the members of the family, the Lord's mercy was needed by all.

(3) Onesiphorus was no longer alive (having been executed?). Hence, Paul expresses the wish that the Lord might grant mercy to *his household!* (But if this be true, it would seem somewhat strange that not a word is

mentioned concerning the death of this hero. However, even for that fact — if it was a fact — a reason can be suggested.)

The very enumeration of some of the possibilities indicates that we are here in the realm of conjecture. We just do not know.

Paul states that Onesiphorus had *refreshed* him, *had, as it were, caused him to breathe more easily.* And Onesiphorus had done this not only once but frequently. Just how the visitor had carried out this bracing and cheering ministry is not stated. Perhaps by his very presence, a presence which implied self-sacrifice and love; furthermore, by bringing news to Paul concerning individuals and churches; by encouraging him on the basis of God's promises; by bringing him food, drink, literature. One is reminded of the services which, with great danger to himself, Jonathan rendered to David (I Sam. 18, 19, 20). Even Paul, a man of dauntless courage and amazing faith, could use encouragement at times. That was true also with respect to David, Elijah, Jeremiah, and John the Baptist. It is comforting to know that though the treatment which the apostle received was far less considerate than that which was accorded him during his first imprisonment, the privilege of receiving visitors and "refreshments" had not been completely taken away. Cf. II Tim. 4:13.

The fact that Onesiphorus had not been ashamed of Paul's *chain* filled him with gratitude. In all probability this *chain* must be taken literally; at least the literal meaning must be *included* (cf. Mark 5:3, 4; Luke 8:29; Acts 12:6, 7; 21:33; 28:20; Eph. 6:20; Rev. 20:1). Note in this chapter the meaningful recurrence of the expression "not ashamed." Timothy must not be ashamed (verse 8). Paul is not ashamed (verse 12). Onesiphorus was not ashamed (verse 16). Readiness to suffer, if need be, for the cause of Christ is the mark of the Christian (II Tim. 3:12; then John 16:33; Rom. 8:17).

17. Far from being ashamed, Onesiphorus had conducted himself in the very opposite manner. Hence, Paul says: **On the contrary, when he was in Rome he diligently searched for me and found me!** As soon as Onesiphorus had arrived in Rome he started the search for Paul. But why did he have to *search* for him? Several answers are given, and in some or all of them there is no doubt an element of truth. For example, a. Onesiphorus had never been in Rome; hence, did not know his way around. b. Part of the city had been destroyed by the great fire. This caused confusion. c. For a while the place of Paul's imprisonment was not known even to believers in Rome. d. Believers in Rome had been greatly reduced in numbers due to persecution and flight, and not even all who were left were eager to disclose "to a stranger" their spiritual affinity with "the prisoner of the Lord." And so one could continue. However that may be, it required *diligent* searching to find Paul. The words, "and he found me" sound like an exclamation.

Having located the "prison," it may not have been easy for Onesiphorus to gain immediate access to Paul. The present imprisonment was grim (cf. II Tim. 1:9). All the more credit to Onesiphorus! Hence, Paul continues:

18. May the Lord grant him to find mercy from the Lord in that day!

The apostle utters a devout wish that *on the great day of judgment* (see verse 12 above; cf. II Tim. 4:8; then II Thess. 1:10) the Lord (Jesus Christ) may grant that the man who had gone to a great deal of trouble to *find* Paul may, in turn, *find* mercy (note wordplay), and this "from the Lord," which probably means, "from God the Father." [123]

Does the fact that Paul expresses the wish that Onesiphorus may find mercy "in that day" (contrast what is said about *the household* of Onesiphorus, verse 16) mean that this true and loyal friend had already departed from this earth, so that he could no longer receive mercy in *this* life? It is possible, but in view of the fact that the apostle does at times express the wish that eschatological blessings be granted to those who, while the apostle is writing, are still living on earth (for example, I Thess. 5:23b), the conclusion that Onesiphorus had actually died is not necessary. Here again we must confess our ignorance.

In reviewing the services which Onesiphorus had rendered, Paul begins with the most recent ones ("he often refreshed me," verse 16), then moves back the clock of his memory ("when he was in Rome he diligently searched for me and found me!" verse 17), and now (verse 18b) moves it back still farther: **And what services he rendered in Ephesus you know better (than I).**[124] Even before he went on his mission to Rome, Onesiphorus, still in Ephesus, had rendered many valued services to the cause of the gospel. This labor of love had been performed under the very eyes of Timothy. Hence, Paul says, "You know better than I."

Timothy, then, should show similar stedfastness, loyalty, and courage!

---

[123] I cannot follow Lenski's reasoning here (*op. cit.,* p. 775). If Paul had meant to say, "May the Lord grant unto *him* (Onesiphorus) to find mercy from the Lord in that day," with "Lord" referring to Jesus Christ in both cases, he could very well have substituted "from *him*" for "from *the Lord.*" This substitution of a pronoun (this time in a different case than a moment before) would not have been ambiguous. Onesiphorus certainly could not find mercy "from *himself.*" The true antecedent, namely, "Lord" (Jesus Christ) would have been obvious.

[124] For *better* the original has βέλτιον. Cf. τάχιον in the sense of "faster" (John 13:27; 20:4). Nevertheless, the elative use of βέλτιον here in II Tim. 1:18 (see also Acts 10:28 in D) cannot be entirely ruled out. Timothy knows "very well" what services Onesiphorus had rendered in Ephesus. See also M.M., 1. 108.

Synthesis of Chapter 1

See the Outline at the beginning of the chapter.

After another "grace, mercy, and peace" salutation, Paul acknowledges gratitude to the God of the forefathers who is also Paul's and Timothy's God. He tells his "beloved child" that his heart yearns to be filled with the joy of seeing him again; and that this yearning has been strengthened by the memory of the latter's tears shed when the two last separated, and by a recent reminder of his unfeigned faith in Christ.

As to that *faith,* Paul "recognizes" it, for he has seen it first in Timothy's grandmother *Lois* and mother *Eunice.* Let *Timothy* then cling to it as *they* had done. Yes, let him stir into a living flame the divine gift which he had received. Does Timothy love Paul? Of course, he does. Let him then bear in mind that at the time of his ordination *Paul's* hands, too, had rested upon him, as a symbol of the impartation of the gift of the Spirit; and that the latter is the Spirit not of timidity but of power and love and self-discipline.

Let Timothy then hold on to his faith as *Paul* had done and is still doing. Let him never be ashamed of the gospel, nor of "the Lord's prisoner" (note: *not* "Nero's prisoner"!), as the writer calls himself.

For the sake of the gospel Timothy must be willing to bear ill treatment along with Paul. God's infinite power will sustain him, for it was this very God who had included both Paul and Timothy (along with all the chosen ones) in his gracious purpose from eternity. Their salvation, the precious treasure which through the effective gospel-call has become their possession, can never be taken away from them. Reason: it rests not on *human works* but on *divine grace.* And this grace "was given to us in Christ Jesus before times everlasting, but has now been displayed through the appearing (First Coming) of our Savior Christ Jesus." And for his own comfort and strengthening, Timothy should bear in mind that it was this very Christ who on the one hand utterly defeated *death,* and, on the other hand, brought to light *life and incorruptibility* through the gospel. Let Timothy then look forward with joy to the prospect of one day entering upon the possession of this incorruptible life for both soul and body. Paul himself rejoices in the fact that with respect to the good news he has been appointed herald and apostle and teacher. To be sure, loyalty to such a commission results in suffering. Reflecting on this, Paul exclaims, "But I am not ashamed, for I know whom I have believed . . ." Prof. E. K. Simpson writes (*op. cit.,* p. 127) that when Dr. James Alexander of Princeton lay on his death-bed, his wife quoted these words inexactly — "I know *in* whom I have believed" — ; and that the dying man then gently corrected her version, because he was unwilling to let even a preposition creep between his soul and his Savior.

Paul continues, "and am convinced that he is able to guard with a view to that day that which I have entrusted to him." The apostle has deposited his soul and his complete salvation with God for safe-keeping. In that respect, too, he was following the example of Jesus who committed his spirit into the Father's hands (Luke 23:46). On the third day the deposit was returned to Jesus, as it were "with interest": a glorious spirit housed in a now glorious body. So, too, on *that* great day, namely, the day of the final judgment, Paul's soul, having been kept in safety in the Father's mansions above, would be clothed with a body like unto Christ's glorious body. Immortal life, in its full meaning (that is, for both body and soul) would take over from then on.

Encouraged by the certainty of a future so glorious, let Timothy then *hold on* to the pattern of sound words which Paul has given him; and let him do it in the spirit of faith and love centering in Christ Jesus. Yes, let him once for all guard the precious deposit of the gospel-ministry which God has left with him. The indwelling Holy Spirit will qualify him.

Another excellent example for Timothy to copy is *Onesiphorus*. When the apostle thinks of him, he exclaims, "May the Lord grant mercy to his house," and a little later, "May the Lord grant him to find mercy from the Lord in that day." When all those in Asia turned away from Paul, no one — not even Phygelus and Hermogenes — being willing to come to Rome in order to appear on the witness-stand in his favor, Onesiphorus had come, perhaps even before being asked. In various ways he had often refreshed Paul, not being ashamed of the apostle's chain. On arriving in Rome, Onesiphorus had searched for the prisoner and after considerable difficulty had found him. And even before starting out for Rome from Ephesus, this wonderful "profit-bringer" had rendered many valuable services to the gospel, as Timothy, in Ephesus, knew even better than Paul.

Outline of Chapter 2

Theme: *The Apostle Paul Tells Timothy What To Do in the Interest of Sound Doctrine*

   Teach It   "Suffer hardship along with (us)"

2:1-13 Though this teaching brings hardship, it also brings great reward.

2:14-26 Vain disputes, on the contrary, serve no useful purpose.

CHAPTER II

II TIMOTHY 2:1, 2

2 1 You then, my child, be strengthened in the grace (that is) in Christ Jesus; 2 and the things which you have heard from me among many witnesses, these things entrust to reliable men, such as will be qualified to teach others as well. 3 As a noble soldier of Christ Jesus suffer hardship along with (us). 4 No soldier on active duty gets himself entangled in the business-pursuits of civilian life, since his aim is to please the officer who enlisted him. 5 Again, if anyone is competing in an athletic event, he does not receive the victor's wreath unless he competes in compliance with the rules. 6 The hard-working farmer should be the first one to take his share of the crops. 7 Put your mind on what I say, for the Lord will give you understanding in all matters. 8 Keep in memory Jesus Christ as raised from the dead, of the seed of David, according to my gospel, 9 for which I suffer hardship even to bonds as an evil-doer; but the word of God is not bound. 10 On account of this I endure all things for the sake of the elect, in order that also they may obtain the salvation (which is) in Christ Jesus with everlasting glory.

11 Reliable is the saying:
For if we have died with (him), we shall also live with (him);
12 if we endure, we shall also reign with (him);
if we shall deny (him), he on his part will also deny us;
13 if we are faithless, he on his part remains faithful,
for to deny himself he is not able.

2:1-13

1, 2. You then, my child, be strengthened in the grace (that is) in Christ Jesus; and the things which you have heard from me among many witnesses, these things entrust to reliable men, such as will be qualified to teach others as well.

In view then of all that has been said in chapter 1 — the examples of faith and stedfastness (Lois and Eunice, Paul himself, Onesiphorus), the Holy Spirit's gift to Timothy, the great salvation that awaits him who perseveres, the wonderful calling — let Timothy *be strengthened* (cf. II Tim. 1:6-8, 14; and for the word itself see Acts 9:22; I Tim. 1:12; II Tim. 4:17, then Rom. 4:20; Eph. 6:10; Phil. 4:13) in that Christ-centered grace which, as was pointed out, had been given to him "before times everlasting" (see on II Tim. 1:9). Timothy's strength in the sphere of grace will grow if he culti-

2:1, 2   II TIMOTHY

vates *the gift* which grace has bestowed on him. The appeal is again couched in the language of the tender affection of a father for his son; note the emphasis *"you* then," and the appeal to *the heart,* "my child" (see on II Tim. 1:2). What the (spiritual) father (Paul) wants the child (Timothy) to do is found in verses 1-7. What the father, as the child's example, is doing is described in verses 8-10a. What *all believers* should constantly remember with respect to the manner in which faithfulness to Christ is rewarded, and unfaithfulness punished, is stated most clearly in verses 10b-13, and is already implied in verses 4-6.

Now, *one* sure way of being strengthened in grace is to transmit to others the truths which have embedded themselves in one's heart and have become enshrined in the memory. Accordingly, let Timothy be a teacher. Even more, let him produce teachers! Timothy needs this experience, and what is far more important, the church needs the teachers! Paul is about to depart from this life. He has carried the gospel-torch long enough. Hence, he hands it to Timothy, who, in turn, must pass it on to others. The *deposit* which was entrusted to Timothy (I Tim. 6:20; II Tim. 1:14) must be deposited with *trustworthy* men. They must be men, moreover, who will be *qualified to teach* others (cf. I Tim. 3:2), so that these others *as well* as their teachers will have been instructed in God's redemptive truth.

This redemptive truth or gospel of salvation, which Timothy is asked to transmit, is here described as "the things which you have heard from me among many witnesses." This expression undoubtedly refers to the entire series of sermons and lessons which the disciple had heard from the mouth of his teacher during all their association from the day when they first met.

Many had been *the witnesses* [125] of this preaching and teaching. Let Timothy bear in mind that the message which he has heard from the mouth

---

[125] The word used in the original has various shades of meaning. The exact connotation is sometimes difficult to determine. At times not much more than *a spectator and/or auditor* seems to be meant; one, however, who is able, if he so desires, to give competent testimony (cf. I Tim. 6:12). Then again, the idea of *actually giving testimony* of that which one has seen and/or heard seems to be reached. Similarly, in our own language a "witness" may be a. a person who is competent to give testimony whether or not he does it, or b. a person who actually gives testimony. In the present passage (II Tim. 2:2) the latter is probably the sense in which the word is used. The *witnesses* of whom Paul speaks were not merely silent observers and listeners. They were obedient to the exhortation, "Let the redeemed of Jehovah *say* so." It is easy to see how the legal sense in which the term *witness* is used is related to this meaning (see Acts 6:13; 7:58). Finally, the word may signify a *martyr* (see also N.T.C. on John, Vol. I, p. 7), one who has sealed his testimony with his blood. Thus, for example, Stephen and Antipas were *martyrs.* Nevertheless, even when these are called μάρτυροι, the question is debatable: In Acts 22:20 and Rev. 2:13 should we choose as English equivalent the word *witness* or *martyr?* Often, as in their case, the faithful *witnesses* became *martyrs.* This also applies to the *witnesses* mentioned in Rev. 11:3; see verse 7; and in Rev. 17:6.

of Paul had been given *among* or *in the midst of* [126] many persons who were ever ready *to lend their support* to the apostle's testimony.

3. The business of entrusting the gospel to reliable men (and, in fact, the gospel-ministry in general) entails *hardship* (verse 3). Yet, when a man fights wholeheartedly for the good cause, competes according to the rules, and works energetically, he will receive a glorious reward (verses 4-6; cf. 10b-13).

Says Paul: **As a noble soldier of Christ Jesus, suffer hardship along with (us).**

Timothy, then, as a *noble* or *excellent soldier* of Christ Jesus, belonging to him and engaged in that warfare in which "the cross of Jesus" is ever "going on before," must not shrink back but must be willing to *suffer hardship* (see on II Tim. 1:8; 2:9), which in this connection means even more than to "rough it" as soldiers do. It implies *suffering persecution* (II Tim. 3:12). He must be willing to endure this, says Paul, "along with. . . ." The question arises: along with *whom?* In view of the fact that in the preceding verse Paul has just referred to himself and the many witnesses, it is best to translate: "along with *us*," and not "along with *me*," as in II Tim. 1:8.[127]

4, 5, 6. These verses contain a threefold figure, beginning with the soldier-simile, continued from verse 3. The three illustrations clearly belong together, and must be seen as a unit in order to be understood:

(a) **No soldier on active duty gets himself entangled in the business-pursuits of civilian life,**[128] **since his aim is to please the officer who enlisted him.**

---

[126] I cannot follow Gealy (*The Interpreter's Bible*, Vol. II, pp. 478, 479) on this passage. Certainly διά does not have to mean *through*. The meaning *among* or *in the midst of* is easily accounted for. The preposition seems to have been derived from the number *two* (cf. δύο and διά). From this it developed into *be-tween* ("by two's"), which, slightly modified in meaning, easily slides into *among* or *in the midst of* (and by a different semantic shift, into *through*). Cf. the use of διά in II Cor. 2:4. In this connection it should be noted that the meaning *in the midst of* is not only "late Greek," as is sometimes maintained. Homer already uses the preposition in that sense (*Iliad* IX, 468; *Odyssey* IX, 298). — In this note I have indicated only a few semantic shifts. It is high time that more intensive study be devoted to the origin and evolution of New Testament prepositions. I have tried to do this with respect to ἀντί. See my doctoral thesis *The Meaning of the Preposition ἀντί in the New Testament*, Princeton Seminary Library. For διά what is found in Gram. N.T., pp. 580-584 is a good *beginning*.
[127] A.V., "endure hardness" rests on an inferior reading. A.R.V., "Suffer hardship with *me*," adds the wrong pronoun. The context favors *us*. Another translation (R.S.V. and others), "Take your share of suffering," though somewhat less literal, is good.
[128] This, by necessity, is a somewhat free translation. Literally the passage reads: "No one soldiering entangles himself (or "gets entangled") in the business-pursuits

2:4, 5, 6 **II TIMOTHY**

(b) **Again, if anyone is competing in an athletic event, he does not receive the victor's wreath unless he competes in compliance with the rules.**

(c) **The hard-working farmer should be the first to take his share of the crops.**

Paul compares the Christian minister (here with particular reference to Timothy, but cf. Phil. 2:25; Philem. 2) to a soldier, an athlete, and a farmer. I Cor. 9:6, 7, 24-27 presents the same threefold figure but with a different application. The resemblance, here in II Tim. 2, is as follows:

a. First, like a soldier on active duty, perhaps even engaged in a campaign, Timothy must perform his task *wholeheartedly.* If a soldiering person should pursue a business on the side, one that would really absorb his interests, so that he becomes "implicated" in it, he would not be able to really "give" himself to his appointed task as a soldier.[129]

The soldier in the field has just *one* purpose, namely, to satisfy the officer who enlisted him. Similarly, Timothy — and, for that matter, any "minister" — must realize that his exalted task "demands his soul, his life, his all." *One* holy passion must fill his frame. He must devote himself completely to his Lord who appointed ("enlisted") and qualified him for his task. Every true and faithful servant of Christ Jesus will *actually* devote himself thus wholeheartedly to his task, in order *to please* his Master (cf. I Cor. 7:32-34; cf. I John 3:22; and see N.T. on I Thess. 2:4). "No enlisted soldier," says Paul, will do differently!

The thought is implied: by way of reward, Timothy's Superior will surely provide for him! That implied thought is expressed with increasing clarity in the figures which follow:

b. *Wholehearted devotion* is not all that is required. *Rules* must be obeyed. In this respect the best figure is always that of a man who is competing in an athletic event. Paul pictures him in the very act of competing.[130] Now, unless such an athlete (for a fuller description see on I Tim.

(or, "in the affairs") of the βίος." M.M., p. 532, shows that πραγματεία may have either the more restricted meaning "business which provides a livelihood," or the wider meaning "matter," "affair." The word βίος may have one of several meanings depending on the context: mode of life, livelihood, the world we live in, biography, settled or civilian life, etc. Here in II Tim. 2:4 the context seems to draw a contrast between military and civilian life; hence, the rendering *civilian life* seems best. It is either that or "livelihood." In the latter case the entire phrase would be, "business of making a livelihood."

[129] It is true that Paul made tents, but this was not a business-pursuit in which he was engaged in order to *establish* himself financially. His heart was in his one, great endeavor. In order to gain the best results for Christ and his kingdom, he made good tents. See N.T.C. on I and II Thessalonians, p. 66.

[130] With respect to the grammatical implications of the tenses in this sentence, I beg to differ (respectfully, of course!) with two authorities: First, I do not believe that the present active subjunctive (ἀθλῇ) necessarily implies that the apostle has in mind *a professional athlete.* It is true that he *may* have been thinking of such

4:7b, 8) competes *lawfully,* that is, in accordance with the established rules, he does not receive *the victor's wreath,* the chaplet of leaves or of leaflike gold. Similarly, unless the man who performs special service in God's kingdom observes the rules — for example, to preach and teach *the truth,* and to do this in *love;* to exercise discipline in the same spirit; and see especially verses 10-12 below —, he will not receive the wreath of righteousness (II Tim. 4:8) and of glory (I Thess. 2:19; cf. I Peter 5:4; James 1:12; Rev. 2:10; see A. Deissmann, *op. cit.,* pp. 309, 369).

c. Timothy, then, must *fight wholeheartedly* for the good cause. He must also *compete according to the rules.* And now, thirdly: *he must toil energetically,* like *the* (generic use of the article) hard-working farmer (cf. I Cor. 3:9). He must be the very opposite of the "sluggard" pictured vividly in Prov. 20:4; 24:30, 31. If the farmer works hard, he should be the first to take his share of the crops (Deut. 20:6; Prov. 27:18). Similarly, if Timothy (or any worker in God's vineyard) exerts himself to the full in the performance of his God-given spiritual task, he, too, will be the first to be rewarded. Not only will *his own* faith be strengthened, his hope quickened, his love deepened, and the flame of his gift enlivened, so that he will be blessed "in his doing" (James 1:25), but in addition he will see in the lives of *others* (Rom. 1:13; Phil. 1:22, 24) the beginnings of those glorious fruits that are mentioned in Gal. 5:22, 23. See also Dan. 12:3; Luke 15:10; James 5:19, 20.

7. Put your mind on what I say, for the Lord will give you understanding in all matters.

Since several beautiful thoughts had been compressed into a terse threefold figure, and no explanation had been furnished, Timothy is told to *put his mind on* (νόει present, active imperative of νοέω; cf. νοῦς *mind*) that which [131] Paul has just said (in verses 4, 5, 6). Mere *reading* is not enough. What has been written must be *pondered.* What has been spoken must be *digested* (cf. Matt. 11:29; 13:51; 15:17; 16:9, 11; I Cor. 10:15; and especially Rev. 10:9, 10). Timothy need not fear that such mental activity will be fruitless. Has not the Lord given his definite promise? See Luke 19:26; John 14:26; 16:13. Surely in all matters with respect to which Timothy is

---

a person, but the present tense could also be used of anyone else. It simply pictures the action as *in progress.* For the opposite view see Bouma, *op. cit.,* p. 273.

Secondly, I do not believe that the first aorist active subjunctive (ἀθλήσῃ) necessarily means, "unless in a particular contest he contends," as A. T. Robertson maintains (*Word Pictures,* Vol. IV, p. 617). The aorist tense simply summarizes the action, takes a snapshot of it, instead of picturing it as being in progress. It is only fair to add that elsewhere Robertson himself states this; see Gram. N.T., p. 832.

[131] The textual apparatus in N.N. clearly indicates that ὅ is to be preferred here to ἅ. It also shows that "will give" (δώσει) is the best reading. It is not difficult, moreover, to account for the variants.

in need of understanding (σύνεσις, comprehension, insight), it will be given to him if he will but apply himself. Let Timothy then compare a scripture with scripture. Let him pray for wisdom (James 1:5). Let him reflect on his own past experience and the experience of other children of God. Let him listen to what these others have to say. By such means as these the Holy Spirit will give him all the guidance he will need in the performance of his task. He will be able to apply to himself and his office the rich meaning of the threefold figure, and he will derive from it the comfort which it affords.

8. In view of raging persecution, comfort was certainly needed. Faithful adherence to duty meant hardship (verses 3-6). Let Timothy not lose courage. Let him not even fear death. Let him rest his confidence on One who "utterly defeated" this terrible enemy (II Tim. 1:10). Accordingly, Paul continues, **Keep in memory Jesus Christ as raised from the dead, of the seed of David, according to my gospel.**

Note here "Jesus Christ," instead of "Christ Jesus" as elsewhere in II Timothy. If this be more than a stylistic variation, the possible reason for it may well have been this, that the apostle wished to turn Timothy's attention first of all to the historical, curse-laden *Jesus* (Gal. 3:13; 4:4, 5), in order that next he may remind him of the fact that this Jesus "was made" (was openly revealed as) *Christ* as a reward for his obedience unto death, yea the death of the cross (Acts 2:36; Phil. 2:5-11; see also footnote 19). Let Timothy then rivet his attention upon the resurrection; nay rather, let him keep his thought concentrated on *the resurrected Lord himself.* "Keep in memory Jesus Christ as raised from the dead," says Paul. Having been raised once for all from the realm in which death reigns, Jesus Christ now remains forever the risen One; hence, the living One (Rev. 1:17, 18). Co-ordinated with this exhortation is the one: "Keep in memory Jesus Christ as the seed of David." This follows very naturally; for, *the risen One* is surely also *the reigning One!* (cf. Matt. 28:18; I Cor. 15:20-25; Heb. 2:9; Rev. 22:1-5). Notice how also in verses 11 and 12 *living* and *reigning* follow one another.

Jesus Christ is "of the seed of David" (II Sam. 7:12, 13; Ps. 89:28; 132:17; Acts 2:30; Rom. 1:3; Rev. 5:5; and cf. Matt. 1:20; Luke 1:27, 32, 33; 2:4, 5; John 7:42).[132] He is "the Son of David" (Matt. 1:1; 9:27; 12:23; 15:22; 20:30, 31; 21:9, 15; 22:42-45; Mark 10:47, 48; 12:35; Luke 18:38, 39; 20:41). It is as the rightful, spiritual heir of David, David's glorious Antitype, that he sits enthroned at the Father's right hand.

The implied comfort is: "Timothy, if you and I and all other believers have died with him, we shall also *live with him.* If we endure, we shall

---

[132] I have discussed the genealogical problem with respect to the Davidic origin of Christ's human nature, in my *Bible Survey*, pp. 135-139.

also *reign with him."* What is *implied* here is *expressed* in verses 11 and 12.

More than this, however, is implied, namely, "Timothy, constantly remember that, as living and reigning Lord, Jesus Christ is able as well as willing to help you and to carry you through. Not Nero but Jesus Christ, exalted at the right hand of the Father, has the reins of the universe in his hands and will continue to govern all things in the interest of the church and unto the glory of God. Hence, whatever happens, never lose courage. We know that to them that love God all things work together for good."

Now this presentation of Jesus Christ as the ever-living and reigning One is "according to (or "in harmony with") my gospel," says Paul. It was *Paul's* gospel, for: a. he had received it by immediate revelation (Gal. 1:12); b. he continues to proclaim it even in this letter, for he had been appointed its herald, apostle, and teacher (II Tim. 1:11); and c. he still clings to it with his whole heart, even now that he is facing death.

9. Exactly as in II Tim. 1:10-12, so also here the mention of Paul's *gospel,* is immediately followed by a statement about his *suffering.* Says Paul, **for which I suffer hardship even to bonds as an evil-doer.** Note in the preceding chapter "suffering" (verse 12), here "suffer hardship" (cf. II Tim. 1:8). The hardship which Paul is now suffering extends "even to bonds as an evil-doer." The rendering "bonds" (A.V., A.R.V.) has the same flexibility of meaning as has the word used in the original. It may refer to literal *shackles, chains,* or *fetters* (Luke 13:16; Acts 16:26); but also to all the hardship of *imprisonment* (Acts 20:23; 23:29; 26:31; Col. 4:18; Philem. 10, 13). Paul generally uses it in the latter, more general, sense. Nevertheless, the "chain" is certainly *included* in the meaning of the term (II Tim. 1:16), as used here. It would have been impossible for the apostle not to think of it!

"Even to bonds as an evil-doer," says Paul. "Evil-doer" (or "evil-worker," *"malefactor"*) is a good, literal translation. A free rendering would be *criminal.* One thinks immediately of the "malefactors" who were crucified with Jesus (Luke 25:32, 33). This second imprisonment of Paul must have been very harsh!

However, in the midst of all his suffering and shame, there were two considerations which afforded him much comfort: First, "The way of the cross leads home," for the watchful eye of Jesus Christ who lives and leads is constantly upon me. He is able to guard my deposit with a view to that day (II Tim. 1:12). Secondly, Though I am bound, **the word of God is not bound.** Others will carry on when I leave this earthly scene. The authorities have put *me* in this dungeon, but they cannot imprison *the gospel.* It will triumph. It will perform its pre-ordained mission on earth. No enemy can thwart it. See the beautiful commentary which Scripture

2:9 **II TIMOTHY**

itself supplies in such well-known passages as Is. 40:8; 55:11; Phil. 1:12-14; and II Tim. 4:17.

One is reminded of Luther's immortal hymn *Ein feste Burg ist unser Gott*, the last two stanzas:

The German:	Translation by Thomas C. Porter:
Und wenn die Welt voll Teufel wär'	Did devils fill the earth and air,
Und wollt uns gar verschlingen,	All eager to devour us,
So fürchten wir uns nicht zu sehr	Our steadfast hearts need feel no care,
Es soll uns doch gelingen.	Lest they should overpower us.
Der Fürst dieser Welt,	The grim Prince of hell,
Wie sau'r er sich stellt,	With rage though he swell,
Thut er uns doch nichts;	Hurts us not a whit,
Das macht, er ist gerecht't;	Because his doom is writ:
Ein Wörtlein kann ihn fällen.	A little word can rout him.
Das Wort sie sollen lassen stan	The Word of God will never yield
Und kein'n Dank dazu haben.	To any creature living;
Er ist bei uns wohl auf dem Plan	He stands with us upon the field,
Mit seinem Geist und Gaben	His grace and Spirit giving.
Nehmen sie den Leib,	Take they child and wife,
Gut, Ehr', Kind und Weib;	Goods, name, fame, and life,
Lass fahren dahin,	Though all this be done,
Sie haben's kein'n Gewinn;	Yet have they nothing won:
Das Reich muss uns doch bleiben.	The kingdom still remaineth.

10. The triumph of the gospel causes Paul to continue with these courageous words, **On account of this I endure all things for the sake of the elect.** Even more literally one might translate: "*On account of* (διά) this I endure all things *on account of* (again διά) the elect." *On account of* the fact that the word is not bound, Paul does not lose courage but perseveres in faith and witness-bearing even in the midst of bitter trial. And this all the more *on account of* the elect, that they may obtain salvation. The two considerations which cause him to continue stedfastly in the course which he is pursuing are really *one:* the glorious and deeply-rooted conviction that the word of God will certainly triumph in the lives and destinies of the elect! Though Paul is in this dungeon, he does not despair. Victory is written on his banner.

The apostle endures *all things*, that is, all his manifold trials, for the sake of the gospel (cf. II Cor. 11:16-33; cf. Rom. 8:35-39; note "all these things," Rom. 8:37). He *endures* them, that is, he exercises the bravery of *bearing up under* them, the courage of positive perseverance and stedfastness even then when all things seem to be against him (cf. I Cor. 13:7). *To endure*

252

means more than *not to complain*. It means more than *acquiescence*. It means going right ahead (believing, testifying, exhorting) though the load under which one is traveling on life's pathway has become very heavy. See further N.T.C. on I and II Thess. pp. 49, 50.

The apostle, then, endures all things "for the sake of the elect." (For a summary of Paul's doctrine of election see N.T.C. on I and II Thessalonians, pp. 49, 50. Cf. N.T.C. on John, Vol. II, p. 307.) *These elect are those on whom God has set his peculiar love from eternity.* Cf. Col. 3:12. They are the objects of his sovereign goodpleasure, chosen not because of their foreseen goodness or faith but because God so willed. It was not man's faith which caused election; but election which caused man's faith. If anyone wishes to see this for himself he should read such passages as the following: Deut. 7:7, 8; Is. 48:11; Dan. 9:19; Hos. 14:4; John 6:37, 39, 44; 10:29; 12:32; 17:2; Rom. 5:8; 9:11-13; I Cor. 1:27, 28; 4:7; Eph. 1:4; 2:8; I John 4:10, 19.

These references clearly teach that God did not choose his own because they are more numerous, but *for his own sake;* that he loves them *freely;* that they are *given* to the Son by the Father, *drawn* by the Father and the Son; and that with respect to them God exercises *his own* very unique kind of love. They teach that this predestinating love has as its objects *sinners,* viewed in all their foolishness and weakness; that it bestows its favor on those who have *nothing* and will never have anything except what they *receive;* on those who differ from other people for the simple reason that God in effectuating his decree of election *causes them to differ;* on those who, far from being chosen on account of their unblemished character, are chosen *in order that they may be* without blemish and unspotted before him; yes, *on those who will love him because he first loved them!*

Instead of *condemning* this doctrine, a person should first of all prove that it is not scriptural! It fits beautifully into the present context. Paul courageously endures all things because he knows that the word of God will certainly triumph in the hearts and lives of the elect. Cf. Eph. 3:13; Phil. 2:17. If it were true that their salvation had its deepest root in *their own works,* would the apostle have been able to face death with such fortitude? [133]

But even though for the elect, salvation is certain from all eternity, *it must be obtained.* The scriptural doctrine of election, far from putting

---

[133] Lenski, *op. cit.,* p. 791, in connection with the present passage, assails the Calvinistic doctrine. It is to be commended in him that he shows where he stands. But he does not furnish proof that this doctrine is unscriptural. Besides, if his attack on the Calvinistic position means that the Calvinist fails to point out that believers "should make their calling and election sure (II Peter 1:10)," then we answer that this is a point which the well-balanced Calvinist *emphasizes.* See L. Berkhof (surely a Calvinist!), *The Assurance Of Faith,* Grand Rapids, Mich. 1928, the whole book!

any restrictions on the exercise of human freedom, points to the One who makes man free indeed! The God who in his sovereign love chooses a person, in time powerfully influences his will, illumines his mind, floods his heart with love in return for God's love, so that these "faculties," under the constant guidance of the Holy Spirit, begin to function to God's glory in their own right. The decree of election includes the means as well as the end. God chose his people to salvation "through sanctification by the Spirit and belief in the truth." And to this salvation they are "called through our gospel" (see N.T.C. on II Thess. 2:13, 14).

Hence, the apostle, here as so often combining the divine decree and human responsibility, continues, **in order that also they may obtain the salvation (which is) in Christ Jesus with everlasting glory.**

Paul is interested not only in his own salvation (II Tim. 1:12) but *also* in that of others, namely, in the salvation of those who even now (while he is writing) are believers in Christ, and those who will afterward be brought to believe. He endures in order that *also they* may obtain that salvation which was merited by Christ, proclaimed by him, and experienced in living communion with him (hence, "the salvation *in* — or *centering in* — Christ Jesus"). He has in mind nothing less than *full salvation*. (For the meaning of *salvation* see on I Tim. 1:15.) Though believers even in this life enjoy salvation *in principle* (II Tim. 1:9; cf. Luke 19:9), they will not receive it in perfection (for both body and soul) until the great day of the consummation of all things (see on II Tim. 1:10-12; cf. Rom. 13:11). And this word *salvation* has two modifiers: a. it is a salvation "in Christ Jesus," as already explained; and b. it is a salvation "with everlasting glory" (Col. 1:27; 3:4). The second follows from the first. Union with Christ Jesus makes one *radiant,* both as to the *soul* (as explained in II Cor. 3:18) and as to the *body* (as set forth in Phil. 3:21). And this glory, in connection with the eternal One, never ends (John 3:16). Both in quality and in duration it differs from earthly glory.

11-13. Accordingly, Paul is willing to endure *all things* — hardship even to bonds, with the prospect of death — in order that through his stedfast ministry the elect may obtain their full, everlasting, Christ-centered salvation (see verses 3, 9, 10). It is necessary to keep this connection in mind. Otherwise what follows may be misinterpreted.

In harmony with what the apostle has just stated, he now introduces the fourth of five "reliable sayings" (see on I Tim. 1:15). The opinion that the lines which he quotes were taken from an early Christian hymn, a cross-bearer's or martyr's hymn, is probably correct. It is evident that he does not quote the entire hymn (unless γάρ here is not "for"; but in the present case "for" is probably right). Now, the word "for" indicates that in the hymn something preceded. The probability is that the unquoted line which preceded was something like, "We shall remain faithful to our Lord even to death," or, "We have resigned ourselves to reproach and suffering and even to death for Christ's sake." In either case the next line, the first one quoted by Paul, could then be: *"For,* if we have died with (him), we shall also live with (him)." Note that this feature of the quotation is similar to that which we encountered in connection with the lines quoted in I Tim. 3:16. Also in that case something that was not quoted must have preceded the quoted portion. In that case the line which presumably immediately preceded the beginning of the quotation probably ended with the word Logos or Christos or Theos (see on that passage).

Here in II Tim. 2:11-13, after the introductory formula (explained in connection with I Tim. 3:16):

Reliable is the saying,

the quoted lines are as follows:

> **For if we have died with (him), we shall also live with (him);**
> **if we endure, we shall also reign with (him);**
> **if we shall deny (him), he on his part will also deny us;**
> **if we are faithless, he on his part remains faithful.**[134]

In the first two lines the if-clause describes the attitude-and-action which proceeds from *loyalty* to Christ: we have died with (him), we endure (re-

---

[134] Grammatically the four lines are similar in that all are First Class Conditional Sentences. In this case the condition *is assumed to be* true to fact. Whether it is *actually* a fact has nothing to do with the form of the conditional clause.

In this kind of sentence we find εἰ with any tense of the indicative in the protasis. In the four lines which are quoted the apodosis, too, is constantly in the indicative. However, in the first three lines the apodosis is in the form of a prediction (future tense); in the last it is in the form of a statement of fact (present tense).

Summary:

	Protasis	Apodosis
Line 1:	First person plural aorist indicative.	First person plural future indicative
Line 2:	First person plural present indicative.	First person plural future indicative
Line 3:	First person plural future indicative.	First person singular future indicative
Line 4:	First person plural present indicative.	Third person singular present indicative

I do not agree with Lenski, *op. cit.,* p. 793, when he maintains that the use of the aorist tense shows that, since neither the apostle nor Timothy had as yet died physically, Paul in writing "If we have died with him," cannot have been thinking of physical death. The aorist tense does not necessarily indicate that an action has taken place in the actual past. It simply views an action *as a whole.* Accordingly, the interpretation, "For if at any time we have (or "shall have") died with (him), we shall also live with him," is not grammatically impossible.

main stedfast). *In the last two lines* the if-clause describes the attitude-and-action which proceeds from *disloyalty*.

The first two lines are clearly illustrations of synthetic or constructive parallelism. They do not express an identical thought, but there is progressive correspondence between the two propositions. As to the if-clauses, the persons who are assumed to have died with Christ are also the ones who endure, being faithful to death. And as to the conclusions, not only will such persons *live* with Christ, but they will also *reign* with him. These two go together. Note that in all the four clauses of these two lines the subject is *we* ("we . . . we . . . ; we . . . we").

The last two lines, describing the course of disloyalty, differ *in form* from the first two. Here we have not "we . . . we," but twice "we . . . *he*." In the third line ("If we shall deny him, he on his part will also deny us"), the conclusion is the *expected* one (just as in lines one and two). In the fourth line, however, the conclusion comes as somewhat of a surprise. It takes careful reflection before we realize that the surprising conclusion is, after all, the only possible one. Once we grasp its meaning, we understand that also lines three and four express a parallel thought, and are illustrations of synthetic parallelism.

Before a detailed analysis of these four lines is attempted, it should be stressed that taken as a whole they convey *one* main thought, namely, *Loyalty to Christ, stedfastness even amid persecution, is rewarded, and disloyalty is punished.* This is in harmony with the idea of the entire chapter (see the Outline).

The meaning of the individual lines:

Lines 1 and 2:

After the connective "For," which has been explained, *line 1* immediately confronts us with a difficulty. There are *two main* lines of interpretation — there are also others which we shall pass by because even on the surface they are unreasonable — ; and the first of these two main lines is subdivided into two main branches or forms:

The first main line of interpretation, *in its first form,* is as follows: "If we have (that is, "If we shall have," or, "If at any time we have") experienced physical death, having been put to death because of our loyalty to Christ, we shall also live with him in glory." The reference in the if-clause would then be to a violent death, the kind of death Christ also suffered. In the case of believers this would be *the martyr's death*.[135]

This interpretation is surely possible. It does not clash with the context. The apostle desires that Timothy be willing to endure bonds along with

---

[135] Bouma, *op. cit.*, pp. 283, 284, interprets the passage in this manner.

other faithful servants of God (verse 3). Paul has just stated that he himself is suffering hardship even to bonds as an evil-doer, and that he endures all things for the sake of the elect (verses 9, 10). All this suffering has been imposed from without. Hence, when now in verse 11 he continues, "For if we *have died* with (him)," he could well have been thinking of that final form of physical affliction (the martyr's death) which may at any time be imposed upon Christ's loyal servants.

It is possible, however, that this interpretation is in need of some modification. This brings us to *the second form* in which the first main line of interpretation presents itself. Here, too, just as in the first form of this main line, *the martyr's death* is in the picture. But according to this view the sense would not be that believers (including Paul and Timothy) are pictured as having at any time already experienced the martyr's death but rather as being fully resigned to it and to all the afflictions which precede it. Paul then would be saying, "For Christ's sake and in harmony with his example we have given ourselves up once for all to a life that involves exposure to pain, torture, reproach, and finally to the martyr's death. We have, accordingly, *died to* worldly comfort, ease, advantage, and honor. If, then, we have in that sense died with (him), we shall also live with (him), here and now, even more by and by in heavenly glory, and especially after the Judgment Day in the new heaven and earth." Along this line Calvin, Ellicott, and Van Andel (for titles see Bibliography).

In favor of this interpretation are the following considerations:

(1) This also is not in conflict with the context which, as was noted, describes deprivation to which believers are exposed.

(2) It is in complete harmony with the line which immediately follows, for the person who has given up earthly ambition and has resigned himself for Christ's sake to reproach, suffering, and if need be to violent death, is the very man who "endures," that is, who "remains stedfast to the end."

(3) It is in agreement with Paul's thought as expressed elsewhere. See especially II Cor. 4:10: *"always* bearing about in the body the *dying* of Jesus, so that *the life* of Jesus may also be manifested in our bodies." With this compare I Cor. 15:31, "I die daily" (explained by verse 30: "we stand in jeopardy every hour").

If this be the correct interpretation — and I believe that it has much in its favor —, the thought which Paul, in quoting from the hymn, is conveying, is the one with which we ourselves are familiar. It has been expressed poetically in the beautiful lines:

> "Hence with earthly treasure!
> Thou art all my pleasure,
> Jesus, all my choice.
> Hence, thou empty glory!

> Naught to me thy story,
>   Told with tempting voice.
> Pain or loss or shame or cross
>   Shall not from my Savior move me,
>   Since he deigns to love me.
>
> Hence, all fear and sadness!
> For the Lord of gladness,
>   Jesus enters in.
> Those who love the Father,
> Though the storms may gather,
>   Still have peace within.
> Yea, whate'er I here must bear,
>   Thou art still my purest pleasure,
>   Jesus, priceless treasure."
>   (Johann Frenck, 1653; translated by Catherine
>   Winkworth, 1863)

The interpretation given, in either of its two forms, is surely preferable to *the second main line of interpretation,* according to which here in II Tim. 2:11 the apostle is referring *in general* (without any reference to the martyr's death) *to the process of dying unto sin,* that process of conversion and sanctification which is symbolized by the rite of baptism. This is a very popular view, in support of which an appeal is usually made to the similar-sounding passage, Rom. 6:8.[136]

But the present passage, II Tim. 2:11, *occurs in an entirely different context.* Romans 6 deals, indeed, with "death unto sin." The theme of the beginning of that chapter is that of spiritual renewal ("What shall we say then? Shall we continue in sin that grace may abound? God forbid. We who died to sin, how shall we any longer live in it? . . . Our old man was crucified with him that the body of sin might be destroyed," etc.) And from verse 10 on to the end of that chapter the word *sin* (noun or verb) or its synonym occurs in every verse!

Accordingly, the contexts of the two passages (Rom. 6:8; II Tim. 2:11) are entirely different. The one deals with sanctification in general; in the other cross-bearing and the martyr's death are in view. — Things which differ should not be confused!

Line 2 is not difficult once line 1 has been correctly interpreted. It means, "If we *remain stedfast* to the very end (for the meaning of *endurance*

---

[136] Among the many commentators who share this view, in one form or another, are Barnes, Gealy (in *The Interpreter's Bible*), Lenski, Lock (in *The International Critical Commentary*), Scott (in *The Moffatt New Testament Commentary*), Van Oosterzee (in *Lange's Commentary*), and White (in *Expositor's Greek Testament*).

II TIMOTHY 2:11-13

see N.T.C. on I and II Thessalonians, p. 198), we shall be kings in close association with him."

If Interpretation 1, Form 1, is adopted, the living and reigning would have to refer solely to the believer's existence *after* death. If Interpretation 1, Form 2, is preferred, the living and reigning pertains in principle even to the period before death, but comes to fruition immediately after death (cf. Matt. 10:32; Rev. 20:4), reaching its everlasting climax on and after the Judgment Day, when the saints will live and reign with Christ with respect to both body and soul (Dan. 7:27; Matt. 25:34; Rev. 22:5).

To live with Christ means *to be* with him, to have fellowship with him, to delight in him, to be like him, to love him, and to glorify him (see, for example, John 17:3; Phil. 2:5; Col. 3:1-4; I John 3:2; 5:12; Rev. 14:1; Rev. 19:11, 14; 22:4).

To reign with Christ means to experience in one's own life the restoration of the royal office. By virtue of creation man held the threefold office of prophet, priest, and king. As prophet his *mind* was illumined so that he knew God. As priest his *heart* delighted in God. As king his *will* was in harmony with God's will. This threefold office, lost through the fall, is restored by God's grace. The joyful response of the believer's will to the will of Christ, that response which is true freedom, is the basic element in this *reigning* with Christ. Moreover, even during the period before death Christians rule the world by means of their prayers, in the sense that again and again judgments occur in answer to prayer (Rev. 8:3-5). In heaven they are even closer to the throne than are the angels (Rev. 4:4; 5:11). In fact, they sit with Christ on his throne (Rev. 3:21), sharing his royal glory. And when Christ returns, the saints sit and judge with him (Ps. 149:5-9; I Cor. 6:2, 3).

Lines 3 and 4:

Having stated in the first two lines what will happen to those who endure or are willing to endure hardship even to violent death, the last two lines of the quoted portion of the hymn take up the case of those who, having confessed Christ (at least with the lips), become disloyal to him. "If we shall *deny* (cf. I Tim. 5:8) him, he on his part will also deny us." When a person, because of unwillingness to suffer hardship for the sake of Christ and his cause, *disowns* the Lord ("I do not know the man!"), then, unless he repents, *he will be disowned* by the Lord in the great day of judgment ("I do not know you"). See Matt. 26:72; then Matt. 25:12; also Matt. 10:33.

To deny Christ means *to be faithless*. (The parallelism and also the conclusion — "he . . . remains faithful" — show that here the meaning of the verb used in the original cannot be: to be unbelieving.) Hence, the hymn continues: "If we are faithless, he on his part . . . ," but obviously the con-

2:11-13 **II TIMOTHY**

tinuation cannot be "will also be faithless." One *can* say, "If we shall deny him, he on his part will also deny us," but one *cannot* say, "If we are faithless, he on his part will also be faithless." Nevertheless, the conclusion of the fourth line corresponds *in thought* with that of its parallel, the third line; for, the clause "he on his part remains faithful" (line four) is, after all, the same (even more forcefully expressed!) as, "he on his part will also deny us," for *faithfulness* on his part means carrying out his threats (Matt. 10:33) as well as his promises (Matt. 10:32)! Divine faithfulness is a wonderful comfort for those who are loyal (I Thess. 5:24; II Thess. 3:3; cf. I Cor. 1:9; 10:13; II Cor. 1:18; Phil. 1:6; Heb. 10:23). It is a very earnest warning for those who might be inclined to become disloyal.

It is hardly necessary to add that the meaning of the last line cannot be, "If we are faithless and deny him, nevertheless he, remaining faithful to his promise, will give us everlasting life." Aside from being wrong for other reasons, such an interpretation destroys the evident implication of the parallelism between lines three and four.

The final clause of verse 13 is probably to be regarded as a comment by Paul himself (not a part of the hymn): **. . . for to deny himself he is not able.** If Christ failed to remain faithful to his threat as well as to his promise, he would be denying *himself,* for in that case he would cease to be The Truth. See also Num. 23:10; Jer. 10:10; Titus 1:2; Rev. 3:7. But for him to deny himself is, of course, impossible. If it were possible, he would no longer be God!

---

14 Remind them of these things, charging them in the presence of the Lord not to wage thoroughly useless word-battles, which upset the listeners. 15 Do your utmost to present yourself to God approved, a workman who has nothing to be ashamed of, rightly handling the word of the truth. 16 But profane empty-chatter shun, for they (who indulge in it) will advance to an increase of ungodliness. 17 And their word will devour like a gangrene. Among them are Hymenaeus and Philetus, 18 the kind of people who have wandered away from the truth, saying that (the) resurrection has already occurred, and they upset the faith of some. 19 Nevertheless, the solid foundation of God stands firm, having this seal:
        The Lord knows those who are his,
                and
    Let every one who names the name of the Lord stand aloof from unrighteousness.

20 But in a large house there are not only gold and silver utensils, but also wooden and earthen, and some (are) for honor, some for dishonor. 21 So, if anyone will effectively cleanse himself from these, he will be a utensil for honor, sanctified, very useful to the Master, prepared for every good work. 22 But from the desires of youth flee away, and run after righteousness, faith, love, peace with those who call upon the Lord out of pure hearts. 23 But those foolish and ignorant inquiries reject, knowing that they breed quarrels. 24 And the Lord's servant must not quarrel, but be gentle to all, qualified to teach, patient under injuries, 25 with mildness correcting the opponents, in the hope that possibly God may grant them

conversion (leading) to acknowledgment of (the) truth, 26 and they may return to soberness, (being delivered) out of the snare of the devil, by whom they had been taken captive to (do) his will.

2:14-26

14. The subject of verses 1-13 is continued, the difference being that what was stated positively in the previous paragraph is stated negatively now (cf., for example, verse 2, "These things entrust to reliable men, such as will be able to teach others as well," with verse 14, "charging them . . . *not* to wage thoroughly useless word-battles"; see also verses 16, 21, 22, 23, 24).

Says Paul, **Remind them of these things, charging them in the presence of the Lord not to wage thoroughly useless word-battles** [137] **which upset the listeners.**

Timothy is told to remind the "reliable men" ("ministers") to remain stedfast in the performance of their God-given tasks of teaching, preaching, etc. Amid their many afflictions let them always look up to Jesus Christ, the risen and reigning Savior, who imparts strength to his faithful ones, and rewards them. It is clear that the expression "these things," refers especially to the entire preceding paragraph (verses 1-13), and perhaps even more directly to verses 8-13.

Timothy, then, has a "charge" for these leaders, just as Paul had a charge for Timothy. In both cases it was a charge "in the presence *of God*" or (in the present instance) "*of the Lord*" (see on I Tim. 5:21; II Tim. 4:1). Thus solemnly Timothy must warn the ecclesiastical leaders of "The District Ephesus and Surroundings" not to wage thoroughly useless word-battles (literally, "not to-wage-word-battle for nothing useful"). For such word-quibbling see on I Tim. 6:4 (*there* the noun is used; *here* the infinitive; in both cases the only instance of its use in the New Testament). Such word-battling is "unto the catastrophy (up-setting) of the listeners." Paul is referring, of course, to the quarrels arising from investigations into "endless

---

[137] *Note on the textual variants in II Tim. 2:14.* Though N.N. favors τοῦ θεοῦ instead of τοῦ κυρίου, the textual evidence in favor of the former is not sufficiently preponderant to rule out the idea that it may have been substituted for τοῦ κυρίου to bring the phrase into exact, verbal agreement with I Tim. 5:21; II Tim. 4:1. But essentially the difference is unimportant.

As to the remaining variants, the readings adopted by N.N. are probably the best. The *infinitive* (λογομαχεῖν) is natural in the present construction. As to the difference between the two ἐπί -phrases, the first followed by *the accusative* (an adverbial phrase: "to-wage-word-battles *for nothing useful*"), the second by *the dative* (indicating result: "unto the catastrophy of the listeners"), the attempts to eliminate this difference in construction after the same preposition (either by causing ἐπί to be followed by the dative both times, or by substituting εἰς for the first ἐπί) evidently stem from a desire for less rugged syntax.

2:14 **II TIMOTHY**

myths and genealogies" (I Tim. 1:3, 4), "profane and old-womanish myths" (I Tim. 4:7a), the kind of drivel that was exposed earlier (see on I Tim. 1:3-7; 4:7a; 6:3-10). It is evident that during the period which had elapsed between the writing of the two epistles to Timothy religious conditions in the Ephesus region had not improved! The leaders and future leaders had to be warned not to be sidetracked into the devious by-ways of futile debates.

15. Timothy's personal example must serve as a powerful weapon against error: **Do your utmost to present yourself to God approved.** Timothy must exert every effort so to conduct himself that even now *before the bar of God's judgment* [138] he stands *approved,* that is, as one who, after thorough examination by no one less than the Supreme Judge, has the satisfaction of knowing that the latter is well-pleased with him and commends him (note synonyms in Rom. 14:18 and II Cor. 10:18). Now this happy result will be achieved if Timothy is found to be:

a. a workman who has nothing to be ashamed of,
accordingly also:
b. rightly handling the word of the truth.

Timothy, then, must be a *workman,* not a *quibbler.* His work, moreover, must be such that it does not reflect shame on him and that he does not need to fear that shame will cover him when he hears the divine verdict with respect to it.

This means, of course, that he is the kind of leader who is engaged in "rightly handling the word of the truth." This word of the truth is "the testimony concerning our Lord" (II Tim. 1:8), "the gospel" (same reference and see Eph. 1:13), "the word of God" (II Tim. 2:9). It is God's redemptive truth. The modifier "of *the truth*" emphasizes the contrast between God's unshakeable special revelation, on the one hand, and the Ephesian errorists' worthless *chatter* on the other.

The expression "rightly handling" has caused much controversy. It is true that "to cut" is the primary meaning of the main element (the *base*) of the composite verb from which this present masculine participle (ὀρθοτομοῦντα) is derived. Nevertheless, the view that *the composite verb* retains either this literal sense or the near-literal sense "divide" (A.V.) is debatable. In a composite verb the meaning-emphasis may shift to the prefix, until in the semantic process the literal sense of the base is lost. Thus straight-*cutting* begins to mean *straight*-handling, handling *aright.* It is not so strange that, by an easy transition from the physical to the moral sphere,

---

[138] The word παρίστημι seems to have the judicial sense here (and also in Acts 27:24; Rom. 14:10; I Cor. 8:8) which it has at times in the papyri. See M.M., pp. 494, 495.

some such notion as "cutting a straight road or path" led in the course of time to the exclusively moral use of the term. Thus Prov. 11:5 (LXX) informs us that "the righteousness of the perfect *cuts his way straight*," meaning: *"keeps his way straight,"* causes him to do what is *right*. Cf. Prov. 3:6 (LXX). Thus it is understandable that here in II Tim. 1:15 the meaning is, "handling aright." [139]

That the base ("to cut") should lose its original, literal meaning when a prefix ("straight") is added is not strange. Even *without* any affix the word "to cut" is frequently used in a non-literal sense. Thus, the Greek speaks of *"cutting* (taking) an oath," *"cutting* (diluting) a liquid," *"cutting* (working) a mine,"* etc. He also uses the expression "cutting short" (bringing to a crisis), and "cutting the waves," just as we do today. And compare our idioms "cutting a strange figure," "cutting droll capers," "cutting a pack of cards," etc.

Returning to the *composite verb*, I would emphasize that *the context* confirms the meaning which nearly all authorities ascribe to it. In the light of verses 14 and 16 the idea which Paul wishes to convey is clearly this, *"Handle* the word of the truth *rightly* instead of waging thoroughly useless word-battles which upset the listeners, and instead of paying any attention to profane, empty-chatter."

The man who handles the word of the truth properly does not change, pervert, mutilate, or distort it, neither does he use it with a wrong purpose in mind. On the contrary, he prayerfully interprets Scripture in the light of Scripture. He courageously, yet lovingly, applies its glorious meaning to concrete conditions and circumstances, doing this for the glory of God, the conversion of sinners, and the edification of believers.

16-18. The proper handling of the word of the truth implies the rejection of whatever is in conflict with its contents and meaning. Hence, Paul continues: **But profane empty-chatter shun, for they (who indulge in it) will advance to an increase of ungodliness. And their word will devour like a gangrene.**

This "profane empty-chatter" has been dealt with earlier (see on I Tim. 1:4; 4:7a; 6:4, 20). The term refers to the unholy, useless disputes about fictitious genealogical histories ("old womanish myths") and hair-splitting

---

[139] One possible reason why this verb has caused some difficulty to English readers may have been that *in English* the expression "cutting straight" or even "rightly dividing" is not immediately clear as an idiom which must be interpreted figuratively. On the other hand, those who are familiar with *the Dutch Bible* (Statenvertaling) experience no difficulty, for that language has the idiom: "die het Woord Gods *recht snijdt*," "he who cuts the Word of God straight," which is immediately understood to mean, "he who handles the Word of God in the proper, straightforward manner."

2:16-18 **II TIMOTHY**

debates about niceties in the law of Moses. Verse 18 seems to indicate that the men who were afflicted with this disease subjected the teachings of Paul to the same abuse. They began to "interpret" them into oblivion, just as is happening even in our own day and age.

Here, as in I Tim. 6:20, Paul uses the plural, so that one might translate "empty-jabberin*gs*." Whenever Timothy encounters them, he must *turn himself about* in order *to avoid* them. Engaging the errorists in debate will make them worse, for *they* (not the jabber*ings* but the jabber*ers,* as the rest of the sentence shows) will *advance!* Do these would-be teachers claim to be advancing, to be making progress? "True," says Paul! "They will advance ... *to more of ungodliness!"* A strange way to advance! They will "chop forward" steadily, removing every obstacle, making for the goal: *an increase of wickedness!* Paul surely knew how to use *irony* effectively!

And their *word* or *talk* will *devour.* It will "have pasture," [140] just like cattle "have pasture," eating away in every direction. The foolish disputes of the jabberers will resemble a *gangrene* or *malignant tumor.* Not only does the cancer eat away the healthy tissue, but in doing so it also aggravates the condition of the patient. Similarly heresy, advertised by too much attention, will develop both extensively and intensively. By adversely affecting an ever-increasing proportion of the membership it will tend to destroy the organism of the church.

The ringleaders are now mentioned by name: **Among them** (literally, "among whom") **are Hymenaeus and Philetus, the kind of people who have wandered away from the truth, saying that the resurrection has already occurred, and they upset the faith of some.**

The Dangerous Error of Hymenaeus and Philetus. The facts with respect to them may be summarized as follows:

(1) They were teachers of heresy in the Ephesian district.

(2) Hymenaeus was possibly the leader. At least, in both passages in which he is mentioned, his name occurs first. In I Tim. 1:19, 20 (see on that passage) Paul associates him with Alexander; here in II Tim. 2:16-18, with Philetus. We do not know why Alexander is no longer mentioned along with Hymenaeus. Had he moved away? Had he died? Had he repented? About Philetus (meaning "beloved") nothing is known except what is found here.

(3) Hymenaeus and Philetus were *the kind of* (οἵτινες) people who had *wandered away* (see on I Tim. 1:6; 6:21) from *the truth,* that is, from the true doctrine of salvation in Christ. It is immediately evident that Paul is not discussing a minor difference of opinion among men who basically thought alike. On the contrary, he refers to capital error.

---

[140] This looks like a medical term. Cf. II Tim. 4:11: *Dr.* Luke was with Paul!

(4) Their error consisted in this, that they said, "The [141] resurrection has already occurred." In this they resembled those present-day liberals who, while refusing to be caught saying, "There is no resurrection," allegorize the concept. Now it must be admitted that Paul, too, believed in a *spiritual* resurrection, the act of God whereby he imparts the new life to those who are dead in sins and trespasses (Rom. 6:3, 4; Eph. 2:6; Phil. 3:11; Col. 2:12; 3:1; and cf. Luke 15:24). But the apostle also most definitely taught *the resurrection of the body* (I Cor. 15; Phil. 3:21), just as Jesus had done (John 5:28). According to Paul's teaching, *denial of the bodily resurrection implies the complete overthrow of faith,* for "if there is no resurrection of the dead, then Christ has not been raised either; and if Christ has not been raised, then our preaching is in vain, y o u r faith is in vain, . . . and y o u are still in y o u r sins" (I Cor. 15:13, 14, 17).

(5) What made matters worse was that Hymenaeus and Philetus professed to be Christians. The context — see verse 19b — seems to indicate that they were among those who "named the name of the Lord." Until their excommunication (for which cf. I Tim. 1:20) they had been members of the church!

In fact, these false prophets pretended to be "experts" in all matters touching religion. They yearned to be law-teachers, although "they understood neither the words which they were speaking neither the themes on which they were harping with so much confidence" (I Tim. 1:7). They perverted both the law and Paul's teaching.

(6) Their denial (by implication at least) of the bodily resurrection probably stemmed from pagan dualism, according to which whatever is spiritual is good, and whatever is material is evil. Their reasoning may well have been: "Since matter is evil, our bodies must be evil. Hence, they will not be raised." The same basic error would lead to other erroneous deductions (see on I Tim. 4:3).

(7) In view of their conviction that in their own case "the resurrection" — the only one they recognized, namely, from sin to holiness, from error to knowledge — had already occurred, why should they worry any longer about *sin?* They were self-righteous and conceited ("puffed up"). Hence, God's law did not "crush" them. They used it as an instrument for adding to their fame as teachers, as has been explained (see on I Tim. 1:9).

---

[141] It is true that the textual evidence somewhat favors the omission of the article. Nevertheless, the context shows that pernicious, fundamental error is meant. Had Hymenaeus and Philetus merely taught that there was *a* resurrection which was past already, the apostle would not have been disturbed in the least, for that would have been a thoroughly scriptural (also *Pauline*) doctrine. But these heresy teachers totally denied the physical resurrection. Hence, as to the article, either: we must accept the reading of A.C., Koine text, D pl., or we must assume that ἀνάστασις can be definite even without the article.

2:16-18 II TIMOTHY

(8) This indifference to sin resulted in their "advance" from ungodliness to "more of ungodliness" (see the context, verse 16; and cf. verse 19b, "unrighteousness").

(9) For example, they even *blasphemed* — railed at — the true gospel (I Tim. 1:20).

(10) Their false teaching "incipient gnosticism") was contagious. "They *upset* the faith of some." They "turned upside down" (see N.T.C. on John 2:15, Vol. I, pp. 122, 123) the religious convictions of these church-members. Perhaps, as yet *not many* had been infected with this terrible heresy (note, *"of some"*), but this was only the beginning. As a malignant tumor eats away the healthy flesh, so this wicked teaching eats away the Christian "faith."

19. Does this mean then that God's true church can be destroyed? Says Paul, **Nevertheless, the solid foundation of God stands firm, having this seal:**
The Lord knows those who are his,
and
Let everyone who names the name of the Lord stand aloof from unrighteousness.

False prophets shall lead many astray (Matt. 24:11). In fact, if it were possible, they would lead astray even the elect (Matt. 24:24). But the Good Shepherd *knows* his sheep, and gives everlasting life to them, and *they* shall certainly never perish, and no one shall snatch *them* out of his hands (John 10:14, 28). Since God is in the midst of her, God's city shall not be moved (Ps. 46:5). His kingdom cannot be shaken (Heb. 12:28). Though Paul has just pointed out that certain individuals have wandered away from the truth and have upset the faith of some (verse 18), it must ever be borne in mind that they are not all Israel that are of Israel (Rom. 9:6), and that, in spite of defections, "all Israel" shall be saved (Rom. 11:26; cf. I John 2:19).

In similar vein he now writes, "Nevertheless, the *solid* (or *compact;* cf. I Peter 5:9; Heb. 5:12, 14) foundation of God *stands firm*" (ἕστηκεν third per. sing., perfect indicative). But what is meant by this "solid foundation"? Among the many answers that have been given — such as, the Old and New Testaments, the bodily resurrection, the Christian religion, etc. — the following are, perhaps, the most important: (1) Election from eternity; (2) Christ himself; (3) the church.[142]

---

[142] For the first view see on this passage Calvin; also J. L. Koole; for the second, C. Bouma; for the third, Gealy, Lenski, Van Dyk, White, and Wuest. For titles see Bibliography. Bouma, commenting on II Tim. 2:19, flatly rejects the idea that *the foundation* indicates the church, *op. cit.,* p. 297 (even more definitely in his *Korte Verklaring,* p. 150). Nevertheless, *op. cit.,* p. 146, commenting on I Tim. 3:15, he states, "The Church of the Lord is a pillar; what is more, it is a foundation."

With respect to (1): This idea cannot be altogether discarded. Paul has just made mention of election (verse 10). No doubt the idea of the divine predestinating love does enter in — notice especially the words, "The Lord knows (from everlasting) those who are his" —; nevertheless, nowhere else does the apostle call election a *foundation*. Besides, the second inscription on the seal (verse 19b) is hardly in keeping with this interpretation, and the context does not demand it.

With respect to (2): It is true that Christ is called the *foundation* in I Cor. 3:10-12. Nevertheless, this does not settle the matter. One cannot always ascribe exactly the same meaning to Paul's metaphors. Thus, in Eph. 2:20 Christ is not called the foundation but "the chief cornerstone." Here in II Tim. 2:19 there is nothing to suggest that Christ is regarded as the foundation.

With respect to (3): I consider this view to be correct. *The church, established upon the bedrock of God's predestinating love, is his foundation, his building well-founded.* Reasons for adopting this view:

a. This harmonizes most beautifully with the context: God's *true* church consists of those who are his, those who stand aloof from unrighteousness (note the seal!). By calling the church "God's *solid foundation*," Paul stresses its permanency and immobility. Some, indeed, have wandered away, etc., but the *true church* is immovable!

b. This is consistent with I Tim. 3:15. There, too, the church is called "the *foundation*" or "the *support*" (there ἑδραίωμα, here in II Tim. 2:19 θεμέλιος).

God's foundation has *a seal* (not *merely* an inscription!). Now a seal may *indicate authority* and thus may *protect* or at least *warn* against all tampering. Thus, the tomb of Jesus was sealed (Matt. 27:66). Again, it may be *a mark of ownership*. "Set me as a seal upon thy heart" (Song of Solomon 8:6). Or it may *authenticate* a legal decree or other document, *certifying* and *guaranteeing* its genuine character. Thus, the decree of Xerxes was sealed (Esther 3:12; cf. I Cor. 9:2).

When we now read that God's solid foundation, the church, has a seal, it is probably unwarranted to apply only *one* of these three ideas to *this* seal. The seal by which believers are sealed protects, indicates ownership, and certifies, all three in one! [143] Cf. Rev. 7:2-4. God the Father *protects* them, so that none are lost. He has *known* them as his own from all eternity (the context calls for this idea). God the Son *owns* them. They were *given* to him. Moreover, he *bought* or *redeemed* them with his precious blood. This idea of ownership is clearly expressed here ("the Lord knows *those who are his*"). And God the Holy Spirit *certifies* that they are,

---

[143] Thus also D. M. Edwards in his excellent article "Seal" in I.S.B.E.

indeed, the sons of God (Rom. 8:16). This divine protection, ownership, and certification *seals* them!

But how do believers experience the comfort of the seal? The answer is: by taking to heart what is written on the seal! The seal bears two closely related inscriptions. *God's* decree and *man's* responsibility receive equal recognition:

The first inscription deals the deathblow to *Pelagianism;* the second, to *fatalism.*

The first is dated *in eternity;* the second, *in time.*

The first is a declaration which we must *believe;* the second, an exhortation which we must *obey.*

The first exalts *God's predestinating mercy;* the second emphasizes *man's inevitable duty.*

The first refers to the *security;* the second to the *purity* of the church (Wuest, in agreement with Vincent).

Between the two there is a very close connection. That connection is interpreted beautifully in I Cor. 6:19b, 20: "Y o u are not y o u r own, for y o u were bought with a price (cf. the first inscription); glorify God therefore in y o u r body" (cf. the second inscription).

The close relationship between the two inscriptions is evident also from the fact that the words of both were probably derived from the same Old Testament incident; namely, the rebellion by Korah, Dathan, and Abiram (Numbers 16). Hymenaeus and Philetus, in their rebellion against true doctrine and holy living, resembled these wicked men of the old dispensation. In both of these instances of rebellion against constituted authority there was disbelief of what God had clearly revealed. In both cases the leaders involved others in their crime. The implication is that just as the rebellion under Korah, etc., ended in dire punishment for those who rebelled and for their followers, so also will the present rebellion of Hymenaeus and Philetus terminate in disaster for them and their disciples, unless they repent.

The similarity between the Old Testament references and Paul's words will be seen by placing them in parallel columns:

Numbers 16:5, 26 (LXX):	II Tim. 2:19:
"God . . . knows those who are his."	"The Lord knows those who are his."
"Separate yourselves from the tents of these wicked men . . . lest y o u be destroyed along with them in all their sin."	"Let everyone who names the name of the Lord stand aloof from unrighteousness."

It is probable, however, that in addition to the story of rebellion so vividly portrayed in Numbers 16, Paul was thinking of other Old Testament references. Thus, the following (and other similar passages) may also have served as a basis for the first inscription: the Lord *knows* Abraham (Gen. 18:19), Moses (Ex. 33:12, 17), those who take refuge in him (Nah. 1:7). The aorist tense here in II Tim. 2:19, "The Lord *knows* or *knew* (ἔγνω)," may be called *timeless*. *By virtue of his sovereign grace he from eternity acknowledged them as his own, and consequently made them the recipients of his special love and fellowship (in the Spirit).* Cf. John 10:14, 27; Rom. 8:28. Hence, they are perfectly safe. They can never be lost (John 10:28).

But this security does not become their possession in any arbitrary or mechanical fashion. *The first inscription has no meaning at all apart from the second, nor the second apart from the first.* The Lord will tell *the wicked* that he has never *known* them (Matt. 7:23; Luke 13:27). The two inscriptions always go together if anyone is ever to become a truly *sealed* person. Security and purity dovetail. Read in this connection, II Thess. 2:13: "God chose y o u from the beginning to salvation through sanctification by the Spirit and belief of the truth." Cf. I Peter 1:1, 2: "Elect . . . according to the foreknowledge of God the Father, in sanctification of the Spirit, unto obedience," etc.

Hence, the second inscription follows hard upon the first. On the seal the two stand next to each other; or *one* on one side, *the other* on the other side. Compare an American coin, with its two sides, an inscription upon each, one pointing to God as the source of our liberty, the other reminding us of the fact that though there are many States, yet there is only one nation, and implying that all should co-operate. *Obverse:* IN GOD WE TRUST; *Reverse:* E PLURIBUS UNUM.

Basic to the words of the second inscription ("Let everyone who names the name of the Lord stand aloof from unrighteousness") are, in addition to Num. 16:26, such Old Testament passages as Is. 26:13 (LXX: "We name thy name"); Ps. 6:8; and Is. 52:11; cf. II Cor. 6:17 (exhortations to depart from evil and from evil-workers). Whether the apostle derived the thoughts embodied in the two inscriptions *directly* from the Old Testament, or whether they had first become embodied in a Christian hymn, as some think, is a question that cannot now be answered, and is of little importance.

The meaning of the second inscription is this: expressed reliance on God must reveal itself in a life that is consecrated to God's glory. A person's confession must exemplify itself in a holy walk and conduct. The person who in prayer and praise "names the name of the Lord" thereby declares that he embraces God's revelation of himself in the realm of nature (Ps. 8) and of redemption (John 16:24). Such a person must be consistent! That very consistency is what Hymenaeus and Philetus lacked. They named the name of the Lord, and promoted unrighteousness! Literally Paul says "Let everyone who names the name of the Lord *apostatize*." But in this connection it must be borne in mind that the Greek uses this verb (to apostatize, stand aloof, withdraw oneself from) both in a favorable and in an unfavorable sense. Let him *apostatize* . . . not from *the faith* (I Tim. 4:1), but from *unrighteousness* of every variety.

20. But, although God's elect never perish, **in a large house there are not only gold and silver utensils, but also wooden and earthen, and some for honor, some for dishonor.**

Timothy must not be surprised about the fact that there is such a thing as defection! He must bear in mind that it is with the *visible* church as it is with "a *large* house." Such a *large* house contains all kinds of *utensils;* that is, furniture, vases, pots and pans, etc., in short, all those material objects which one expects to find in a mansion, the entire "household contents"; hence, not only gold and silver but also wooden and earthen vessels; not only articles to be kept and displayed, but also those which are taken to the dump or junk-yard when they have served their purpose. In passing, note that Paul must say *large* house, because a *small* house might not contain gold and silver utensils. — Similarly, the visible church, as it manifests itself on earth, contains *true believers* (some more faithful, comparable to gold; others less faithful, comparable to silver) and *hypocrites.* Cf. Matt. 13:24-30: wheat and tares. The genuine members are destined for *honor* (see Matt. 25:34-40); the others, for dishonor (see Matt. 25:41-45). Cf. I Sam. 2:30b; Rom. 9:21.[144]

21. How can one be sure of being a utensil for honor? The answer is: **So, if anyone will effectively cleanse himself from these, he will be a utensil for honor, sanctified, very useful to the Master, prepared for every good work.**

Close and intimate association with hypocrites may easily lead to moral and spiritual contamination (I Cor. 15:33; and see N.T.C. on II Thess.

---

[144] Reference to I Cor. 3:10-15 or to I Cor. 12:12-31 only serves to confuse matters. The first discusses building-materials (works, teachings); the second, distribution of talents. But II Tim. 2:20, 21 describes *church-members,* genuine and false. Scott (*op. cit.,* p. 114) says that the writer of II Timothy uses a clumsy simile that becomes more and more confused. Bouma (*Korte Verklaring,* p. 152) thinks of this *house* of verse 20 as built upon *the foundation* mentioned in verse 19. That is *one* reason why he cannot identify the foundation with the church, for how can the church be built upon the church? But verse 20 does not say that *the house* of verse 20 is built on *the foundation* of verse 19. Both of these interpreters fail to do justice to the fact that each metaphor must be given its own distinct interpretation. This is often the case in Scripture. The church is *both* a house *and* a foundation (thus also in I Tim. 3:15, though the words used in the original vary slightly from those used here in II Tim. 2:19, 20). In *one* sense it is like a house; in another sense it is like a foundation. Thus also in John 10 Jesus is both the door and the Good Shepherd. His enemies are strangers, thieves, *and* hirelings. And in the book of Revelation the church is *both* a bride *and* a city. See N.T.C. on John, Vol. II, p. 102. These are not *mixed* metaphors, but *different* metaphors.

3:14). The temptation to fall into this trap must be avoided. The sin of accepting the doctrines and/or of copying the example of such wicked men (whether the latter be thought of as still in the church or as already out of the church) must be avoided (cf. verse 19b); and if committed, must be confessed, and the evil must be overcome with good. Thus, a person must "effectively" or "thoroughly" cleanse himself "from these," that is, from evil men ("utensils for dishonor") and their defiling doctrines and practices; from such men as Hymenaeus and Philetus and their disciples, and from their false teachings and evil habits.

Now if anyone will thus effectively cleanse himself, he will be a utensil for honor.[145] The reality rises above the figure: a cheap dish will always remain a cheap dish, but God's grace enables a sinner to become a saint, "a utensil for honor." Such a person, having cleansed himself, is *sanctified*. Through the purifying operation of the Holy Spirit he has now become "a saint in experience as well as position" (K. S. Wuest, *Golden Nuggets*, p. 72), having been wholly *set apart* for the Lord and his work, and this abidingly. Accordingly, he is now "very useful" to his *Master*, the One who exercises full authority over him (cf. I Tim. 6:1, 2; Jude 4; Rev. 6:10), namely, Jesus Christ. Once for all he is *prepared* for *every* good work (cf. II Tim. 3:17; Titus 1:16; 3:8, 14; then II Cor. 9:8).[146]

22. The way to cleanse oneself is to become *de*tached from that which is evil and *at*tached to that which is good. Hence, Paul continues: **But from the desires of youth flee away, and run after righteousness, faith, love, peace with those who call upon the Lord out of pure hearts.**

When Paul wrote these words, Timothy must have been 37-42 years of age (see on I Tim. 4:12). He was still rather young, especially in relation to the position of trust and responsibility which he occupied. So the apostle warns him against "the (or "those well-known," note the article) *desires of youth*." But just what does he mean?[147]

---

[145] The construction is regular: a future more vivid conditional sentence, using ἐάν with the aorist subjunctive in the protasis, and the future indicative in the apodosis. The condition is conceived as a probable future reality. See N.T.C. on John, Vol. I, pp. 42, 43. The expression "utensil for honor" has three modifiers: "sanctified" and "prepared" are perfect passive participles; "very useful" is an old verbal adjective.
[146] This, however, does not necessarily mean that the "utensils for *dis*honor" serve no useful purpose in the church. They *do,* and this in spite of themselves! Study Rom. 9:17, 22, 23. Even Pharaoh was of some use (Ex. 7:4, 5; 9:16; 10:1, 2). Cheap dishes serve a useful purpose even though they are soon discarded!
[147] The word "desire" (ἐπιθυμία) has the following uses: (1) Legitimate desire: Luke 22:15 (Christ's desire to eat the Passover with his disciples); Phil. 1:23 (Paul's desire to depart and be with Christ); I Thess. 2:17 (the desire of Paul, etc., to re-visit the Thessalonians).
(2) Illegitimate or sinful desire (the desire for wrong things, or simply the wrong kind of desire):

The word *desire* that is used in the original, whether in a favorable or unfavorable sense, always indicates *strong yearning*. As the footnote indicates, it is used far more often in an unfavorable than in a favorable sense. In the present passage, it is definitely *sinful* desire that is meant ("From the desires of youth *flee away*"). Such sinful desires, as the footnote also proves, can be classified more or less after the manner of modern psychology (though here these yearnings would hardly be called *sinful*), as follows:

(1) *P*leasure, etc., the inordinate craving for the satisfaction of the physical appetites: the "lust" for food and drink, pleasure-madness, uncontrolled sexual desire (Rom. 1:24; Rev. 18:14, etc.)

(2) *P*ower, etc., the ungoverned passion to be Number 1, the lust to "shine" or be dominant. This results in envy, quarrelsomeness, etc. This sinful tendency is included prominently in such references as Gal. 5:16, 24; II Peter 2:10, 18; Jude 16, 18.

(3) *P*ossessions, etc., uncontrolled yearning for material possessions and for the "glory" that goes with them (see I Tim. 6:9 in its context).

Objectively speaking, Christ triumphed over the first when in the first temptation he said, "Man shall not live by bread alone, but by every word that proceeds out of the mouth of God" (Matt. 4:1-4); over the second, when in the second temptation he refused to cast himself down from the pinnacle of the temple (Matt. 4:5-7); and over the third, when in the third temptation he refused to receive as a gift out of Satan's hand "the king-

---

a. With the emphasis definitely on sins in the realm of sex: (Rom. 1:24; I Thess. 4:5).

b. With the emphasis more general, the context at times indicating one or more of the following: the closely related sins of sex and of idolatry, the liquor-mania, inordinate craving for material possessions, self-assertiveness (hence, quarreling, jealousy, vanity, the lust to dominate): Mark 4:19 (the "thorns" which choke the good seed); John 8:44 (Satan's desires); Rom. 6:12 (unrighteous desire versus righteousness); Rom. 7:7, 8 (covetousness); Rom. 13:14 (note synonyms); Gal. 5:16, 24 (sex, idolatry, self-assertiveness in several manifestations, drunkenness, etc.); Eph. 2:3 (with probably the same mental context as Gal. 5:16, though *there* the context is more specific); Eph. 4:22 (versus "righteousness, holiness, and truth"); Col. 3:5 (cf. Gal. 5:16); I Tim. 6:9 (money-lust and its results); II Tim. 2:22 (the passage under discussion); II Tim. 3:6 ("various impulses," see on that passage); II Tim. 4:3 (very general: desiring "teachers after their own lusts"); Titus 2:12 ("worldly passions"); Titus 3:3 ("malice, envy," etc.); James 1:14, 15 (probably the same mental context as Gal. 5:16); I Peter 1:14; 2:11 (for context see I Peter 2:1: "wickedness, guile, hypocrisy, envy, evil speaking"); I Peter 4:2, 3 (sins of sex and idolatry, drunkenness and its results); II Peter 1:4 (very general); II Peter 2:10, 18 (sex, self-assertiveness and kindred sins); II Peter 3:3 (emphasis on mockery); I John 2:16, 17 ("lust of the flesh and lust of the eyes"); Jude 16, 18 (mockery, sinful desire for advantage, animal-desires, the dissatisfied spirit, arrogance); Rev. 18:14. Probably this also belongs here (inordinate desire for ripe fruits, crowding out desire for spiritual things).

R. C. Trench, *op. cit.*, par. lxxxvii, has shown that while πάθος represents the more passive aspect of evil desire, ἐπιθυμία expresses the active side, and is also far more comprehensive in its *New Testament* usage.

doms of the world and their glory" (Matt. 4:8-10). As a result of his triumph he in a far more glorious sense received from his heavenly Father the very things with which the devil had tempted him. (In *Christ's* case, however, the temptations were entirely *objective;* there were no *subjective,* sinful tendencies.)

Since these inordinate desires often assert themselves more turbulently in youth than in old age — as he grows older a Christian rises above them through the sanctifying grace of the Holy Spirit, bringing him gradually to spiritual *maturity* —, they are here fittingly called "the desires *of youth*" (literally, "the youthful desires").

Two extremes should be avoided. First, it is wrong to construe the reference to be, either exclusively or predominantly, to uncontrolled *sexual* desire. Secondly, it is not necessary to exclude this evil entirely from view. The term, as here used, must probably be taken in its most general sense, as indicating *any sinful yearning to which the soul of a young or relatively young person is exposed.* If, within this general connotation, any element of special emphasis must be found, it should be derived from the context. In the present case there was, perhaps, the tendency of the younger man to be somewhat impatient with those who stood in the way. Timothy's high moral character, coupled with his youthful years, might induce him to act somewhat inconsiderately toward those who were opposing the truth. A person of natural reserve, timidity, and general amiability, such as Timothy, can at times act rather impulsively when at last, contrary to his natural tendency, he is aroused to action. But whether or not in Paul's mind there was any special reference to *this* particular danger of youth cannot now be determined. The sinful desires of youth may best be regarded in the most general sense, and thus as the antonyms of the virtues now mentioned: "righteousness, faith, love, and peace."

Grammatically it is also possible to interpret Paul's words as meaning no more than this: "Timothy, continue to do exactly as you have always been doing. Keep on in your present course, fleeing away from the desires of youth and pursuing righteousness, faith, love, peace," etc.[148] But, though the tense used in the original *permits* this interpretation, it does not *require* it. It is, moreover, in line with Paul's very practical bent of mind to assume that these crisp commands bear some reference to reality, and were warnings that were actually needed, yes needed even by Timothy because of certain character-weaknesses, however unpronounced they may have been. In our desire to do full justice to the beauty of Timothy's character, let us not equip him with wings!

Paul's youthful associate, then, must constantly flee away from the sinful propensities of youth, and must cultivate the habit of running after the

---

[148] Lenski interprets along this line, p. 812.

2:22

virtues that are here enumerated. Note the alliteration — *"run after right-eousness"* (here as in I Tim. 6:11) — and the *chiastic* sentence-structure, with *the vices and the virtues* (the last one, "peace," expanded into a compound phrase) at either end of the sentence; and *the opposite actions* — "flee away from," "run after" — next to each other in the middle.

Since most of the concepts here mentioned have occurred before, the reader is referred to the more detailed explanation in I Tim. 4:12 and I Tim. 6:11. Briefly, then, what Paul has in mind may be paraphrased as follows:

From the sinful tendencies of youth flee away, and *run after* (steadily pursue) the following: a. that state of heart and mind which is in harmony with God's law ("righteousness"); b. humble and dynamic confidence in God ("faith"); c. deep personal affection for the brothers, including in your benevolent interest even the enemies ("love"); and d. undisturbed, perfect understanding ("peace") with all *Christians* (those who in prayer and praise "call upon" the Lord Jesus Christ — cf. Joel 2:32; Rom. 10:12; I Cor. 1:2 — out of pure hearts). The "pure hearts" (the original has the singular where English prefers the plural) are the inner personalities of those who "stand aloof from unrighteousness" (verse 19) and "have effectively cleansed themselves" (verse 21).

23. To the admonition of verse 22 a second is now added: **But those foolish and ignorant inquiries reject, knowing that they breed quarrels.**

See what has already been said with reference to this in our comments on verse 14 above, and on I Tim. 1:4; 4:7; 6:4; cf. also Titus 3:9. Not only must Timothy refrain from waging thoroughly useless word-battles (verse 14), but he should even refuse, politely but definitely, to bother with *the* well-known (note the article) *enquiries* that would result in such word-battles. Such enquiries are *foolish*. They are senseless, the kind of investigations which one associates with morons. They are *ignorant*, "uneducated" or "uninstructed"; that is, they are the work and the mark of ignorant men. The person who has been *properly* educated in God's redemptive truth is able to distinguish between the worth-while and the worthless, and does not conduct such worse than useless enquiries (into genealogical and other Jewish-tradition lore). Timothy must *constantly refuse* to have anything to do with them, for he knows that they breed or generate *quarrels*.

24-26. These three verses clearly form a unit. The mention of *quarrels* in verse 23 leads Paul to re-inforce his admonition that Timothy must refuse to become involved in foolish and ignorant enquiries. Such enquiries breed quarrels, which are exactly the obstacles which ministers must avoid. Says Paul:

And the Lord's servant must not quarrel, but be gentle to all, qualified to teach, patient under injuries, with mildness correcting the opponents,

in the hope that possibly God may grant them conversion (leading) to acknowledgment of (the) truth, and that they may return to soberness, (being delivered) out of the snare of the devil, by whom they had been taken captive to (do) his will.

Timothy is *the servant* (this is a better rendering than *slave;* see N.T.C. on John, Vol. II, footnote 184) *of the Lord* (Jesus Christ; cf. Rom. 1:1; Phil. 1:1; then also James 1:1). As such he should resemble his Lord, who was meek, lowly, restful; who did not cry or lift up his voice or cause it to be heard in the street; who when he was oppressed and afflicted opened not his mouth, but was like a lamb that is brought to the slaughter; and who refused to revile those who reviled him (Is. 42:2; 53:7; Zech. 9:9; Matt. 11:29; 12:19; 21:5; I Peter 2:21-24). True, *the Lord's servant* — the term and the admonition apply not only to Timothy but to every "minister" — must be *an excellent soldier* (see verses 3 and 4 above), but he must *not be a quarreller,* a mere *quibbler* about farcical questions regarding family-trees and rabbinical law-interpretations.

Instead of finding in these words additional proof that Paul cannot have written the Pastorals, one should find in them the very opposite. It was *Paul* who also wrote I Thess. 2:7-12!

The Lord's servant, then, must be *gentle* (this is the best reading, both here and in I Thess. 2:7, the only New Testament occurrences), that is, affable, easy to speak to, approachable in his demeanor; *not* irritable, intolerant, sarcastic, or scornful, not even toward those who err. He must try to *win* them. Hence, he must be gentle *to all!*

Gentleness is necessary, for the Lord's servant must be *qualified to teach,* capable of imparting counsel and instruction.

His gentleness will, however, not always be reciprocated or even appreciated. His teaching will at times meet with ridicule and abuse, with insult and injury. When this happens, he must be *patient under injuries.* He must *hold up under evil* (cf. I Peter 2:21-24).

Not only must he be *gentle* in outward demeanor; he must also be *mild* or *meek* in inner attitude or disposition, "with *mildness* (see also Titus 3:2; then I Cor. 4:21; II Cor. 10:1; Gal. 5:23; 6:1; Eph. 4:2; Col. 3:12; James 1:21; 3:13; I Peter 3:15) correcting the opponents"; cf. Christ's example (Matt. 11:29). Note here the play on words in the original. The *opponents* ("those who are constantly placing themselves in opposition") never ceased to come up with ignorant or *"uninstructed"* enquiries (verse 23). So the apostle tells Timothy to instruct these uninstructed ones, to educate the uneducated, to discipline (in this case, with the discipline of *teaching;* contrast I Tim. 1:20) the undisciplined, to inform the uninformed. Instead of entering into their foolish enquiries, he must gently show them why one should not even bother with these things, and he must then immediately

2:24-26

proceed to impart positive instruction, so that the opponents may thus receive *correction.*

The purpose of all this didactic and pastoral work is now stated: "in the hope that possibly God may grant them *conversion,* leading to acknowledgment of the truth, and they may return to soberness . . ." This hope may have been expressed in such a hesitant manner ("possibly . . . may grant") because with the errorists *contradicting* had become a habit. It had become hard for them even to listen to the truth. If there was to be a change, no one less than *God* would have to bring it about. It is Paul's earnest longing that this great transformation may still be effected.

The word used in the original to indicate this basic change (μετάνοια) means more than *repentance.* It is *conversion* (cf. II Cor. 7:8-10), a term which looks forward as well as backward, whereas *repentance* mainly looks backward. *Conversion,* moreover, affects not only the emotions but also the mind and the will. In fact, it *is first of all* (as the derivation of the word implies) *a complete change-over in mental and moral outlook.* It is *a radical change of view that leads to a radical change of life.* Thus, it is here described as leading to "acknowledgment of (the) truth." Paul hopes that the adherents of false doctrine will be converted from their habit of majoring on minors, and that they will recognize and confess the great and wonderful truth as revealed in the gospel and as centered in Christ.

He hopes, accordingly, "that they may return to soberness" (ἀνανήψωσιν). (This is the only occurrence of this compound verb in the New Testament. But see also footnote 193.) Through the work of the ministry may the adversaries be brought back to their senses; may they be aroused from their dull stupor, being delivered "out of the snare of the devil," that is, out of the snare set by the devil, the snare into which he had lured them, that they might do his will (see on I Tim. 3:7). That this is the meaning is clear from the words which immediately follow: "by whom they had been taken captive to (do) his will" (literally, "having been taken captive by *him* (that is, by the devil), for *that one's* (the devil's) will").[149]

True conversion, then, is a radical change:

(1) from ignorance to acknowledgment of the truth (verse 23, verse 25);

---

[149] It is difficult to see why there is so much disagreement about the pronouns αὐτοῦ and ἐκείνου. The antecedent of αὐτοῦ is naturally the nearest noun *(the devil);* and the antecedent of ἐκείνου is the nearest pronoun *(him, that is, the devil).* This makes excellent sense. It is the devil who captures men, and endeavors to hold on to them. Note the perfect passive participle: "having been captured (primary meaning: *caught alive)* once for all." The devil does not intend to release them! Attempts to connect these pronouns with remote antecedents in order to prove that one or both of them refer to *God* or to *the Lord's servant* impress me as being unsuccessful. Hence, I cannot agree here with Robertson, *op. cit.,* p. 622; Lenski, *op. cit.,* p. 818; Scott, *op. cit.,* p. 117; Lock, *op. cit.,* p. 103; etc.

(2) from intoxication and stupor to soberness (verse 26a); and
(3) from slavery to freedom (verse 26b).

Synthesis of Chapter 2

See the Outline at the beginning of the chapter.

In view, then, of the examples and of the gift which he has received, let Timothy — Paul's "child" — be strengthened in the grace that is in Christ Jesus. In order to become strong himself and to benefit the church, let him *teach* men who, in turn, are qualified to teach others. To such men let him entrust those teachings which he — among many others, "witnesses" all — has heard from the lips of Paul throughout their years of association with each other.

Now this activity of *teaching* — in fact, *all* the work of the ministry — will not be easy, but will result in hardship for Timothy. Let him then be a noble soldier and suffer hardship along with Paul and the witnesses just mentioned. Let him be encouraged by the fact that only the soldier who fights wholeheartedly, only the athlete who competes according to the rules, and only the farmer who works hard, will receive their reward. Thus also Timothy will receive *his* reward. Let him rely on his Lord, who will give him understanding in all matters. Let him, moreover, keep in memory Jesus Christ. He, too, performed his task *wholeheartedly, obediently* — never breaking any divine rule — , and *diligently*. And did he not receive his reward? Was he not raised from the dead, and does he not reign on high as the rightful spiritual heir of David? Is this not true according to the gospel which Paul cherishes as his very own (*"my* gospel")?

For this gospel Paul suffers hardship, even to bonds, as if he were a criminal. But he is greatly comforted by the fact that though he himself is bound, the word of God which he proclaims is not bound but accomplishes God's pleasure in the hearts and lives of all the elect, in order that they may obtain the salvation which centers in Christ Jesus with everlasting glory.

Four lines of what was probably an early-church hymn are now quoted. These show that *loyalty* to Christ and stedfastness even in the midst of bitter persecution are ever rewarded by the privilege of living and reigning with Christ; while, on the contrary *denial and disloyalty* are punished by being rejected by him who ever remains faithful to his threats as well as to his promises, *not being able* (adds Paul) to do otherwise.

In the second part of this chapter the apostle shows that word-battles, profane empty-chatter, and foolish inquiries serve no useful purpose and breed quarrels. Timothy must do his utmost to win God's approval, as a workman who has nothing to be ashamed of, one who rightly handles the word of the truth. The errorists will make progress, indeed, but what kind of progress? They will advance . . . to an increase of ungodliness! Their word will "have pasture," eating its way like a malignant tumor. Among the ring-leaders of these false teachers are Hymenaeus and Philetus, men who teach that the only resurrection is the spiritual one, which, they say, *has already occurred!* But though these do upset the faith of *some,* God's *true* church remains stedfast. It is his solid foundation. Its members are protected by the Father, owned by the Son, and certified by the Spirit. In other words, they are *sealed.* And on that seal there are two inscriptions, one stressing the *divine* side of their salvation: "The Lord knows who are his"; and the other bringing out the *human* side: "Let every one who names the name of the Lord stand aloof from unrighteousness."

With the visible church, however, it is as with a large house: not everything in it is equally valuable: some "vessels" are destined for honor; others for dishonor. Hence, it should not cause any surprise that men like Hymenaeus and Philetus have a following. But if anyone will effectively cleanse himself from men of this type and their evil influences, he will be . . . very useful to the Master, prepared for every good work. This applies also to Timothy.

Now in order to become thus thoroughly qualified, Timothy must also flee away from the sinful desires that pertain to the younger generation. Positively, he should stedfastly pursue faith, love, etc. He must not be quarrelsome but gentle to all. Only in this way will he be *qualified to teach.* Such teaching will require that he exercise great patience, even under injuries. When opposed, he should correct his opponents with mildness, in the hope that possibly God may grant them conversion, a complete mental, moral, and spiritual turn-about which leads to acknowledgment of the truth and to soberness. Thus they will have been delivered from the snare set by the devil, by whom they had been taken captive to do *his* (that is, the devil's) will.

Outline of Chapter 3

Theme: *The Apostle Paul Tells Timothy What To Do in the Interest of Sound Doctrine*

    Abide in It　　　　　　　　"Grievous times will come"

3:1-9　Knowing that enemies will arise, who have its form, not its power.

3:10-17　Knowing that it is based on the sacred writings, as you learned from trustworthy persons.

CHAPTER III

II TIMOTHY   3:1

3 1 But understand this, that in (the) last days grievous seasons will set in; 2 for the people will be self-loving, money-loving, boasters, overbearing, blasphemers, disobedient to (their) parents, unthankful, unholy, 3 unfeeling, unforgiving, slanderers, unrestrained, untamed, unloving toward the good, 4 traitors, reckless, blinded with conceit, pleasure-loving rather than God-loving, 5 having a form of piety but denying its power; and from such people turn away.

6 For out of these circles come those who are infiltrating the homes and are taking captive weak-minded women loaded down with sins, swayed by various impulses, 7 ever learning and never able to arrive at the acknowledgment of (the) truth. 8 And just as Jannes and Jambres opposed Moses, so do also these men oppose the truth, men corrupt in mind and reprobate with respect to the faith. 9 But they will not get very far, for their folly will be obvious to everyone, as also that of those (two men) got to be.

3:1-9

1. To be gentle, patient, and mild (see II Tim. 2:24-26) will not be easy, as the apostle now proceeds to show: **But understand this, that in (the) last days grievous seasons will set in.**

There are two things which Paul wants Timothy to do, according to the lengthy sentence which extends all the way from 1:1 to the end of verse 5. He tells his dearly-beloved representative that he:

a. must constantly realize that in the last days grievous seasons will set in; and

b. must constantly turn away from the kind of people who will make these seasons so grievous.

These two commands are connected by the conjunction "and." Hence, when most of the explanatory material that intervenes between the commands is omitted, there remains this: "But *understand* this, that in (the) last days grievous seasons will set in; for the people will be self-loving ... *and* from such people *turn away*."

Once this connection is understood, it also becomes clear that the expression "in the last days," as here used, cannot be limited to the days which will immediately precede Christ's second coming.[150] It would have been

---

[150] Scott *op. cit.*, p. 118, simply states that this is the meaning, but does not offer any proof or any word-study of the concept. Bouma, *op. cit.*, p. 311, who inter-

senseless to tell Timothy to avoid people who would never bother him at all! And it is not warranted to "solve" the difficulty by saying: "The writer expected Christ's return any moment!" (See N.T.C. on II Thess., chapter 2). — The key to the correct interpretation is the contextual explanation of the expression "in the last days."

Now in the Old Testament this expression (Gen. 49:1; Num. 24:14; Deut. 4:30; Is. 2:2; Jer. 23:20; 30:24; 48:47; 49:39; Ezek. 38:16; Dan. 2:28; 10:14; Hos. 3:5; Mic. 4:1) refers to "the days to come," "the future." What is included in that "future" must be determined in each separate instance by the context.[151] That it cannot in every instance refer exclusively to the days that will immediately precede Christ's second coming is clear at once from the context of such a passage as Gen. 49:1. Jacob, in blessing his sons, was not thinking primarily of what would happen at the end of the world, nor was he even thinking of a period which for each tribe would begin at the Messiah's first advent. On the contrary, he was describing the events that were to take place in the lives of his sons and in the history of the tribes of Israel. And even from the context of such a passage as Dan. 2:28 it is evident that the expression "in the last days" covers a period which *begins* with the Babylonian sovereignty, long before the days of Christ's first advent, and which includes also the entire new dispensation. In fact, in a sense, the period covered never ends, for a kingdom is predicted "which will last forever."

As the context shows, in passages such as Is. 2:2; Micah 4:1 (cf. 5:2) the expression "in the last days" refers to *the age ushered in by Christ's appearance on earth*. This is the age of the fulfilment of the Messianic promises, promises which attain their even more glorious realization at the consummation.[152]

This is clearly also the meaning in Acts 2:17 (quotation from Joel 2:28), where the events that occurred on the day of Pentecost are included in "the last days." (Cf. the use of the expression in James 5:3, variously interpreted.) The rather similar expression "at the end of these days" in Heb. 1:2 (see context) also clearly refers to a period which began with the coming of Christ into the flesh. Moreover, the apostle John knew that "the last hour" *had already arrived* (I John 2:18).

Accordingly, Paul's words here in II Tim. 3:1 are best interpreted as meaning, "Timothy, constantly realize that in these last days — this lengthy dispensation — *in which we are now living* there will be grievous seasons."

---

prets similarly, states that John in his Gospel often uses this expression. But this is incorrect. Christ's "at the last day" (sing., see John 6:39, 40, 44, 54; 11:24; 12:48) must not be confused with Paul's "in the last days" *(plural)*.

[151] See G. Ch. Aalders, *Het Herstel Van Israel Volgens Het Oude Testament*, pp. 13, 14, 39, 46.

[152] The Old Testament, however, does not sharply distinguish between the two comings, but treats them as if they were one.

These seasons will come and go, and the last will be worse than the first. They will be seasons of ever-increasing wickedness (Matt. 24:12; Luke 18:8), which will culminate in the climax of wickedness, the revelation of "the man of lawlessness" (II Thess. 2:1-12; cf. Matt. 24; Mark 13; Luke 21).

"There will *set in* (approaching like a thunder-storm, until fully present) seasons grievous." Thus the passage reads literally, with some emphasis on the adjective *grievous, hard* or *painful* (to endure). These *seasons,* then, are eras of duress for the true church, difficult time-periods of the new dispensation, definitely marked out in God's eternal decree.

As was true with respect to the closely related "later seasons" prophecy (I Tim. 4:1-5), so also the present prediction has "multiple fulfilment." But while I Tim. 4:1-5 warned against the coming of *Ascetic* Gnostics and their followers throughout the course of history, the present prophecy deals more emphatically with the coming of *Antinomian* or *Licentious* Gnostics and with those throughout the centuries who, although dropping some of their weird basic theories, copy their worldly example.

2-5. Grievous seasons will set in, **for the people will be. . . .** It is *the people* (the members of the human race; *the men* generically, not the "men" as distinguished from the "women") living during these grievous seasons who will cause all the grief. A catalogue of their sinful characteristics follows. It should be compared with the list in Rom. 1:29-31. Note in both lists: a. *boasters, overbearing* (or *haughty*); b. *unsubmissive* or *disobedient to parents;* and c. *unfeeling* (or *without natural affection*). Note also synonyms: Romans has *whisperers* and *defamers* ("backbiters"); II Timothy, *slanderers;* Romans, *haters of God;* II Timothy, *pleasure-loving rather than God-loving;* Romans *unmerciful;* II Timothy, *unforgiving* (or *implacable;* literally; *admitting of no truce*); etc.

Here in II Tim. the list has nineteen items (if the modifiers "pleasure-loving rather than God-loving," and "having a form of piety but denying its power" each be regarded as *one* item).[153] Whether Paul had any division in mind, so that the nineteen can be divided into groups, each group emphasizing one central idea, cannot be determined. It is true, however, that items 6-10 form an unbroken series, in the sense that all of these begin with the prefix *un-* or *dis-* (ἀ -privative in the original). This would divide the entire catalogue into three groups (items 1-5; 6-10; 11-19), structurally considered. Note, however, that three of the items in the last group also begin with the negative prefix.[154]

---

[153] I cannot follow Lenski's arithmetic, *op. cit.,* p. 821. He counts "eighteen" items, and then seems to divide these 18 into three groups, containing respectively 5, 3, and 12 items. But that would make 20 in all, not 18! Hence, his allegorical interpretation of the figures (5, three 4's, and a final 3) also looks rather dubious.
[154] It is true, of course, that ἀ -privative does not need to be rendered by a similar negative prefix like *un-* or *dis-* or *in-* or *non-*. One may try the suffix *-less;* or one

3:2-5   II TIMOTHY

The list, then, is as follows:

self-loving, money-loving, boasters, overbearing, blasphemers, disobedient to (their) parents, unthankful, unholy, unfeeling, unforgiving, slanderers, unrestrained, untamed, unloving toward the good, traitors, reckless, blinded with conceit, pleasure-loving rather than God-loving, having a form of piety but denying its power.

These people, then, are, first of all *self-loving.* Cf. Titus 1:7: "self-pleasing." Trench (par. xciii) borrows the illustration of the hedgehog which a. rolls itself up in a ball, keeping the soft, warm wool for itself (φίλαυτος, self-loving, selfish); and b. presents the sharp spines to those without (αὐθάδης, self-pleasing, arrogant).

Since they are self-loving, they are naturally also *money-loving* (lovers of silver). Think of the Pharisees as described in Luke 16:14.

They are *boastful* or *boasters* (cf. Rom. 1:30). This word originally referred to a person who wanders about the country. He may be peddling medicine, boasting about its healing virtue; hence, a "quack." But in the present passage boasting in general is meant.

While boasting about themselves and their "wares," accomplishments, or talents, these people are *overbearing* (cf. Rom. 1:30; then Luke 1:51; James 4:6; I Peter 5:5) in their attitude to others. They are the *haughty* type, "uppish."

It is not surprising that such people are also described as being *blasphemers.* When they *speak,* they *hurt* or *injure.* They use scornful language, insulting God and man (see on I Tim. 6:4). The group of words formed around this stem has many examples in the New Testament. For the adjective *blasphemous* (here in II Tim. used as a substantive, *blasphemers*) see also Acts 6:11; II Peter 2:11 (cf. Jude 9). For the related verb *(to blaspheme)* see on I Tim. 1:20; for the related noun *(blasphemy),* see on I Tim. 6:4.

These people are *lacking* in such excellent qualities as submissiveness, thankfulness, holiness, affection for their own families, and the forgiving attitude. It is implied that in each case they possess the very opposite attitude; that is, they are not only *disobedient* but definitely *rebellious;* not only *untamed* but *fierce;* not only *unholy* but *wicked,* etc. Taking these five characteristics one by one, these people are described as being, first of all, *disobedient* toward their parents (cf. Rom. 1:30; then Luke 1:17; Acts 26:9; Titus 1:16; 3:3).

This shows that they are *unthankful* (cf. Luke 6:35), not appreciative of the many acts of kindness which their parents have bestowed upon them,

---

may even substitute a positive for a negative word; for example, "fierce" for "untamed." I have chosen *un-* or *dis-* for all the ἀ -privatives in the list in order to remain as close as possible to the flavor of the original without changing the sense of the entire word.

and not appreciative toward other people either, nor toward God (cf. Rom. 1:21, "neither gave thanks"). Though blessings are common enough, there is in this world no "common gratitude." "Common *grace*" (God's kindness toward all his creatures, Ps. 145:9, 17; Jonah 4:10, 11; Matt. 5:43-45; Luke 6:35), yes; "common *gratitude,*" no!

With respect to things which have divine sanction, they are *unholy* or *impious* (cf. I Tim. 1:9). They do not reverence the established sanctities. This implies that they are *unfeeling,* or *unsympathetic, heartless, lacking* even in natural affection such as parents have for their children, and children for their parents (cf. Rom. 1:31).

They show that same callousness all around, also in their relation to their fellowmen. Their feuds never end. In their camp no libation is ever poured out to signify that those who had been at variance with each other have consented to a truce. They are *implacable, irreconcilable.*

The final group shows how these inner attitudes or deficiencies express themselves outwardly in words of hatred and deeds of cruelty.

These people, then, hurl false and/or hostile epithets and charges at each other. They are *slanderers, false accusers,* imitators of the great Diabolos (I Tim. 3:6, 7; Eph. 4:27; 6:11; etc., a word of frequent occurrence in the New Testament). They have never learned to control themselves; hence, are *unrestrained,* "uninhibited," thoroughly lacking in self-control, devoid of power to check their own drives and impulses. Having never "settled down," they are *untamed, savage, fierce.* They despise virtue, are *unloving toward the good.* By them their associates, even *before* the latters' ruin is evident, have been *given over* to the enemy. They are *traitors,* therefore, receiving their pay beforehand, just like Judas (cf. Luke 6:16; Acts 7:52). Nothing stops them. Rashly they plunge ahead in their wickedness, being *reckless* or *precipitate* in their deeds of violence (cf. Acts 19:36). No one can tell them anything, for they "know it all," so *blinded with conceit* (see on I Tim. 3:6; 6:4) are they. This blindness, moreover, has a moral, spiritual cause. Its root is in the heart and in the will, for these people are utterly selfish (note how the description in reaching a climax returns to its starting-point: "self-loving"). They are *pleasure-loving rather than* (or *more than*) *God-loving.* This definitely does not mean that they also love God to some extent. It means that they do not love God at all (for "rather than" or "more than" in this sense see also John 3:19; 12:43; Acts 4:19; 17:11; I Tim. 1:4; cf. somewhat similar idioms in Luke 15:7; 18:14). Not only does one find these people outside of the church. They have infiltrated the church (and not only the church, see verse 6). And even should they be excommunicated, they will still pretend to be eminent Christians. They are described as having a *form,* a mere *semblance* or *appearance* (cf. Rom. 2:20) of *piety* (see on I Tim. 2:2; 3:16; 4:7, 8; 6:3, 5, 6, 11), but *denying* (literally, "having once for all denied") its power.

These people lack spiritual dynamite. They have no love for God, nor for his revelation in Jesus Christ, nor for his people. Hence, since they are not Spirit-filled men, it is not surprising that they lack power.

And from such people turn away, says Paul (for explanation see pp. 281, 282). Cf. II John 10.

6, 7. The reason why Timothy must turn away from such people is now pointed out: **For out of these circles come those who are infiltrating the homes and are taking captive weak-minded women.**

Out of the circles (for the Greek idiom see N.T.C. on John 1:24) of the men described in verses 1-5 come those false prophets who specialize in the art of captivating *women*. They are not successful with *all* the women, of course. Many women are far too sensible to become the dupes of false prophets. Paul thought very highly of such noble women and made good use of their talents (see on I Tim. 3:11; and on I Tim. 5:9, 10). But every age also has its *fickle* women (see on I Tim. 5:13), and these are found both *in* the church and *outside* of it.

Probably when their husbands are not at home, the women are visited by these peddlers of strange doctrines. There was a beginning of this evil practice in Paul's day — or shall we go back all the way to Paradise? (Gen. 3:1-6a) — ; it was going to become worse in days to come. We of the twentieth century know that exactly this practice is going on today, and that the false prophets who engage in it show a close resemblance to those of Paul's day and age. Also today, as many can testify, the men who visit the women in order to ensnare them fail to take sin seriously, often deny everlasting punishment, and in general proclaim a religion which satisfies "the flesh."

These men, then, worm their way into *the homes* (pl. of οἰκία, *dwelling;* then *home, household, family*). Why is it that they seek out *women?* Is it because they know that women (especially women of this particular brand) are easier to mislead than men? Is it that they reason thus: Once we have the women on our side, the men will come of their own accord? (Again see Gen. 3.) By methods either fair or foul these men *are getting into* (not necessarily in every case: are sneaking into) the family-units. By means of the very novelty of their doctrines, which offer "an easy way out" for anyone who is bothered by sin, these infiltrators *are taking captive* (original sense: *taking with the spear;* but here more general and metaphorical, *captivating*) *weak-minded women*. To describe these women, the original uses a diminutive with contemptuous meaning. This is hard to reproduce in English. Cf. the German *Weiblein,* and the Dutch *vrouwtjes;* "little women" would hardly do. Probably "weak-minded women" or "weak-natured women" or "silly women" (A.V., A.R.V.) will do; cf. the colloquial "softies." These are, at any rate, women "who do not amount to much," "easy marks" for the false prophets.

By means of three participial phrases, the last one a compound phrase, these weak-minded women are further described: **loaded down with sins, swayed by various impulses, ever learning and never able to arrive at the acknowledgment of (the) truth.**

First of all, then, these women are "heaped up with sin" (for the verb see Rom. 12:20). They are *very wicked,* and the fact that they welcome the smooth talkers seems to indicate that their sins have given them an uneasy feeling, though not in the sense of Rom. 7:24. These women are probably *afraid* of the consequences of their sins, but are not necessarily *ashamed* of them.

Secondly, they are "swayed by various *impulses*" (or *"desires,"* see explanation of II Tim. 2:22 for word-study). What these evil incentives are is not stated. Perhaps we may think of such things as the following: the desire to find an easy way out of their guilt-complex, the desire to gain recognition, to be considered "well-informed," to satisfy their curiosity, to have attention bestowed upon them by "prominent" representatives of the opposite sex, etc.

Thirdly, these weak-minded women are *ever learning.* Eager disciples are they, "taking it all in," as with rapt attention they sit down to listen to their licentious teachers and to admire them. But their unwillingness openly to confess and to resist the evil promptings of their nature results in their being *"never able* to arrive at the acknowledgment of (the) truth" as revealed in the gospel (cf. I Tim. 2:4; II Tim. 2:25).

By making propaganda for their nefarious doctrines, going from home to home in order to enlist women-disciples and women-helpers, these false teachers become manifest to all true believers as adversaries of God and of his truth. This also has its present-day fulfilment, for the well-known "witnesses" (or by whatever name they may be called) are always denouncing the orthodox churches and their ministers.

8. Says Paul, **And just as Jannes and Jambres opposed Moses, so do also these men oppose the truth, men corrupt in mind and reprobate with respect to the faith.**

When Moses told Pharaoh, "Let my people go" (Ex. 5:1), and when he proved his divine commission by performing genuine miracles through the power of God (Ex. 7:10, 20, etc.), Pharaoh's magicians performed their counter-miracles (Ex. 7:11, 22; 8:7; but see also 8:18, 19). From Jewish tradition,[155] with which Paul was very familiar (having been a student of

---

[155] The names Jannes and Jambres occur frequently in late Jewish, pagan, and early Christian literature. For specific references see the article "Jannes and Jambres" in *The New Schaff-Herzog Encyclopaedia of Religious Knowledge,* Vol. VI, p. 95.

Gamaliel, Acts 22:3), he cites the example of those two ring-leaders among the magicians who, whatever their real names may have been, were known to the Jews as "Jannes and Jambres" (Aram. probably: "he who seduces and he who makes rebellious"). The apostle had in mind the following comparison:

Just as Jannes and Jambres *opposed* God's representative, Moses, so do also these licentious leaders *oppose* the truth of God as revealed in his Word and as proclaimed by Paul, Timothy, etc.

This point of comparison is definitely stated. (For another undoubted third of comparison see below, on verse 9.) Whether here in verse 8 any further resemblances are implied cannot be proved. The following are mere possibilities:

(1) Jannes and Jambres were deceivers; so are the purveyors of strange doctrine against whom Paul warns Timothy.

(2) If Jewish tradition can be credited in this respect, Jannes and Jambres became proselytes, faking "conversion" to the Jewish religion. When they saw that they could not prevent Israel's exodus from Egypt, they are said to have joined the departing multitude. Later (according to Jewish tradition!) *they* were the ones who induced the people to make a golden calf and to worship it. They were pretenders, therefore; hypocrites, and as such very dangerous. — Similarly, the false leaders whom Paul describes are all the more dangerous because they pretend to be genuine converts to the Christian religion.

Paul calls the men whom he is describing "corrupt in mind" (perfect passive participle; cf. I Tim. 6:5). In their case the very organ that was given to men in order that he might be able to receive and reflect on spiritual realities has become thoroughly and permanently defiled. As a result, with respect to "the faith" (objective sense), these men have been found to be worthy of emphatic disapproval; hence, *reprobate,* condemned as worthless, unfit, disqualified, utterly *rejected.*

9. There is, however, one reason for encouragement. Says Paul: **But they will not get very far, for their folly will be obvious to everyone, as also that of those (two men) got to be.**

To be sure, the enemies of the faith advance to constantly increasing ungodliness, and their word devours like a gangrene (II Tim. 2:16, 17), so that for a while it may seem that their purpose is going to be achieved and that the entire organism of the church will be destroyed. But this never happens, not in any of the many periods of the church's history, not even toward the end of the age. The purpose is always to lead astray: *if possible,* even the elect (Mark 13:22), but this is ever *impossible!* The thought here is like that in II Tim. 2:17, 18, followed by the comforting verse 19. God's solid foundation remains standing. And in that sense it is true that the errorists *"will not get very far"* (for ἐπὶ πλεῖον in this sense consider also Acts 20:9). Their *folly* (lack of understanding, senselessness) will become *entirely clear to all.* No doubt, God's true children see this folly first of all. Afterward, others too will see it; for worldly people have a tendency to follow first one deceiver, then another. For example, those who yesterday *glorified* Stalin, today *condemn* him in no uncertain terms! Exactly that same thing happened in the case of Jannes and Jambres.

---

10 **You, however, followed my teaching, my conduct, my purpose, my faith, my longsuffering, my love, my endurance, 11 my persecutions, my sufferings, what kind of things happened to me at Antioch, at Iconium, (and) at Lystra, what kind of persecutions I underwent;** yet from them all the Lord rescued me! 12 In fact, all who desire to live devoutly in Christ Jesus will be persecuted. 13 Evil men and impostors, moreover, will proceed from bad to worse, deceiving and being deceived. 14 **You,** however, must continue in the things which you have learned and of which you have become convinced, knowing from w h o m you learned (them), 15 and that from infancy you have known (the) sacred writings, which are able to make you wise for salvation through that faith (which is) in Christ Jesus. 16 All scripture (is) God-breathed and useful for teaching, for reproof, for correction, for training in righteousness, 17 that the man of God may be equipped, for every good work thoroughly equipped.

3:10-17

10, 11. Now in view of the fact that grievous seasons will set in, in which wicked men and impostors will proceed from bad to worse, Timothy, who has hitherto followed Paul's teaching, etc., should exert himself the more to *abide in* this sound doctrine, which he has learned from trustworthy persons and which is based upon those divinely inspired writings in which from the days of infancy he has been instructed. Says Paul, **You, however, followed my teaching, my conduct, my purpose, my faith, my longsuffering, my love, my endurance, my persecutions, my sufferings, what kind of things happened to me at Antioch, at Iconium, (and) at Lystra, what kind of persecutions I underwent.**

Between the false teachers and Timothy there had been a sharp contrast, so that Paul is able to exclaim, *"You* (with great emphasis on this pronoun), however, followed my teaching," etc. The verb *followed,* in Greek as well as in English, when it is used in a figurative sense, can mean either *watched, observed, investigated* (cf. Luke 1:3); or *took as a model, adhered to, copied.* Though the latter meaning will do very well when associated with "my teaching, my conduct, my purpose, my faith," etc., it will not do nearly as well with "the things which happened to me at Antioch," etc. Probably what the apostle means is this, "Timothy, in contrast with our opponents, *you* took a deep, sympathetic interest in my teaching, my conduct," etc. So interpreted, the verb implies that Timothy had actually taken Paul as his model, and had also listened to him with keen interest when he related his experiences, in some of which (for example, those at Lystra) the younger man had become intimately involved.

Paul, soon to die, clearly is looking back upon his whole life of service to Christ, especially upon that part of it which began with his first missionary journey and extended to this very day here in the Roman dungeon. With respect to that entire long journey he says, in summary, "You ... followed my teaching, conduct," etc.[156]

In the original each of the particulars with respect to which Timothy has "followed" Paul is definite. Hence, the correct rendering is not "my teaching, conduct, purpose," etc. (A.V. and A.R.V.), but "my teaching, my conduct, my purpose," etc., with "my" repeated before each item.

Does the list of nine particulars show any definite order or grouping? It is impossible to answer this question categorically. Surely, if any sequence is pointed out, it should be a natural one, characteristic (at least to some extent) of Paul.[157] An arbitrary division is of no help whatever. It must be admitted, however, that we today cannot be sure that *our* attempt to point out why one item in the list follows another corresponds with *Paul's own* reasoning. If it be permissible, nevertheless, to make such an attempt — with the definite understanding that it is merely an attempt, which may or may not be entirely successful — I would suggest the following:

All the items express or imply *obedience to the Lord*. The seven items in verse 10 are the manifestations of *active* obedience (even *endurance*, that is, "stedfast perseverance," is active; and so is *longsuffering*, "the exercise of patience toward others"). The two items in verse 11 are the manifestations of a more *passive* type of obedience: a person is *persecuted*; as a result, he *suffers*.

In the first group of seven there are four items which probably go together ("my faith, my longsuffering, my love, my endurance"). The linking of *faith, love,* and *endurance* is characteristic of Paul (I Thess. 1:3; I Tim. 6:11; Titus 2:2). Sometimes *hope* appears in the place of *endurance*, the latter being the fruit of the former: Col. 1:4, 5 ("faith, love, hope"); I Cor. 13:13 ("faith, hope, love"). Here in II Tim. 3:10 it is not strange to find *longsuffering* in a subdivision which also lists *endurance*. In both of these the Christian's *patience* is expressed (for the distinction see below).

---

[156] This, it would seem to me, is a more natural explanation than that favored, among others, by Bouma, *op. cit.*, p. 323, according to which the aorist would be ingressive, and would mean, "You *became* my follower when you changed from the Jewish to the Christian faith."

[157] Hence, I cannot agree with the grouping presented by Lenski, *op. cit.*, p. 831. Paul would not thus separate *faith* and *love*.

We arrive, accordingly, at the following grouping which *may* have been in the author's mind:

A. *Expressions of Active Obedience* (verse 10)

1. my teaching, my conduct, my purpose (as to the possible relation of these three see below)
2. my faith, my longsuffering, my love, my endurance

B. *Expressions of Passive Obedience* (verse 11)

my persecutions (those which I experienced), my sufferings.

As to the separate items, note the following:

a. *my teaching*. Logically this comes first, for it was *the teaching* of Paul, *the gospel* which he preached, which had first of all impressed Timothy, and had been sanctified to his heart unto conversion (cf. Acts 14:12). On this word *teaching* see also pp. 6, 7, 9.

b. *my conduct*. Paul's consecrated walk of life (cf. I Cor. 4:17), his completely unselfish behavior, giving all honor to God and refusing to receive any honor for himself, had also left its imprint upon Timothy (cf. Acts 14:13-18). Moreover, not only at the beginning but throughout their association with each other Paul's teaching and his conduct in harmony with that teaching had constantly been watched with sympathetic interest by the younger man. In his own life these two (teaching and conduct) had borne fruit.

c. *my purpose*. A man's real, inner purpose is not clearly evident the first time you meet him. Though his words may be very fine, he may be a deceiver. But when, as in the case of Paul, teaching and conduct are in beautiful harmony, no legitimate doubt remains as to the purpose of one's life. Already at the time of Paul's first visit to Lystra, Timothy, no doubt, had become persuaded about this purpose and had made it his own. The apostle's subsequent heroic return (on this same first missionary journey) to the very city which had stoned him almost to death must have made that glorious purpose even clearer (see especially Acts 14:22), and even more a matter to be copied. Later experiences had served to further clarify and intensify this "aim in life."

Turning now to the group of four items which seem to belong together (as has been shown), the one first in this list is:

d. *my faith*. Occurring between "my purpose" and "my longsuffering," the expression "my faith" is best interpreted in the subjective sense, "the faith in God (and in his redemptive truth) which I exercise." This, too, had exerted its powerful effect upon Timothy and had been reproduced in his own heart and life.

e. *my longsuffering*. This "patience with respect to *people*" (as distinguished from *endurance,* which is "patience amid *adverse circumstances,*" see N.T.C. on I and II Thess., p. 198), yes even with respect to *persecutors,* Paul had exhibited again and again, from the very day when Timothy had first met him at Lystra.

f. *my love,* probably in this connection especially with respect to *people,* including *enemies.*

g. *my endurance.* For definition see under e. above. Stedfast perseverance amid trying circumstances, the grace to hold up under, had been characteristic of Paul throughout his glorious missionary-career. To a certain extent, Timothy had caught the spirit.

As to Paul's passive obedience (also reflected in Timothy), the apostle continues:

h. *my persecutions,* those which I endured; and last of all, their natural effect or consequence:

i. *my sufferings,* for the sake of Christ, of course (Rom. 8:17, 18; II Cor. 12:10; Col. 1:24). To see what kind of persecutions and sufferings Paul endured one should read the list in II Cor. 11:21-33. In some of these Timothy had shared.

It is not at all surprising that in connection with persecutions and sufferings Paul says, "what kind of things happened to me at Antioch, at Iconium, (and) at Lystra," for these were the very places which he had visited on his first missionary journey, the journey on which Timothy had first met the apostle and had been converted. Timothy had heard Paul's preaching at Lystra, had probably witnessed the miraculous cure of the born-cripple, the manner in which Paul (and Barnabas) had restrained the multitude from worshipping him, and the stoning. Very vividly Timothy must have recalled how the people, believing that Paul was dead, had dragged him out of the city (*Timothy's* native city, in all probability). Read Acts 14. On this occasion or shortly afterward the new convert must also have learned about the tribulations which the missionaries had endured just before entering Lystra, namely, at Antioch (expulsion), and at Iconium (the minds of the Gentiles poisoned against them by the Jews, and the threat of physical harm). By saying "what kind of things happened to me," and "what kind of persecutions I underwent," the apostle indicates: a. the character or nature of these woeful experiences (they were very severe, very bitter), and probably b. the fact that many similar hardships for the sake of the gospel had followed in their train, until this very moment.

The vivid recollection of these afflictions, which march in rapid procession before Paul's mind's eye, causes him by way of contrast to exclaim, **Yet** (καί is undoubtedly adversative here) **from them all the Lord rescued me!** Let timid Timothy take this to heart (Ps. 27:1-5; Ps. 91; Ps. 125; Is.

43:2; Nah. 1:7). The Lord *ever* rescues his people, frequently *from* death, sometimes *by means of* death. Either way, nothing ever separates them from his love (Rom. 8:38, 39).

12. The fact that believers are intimately united with Christ means that *essentially* (though not in degree) *all* must suffer Christ's reproach. Says Paul, **In fact, all who desire to live devoutly in Christ Jesus will be persecuted.**

The idea of the godly, pious, or devout life occurs again and again in the Pastorals (see p. 10; then for the noun also on I Tim. 2:2; 3:16; 4:7, 8; 6:3, 5, 6, 11; II Tim. 3:5; Titus 1:1; for the related verb see I Tim. 5:4. Here in II Tim. 3:12 and also in Titus 2:12 the adverb is used). But though the words built on this stem occur at times in a very general sense and are applied also to pagan religious life (see M.M., pp. 265, 266), Paul speaks distinctly about those who desire to live devoutly *in Christ Jesus*. The people whom he has in mind have made it their earnest resolution, with God's help and by his grace, to live the life of devotion *to Christ*. They live in close fellowship *with him* (John 15:4, 5; Gal. 2:20; Phil. 3:10).

Now the apostle makes the definite statement that *all* those who desire to live devoutly in Christ Jesus *will be persecuted*. Paul's own experience (see verse 11 above) is by no means peculiar. Scars are the price which *every* believer pays for his loyalty to Christ. They are also his *credentials* before God.

The reason why persecution awaits all those who are firmly resolved to adorn their confession with a truly Christian life is that in the midst of contradictions coming from every side they refuse either to stop their ears or to cringe and compromise. Instead, they face the foe and challenge him to combat. They go right ahead, boldly defending the faith against every attack, and courageously assaulting the fortress of unbelief. The result is persecution, at times very bitter.

This inescapable character of persecution is a truth which Scripture proclaims everywhere (especially in such passages as Matt. 5:10-12; 10:28; John 15:17-20; 16:1-4, 33; I Thess. 3:4). The fact that Timothy knows beforehand that also this is included in God's decree and takes place within the realm of God's providence which is ever causing good to come forth out of evil, should be a source of comfort to him and to all true believers. The comfort becomes even greater when verse 12 is read in the light of the immediately preceding verse: even in the midst of bitter persecution the interests of every believer are perfectly secure with him whose name is Rescuer.

13. Between verses 12 and 13 there is no contrast. Not until verse 14 is reached is a contrast introduced, similar in nature to that which is found at the beginning of verse 10 (in both cases, *"You,* however") — Persecution is the lot of every believer; hence, will continue. That is the idea which the apostle has conveyed in verse 12. And now the reason why it continues is stated: the wicked will never desist, but will increase in wickedness. Says Paul, **Evil men and impostors, moreover, will proceed from bad to worse, deceiving and being deceived.** These "wicked men" and "impostors" are the ones described in verses 2-9. They must not be thought of as two mutually exclusive groups (one group consisting of nothing but "wicked men," the other of nothing but "impostors"). It is *one and the same* group, *one* predicate applying to everyone included in the group, though in the subject *two* descriptive terms are used to characterize this group. These persons are called: a. *evil men* (cf. I Cor. 5:13; II Thess. 3:2), men whose attitudes, desires, words, and works are wicked (see verses 1-9), and whose master is "the evil one" (II Thess. 3:3; then Matt. 6:13). b. These persons are also called *impostors* (γόητες, used only here in the New Testament). They are deceivers, shrewd and crafty individuals. In that respect — not necessarily in the ability to work magic — they remind one of Jannes and Jambres (see on verse 8 above).

These evil men and impostors, who persecute sincere believers and who strive to lead everyone astray, "will proceed from bad to worse," that is, *inwardly:* morally and spiritually, "deceiving (see on verses 6-8) and being deceived." [158] The implication may well be that while they are engaged in deceiving others, they themselves are being deceived. A "deluding energy" is the punishment which those receive who would delude others. Delusion is their weapon; by delusion they are slain. They believe, or try to make themselves believe, that the falsehoods by means of which they would ensnare others will gain for themselves complete happiness and ultimate victory. In this they will be bitterly disappointed. (See N.T.C. on II Thess. 2:11.) Nevertheless, the emphasis in the present passage is not on "being deceived" but on "deceiving," as is clear from the words which immediately follow. While some fall for this deception, let Timothy be on his guard. Let *him* remain firm and stedfast. Says Paul:

---

[158] The expression is almost proverbial. Cf. Philo, *On The Migration Of Abraham,* XV, "intending to deceive, they are deceived." Ovid, *Metamorphoses,* XIV. 81, "Being herself disappointed, she disappointed all." Augustine, *Confessions,* VII. 2, "deceived deceivers."

Having erected an instrument of death for Mordecai, Haman discovers too late that it is going to be the instrument for his own execution. Perillos of Athens, desiring to bake others to death by means of his "metal bull" is himself baked to death in it. Hugues Aubriot, having built the Bastille for the imprisonment of others, is himself the first one to be confined in it. The bishop of Verdun, having invented the Iron Cage for the punishment of others is himself the first man to be shut up in it. And Rebent Morton is the first to lose his head to The Maiden (a kind of guillotine) which he himself devised for the decapitation of others.

14, 15. *You, however, must continue in the things which you have learned and of which you have become convinced.*

You (note emphatic position in the original, at the very head of the sentence, just as in verse 10) must pursue a course which is the very opposite of that which was followed by the false teachers and their adherents. Timothy, then, is here admonished *to continue* or *abide* in "the things" (the doctrines based on Holy Writ, see verses 15, 16) which he has learned and of which he has become convinced. When did he learn them? And when had he become convinced of them? The tense used in the original does not specify. It simply *states* the historical fact that Timothy has learned and has become convinced.[159] From the context (verse 15) we gather that the two activities (learning and becoming convinced) had begun already in very early childhood. It is natural to suppose that they had continued up to this very moment while Paul is admonishing him to remain in these things. Learning had increased throughout the years, and conviction had been deepened.

Note that *learning* is not enough. What has been learned must be applied to the heart by the Holy Spirit, so that one also *becomes convinced,* with a conviction that transforms life.

According to the most natural grammatical construction, Paul states *two* reasons why Timothy must continue in the things which he learned and of which he became convinced. *In reality* the two reasons are only *one,* for the testimony of human beings with respect to matters of faith means nothing apart from the Word; nevertheless, since it pleased God *by means of devout human individuals* to convey to the mind and heart of Timothy the message of the Word, it is entirely proper to speak of *two* reasons:

a. The trustworthy character of those who had instructed Timothy in these doctrines (verse 14b); and

b. The super-excellence of the sacred writings on which these doctrines are based (verse 15).

The first reason is expressed in these words: **knowing from whom you learned them.** Timothy must never forget that he had learned these things from no less a person than Paul himself (see verses 10 and 11 above) and, going back even farther, from those highly esteemed worthies: grandmother Lois and mother Eunice (II Tim. 1:5), women who, before their conversion to the Christian faith, had instructed the little child Timothy in "the sacred writings," and who, having once accepted Jesus as their Lord and Savior, had been used as instruments in God's hand to co-operate with

---

[159] The theory of some interpreters, namely, that the aorist tense expresses that Timothy had learned and had become convinced of these things at a definite time (for instance, "before he became a Christian," Bouma, *op. cit.,* p. 328) is questionable. Far better is the view of Lenski, *op. cit.,* p. 836: both aorists are simply constative. They simply summarize the past, without indicating any definite time.

3:14, 15   **II TIMOTHY**

Paul in the important task of leading the young man to see in Christ the fulfilment of the Old Testament promises.

It is clear that Paul, Lois, Eunice, and any others who may have nurtured Timothy, are not viewed as independent authorities, apart from the Word, but as secondary or intermediate sources of knowledge, avenues of instruction, and even this *only because they accepted Scripture!* — Hence, not Tradition *and* Scripture (which really means Tradition *superimposed upon* Scripture) are here viewed as *basically* authoritative. *Scripture alone* (see verses 15 and 16) *is final authority,* and Tradition is important only in the measure in which it adheres to and imparts Scripture. When it does this, then it is of considerable significance, and this especially in the education of children who as yet are not able to read and/or interpret Scripture itself!

Accordingly, the second — the only really *basic* — reason why Timothy should abide in the things which he learned and of which he had become persuaded is: **And that from infancy you have known (the) sacred writings, which are able to make you wise for salvation through that faith (which is) in Christ Jesus.**

Principles and Methods of Education in Israel
Background for the Understanding of II Tim. 3:15

(1) Among the Jews education was definitely *God-centered* as to principles, contents, and methods. *The devout Israelite taught his children because Jehovah commanded him to do so.* And he instructed them *with respect to* the *verba et gesta Dei* (words and deeds of God), *as recorded in "the* sacred writings." This is evident throughout the Old Testament (Gen. 18:19; Ex. 10:2; 12:26, 27; 13:14-16; Deut. 4:9, 10; 6:7, 9; 11:19; 32:46; Is. 38:19; and many other passages; cf. also Josephus, *Antiquities,* IV. viii. 12).

(2) Naturally *the content* of this body of God-centered education was, "The fear of Jehovah is the beginning of (knowledge and of) wisdom, And the knowledge of the Holy One is understanding" (Prov. 1:7; 9:10). That was also its *purpose:* "This is the end of the matter . . . Fear God and keep his commandments; for this is the whole duty of man" (Eccl. 12:13).

(3) *At first,* as is clear from many of the passages cited, the physical-mental-moral-spiritual nurture of the child was centered *solely in the home,* both father and mother taking part in this. Little children, both boys and girls, were taught by their mother, to whom also the education of the older girls was entrusted. The boys, on the other hand, were soon placed under the care of the father. *Even in later times* (when father and mother received outside help in the rearing of their children; see (14)) the influence

of godly parents and their efforts to train their children in the fear of the Lord remained paramount.

(4) *Children,* in turn, were admonished to give heed to their father's instruction, and not to reject their mother's teaching (Prov. 1:8; 6:20). They *were taught to honor and obey* their parents (Ex. 20:12; 21:15-17; Lev. 20:9; Deut. 21:18; Prov. 30:17; cf. Eph. 6:1-3). The soul-destructive falsehood that the child should be permitted to do "just as he pleases" is refuted by Scripture. Godly parents did not inflict this cruelty upon their immature offspring!

(5) The reason why everything was not simply left to the child was that *the little one was viewed as being* not only immature (that were reason enough in itself) but also *sinful by nature,* hence incapable of itself to choose the good (Ps. 51:5).

(6) Realizing that no human wisdom or piety is ever able to cope with the tremendous ravages of sin, *godly parents committed their children to God* and to his kindly care (Job 1:5).

(7) In Israel God-centered education was begun when the child was still very, very young (I Sam. 1:27, 28; 2:11, 18, 19; cf. Josephus, *Against Apion,* I. 12; Susanna 3; IV Macc. 18:9). The purpose of beginning early is expressed beautifully in the words of Prov. 22:6, "Train up a child in the way he should go (literally, "according to his way"), And even when he is old he will not depart from it."

(8) In the midst of the difficult task of properly training their children, *Israelites received much encouragement from God's covenant-promise:* "I will establish my covenant between me and thee and thy seed after thee throughout their generations for an everlasting covenant, to be a God unto thee and to thy seed after thee" (Gen. 17:7; Ps. 74:20; Ps. 105:8, 9), a promise which is organically realized in the hearts and lives of all those who through the enabling power of God's sovereign grace are firmly resolved to surrender themselves completely to him. (Cf. Acts 2:38, 39; Gal. 3:9, 29.)

(9) In view of the fact that the child was regarded as by nature sinful but by grace capable of inner change, *discipline was not cast aside* as unprofitable or unjust. The rod of correction was not spared, yet was used with discretion, since wise reproof was considered generally better than a hundred stripes (Prov. 13:24; 23:13, 14; then 17:10).

(10) Above all, *parents loved their children,* and nurtured them in the spirit of love (Ps. 103:13). Jewish children were not forced to devote all their time to work and study. They had their games (Zech. 8:5; Matt. 11:16-18).

(11) Though *godly Israelites* made many decisions *for* their children, they *prepared them to choose for themselves* (Josh. 24:15).

(12) *Education* in Israel *was of a very practical* character. It would seem

3:14, 15   **II TIMOTHY**

that even the smaller children were in many cases taught to read and write (Is. 10:19; cf. Josephus, *Against Apion.* II. 25), though it is impossible to determine the extent of this ability (cf. Is. 29:11, 12). That boys were taught an occupation, and that craftsmanship was encouraged is well-known.

(13) As to methodology, the Israelites were not, as a rule, afflicted with memorization-phobia. To a certain extent, necessity even demanded and common sense dictated that committing to memory receive its prominent place in the system of education (Is. 28:10). At times this method may have received undue emphasis, just as today it certainly receives *too little* emphasis.

The notion that educators should merely ask questions to which no one except the child (!) has the right to supply answers was favored only by men like Eli ("Why do y o u do such things?" I Sam. 2:23), who failed miserably in the task of bringing up his children. *God demanded that when questions were asked, definite answers should be given* (Ex. 13:8; Deut. 6:7; 6:20-25; 11:19; Josh. 12:26-28); that children should be *taught* Jehovah's statutes; that a body of truth with respect to the words and deeds of Jehovah should be handed down from generation to generation.

(14) Although at first the education of the child was viewed as the sole task and responsibility of the parents, at a later period priests and Levites, prophets, special tutors (especially in the case of the well-to-do, Numbers 11:12; II Sam. 12:25; II Kings 10:1; I Chron. 27:32; Is. 49:23), "wise men," scribes, and rabbis, all contributed their share in raising the cultural level of youth and of the nation.

After the Exile (especially from the time of Simon ben Shataḥ, about 70 B. C.), due to scribal influence, a new order of educational institutions or "schools" gradually arose. The school was called a "house" or "place" (Hebrew *Beth*). The lower or elementary school was called *Beth Ha-Sefer* ("place of writing"), the school attended by talented youths was called *Beth Ha-Midrash* ("place of study"), while for the masses there arose the *Beth Ha-Keneseth* ("place of assembly"). In course of time this "place (or "house") of assembly" began to be known by its Greek name, of similar meaning, "synagogue."

(15) That the system of home-centered religious nurture, both *formal* (imparting specific, systematic instruction) and *informal* (teaching *by example*) — in connection with the feasts, formal and informal education coalesced —, actually "worked" is evident from the book of Daniel. Even in the lands of the exile, youths who had been brought up in Jehovah's ways refused, at the risk of losing their lives, to defile themselves or to render homage to anyone or anything other than the God of their fathers. Thus, throughout the dark night of the captivity and foreign domination, the example of parental piety, the indoctrination in Jehovah's statutes (Ps

II TIMOTHY 3:14, 15

119:33), served as a lamp unto the feet and a light upon the path (Ps. 119:105). It also served to bind the people together, and wherever it was practised diligently, it prevented them from losing their spiritual distinctiveness, and made them, in many instances, a blessing to their heathen neighbors.[160]

Accordingly, in the manner of devout Israelites, grandmother Lois and mother Eunice had instructed "little" Timothy (II Tim. 1:5). Note the expression "from infancy." Literally Paul says, "from *an infant*." In some passages the word used in the original refers to *an unborn child* (Luke 1:41, 44); elsewhere simply to *a very small child,* a babe or infant (Luke 2:12, 16; 18:15; Acts 7:19; I Peter 2:2). Nevertheless, when Paul writes, *"You,* however, must continue in the things which you have learned and of which you have become convinced because . . . *from infancy* you have known (the) sacred writings," he is not thinking only of Timothy's *early childhood,* but is referring to Timothy's life from the days of his infancy *to this very*

---

[160] In addition to Scripture itself the following references with respect to education among the Jews have been consulted:
Abrahams, Israel (editor), *Hebrew Ethical Wills,* Philadelphia, 1926, esp. ch. III, "A Father's Admonition" (by Judah ibn Tibbon).
Bavinck, H., *Paedagogische Beginselen,* Kampen, 1904, esp. pp. 26, 27.
Benzinger, I., art. "Family and Marriage Relations," esp. par. 15, *The New Schaff-Herzog Encyclopaedia of Religious Knowledge,* Vol. IV, p. 277.
Berkhof, L., *Biblical Archaeology,* Grand Rapids, Mich., 1915, p. 68.
Day, E., *Social Life of the Hebrews,* New York, 1901.
Drazin, N., *History of Jewish Education from 515 B.C.E. to 220 C.E.,* Baltimore, 1940.
Edersheim, A., *The Life and Times of Jesus the Messiah,* two volumes, New York, 1897, esp. Vol. I, pp. 226-234.
Finkelstein, Louis (editor), *The Jews, Their History, Culture, and Religion,* New York, two volumes; see especially Vol. II, chapter 21, "The Role of Education in Jewish History" (by Julius B. Maller).
Gispen, W. H., "Bijbelsche Archaeologie," in *Bijbelsch Handboek,* two volumes, Kampen, 1935; see Vol. I, pp. 252, 253.
Guignebert, Charles, *The Jewish World in the Time of Jesus,* translated by S. H. Jooke, London, 1938.
Kuiper, A., Jr., "De Opvoeding in het Huisgezin," in *Christendom En Opvoeding* (composite authorship), Baarn, pp. 33-75.
Leipziger, *Education of the Jews,* New York, 1890.
Mackie, G. M., *Bible Manners and Customs,* London, 1898.
Marcus, Samuel, *Die Paedagogik des israelitischen Volkes,* two volumes, Vienna, 1877.
Meyer, H. H., art. "Education" in I.S.B.E.
Miller, M. S. and J. L., *Encyclopedia of Bible Life,* New York and London, 1944, pp. 390-392.
Schuerer, Emil, *A History of the Jewish People,* Edinburgh, 1893, esp. Vol. II, "The Scribes," "School and Synagogue."
Seeley, *History of Education,* New York, Cincinnati, Chicago, 1914, Chapter V, "The Jews" (pp. 44-49).
Strack, Hermann L., *Introduction to the Talmud and Midrash,* Philadelphia, 1931.

moment. Throughout that entire period Timothy had known the sacred writings, having learned to know them better and better right along.

This also indicates that the term "sacred writings" does not merely mean "the ABC which you learned from the Bible when you were a little child" (as several commentators interpret it). By "sacred writings" the apostle simply means *The Old Testament.* Words have a history. The fact that γράμμα has the primary meaning "that which is drawn or traced," hence, *character, letter, script,* does not in any way compel us to accept that meaning *here.* See N.T.C. on John 7:14, 15. In Josephus "sacred writings" means The Old Testament (*Antiquities,* X. x. 4; *Against Apion,* I. 10). He gives the list of the books belonging to it in *Against Apion,* I. 8. This list shows that his Old Testament was the same as ours (see the explanation in my *Bible Survey,* pp. 19, 20).

Paul uses the expression "sacred writings" here in verse 15, but "all scripture" in verse 16, for the simple reason that he wishes to draw a distinction between the Old Testament (verse 15) and *whatever* has a right to be called divinely inspired scripture (verse 16). The latter comprises more than the former. Yet, Paul would have been incorrect had he said that Timothy had been instructed in *"all* scripture" *from the days of his infancy,* for when he was a small child Lois and Eunice knew only the Old Testament. But it was definitely true that from very early childhood until the moment when Paul is writing these words Timothy had been constantly adding to his knowledge of *the Old Testament.* Let him then remain firm in the faith. Let him keep clinging to that which he has learned so thoroughly and of which he has become persuaded in his heart!

That this is the correct explanation is also clear from the words which follow, namely, "the sacred writings ... which are able to make you wise for salvation." Letters of the alphabet (even when they are learned from the Bible!), the mere ABC, cannot make one wise for salvation; the sacred writings can! It is "the testimony of Jehovah" and his "commandments" which *make a man wise* (Ps. 19:7; 119:98; in both cases the same verb is used in the Septuagint as is used here in I Tim. 3:15; see LXX Ps. 18:8; 118:98). It is these that lead a person to choose the best means in order to achieve the highest goal. And *that* is real wisdom! Note: "wise *for salvation"* (Rom. 11:11; Phil. 1:19; 2:12, etc.). What is included in this rich concept has been explained in connection with I Tim. 1:15.

Now this wonderful work of God whereby sinners are emancipated from the greatest evil and made possessors of the highest good is not brought about in a mechanical fashion, through the mere hearing, reading or study of "the sacred writings." One must learn to see Christ Jesus in the Old Testament. One must *surrender his life* (note: "through the faith") to the Anointed Savior, apart from whom "the sacred writings" have no meaning (on Christ as the fulfilment of the Old Testament see Luke 24:27, 32,

44; John 5:39, 46; Acts 3:18, 24; 7:52; 10:43; 13:29; 26:22, 23; 28:23; I Peter 1:10).

16, 17. Paul now expands the idea which he has just expressed. He does this in three ways:
  a. Not only are "the sacred writings" (verse 15) of inestimable value; so is also *"all* scripture."
  b. Not only does this sacred literature "make wise for salvation" (verse 15) but it is definitely God-breathed and as such capable of thoroughly qualifying a person "for every good work."
  c. Not only will it benefit *Timothy* (verse 15), but it will do the same for *every* "man of God."

Accordingly, Paul writes, **All scripture** [161] **(is)** [162] **God-breathed and useful for teaching, for reproof, for correction, for training in righteousness.**

All scripture, in distinction from "(the) sacred writings" (for which see on verse 15) means everything which, through the testimony of the Holy Spirit in the church, is recognized by the church as canonical, that is, authoritative. When Paul wrote these words, the direct reference was to a body of sacred literature which even then comprised more than the Old Testament (see on I Tim. 5:18; also footnote 160). Later, at the close of the first century A. D., "all scripture" had been completed. Though the history of the recognition, review, and ratification of the canon was somewhat complicated, and virtually universal acceptance of all the sixty-six books did not occur immediately in every region where the church was represented — one of the reasons being that for a long time certain of the smaller books had not even *reached* every corner of the church — , it remains true, nevertheless, that those genuine believers who were the original recipients of

---

[161] It is not true that the absence of the article compels us to adopt the translation of the A.R.V., "Every scripture." The word Scripture can be definite even without the article (I Peter 2:6; II Peter 1:20). Similarly πᾶς Ἰσραήλ means "all Israel" (Rom. 11:26). See Gram. N.T., p. 772. But even if the rendering "every scripture" be accepted, the resultant meaning would not differ greatly, for if "every scripture" is inspired, "all scripture" must be inspired also.

[162] The most natural rendering of θεόπνευστος καὶ ὠφέλιμος is "God-breathed and useful." I can see no compelling reason for inserting a copula between the two modifiers, resulting in: "God-breathed *is also* useful." Moreover, if *God-breathed* is attributive, καί in the sense of *also* would be superfluous: "All scripture God-breathed is useful," etc., would suffice.

In the abstract, another possibility presents itself, namely, that we adopt the rendering "God-breathed and useful," but regard both as attributive; hence, "All scripture God-breathed and useful for teaching," etc. However, when this is done, the sentence dangles. It "hangs in the air," having no predicate.

It is clear, therefore, that with respect to grammatical construction there is no solid reason for departing from the view which forms the basis of the A.V. Though not the only possible view, it seems to be the most natural. Its translation, "All scripture is given by inspiration of God," is excellent. So is also the almost identical rendering found in the text of the R.S.V.

the various God-breathed books regarded them at once as being invested with divine authority and majesty. What should be emphasized, however, is that not because the church, upon a certain date, long ago, made an official decision (the decision of the Council of Hippo, 393 A. D.; of Carthage, 397 A. D.), do these books constitute the inspired Bible; on the contrary, the sixty-six books, by their very contents, immediately attest themselves to the hearts of all Spirit-indwelt men as being the living oracles of God. Hence, believers are filled with deep reverence whenever they hear the voice of God addressing them from Holy Writ (see II Kings 22 and 23). All scripture is canonical because God made it so!

The word *God-breathed,* occurring only here [163] indicates that "all scripture" owes its origin and contents to the divine breath, the Spirit of God. The human authors were powerfully guided and directed by the Holy Spirit. As a result, what they wrote is not only without error but of supreme value for man. It is *all* that God wanted it to be. It constitutes the infallible rule of faith and practice for mankind.

The Spirit, however, did not suppress the personality of the human writer, but raised it to a higher level of activity (John 14:26). And because the individuality of the human author was not destroyed, we find in the Bible a wide variety of style and language. Inspiration, in other words, is organic, not mechanical. This also implies that it should never be considered apart from those many activities which served to bring the human author upon the scene of history. By causing him to be born at a certain time and place, bestowing upon him specific endowments, equipping him with a definite kind of education, causing him to undergo predetermined experiences, and bringing back to his mind certain facts and their implications, the Spirit prepared his human consciousness. Next, that same Spirit moved him to write. Finally, during the process of writing, that same Primary Author, in a thoroughly organic connection with all the preceding activity, suggested to the mind of the human author that language (the very words!) and that style, which would be the most appropriate vehicle for the interpretation of the divine ideas for people of every rank and position, age and race. Hence, though every word is truly the word of the human author, it is even more truly the Word of God.[164]

Though the word *God-breathed* — that is, inspired by God — occurs only here, the idea is found in many other passages (Ex. 20:1; II Sam. 23:2; Is. 8:20; Mal. 4:4; Matt. 1:22; Luke 24:44; John 1:23; 5:39; 10:34, 35;

---

[163] θεόπνευστος does not mean "God-breathing," "breathing the divine spirit," but is passive: "God-breathed." Cf. II Peter 1:21. See the detailed argument in B. B. Warfield, *The Inspiration and Authority of the Bible,* Philadelphia, Pa., 1948, pp. 245-296.
[164] See I. Orr, *Revelation and Inspiration,* London, 1910; H. Bavinck, *Gereformeerde Dogmatiek,* third ed., Vol. I, p. 464.

14:26; 16:13; 19:36, 37; 20:9; Acts 1:16; 7:38; 13:34; Rom. 1:2; 3:2; 4:23; 9:17; 15:4; I Cor. 2:4-10; 6:16; 9:10; 14:37; Gal. 1:11, 12; 3:8, 16, 22; 4:30; I Thess. 1:5; 2:13; Heb. 1:1, 2; 3:7; 9:8; 10:15; II Peter 1:21; 3:16; I John 4:6; and Rev. 22:19).

Now by virtue of the fact that "all scripture" is God-breathed, it is *useful* or *beneficial* or *profitable*. It is a very practical, yes an indispensable, instrument or tool *for the teacher* (implied here). Timothy should make good use of it:

a. *for teaching*. What is meant is the activity of imparting knowledge concerning God's revelation in Christ. See on I Tim. 5:17. This is ever basic to everything else.

b. *for reproof* (cf. Ps. 38:14; 39:11). Warnings, based on the Word, must be issued. Errors in doctrine and in conduct must be refuted in the spirit of love. Dangers must be pointed out. False teachers must be exposed (cf. I Tim. 5:20; Titus 1:9, 13; 2:15; then Eph. 5:18; and see N.T.C. on John 16:8-11).

c. *for correction* (see M.M., p. 229). If *reproof* stresses the negative aspect of pastoral work, *correction* emphasizes the positive side. Not only must the sinner be warned to leave the wrong path, but he must also be directed to the *right* or *straight* path (Dan. 12:3). This, too, "all scripture" is able to do. The Word, especially when it is used by a consecrated servant of God who is diligent in the performance of his pastoral duties, is *restorative* in character (cf. John 21:15-17).

d. *for training in righteousness* (cf. II Tim. 2:22). The teacher must train his people. Every Christian needs to be disciplined, so that he may prosper in the sphere where God's holy will is considered normative. Such is the character of *training in righteousness* (cf. Titus 2:11-14).

The teacher (in this case Timothy, but the word applies to everyone to whom the souls of men are entrusted) needs "all scripture" in order to enable him to perform his fourfold task (teaching, administering reproof, correction, training in righteousness), with a glorious purpose in mind, a purpose which in his own way and at his own time God will cause to be realized in the hearts of all his people: **that the man of God may be equipped, for every good work thoroughly equipped.**

The man of God (see on I Tim. 6:11) is the believer. *Every* believer, viewed as belonging to God, and as invested with the threefold office of prophet, priest, and king, is here given this title. To function properly in this threefold office the believer must become *equipped* (note the emphasis of the original; literally, ". . . that equipped may be the man of God"); yes, once for all *thoroughly equipped* (cf. Luke 6:40) "for every good work" (I Tim. 5:10; II Tim. 2:21; Titus 3:1). Paul (and the Holy Spirit speaking through him) is not satisfied until the Word of God has fully accomplished its mission, and the believer has reached "the measure of the stature of the fulness of Christ" (Eph. 4:12, 13).

The ideal to be realized is glorious, indeed! The power to reach it is from God. Hence, let Timothy remain stedfast. Let him *abide* in the true doctrine, applying it whenever opportunity presents itself.

Synthesis of Chapter 3

See the Outline at the beginning of this chapter.

Timothy must *abide* in the sound doctrine. He must put forth every effort to do so in view of the fact that in these last days — that is, in the age ushered in by Christ's First Coming — grievous seasons will set in. Let him realize this. Are not the peddlers of sinister falsehoods beginning to make their appearance even now? Such individuals are characterized by love of *self* and of their own pleasures instead of love for *God,* by disobedience toward their superiors, unthankfulness with respect to their benefactors, an unforgiving attitude to those whom they dislike, and an unwillingness to restrain their own evil desires. Yet, they put on a religious front. They are fakers, for though they maintain a facade of religion, they deny its power. From such people Timothy should turn away.

Out of circles such as these come the men who worm their way into the homes of church-members with the purpose of making a prey of weak-minded women, women who are burdened with an evil conscience, yet are impenitent, being swayed by various impulses; and who, in spite of all the "instruction" they receive, are never able to arrive at the acknowledgment of the truth.

As to these women-baiters and the other men who belong to the same circles, they remind one of Jannes and Jambres, men who according to tradition were the two ringleaders among Pharaoh's magicians. As they *opposed* Moses, so these *oppose* the truth. They are corrupt in mind and utterly useless and disqualified as far as the faith is concerned. However, they will not get very far, for their folly will become as obvious to everybody as did that of Jannes and Jambres.

Another reason why Timothy must by all means endeavor to *abide* in the sound doctrine is the fact that it is based on the most reliable foundation, as he has learned from trustworthy persons. Has not Timothy had the apostle as a model of obedience both active ("*my* teaching, *my* conduct," etc.) and passive ("*my* persecutions, *my* sufferings")? Has he not taken a keen interest in the persecutions which Paul underwent, beginning with the first missionary journey — Antioch, Iconium, and Lystra! — , the journey which had meant so much to Timothy himself? How vividly Paul recalls especially this fact, which should encourage Timothy, namely, that though persecution is the lot of everyone who desires to live a sincere Christian life, inasmuch as evil men and impostors proceed from bad to worse, deluding and being deluded, nevertheless the Lord protects his faithful ones! Did he not rescue Paul from all these persecutions? Let Timothy then *abide* in the things he has learned and of which he has become convinced, constantly bearing in mind from what kind of people his knowledge has come, namely, from those who had been his wise monitors from the days of his earliest infancy. From infancy until this very day he had known the sacred writings — the Old Testament —, having learned to know them better right along. These are the writings which are able to make a man wise for salvation through faith in Christ Jesus. This, moreover, holds not only with respect to the inspired writings of the Old Testament but also with respect to God's further special revelation that has been deposited in written form. In fact, *all* such scripture (today we would say: both the Old and the New Testament) is God-breathed and *useful* — indispensable to the teacher! — for teaching, for warning the sinner to depart from unrighteousness, for leading him in the path of righteousness; hence, for training him in righteousness; in order that, as a result, "the man of God," that is, the believer, thus instructed and guided, may be equipped, yes *fully* equipped for every good work.

Outline of Chapter 4

Theme: *The Apostle Paul Tells Timothy What To Do in the Interest of Sound Doctrine*

    Preach It   "I charge you"

4:1-8   In season, out of season, for apostasy is coming.
          Remain faithful in view of the fact that "I am about to set sail."

4:9-22 Items of personal information, requests, greetings.

CHAPTER IV

II TIMOTHY   **4:1**

4 1 I charge you in the sight of God and of Christ Jesus, who will judge the living and the dead, and by his appearing and his kingdom: 2 herald the word; be on hand in season, out of season; reprove, rebuke, admonish, with all longsuffering and teaching. 3 For the season will arrive when men will not endure the sound doctrine, but, having itching ears, will accumulate for themselves teachers to suit their own fancies; 4 and will turn away their ears from the truth, and will turn aside to the myths.

5 As for yourself, however, be sober in all matters, suffer hardship, do the work of an evangelist, your ministry discharge to the full.

6 For I am already being poured out as a drink-offering, and the season of my departure has arrived. 7 The grand fight I have fought, the race I have finished, the faith I have kept. 8 For the future, there is safely stored away for me the wreath of righteousness, which the Lord, the righteous Judge, will award to me on that day, and not to me alone but to all who have loved his appearing.

4:1-8

1. Underlying the thought expressed in the opening paragraph of chapter 4 are the "grievous seasons" of departure from the faith, which were described in chapter 3. Though, in a sense, these seasons are certainly future (3:1; 4:3, 4), they must not be thought of as wholly separate from and unrelated to conditions present even now, while Paul is writing. The very fact that Paul admonishes Timothy to fulfil his ministry, reproving and rebuking whenever this is necessary, and remaining sober in the midst of all untoward circumstances, shows that future heresy is viewed as the outgrowth of present error. The coming apostasy is a further stage in the development of the already present deviation from the truth.

But though the background of chapters 3 and 4 is the same, a difference of approach is, nevertheless, discernible. Chapter 3 stresses the fact that Timothy, confronted with developing opposition to the truth, must *abide* in the true doctrine. Chapter 4 brings into prominence Timothy's duty *to proclaim* this doctrine. Let him "speak out" while people are still willing to listen. They will not always be willing. Let the "herald" of the gospel discharge his ministry to the full!

Accordingly, Paul writes, **I charge you in the sight of God and of Christ Jesus, who will judge the living and the dead, and by his appearing and his kingdom.**

For the meaning of "I charge [165] you in the sight of God and of Christ Jesus" see on I Tim. 5:21. It is on the eve of his death that Paul delivers this final, most solemn charge. He directs Timothy's attention to God and to Christ Jesus, in whose presence the charge is issued and received. He places Timothy under oath to comply with the charge. It is to God and to the Anointed Savior that Timothy (Paul, too, of course!) will have to render an account. And this is the Christ who "is about to" judge! In a sense, even now his approaching footsteps can be heard. He is on the way. Paul stresses the certainty of his coming and its impending character, but does not fix any date.

Now this Christ Jesus will judge "the living," that is, those who will still be living on earth at the moment of the Second Coming, and "the dead," that is, those who will have died by that time. (See also Matt. 25:31-46; Luke 18:8; John 5:27-29; I Cor. 15:51, 52; I Thess. 4:13-18; Rev. 20:11-15.)

The idea that Christ is coming to judge is of frequent occurrence in Paul (Rom. 2:16; I Cor. 4:5; II Cor. 4:5; II Thess. 1:7-9; cf. Acts 17:31). The expression, "He will judge the living and the dead" may already have become a fixed formula, as would appear from similar statements in Acts 10:42 and I Peter 4:5. It was probably part of a baptismal confession, explained to the catechumens and afterward confessed by them at baptism. Out of such formulas as these *The Apostles' Creed* arose.[166]

Paul furthermore adjures Timothy by Christ's future, glorious *appearing*, that is, by his brilliant Second Coming, viewed as the rising of the sun (see also verse 8; I Tim. 6:14; Titus 2:13; see on II Tim. 1:10; also N.T.C. on II Thess. 2:8; and cf. Mal. 4:2), and *by* [167] his *majestic kingship*, the rulership into which he will then fully enter. (With reference to this perfected reign see also verse 18; then N.T.C. on I Thess. 2:12 and on II Thess. 1:5, especially footnote *e*.) If Timothy obeys, he will share in (and if he disobeys, he will miss) the glory of the Epiphany and of the Reign (I Thess. 4:13-18; cf. 3:13; II Tim. 2:12; Rev. 3:21; 22:5).

2. By means of five brisk imperatives (all of them aorists) the content of the charge is now set forth: **herald the word; be on hand in season, out of season; reprove, rebuke, admonish, with all longsuffering and teaching.**

---

[165] The rendering "charge" (A.V., A.R.V., R.S.V.) is correct. The context requires this rendering *charge* or *adjure*, not *solemnly testify*; for what follows (in verse 2) *is a charge*, not a *testimony*. For the opposite view see Robertson (*Word Pictures*, Vol. 4, p. 629), and Lenski, *op. cit.*, p. 850.
[166] See P. Schaff, *Creeds of Christendom*, three volumes, New York and London, edition 1919, Vol. I, pp. 16-23.
[167] The accusative of the nouns *epiphany* and *kingdom* (or "kingship") has been called that of "adjuration" or "conjuration" (cf. Mark 5:7; Acts 19:13; I Thess. 5:27; cf. LXX on Deut. 4:26; 30:19; 31:28).

a. "Herald [168] the word." This is basic to the other four imperatives. The rendering *"Preach the word"* is entirely correct, *if* the verb *preach* be understood in its primary, etymological meaning (from the Latin *praedicare*): *to proclaim before the public,* and not in the weakened sense which today is often attached to it: "to deliver a moral or religious discourse of any kind and in any way." The word employed in the original means *proclaim* (cf. Matt. 10:27); literally, *herald,* make known officially and publicly a matter of great significance. Of course, all preaching should be heralding (Rom. 10:14, 15). Paul calls himself a *herald* (see footnote 168). By order of his Superior he made an authoritative, open, forceful declaration. He here commands Timothy to be a herald also.

According to Scripture, then, *"heralding" or "preaching" is generally the divinely authorized proclamation of the message of God to men. It is the exercise of ambassadorship.*[169]

This is evident from the following examples. These men are all said to have "heralded":

Noah

"God will destroy the world. Turn away from y o u r sins!" Or similar words (II Peter 2:5; cf. I Peter 3:19).

Jonah

"Yet forty days, and Nineveh shall be overthrown!" (Jonah 3:4; Matt. 12:41; Luke 11:32).

John the Baptist

"Repent, for the Kingdom of heaven is at hand!"
"Look, the Lamb of God, who is taking away the sin of the world!" (Matt. 3:1, 2; John 1:29).

The Healed Gerasene Demoniac

"God has done great things for me!" (Luke 8:39).

---

[168] In Paul *the verb* "to herald" (κηρύσσω) occurs in the following passages: Rom. 2:21; 10:8, 14, 15; I Cor. 1:23; 9:27; 15:11, 12; II Cor. 1:19; 4:5; 11:4; Gal. 2:2; 5:11; Phil. 1:15; Col. 1:23; I Thess. 2:9; I Tim. 3:16; II Tim. 4:2. It is also of frequent occurrence in the Synoptics and in Acts. It is found once in Peter (I Peter 3:19); once in Revelation (5:2). *The noun* "herald" (κῆρυξ) is found in I Timothy 2:7 and II Tim. 1:11. In the New Testament outside of Paul it occurs only in II Peter 2:5. "Proclamation by the herald" or "heralding" (κήρυγμα) is found in Rom. 16:25; I Cor. 1:21; 2:4; 15:14; II Tim. 4:17; Titus 1:3. In addition to its occurrences in Paul this noun also occurs in Matt. 12:41 and in Luke 11:32.

Synonyms are εὐαγγελίζω (to announce good tidings), and in certain contexts καταγγέλλω (to proclaim, declare).

[169] Words have a history. It is, therefore, not surprising that also this verb, like so many others, is at times used in a more general sense, namely, with respect to a proclamation or heralding that is *not* divinely authorized, Mark 1:45; 7:36.

The Apostle Paul

"Jesus is the Christ!" (Acts 9:20).
"Far be it from me to glory, except in the cross of our Lord Jesus Christ!" (Gal. 6:14).
"But now has Christ been raised from the dead, the first-fruits of them that are asleep!" (I Cor. 15:20; cf. verses 55-58; I Thess. 4:13-18).

Similarly the twelve, Philip the evangelist, Peter at Cesarea, "a strong angel," etc., are said to have "preached" ("heralded"). The verb is even used in connection with Christ, for he, too, was bringing God's message to man.

The herald brings *God's* message. Today in the work of "heralding" or "preaching" careful exposition of the text is certainly included. But genuine heralding or preaching is lively, not dry; timely, not stale. *It is the earnest proclamation of news initiated by God. It is not the abstract speculation on views excogitated by man.*

The somewhat timid Timothy must never be afraid to herald *the word*, that is, *the gospel* (see on II Tim. 2:8, 9; cf. Mark 1:14; 16:15; I Thess. 2:9). It is *the true* message of redemption in Christ, and as such stands over against all *falsehood* (see verse 4). Moreover, in sharp contrast with the oft stealthy *infiltration* practised by Satan and his servants (II Tim. 3:6) is this open-and-above-board *proclamation* by one who brings good tidings and publishes peace (Nah. 1:15; Rom. 10:15).[170]

How this heralding must be done is indicated by the four imperatives which follow:

b. "Be on hand in season, out of season." Welcome or not welcome, Timothy must ever be "on the spot" [171] with the message from God. He must "buy up the opportunity" (Eph. 5:16).

---

[170] One must not ascribe qualities to "heralding" which do not properly belong to it. The view — held by some (see, for example, Alan Richardson, article "Preach, Teach" in *A Theological Word Book of the Bible,* New York, 1952, pp. 171, 172) — that the term "heralding" and its synonyms have nothing to do with the delivery of sermons to the converted, but always indicate the proclamation of the good news to *the non-Christian world,* is incorrect. To be sure, when the church was still in its infancy, and when even in the Roman world most people had never heard of the gospel, great emphasis was placed on missionary-activity. And the missionary's audience would naturally consist exclusively or largely of unbelievers, whether Jews or Gentiles. But this does not mean that when *believers* are being established in the faith, the message which they hear ceases to be "kerugma" (see Rom. 16:25), and that the messenger ceases to be a "herald."
[171] Since everywhere else in the New Testament the verb has the sense "arrive," "come near," "be present," "be on hand," (or the very closely related meaning "come upon," "come on"), a meaning which also suits the present context, I see no reason to adopt a different sense here (like "keep on," or "be urgent").

c. "Reprove" or "Convict." See on II Tim. 3:16 for the related noun. Sin must be brought home to the sinner's consciousness in order that he may repent. See the detailed discussion of this verb in N.T.C. on John 16:8, especially footnote 200.

d. "Rebuke." In the process of reproving or convicting the sinner, the latter must be sharply reprimanded. His sin must not be toned down.

e. "Admonish." Nevertheless, the demands of love must be fully satisfied. Hand in hand with pertinent rebuke there must be tender, fatherly admonition. See N.T.C. on I Thess. 2:7-12, and for detailed explanation of the verb "admonish" see on I Tim. 5:1.

Modifying each of the three imperatives is the beautiful phrase, "with all longsuffering and teaching," meaning "with utmost longsuffering and with most painstaking teaching-activity." Cf. a similar combination in II Tim. 2:24, "gentle to all, qualified to teach."

Such longsuffering is a distinctly Christian virtue (II Cor. 6:6; Eph. 4:2; Col. 1:11; 3:12; and see N.T.C. on I Thess. 5:14), as well as (elsewhere) a divine attribute (Rom. 2:4; I Tim. 1:16). Note that *longsuffering* (slowness to wrath, gentle patience with people who have erred) and *teaching-activity* go together. Neither is complete without the other. The manner in which Paul dealt with the Corinthian fornicator illustrates what he means by "reprove, rebuke, admonish, with all longsuffering and teaching" (I Cor. 5:1-8, 13; II Cor. 2:5-11). A much earlier example is Nathan's treatment of David (II Sam. 12:1-15).

3 and 4. A reason is now given, showing why Timothy must be diligent in the work of heralding the gospel and of reproving, rebuking, and admonishing: **For the season will arrive when they will not endure the sound doctrine.**

In every period of history (see on II Tim. 3:1) there will be a season during which men refuse to listen to sound doctrine. As history continues onward toward the consummation, this situation grows worse. Men will not endure or tolerate the truth, the doctrine which because it promotes spiritual health is called *sound* (see on I Tim. 1:10). **But, having itching ears, will accumulate for themselves teachers to suit their own fancies.** It is not the herald of the gospel that is at fault, but *the hearing* of the fickle men who make up the audience! They have ears that *are itching* (from a verb which in the active means *to tickle;* hence, in the passive, *to be tickled,* and thus *to itch,* fig. "to have an irritating desire"). Their craving is for teachers to suit their *fancies* or *perverted tastes* (see on II Tim. 2:22). So great is that hankering that they pile up teacher upon teacher. This reminds one of Jer. 5:31, "The prophets prophesy falsely . . . and my people love to have it so," and of Ezek. 33:32, "And lo, thou art unto them as a very lovely song of one who has a pleasant voice and can play well on an instrument; for they hear thy words, but they do them not." The people here pictured are more interested in something different, something sensational, than they are in sober truth. And when sober truth is presented (as it surely was by Ezekiel), they are not interested in the truth itself, but only in *the way* in which it is presented, the preacher's "style," "oratory," ... the preacher *himself*, his voice, bearing, looks, mannerisms. Here in II Timothy 4:3, 4 the emphasis is on the craving for fascinating stories and philosophical speculations: **and will turn away their ears from the truth, and will turn aside to the myths.** God's redemptive truth, which deals with sin and damnation, with the necessity of inner change, etc. (cf. II Tim. 3:15-17) they cannot stomach. They *turn away* (as in II Tim. 1:15) from it, and *turn aside* (as in I Tim. 1:6) to "the myths," those familiar old womanish myths mentioned earlier (see on I Tim. 1:4, 7; 4:7; Titus 1:14; cf. II Peter 1:16) or anything similar to them. There are always teachers that are willing to "scratch and tickle the ears of those who wish to be tickled" (Clement of Alexandria, *The Stromata*, I. iii).

5. As for yourself, however ... Cf. 3:10, 14. Note the sharp and double contrast. Verse 5 is both the climax of verses 1-5 and the introduction to verses 5-8. *As a climax,* it draws a contrast between Timothy and the fickle multitude described in verses 3 and 4. *As an introduction,* it draws a contrast between Timothy, still in the thick of the fight, and Paul who *has fought* the grand fight. In the beginning of the verse the first of these two contrasts predominates; at the end, the second.

Paul writes, **be sober in all matters, suffer hardship, do the work of an evangelist, your ministry discharge to the full.** The sober person is calm, steady, and sane (cf. I Peter 4:7; see N.T.C. on I Thess. 5:6, 8). He is not intoxicated with morbid craving for whatever is sensational or sentimental. He does not turn away his ears from the truth and turn aside to the myths. The apostle demands that Timothy shall show this calm and well-balanced attitude "in all matters." This means, of course, that also with respect to suffering for the sake of the gospel Timothy must neither court such suffering, on the one hand, nor complain about it, on the other. He must simply "do the work of an evangelist" (gospel-preacher, Acts 21:8; Eph. 4:11), perfectly willing to bear ill-treatment whenever it is his lot so to suffer, even rejoicing that he is counted worthy to suffer dishonor for the name of Christ (Acts 5:41; on the verb see II Tim. 2:9; cf. the similar verb in II Tim. 1:8). He must permit nothing to stop him, but must discharge his gospel-ministry *to the full:* heralding the word, being on hand in season, out of season, reproving, rebuking, admonishing, with all longsuffering and teaching.

6-8. Timothy, then, must "preach the word," etc., not only because apostasy is coming (verses 1-4), but also in view of the fact that Paul is about to set sail to the shores of eternity. When the older man is called to higher spheres, the younger man must fill the breach. He must take the torch and carry it onward. This second thought explains the conjunction "for" at the beginning of verse 6.

In one of the most sublime and moving passages, which with respect to grandeur of thought and stateliness of rhythm is probably unsurpassed anywhere in Paul's epistles, the apostle lifts this letter — and his apostolic career — to its wonderful finale:

For I am already being poured out as a drink-offering, and the season of my departure has arrived.

The grand fight I have fought, the race I have finished, the faith I have kept.

For the future there is safely stored away for me the wreath of righteousness, which the Lord, the righteous Judge, will award to me on that day, and not to me alone but to all who have loved his appearing.

A possible theme for this passage would be:

In Three Tenses Paul, the Lord's Prisoner, Triumphantly
Expresses His Faith

This is divided as follows:
1. Verse 6: His Faith-Appraisal of the Present
2. Verse 7: His Faith-Summary of the Past
3. Verse 8: His Faith-Exultation regarding the Future

1. *His Faith-Appraisal of the Present*

When Paul writes, "For I am already being poured out as a drink-offering," he is making a *profession of faith*. He does not call his present horrible imprisonment, with the issue no longer in doubt, *death,* but a *drink-offering,* comparable to the libation of wine which was poured out beside the altar. According to the law (Num. 15:1-10), when a lamb was sacrificed, the drink-offering consisting of one-fourth of a hin of wine (1 hin = slightly more than 1 gallon); when the offering was a ram, the prescribed libation was one-third of a hin; and for a bull it was one-half of a hin. Since this wine *was gradually poured out,* was *an offering,* and was *the final act* of the entire sacrificial ceremony, it pictured most adequately *the gradual ebbing away* of Paul's life, the fact that he was presenting this life to God as *an offering,* and the idea that while he viewed his entire career of faith as "a living sacrifice" (Rom. 12:1; cf. 15:16), he looked upon *the present* stage of this career as being *the final sacrificial act*.

Similarly, when the apostle adds, "And the season of my departure has arrived," he is again making a *profession of faith*. The word *season* (καιρός)

4:6-8 **II TIMOTHY**

is entirely proper in this connection, for: a. the apostle is thinking not only of the moment of execution but of this entire final imprisonment which was about to end in execution; and b. he views this final period under the symbolism of the unmooring of a ship which in its coming and going is bound to the seasons (cf. Acts 27:12).

Now this appropriate time or season is here called "the season of my departure." The primary meaning of the phrase used in the original is "of my *loosening*" or "of my *release*." Think of the loosening of the ropes or cables of a ship when weighing anchor. Hence, the word *loosening* acquired the secondary meaning *departure* (cf. M.M., p. 36). Accordingly, Paul says that the season of his departure *has arrived* (perfect tense of the verb that was used in verse 2, where it was rendered "be on hand," see footnote 171). Even now *the season* is already here. The weighing of the anchors and the loosening of the ropes has begun. Soon the blast of the wind will be in the sails, and then, almost immediately, the haven of everlasting bliss will have been reached.

It is only by faith that *present circumstances* can be so appraised. Similarly, in other passages the apostle speaks of the believer's demise as: a departure to be with Christ (Phil. 1:23), and to be at home with the Lord (II Cor. 5:8); gain (Phil. 1:21); very far better (Phil. 1:23); a falling asleep in Jesus (I Thess. 4:14).

Elsewhere Scripture calls it: precious in the sight of Jehovah (Ps. 116:15); a being carried away by the angels into Abraham's bosom (Luke 16:22); a going to paradise (Luke 23:43); a going to the house with many mansions (John 14:2).

2. *His Faith-Summary of the Past*

When the apostle continues, "The grand fight I have fought," he is again using the language *of faith;* for it is clear that an unbeliever, describing Paul's post-conversion life, would have characterized it as "foolish" or even "insane," sheer "madness" (cf. Acts 26:24), certainly not "the *grand* fight." But Paul, by means of the very word-order which he selects (placing each of the three objects before its verb; see my translation), emphasizes that it was, indeed, *the* "beautiful," *grand,* or noble, *fight* which he had fought; that it was not the path of chance but *the scheduled race* which he had run; and that this life of his, now viewed as finished, had been ruled not by the whim or caprice of the moment but by *that personal faith* which by God's grace he had kept to the very end.

When Paul thus summarizes his past, he is not boasting, except "in the Lord." He is recording what grace has achieved in the heart of "the chief of sinners." Hence, not on the pronoun "I" does he place the emphasis — as one might mistakenly infer from the usual translation, which causes each of the three brief clauses to begin with *"I"* —, but on "the grand fight," "the race," "the faith."

When the apostle summarizes his life as a Christian under the symbolism of "the grand fight," the underlying figure is probably a wrestling-match, boxing-bout, or similar contest (see on I Tim. 4:7b, 8; 6:12). The third of comparison is prodigious exertion of energy against a very powerful foe.

It had been a fight against Satan; against the principalities and powers, the world-rulers of this darkness in the heavenlies; against Jewish and pagan vice and violence; against Judaism among the Galatians; against fanaticism among the Thessalonians; against contention, fornication, and litigation among the Corinthians; against incipient Gnosticism among the Ephesians and Colossians; against fightings without and fears within; and last but not least, against the law of sin and death operating within his own heart.

But triumphantly Paul is able to say, "the grand fight *I have fought.*" It is vain to say that this is not strictly true because Paul had not as yet actually reached the execution-block. When death is very near and very certain, it is easy for the mind to project itself into that near-by future moment from which it then looks back upon the past, and rejoices not only in that past but in the present blessing which that past has produced.[172] Our Lord used similar language, which must be explained similarly (see N.T.C. on John 17:4).

When the apostle adds, "the race I have finished" — an obstacle-race, indeed! —, he stresses the fact that in his life as a believer he has fully accomplished that ministry to which the Lord had called him (the passage which sheds light on this is Acts 20:24); his eye, like that of a skilled runner, having been riveted at all times upon the finishing post: the glory of God by means of the salvation of sinners (Gal. 2:2; 5:7; Phil. 2:16; cf. Heb. 12:1, 2).

That Paul was, indeed, a man with *this one holy passion,* with *this* one objective in mind, so that the figure of *the race* is very appropriate, is evident from such words as the following:

"I have become all things to all men, *that I may by all means save some* . . . Even so *run* that y o u may attain . . . Therefore, whether y o u eat or drink, or whatever y o u do, do it all to *the glory of God* . . . just as I also please all men in all matters, not seeking my own profit but the profit of the many, *that they may be saved.*" (I Cor. 9:22-24; 10:31-33) And cf. 3:7-14.

In summarizing the past, Paul finally drops every metaphor, and writes,

---

[172] Hence, I cannot agree with Lenski (*op. cit.,* p. 860) who criticizes Robertson's graph (Gram. N.T., p. 895) for the three perfect tenses in "I have fought, I have finished, I have kept."

"The faith I have kept." Here, as in I Tim. 6:12, the meaning is probably not, "I have kept the pledge" (or "fidelity") nor "I have maintained *the true doctrine*" ("faith" in the objective sense), but, in harmony with the present context, "I have retained my personal trust in God, my confidence in all his Christ-centered promises. In the spiritual arena of life I have not only *fought hard* and *run well*, but I have also been sustained to the end by the deeply rooted *conviction* that I shall receive the prize, the glorious reward" (see next verse).

3. *His Faith-Exultation regarding the Future*

Having discussed the present and the past, Paul turns his eye to the future. This, as has become evident, is altogether natural; for, the noble fight, successfully waged, the race satisfactorily run, and the faith stedfastly exercised, call for the reward of grace. Accordingly, the apostle writes, "*For the future,*[173] and then tells us what he confidently expects. Says he, "There is *safely stored away for me* (note the force of the compound Greek verb ἀπόκειται), so that no enemy will ever be able to deprive me of it, *the wreath* — the *victor's* wreath (see on II Tim. 2:5) — *of the righteousness,*[174] that is, the wreath to which I am *entitled* as a reward for the life which in principle has been in conformity with God's law (see on I Tim. 6:11; II Tim. 2:22; 3:16; Titus 3:5). That this wreath is Paul's *by right*, a right founded upon grace, is evident; for:

a. To those who fight the grand fight, run the race, and keep the faith (in other words, to Paul and others like him) *God has promised* to give the wreath (I Tim. 6:12; James 1:12; I Peter 5:4; Rev. 2:10).

b. *Christ has earned* it for them (see on Titus 3:5, 6).

Now the present passage simply states that the wreath or award is a righteous one, but does not indicate its nature. From other passages we

---

[173] The objection advanced by Lenski against the futuristic rendering of ἀπόκειται (*op. cit.,* p. 862), namely, that the verb which is here introduced is present tense with perfect meaning ("there has been laid up"), is not valid. It is the sense of the entire verse (verse 8), and not of the one verb, that determines the meaning of the adverb. English, too, allows such usage; for example, "As to the future, a job *has been* provided for me!" For other examples of λοιπόν (with or without the article) in the futuristic sense see Acts 27:20; I Cor. 7:29; Heb. 10:13. The meaning "for the rest" is represented by the following passages: a. without the article: I Cor. 1:16; 4:2; I Thess. 4:1; b. with the article: Phil. 3:1; 4:8.

[174] This is "a righteous wreath," a wreath *justly* bestowed upon the righteous. It *springs from* righteousness, just like in I Thess. 1:3 work springs from (results from) faith, exertion springs from (is prompted by) love, and endurance springs from (is inspired by) hope. For this *genitive of source* see N.T.C. on I and II Thessalonians, pp. 46, 47, footnote 35. Others (e.g. Robertson, *op. cit.,* p. 631) consider this to be a *genitive of apposition*, which, however, yields a very difficult meaning in the present context.

learn that it means *everlasting life* (I Tim. 6:12; cf. James 1:12; I Peter 5:4; Rev. 2:10), here (in II Tim. 4:8) as possessed and experienced in the new heaven and earth.

The apostle continues, "which the Lord, the righteous Judge, will award to me on that day." This Lord and Judge is Christ Jesus (see on verse 1). And this Judge or Umpire respects the contest-rules which he himself has laid down. He is the *righteous* Judge, who on that notable day, the day of his return (see on II Tim. 1:12, 18; cf. II Thess. 1:10) *will give whatever is due* (note the verb used in the original, on which such passages as Matt. 20:8, 13; Rom. 2:6 shed much light). For all such people who, like Paul, are unjustly condemned, the idea of the coming judgment day when they will be vindicated by a *just* Judge is full of comfort.

This righteous Judge, says Paul, will award the wreath of righteousness *to me.* Yet, not to me alone, but *to all who love his appearing,* his brilliant second coming (as in verse 1). Note the word *love,* not *fear,* for perfect love casts out fear (I John 4:18). When the Spirit and the bride say, "Come," every person who really loves the Lord will also say, "Come." And when the Lord answers, "I am coming quickly," the immediate reply will be, "Amen, come, Lord Jesus." Of all the indications that one loves the Lord, this earnest longing for his return is one of the best, for such a person is thinking not only of himself and of his own glory but also of his Lord and of the latter's public vindication. For all such persons the wreath is waiting. And *this* wreath, unlike earthly wreaths, is imperishable (I Cor. 9:25).

---

9 Do your best to come to me quickly; 10 for Demas has deserted me, because he fell in love with the present world, and has gone to Thessalonica; Crescens (has gone) to Galatia, Titus to Dalmatia. 11 Luke is the only one with me. Pick up Mark and bring him with you, for he is very useful to me for (the) ministry. 12 Now Tychicus I am commissioning for Ephesus. 13 The cloak which I left in Troas with Carpus bring along when you come; also the books, especially the parchments.

14 Alexander, the metal-worker, did me much damage. The Lord will repay him in accordance with his deeds. 15 You, too, be on your guard against him, for he vigorously opposed our words.

16 At my first defence no one was at my side, but all deserted me; may it not be charged against them! 17 But the Lord stood at my side, and gave me strength, in order that through me the message might be fully heralded, and all the Gentiles might hear it, and I was rescued out of (the) mouth of (the) lion. 18 And the Lord will rescue me from every evil work, and save me (bringing me) to his heavenly kingdom; to him (*be* or *is*) the glory forever and ever. Amen.

19 Greet Prisca and Aquila and the family of Onesiphorus. 20 Erastus remained at Corinth, but Trophimus I left at Miletus sick. 21 Do your best to come before winter. Eubulus greets you, as do Pudens and Linus and Claudia and all the brothers.

22 The Lord (be) with your spirit. Grace (be) with y o u.

4:9-22

The present paragraph consists, in general, of items of personal information, requests, and greetings. It can be divided into five sub-paragraphs, as follows:

a. verses 9-13: Paul gives expression to the loneliness which he feels, and the need of more kingdom-workers, asks for his cloak, for books and parchments, and for the speedy arrival of Timothy.

b. verses 14, 15: He warns Timothy against Alexander, the metal-worker.

c. verses 16-18: From the manner in which the Lord had strengthened him during his "first defence" Paul derives comfort for the present and for the future.

d. verses 19-21: Greetings to and from certain individual believers, items of information with reference to others, repetition of request for Timothy's speedy coming.

e. verse 22: Benediction.

9, 10, 11a. Do your best to come to me quickly.

Paul, writing from a cold, dank dungeon in Rome, and facing death, longs for the presence of his "beloved child" Timothy. He wants him to come quickly, that is, "before winter" (see on verse 21). The reason for the apostle's feeling of loneliness is as follows: **for Demas has deserted me, because he fell in love with the present world, and has gone to Thessalonica; Crescens (has gone) to Galatia, Titus to Dalmatia. Luke is the only one with me.**

Demas had at one time been Paul's assistant in the gospel-ministry (Philemon 24). During the first Roman imprisonment Demas, too, had been in Rome. Twice the apostle had mentioned him in one breath with Luke, the beloved physician (Col. 4:14; Philemon 25). It would seem to be a safe inference from the present passage that also during the second Roman imprisonment Demas had been in Rome, and had rendered service in the kingdom. Hence, all the more pathetic are these plaintive words, "Do your best to come to me quickly, for Demas has deserted me." The verb used in the original implies that Demas had not merely *left* Paul (on this or that legitimate mission), but had *left him in the lurch,* had abandoned, forsaken him. The separation was not merely local but spiritual. Paul is deeply disappointed with Demas. Demas left *because he fell in love*[175] with the present age, the "world" on this side of the grave, the transitory era which, in spite of all its pleasures and treasures, will soon be past (see

---

[175] By means of the translation, "because he fell in love," I have tried to do justice to two facts: a. the participle used in the original is aorist, and b. it is undoubtedly causal in the present connection.

on I Tim. 6:17). Much can be said in support of the view that Demas, in love with the present world, never belonged to the company of those who love Christ's appearing. Note the sharp and probably intentional contrast between the lover of the present world (verse 9) and the lovers of the Epiphany (verse 8). Moreover, nowhere is there a word about the restoration of Demas. Demas should probably not be placed in a class with Mark! Though we have no solid ground for speaking with certainty about this matter, nevertheless, the spirit of the present passage and of its context rather points in the direction of Matthew 7:22, 23, as a general indication of the class to which Demas belongs. Just why Demas went *to Thessalonica*, and not to some other place, is not known. Perhaps he thought that the deepest desires of his soul could be better satisfied there than elsewhere. Did he leave Rome because this capital was at that time the most dangerous place for a Christian to be? Did he have business, friends, or relatives in Thessalonica? We do not know.

Paul adds, "Crescens (has gone) to Galatia." Instead of *Galatia* another reading has *Gallia*. This would then be the region which today is called France plus certain surrounding territories. It is impossible to determine which of these two readings is correct. Hence, we do not know where Crescens went.[176] Nor do we have any *reliable* information about Crescens except that which is supplied by the present passage.

---

[176] The problem with reference to *Galatia* or *Gallia* is complicated. About the year 400 B. C. certain Gauls or Celts migrated to northern Italy. Some of the tribes moved farther eastward, entering Macedonia and Thrace. In the year 278 B. C. 20,000 Gauls crossed the Hellespont and moved into Asia Minor. Here they prospered and increased greatly in numbers. Though subsequently subjugated by the Romans, they were permitted to keep their own kings. The Roman province *Galatia*, named after them, comprised: a. the territory in central and northern Asia Minor in which most of *these* Gauls were now living, and b. certain districts to the south of this Celtic territory.

Since Paul must be regarded as the author of the Pastorals, and he was in the habit of using the official names of Roman political units or provinces — "Asia" (I Cor. 16:19); "Achaia" (II Cor. 1:1); and "Macedonia" (II Cor. 8:1) — I believe that in I Cor. 16:1; Gal. 1:2; and also in our present passage (II Tim. 4:10) *if the reading "Galatia" is here authentic*, it is the Roman province of Galatia (in Asia Minor) that is meant. (The fact, mentioned by several commentators, that certain Greek writers — Polybius, Plutarch, etc. — use the term "Celtic Galatia" to designate Gaul proper, has nothing to do with the argument. It is *Paul's* usage that interests us.) *The Constitutions of the Holy Apostles*, VII. xlvi (see the context) favors Galatia in Asia Minor as the province to which Crescens was sent.

However, if the reading "Gallia" is, after all, authentic, it becomes easier to account for the tradition which ascribed to Crescens the founding of the church at Vienne near Lyons. Eusebius, moreover, says that Crescens was sent to Gaul, *Ecclesiastical History*, III. iv. The possibility that it was Gaul in Europe and not Galatia in Asia must be granted. On the assumption that Paul had visited Spain, it is logical to believe that he may also have established churches in Southern Gaul, and that Crescens may have been sent to strengthen what had been started there. Accordingly, the answer to the question, "Where did Crescens go?" depends on

"Titus (has gone) to Dalmatia," continues Paul. It seems that after Titus' visit to Jerusalem as a test-case (Gal. 2:21), all his missions were to provinces in Europe. Whenever, away from Paul, he was on a mission, he was never very far from the east coast of the Adriatic Sea or its southern extension, the Ionian Sea. Being able, courageous, and consecrated, he knew how to handle the quarrelsome Corinthians, the mendacious Cretans, and the reputedly pugnacious Dalmatians. Cf. Rom. 15:19. In contrast with Demas who had deserted Paul, we must believe that both Crescens and Titus had gone where duty called them. See also on Titus 3:12.

"Luke is the only one with me." The author of the third Gospel was a remarkable person. He was "the beloved physician" (Col. 4:14), always loyal to Paul, to the gospel, to the Lord. Frequently he had been Paul's companion in travel, as is indicated by the "we" sections in Acts (16:10-17; 20:6-16; 21; 27; 28). He had been with Paul on the second missionary journey, at Troas and at Philippi. He had evidently been left behind at the latter place (Acts 16:17-19). Toward the close of the third tour he seems again to have joined Paul at Philippi (Acts 20:60), and he accompanied him to Jerusalem. For a while we do not see him. But suddenly he re-appears, for he is in Paul's company on the long and dangerous sea-journey from Palestine to Rome (Acts 27). He is with the apostle during both the first and the second Roman imprisonments (Col. 4:14; Philemon 24; II Tim. 4:11). Paul needed a doctor and a friend. Luke was both, and *directly or indirectly* may also have served in the capacity of Paul's secretary.

Luke and Paul had much in common. Both were educated men, men of culture. Both were big-hearted, broad-spirited, sympathetic. Above all, both were believers and missionaries.[177]

But if Luke was such a wonderful friend, why does Paul say, "Luke is the only one with me"? The following answer may be suggested: a. The very presence, off and on, of no one else besides Luke made the absence of all the others all the more conspicuous, especially in contrast with Paul's circumstances during the *first* imprisonment when he was permitted to

---

the answer to that other question, "What is the correct reading here in II Tim. 4:10?" Is it "Galatia" or is it "Gallia"? And the textual evidence is too nearly even to answer this question with any degree of finality.

[177] Several authors have attempted to write a Biography of Luke; for example, W. Ramsay, *Luke The Physician*; A. T. Robertson, *Luke The Historian In The Light of Historical Research*, New York, 1923, chapter II: "A Sketch of Luke's Career"; D. A. Hayes, *The Most Beautiful Book Ever Written*, New York, 1913, pp. 3-54. The accounts are all very interesting; nevertheless, there is scarcely enough reliable first-hand information for a biography. There are many possibilities and some probabilities, but there are few certainties. Authorities are not even in agreement on the place of Luke's birth, though much can be said in favor of Antioch in Syria. See *The Anti-Marcionite Prologue to the Third Gospel*.

receive all who came to him (Acts 28:30). Also, b. There may be more here than an expression of *loneliness*. It is entirely possible that the apostle also wishes to stress the fact that he is short on help, that there were not enough reapers; perhaps not even a sufficient number to provide adequately for the spiritual needs of those believers who were still in Rome.

It must be emphasized that whatever is stated in verse 10 and 11a, in connection with Demas, Crescens, Titus, and Luke, has the purpose of urging Timothy to do his best to come quickly.

11b, 12, 13. With a view to this coming of Timothy, the apostle continues, **Pick up Mark and bring him with you, for he is very useful to me for (the) ministry.** The home of Mark was in Jerusalem (Acts 12:12). It was he who had deserted Paul and Barnabas on the first missionary journey. Paul, therefore, had refused to take Mark with him on the second tour. So Barnabas had taken Mark and had sailed away to Cyprus (Acts 15:36-41). Subsequently, however, we find Mark again in the company of Paul at Rome during the apostle's first imprisonment (Col. 4:10; Philemon 24). Afterward he is with Peter in Rome (I Peter 5:13). Tradition supports the idea that there was a close connection between Peter's preaching in Rome and the writing of Mark's Gospel. After Peter's martyrdom Mark seems to have become *Paul's* assistant once more. At Paul's request and in co-operation with Timothy he may have been making a tour of the churches in Asia Minor while Paul was writing II Timothy. Timothy, leaving for Rome, is urged to "pick him up," because Paul knows that by this time Mark is very useful to him "for ministry." The implication is probably this: since Mark has experienced a change for the better, having taken to heart the lesson which his earlier failure had taught him, and since he is well acquainted with Rome and with the condition of the church in that city, hence *in Rome* he will be the right man in the right place. The context indicates that when Paul uses the term *ministry* or *service*, he is thinking of kingdom-work, service in the interest of the gospel, and does not merely mean, "He can perform certain duties to make life easier for me personally."

Continuing, then, along this same line, the man who even in the dungeon is the great superintendent of missions adds, **Now Tychicus I am commissioning** (probably an epistolary aorist) **for Ephesus.** Tychicus (Greek proper name, meaning "fortuitous") was a beloved brother, faithful minister and fellow-servant in the gospel, a man worthy of all confidence. He was one of several intimate friends who had accompanied the apostle when at the close of his third missionary journey he was returning from Greece through Macedonia into Asia, with the purpose of going to Jerusalem on a charitable mission (Acts 20:4). Also later, during the first Roman imprisonment, Tychicus had been with Paul. He had been commissioned by the apostle to carry to their destinations the epistle to the Ephesians, the one to the Colossians, and probably also the one to Philemon. He was, moreover, the right person to supply the necessary "atmosphere" — more detailed information about Paul's circumstances —, so that the letters which he delivered could be understood all the more readily (Eph. 6:21; Col. 4:7). During the interval between the first and second Roman imprisonments Tychicus is again (or *still*) working in close cooperation with Paul (see on Titus 3:12). And now, during the second Roman imprisonment, Paul finds that Tychicus is the logical person to send to Ephesus with this letter (II Timothy). In addition, he is also the right man to serve for a while as director of affairs in the churches of Asia Minor, as a substitute for Timothy during the latter's absence, which would be of rather lengthy duration, since Timothy would not be able to return to Ephesus until at least April (see on verse 21).

Timothy, then, must not hesitate to leave Ephesus. Under another trusted leader, namely, Tychicus, the work will be continued. The *cause* will not have to suffer. When Timothy leaves for Rome, he must, moreover, take with him a few things needed by Paul: **The cloak which I left in Troas with Carpus bring along when you come; also the books, especially the parchments.**

The word translated "cloak" (φαιλόνης = , by metathesis from φαινόλης, a transliteration of the Latin *paenula*) indicates a kind of blanket of coarse wool that was used as an outer garment to protect against the cold and the rain. It had a hole in the middle for the head to pass through. There were no sleeves. In Latin this is the more usual (though not the only) meaning of the word. In Greek it is this meaning that has abundant papyri support. The connotation *briefcase, bookwrap,* or *satchel,* a receptacle for important documents and/or "books," is found at times, and there have always been those who assign this meaning to the word in the present passage.[178] But the apostle does not seem to be asking for his "satchel with documents" but for two different kinds of articles: a. "the paenula," and b. "the books, especially the parchments." It is possible that both a. and b. were in one class in *this* sense only, that they were rather troublesome to carry along at all times; for example, in hot weather. So, Paul may have left them with Carpus (otherwise unknown to us), intending soon to return in order to pick them up. Whatever may have been the reason

---

[178] Milligan formerly defended this view, but changed his opinion (M. M., p. 665). A recent defender is A. Sizoo, in his own, very interesting, manner. See his valuable book, *De Antieke Wereld En Het Nieuwe Testament,* Kampen, 1948, pp. 90, 91. His argument in defence of the position that here the word can hardly mean "cloak" is that Paul, the great traveler, would not have left his rain-coat behind, an article which was necessary not only in winter but in certain regions also during the summer. — However, for reasons unknown to us, it may not have been feasible or even possible for Paul to get his belongings together.

why this was not done, the apostle in his cold, damp dungeon, with winter just around the corner, feels the need of this cloak, and asks Timothy to bring it along when he comes. Troas was not far from Timothy's headquarters at Ephesus.[179]

And let Timothy also bring "the books, especially the parchments." The "books" were in all probability papyrus-rolls; the "parchments" or "membranes" were skins of sheep, lambs, goats, or calves, especially prepared for writing. Paul wants the books but above all the parchments! What was written in these books and parchments? Is it not natural to assume that the Lord's prisoner desired above all else to spend his few remaining weeks or months in meditating upon the Word of God? For the rest, as to exact contents, we simply do not know, and it is useless to add to the guesses that have been made.[180]

It is clear that the believer in his yearning to provide for his intellectual and spiritual needs (books, parchments) is not called upon to ignore the needs of the body ("the cloak"). One is reminded of the very similar entreaty which, under analogous circumstances, was penned by another notable warrior of the cross many centuries later. It was William Tyndale, the well-known Bible translator, who from his cold prison-cell at Vilvoorde made request that *in view of the approaching winter* (how like Paul!) a cloak, woollen shirt, warm cap, and most of all, his Hebrew Bible, grammar, and vocabulary be brought to him.

14, 15. We come now to the second sub-paragraph (see p. 318), a warning against a bitter enemy of the faith: **Alexander, the metal-worker, did me much damage.**

It is not easy to reconstruct the circumstances under which Alexander

---

[179] On the basis of the reference to Troas, Scott argues that these verses must be assigned to a much earlier letter, because Paul had not been in Troas for several years (*op. cit.*, p. 138). But Scott's argument has value only if the book of Acts (see 16:8; 20:5) and Paul's other epistles (see II Cor. 2:12) give us a complete itinerary. Specifically, it has value only if there cannot have been a release from a first Roman imprisonment and, following upon this release, a second Roman imprisonment. Such assumptions, are precarious.

[180] There are those who think that *the rolls* contained portions of the Old Testament, or Jewish commentaries, or copies of his own letters, or of certain writings of pagan philosophers or poets. The following are a few among the many conjectures with respect to *the parchments:* the Septuagint, the words of Jesus which preceded the Gospels, Paul's own notations, legal documents or certificates (for example, a certificate of Roman citizenship) which the apostle needed for his coming (?) trial, etc. This last view is especially in favor among those commentators who are convinced that verses 16-18 imply that Paul is still awaiting a formal trial. Thus the reader is being gradually conditioned for what I consider to be a rather questionable interpretation of these verses. There are also those who adopt the view that neither books nor parchments had any writing on them. The apostle, then, is simply asking for something to write on!

4:14, 15 **II TIMOTHY**

opposed Paul and the good cause which the latter represented. It can, however, be stated with well-nigh certainty that there had been a trial (this, in the light of the trial-context; see verse 16, though the trial referred to there is probably not the same as the one in which Alexander was involved; see on that verse). In this trial Alexander had been an accuser or a witness for the prosecution. Who was this Alexander? His name was as common then as are the names Brown, Jones, or Smith today (Mark 15:21; Acts 4:6; 19:33, 34; I Tim. 1:19, 20; II Tim. 4:14, probably five different Alexanders). From the context it would appear that *this* Alexander is living in Rome; for it stands to reason that it was especially in Rome that he was able to oppose Paul, who was also in that city. Now if that inference be correct, he must probably not be identified with the Alexander mentioned in I Tim. 1:20 nor with the one to whom Acts 19:33, 34 refers, for these Alexanders lived in the Ephesus region.[181]

---

[181] A. Those who, nevertheless, favor the identification of "Alexander the metal-worker" or "metallurgist" (II Tim. 4:14, 15) with "Alexander the Ephesian heretic" (I Tim. 1:19, 20) base this theory upon the supposition that what Paul means in the passage now under discussion is, "On my recent visit to Ephesus, Alexander the metal-worker did me much damage by vigorously opposing my proclamation of the gospel. So, Timothy, as long as you remain in Ephesus, be on your guard against him." Cf. John Rutherford, art. "Alexander," in I.S.B.E., Vol. I., see esp. p. 91. *Objections:*

(1) If the Alexander of II Tim. 4:14, 15 is the one of I Tim. 1:19, 20, Timothy would know him. If any further description were needed, in addition to the mention of his name, would it not be in terms of the passage in the earlier epistle? The addition "the metal-worker" points *away from* the Alexander mentioned in I Tim. 1:19, 20.

(2) As the context indicates (see verse 16), the apostle is not now thinking principally about opposition to the proclamation of the gospel but about opposition to "words" of defence in the court-room.

(3) The setting in our present passage is Rome, not Ephesus.

B. Those who favor identification of "Alexander the metal-worker" (II Tim. 4:14, 15) with "Alexander the Jew" thrust forward, in connection with a riot, to shield the Ephesian Jews (Acts 19:33, 34), an identification favored, among others, by F. W. Grosheide, *Korte Verklaring, Handelingen*, Vol. II, p. 100, do so because they like to associate Demetrius *a silversmith* (Acts 19:24) with Alexander *the coppersmith*. On the basis of this theory an interesting story can then be fabricated. For example, at the occasion of the Ephesian riot Alexander can be imagined to say, "We Jews are not guilty of opposing Diana of the Ephesians. Why, I myself, as a coppersmith, make the shrines which Demetrius plates with silver. So, please do not take this out on us. Punish this fellow Paul and his companions Gaius and Aristarchus." The *possibility* that the two ("Alexander the metal-worker" and "Alexander the Ephesian Jew") were the same person must be granted, but the belief that this is more than a mere *possibility* is faced with the following difficulties:

(1) The account in Acts tells us nothing about the occupation of *that* Alexander.

(2) In order to clinch this identification, Alexander the Jew of Ephesus must be brought to Rome. Now, of course, this may have happened; but there is nothing in the account to raise this mere possibility to the level of a probability. — Or else the *opposition* of which Paul speaks (II Tim. 4:14, 15) must be regarded as having taken place in Ephesus. This would seem to be in conflict with the present context.

The present Alexander, then, is probably a different person. He is *the metal-worker* (primary meaning is *coppersmith;* then *metal-worker* in general; cf. Gen. 4:22 LXX). Now, in connection with the trial, Alexander, by means of *deeds* (verse 14) and *words* (verse 15), had succeeded in damaging Paul. No doubt he had helped to bring about an adverse court-decision with respect to the apostle, though we do not know whether the sentence, "Condemned to death" had already been announced or conveyed to the apostle. We *do* know, however, that this sentence was now *certain,* and that Paul knew this. He knew that he was about to die (see on 4:6, 7, 8; also on verse 18). But instead of avenging himself upon Alexander, he leaves the matter of retribution entirely to the Lord (Deut. 32:35; cf. Rom. 12:17-19; I Peter 2:23). Hence, he immediately adds, **The Lord** *will repay* (best reading) **him in accordance with his deeds.** When Christ returns to judge (see on verses 1 and 8), he will not forget what Alexander has done, but *will give him his due* (same verb as in verse 8, where it is used in a favorable sense). See Ps. 62:12; Prov. 24:12; Matt. 25:31-46; John 5:28, 29; Rom. 2:6; II Cor. 11:15; Rev. 2:23; 20:13.

Paul continues, **You, too, be on your guard against him, for he vigorously opposed our words.** "Forewarned is forearmed." Let Timothy, in coming to Rome, be constantly on his guard against this wicked Alexander, who will try his utmost to harm the disciple even before the latter has reached his master. Let him take the necessary precautions so that he will know what to say and what to do if and when he should be confronted with Alexander. And, prayer being at all times the best prophylactic, let him pray about this matter, in order that the proper words may be given to him when he needs them, and the proper actions may be suggested to him.

This Alexander was a relentless persecutor, one who *vigorously* (upon this word rests the emphasis) *stood over against* — hence, *resisted, opposed* (Matt. 5:39; Luke 21:15; Acts 6:10; 13:8; Rom. 9:19; Gal. 2:11; Eph. 6:13; II Tim. 3:8; 4:15; James 4:7; I Peter 5:9) — "our words," that is, the arguments for the defence, a defence in which the apostle had been assisted by others (Onesiphorus, Luke?; see on II Tim. 1:15, 16; 4:11), as the modifier *our* indicates.

16-18. That word *our* ("our words"), instead of *my,* brings up the past. There had been another trial. In that *first* defence no one had taken Paul's side. It is readily understood why Paul speaks of the trial as a *defence* (literally "apology" in the sense of speech in vindication from accusation), for that had been *his* part in it. In that former trial, then, Paul had stood alone. *Entirely* alone? No, for the Lord had caused *his* presence to be felt in a remarkable manner. From the way in which the Lord had then strengthened him Paul derives comfort for the present and for the fu-

4:16-18 **II TIMOTHY**

ture. Let Timothy also take courage. — This, in general, is the sense of the third sub-paragraph (see p. 318) which follows.

I shall treat it first *positively,* giving the interpretation which by many is considered to be "the most natural one," even though today it is not the most widely accepted one; then *negatively,* stating the difficulties which beset the opposite interpretation.

At my first defence no one was at my side, but all deserted me.

Paul, being in a reminiscent mood, as one is prone to be when he reaches the end of his life here on earth and has an opportunity to look back, vividly recalls this other trial, the one which, if these interpreters are correct, had taken place a few years earlier. At that time no one had come to *stand beside* him in his defence. That was during the period of the first Roman imprisonment. What a difference between then and now, *as to the actual trial! Now,* during this second Roman imprisonment, *Demas* had *deserted* him (see on verse 10), and "all those in Asia" had *turned away from* him (see on II Tim. 1:15). But Onesiphorus had come from Asia, and Luke had remained faithful. But during that previous imprisonment *not a single person* had presented himself as a witness for Paul's defence. *All had deserted.* Why? Had fear held them back? Or possibly the feeling: The apostle does not need us, for the Romans are favorably inclined to him, and no accuser has appeared in order to press his charge? See pp. 26, 27. However that may be, to a certain extent Paul had suffered a disappointment. But he knows how to forgive. Hence, he continues: **May it not be charged against them.** This prayerful wish is entirely in harmony with the spirit of Christ (Luke 23:34), of Stephen (Acts 7:60) and . . . of Paul himself (I Cor. 13:5).

But the Lord stood at my side and gave me strength. That, during his first imprisonment, this had indeed been Paul's blessed experience is clear from Phil. 4:13. The Lord (Jesus Christ) had stood by him and *had strengthened* (cf. I Tim. 1:12; the same word as in Phil. 4:13; and cf. Acts 9:22; Rom. 4:20; Eph. 6:10) him, and this not only *during* that imprisonment but even *on his way* to it (Acts 23:11; 27:23). And the purpose had been: **in order that through me the message might be fully heralded** (literally, "in order that through me *the heralded message* — or "preaching," "kerugma," see on verse 2 — *might be fulfilled* or accomplished"), **and all the Gentiles might hear it.**

The following interpretation is natural: I was set at liberty in order that after my acquittal I might complete my task of heralding the gospel of salvation, so that not only the Gentiles *east* of Rome but also those *west* of Rome might hear it. — Paul's gospel-message, the heralded word as spoken by him, must reach the limits of the West. Spain could not be omitted (Rom. 15:24, 28).

And I was rescued out of (the) mouth of (the) lion. Probably this is simply an idiomatic way of saying, "I was delivered out of the jaws of death" (*ex faucibus mortis,* Calvin), and not a specific reference to Satan, Nero, or a literal lion of the amphitheater. In all probability this, as is clear from Ps. 22:21, 22 (the passage upon which Paul's figurative expression is based) means *complete* deliverance. Paul had been enabled to declare the name of the Lord far and wide. His first Roman imprisonment had ended in full acquittal and in more missionary journeys.

From this experience of the past the apostle draws encouragement: **And the Lord will rescue me from every evil work, and save me (bringing me) to his heavenly kingdom.**

Note the parallel:

At my first defence *all deserted* me (verse 16). Now Demas *has deserted* me (verse 10). Same verb in both cases.

At my first defence *I was rescued* (verse 17). Now, "the Lord *will rescue me*" (verse 18). Again the same verb both times.

The stress falls on this divine rescuing activity. *In the past* there had been danger. *Now,* too, there was that which men would consider danger. But in the past the Lord had intervened; now again he will *intervene decisively for deliverance* (which is the meaning of *rescue,* as in I Thess. 1:10). In the past Paul had been rescued *from* death. Now he will be rescued *by means of* death. In neither case does his soul perish. He is never separated from the love of God in Christ.

To destroy Paul spiritually and to annihilate the kingdom of Christ is, nevertheless, at all times exactly what Satan intends to do. All the efforts which he puts forth to achieve this sinister purpose constitute his *evil work*. But Paul is convinced that, as in the past so also now, "the Lord will rescue me from every evil work," though not from all physical harm. The man who wrote II Cor. 11:22-33 does not expect immunity from injury to the body! But *the Lord* (Jesus Christ) *will save me to* (this is either a pregnant expression meaning "will save me, bringing me to," or means "will save me *for*," the two interpretations yielding about the same resultant sense) *his heavenly kingdom.* The Lord is going to bring Paul to heaven, that is, to that kingdom which, though seen on earth in shadow, has its seat in heaven, and belongs to heaven as to its essence and fulness (see on verse 1).

The expression "the Lord . . . will save me to (or *for*) his heavenly kingdom" implies that Paul expected to go to heaven immediately upon death. This is Scripture's doctrine throughout. Thus, the psalmist expects to be welcomed into the realm of glory when he dies (Ps. 73:24, 25). "Lazarus" is immediately carried by the angels into Abraham's bosom (Luke 16, see especially verse 22). The penitent thief enters Paradise at once, together with his Lord (Luke 23:43). Paul is convinced that when the earthly tent is destroyed, the building from God, "eternal in the heavens" will be ready

4:16-18   II TIMOTHY

to receive the believer (II Cor. 5:1); that death is "gain" (Phil. 1:21), which would not be true if it meant extinction of being or passing into oblivion; and that to depart from this earth means to be with Christ, a condition which is "better by far" than continued life here below (Phil. 1:23). And the book of Revelation pictures the souls of the martyrs as having been translated immediately into heaven, and as being very happily and busily occupied in that region of bliss (Rev. 7:13-17).

Not filled with dismay is Paul when he thinks of imminent departure from this earth. On the contrary, since this departure is better by far than remaining on earth, his soul is filled with rapture. Hence, not surprising is the doxology: **To him the glory forever and ever. Amen.** Cf. Gal. 1:5; but here in II Tim. 4:18 the never-ceasing glory is ascribed to *Christ, the Lord.* Cf. Rom 9:5; 16:27. By adding the word of solemn affirmation or confirmation, "Amen" (on which see N.T.C. on John, Vol. I, p. 111, footnote 51), the apostle shows that he most heartily *desires* (if the omitted verb is "be") or definitely *declares* (if "is" must be understood, as in I Peter 4:11 and in those texts of Matt. 6:13 which contain the doxology of the Lord's prayer) that Christ's *glory* — the radiating splendor of all his marvelous attributes — be (or "is") his possession world without end.

The interpretation that has been presented, according to which the expression "my first defence" refers to the first Roman imprisonment, particularly to the trial which then took place and which resulted in Paul's acquittal and more journeys, is supported by the testimony of tradition. That Eusebius thus interprets the passage is clear from the quotation which has been given (see p. 27). Cf. also Chrysostom (Hom. XI).[182]

Many commentators, however, favor an interpretation which differs radically from the one supported by tradition. They feel that the latter is out of harmony with the favorable conditions of the imprisonment recorded in the book of Acts. Their view may be briefly summarized as follows:

(1) "My first defence" means: "my first appearance in court," "the preliminary investigation" (prima actio) in *the present trial.*

(2) "No one was at my side" means: no *patron* ("friend" at court, a man of importance in the eyes of the Romans) accompanied me to the courtroom, attesting by his very presence that I am a respectable person.

Similarly, "all deserted me" means: all those potential *patrons* abandoned me.

(3) The sentence, "But the Lord stood at my side and gave me strength, in order that through me the message might be fully heralded" means: the

---

[182] Among others who have accepted this view or, while admitting some doubt, have expressed a preference for it, are the following: Barnes, Bouma, Lock, Zahn (for titles see Bibliography).

Lord strengthened me in order that by means of my defence in the courtroom my message might reach its climax (or: so that by that means it got to be fully completed).

(4) "And all the Gentiles might hear it" means: and in order that the crowd of Roman grandees in the court-room, as representing the entire heathen world, might hear my defence (or: so that this crowd got to hear my defence).

(5) "And I was rescued from the mouth of the lion" means: and I was kept from being executed that day.[183]

In fairness to those who favor this view it must be said that some, though wishing to be counted among its defenders, express serious misgivings and doubts about it. This is not surprising. Note the following:

With respect to point (1) above. The fact that the statement, "Alexander, the metal-worker, did me much damage" is followed by *"At my first defence* no one was at my side," may imply that the damage wrought by Alexander was *not* done "at my first defence," but more recently. Paul may be comparing the present with the past. *If so, he is retracing his steps,* drawing lessons and analogies from the experiences of former years. *This, at any rate, is entirely in line with what he is doing in other passages of the same epistle* (1:5; 2:2; 3:14, 15; 4:7).

With respect to (2). Paul mentions Luke who is with him, and Demas who has deserted him. About "patrons" not a word. Also, if there has been a trial of any kind ("preliminary" or otherwise) *during this present imprisonment,* it is hard to believe that Paul intended to say that Luke was either absent or not qualified to serve as patron.

With respect to (3). The idea that *the fully accomplished proclamation* refers simply to a court-room defence does not seem as reasonable as is the view that it refers to the hope of *proclaiming the gospel* to the whole world, that is, to the West (Spain) as well as to the East.

With respect to (4). To say that the clause, ". . . and that all the Gentiles might hear it" means no more than, "and that the whole court-room crowd might hear it" would seem to do violence to the text (as Gealy admits). To view this crowd as *representing* "the entire heathen world" looks like forced exegesis in the interest of a theory.

And finally, with respect to (5). In the light of the passage of which Paul, no doubt, was thinking, namely, Ps. 22:21, 22, which describes a deliverance of the most thorough-going character, it can be said with little possibility

---

[183] Among those who accept or lean toward this view are the following, with individual variations as to details of interpretation: Dibelius, Ellicott, Feine, Gealy, Jülicher, Lenski, Robertson, Scott, Simpson, and White (see Bibliography for titles). It must be stressed, however, that the summary which has been given does not necessarily do full justice to the view of any one particular interpreter. See the separate Commentaries and Introductions for more complete information.

4:16-18　　　　　　　　　　II TIMOTHY

of successful contradiction that rather unsatisfactory is the view according to which *rescue from the lion's mouth* means nothing more than this, namely, that immediately after his preliminary hearing Paul, instead of being executed, was led back, as a chained prisoner, to his horrible dungeon, there to await *certain* death (cf. II Tim. 4:6).

It is safe to say, therefore, that if there be a better interpretation than that which was offered by the early church, it has not yet been presented. It must be freely admitted that the traditional view has its difficulties. But are not the difficulties with which the opposite view is confronted even more formidable?

19. The fourth sub-paragraph (greetings, etc., verses 19-21; see p. 318) begins as follows: **Greet Prisca and Aquila and the family of Onesiphorus.**

As to Prisca and Aquila, note that in four of the six references to this wonderful team the name of the wife precedes (Acts 18:18; 18:26; Rom. 16:3; and here in II Tim. 4:19). In two references the order is reversed (Acts 18:2; I Cor. 16:19). Guesses as to the reason why Aquila is usually mentioned *last* (and Prisca *first*) are:

a. Prisca excelled her husband in loyalty and zeal with respect to the work of the Lord.

b. Prisca sprang from a more distinguished family.

c. Prisca had been the "noble hostess," and as such had bestowed much sympathetic care upon Paul and his helpers.

If the underlying assumption be correct, namely, that a writer bestows special honor or higher rating upon the person whom he most often mentions first — an assumption which is *not* granted by all! — then the last-mentioned reason might well be the correct one; but we do not know.

Note also that Paul says *Prisca* ("earnest — or *old* — woman"), but Luke says *Priscilla* (same meaning with "little" added as a suffix; cf. Dutch "oudje"). *Aquila* means *eagle*. These are Latin names.

Aquila was "a man of Pontus by race," who had lived for a while in Rome. As a result of an outburst of anti-Semitism on the part of emperor Claudius, Aquila and his wife had left Rome and had settled in Corinth. He was a tentmaker as was Paul. Soon the two men were working together. (Acts 18:1-3.) The inference would seem to be justified that it was through Paul that his host and hostess were brought to Christ. When, homeward bound from the second missionary journey, the apostle made a brief stop at Ephesus, Aquila and Prisca were traveling with him, and "he left them there" (Acts 18:18, 19). It was here that they proved to be a God-send to that fervent preacher Apollos, to whom "they expounded the way of God more accurately" (Acts 18:24-26). When Paul on his third missionary journey sends I Corinthians from Ephesus, he appends a fervent greeting from Aquila and Prisca and from "the church that is in their house" (I

Cor. 16:19). When on this same journey Paul finally arrives in Corinth and sends a letter to the Romans, he causes the salutation to Prisca and Aquila to be the first of a lengthy list. (The theory that this list does not belong here, though strongly argued, has never been proved. I cling firmly to the belief that it is an authentic part of the epistle to the Romans.) Not only is this greeting the first, it is also the fullest and the warmest. It now appears that the devoted couple had "risked their necks" for Paul. Once more, as in Ephesus, the home of Aquila and Priscilla, who are now back in Rome, is the meeting-place for the Christian congregation (Rom. 16:3-5). Finally, it appears from our present passage (II Tim. 4:19) that the two have again left Rome and have returned to Ephesus. The reason for this return to Ephesus may have been the Neronian persecution. With what warmth of feeling Paul must have sent this greeting — penning it with his own hand! See on II Thess. 3:17 — to his loyal friends and fellow-workers Aquila and Prisca!

The apostle also sends greetings to "the family of Onesiphorus" (see on II Tim. 1:16).

20. Paul is about to convey "best regards" from certain believers here in Rome with whom he had maintained a degree of contact (see verse 21), no doubt through Luke (see on verse 11). Before he does this, however, he is careful to indicate the reason why two persons have been prevented from sending greetings. This reason is that they are not in Rome. The apostle wants Timothy to know this, so that he may not begin to wonder about the omission. Says Paul: **Erastus remained at Corinth, but Trophimus I left at Miletus sick.** Since in the book of Acts both of these *names* occur in close proximity, in connection with Paul's third missionary journey, a journey in which he was accompanied by Timothy much of the way (see pp. 35, 36), and since here in II Tim. 4:20 the apostle mentions these names as those of men well-known to Timothy, so that no further designation is necessary, it may be safely assumed that Erastus is the one who on the third missionary journey (outward bound) was sent *with Timothy* to Macedonia (Acts 19:22),[184] and that Trophimus was the one who on that same journey

---

[184] Whether the Erastus mentioned in Rom. 16:23 was the same person as the one mentioned in the other two references (Acts 19:22 and II Tim. 4:20) cannot be determined. Those who reject the identification reason that the treasurer of the city of Corinth would not have been able to find time to be Paul's constant assistant, so as to be with him in Ephesus, ready to be sent on various missions.

Those who favor the identification answer:

a. Timothy and Erastus are sent by way of Macedonia *to Corinth* (cf. Acts 19:22 with I Cor. 16:10), and according to Rom. 16:23 Erastus is "the treasurer of the city," that is *of Corinth*.

b. Also, according to both Rom. 16:23 and II Tim. 4:20 Erastus has something to do with *Corinth*. According to the first, he is Corinth's treasurer; according to the second, he "remained at Corinth."

(homeward bound), *with Timothy* accompanied Paul (Acts 20:4, 5). It was this same Trophimus, an Ephesian, who became the innocent cause of Paul's seizure by the mob in Jerusalem (Acts 21:29).

It is reasonable to assume that, in his notes regarding Erastus and Trophimus, the apostle is recounting recent experiences. It was only shortly ago, while Paul, perhaps returning from Spain, was traveling east, then north, then west (via Miletus, Troas, Corinth, to Rome; see a map; also pp. 39, 40) that Erastus had remained at Corinth, and that Trophimus had been left at Miletus sick. Hence, neither of these men is now able to send greetings from Rome.

It must have been hard for Trophimus to be left behind at Miletus, only thirty-six miles south of his home at Ephesus. And it must have been a sorrowful experience for Paul to discover that he did not at this occasion receive from his Lord the power to heal. In God's sovereign providence believers, too, become ill (Elisha, II Kings 13:14; Hezekiah, II Kings 20:1; Paul, Gal. 4:13; Epaphroditus, Phil. 2:25-27; Timothy, I Tim. 5:23; Trophimus, II Tim. 4:20). They even die! The passage, "With his stripes we are healed," does not mean that they have been exempted from the infirmities of the flesh. Often, to be sure, it pleases God to heal them, a blessing which arrives in answer to prayer (James 5:14, 15). But even if God's will be otherwise, theirs is ever the comfort of such passages as Ps. 23; 27; 42; John 14:1-3; Rom. 8:35-39; Phil. 4:4-7; II Tim. 4:6-8; Heb. 4:16; 12:6, to mention only a few among many references.

21. For a true appreciation of the depth of feeling, the pathos, which underlies the request which now follows, one must bear in mind that to the list of *absent fellow-workers* mentioned in verse 10 those which have just now been named (Prisca, Aquila, Erastus, Trophimus, and where was Onesiphorus? still on earth?) must now be added. Hence, not at all surprising are the words: **Do your best to come before winter.** The winter-season (Feast of Tabernacles to Feast of Passover; in other words, October to April) was approaching. Then navigation ceased, or, if attempted at all, became very dangerous, as Paul knew by experience (read Acts 27). Besides, the apostle was aware that the day of execution was fast approaching (II Tim. 4:6). If Timothy delayed his coming, the two would never

---

c. On his third missionary journey Paul *was collecting funds* to help the needy brothers in Jerusalem. A man such as the Erastus of Rom. 16:23, expert in financial affairs, would therefore be the right person to go along with Timothy (Acts 19:22).

d. It is not impossible that a man who traveled with Paul as financial expert could become city-treasurer, perhaps for one year. This office, moreover, was not regarded as one of great prominence. Even a slave or freedman could become city-treasurer.

On the entire question see also H. J. Cadbury, "Erastus of Corinth," *JBL* 50 (1931), 42-58. For myself the matter remains in doubt.

meet again on earth. And, with winter approaching, Paul needed his cloak (see on verse 13).

Probably through Luke as go-between, certain believers who have resisted the urge to flee away from Rome and its bloody persecution ask to be remembered: **Eubulus greets you, as do Pudens and Linus and Claudia and all the brothers.** Even legend has nothing to say with reference to *Eubulus*, a Greek proper name meaning "good counselor," "prudent person." Among the Greeks *Linus* (meaning "flaxen-haired") was the name of a mythical minstrel. The Linus to whom Paul refers seems to have been simply a believer in Rome, not a past companion of Paul. Tradition has it that after Peter's death this man was appointed to the bishopric of the church at Rome (Irenaeus, *Against Heresies* III. iii. 3; Eusebius, *Ecclesiastical History* III. iv). Whether this tradition rests upon any basis of fact is open to doubt. The apostle does not seem to regard him quite so highly. According to legend *Pudens* ("modest") was a Roman senator converted by Peter; and *Claudia* ("lame") was the mother of Linus. These last two (Pudens and Claudia) are common Latin names. Except for these brief notices here in II Tim. 4:21, we have no definite and reliable knowledge about any of the four persons mentioned here.[185] Neither do we know who are meant by "all the brothers." For example, we do not know whether these brothers belonged to the original, predominantly Gentile congregation or to one of the subsequently established assemblies of believers drawn from the Jewish element in Rome.[186]

22. The closing salutation, which is the fifth sub-paragraph (see p. 318) has two parts. The first part is addressed to Timothy alone: **The Lord (be) with your spirit.** "The Lord" means "the Lord Jesus Christ" (cf. Gal. 6:18; Phil. 4:23). The predicate "(be) with your spirit" implies that the spirit of Timothy needs to be strengthened, so that he will fully discharge his ministerial task and in the fulfilment of his duties will even be able to endure suffering for the sake of Christ, and this without protest. The second part is addressed not only to Timothy but also to all those who will hear or read the letter: **Grace (be) with y o u.** See on I Tim. 6:21.

Synthesis of Chapter 4

See the Outline at the beginning of this chapter.

Timothy must *preach* the sound doctrine. This is the final, most solemn charge which the apostle issues as he directs his assistant's attention to God and to Christ Jesus, who will judge the living and the dead, and in whose

---

[185] For the unreliable legends with respect to Pudens and Claudia see Edmundson, *The Church in Rome,* note C.
[186] See my *Bible Survey,* pp. 427-432.

presence the charge is issued and received. Thus he places Timothy under oath to comply with the charge. If Timothy obeys, he will share in (and if he disobeys he will miss) the glory of Christ's Epiphany and Reign.

Timothy, then, must be a herald. He must forcefully and faithfully proclaim the divinely authorized message of salvation. Welcome or not welcome, he must ever be on hand with his good news. In this connection, he must reprove, rebuke, and admonish, doing all this with utmost longsuffering and painstaking teaching-activity. Let him bear in mind that the season will arrive — every age has such a season, but these seasons grow progressively worse — when men will not tolerate the sound doctrine. To be sure, they will still want to have teachers; in fact, "heaps of them." But these teachers will be the kind that suit the fancies of men whose ears itch to hear interesting stories instead of the truth. Let Timothy then be sober, willing to suffer hardship, while he discharges to the full his evangelistic ministry. Let him do this all the more in view of the fact that Paul, who has fought the grand fight, has finished the race, and has kept the faith, is about to depart to the shores of eternity, in order that he may receive the wreath which he can justly claim as his own, and which the Lord, the righteous Judge will award to him on the day of judgment, and not to him alone but to all those who have been looking forward with love and longing to the moment of their Lord's appearing, his brilliant second coming.

The closing paragraph (4:9-22) has been summarized on p. 318.

Commentary on Titus

Outline of Titus

Theme: *The Apostle Paul, Writing to Titus, Gives Directions for the Promotion of the Spirit of Sanctification*

Chapter 1: In Congregational Life.
    A. The Address and Salutation.
    B. Well-qualified elders must be appointed in every town.
    C. Reason: Crete is not lacking in disreputable people who must be sternly rebuked.

Chapter 2: In Family and Individual Life
    A. All classes of individuals that compose the home-circle should conduct themselves in such a manner that by their life they may adorn the doctrine of God, their Savior.
    B. Reason: to all, the grace of God has appeared unto sanctification and joyful expectation of the appearing in glory of our great God and Savior, Jesus Christ.

Chapter 3: In Social (i.e. Public) Life
    A. Believers should be obedient to the authorities. They should be kind to all men, since it was the kindness of God our Savior — not our own works! — which brought salvation.
    B. On the other hand, foolish questions should be shunned, and factious men who refuse to heed admonition should be rejected.
    C. Concluding directions with respect to kingdom-travelers (Artemas or Tychicus, Titus, Zenas, Apollos) and Cretan believers in general. Greetings.

Outline of Chapter 1

Theme: *The Apostle Paul, Writing to Titus, Gives Directions for the Promotion of the Spirit of Sanctification*

In Congregational Life

1:1-4	The Address and Salutation.
1:5-9	Well-qualified elders must be appointed in every town.
1:10-16	Reason: Crete is not lacking in disreputable people who must be sternly rebuked.

CHAPTER I

TITUS   1:1

1   1 Paul, a servant of God and an apostle of Jesus Christ in the interest of (the) faith of God's elect and of (their) acknowledgment of the truth which accords with godliness, 2 (based) on the hope of life everlasting, which the never-lying God promised before times everlasting 3 — but in due season he revealed his word by that proclamation which by order of God our Savior was entrusted to me —; 4 to Titus (my) genuine child in terms of (the) common faith; grace and peace from God (the) Father and Christ Jesus our Savior.

1:1-4

1. Paul, a servant of God and an apostle of Jesus Christ in the interest of (the) faith of God's elect and of (their) acknowledgment of the truth which accords with godliness.

These are the opening words of a lengthy salutation. In Paul's epistles only two are longer. For the sake of comparison note the following list which, arranged in an ascending series, indicates the number of words *in the original* for each salutation:

I Thessalonians	19	II Corinthians	41
II Thessalonians	27	Philemon	41
Colossians	28	I Corinthians	55
Ephesians	28 (or 30)	**Titus**	**65**
II Timothy	29	Galatians	75
Philippians	32	Romans	93
I Timothy	32		

The present salutation (verses 1-4) resembles that in Romans more than it does any other. Here as in Romans Paul calls himself both *servant* and *apostle* (cf. II Peter 1:1), and speaks about a *promise* now fulfilled. Also, as in Romans and in several other epistles, he traces *grace* and *peace* (not "grace, mercy and peace" as in I and II Timothy) to the same twofold source, though the wording varies.

Here as elsewhere (especially in lengthy salutations) the salutation is in line with the character and purpose of the epistle. Thus, it comes as no surprise that in Titus, which stresses the idea that *sound doctrine goes hand in hand with the life of sanctification and the doing of good works,* the very salutation already mentions *godliness* ("the truth which accords with godliness"), and over against the *mendacious* character of the Cretans (Titus 1:12) makes mention of the *never-lying God*.

Paul is *God's servant* [187] ("servant" also in Rom. 1:1; Phil. 1:1; cf. James 1:1; II Peter 1:1, but note variation in modifiers), and has received his authoritative commission directly from *Jesus Christ,* being therefore his *apostle*.

The service and apostleship are exercised "in the interest of" (that seems to be the meaning of κατά here; cf. John 2:6; II Cor. 11:21) the faith of God's elect and (their) acknowledgment of the truth which accords with godliness; that is, they are carried out *in order to further or promote* the reliance of God's chosen ones upon him, and their glad recognition or confession of the redemptive truth which centers in him; a truth which, in sharp contrast with the vagaries of false teachers, *accords with* (or here also "is in the interest of," "promotes") godliness, the life of Christian virtue, the spirit of true consecration.[188]

2. Now *all* that has been said so far — Paul's service and apostleship in the interest of the faith of God's elect and of their acknowledgment of the truth which accords with godliness — rests **on the hope of life everlasting, which the never-lying God promised before times everlasting.**[189] This hope is an

---

[187] Translators and commentators will probably never reach agreement with respect to the question whether δοῦλος, as used here and in similar passages, should be rendered *slave* or *servant*. In favor of *slave* is the fact that Paul's Master *has bought* him, hence *owns* him, and that the apostle *is completely dependent* upon this Master, a relation of which he is fully aware. On the other hand, this very rendering is jarring to our ears because the word "slave" generally conveys to our minds the idea of *involuntary service* and *harsh treatment*. All in all, it would therefore seem that if the choice is between *slave* and *servant*, the rendering *servant* deserves the preference here. See also N.T.C. on John, Vol. II, p. 306, footnote 184. However, it must be admitted that here, as happens frequently, no translation is able *in one word* to convey the full, rich meaning of the original.
[188] Various concepts in this verse have been discussed more fully elsewhere. For the idea of *apostleship* see on I Tim. 1:1. For the idea of *election* see N.T.C. on I Thess. 1:4. For the expression "Jesus Christ" see the comments on I Tim. 1:1; cf. N.T.C. on I Thess. 1:1. And for *godliness* see on I Tim. 2:2; 3:16; 4:7, 8; 6:3, 5, 6, 11; and II Tim. 3:5.
[189] Does the expression "on the hope of life everlasting" really modify the entire first verse? In other words, is *hope* here viewed as a kind of energizing cause both of Paul's apostolic ministry and of the elect's complete devotion to God? This would seem to be the most natural view. Also, it harmonizes with Paul's teaching elsewhere:

Thus, with respect to a. *hope viewed as a spur to faithfulness in the performance of his own task* (and that of Timothy), he says, "For to this end we toil and strive, because we have our hope set on the living God" (see on I Tim. 4:10).

And with respect to b. *hope viewed as an incentive for holy living of believers in general,* the passage Titus 2:11-14 is very clear. (Other passages proving a. or b. or both are the following: I Tim. 1:16; 6:19; II Tim. 1:12; 2:5, 11, 12; 4:1, 7, 8, 18; then also Acts 26:6, 7; Rom. 4:18; 8:20; I Cor. 9:10; 15:58; I Thess. 1:3, 9, 10; 2:12; 4:13.) Surely, if even Jesus "for the joy that was set before him" endured the

earnest yearning, confident expectation, and patient waiting for "life everlasting," salvation in its fullest development (cf. John 17:24; Rom. 8:25). It was this salvation which the God *who cannot lie* (I Sam. 15:29; Heb. 6:18; cf. II Tim. 2:13; contrast Titus 1:12) "promised before times everlasting."

Just as God's grace was given to us in Christ Jesus "before times everlasting" (II Tim. 1:9), so also everlasting life was promised "before times everlasting." Before the ages began to roll along in their never-ending course, that is, "before the world began" (A.V.), hence "from eternity," the grace was given and the life was promised. When God decides to call into being a people for his own possession, the fulfilment of this decree is so certain that the grace which they will receive can be spoken of as having been already given, just as the life is described as having been already promised. Besides, strictly speaking, the text does not say, "God promised *to them,*" but simply, "God *promised.*" Nevertheless, the context (see verse 1) definitely implies that it is *for the benefit of the elect* out of Jews and Gentiles that this promise is made. That in the covenant of redemption from eternity such a promise (of the Father to the Son in the interest of all the elect) was actually made is clearly implied in the fact that believers are viewed as "given" to Christ by the Father, in order that they may inherit life everlasting in its most glorious manifestation (John 17:6, 9, 24; cf. also Ps. 89:3, based on II Sam. 7:12-14; cf. Heb. 1:5). Note especially John 17:24, "Father, I desire that they also, whom thou hast given me, be with me where I am, in order that they may gaze on my glory which thou hast given me, for thou lovest me *before the foundation of the world"* (John 17:24).

This "before the foundation of the world" doctrine, the exact phrase-

---

cross (Heb. 12:2), believers have a right to regard their future salvation as a legitimate (though not as the only!) incentive for a life of consecrated service here below.

But several commentators accept only a. as far as the present passage is concerned. They interpret as follows:
Paul's ministry and apostleship are:
(1) "in the interest of the faith of God's elect," etc.,
and
(2) "based on the hope of life everlasting, which," etc.
The phrases (1) and (2) are viewed as co-ordinate modifiers of "Paul, a servant of God and an apostle of Jesus Christ."
Though this view may be correct, it would seem to be exposed to the following objections, making it less probable:
In the first place, in that case would not (2) be more naturally introduced by some specifying particle?
Secondly, thus narrowly conceived, is not the antecedent of the expression "(which is based) on the hope" rather remote?
Thirdly, when the words which immediately precede this expression mention other things (furtherance in faith, acknowledgment of the truth, the exercise of godliness) which according to Paul's consistent teaching are *also* stimulated by this living hope, as has been shown, what good reason is there to say that *only* Paul's apostolic ministry is based on it?
Other views of the construction are even less satisfactory.

ology, is not only Johannine but also definitely Pauline. Note Eph. 1:4, "He elected us for himself in him (i.e., in Christ) *before the foundation of the world."*

Thus interpreted, Titus 1:2 is entirely in harmony with Pauline thinking, which regularly traces the salvation of believers to its origin in God's redemptive plan from eternity (besides II Tim. 1:9 and Eph. 1:4 see also Rom. 8:29, 30; I Cor. 2:7; II Thess. 2:13; and see N.T.C. on I Thess. 1:4 [190]).

3. Verse 3 is really a parenthesis: — **but in due season he revealed his word by (that) proclamation which by order of God our Savior was entrusted to me** — .

From eternity God *promised* life everlasting, but "in due season" (here used as in I Tim. 2:6; 6:15; see footnotes 102 and 105; cf. also Gal. 4:4) he *revealed* it. Strictly speaking, however, it was not life everlasting itself in its glorious heavenly phase that was revealed to earth-dwellers (how could it be?), but *the word* of God with respect to it. Hence, the change from "life everlasting" in verse 2, to "his word" in verse 3. In the form of (or: by means of) the *good news* which Paul proclaimed and which by order of "God our Savior" (see on I Tim. 1:1) had been *entrusted* to him (see on I Tim. 1:11-13), this *word* or *message* of God with respect to Christ and his gracious gift had now been made manifest.

This parenthetical statement is in complete harmony with Paul's teaching throughout. That teaching may be summarized as follows:

Full salvation in Christ for both Jew and Gentile, considered as equals, a salvation viewed as based solely upon Christ's merits appropriated by faith, was:

a. objectively *given* and *promised* from eternity (I Cor. 2:7; Eph. 1:4; II Thess. 2:13; II Tim. 1:9; Titus 1:2);

b. *hidden* — i.e., the message with reference to it was hidden — in preceding ages and from the eyes of former generations (Rom. 16:25; Eph. 3:5, 6, 9; Col. 1:26a); hidden, namely, in the sense that it was not *fully* proclaimed, nor *fully* realized, nor *fully* understood by the men of the old dispensation, though it had been foreshadowed (Gen. 3:15; 12:3; cf. Gal. 3:8; Is. 60; 61;

---

[190] The objections that have been raised against this explanation are as follows:
(1) It cannot be truly said that life everlasting *was promised* from all eternity. This objection has already been answered.
(2) He who in this connection thinks of God's eternal decree is forced to conclude that God gave the promise *before eternity.*
Answer: Not at all; he gave it *"before* times everlasting," that is, *"from* eternity."
(3) The verb *promised* is in the *aorist tense* (middle voice). Hence, it must refer to just one event, probably to the promise in Gen. 3:15.
Answer: It is not true that the aorist tense necessarily refers to only one *event*. Rather, its function is to summarize, to give a "capsule view." But even if it did refer to only one event, that event could be the (humanly conceived) promise of God in the covenant of redemption.

Joel 2:28, 29; Amos 9:11, 12; Micah 4:12; Mal. 1:11; also Ps. 72:8-11, 17; 87);

c. now fully *manifested* — i.e., the message with reference to it was fully manifested — by means of universal gospel-proclamation (see on II Tim. 1:10, 11; cf. Rom. 16:26; Eph. 3:3-9; Col. 1:26b-29). For "proclamation" or "preaching" (literally "heralding," "kerugma") see on II Tim. 4:2.

The glorious fact that the proclamation of the good news concerning life everlasting had actually been entrusted to one so unworthy as Paul, a fact which caused the heart of the apostle to overflow with gratitude, accounts for this interruption in the steady flow of the sentence.

4. To Titus (my) genuine child in terms of (the) common faith; grace and peace from God (the) Father and Christ Jesus our Savior.

The words of address closely resemble those in II Tim. 1:2 and even more closely those in I Tim. 1:2. Note how here, too, apostolic authority (Titus 1:1) and tender love ("my genuine child") are beautifully blended.

Titus was Paul's *child* because it was to the apostle as a means in God's hand that he owed his spiritual life, though the time, place, and circumstances of his conversion have not been revealed (see p. 37). The designation *child* is a happy one, for it combines two ideas: "I have begotten you," and "You are very dear to me." Titus was, moreover, a *genuine* child, natural (not adopted), not a bastard son, not merely a nominal believer. Paul considers himself the father of Titus, not in the physical sense but "in terms of the common faith," that is, with respect to the faith common to Paul and Titus. The phrase "in faith" ("my genuine child in faith") in I Tim. 1:2 has virtually the same meaning. It is probably best to take *faith*, as here used, in the subjective sense, a true knowledge of God and of his promises revealed in the gospel and a hearty confidence in him and in his redemptive, Christ-centered love.

Upon this genuine child the apostle now pronounces *grace and peace* (cf. "grace, mercy, and peace" in I Tim. 1:2 and in II Tim. 1:2). *Grace* is God's unmerited favor in operation in the heart of his child. It is his Christ-centered pardoning and strengthening love. *Peace* is that child's consciousness of having been reconciled with God through Christ. *Grace* is the fountain, and *peace* is the stream which issues from this fountain (cf. Rom. 5:1).

This grace and this peace have their origin in God the Father, and have been merited for the believer by Christ Jesus. These two are the *one* source of grace and peace (the preposition *from* is not repeated). But though in all the other salutations of Paul (Rom. 1:7; I Cor. 1:3; II Cor. 1:2; etc., including the Pastorals: I Tim. 1:2; II Tim. 1:2) Christ is called *Lord,* he is here called "our Savior." For the meaning of this word *Savior,* which occurs as often in Titus as in all the other Pauline epistles put together (six times: Titus 1:3, 4; 2:10, 13; 3:4, 6), and in this letter is used both with reference to "God" and to "Christ," see on I Tim. 4:10. Here in Titus 1:4 the term is used in its full, redemptive meaning. Christ Jesus is the One who rescues from the greatest evil and bestows upon the rescued ones the greatest good. For the meaning of *salvation* see on I Tim. 1:15.

In view of the close similarity between Titus 1:4 and I Tim. 1:2, the reader is referred to the explanation of I Tim. 1:2 for a more detailed discussion. And see also N.T.C. on I and II Thessalonians, pp. 37-46.

---

5 For this reason I left you behind in Crete, that you might straighten out the things that remain to be done, namely, that you might appoint elders in each city in such a manner as I gave you directions. 6 A person (can be appointed) if he is blameless, one wife's husband, having believing children (who are) not open to the charge of dissolute behavior nor unsubmissive. 7 For the overseer, as God's steward, must be blameless, not self-pleasing, not hot-tempered, not (one who lingers) beside (his) wine, not given to blows, not greedy of shameful gain, 8 but hospitable, loving the good, self-controlled (or sensible), fair, pious, master of himself, 9 holding on to the trustworthy word which is in line with the doctrine, in order that he may be able both to encourage (others) by means of his sound teaching and to refute those who contradict (it).

1:5-9

5. In order that congregational life in the various cities of Crete may flourish, well-qualified elders must be appointed: **For this reason I left you behind in Crete, that you might straighten out the things that remain to be done, namely, that you might appoint elders in each city in such a manner as I gave you directions.**

Evidently, on a certain journey by sea Paul and Titus had been together in Crete. The gospel had been proclaimed, little groups of disciples had been gathered, meeting-places had been arranged, but no official organization had been effected, or, if anything worthy of this name had been initiated, it had been left far from finished.

If the *conjecture* be correct that the stop-over in Crete occurred immediately after Paul's release from his first Roman imprisonment, the following problem had at that time presented itself:

a. After a lengthy absence from his friends the apostle was anxious to see the old familiar faces and to revisit the churches previously established. This is understandable, for he was an intensely human, warm-hearted person. Also, he loved his Lord and longed to promote the good cause in every possible way. Moreover, he had made what might be considered *promises* of early visits (Philemon 22; Phil. 1:25, 26). Accordingly, for Paul himself a lengthy delay in Crete was out of the question.

b. Nevertheless, in Crete the business of organizing the various churches was far from finished, and undue haste in appointing men to office was contrary to Paul's principles (I Tim. 3:6; 5:22).

The solution was: Paul must be on his way, and Titus must be *left behind* (cf. II Tim. 4:13, 20) in the island to straighten out the things that remained to be done, *namely* (κατά here used in that sense), to establish presbyteries. The apostle, who likes to stress the fact that *God* does not leave *his* work of grace unfinished (Phil. 1:6; I Thess. 5:23), is a true imitator of God also in this respect; for Paul, too, abhors unfinished business (see I Tim. 1:3 and I Thess. 3:10 for different applications of this same principle). And with respect to Titus, one could almost say that for him no task was too difficult to be attempted and no challenge too formidable to be met, in dependence on divine strength and wisdom (see pp. 36, 39).

The text implies that the apostle had given directions as to *just how* (ὡς = abbreviation for *in such a manner as*) elders must be appointed. This refers to *the requirements for office* which must be considered in appointing men to office. Since the verses which follow refer only to *elders* but it is clear from I Timothy 3 that it was Paul's conviction that (at least in course of time) a church would also need *deacons,* we may assume that the apostle means that when the work to be done became too heavy for the elders, deacons should be appointed similarly (cf. Acts 6:1-6).

Accordingly, the directions as to the requirements for the office of presbyter or elder are here re-stated. They had been given orally while Paul and Titus were still together in Crete, and they are now repeated in written form: *"For this reason* (anticipative τούτου χάριν followed by ἵνα, as in Eph. 3:1, 14-16) I left you behind in Crete, that you might . . . appoint elders *in each city"* ("down the line," hence, "city by city"). For the practice see Acts 14:23, and for this use of the preposition see Luke 8:1; Acts 10:23.

Possible reasons for the repetition in written form of a directive which earlier had been given orally:

(a) For the convenience of Titus, to assist his memory;

(b) For the confirmation of his authority in the event that this should be disputed;

(c) For future ages.

Though Paul says, "that *you* might appoint," he by no means excludes the responsible co-operation of the individual congregations (see Acts 1:15-26; 6:1-6, note same verb in Acts 6:3).

6-9. The list of requirements for elders or presbyters is introduced by the words: "If anyone is . . ." We have here another instance of *abbreviated discourse* (see N.T.C. on John 5:31, Vol. I, p. 206). Here as in I Tim. 5:10 it is not difficult to fill in the implied words. The meaning, as required by the preceding context, is, "If anyone is blameless, etc. . . . , *he can be appointed,"* or as I have translated: **A person (can be appointed) if he is,** etc.

The requirements listed occur in three groups:

(1) The person who is going to occupy such an important post must be of deservedly high reputation and if married (which will generally be the case) a good family-man (verse 6).

(2) He must *not* be the type of person who in his desire to please himself has lost interest in other people (except to vex them!) and who, if embroiled in a quarrel, is ever ready with his fists. A list of *negative* characteristics is given: qualities which the overseer must *not* have (verse 7).

(3) All his actions must give evidence of the fact that both in *deed* and in *doctrine* he wishes to be a blessing to others. A list of *positive* characteristics is given: qualities which the overseer must have (verses 8 and 9).

The three groups of requirements pertain to people who as to their age and dignity are called *elders,* and as to their task are called *overseers.* Though it is true that the text has the singular "the overseer," this "the" is generic, one member representing the entire class viewed from the point of view of a definite characteristic (see N.T.C. on I and II Thessalonians, p. 55, footnote 41). One might paraphrase the meaning as follows, "For, *any* overseer, by reason of the very fact that he should live up to his name of *overseer* and should manage God's own house, (being God's *steward;* see on I Tim. 1:4; cf. I Cor. 4:1; I Peter 4:10), must be blameless," etc. That for the author of the Pastorals the terms *elder* and *overseer* indicate the same person also follows from the fact that essentially the same requirements for an elder as are given here in Titus 1:5, 6 — that he be blameless, one wife's husband, and have well-behaved children — are listed with reference to the *overseer* in I Tim. 3:2, 4. The hierarchical idea — the *several* "priests" and their "parishes," outranked and governed by the *one* "bishop" and his "diocese" — is foreign to the Pastorals.

To avoid unnecessary duplication and at the same time to show the relation between the two rather similar lists of requirements (Titus 1 and I Timothy 3), I give the explanation of verses 6-9 in the form of a Table. *Whenever the stipulated requirement has already been treated elsewhere (particularly in I Tim. 3) the reader is referred to the fuller explanation which can be found there.*

Column 1 contains the list of requirements for elders or overseers as found in Titus 1. Column 2 gives the meaning in brief of each of these requirements. Column 3 lists those requirements *of the Titus 1 list* which are paralleled (either exactly or by means of a synonym) in *the overseer-requirements-list* as found in I Tim. 3. Column 4, similarly, shows the parallels in *the deacon-requirements-list* of I Tim. 3. And Column 5 lists antonyms of four overseer-requirements which find no parallel in I Tim. 3. These antonyms occur in the II Tim. 3 list of character-traits of people living "in the last days" (see the explanation of II Tim. 3:1-5).

1 Titus 1 *Elders*	2 Meaning	3 I Timothy 3 - Overseers	4 I Timothy 3 - Deacons	5 II Timothy 3
blameless	not to be called to account (particularly with respect to the points to be mentioned in verses 6-9)	cf. above reproach (verse 2)	blameless, (verse 10)	
one wife's husband	faithful in the marriage-relationship	one wife's husband (verse 2)	one wife's husband, (verse 12)	
having believing children (who are) not open to the charge of dissolute behavior nor unsubmissive	having children who share the Christian faith of their fathers and who adorn that faith with a godly conduct. A man whose children are still pagans or behave as pagans must not be appointed elder. cf. Eph. 5:18	cf. managing well his own household, with true dignity keeping his children in subjection, etc. (verses 4, 5)	cf. managing well his children and his household (verse 12)	
Overseers				
For the overseer as God's steward must be blameless, (This has already been explained.) **not self-pleasing**	(explanation of "not self-pleasing") not self-indulgent to the point of showing arrogance to others (cf. II Tim. 3:2 and II Peter 2:10)			contrast and cf. "self-loving" (verse 2)
not hot-tempered	not given to outbursts of wrath		cf. not given to blows, not contentious (verse 3)	

| 1
Titus 1 | 2
Meaning | 3
I Timothy 3-
Overseers | 4
I Timothy 3-
Deacons | 5
II Timothy 3 |
|---|---|---|---|---|
| not (one who lingers) beside (his) wine | no wine-bibber, tippler, or drunkard | not (one who lingers) beside (his) wine (verse 3) | cf. not addicted to much wine (verse 8) | |
| not given to blows | not eager to use his fists, not bellicose, no spitfire | not given to blows (verse 3) | | |
| not greedy of shameful profit | no embezzler, pilferer, Simonite (cf. Titus 1:11; also cf. I Peter 5:2 adverb) | cf. not fond of money (verse 3) | not greedy of shameful profit (verse 8) | |
| but hospitable | "loving strangers"; here, especially, ready to befriend and to lodge destitute, traveling, or persecuted believers (cf. I Peter 4:9) | hospitable (verse 2) | | |
| loving the good | loving goodness, virtuous, ready to do what is beneficial to others | | | contrast and cf. "unloving toward the good" (verse 3) |
| self-controlled or sensible | of sound mind, discreet, sane (cf. Titus 2:2, 5) | self-controlled (verse 2) | | |
| fair | performing one's duty toward man | | | |
| pious (or "holy") | performing one's duty toward God (cf. I Tim. 2:8) | | | contrast and cf. "impious" or "unholy" (verse 2) |

master of himself	possessing *the moral strength* to curb or master one's sinful drives and impulses (cf. Gen. 39:7-9; 50:15-21)	contrast and cf. "unrestrained" (verse 3)
holding on to the trustworthy word which is in line with the doctrine	clinging to and applying himself to the sacred tradition which is in harmony with the sound doctrine, that is, with the doctrine which, in turn, is based on Scripture	cf. keeping hold of the mystery of our faith with a pure conscience (verse 9)
in order that he may be able both to encourage (others) by means of his sound teaching and to refute those who contradict it	to the end that every overseer may be able by means of his sound teaching to incline will and heart to the joyful service of God, and to expose the errors of those who rebel; that is, to withstand these opponents, if at all possible bringing *them* to an acknowledgment of their error and to repentance; at least, convincing *believers* that these adversaries are wrong. Not all the overseers or elders are actually called upon to perform this task (see on I Tim. 5:17), but *all must be able* to perform it.	qualified to teach (verse 2)

10 For there are many insubordinate men, futile talkers and mind-deceivers, especially those of the circumcision-party, 11 whose mouths must be stopped, since (they are) such as upset entire families by teaching, for the sake of shameful profit, what is not proper. 12 One of them, a prophet of their own, made the statement:

"Cretans (are) always deceivers, evil brutes, bellies inactive."

13 This testimony is true. Therefore reprove them sharply in order that they may be sound in the faith 14 instead of devoting themselves to Jewish myths and injunctions of men who turn their backs on the truth.

15 All things (are) pure to those who are pure; but to those who are contaminated and unbelieving nothing (is) pure; on the contrary, contaminated are even their minds and their consciences. 16 God they profess to know, but by their actions they deny (it), because they are despicable and disobedient and for every good work unfit.

1:10-16

10. The reason why men so highly qualified for spiritual office are *especially* necessary in Crete is now stated:

For there are many insubordinate men, futile talkers and mind-deceivers, especially those of the circumcision-party.

This group (verses 10-14a) is the same as is mentioned in I Tim. 1:3-11; note similarities:

Titus 1	I Timothy 1
insubordinate men (verse 10)	insubordinate men (verse 9)
futile talkers (verse 10)	certain individuals . . . have turned aside to futile talk (verse 6)
teaching what is not proper (verse 11)	in order that you may charge certain individuals not to teach differently (verse 3); cf. 6:3
always liars (verse 12) in order that they may be sound in the faith (verse 13)	liars (verse 10) contrary to the sound doctrine (verse 10); cf. 6:3
devoting themselves to Jewish myths (verse 14)	not to devote themselves to endless myths and genealogies (verse 4); cf. 4:7a.

These men are present here in Crete *in alarming numbers* ("many insubordinate men"; contrast the "certain individuals" in I Tim. 1:3). This may have been due to the fact that their peculiar faults were in line with the Cretan national character and that they were under the strong influence of Jewish rabbis (*outsiders,* verses 14b-16). They are *insubordinate;* that is disobedient to the Word of God. Also, they are *futile talkers,* achieving no *useful* purpose, with their fictitious tales about Adam, Moses, Elijah, etc., and with their legalistic hair-splitting (cf. I Tim. 1:6); yet *deceiving the minds* (see M.M., p. 675) of the weak. Especially "those of the circumcision-party," that is, Jewish church-members (cf. Acts 10:45; Gal. 2:12), belong to the class of futile talkers and mind-deceivers. They probably regarded their circumcision as a mark of superior excellence, entitling them to be heard and looked up to by others.

11. But Paul, disagreeing sharply with their opinion of themselves, says with respect to them and also with respect to the rest of the futile talkers and mind-deceivers: **whose mouths must be stopped, since (they are) such as upset entire families by teaching, for the sake of shameful profit, what is not proper.**

In telling Titus what should be done with such people, Paul uses a rare verb (see M.M., p. 246) which has as its primary meaning "to stop the mouth by means of a bridle, muzzle, or gag." The deceivers, then, must not be tolerated but be silenced, and this should be done *by Titus and by the elders,* as the context would seem to indicate (verses 5-9).

Just *how* this silencing should be done is not indicated in the present passage. See, however, on I Tim. 1:3, 4; 1:20; 4:7; II Tim. 2:16, 21, 23; 4:2; Titus 1:13b; 3:10. At first the errorist should be tenderly admonished so that he may be won for the truth. If he refuses, he must be sharply reprimanded and told to desist. The person who persists in his evil ways must be shunned by the church and disciplined. The supreme measure, excommunication, may have to be employed in order to safeguard the church and in order to bring the sinner to repentance. In the church of God there is no such thing as "freedom of *misleading* speech." Reason: it would be too dangerous. The teachers of false doctrine "upset (cf. John 1:15) entire families," causing them to wander away from the truth (see on II Tim. 3:6). They do this by teaching "what is not proper," that is, "Jewish myths and injunctions of men" (see on verse 14). And their purpose is to acquire *shameful profit,* profit that is shameful because the men who are after it are anxious to enrich themselves even at the expense of the downfall of others. They are utterly selfish, aiming at nothing but money and prestige. (Cf. I Tim. 3:3, 8; 6:5; Titus 1:7; and on the entire subject of remuneration for spiritual work see N.T.C. on I Thess. 2:9.)

12. These *Jewish church-members* of the Pharisaic type and tinged with incipient gnosticism, which led at times to licentiousness and at times to asceticisms (see on I Tim. 4:3, 4), were *Cretans* — there were many Jews in Crete (cf. Acts 2:11) — , and, in addition to being influenced by unbelieving Jews (see on 14b-16), had absorbed the worst character-traits of their non-

Jewish countrymen. This had not been a chore, for the Jew and the Cretan had something in common. The employment of trickery or deception for selfish advantage characterized both (cf. John 1:47 with Titus 1:12). An honest Jew or an honest Cretan seems to have been an exception. And certainly the combination *Cretan-Jew* was not a happy one.

As to the Cretans, they were condemned "out of their own mouth." Says Paul, **One of them, a prophet of their own, made the statement:**
Cretans (are) always deceivers, evil brutes, bellies inactive.

A prophet *of their own* would be more apt *to brag* about his countrymen to others than *to condemn* them. Yet, condemn them is exactly what their own prophet had done. By Clement of Alexandria (*Stromata* I. xiv. 59) and by Jerome the devastating characterization is attributed to a poet and reformer whose date is variously given as somewhere between 630 and 500 B. C. His name was Epimenedes, a native of Cnossus near Iráklion (= Candia) on Crete's northern shore, where even today one can visit the museum that contains the unique treasures of the Minoan Age. In a hymn "To Zeus" Callimachus (about 300-240 B. C.) had quoted the first words, "Cretans (are) always deceivers." To the question whether or not Paul himself *had actually read* Epimenedes not all give the same answer. Some hold that since the quotation is really a proverb, it may have been derived by Paul from widely disseminated oral tradition. Others believe that it is not necessary to confine Paul's *reading*-knowledge within such *narrow* limits.[191]

Now by the ancients Epimenedes was considered *a prophet,* "a divinely inspired man" (thus Plato), "a man dear to the gods" (thus Plutarch). Paul does not mean to say that the Cretan reformer was actually a prophet in the Scriptural sense. He means, "a man who by them and by others was considered a prophet, a spokesman of the gods." With reference to Epimenedes' so-called *prophetic* activity Plato (*Laws* I. 642 D and E) wrote as follows:

"That divinely-inspired man Epimenedes . . . was born in Crete, and ten years before the Persian War, in accordance with the oracle of the god, went to Athens . . .; and when the Athenians were filled with fear by reason of the Persians' expeditionary force, he made this prophecy: They will not come for ten years, and when they do come, they will turn back again, having accomplished nothing that they had hoped (to accomplish), and having suffered more woes than they will have inflicted."

By many Epimenedes was regarded as one of "the seven wise men" of the ancient world. These seven were: Bias of Priene, Chilon of Sparta, Cleobulus of Lindus, Pittacus of Mitylene, Solon of Athens, Thales of

---

[191] Cf. R. Stob, *Christianity and Classical Civilization*, Grand Rapids, 1950, pp. 61, 62, and A. T. Robertson, "Paul the Apostle," in I.S.B.E., especially IV, 3.

Miletus, and Epimenedes of Crete or Peiander of Corinth or Anacharsis the Scythian (see Plutarch, *Lives, Solon* XII. 4-6; cf. Clement of Alexandria, *Stromata* I. xiv).

It was this same Epimenedes who according to Diogenes Laertius advised the Athenians to sacrifice "to the appropriate god," which advice may have led to the erection of that well-known "altar to an unknown god" which provided a starting-point for Paul's proclamation of *the living God* (Acts 17:23).

The quotation from Epimenedes here in Titus 1:12 is a line which consists of six metrical feet (hexameter verse), somewhat like Longfellow's (*Evangeline*):

"This is the forest primeval. The murmuring pines and the hemlocks . . ."

I have tried to preserve the rhythm, and have therefore rendered the line as follows:

"Cretans are always deceivers, evil brutes, bellies inactive."

Their representation as *deceivers* or *liars* may have arisen from their claim that they had on their island the tomb of Zeus. But the reputation of the Cretans for telling lies for selfish purposes (notice context, verse 11) was so widely spread that it had given rise to the noun "Cretism," meaning "Cretan behavior," that is, "lying" (Plutarch, *Aemilius* 26); and to the verb "to Cretize" or "to speak like a Cretan," which meant "to tell lies," "to deceive" (e.g. Polybius VIII. 19). Cf. "to Corinthianize," meaning "to live a profligate life like a Corinthian."

The expression "evil brutes" describes the savage and cruel character of the Cretans of the days of Epimenedes and of the days of Paul and Titus. They would push everyone out of the way in order to gain an advantage for themselves. Some see in this descriptive epithet an allusion to the mythical Cretan Minotaur, half bull half man, whom Minos hid in the Cretan labyrinth, where, until Theseus slew this monster, he devoured the Athenian youths and maidens sent as a tribute every nine years.

"Bellies inactive" marks the Cretans as lazy gluttons, sluggish and sensual gormandizers.

The Cretans, then, are *untruthful, selfish,* and *pleasure-loving.* Now some writers consider the action of Paul in quoting this devastating verdict with respect to the character of the Cretans as singularly untactful, a "smear" upon the good name of an entire population. However, the character of the Cretans displayed itself so clearly that confirmation of the severe judgment comes from every direction and is not limited to a single century. The reader should see this for himself. In addition to the noun "Cretism" = *lie,* and to the verb "to Cretize" = *to deceive, to tell lies,* we have the following (the dates given are mostly approximate):

Polybius, Greek historian (203-120 B. C.):

"So much in fact do love of shameful profit and greed prevail among them that among all men Cretans are the only ones in whose estimation no profit is ever disgraceful" (*The Histories* VI. 46).

Cicero, Roman orator, statesman, and philosopher (106-43 B. C.):

"Indeed, (men's) moral principles are so divergent that the Cretans . . . consider highway-robbery (or "brigandage") to be honorable" (*Republic* III. ix. 15).

Livy, Roman historian (59 B. C.-A. D. 17):

"The Cretans followed (Perseus) in hope of cash" (XLIV. xlvi).

Plutarch, Greek essayist and biographer (A. D. 46-120):

"Of his soldiers (only) the Cretans followed him, not through being favorably disposed (toward him), but because they were as devoted to his riches as are bees to their honeycombs. For he was carrying along vast treasures, and he had handed out for distribution among the Cretans drinking-cups and mixing bowls and other utensils of gold and silver, valued at fifty talents" (*Aemilius Paulus* XXIII. 4). Werner Keller, *The Bible as History,* New York, 1956, pp. 172, 173, hints that the ancient Cretans were "powerful drinkers" and submits interesting archaeological evidence: the fact that large numbers of wine cups and beer mugs, the latter fitted with filters, were found in the settlements of the Philistines who, as Scripture says (Amos 9:7), came from Caphtor, that is, Crete.

13 and 14. It is not surprising therefore that Paul says, **This testimony is true.** The character of the mendacious, grasping Cretans was so clearly displayed by their actions that Paul cannot do anything else than confirm the judgment that was expressed in Epimenedes' hexameter.

An attempt has been made to show that the verdict of Epimenedes and of Paul is really a self-contradiction. This is done by means of the following bit of sophistry:

"A Cretan, Epimenedes, said that Cretans always lie. He must therefore himself have lied when he said this. Therefore it is not true that the Cretans always lie. Or (even worse): Therefore, the Cretans do not lie. But if the Cretans do not lie, then Epimenedes, a Cretan, must have spoken the truth. But then he, too, being a Cretan, was a liar when he said that Cretans always lie." And so we are back at the place from which we started.

But certainly all that was meant by Paul was that *Crete was notorious for its many constant liars.* His statement leaves ample room for the following propositions:

   a. Even Cretan liars sometimes speak the truth.

   b. Some Cretans are not outstanding liars.

   c. This particular Cretan, namely Epimenedes, spoke the truth when he described Cretans as being, generally speaking, constant liars.

Therefore reprove them sharply in order that they may be sound in the faith. The errorists and those who listen to them must be *reproved* (cf. II Tim. 4:2) *sharply* (cf. II Cor. 13:10), decisively, and this not only by the elders (see on verse 9 above) but also by Titus himself, in order that they may be (that is, *may become*) what at present they are not, namely, *sound* (cf. I Tim. 1:10) in their stand with respect to the truth as revealed in Christ.

Paul continues: **instead of devoting themselves to Jewish myths and injunctions of men who turn their backs upon the truth.**

To escape the impact of the law of God the errorists were devoting themselves (see on I Tim. 1:4) to "Jewish myths," that is, to fanciful stories about ancestors; and to "injunctions of men," that is, to man-made commands. These, too, were probably to a large extent Jewish in character. To the extent in which they were, *they were said to be* based on the law of God. *Actually,* however, they obscured the real intent and meaning of the law. Cf. Matt. 5:43; 15:3, 6, 9; Mark 7:1-23; Luke 6:1-11; and see N.T.C. on John 5:1-18.

The Cretan deceivers, accordingly, busied themselves with Talmudic anecdotes and hair-splitting legal decisions for which the claim was made that they were derived from the law. The injunctions which they praised and tried to force upon others were actually the commands of "men who turn their backs upon the truth." By these men *the Jews* are meant, particularly Jewish rabbis and scribes. The situation, then, was as follows:

The stedfast believers in the island of Crete mingled daily with other church-members who were not so stedfast but were willing to lend an ear to loud-mouthed Judaistic deceivers, tinged with gnosticism. These false teachers, in turn, were under the influence of men who stood entirely outside the church, namely, Jews, Pharisaic propagandists, who completely rejected Christ, turning their backs upon God's redemptive truth as revealed in his Son.

15. The nature — at least in part — of the subversive doctrine that was literally being *sold* (taught by false teachers with a view to "shameful profit") in Crete is suggested by the words of verse 15. The deceivers, who in turn were being deceived by outside-deceivers, namely, by the Jews, were *denying* that: **All things (are) pure to those who are pure; but to those who are contaminated and unbelieving nothing (is) pure; on the contrary, contaminated are even their minds and their consciences.**[192]

---

[192] In agreement with most commentators I regard the proverb "All things (are) pure to those who are pure" to be part of Paul's own teaching. It was either coined by himself or else it had been phrased by another (perhaps by Jesus Christ himself; cf. Luke 11:38-41) and then taken over by him and quoted over against the Jewish differentiation between "pure" and "impure."

Other interpreters (for example, J. Van Dijk, *Paraphrase Heilige Schrift, Tim-*

1:15   **TITUS**

The false teachers inside the churches of Crete were trying to reconcile Jewish bondage (ceremonialism) with Christian freedom. Many of them, no doubt, had been trained from early childhood in the religion of the shadows, and it was hard for them to understand that with the coming and death of the Lord these shadows had disappeared. Influenced, as they certainly were, by the impenitent Jews outside the church, they attach a degree of *saving* value (a value which even the law itself had never taught) to ceremonial ordinances — and even more to Pharisaic refinements of these ordinances — concerning what was "clean" and what was "unclean" with respect to articles of food, pieces of furniture, the human body, etc. They regarded purity as being an attribute not of the mind and conscience of man but of material things. As was shown in connection with I Tim. 4:3, they were probably also strengthened in this error by pagan dualism which regarded matter as being sinful in itself. But the main sinister influence here in Crete seems to have come from the Jews.

Jesus had combated this error vigorously. He had said, "Not what goes into a man but what comes out of him defiles him, for from within come evil thoughts" (see Matt. 15:11, 15-20; Mark 7:14-22; Luke 11:38-41; and cf. Prov. 4:23). The early church had followed where Christ had led (as is implied in Acts 10:9-16; 11:1-18; 15:20). Paul, too, in his other epistles had consistently defended the thesis that "nothing is unclean in itself" (Rom. 14:14, 20; cf. I Cor. 6:12; 10:23; Gal. 2:11-21; Col. 2:16-23), and that it is the disposition of the heart and the purpose of the mind which render a matter clean or unclean (Rom. 14:23; I Cor. 10:31). In Romans and I Corinthians this basic truth had been applied in one direction (to eat without regard to the weaker brother is sinful); here it is applied in another direction (to eat with an unbelieving mind or contaminated conscience is defiling).

"All things (are) pure to those who are pure; but to those who are contaminated and unbelieving nothing (is) pure." The expression "all things" is best explained by Paul himself. It amounts to "every creature of God" (I Tim. 5:5), that is, everything that was created by God for consumption as food. It is not the impure thing which makes men impure, as the Jews erroneously held (see N.T.C. on John 18:28), but it is impure men who make *every* pure thing impure, a truth foreshadowed in Hag. 2:13.

Pure men are those who have been cleansed from their guilt by the

---

otheus, Titus en Philemon, p. 68) regard it as a saying of the false teachers as an excuse for their immoral teaching and conduct.

But that view fails to reckon with the fact that these errorists were for the most part "of the circumcision" (verse 10), people who esteemed very highly the Jewish *Halacha* (verse 14; cf. also verse 16 and 3:9). Their rules regarding morals were far more likely to be rigid than loose (see I Tim. 4:3; cf. Col. 2:21). — Besides, if Rom. 14:14, 20 and I Tim. 4:4, 5 contain positive Pauline teaching, why not Titus 1:15?

blood of Christ and, having been regenerated by the Holy Spirit, are being constantly cleansed by that same Spirit from the pollution of their sins (see on Titus 3:5; then Matt. 5:8; John 3:3, 5; I Cor. 6:11; Eph. 1:7; 5:26, 27; I John 1:7, 9; see also N.T.C. on John 13:10; 15:3). These are the ones who do not reject what God has created as good foods but "partake of them with thanksgiving" (see on I Tim. 4:3, 4).

On the other hand, those who are contaminated, befouled, or polluted, namely, the Jews, and having rejected Christ are at the same time unbelieving, have thereby defiled *all* of God's pure gifts. Even their *minds,* those organs which reflect on things spiritual and guide the will, and their *consciences,* that is, their moral selves in the act of passing judgment upon their deeds, *are* — and unless God's grace intervenes, *remain;* note perfect passive indicative — *contaminated.* (For the concept *conscience* see on I Tim. 1:5.) This is evidenced by the fact that their moral judgments are perverted and that they do not arrive at godly sorrow.

16. The description of "men who turn their backs upon the truth," a description begun in verse 14b, continues. Referring, then, to *the Jews* (particularly, the Pharisaic leaders who, though outsiders, are exerting a sinister influence upon the false leaders within the churches of Crete), Paul adds: **God they profess to know.** As did their fathers long ago (Deut. 6:4), so also these Jews proclaim to all who are willing to listen that they know the one true God as their own God (see N.T.C. on John 8:54, 55; and cf. Rom. 2:17). "We know him," they declare; and they mean, "with a knowledge intuitive and direct" (note the verb used in the original).

Now it was indeed true that to their forefathers God had revealed himself in a very special way, as to no other nation (Ps. 96:5; 115; 135; 147:19, 20; Amos 3:2; Rom. 3:1, 2; 9:1-5); but instead of realizing that greater opportunity implies greater responsibility, especially with respect to those *who do not know God* (cf. Gal. 4:8; I Thess. 4:5), they had become boastful and had completely rejected the Messiah. Hence, Paul is able to assert that though these Jews profess to know God, yet **by their actions they deny (it).** Their actions *belie* their profession. (The verb *deny,* though not occurring in the earlier epistles of Paul, is found again and again in the Pastorals; see on I Tim. 5:8; II Tim. 2:12, 13; 3:5; Titus 2:12.) For a vivid account of the actions of the Jewish leaders whom Paul has chiefly in mind see Matt. 23. These actions may be summarized in two words: hypocrisy and rejection of the Christ. By wrongly influencing false teachers in Crete they are continuing to reject him.

The reason why they commit these evil acts is now stated: **because they are despicable and disobedient and for every good work unfit.**

They *do* what they do because of what they *are* in their inner nature. It is not surprising that Paul characterizes those who are "defiled in mind and conscience" (see on verse 15) as being *despicable, detestable,* or *abominable* in the eyes of God. Again, they are despicable because, *in spite of* being such sticklers for man-made rules and regulations (cf. Is. 1:12-15; Jer. 6:20; Amos 5:21-23; Matt. 23:23-33; Luke 18:11, 12) — or shall we not rather say: *because* of this very fact? — they are *disobedient* to *God's* holy law. Hence, instead of being "men of God for every good work thoroughly equipped" (see on II Tim. 3:17; cf. II Tim. 2:21), they are the very opposite: "for every good work *unfit*" (after testing rejected as worthless), completely incapable of performing any work that proceeds from faith, is done according to God's law, and redounds unto his glory.

Synthesis of Chapter 1

See the Outline at the beginning of this chapter.

In addressing this letter to Titus, here described as Paul's genuine child in terms of the common faith, the apostle introduces himself as a servant of God and an apostle of Jesus Christ. He declares that he fulfils this mission in order to promote the faith of God's elect and their acknowledgment of the truth which harmonizes with (or: which furthers) the life of Christian devotion. He regards *his* apostleship and *their* devotion as being based on the hope of life everlasting. It is that hope which encourages both Paul and believers in general to be true to their calling. The God who, in sharp contrast with the Cretans, never deceives anyone, promised life everlasting before the never-ending time-process began; that is, he made that promise "from eternity." In due season his word with respect to this great salvation began to be fully and authoritatively proclaimed in the "preaching" (kerugma, proclamation) of Paul, to whom it had been entrusted.

Upon Titus, Paul pronounces "grace and peace from God the Father and Christ Jesus our Savior."

It was in the interest of promoting the spirit of sanctification in the life of the congregations that Paul had left Titus behind in the island of Crete. With this purpose in mind Titus is now being reminded *in writing* of the order which previously had been given to him *orally,* namely, that he should straighten out what remained to be done, and should accordingly appoint elders in each city. The requirements for the office of elder have been summarized on pp. 345-349.

That the idea of *sanctification* in congregational life is, indeed, uppermost in the apostle's mind as he pens this chapter is clear from *the reason* which he gives, showing why men so highly qualified for office are *especially* necessary in the churches of *Crete*. He speaks of *false teachers* within the bosom of the churches, insubordinate men, futile talkers, mind-deceivers, men interested in shameful profit; of *Cretans* whom he describes as "always deceivers, evil brutes, bellies inactive"; and of a certain class of *Jews* whom he pictures as "men who turn their backs upon the truth," and are *"contaminated* in mind and conscience." Accordingly, wise leadership and saving discipline is a "must," in order that *sanctification* may replace *contamination.*

Interesting recent articles on Crete are the following: "Greece, The Birthplace of Science and Free Speech," in *Everyday Life in Ancient Times,* published by The National Geographic Society, Washington, D. C., 1953, see especially pp. 189, 191, 202, 203; and "Crete, Cradle of Western Civilization," in The National Geographic, November, 1953, pp. 693-706. See also E. G. Kraeling, *op. cit.,* p. 463.

Outline of Chapter 2

Theme: *The Apostle Paul, Writing to Titus, Gives Directions for the Promotion of the Spirit of Sanctification*

In Family and Individual Life

2:1-10   All classes of individuals that compose the home-circle should conduct themselves in such a manner that by their life they may adorn the doctrine of God, their Savior.

2:11-15   Reason: to all the grace of God has appeared unto sanctification and joyful expectation of the appearing in glory of our great God and Savior, Jesus Christ.

CHAPTER II

TITUS 2:1

2 1 But as for you, speak what is consistent with the sound doctrine: (2) (urge) aged men to be temperate, dignified, self-controlled, sound in their faith, in their love, (and) in their endurance; 3 (urge) aged women similarly (to be) reverent in demeanor, not slanderers and not enslaved to much wine, teachers of that which is excellent, 4 so that they may train the young women to be loving toward their husbands and loving toward their children, 5 self-controlled, chaste, workers at home, kind, submissive to their own husbands, in order that the word of God may not be reviled. 6 Similarly urge the young(er) men to exercise self-control in every respect, 7 showing yourself a model of noble deeds; in your teaching (showing) incorruptibility, dignity; (8) (your) speech (being) sound, incensurable, so that he that is on the opposite (side) may be put to shame, having nothing evil to report concerning us. 9 (Urge) slaves to be submissive in every respect to their own masters, to be eager to please (them), not talking back, 10 not pilfering, but evincing the utmost trustworthiness, so that in every respect they may adorn the doctrine of God our Savior.[193]

2:1-10

1. Directions for the promotion of the spirit of sanctification in *congregational life* have been given. Titus has been urged to complete the organization of the various churches in the island, in order that, by means of the work of truly consecrated elders, the voice of persons who by their false doctrines and practices were defiling the churches might be silenced, and congregational life might flourish. That was the substance of chapter 1.

Now in chapter 2 Paul focuses the attention of Titus upon *family and individual life*. He issues commands relative to the proper conduct of five classes of individuals: *aged men, aged women, young married women, young men* (Titus himself to set the example), *and slaves*. The emphasis upon *the family* is evident especially from verses 4 and 5: "so that they (the aged women) may wisely train the young women to be loving toward their husbands, loving toward their children," etc.

For Paul's teaching with respect to The Christian Family see also I Tim. 5:1-8; then Gal. 3:28; Eph. 5:22-6:4; Col. 3:18-21. On Slaves and Their

---

[193] Because of its length this footnote has been placed at the end of the chapter.

2:1   **TITUS**

Masters (considered members of the family) see also I Tim. 6:1, 2; then Eph. 6:5-9; Col. 3:22-4:1; Philemon.[194]

Since Titus is the man who must deliver Paul's instructions with respect to the five groups, the apostle begins by writing, **But as for you, speak what is consistent with the sound doctrine.** Note the word of contrast, "*But,* as for you." Cf. a similar contrast in I Tim. 6:11; II Tim. 3:10, 14; 4:5. The life and teaching of Titus must contrast sharply with that of "the contaminated and unbelieving" enemies of the faith who were doing such damage in Crete (as shown in chapter 1). Not only must these errorists be reproved sharply (Titus 1:13), but *evil must be overcome with good.* Not only must *the elders* do their duty over against teachers of false religion (chapter 1), but *Titus himself* must give the example! Even in his informal daily *conversation* he must "speak" what is consistent with sound doctrine. Note the verb "speak" or literally "talk" (λάλει), which indicates informal vocal utterance.

Now to talk "what is consistent with (or "proper to," cf. I Tim. 2:10; Eph. 5:3) the sound doctrine" certainly means that, as the author conceives of it, *doctrine and life must harmonize.* This is the key to all that follows in verses 2-10. Accordingly, the position defended by some, namely, that the morality urged here is *in no sense* specifically Christian, is in conflict with Paul's declaration. It is true, of course, that even outside of the church some of the character-traits here mentioned — for example, *being temperate or sober, being self-controlled or sensible* — are given in lists of moral requirements for those who occupy certain important positions in life: the Stoic philosopher, the general, etc.[195] Even an unbeliever has "some regard for virtue and for good outward behavior," a truth which should never be denied (see on I Tim. 3:7; and *Canons of Dort,* Third and Fourth Heads of Doctrine, art. 4; note, however, the qualification at the end of that article). But when these same qualities are mentioned here in this letter (or in I Tim. 3), they must not be lifted out of their context, nor must they be dissociated from the general teachings of Scripture. Titus 2:1, 2 must not be separated from Titus 2:12, 13. As soon as the question is asked, "What is the source of these virtues, how are they motivated, according to what standard is their exhibition to be judged, and for what purpose are they to be used?" the great contrast immediately appears. Accordingly, the qualities that are mentioned in the verses which follow are *specifically Christian* virtues in this sense, namely, that they presuppose the

---

[194] For a fine summary of biblical teaching with respect to The Christian Home one may consult (in addition to various works on Ethics, Encyclopedia-articles, and special treatises) the excellent topical outlines in the Index of Thompson's *New Chain Reference Bible,* pp. 62-66, article "Home."
[195] See the lists on p. 201 of Burton Scott Easton's *The Pastoral Epistles,* New York, 1947.

dynamic of God's grace working in the heart, are motivated by the example of Christ, are measured by God's holy law, and have God's glory as their goal.

2. The first rule has reference to "aged men." [196] Says Paul, **that aged men be temperate, dignified, self-controlled, sound in their faith, in their love, (and) in their endurance.**

The greybeards should have the same moral characteristics as the elders and the deacons. Titus must *urge* (here in verse 2 the verb of verse 6 is probably implied) them to be *temperate* or *sober,* that is, moderate with respect to the use of wine (see verse 3) and in all their tastes and habits (cf. I Tim. 3:2, 11). They must also be *dignified,* that is grave, venerable, serious, respectable (cf. I Tim. 3:5, 8, 11); *self-controlled* or *sensible,* that is, men of mature judgment and proper restraint (cf. Titus 1:8; then I Tim. 3:2); and *sound* (see on verse 1; especially footnote 193); not *morbid* (cf. I Tim. 6:4; then Rom. 14:1), but healthy and even health-imparting: spreading health, moral and spiritual, in every direction (cf. Titus 1:9, 13; then I Tim. 1:10; 6:3; II Tim. 1:13; 4:3).

This soundness must be shown with respect to *the* faith, *the* love, and *the* endurance. Here the article is perhaps best rendered by the possessive *their . . . their . . . their.* Their faith, in order to be sound, must be neither luke-warm nor mixed with error (cf. Titus 1:14). Their love must not deteriorate into sentimentality nor must it be permitted to wax cold (Matt. 24:12; Rev. 2:4). And their endurance must not be replaced by either faint-heartedness on the one hand or obstinacy on the other.

In their attitude *toward God* let the aged men show *soundness in their faith.* Let them rely wholly on him and his revealed truth. In their attitude *toward the neighbor* let them evince *soundness in their love.* And in their attitude *toward bitter trials* let them reveal *soundness in their endurance* or *stedfastness* (for a word-study of this term see N.T.C. on I and II Thessalonians, pp. 136-137 — footnote 108 —; 155, 156; and pp. 197, 198).

---

[196] Titus has the sequence: *aged men, aged women, young women, young(er) men,* a chiastic arrangement. I Tim. 5:1, 2 has: *old(er) man, young(er) men, old(er) women, young(er) women.* Note that three of the words in the first list differ from the three corresponding words in the second list. "Aged man" (πρεσβύτης cf. Philem. 9) cannot mean church-elder, but the word which in I Tim. 5:1 has been rendered "old(er) man" (πρεσβύτερος) has elsewhere in the Pastorals the meaning church-elder (I Tim. 5:17, 19; Titus 1:5). "Aged woman" (πρεσβῦτις) is fem. of πρεσβύτης, the prose form of πρέσβυς, but "old(er) woman" is compar. adj. as subst. Finally, "young woman" is the adj. *young, youthful,* with fem. ending, as subst.; but "young(er) woman" is the compar. of the same adj. However, as remarked in connection with I Tim. 5:1, at times the comparative idea seems to have almost vanished.

3. To the four requirements for aged men four somewhat similar requirements for aged women are now added: **(urge) aged women similarly (to be) reverent in demeanor, not slanderers and not enslaved to much wine, teachers of that which is excellent.**

In their entire bearing (hence, not only in their *dress,* I Tim. 2:9) as well as in their deportment, aged women must be *reverent,* conducting themselves as if they were servants in God's temple, for such, indeed, they are! Cf. Rev. 1:6. The theme-song of these aged women (as well as of all members of the Christian family) must ever be:

> "Fill thou my life, O Lord my God,
> In every part with praise,
> That my whole being may proclaim
> Thy being and thy ways.
> Not for the lip of praise alone,
> Nor e'en the praising heart,
> I ask, but for a life made up
> Of praise in every part.
>
> "Praise in the common words I speak,
> Life's common looks and tones,
> In intercourse at hearth or board
> With my beloved ones,
> Enduring wrong, reproach, or loss,
> With sweet and stedfast will,
> Loving and blessing those who hate,
> Returning good for ill."
>
> (Horatius Bonar, 1866)

Note how "not *slanderers*" (on which see I Tim. 3:11) and *"not enslaved by much wine"* are combined. Wine-drinking and malicious gossip often go together. (For *wine-drinking* see the remarks on I Tim. 3:8 and on I Tim. 5:23.) Aged women, then, must be temperate, just like aged men. They must not become *enslaved to* (for this figurative sense see also Rom. 6:18, 22; I Cor. 9:19; Gal. 4:3) much wine. On the contrary, by their godly example they must be "teachers of that which is excellent" (cf. I Peter 3:1, 2).

4 and 5. Such "teaching by way of example" has as one of its purposes the "training" of the younger married women. Hence, Paul continues: **so that they may train the young women to be:**
  a. **loving toward their husbands** (or **husband-lovers**) **and**
  b. **loving toward their children** (or **children-lovers**),
  c. **self-controlled,**
  d. **chaste,**

e. **workers at home,**
f. **kind,**
g. **submissive to their own husbands.**

One understands immediately that no one — not even Titus — is better able to train a young woman than an experienced, older woman. Note the emphasis on *love*. The Christian young woman must be trained *to love* her husband and *to love* her children. Was it not *love* that saved her? See John 3:16. This love, coming from heaven, being shed abroad in the heart, must "flow out" toward others; and certainly among those "others" a young woman's own husband and her own children should occupy a very prominent place. Moreover, the Christian virtue of *self-control* — that same virtue which is demanded not only of overseers (Titus 1:8; then I Tim. 3:2) but also of aged men in general (verse 2 above), and which is implied in what is demanded of aged women (verse 3 above) — is a most necessary requirement for any practical Christian wife and mother. Such younger women must scrupulously avoid any immorality in thought, word, and action. Their attention, moreover, must be concentrated on their own families. Hence, not only must they be *chaste* but also *workers at home* (see on I Tim. 2:10 and especially on I Tim. 5:13). The two virtues quite obviously are related. Now, while performing their tasks in the family, these young women must take care that the constant strain of domestic duties does not make them irritable or cruel. They must pray for grace to remain *kind,* and this not only to husbands and children but also to slaves.[197] Moreover, lest Christian women should begin to think that their equality in spiritual standing before God and the great liberty which has now become their portion as believers (Gal. 3:28) entitles them to forget about God's creation-ordinance regarding the relation to their husbands (Gen. 3:16), Paul, inspired by the Holy Spirit, adds that they must be "submissive to their own husbands" (see also on I Tim. 2:11-15, and cf. Rom. 7:2; I Cor. 7:4; 14:34, 35; Eph. 5:22-24, 33; Col. 3:18; I Peter 3:1-6). Surely, in the light of Gen. 24:67; Eph. 5:22-33; Col. 3:19; I Peter 3:7, when the husband too is a believer, this is not a burden. And when he is not, then "as unto the Lord" makes the burden bearable.

A purpose-clause, in all probability qualifying not only the last requirement but all seven, is now added: **in order that the word of God may not be reviled.** See on I Tim. 6:1. This is characteristically Pauline language; cf. Rom. 2:24. He, in turn, borrowed it from the Old Testament (Is. 52:5).

---

[197] It is possible to accept a different punctuation, so that instead of the rendering "workers at home, kind," we would have to translate (with Bouma and others): *"good workers* at home." But the former is more in keeping with the entire list of requirements. Note that none of the four preceding ones has a modifier; each is a single word: loving-toward-their-husbands (just one word), loving-toward-their-children (again only one word in the original), self-controlled, chaste.

Wrong conduct on the part of the young married women would easily lead to slanderous remarks with respect to the gospel. Not only do *the Greeks* judge a doctrine by its practical effect upon everyday life (Chrysostom), but so does the world in general. If young mothers, professing to be Christians, should manifest lack of love for their husbands and for their children, lack of self-control, of purity, domesticity, kindness, and submissiveness, they would cause the message of salvation to be evil spoken of by outsiders. It must be borne in mind, moreover, that when Paul says "in order that the word of God *may not be reviled*," he means, "in order that the word of God *may be honored*." This, too, as noted earlier, is a typically Pauline way of speaking (see pp. 14, 15).

6. The admonition which must be passed along to "the young(er) men" of the various congregations is brief, but in its very brevity it is all-inclusive: **Similarly urge the young(er) men** [198] **to exercise self-control in every respect.** The fact that this admonition is very brief makes it all the more probable that the phrase "in every respect" belongs here and must not be construed with verse 7. *In every respect*, therefore, whether the attention is focused upon morals or upon doctrine, *young men* must place themselves under the discipline of the gospel, and must guard themselves against being led astray either by the evil promptings of their own sinful nature or by the opinions and customs which prevail in the pagan world round about them. Let them never place their own conclusions, feelings, or ambitions above the will of God (cf. Rom. 12:3; cf. II Cor. 10:5). Let them learn to master themselves. The verb translated "to exercise self-control" is from the same stem as the adjective rendered "self-controlled." Hence, young men are here urged to exercise the same virtue which is demanded of the overseer (Titus 1:8; cf. I Tim. 3:2), of aged men (Titus 2:2), of the young women (verse 4), and, by implication, of aged women (verse 3).

7 and 8. Since Titus, though not as young as Timothy (see p. 38), must probably still be reckoned among the "young(er) men," it is logical that Paul urges him to be an example for the group mentioned in the preceding verse. Says Paul: **showing yourself a model of noble deeds; in your teaching (showing) incorruptibility, dignity; (your) speech (being) sound, incensurable.**

---

[198] What age-limit does the apostle have in mind when he refers to these "young(er) men"? Is he thinking only of those under forty? (See on I Tim. 4:12 and II Tim. 2:22.) But then, if by "aged men" those of 60 and over are indicated, there would remain a large group — those of 40-60 — for which he has no admonition at all. Hence, "young(er) men" may here indicate all those under 60; or else the age-limit separating the two classes — "aged" and "young(er)" — may have to be lowered somewhat, say to 50 years of age. See Irenaeus, *Against Heresies* II. xxii, 5; also John 8:56, 57.

A similar admonition was addressed to Timothy. He also had been admonished to be *the believers' model* (in speech, in conduct, in love, in faith, in purity). The word *model*, too, is exactly the same; hence, see on I Tim. 4:12 (cf. II Thess. 3:9; Phil. 3:17). Note the beautiful co-ordination: Titus must a. *admonish* the young(er) men (verse 6), and b. *give them a good example* (verses 7 and 8). *Precept and example must go hand in hand.* Precept alone will never do, for often *"Example* draws where *Precept* fails." [199] The young(er) men of the various congregations entrusted to the care of Titus must be able to see in their leader what *noble deeds* really are. Note the constant emphasis in the Pastorals on these *noble deeds* or *good works.* May this not be considered a reaction, on the part of Paul, to the misrepresentation and abuse of his doctrine of "salvation by grace"?

In his teaching, Titus must show *incorruptibility.* He must give such clear and courageous instruction in the well-balanced truth of the gospel that it is evident to all that he has not been and cannot be *infected* with the lies and distortions of the adversaries. Moreover, his attitude and the manner in which he presents his teaching must be that of *dignity* or *seriousness.* Not only must his more formal teaching be characterized by purity of contents and gravity of method, but his entire *speech* (his *word* whenever and wherever it is spoken), whether it is uttered in the form of a sermon, a lesson, a message of consolation, or even an ordinary daily conversation, must be *sound* and *incensurable,* that is, not open to just rebuke (cf. synonym in I Tim. 6:4).

Now the intended result or purpose of such conduct is: **so that (or: in order that) he that is on the opposite (side) may be put to shame, having nothing evil to report concerning us.** As to the expression "on the opposite (side)" or "of the opposite (party)" — the ellipse is obscure — , note that it was the centurion who stood "over against" or "facing" Jesus on the cross (Mark 15:39). We read of *contrary* winds (Matt. 14:24; Mark 6:48; Acts 27:4). In the passage under discussion the ἀντί-compound is used in a metaphorical sense; opposition here amounts to *hostility* (cf. Acts 26:9; 28:17; I Thess. 2:15). The one on the opposite (side) is the spiritual *adversary* (cf. I Tim. 5:14; II Tim. 2:25). The reference is especially to any one of the Cretan errorists described in Titus 1:10-16.

Now when the opponent begins to notice that his shrewd little plan of spreading malicious gossip about Titus or of preferring formal charges against him miscarries, because the irreproachable conduct of Paul's representative completely disproves the insinuations and accusations that were aimed against him, this enemy of the truth will be put to shame (as in

---

[199] Nam parum alioqui autoritatis habebit doctrina, nisi in vita episcopi, tanquam in speculo, vis eius et maiestas eluceat. Vult ergo doctorem esse exemplar, cui se discipuli conforment (John Calvin on this passage).

2:7 and 8 **TITUS**

II Thess. 3:14; I Cor. 4:14). He will look foolish, "having nothing *evil* (cf. II Cor. 5:10) to report concerning" . . . here we expect that the next word will be "you" (Titus), but it actually is "us," for the antagonism is directed not against Titus as a separate individual but against him as a disciple of Christ; hence, really against Christ himself and all his messengers.

9 and 10. To the family belonged also *slaves*. In his first epistle to Timothy the apostle distinguishes between slaves who had believing masters and those who did not (I Tim. 6:1, 2). Here in Titus no such distinction is made. The command is to be transmitted to all slaves who hear the gospel; no doubt especially to all *believing* slaves. Says Paul, **(Urge) slaves to be submissive in every respect to their own masters, to be eager to please (them), not talking back (or: not rebellious), not pilfering, but evincing the utmost trustworthiness.**

For a discussion of the slavery-question in Paul's day see on I Tim. 6:1, 2. Had all masters and slaves everywhere taken to heart the inspired words of Paul anent slavery, this institution would have perished from the earth without blood-baths. — A superficial glance at the passage now under discussion might cause one to think that their author is hardly fair to the slave, neglecting to point out the equality of slave and master before God, and apparently condoning the sins of the master. But this inference would be erroneous, for it overlooks two important facts: a. Titus 2:9, 10 contains only *part* of Paul's teaching with respect to the master-slave relationship (see also Eph. 5:8, 9; Col. 3:25; 4:1; Philem. 16); and b. even here in the Titus-passage the immediately following context (note particularly verse 11) stresses the full equality of *all* believers, bond and free, from the aspect of God's redeeming grace.

The verb of verse 6 is again implied; hence, *"Urge* or *admonish* slaves." The three points with respect to which slaves must be admonished are:

(1) *Deportment.*

The slave must comply with the wishes of his master, and this "in every respect" (cf. Col. 3:22; then Eph. 5:24). From morning until evening and in every category of work the slave must be submissive to his master. It is hardly necessary to add that this phrase "in every respect" must not be taken in the absolute sense, as if the apostle meant to say that even then when the master demanded of the slave that he tell a lie or commit thievery, adultery, or murder, the latter must obey. The purpose-clause at the close of verse 10 implies a restriction, for surely by agreeing to sin the slave would never be able to "adorn the doctrine of God our Savior." And see also Acts 4:19; 5:29; Eph. 5:21.[200]

---

[200] I see no need, therefore, of adopting the view of Bouma and others, that ἀγαθήν (verse 10, the best text) is a limiting word and must be translated "with respect to

(2) *Disposition*

External compliance with the will of the master is not enough, however. Growling and grumbling underneath are also forbidden. The sullen disposition has never yet won a soul for Christ. Slaves, accordingly must be *eager to please, well-pleasing*. This adjective is typically Pauline: elsewhere the apostle uses it no less than *seven* times, while in all the rest of the New Testament it occurs only *once* (Heb. 13:21). And even if we add to this one occurrence the number of times Hebrews employs the cognate verb and adverb (fairness requires that we make this addition!), the frequency-ratio is still 7-5 (or if the reference in Titus is included 8-5) in favor of Paul.

The negative aspect of being well-pleasing is *not talking back*. This ἀντί-compound occurs nine times in the New Testament: Luke 2:34; 20:27; John 19:12; Acts 13:45; 28:19; 28:22; Rom. 10:21; Titus 1:9; 2:9. The cognate noun occurs in four passages: Heb. 6:16; 7:7; 12:3; and Jude 11. Although the basic meaning is that of *talking back,* it often conveys the overtone of *active disobedience, resistance, rebellion, strife*. See, for example, Rom. 10:21; Heb. 12:3; Jude 11. It probably has that coloring here also. Thus interpreted, the two expressions make a fitting pair: "well-pleasing" and "not rebellious" in disposition.

(3) *Dependability*.

When the master's back was turned, petty larceny was often committed. Such pilfering or purloining, whereby the slave secretly *holds back* (cf. the use of the verb in Acts 5:2, 3) or *withdraws* (sets apart for himself) a portion of that which belongs to his master, must not be excused by saying, "The master owes me much more than this, for he has taken away my freedom and he is robbing me of my strength and talents, all without adequate compensation." The slave must show "the utmost *trustworthiness*" (or "fidelity," Rom. 3:3b; cf. I Tim. 5:12; then Gal. 5:22).

Now the reason for the demand that slaves display a submissive deportment, an ingratiating disposition, and utmost dependability is this: **so that in every respect they may adorn the doctrine of God our Savior.** A sanctified life, which brings into clear perspective all the fruits of transforming grace — obedience, cheerfulness, integrity, etc. — scintillating like so many precious jewels, is an ornament to "the doctrine of *God our Savior*" (see on I Tim. 1:1), the Christian faith. It should cause masters to exclaim, "If the Christian religion does this even for slaves, it must be wonderful!"

---

that which is good." More natural would seem to be the construction which gave rise to the rendering found in the A.V. and A.R.V.: "showing all good fidelity." One might regard the original as an idiom for "evincing the utmost trustworthiness." Cf. the original in Titus 3:2; II Tim. 4:14.

2:11-14 **TITUS**

11 For the grace of God has appeared, bringing salvation to all men, 12 training us in order that, having renounced ungodliness and those worldly passions, we in the here and now may live lives of self-mastery and fairness and devotion, 13 while we are waiting for the blessed hope, the appearing of the glory of our great God and Savior Christ Jesus, 14 who gave himself for us in order to redeem us from all lawlessness and to purify for himself a people, his very own, with a zest for noble deeds.

15 These things keep on telling (them) and urging (upon them) and reproving with all authority. Let no one slight you.

2:11-15

11-14. *The grace of God considered as the reason why every member of The Christian Family can and should live a Christian life,* this is the theme of one of the richest passages of Holy Writ. Note the four main thoughts:

1. verse 11   *The Grace of God in Christ is the Great Penetrator, Dispelling the Darkness for All and Bringing Salvation to All.*

Says Paul, **For the grace of God has appeared, bringing salvation to all men.**

God's grace is his active favor bestowing the greatest gift upon those who have deserved the greatest punishment. (For a word-study of the concept *grace* see N.T.C. on I Thess. 1:1.) This grace has *penetrated* our moral and spiritual darkness. It "has appeared." The verb used in the original is related to the noun *epiphany,* that is, *appearing* or *manifestation* (for example, of the sun at sunrise). Upon those sitting in the darkness and in the shadow of death the grace of God had suddenly dawned (see also Mal. 4:2; Luke 1:79; Acts 27:20; and Titus 3:4). It had arisen when Jesus was born, when words of life and beauty issued from his lips, when he healed the sick, cleansed the lepers, cast out demons, raised the dead, suffered for man's sins, and laid down his life for the sheep in order to take it again on resurrection-morning. Thus, grace had "shed on the world Christ's holy light" and had "chased the dark night of sin away." The sun of righteousness had arisen "with healing in its wings." The grace of God had appeared *"saving* (σωτήριος) for all men." Everywhere else in the New Testament this word *saving,* when preceded by the article and used as a noun, means *salvation* (Luke 2:30; 3:6; Acts 28:28; Eph. 6:17), in the spiritual sense of the term. Hence, also here in Titus 2:11 the meaning is: God's grace made its appearance "salvation-bringing." Grace came to rescue man from the greatest possible evil, namely, the curse of God upon sin; and to bestow upon him the greatest possible boon, namely, the blessing of God for soul and body throughout all eternity. (For a word-study of the concept *salvation* see on I Tim. 1:15.)

It brought this salvation to "all men." For a detailed explanation of this

370

expression see on I Tim. 2:1. Here in Titus 2:11 the context makes the meaning very clear. Male or female, old or young, rich or poor: *all* are guilty before God, and from them *all* God gathers his people. Aged men, aged women, young women, young(er) men, and even slaves (see verses 1-10) should live consecrated lives, *for* the grace of God has appeared bringing salvation to men of *all* these various groups or classes. "All men" here in verse 11 = "us" in verse 12. Grace did not bypass the aged because they are aged, nor women because they are women, nor slaves because they are merely slaves, etc. It dawned upon *all,* regardless of age, sex, or social standing. Hence, no one can derive, from the particular group or caste to which he belongs, a reason for not living a Christian life.

2. verse 12 *The Grace of God in Christ is the Wise Pedagogue.*

The words which convey this thought are: **training us in order that, having renounced ungodliness and those worldly passions, we in the here and now may live lives of self-mastery and fairness and devotion.**

Grace *trains.* See on I Tim. 1:20. The verb used in the original is from the same stem as is the noun *pedagogue.* A pedagogue leads children step by step. Thus, grace, too, gently leads and guides. It does not throw things into confusion. It does not suddenly and forcefully upset the social order. For example, it does not abruptly order masters to free their slaves; nor does it unwisely command slaves to rebel forthwith against their masters. On the contrary, it gradually causes masters to see that the encroachment upon the liberty of their fellows is a great wrong, and it convinces slaves that resort to force and vengeance is not the solution to every problem. Grace *trains* by teaching (Acts 7:22; 22:3), chastening (I Tim. 1:20; II Tim. 2:25; then Luke 23:16, 22; I Cor. 11:32; II Cor. 6:9; Heb. 12:6-11; Rev. 3:19), counseling, comforting, encouraging, admonishing, guiding, convicting, rewarding, restraining, etc.

The purpose of all this is stated first negatively, then positively (which is a Pauline style-characteristic). *Negatively,* it induces us to *renounce* or *reject* (the verb has here the same meaning as in Acts 3:13; 7:35) *ungodliness,* impiety, wickedness (see on II Tim. 2:16). Study the vivid description of "ungodliness" in Rom. 1:18-32 (note the very word in Rom. 1:18; cf. 11:26). Such ungodliness is *idolatry* plus *immorality,* both terms taken in their most comprehensive meaning. When grace takes over, the sinner repudiates ungodliness. This repudiation is a definite act, a decision to give up that which is displeasing to God. No one *sleeps* his way into heaven. Rejecting ungodliness implies the renunciation of "those worldly passions" — strong, sinful desires — as well. (See word-study of the term *passion* or *desire* in connection with the exegesis of II Tim. 2:22.) According to scriptural usage, such worldly or sinful desires include the following: inordinate sexual desire, the liquor-mania, excessive yearning for material possessions, self-assertiveness (hence, quarrelsomeness, vanity, the lust to dominate), etc. Briefly, it refers to inordinate longing for pleasure, power, and possessions. See also I John 2:16, and on Titus 3:3.

Positively, grace trains us in order that "in the here and now" (*this present age;* cf. I Tim. 6:17; II Tim. 4:10; then Rom. 12:2; I Cor. 1:20; II Cor. 4:4; contrasted with *the coming age* in Eph. 1:21; cf. Mark 10:30) we may live lives which display a changed relation:

a. *to oneself:* "selfmastery," making the proper use of such desires or drives as are not sinful in themselves, and overcoming those that are sinful;

b. *to the neighbor:* "fairness," honesty, justice, integrity in dealing with others;

c. *to God:* "devotion," godliness, true piety and reverence with respect to him who alone is the proper Object of worship.

3. verse 13 *The Grace of God in Christ is the Effective Preparer.*

We — aged men, aged women, young women, young men, slaves, etc. — should live a Christian life because through the power of God's grace **we are waiting for the blessed hope, the appearing of the glory of our great God and Savior Christ Jesus.**

The grace of God trains us in order that we may *live* consecrated lives, *while we are waiting for* [201] the blessed hope. The *waiting for* or *patient looking forward to* modifies the *living,* of which it is an attendant circumstance or further explication. It is "the blessed hope" for which believers are waiting. This is metonymy for *the realization of that hope* (that is, the realization of our earnest yearning, confident expectation, and patient waiting). We find a similar metonymy in Gal. 5:5; Col. 1:5 (to which some interpreters would add Heb. 6:18).

This hope is called *blessed.* It imparts bliss, happiness, delight, and glory. The adjective *blessed* is used in connection with *God* in I Tim. 1:11; 6:15; see on these passages.

Now, even *the possession* of the hopeful spirit and *the exercise* of hope is blessed, because of hope's:

(1) immovable foundation (I Tim. 1:1, 2; then Rom. 5:5; 15:4; Phil. 1:20; Heb. 6:19; I Peter 1:3, 21);

---

[201] The present participle προσδεχόμενοι is here used in a sense in which Luke often (and Paul never elsewhere) employs the word (Luke 2:25, 38; 12:36; 23:51). Paul uses it in the sense of *receiving favorably, welcoming* (Rom. 16:2; Phil. 2:29; thus also Luke in Luke 15:2). But this is no valid argument against the Pauline authorship of the Pastorals or the Lucan authorship of Luke 15:2. Luke and Paul were friends. Besides, if Paul's nephew could use the word in the sense of *waiting for* (Acts 23:21), why not Paul himself? And, if the answer to this should be, "But it is Luke, and not Paul's nephew, who is responsible for the word in Acts 23:21," the reply to this is once again, "Luke and Paul were friends!"

(2) glorious Author (Rom. 15:13; cf. II Thess. 2:16);

(3) wonderful object (everlasting life, salvation, glory: Titus 1:2; 3:7; then I Thess. 5:8; then Rom. 5:2; Col. 1:27);

(4) precious effects (endurance, I Thess. 1:3; "boldness of speech," II Cor. 3:12; and purification of life, I John 3:3);

(5) and everlasting character (I Cor. 13:13).

Then surely *the realization* of this hope will be blessed, indeed! Read Dan. 12:3; Matt. 25:34-40; Rom. 8:20b; I Cor. 15:51, 52; I Thess. 4:13-18; II Thess. 1:10; Rev. 14:14-16; 19:6-9. In fact, the certainty of the realization imparts strength to the hope, and results in the graces mentioned under (4) above.

Now the realization of the blessed hope is "the appearing in glory." [202] Note the two appearings. There had been *one* (see on verse 11; cf. II Tim. 1:10). There is going to be *another* (see N.T.C. on II Thess. 2:8; cf. I Tim. 6:14; II Tim. 4:1, 8). It will be the appearing of . . . well, of whom? Throughout the history of interpretation that question has divided grammarians and commentators. Are we waiting for the appearing in glory of *one* Person or of *two Persons*?

Those who endorse the *one-Person* view favor the rendering:

"of our great God and Savior Christ Jesus." (Another reading has "Jesus Christ," but that makes no difference in connection with the point at issue.) Now if that view be correct, those who accept Scripture's infallibility have in this passage an additional prooftext for the deity of Christ; and even those who do not accept Scripture's infallibility but who do accept the *one-Person* rendering must admit that at least the author of the Pastorals (perhaps erroneously, according to them) held Jesus to be one in essence with God the Father. The *one-Person* rendering is favored by the A.R.V. margin, Weymouth, Goodspeed, Berkeley Version, R.S.V., and many commentators: Van Oosterzee, Bouma, Lenski, Gealy, Simpson, etc. The great New Testament grammarian A. T. Robertson has given a strong defence of this view, from the standpoint of grammar, basing his arguments upon Granville Sharp's rule.

Among others, John Calvin was unwilling to choose between the *one-Person* and the *two-Persons* rendering. Yet, he emphasized that on either view the purpose of the passage is to state that when Christ appears, the

---

[202] Literally the text reads "the appearing of the glory." Some (for example, A.V., Berkeley Version, Goodspeed) prefer the rendering "the glorious appearing." Others (for example, Lenski and White) object to this rendering. Yet, I cannot see that the objection is very formidable. If the expression "the steward of the unrighteousness" (Luke 16:8) means "the unrighteous steward," why cannot the phrase "the appearing of the glory" mean "the glorious appearing"? But whether a person translates one way or the other, the resultant meaning is about the same, namely, "the appearing in glory" (as Weymouth renders the phrase and as Bouma and others interpret it). Cf. Matt. 25:31; Mark 13:26; II Thess. 1:10.

greatness of the divine glory will be revealed in him (cf. Luke 9:26); and that, accordingly, the passage can by no means give any comfort to the Arians in their attempt to prove that the Son is less divine than the Father.

The *two-Persons* theory is represented, with minor variations, in the versions of Wyclif, Tyndale, Cranmer, A.V., A.R.V. (text), Moffatt, and R.S.V. (margin). It has been supported by a long list of commentators (among whom are De Wette, Huther, White [in *The Expositor's Bible*], E. F. Scott, etc.) and especially by the grammarian G. B. Winer.

The rendering then becomes:

"of the great God and the (or "and of the") Savior Jesus Christ."

Winer was willing to admit that his endorsement of this view was based not so much upon grammar — which, as even he admitted, *allowed* the one-Person rendering — as upon "the dogmatic conviction derived from Paul's writings that this apostle cannot have called Christ *the great God.*" (Such argumentation encounters difficulty in interpreting Rom. 9:5; Phil. 2:6; Col. 1:15-20; Col. 2:9; etc.) But he should have noticed that even the very context (verse 14) ascribes to *Jesus* functions which in the Old Testament are ascribed to *Jehovah,* such as *redeeming* and *purifying* (II Sam. 7:23; Ps. 130:8; Hos. 13:14; then Ezek. 37:23); and that the word *Savior* is in each of the three chapters of Titus ascribed first to *God,* then to *Jesus* (Titus 1:3, 4; 2:10, 13; 3:4, 6). It is therefore evidently the purpose of the author of this epistle (namely, Paul!) to show that Jesus is fully divine, just as fully as is Jehovah or as is the Father.

The *one-Person* rendering must be considered the correct one. It is supported by the following considerations:

(1) Unless in any specific instance there are strong reasons to the contrary, the rule holds that when the first of two nouns of the same case and connected by the conjunction *and* is preceded by the article, which is not repeated before the second noun, these two nouns refer to *the same person.* When the article is repeated before the second noun, *two persons* are indicated. Examples:

a. The article, preceding the first of two nouns and *not* repeated before the second: "*the* brother y o u r and fellow-partaker." The two nouns refer to *the same person,* John, and the expression is correctly translated, "y o u r brother and fellow-partaker" (Rev. 1:9).

b. *Two* articles, one preceding each noun: "Let him be unto you as *the* Gentile and *the* tax-collector" (Matt. 18:17). The two nouns refer to *two persons* (in this case, each representing a class).

Now, according to this rule the disputed words in Titus 2:13 clearly refer to *one* Person, namely, Christ Jesus, for when translated word for word the phrase reads:

"of *the* great God and of Savior our Christ Jesus." The article before the first noun is not repeated before the second, and therefore the expression must be rendered:

"of our great God and Savior Christ Jesus."

No valid reason has ever been found which would show that the (Granville Sharp) rule does not apply in the present case.[203] In fact, it is generally admitted that the words which in the original occur at the close of II Peter 1:11 refer to *one* Person, and must be rendered, "our Lord and Savior Jesus Christ." But if that be true, then why should not the *essentially* identical idiom in II Peter 1:1 and here in Titus 2:13 be rendered, "our God and Savior Jesus Christ" (or "Christ Jesus")?

(2) Nowhere in the entire New Testament is the term *epiphany (appearing* or *manifestation)* used with respect to more than *one* Person. Also, the *one* Person to whom it refers is always Christ (see II Thess. 2:8; I Tim. 6:14; II Tim. 4:1; II Tim. 4:8; and II Tim. 1:10, where the reference is to the First Coming).

(3) The phraseology here in Titus 2:13 may well have been framed in reaction to the type of language that was often used by the heathen with respect to their own idol-gods, whom they regarded as "saviors," and particularly to the phraseology in connection with the worship of earthly rulers. Was not Ptolemy I called "Savior and God"? Were not Antiochus and Julius Cesar addressed as "God Manifest"?[204] Paul indicates that believers look forward to the Appearing of the One who is *really* God and Savior, yes "our great (exalted, glorious) God and Savior, namely, Christ Jesus."

The real "point" of the passage, in connection with all that has preceded, is that our joyful expectation of the appearing in glory of our great God and Savior Christ Jesus *effectively prepares* us for the life with him. How does it do this? First, because the Second Coming will be so altogether glorious that believers will not want to "miss out on" it, but will want to "be manifested with him in glory" (Col. 3:4). Secondly, because the blissful expectation fills believers with gratitude, and gratitude produces preparedness, by God's grace.

4. verse 14   *The Grace of God in Christ is the Thorough-going Purifier.*

---

[203] See Gram. N.T., pp. 785-787; also same author (A. T. Robertson), *The Minister And His Greek New Testament,* New York, 1923, pp. 61-68. Now if it could be established that not only is σωτήρ a proper name but that in addition Paul generally refers the epiphany to two Persons, we would have something parallel to the expression "of *the* God our and of Lord Jesus Christ" where in spite of the *one* article the reference is in all probability to *two* Persons, and the phrase can be rendered: "of our God and of the Lord Jesus Christ" (II Thess. 1:12). See N.T.C. on I and II Thessalonians, p. 164, the last paragraph, and also footnote 117 on that page. But II Thess. 1:12 and Titus 2:13 are not identical.

[204] See E. Stauffer, *Christ and the Caesars,* Philadelphia, 1955 (reviewed in *WThJ,* XVIII, Number 2 (May, 1956), pp. 171-176. And see also footnote 76.

Our great God and Savior Christ Jesus to whose appearing in glory believers look forward with such hope and joy is the One **who gave himself for us in order to redeem us from all lawlessness and to purify for himself a people, his very own, with a zest for noble deeds.**

For the meaning of "who gave himself for us in order to redeem us" see on I Tim. 2:6, "who gave himself a ransom for all." Anyone who doubts the necessary, objective, voluntary, expiatory, propitiatory, substitutionary, and efficacious character of the act of Christ whereby he gave himself for us should make a diligent, contextual study of the following passages: [205]

Old Testament	New Testament		
Gen. 2:16, 17	Matt. 20:28	I Cor. 7:23	Heb. 9:28
Ex. 12:13	Matt. 26:27, 28	II Cor. 5:18-21	I Peter 1:18, 19
Lev. 1:4	Mark 10:45	Gal. 1:4	I Peter 2:24
Lev. 16:20-22	Luke 22:14-23	Gal. 2:20	I Peter 3:18
Lev. 17:11	John 1:29	Gal. 3:13	I John 2:2
II Sam. 7:23	John 6:55	Eph. 1:7	I John 4:10
Psalm 40:6, 7	Acts 20:28	Eph. 2:16	Rev. 5:12
Psalm 130:8	Rom. 3:25	Eph. 5:6	Rev. 7:14.
Isaiah 53	Rom. 5	Col. 1:19-23	
Zech. 13:1	I Cor. 6:20	Heb. 9:22	

He gave nothing less than *himself,* and this *for us,* that is, in our interest and in our stead. The contemplation of this sublime thought should result in a life to his honor. Furthermore, by his sacrificial death he merited for us the work of the Holy Spirit in our hearts. Apart from that Spirit it would be impossible for us to live the sanctified life.

Christ gave himself for us with a twofold purpose: the first negative (see Ps. 130:8), the second positive (see II Sam. 7:23). Negatively, he gave himself for us "in order to redeem us," that is, in order to ransom us from an evil power. The ransom-price was his own precious blood (I Peter 1:18, 19). And the power from which we are delivered is that of "lawlessness" (see N.T.C. on II Thess. 2:3), that is, indwelling disobedience to God's holy law, in whatever form that disobedience makes itself manifest ("*all* lawlessness").

Positively, he gave himself for us "in order to purify for himself a people," that is, in order by means of his blood and Spirit to purify us (Eph. 5:26; Heb. 9:14; I John 1:7, 9), so that, thus purified, we are fit to be a people, *his very own* (see footnote 193 and cf. Ezek. 37:23). Formerly *Israel* was Jehovah's peculiar people; now *the church* is. And just as Israel was characterized by zeal for the law (Acts 21:20; cf. Gal. 1:14), so now

---

[205] Read also A. A. Hodge, *The Atonement,* Philadelphia, 1867; and L. Berkhof, *Vicarious Atonement Through Christ,* Grand Rapids, Mich., 1936.

Christ purifies his people with this very purpose in mind, namely, that it shall be a people for his own possession "with a zest for noble deeds," deeds which proceed from faith, are done according to God's law and unto his glory (cf. I Peter 3:13).

In summary, verses 11-14 teach us that the reason why every member of the family should live a life of self-mastery, fairness, and devotion is that the grace of God in Christ has penetrated our moral and spiritual darkness and has brought salvation to all men; that this grace is also our Great Pedagogue who leads us away from ungodliness and worldly passions and guides us along the path of holiness; that it is the Effective Preparer who causes us to look forward with eagerness to the Appearing in glory of our great God and Savior Christ Jesus; and, finally, that it is the thorough-going Purifier, so that, redeemed from all disobedience to God's law, we become Christ's peculiar treasure, filled with a zest for excellent deeds.

15. As a fitting conclusion to the entire chapter (in a sense to both chapters) Paul adds: **These things keep on telling (them) and urging (upon them) and reproving, with all authority.**

Titus must never grow slack in his duty. He must continue to do what he has been doing all along. He must constantly *talk* (see on verse 1) about this glorious life of sanctification as a thank-offering presented to God for his wonderful grace in Christ. He must *urge* it upon the people, doing this whenever the occasion presents itself, *admonishing* (see on verse 6) those who are in need of special admonition, and even *reproving* (see on Titus 1:9, 13) those who have merited reproof. All this he must do "with all authority," the authority of Christ whom he represents.

Let no one slight you. Cf. I Tim. 4:12. Titus must conduct himself in such a manner that no one will "think around" him; that is, that no one will in his heart and mind "by-pass," disregard or ignore Titus, thinking, "Never mind what *he* has said about this or that matter." Though this command is addressed *directly* to Titus who must take it to heart, it will also *indirectly* help him in the performance of his duties, namely, when it is read to the various presbyters and congregations.

---

[193] Because of its many words or expressions that occur only once — *hapax legomena* — the second chapter of Titus is among those portions of the Pastorals on which the critics concentrate in order to prove that Paul cannot in any sense have been the author. But do *the facts* support this conclusion? *I am convinced that they do not.* A long list of such words may look very impressive, but in the final analysis it is not the mere *number* of such words that counts but their *nature*.

By means of the summary which follows, I wish to show that *every word* of this chapter is of such a character that no one has a right to say, "Paul cannot have written it." The vocabulary of Titus 2 may be summarized as follows:

(1) Many of the words used in this chapter are more or less common in the Greek language or at least in Koine Greek. Surely, no argument against Pauline authorship can be based upon them.

(2) Then, among the remaining words there are those which elsewhere in the New Testament are used only by Paul. How can they prove that Paul could not have written the Pastorals?

(3) Again, there are those which elsewhere are used only by Paul's frequent companion and close friend, Luke, or elsewhere only by Luke and by Paul. No argument against Pauline authorship can be derived from them either, as is obvious.

(4) Among the words which in the New Testament occur only here in the second chapter of Titus or only in the Pastorals, there are those which are known to have been used by other authors living in or very close to Paul's own time. How can it be argued that Paul could not have used those words which he heard round about him? Or, some of the words were known to Paul because he had found them in the LXX.

(5) There are also words which, though occurring only once or only a few times in the Pastorals, and nowhere else in the New Testament, are close cognates of words used by Paul and/or by Luke. Now if an author has written "nicely," is it impossible for him to use the word "nice"?

In this same connection, there are words which, though occurring only here, follow a typically Pauline pattern. Let us imagine that a certain author, John Brown, in works which by common consent are ascribed to him, has been using a series of substantives in which the word *snow* occurs as a component element; e.g., "snow-field," "snow-flake," "snow-pigeon," "snow-flower," etc. Now, in a writing of disputed authorship the word "snow-ball" is used. Would it be reasonable, in such a case, to argue as follows: "John Brown cannot have written this particular book, for the word *snow-ball* does not occur in any of his recognized literary products"? Would it not be more reasonable to say, "It is surely *possible* that John Brown wrote this book, for he is the very man who is fond of combinations containing the word *snow*"?

Analysis of the Words Occurring in Titus, Chapter 2
A. Words of more or less Common Usage

All the words of verse 1 belong to this class. Such words as "But," "you," "speak," and "the," are, of course, very common.

As to "being sound," this, too, is an expression that is by no means limited to the Pastorals. Luke and John also use it. Much has been made, however, of the following three arguments:

(1) In the Pastorals this word is used in a superphysical sense; elsewhere in a merely physical sense.

(2) In the Pastorals the word has a philosophical meaning. It means "in accordance with reason." It is in that sense that one's teaching or doctrine must be "sound." Hence, *Paul* cannot have written the Pastorals, for he asserted that *his* gospel is not based on human reason but is "foolishness" to the world (I Cor. 2:6, 14). An unknown author borrowed words and concepts from the Hellenistic literature of his own day. (See M. Dibelius, *Die Pastoralbriefe,* second edition, Tübingen, 1931, p. 14.)

(3) In the Pastorals this word is used with great frequency.

But over against this threefold argument against Pauline authorship stands the following:

In answer to (1). See Prov. 13:13 (LXX). Here "being sound" cannot be restricted to man's physical frame.

In answer to (2). In the Pastorals "being sound" is not an antonym of "being irrational" but of "being morally and spiritually perverted," as appears most clearly from Titus 1:12, 13. It is true, of course, that man's intellect, too, is beclouded when he resists the will of God.

In answer to (3). The frequency with which a certain term is used does not necessarily prove difference in authorship. It may simply prove difference in subject-matter and general situation. Is it really impossible to picture *Paul,* the aged, deeply concerned about the question whether the church will remain loyal to "sound" doctrine?

The final word of verse 1 — namely, "doctrine" — is also rather common. Matthew and Mark both use it. So does Paul in Rom. 12:7; 15:4; Eph. 4:14; and Col. 2:22.

Hence, nothing whatever against Pauline authorship can be based upon any of the words found in verse 1. And the same holds with respect to the "more or less common words" used in the rest of the chapter. It would be a waste of time, therefore, to pay any further attention to words of that class in this brief summary.

B. *Words which elsewhere in the New Testament occur only in Paul's Epistles*

Thus, "dignified" or "honorable," aside from its use in Titus 2:2 and I Tim. 3:8, is in the New Testament found only in Phil. 4:8; "appearing" (Titus 2:13; cf. I Tim. 6:14; II Tim. 1:10; 4:1, 8) occurs only in II Thess. 2:8; and the word translated "authority" (Titus 2:15; cf. 1:3; I Tim. 1:1) is found only in Rom. 16:26; I Cor. 7:6, 25; II Cor. 8:8, though the cognate verb also occurs in Mark, Luke, and Acts.

Such words would seem to point *toward* Paul rather than *away from* him.

C. *Words which elsewhere in the New Testament are found only in Luke or only in Paul and Luke*

The word "aged man" (Titus 2:2) is found only in Philem. 9 and in Luke 1:18; "embezzle" or "purloin" (Titus 2:10) occurs only in Acts 5:2, 3; "appeared" (Titus 2:11; cf. 3:4) is found only in Luke 1:79; and "bringing salvation" (Titus 2:11) appears elsewhere only in Eph. 6:17; Luke 2:30; 3:6; Acts 28:28, though in these several instances it is neut. as subst. "salvation."

Interesting, although not entirely confined to Paul and Luke, is also the word "waiting for" (see on verse 13). Does the sense in which it is here used betray Lucan influence?

This group of words offers nothing in support of the theory that Paul cannot have written the Pastorals.

D. *Words which in the New Testament occur nowhere outside the Pastorals, but which do occur in earlier and/or contemporary sources*

Verse 3 contains the word "demeanor." It occurs also in Josephus, *Jewish Antiquities* XV. vii. 5. He makes mention of the alleged intrepid *demeanor* of Mariamne, the wife of Herod the Great. It was one of the causes which led to her death by order of her cruel husband. Plutarch (A. D. 46-120) also has the word.

In verse 7 the word "incorruptness" or "incorruptibility" is used. "Untaintedness" or "purity" would be another good rendering. In the sense of *pure* or *chaste* the cognate adjective is found in Esther 2:2 (LXX): "Let *chaste* maidens (virgins), beautiful in form, be sought for the king."

Verse 14 has the expression "people for his own possession." Here περιούσιος is from the verb περίειμι *to be over and above;* hence, *to be left over.* It indicates that which remains to oneself; for example, after the price has been paid; hence, anything which one can call "his very own." The expression is a quotation which occurs again and again in the LXX (Ex. 19:5; 23:22; Deut. 7:6; 14:2; 26:18). In Deut. 7:6 the Hebrew original on which the LXX is based has 'am ṣ ᵉgullah, "peculiar treasure." As that passage proves, it indicates that Israel is Jehovah's "special possession," his "holy people" because he has chosen it. That act of divine grace raised Israel above all other nations.

Paul was, of course, well acquainted with the LXX. Hence, this quotation (cf. Eph. 1:14; then I Peter 2:9) presents no great problem.

E. *Words which in the New Testament occur nowhere outside the Pastorals, but which follow a Pauline word-pattern*

Nearly all the words which follow could also have been included under D. But in addition to being current in the Greek-speaking world of that day, as most of them were, they follow a Pauline word-pattern, as will be shown:

Verse 3 contains the word "aged woman" (πρεσβῦτις). But this is simply the fem.

of πρεσβύτης. See also footnote 196. Not only is this fem. form found also in IV Macc. 16:14 (LXX) and in several other early and later sources, but Paul has himself used the masc. in Philem. 9 (cf. Titus 2:2).

The same verse (Titus 2:3) also contains the word ἱεροπρεπής, "as is proper for those employed in temple-service" (or *in sacred-service*); hence, reverent, pious. This word is found in the stirring Macabbean story of the mother and her seven sons who were martyred for their loyalty to Jehovah. In connection with the death of the eldest son we read, "And having said this, the *pious* youth died" (IV Macc. 9:25; cf. 11:20; cf. Josephus, *Jewish Antiquities* XI. viii. 5). Although the two expressions do not have exactly the same meaning, nevertheless the one here in Titus ("as is proper for those employed in temple-service") and the one in Eph. 5:3 ("as is proper for saints," and cf. I Cor. 11:13) have enough in common to prevent one from saying that the author of the latter could not have been the author of the former.

Once more turning to verse 3 we find the word καλοδιδάσκαλος, "teacher of that which is excellent." Now it was exactly Paul who loved such compounds, and they were not limited to any particular period of his life as an author. See p. 15. So why could not he who in II Thess. 3:13 wrote *"doers* of that which is excellent" also write *"teachers* of that which is excellent"?

Verse 4 contains the verb σωφρονίζω, to moderate, curb, sober down; then, as here, "to train." It was Xenophon (430-355 B. C.), who, in using as an illustration the training of horses, said, "Fear of the spearmen *curbs* them" (*The Tyrant* X). In the New Testament this verb is found only here. And the cognate περιφρονέω "to slight" is found only in verse 15. Another word from the same stem, which also occurs only once in the entire New Testament, is σωφρόνως, "with self-control," sensibly (verse 12). I might add that the cognate adjective "self-controlled" is found only in I Tim. 3:2; Titus 1:8; 2:2, 5; and that the cognate noun "self-control" is found only in II Tim. 1:7.

But does this mean that Paul could not have written the Pastorals? On the contrary, I find that about half of the words listed separately in the Lexicon, and based upon the stem φρήν, that is, *heart, mind, thought,* occur in one or more of the ten epistles commonly ascribed to Paul. The apostle was very fond of words formed on this stem (see, for example, the original of the following passages: Rom. 2:4; 2:20; 8:6; 12:3; I Cor. 10:15; I Cor. 13:11; I Cor. 14:20; II Cor. 2:2; II Cor. 11:1; II Cor. 11:23; Gal. 6:3; Eph. 1:8; and Phil. 2:3). Is it logical to believe that an author who in Rom. 12:3 used the term ὑπερφρονέω, and who in Phil. 2:3-5 used both φρονέω and ταπεινοφροσύνη could not have used περιφρονέω in Titus 2:15? As to the latter, Plutarch describes Fable as at times obviously *disdaining* to make herself convincing (*Parallel Lives*, Theseus I). The word is also found in IV Macc. 6:9; 14:1 (LXX). But long before this, Thucydides already used it.

Verse 4 also contains the expression φίλανδρος καί φιλότεκνος, here in pl., "loving toward their husbands and loving toward their children." Plutarch used both words in the sense here indicated. And see Deissmann, *Light From the Ancient East,* p. 315. Now the Pastorals contain many composites based on φιλ-, and among them there are several which are not found elsewhere in the New Testament (φιλήδονος, φιλόθεος, φίλανδρος, φιλότεκνος, φιλάγαθος, ἀφιλάγαθος, φιλαργυρία, and φίλαυτος). But this use of words based on φιλ- appears also to have been characteristic of Paul and of Luke. Paul, for example, in his other epistles, *is the only New Testament author* who uses the following: φιλόνεικος, φιλοσοφία, φιλόστοργος, and φιλοτιμέομαι; while his good friend and frequent companion Luke is the only New Testament author in whose writings we find φιλανθρώπως, φιλονεικία, φιλόσοφος, and φιλοφρόνως.

Surely, to say that *Paul* could not have written the Pastorals, because it contains many compounds based on the stem φιλ- is hardly convincing.

Verse 5 contains the noun οἰκουργός, home-worker. (I shall consider this the best reading here, as it seems to agree best with the context.) Now is this really an un-Pauline word, showing that the apostle could not have written the Pastorals? (We can safely permit the medical writer of the second century who also used it to rest in peace.) It was exactly Paul who loved word-formations in ἐργ-, either using them freely wherever he finds them or else perhaps even coining them himself. For ἐργ- compounds in Paul examine the original in the following references, each reference pointing to a different form: Acts 14:17 (Paul speaking); Rom. 4:15; Rom. 15:16; Rom. 16:3; I Cor. 3:9; II Cor. 1:11; II Cor. 12:16; II Thess. 3:11. It surely seems indefensible to say that the only New Testament writer who used πανοῦργος (II Cor. 12:16) could not have written οἰκουργός. — Luke also loved ἐργ- compounds. Luke and Paul were friends!

Similarly verse 8 presents the only instance in the New Testament of the word ἀκατάγνωστος uncensurable, irreproachable. In the sense of *uncondemned* the word occurs in II Macc. 4:47 (LXX): "And him who was the cause of all the evil, Menelaus, he discharged from the accusations; but those luckless men who, if they had pleaded even before the Scythians, would have been discharged *uncondemned*, them he sentenced to death." But why would it be impossible for the same author who in Gal. 2:11 used the verb καταγινώσκω to write ἀκατάγνωστος here in Titus 2:8? An un-Pauline word? Not at all!

Similar reasoning holds with respect to other words which in their New Testament usage occur here in Titus 2 and for the rest only in the Pastorals; such words as *temperate or sober* (Titus 2:2; cf. I Tim. 3:2, 11); *piously* (Titus 2:12; II Tim. 3:12); and *dignity or seriousness* (Titus 2:7; cf. I Tim. 2:2; 3:4). Does anyone really wish to maintain that an author who wrote *impious* (Rom. 4:5; 5:6) and *impiety* (Rom. 1:18; 11:26) could not have written *piously;* that the one who wrote *dignified or honorable* (Phil. 4:8) could not have used the word *dignity;* and that he who wrote *awake to soberness* (I Cor. 15:34) could not have written *sober?*

CONCLUSION: *When all the words in the second chapter of Titus have been examined, this conclusion becomes clear: there is not a single one which Paul could not have written.*

Note also that there are here, in Titus 2, several concepts which, though also found elsewhere in the New Testament, are treated *more fully by Paul* in the ten epistles than by any other New Testament writer. I refer to such concepts as are here in Titus 2 indicated by the words: a. *noble* (or excellent, admirable) *deeds* (Titus 2:7, 14; cf. 3:8; I Tim. 3:1; 5:10, 25; 6:18); with which one should compare the expression *good work(s)* (Titus 1:16; 3:1; cf. I Tim. 2:10; 5:10; II Tim. 2:21; 3:17); b. *grace* (Titus 2:11, etc.); and c. *the here and now* or *the present age* (Titus 2:12, in distinction from *the future or coming age*).

It is true that a synonym is sometimes found in addition to or in the place of the word used in the earlier epistles. Thus, in the Pastorals we meet both *noble deeds* (cf. Mark 14:6) and *good works,* while in the earlier epistles the latter expression alone is found. But to base upon grounds as flimsy as this the assertion that Paul cannot have been the responsible author of the Pastorals is certainly unwarranted. Why would it be impossible to assume either that since both expressions were current, the author, in writing extensively on the subject, as he does here in the Pastorals, chose to vary the terminology; or else that here and there his "secretary" is using his own vocabulary, with Paul's full approval? Even in that case the real and responsible author could certainly be *Paul.*

When to all this the various Pauline style-characteristics of Titus 2 are added, to which I have called attention in the commentary proper — and see also pp. 14-18, it will be evident that the burden of proof rests entirely on him who rejects Pauline authorship.

Synthesis of Chapter 2

See the Outline at the beginning of the chapter.

Sanctification in mutual relationships, with emphasis on the Christian family, is the theme of this chapter. Doctrine and life must agree. Hence, Titus must urge aged men to be temperate, dignified, etc.; aged women to be reverent; young men to exercise self-control (Timothy himself being their model); and slaves to be submissive in their deportment, pleasing in disposition, and of unquestionable dependability. Moreover, he wants the older women to instruct the younger ones to love their husbands and their children, to be self-controlled, chaste, domestic, kind, and submissive to their husbands. All these various classes should be motivated by the desire that the Word of God be honored, the sound doctrine adorned, and the enemy of the truth put to shame.

Not a single class or group of society must fail to come under the sanctifying influence of the Holy Spirit. Has not the grace of God appeared, bringing salvation to them all? This grace is the Great Penetrator, which invaded the realm of darkness and brought light, namely, the light of knowledge, holiness, joy, and peace ("salvation"); the Wise Pedagogue, training us to crucify worldly passions and to live lives of Christian devotion; the Effective Preparer, pointing to the realization of our blessed hope when our great God and Savior Christ Jesus returns in glory; and the Thorough-going Purifier, in Christ redeeming us from all lawlessness and transforming us into a people for Christ's own possession, filled with a zest for noble deeds. Titus must constantly talk about this glorious life of sanctification on the part of everybody. It should be presented to God as a thank-offering for his wonderful grace. Let Titus then see to it that no one slights him or his words.

On the question of slavery and race-relations see also the following: *Everyday Life in Ancient Times,* published by the *National Geographic Magazine,* 1953, pp. 175, 302, 303; J. C. Furnas, *Goodbye to Uncle Tom,* New York, 1956, especially pp. 285-388; note extensive Bibliography on pp. 397-418; Frank C. J. McGurk, "A Scientist's Report on Race Differences," *U.S. News and World Report,* Sept. 21, 1956; and the pertinent articles in *Life* magazine, Sept. 3, 1956.

Outline of Chapter 3

Theme: *The Apostle Paul, Writing to Titus, Gives Directions for the Promotion of the Spirit of Sanctification In Social (i.e. Public) Life*

3:1-8   Believers should be obedient to the authorities. They should be kind to all men, since it was the kindness of God our Savior — not our own works! — which brought salvation.

3:9-11 On the other hand, foolish questions should be shunned, and factious men who refuse to heed admonition should be rejected.

3:12-15 Concluding directions with respect to kingdom-travelers (Artemas or Tychicus, Titus, Zenas, Apollos) and Cretan believers in general. Greetings.

CHAPTER III

TITUS 3:1-8

3 1 Remind them to be in subjection to rulers (and) to authorities, to be obedient, to be ready for every good work, 2 to revile no one, not to be contentious, to be genial, showing all mildness toward all people.

3 For at one time we also were without understanding, disobedient, deluded, enslaved to various passions and pleasures, living in malice and envy, detestable, hating each other. 4 But when the kindness of God our Savior and his love toward man appeared, 5 he saved us, not by virtue of works which we ourselves had performed in (a state of) righteousness, but according to his mercy through the washing of regeneration and renewing by the Holy Spirit, 6 which he poured out upon us richly through Jesus Christ our Savior, 7 in order that, having been justified by his grace, we might become heirs-in-hope of life everlasting. 8 Reliable (is) this saying, and about these matters I want you to speak with confidence, in order that those who have their faith fixed on God may be careful to apply themselves to noble deeds. These matters are excellent and beneficial for (all) people.

3:1-8

To the directions for the promotion of the spirit of sanctification in congregational life (chapter 1) and in family and individual life (chapter 2) are now added:

Directions for the promotion of the spirit of sanctification in public life.

The *positive* part of this section is found in verses 1-8, the *negative* part in verses 9 and 10, while the remaining verses of the chapter form a fitting *conclusion* to the entire letter. As to the positive part (verses 1-8) note:

1. The Reminder: obey the magistrates and be kind to everyone (verses 1 and 2).
2. The Reason: at one time we were like these outsiders, and were it not for the sovereign kindness of God Triune we would be like them today (verses 3-7).
    a. What we were at one time: without understanding, etc.
    b. The sovereign kindness of the Father
    c. The work of the Holy Spirit
    d. The grace of Jesus Christ
    e. The purpose of all this: life everlasting for us.
3. The Re-affirmation: these matters must be asserted with confidence, for they are excellent and beneficial for (all) people (verse 8).

1 and 2. Remind them to be in subjection to rulers (and) to authorities, to be obedient, to be ready for every good work, to revile no one, not to be contentious, to be genial, showing all mildness toward all people.

Although believers, being heavenly-minded, look forward with joy to the day of the glorious appearing of him who bought them with his own precious blood, they must never forget their duty here on earth. Titus must *remind* them of this (cf. II Tim. 2:14), in order that at all times they may be *good citizens* and *good neighbors.*

For the Christian's relation to the State see also on I Tim. 2:1-7; cf. Matt. 17:24-27; 22:15-22; Rom. 13:1-7; I Peter 2:13-17. The expression *"Remind them to be in subjection,"* probably implies that Paul had talked to the Cretans about this important matter while he was with Titus on the island (cf. II Thess. 2:5). Moreover, from the writings of Polybius and of Plutarch it appears that the Cretans were fretting and fuming under the Roman yoke. It is *possible,* therefore, that this circumstance had something to do with the precise nature of the present "reminder." It has been pointed out by several commentators that while *Timothy* at Ephesus was ordered to see to it that believers cease not *to pray* for rulers, *Titus* is told to remind the Cretans *to be in subjection* to rulers. But see also Rom. 13:1-7. At any rate, the Christian message will be ineffective unless, in obedience to the fifth commandment in its broader meaning, believers "render unto Cesar the things that are Cesar's, and unto God the things that are God's."

To those, then, who not only actually *rule* but as such have also been invested with divine *authority* (Rom. 13:1) — hence, "to rulers and authorities" — believers must not only in a general way *outwardly subject themselves* but must even be *inwardly obedient,* carrying out with a willing heart *all the particular commands;* for example, those with respect to paying taxes, being orderly in behavior, displaying honesty in business, etc. (The exception referred to in Acts 5:29 holds whenever any human regulation clashes with the law of God.)

Not only that, but whenever the need presents itself — think of epidemics, wars, conflagrations, etc. — believers must be ready to show their good spirit, in thorough co-operation with the government which protects them. Note same connection in Rom. 13:3. They must not only be "thoroughly equipped" but also "ready" and eager for *every good work* (cf. Titus 3:1 and II Tim. 3:17).

The expression "ready for every good work" forms a natural bridge between the duties which believers owe to their government and those which they owe to their neighbors.

In the five requirements which follow, a climax is clearly observable. It stands to reason that believers should never *revile* any one (see on I Tim. 6:4). Not many believers will even need such a reminder. Insulting and abusive language is surely out of place for anyone, certainly for believers.

A more stringent requirement is the one which demands that believers be not even *contentious* or *quarrelsome* (cf. I Tim. 3:3). But more than the absence of a vice is expected of them. A positive virtue must display itself in all their contacts with those outside the church: Christians must be *genial* (also I Tim. 3:3), that is, ready to yield personal advantage, eager to help the needy, kind to the weak, considerate toward the fallen, always filled with the spirit of sweet reasonableness. The climax is surely reached with the words: "showing *all* mildness (cf. II Tim. 2:25) toward *all* people." Note the play on words,[206] reflected also in the A.V. and A.R.V. renderings. Showing *some* mildness toward *some* people might not be so difficult. Nor showing *all* (that is, *complete, thorough-going*) mildness to *some* people, or *some* mildness to *all* people. But to *show all* mildness to *all* people, even to all those Cretan "liars, evil brutes, and lazy bellies," was an assignment impossible of fulfilment apart from God's special grace!

3. The reason why this *must*, nevertheless, be done (and *can* be done) is stated in the beautiful passage beginning with the words: **For at one time we also were without understanding, disobedient, deluded, enslaved to various passions and pleasures, living in malice and envy, detestable, hating each other.**

Reflection upon our own former condition makes it easier for us to be mild and kind toward others. Note, "For at one time *we* also were . . ." *We* means: I, Paul, who write the letter; you, Titus, who receive it; and further, all believers in Crete, and in fact, all believers everywhere. Paul, too, had been a slave of sin. To be sure, he had been "zealous for the traditions," but at the same time he had been "persecuting the church" (see on I Tim. 1:13; then Gal. 1:11-17). As to what Titus had been, read Gal. 2:2, 3. This merciful inclusion of oneself is very effective and appealing. It causes the reader (Titus) and the hearers (the Cretan believers when the letter is read to them) to feel that the writer is standing on common ground with them and understands them (cf. Titus 1:4; then I Thess. 5:9; Rev. 1:9). Moreover, the sharp contrast between what men *were* in their state of sin and what they *have become* since they entered the state of grace encourages gratitude to God; hence also goodwill toward the neighbor who was made in God's image. (The vivid portrayal of this contrast is characteristic of Paul; see I Tim. 1:12-17; then Rom. 6:17-23; I Cor. 6:11; Eph. 2:2-13; 5:8; Col. 3:7; and cf. I Peter 4:3.)

We are not surprised, then, to notice that over against the seven virtues

---

[206] Translations which go too far in their attempt to "westernize" the New Testament *miss* the play on words in this verse, and then, contrary to the original but in harmony with A.V. and A.R.V., *insert* a play on words in the next verse: "hateful, hating one another." In both cases I have attempted to retain in the translation the flavor of the original.

mentioned in verses 1 and 2, showing *what (Cretan) believers should be,* are placed an equal number of vices (verse 3) showing *what we once were.*

We were *without understanding* ("senseless," I Tim. 6:9), not only ignorant, but by nature actually *unable* to discern the things of the Spirit (I Cor. 2:14; cf. Rom. 1:21; Eph. 4:18).

Disobedient to both divine and human authority (Titus 1:6, 10; 3:1; then II Tim. 3:2; Rom. 1:21, 30), heeding neither the voice of conscience nor the admonitions of parents or the laws of civil magistrates.

Deluded (see on II Tim. 3:13), made to wander from the truth, living in a world of unreality, imagining that license is liberty. Though we considered ourselves to be free, we had become slaves:

Enslaved to various passions and pleasures, allowing these strong evil desires to dominate our life and conduct. (For *passions* see on II Tim. 2:22; 3:6, and for *pleasures* cf. Luke 8:14; James 4:1, 3; II Peter 2:13.) The world apart from Christ passes in review, and what a sorry spectacle it is. Here "we" come: the glutton and the toper, the miser and the spend-thrift, the mad-cap and the dotard, the sports-worshiper and the sluggard, the fraud and the fop, the sadist and the rapist, the "tiger" and the "wolf." Cf. Rom. 1:18-32; Gal. 5:19-21. Some serve one master, some another, but by nature all are slaves to those terrible "drives" which they have never learned to control, and which, according to some modern psychologists they should not even try too strenuously to hold down!

Living (literally "leading," with *a life* understood; cf. I Tim. 2:2) *in malice and envy.* This *malice* is not mere "mischief" as in "With Malice Toward *Some.*" No, it is badness, perversity, wickedness; especially the evil disposition of the mind. One of its most soul-destroying manifestations is *envy,* an evil which, as the probable etymology of the Greek word implies, causes one *to waste away.* Has not envy been called that vice whose rage nothing can allay, "the eldest-born of hell"? Does it not "feed on" the living, never ceasing until they are dead? Is it not "the rottenness of the bones"? (Prov. 14:30). See also what *Paul* says about it elsewhere (I Tim. 6:4; then Rom. 1:29; Gal. 5:21; Phil. 1:15) and cf. Matt. 27:18; Mark 15:10; James 4:5; and I Peter 2:1. Our English word *envy* is from the Latin *in-video,* meaning "to look against," that is, to look with ill-will at another person because of what he is or has. (*Jealousy,* it has been well said, is afraid of losing what it has; *envy* hates to see another person have something. Thus, Mr. A. is *jealous* of his own honor, and is *envious* of Mr. B.'s superior skill.) It was envy which caused the murder of Abel, threw Joseph into a pit, caused Korah, Dathan, and Abiram to rebel against Moses and Aaron, made Saul pursue David, gave rise to the bitter words which "the elder brother" (in the Parable of the Prodigal Son) addressed to his father, and crucified Christ. *Love* never envies (I Cor. 13:4).

Detestable, odious, fulsome, offensive, disgusting, repulsive. In the New

Testament the word used in the original occurs only here, but Philo the Jew (20 B. C.-A. D. 50) also uses it. The unconverted sinner by means of his attitude to God and man causes *loathing*. Hence:

Hating each other. This is the natural result when detestable people in all their gruesomeness are nevertheless forced somehow to live with each other and to meet each other in a hundred different ways.

"Such were we at one time," says Paul. Hence, let us not be too hard on the people who are still in that condition, but let us strive by godly conduct to win them for Christ.

4-6. And let us do this from the motive of gratitude for what we ourselves have received. Hence, Paul continues, **But when the kindness of God our Savior and his love toward man appeared, he saved us.** What a striking contrast, a *double* contrast, in fact! (1) Over against "man's inhumanity to man" pictured in verse 3, is portrayed God's *benignity* (a word used *only* by Paul: Rom. 2:4; 3:12; 11:22, etc.) and *love* for man (cf. Acts 28:2). And (2) upon the Stygian darkness of our *past* (verse 3) *dawns* dramatically the light of the Father's kindliness and pity which brought us into the *present* state of grace. (Here again is that glorious *epiphany* mentioned earlier; see on Titus 2:11.)

This, let it be emphasized, is more than an *argument*. It *is* an argument, to be sure, as has already been pointed out. But it is *more* than that. It is the outpouring (in proverbial language; see on verse 8) of a heart which is glowing with love in return for God's love. It must be borne in mind that Paul writes as one who has in his own life *experienced* all this. He does not stand next to his story, but he is himself part of it. Hence, these words about the kindness of God our Savior and his love toward man are as warm and tender as was the heart of this same apostle, a man who was often seen to weep, and who once wrote very touchingly, "The Son of God loved *me*, and gave himself up . . . *for me!*" (Gal. 2:20).

The expression "the kindness and the love toward man" is *one* concept; hence, the verb in the original is singular. The *expression* as such is found also in the works of pagan moralists, but the *content* as used here in Titus 3:4 is unique. Here is not "the kindness and the love" ascribed to some earthly ruler upon whom the praises of men are being showered, praises which he has hardly deserved; but here is the *real* benignity and love. The expression "love-toward-man" is *one* word, exactly the same word as our "philanthropy." Nevertheless, since in present English usage the term "philanthropy" is often understood as referring only to "the work of practical benevolence," a work of which men are the authors as well as the recipients, it is probably best to retain the beautiful rendering which is found in our common English versions; for certainly, as Paul uses the term it combines both the love itself and its generous outpouring upon mankind. By retaining the rendering *"love* toward man" one is immediately reminded of John 3:16, which beautifully expresses the truth which the apostle had in mind.

It was the kindness and the love of *God our Savior* (see on I Tim. 1:1; Titus 1:3; 2:10) which came to man's rescue. It was he, namely, God the Father, who *saved* us, rescuing us from the greatest evil and bestowing upon us the greatest blessing (see on I Tim. 1:15). He saved *us:* Paul, Titus, in fact all those who in course of time become the recipients of this great blessing.

Now, in order to make us all-the-more-ready to help others who as yet are unsaved, and to prevent us from ever saying, "But they *do not deserve* our help," Paul stresses the fact that we, on our part, did not deserve our salvation either. He does this by pointing out that *negatively* the Father saved us **not by works which we ourselves had performed in (a state of) righteousness,** and *positively* **but according to his own mercy.** So strong is Paul's emphasis upon this completely *sovereign* (that is, by us wholly unmerited) character of our salvation, that (as is clear in the original; and see also the renderings of the A.V. and A.R.V.) he causes this entire lengthy compound phrase to *precede* the verb *saved.* Thus, A.V. has:

"4 But after that the kindness and love of God our Saviour toward man appeared, 5 Not by works of righteousness which we have done, but according to his mercy he saved us . . ."

As concerns the word-order, that rendering is correct. The only objection which many have felt is this, that, unless one pays very close attention to the punctuation, he is in danger of mentally construing the compound phrase as if it were a modifier of the verb *appeared,* and not of the verb *saved.*

"Not *by* (i.e., in consequence of, on the basis of; cf. Gal. 2:16) works which we ourselves had performed in a state of righteousness." The implication is: there were no such works. Neither Paul nor anyone else had ever performed such a work, for before God and his holy law *all* — both Jews and pagans — are by nature "under sin" (Rom. 3:9). Hence, if men are ever to be saved at all, it can only be done "according to his (God's) own mercy." Note, not only are men saved *of* or *by* or *on the basis of* his mercy (all this, to be sure, is implied), but *according to* his mercy, the "wideness of God's mercy" being the yardstick which determines the wideness of their salvation (cf. Eph. 1:7). Other passages of Scripture which similarly emphasize the completely sovereign character of God's grace in saving man are quoted on p. 307 of N.T.C. on John, Vol. II.[207] God's

---

[207] See also Edwin H. Palmer, *The Five Points of Calvinism,* published by The Men's Society of the Christian Reformed Church, 422 E. Exchange St., Spring Lake, Mich.; esp. pp. 21-33.

mercy (for which see on I Tim. 1:2) is his *kindness* and *pity* to those *in need* or *in distress.*

The means employed in saving us is indicated by an additional modifier of the verb *he saved,* namely, **through a washing of regeneration and renewing by the Holy Spirit.** Note "through *a washing*" (λουτρόν, -οῦ), not "through *a laver* or *basin for washing."* The washing referred to is wholly spiritual. It is that of *regeneration and renewing,* regarded as one concept.

The term *regeneration* as applied to *individuals* occurs only in this one New Testament passage. (Matt. 19:28 has reference to the cosmic regeneration.) Literally it means *new birth,* the being born again (*palin* = again, plus *genesia* = birth; hence, *palin-genesia*). But though *the word* occurs only this once, *the idea* is found in many other passages (John 1:13; 3:3, 5-8; I Peter 1:23; I John 2:29; 3:9; 4:7; 5:1, 4, 18; cf. also II Cor. 5:17; Gal. 6:15; Eph. 2:5; 4:24; and Col. 2:13). I know of no better definition than that which is given by L. Berkhof, namely, "Regeneration is that act of God by which the principle of the new life is implanted in man, the governing disposition of the soul is made holy, and the first holy exercise of this new disposition is secured." [208]

The present passage, in connection with its context, places emphasis on the following particulars in connection with this wonderful work of God:

(1) It is the work of *the Holy Spirit.* This stands to reason, for in Scripture it is especially the third person of the Trinity who is represented as the bestower of life; hence, also of *spiritual* life. Also, it is he, the *Holy* Spirit, who takes the lead, as it were, in the work of making men *holy.*

(2) It precedes and gives rise to the process of *renewing.* While the latter is a life-long activity, the former is a single act, an instantaneous change.

(3) It affects the entire man. Note: "he saved *us."*

(4) It is a *radical* change, so that those who beforehand were loaded down with the seven vices mentioned in verse 3 are now *in principle* adorned with the seven virtues mentioned in the verses 1 and 2.

The word *renewing* is found also in Rom. 12:2. That passage indicates that although this work, as well as regeneration, is ascribed to the Holy Spirit, nevertheless, there is this difference: *regeneration* is entirely the work of God, but in *renewing* or *sanctification* man as well as God takes part. While *regeneration* is never directly perceived by man, and becomes known to him only because of its effects, *renewal* requires the *conscious* and *continued* surrender of man's whole personality to the will of God.

For the definition I quote once more L. Berkhof (p. 532 of the work mentioned in footnote 208):

"Sanctification is that gracious and continuous operation of the Holy Spirit, by which he delivers the justified sinner from the pollution of sin,

---

[208] *Systematic Theology,* Grand Rapids, 1949, p. 469.

renews his whole nature in the image of God, and enables him to perform good works."

It is clear from such passages as John 3:3, 5 and especially Eph. 5:26 (cf. Heb. 10:22) that this "washing of regeneration and renewing" stands in some relation to the rite of baptism. Undoubtedly, also here in Titus 3:5 there is an implied reference to this sacrament. However, discussing that problem *here,* while commenting on a passage in which the *water* is not even mentioned, would take us too far afield. See, however, N.T.C. on John 3:3, 5.

Now, in order to place still more emphasis on the fact that believers do not have a reason for falling short in their duty of winning others for Christ through godly conduct, Paul adds the following words, with reference to the kindness of God in saving us and imparting to us his *enabling* Spirit: **which** (or **whom,** namely, this Spirit) **he** (namely, God the Father) **poured out upon us richly through Jesus Christ our Savior.**

Note how in this passage God the Father, God the Spirit, and God the Son are beautifully combined.

God the Father not only gives his Son but also pours out his Spirit. The reference is to Pentecost (Acts 2:17, 18, 33). Organically speaking, the Spirit was poured out upon the church of the present and of the future; for, that Spirit having once established his personal residence in the church, never leaves it again. Hence, Paul can say, "whom he poured out upon *us.*"

The adverb *richly* indicates the rich supply of spiritual gifts which results from this outpouring. No one has any right to say, "I can do nothing in the kingdom, since God has given me nothing." The beautiful phrase "through Jesus Christ our Savior" indicates that the latter through his atoning sacrifice and prayer secured for his people the gift of the Holy Spirit (John 14:16; 16:7).

7. Our former state, described in verse 3, has ended. The blessings described in verses 4-6 have been and are being received. Their purpose and result is now stated: **in order that, having been justified by his grace, we might become heirs-in-hope of life everlasting.**

The process of reasoning which we find in these verses (verses 3-7) is familiar to the student of Paul's epistles. Note the three stages:

We *were* by nature children of wrath — we *have been made* alive — we *now look forward* by faith to the ages to come when we shall receive even greater glory (Eph. 2:1-10);

We *were* idol-worshippers — we *now* serve the true and living God — we *await* the coming of the Son of God from heaven (I Thess. 1:9, 10), and our everlasting fellowship with him (I Thess. 4:13-18).

We *were* ungodly and ruled by worldly passions — we *have renounced* all this and are now living lives of self-mastery and fairness and devotion — we *are waiting for* the realization of the blessed hope (Titus 2:11-13).

Having just mentioned "Jesus Christ our Savior," Paul, still thinking about the grace of God in Christ, continues, "in order that having been justified by *his* grace" (as effective, meriting cause), etc. Note the aorist passive participle *having been justified.* This does not mean "having been made upright." [209] It means *having been declared righteous.* Justification is that act of God the Father whereby he counts our sins to be Christ's, and Christ's righteousness to be ours (II Cor. 5:21). It is the opposite of *condemnation* (Rom. 8:33, 34). It implies deliverance from the curse of God because that curse was placed on Christ (Gal. 3:11-13). It means *forgiveness* full and free (Rom. 4:6-8). It is God's free gift, the fruit of *sovereign grace,* and not in any way the result of human "goodness" or "accomplishment" (Rom. 3:24; 5:5, 8, 9). It brings peace to the soul (Rom. 5:1), a peace that passes all understanding. It fills the heart with such thanksgiving that it produces in the life of the believer a rich harvest of good works. Hence, justification and sanctification, though ever distinct, are never separate but stand in the closest possible relation to each other (Rom. 6:2; 8:1, 2).

The purpose, then, of the work of God in saving us is "that . . . we might become heirs . . . of life everlasting"; that is, that *even now in this present life* we might have the right as children to look forward to the full possession of that which we now possess only *in principle.* When that future day arrives, we shall rejoice in the richest possible (because sinless!) fellowship with God in Christ (see also N.T.C. on John 3:16; 17:3), basking in the sunshine of his love (John 5:42) and partaking, to the fullest extent possible for man, of his joy and glory (John 17:13). That life differs, accordingly, *in essence* from the "life"(?) of the unbeliever, and *in degree* even from the life of the believer here below. It is, moreover, actually *ever-lasting,* that is, *never-ending.* Of that life as it is in principle we are *now* the possessors; and of that life as it will be in perfection we are *even now* the heirs, but heirs-in-hope, hoping heirs. But this hope will *certainly* be realized (Rom. 5:5).

8. Reflecting on the gospel-summary given in verses 4-7 the apostle continues: **Reliable (is) this saying, and about these matters I want you to speak with confidence, in order that those who have their faith fixed on God may be careful to apply themselves to noble deeds.**

This, then (that is, verses 4-7), was the last of the five great "sayings." See on I Tim. 1:15 for the meaning of the introductory formula, "Reliable is the saying." It is about *these* matters — namely, a. the kindness of the

---

[209] See L. Berkhof, *Systematic Theology,* p. 510.

Father and his love toward man; b. the work of the Holy Spirit in regenerating and renewing man; c. the grace of Jesus Christ considered as the effective cause of our justification; and d. the purpose of all this: that we might become what we are today, heirs-in-hope of life everlasting — that Paul wants Titus *to speak with confidence.* Others, to be sure, speak with confidence about frivolous matters; matters, moreover, about which they know nothing (see on I Tim. 1:7; and see on verse 9 below). Let Titus then stress those matters of which he has become firmly and rightfully convinced, the purpose being that those who have their faith fixed on God (note perfect participle, indicating both the past action and the present abiding result) *may be careful to apply themselves* to noble deeds. They should concentrate their *thought* on such deeds of gratitude, *applying* themselves with diligence to their performance, and making this their chief business. **These matters** — that is, the things just mentioned: the kindness of the Father, the work of the Holy Spirit, etc. — **are excellent and beneficial for (all) people.** Not only are these things excellent in themselves, but they are also *beneficial (useful, profitable;* see on I Tim. 4:8; II Tim. 3:16; also in classical Greek and in the papyri). Moreover, when appropriated by faith, they benefit *men in general,* not this or that particular class. They bring life, light, joy, and peace where before there was death, darkness, sadness, and fear.

---

9 But as for foolish inquiries and genealogies and wrangling and skirmishes about the law, shun them, for they are unprofitable and futile. 10 After a first and a second warning have nothing further to do with a factious person, 11 knowing that such an individual is distorted and sins, being self-condemned.

3:9-11

9. A few negative directions are now added: **But as for foolish inquiries and genealogies and wrangling and skirmishes about the law, shun them, for they are unprofitable and futile.**

This is in strong contrast with the preceding: Titus must *do* the one, but *avoid* the other. The order of the words in the sentence (the compound object placed before the verb) and the absence of the article before any of the four nouns, these facts clearly prove that all possible emphasis is placed on the quality and contents of the object. It is exactly *foolish inquiries,* namely, investigations into genealogical lore, that must be avoided. It is precisely *wrangling,* namely, skirmishes about the law, that must be given a wide berth. See also on Titus 1:9, 10, 14. The matters referred to have been described in detail in connection with I Tim. 1:3-7, 19, 20 and I Tim. 6:3-5 (see on these passages). Let Titus then shun (cf. II Tim. 2:16) the Jewish legends and the stipulations, the inquiries and the wrangling.

When he sees them coming, let him turn around and flee! Let him see these things for what they truly are: *unprofitable, futile*. What a sharp contrast between all this *useless* nonsense and the very *useful* matters about which Paul has just spoken in verses 4-7 (see also verse 8). A minister who does justice to the latter will have no time for the former.

10, 11. And what must be the attitude of Titus toward those church-members who are "roped in" by these specialists in genealogical lore and by these law-skirmishers, and who begin to make propaganda for this unworthy cause? Says Paul: **After a first [210] and a second warning have nothing further to do with a factious person, knowing that such an individual is distorted and sins, being self-condemned.**

Paul speaks about a "heretical" person. Originally, the word "heresy" (αἵρεσις) simply meant "that which one chooses for himself," "an opinion." This meaning gave rise to another, namely, "a set of persons professing certain definite principles or opinions," hence a *school* or *party*; for example, the "party of the Sadducees" (Acts 5:17), and "the party of the Pharisees" (Acts 15:5; cf. 26:5).

While in certain contexts this neutral meaning persisted for a while, the term began to be used also in an unfavorable sense. Cf. our English word *faction*. In that sense there were *factions* in Corinth ("I am of Paul," "I am of Apollos," etc.). When Tertullus called Paul "a ringleader of the *faction* (or *sect*) of the Nazarenes," he was not trying to pay him a compliment. Cf. also Acts 24:14 where Paul says, "after the Way which *they* call a *faction* (or *sect*)." And see Acts 28:22.

Accordingly, *a factious person* is here a person who without justification creates division. In the light of the context it is probable that the rendering "a heretic" is not far off. At any rate, the word is moving in that direction. The factious person of whom the apostle is thinking has accepted the sinister philosophy of the Cretan errorists who specialized in foolish inquiries and law-skirmishes (see on verse 9). As has become clear, their error touched both doctrine and life, as is usually the case. It is true, of course, that the term as here used need not be restricted to a particular type of fanatic. *Every* factious person stands condemned here.

The apostle demands that when the time is ripe such a person shall be *rejected*. The expression "Have nothing further to do with" must be taken in the sense of *refuse, reject* (cf. I Tim. 5:11; II Tim. 2:23). There seems to be a reference here to Matt. 18:15-17. Official exclusion from church-membership is probably indicated. This is not surprising, for Titus will know *that such an individual* (cf. Rom. 16:18, etc.), who not only creates division but also after repeated warnings persists in this practice,

---

[210] The Koine often substitutes the cardinal for the ordinal; cf. Matt. 28:1; Mark 16:2.

3:10, 11 TITUS

"is distorted" and is sinning. The word rendered "is distorted" is very descriptive. Such a person is not living and seeing *straight*. He is *mentally and morally turned* or *twisted*. He is even worse than the man who colloquially is sometimes called "a screw-ball." He is actually living in sin. What makes his sin very bad is the fact that *he knows* that he is sinning. If his conscience has not already spoken plainly, he has at least been warned, and that not once but twice. Hence, he sins "being self-condemned."

In this connection the qualification is very important, namely, "After a first and a second *warning* (or *admonition*)." Both this noun and the cognate verb *(to warn, to admonish;* literally *to put in mind)* are used elsewhere only by Paul (for the noun see I Cor. 10:11; Eph. 6:4; for the verb, Acts 20:31: Paul speaking; Rom. 15:14; I Cor. 4:14; Col. 1:28; 3:16; I Thess. 5:12, 14; II Thess. 3:15). The qualification indicates that, according to Pauline teaching, discipline must ever spring from love, from a desire to heal, never from a desire to get rid of an individual. Much patience must be shown. Even when the error is very grievous and dangerous, as in the present instance, every effort must be put forth to win the erring one. If the member, having been lovingly warned, refuses to repent and continues his evil work in the midst of the congregation, the church through its officers and by means of the entire membership must redouble its efforts. There must be a second warning. But if even this remedy fails, he must be expelled. Even this extreme measure has as one of its purposes the reclamation of the sinner. This, however, can never be the only purpose. The welfare of the entire church (cf. Matt. 12:25) unto the glory of God must never be lost sight of. That, after all, is the main objective of discipline (see also N.T.C. on II Thess. 3:14, 15).

---

12 As soon as I shall have sent Artemas or Tychicus to you, do your best to come to me at Nicopolis, for I have decided to spend the winter there. 13 Do all you can to help along on their journey Zenas the law-expert and Apollos, so that they may lack nothing. 14 Besides, let also our people learn to apply themselves to noble deeds for these occasions of imperative need, in order that they may not be unfruitful.

15 All those who are with me send you greetings. Greet those who love us in faith. Grace [211] (be) with y o u all.

3:12-15

12. The *body* of the letter (Titus 1:1-3:11) is finished. Was it written by *an amanuensis* who faithfully reproduced Paul's message, retaining in every instance the latter's style, hence also most of his words, but here and there making use of his own vocabulary, the whole having been subse-

---

[211] Literally "the grace," that is, the grace of God.

quently approved by the apostle? And did Paul then add verses 12-15, writing *them* "with his own hand"? See N.T.C. on II Thess. 3:17. However that may be, fact is that, as could be expected, the concluding section consists almost entirely of words which are also found in the Ten (Paul's epistles apart from the Pastorals).[212]

Says Paul: **As soon as I shall have sent Artemas or Tychicus to you, do your best to come to me at Nicopolis, for I have decided to spend the winter there.**

At this moment Paul is probably somewhere in Macedonia (Philippi?). He is certainly not in Nicopolis, though the subscription found in late manuscripts states that it was from that place that the letter to Titus was sent. If that had been true, Paul could not have written, "I have decided to spend the winter *there*."

The apostle desires to spend the winter with Titus. He has decided upon Nicopolis as the meeting-place. Since this name is mentioned without any further clarification, it probably refers to the most well-known of all the Victory Cities, namely, the one situated on the southwest promontory of Epirus, in Greece. Its site was a few miles north of the modern Preveza. The ancient city of Nicopolis had been founded and had been constituted a Roman colony by Augustus, as a memorial to his *victory* over Antony and Cleopatra at nearby Actium (31 B. C.).

Nicopolis was certainly a suitable meeting-place, and this for one or more of several possible reasons, such as:

It was more or less centrally located: Paul would have to travel almost as far southwest as Titus would have to travel northwest. Consult a map.

It was a fine winter-resort. Moreover, the winter-months were not suitable for sea-travel (see also Acts 27:12; 28:11; I Cor. 16:6; and II Tim. 4:21).

It was an excellent "base of operations" for mission-activity in Dalmatia. It seems probable that Titus actually reached Nicopolis, and performed some evangelistic work in Dalmatia, to which he returned at a later time (see on II Tim. 4:10).

It was a fine stepping-stone to places farther west. Did Paul intend to go from there to Spain as soon as the winter-season was over?

But although Titus must *do his best* (or "do his utmost," cf. II Tim. 2:15; 4:9, 21; Gal. 2:10; Eph. 4:3; I Thess. 2:17) to meet Paul at Nicopolis, Crete must not be left without a good leader. Conditions were too serious to permit even a brief period of vacancy. As soon as a replacement arrives,

---

[212] Note, however, that even in this conclusion "noble deeds" replaces Paul's earlier "good works," and the verb προ-ίστημι is used in a sense which does not attach to it in the Ten. But, as has been noted earlier, the apostle's vocabulary may have changed somewhat. Also, it is not always easy to discover the exact extent of what Paul wrote "with his own hand."

Titus can leave, but not before. Note that Paul does not say, "The Cretans can easily take care of themselves during your absence." He realizes that churches cannot be made "indigenous" over-night. As long as leadership "from the outside" is necessary, it must be provided.

So Paul is going to send either Artemas or Tychicus. Both of these men may be regarded as Paul's co-workers and envoys, performing kingdom-work under his authority and supervision. The name Artemas is probably an abbreviation of Artemidorus, meaning "gift of Artemas," the Greek goddess of hunting, corresponding to the Roman Diana. No further reliable information has come down to us with reference to this man. What is known about Tychicus has been summarized in II Tim. 4:12; see on that passage. His name, meaning "fortuitous" may be connected with that of the Greek goddess Tyche, that is, Fortune ("Fortuna").

There are those who think that when Paul had to make up his mind whom to send to Crete, whether Artemas or Tychicus, he commissioned Artemas for that task. They deduce this from the fact that during his second imprisonment the apostle reports that he has commissioned Tychicus for Ephesus (II Tim. 4:12). This could be a questionable deduction.

13. With reference to the bearers of the letter Paul has a friendly word: **Do all you can to help along on their journey Zenas the law-expert and Apollos, so that they may lack nothing.**

What kind of law-expert was Zenas? Before his conversion to the Christian faith, had he been an expounder of the law of Moses ("teacher of the law," "scribe"), or was he a Roman jurist or "lawyer" with whose assistance a will was made or a lawsuit was instituted? Some prefer the latter view, giving as their reason that the man could hardly have been a Jew since he has a Greek name, a name which is probably an abbreviation of Zenodorus, meaning "gift of Zeus." But there were many Jews with Greek names. Were not *Paulos* and *Apollos Jews* with Greek names? Others, "putting two and two together" in an interesting way, surmise that Zenas as well as Apollos was a Jew, *and* that both of these good Christians who were also experts in Jewish lore were sent to Crete in order to curb the influence of those who specialized in Jewish myths at the expense of the true gospel.

This may be true, but all we really know is that Zenas, in some sense a law-expert, and Apollos, who were in all probability bearers of the letter, were on a journey, and that Titus is ordered to do everything possible *to help them along* (or "set them forth") on this trip. To what ultimate destination? Again, we simply do not know. These men must be provided with food and lodging while in Crete, and must be aided in every way so that, *lacking nothing,* they may be able to continue their travels.

Apollos is a familiar figure. He was a Jew, a native of Alexandria (Acts

18:24), the famous Egyptian library-and-university-city which had been founded by Alexander the Great in the year 332 B. C. He was, moreover, an orator, mighty in the scriptures. Having come to Ephesus, where he spoke boldly in the synagogue, he had been taught the way of God more accurately by Priscilla and Aquila (Acts 18:26). Thus equipped, he had gone to the province of Achaia where he proved to be a great blessing to believers, and powerfully confuted the Jews, and that publicly, showing by the scriptures that Jesus was the Christ (Acts 18:27, 28). Afterward he had returned to Ephesus (I Cor. 16:12). He was a good friend of Paul ("I planted, Apollos watered; but God gave the increase," I Cor. 3:6). We may be sure that both Paul and Apollos were grieved by the party-spirit which plagued the Corinthian church ("I am of Paul," "I am of Apollos," I Cor. 1:12).

14. Titus, then, must help these men along on their journey, but he should not try to shoulder the burden *alone*. Hence, Paul continues, **Besides, let also our people learn to apply themselves to noble deeds for these occasions of imperative need, in order that they may not be unfruitful.**

In the light of the immediate context the meaning must be: Titus, do not fail to encourage *our folks* (see p. 11), that is, the believers on the island of Crete, to co-operate wholeheartedly in all these manifestations of generosity. They should *keep on learning* things of this kind, that is, they should *become experienced* in well-doing (cf. I Tim. 5:4; Phil. 4:11), just as Paul himself had *learned* to be content in whatsoever state he was. This "learning through practice" is the finest self-education anyone could ever desire.

The Cretan believers, then, should learn "to apply themselves to noble deeds" (see on verse 8; cf. verse 1) "for these imperative needs" (thus literally). Cf. Acts 20:34; 28:10. If Paul was at Philippi when he wrote this letter, he did not have far to look in order to point to brilliant examples of men and women who understood this duty and were learning it better and better right along (read Phil. 2:25; 4:16). The purpose is: "in order that they may not be unfruitful" (cf. Matt. 7:15; 13:8, 23; John 15:8; Gal. 5:22). The author of this epistle realizes fully that though grace is *the root* (Titus 3:7; cf. Eph. 2:8), noble deeds are *the fruit* (cf. Eph. 2:10) of the tree of salvation.

15. The farewell greeting consists of three parts: **All those who are with me send you greetings.** All the fellow-workers who are in the company of (μετά) the apostle send greetings to Titus. Cf. II Tim. 4:21; then Acts 20:34. **Greet those who love us in faith.** Titus is asked to convey the greetings of Paul and of his companions to those who are filled with affection for them in the sphere of the Christian faith. **Grace (be) with y o u all.** Upon all the believers who hear this letter when it is read to them "God's favor in Christ for those who have not deserved it" is pronounced. In their *midst* (μετά) it will dwell, filling their hearts with peace and joy. For details see N.T.C. on I Thess. 1:1.

Synthesis of Chapter 3

See the Outline at the beginning of this chapter.

Sanctification in public relations is stressed in the present chapter. Believers should be obedient to the authorities. They should be kind to all men, since it was the kindness of God our Savior — not our own works! — which brought salvation. For the synthesis of the first eight verses see p. 385. On the other hand, foolish inquiries into genealogical lore and skirmishes about the law should be shunned, for they are unprofitable and futile. Factious men who refuse admonition should be rejected. Such people are mentally and morally turned or twisted. Moreover, they *know* that they are sinning, for if their conscience has not already told them this, they have at least been so informed by the church on the basis of the Word. Hence, they sin against better knowledge.

In his *Concluding Directions* Paul tells Titus that he will provide for the vacancy which will arise when the latter leaves Crete. The apostle is going to send either Artemas or Tychicus to replace Titus on the island. As soon as the substitute has arrived, he wants Titus to do his utmost to meet Paul at Nicopolis, probably the one in Epirus, where the apostle has decided to spend the winter. Also he asks that both Titus and the Cretan believers in general do all in their power to help along on their journey the two Christian friends and helpers who were in all probability the bearers of this letter, namely, Zenas the law-expert, and Apollos the famous orator from Alexandria. Note: not only *Titus* must provide for these men but "our people," too, must learn to apply themselves to noble deeds for such occasions of imperative need, in order that they may not be unfruitful. — All the fellow-workers who are with Paul send greetings to Titus, who, in turn, must convey the greetings of Paul and his companions to those who are filled with Christian affection for them. — A brief salutation concludes the letter: "Grace (be) with y o u all."

SELECT BIBLIOGRAPHY

An attempt has been made to make this list *as small as possible.*

Bouma, C., *De Brieven van den Apostel Paulus aan Timotheus en Titus* (in *Kommentaar op het Nieuwe Testament*), Amsterdam, 1942.*

Calvin, John, *Commentarius In Epistolam Pauli Ad Timotheum I, Ad Timotheum II, Ad Titum* (Corpus Reformatorum, vol. LXXX), Brunsvigae, 1895; English translation (in *Calvin's Commentaries*), Grand Rapids, 1948.

Simpson, E. K., *The Pastoral Epistles,* London, 1954.

---

* In the present commentary "Bouma, *op. cit.,*" refers to *this* book, not to Bouma's shorter work on the Pastoral Epistles (in *Korte Verklaring*).

GENERAL BIBLIOGRAPHY

Ante-Nicene Fathers, The, ten volumes, reprint Grand Rapids, Mich., 1950.
Arminius, The Writings of (tr. by James Nichols and W. R. Bagnall), reprint Grand Rapids, Michigan, 1956.
Barnes, A., *Notes on the New Testament, Thessalonians-Philemon,* reprint Grand Rapids, 1949.
Bavinck, H., *Gereformeerde Dogmatiek,* third edition, Kampen, 1918.
Bavinck, H., *The Doctrine of God* (tr. by William Hendriksen), Grand Rapids, Mich., 1951.
Bengel, J. A., *Gnomen Novi Testamenti,* Tübingen, 1742.
Berkhof, L., *The Assurance of Faith,* Grand Rapids, 1928.
Berkhof, L., *Systematic Theology,* Grand Rapids, 1949.
Berkhof, L., *Vicarious Atonement Through Christ,* Grand Rapids, Mich., 1936.
Blackwood, A. W., *The Fine Art of Public Worship,* Nashville, 1939.
Bouma, C., *I, II Timotheus en Titus* (in *Korte Verklaring*), second edition, Kampen, 1953.
Bouma, C., *De Brieven van den Apostel Paulus aan Timotheus en Titus* (in *Kommentaar op het Nieuwe Testament*), Amsterdam, 1942.
Brooks, A. E., "The Problem of the Pastoral Epistles," *JThS* 23 (1922).
Burrows, Millar, *The Dead Sea Scrolls,* New York, 1956.
Calvin, John, *Commentarius In Epistolam Pauli Ad Timotheum I, Ad Timotheum II, Ad Titum* (Corpus Reformatorum, vol. LXXX), Brunsvigae, 1895; English translation (in *Calvin's Commentaries*), Grand Rapids, 1948.
Deissmann, A., *Light From the Ancient East* (tr. by L. R. M. Strachan), New York, 1922.
De Wette, W. M. L., *Kurze Erklärung der Briefe an Titus, Timotheus,* Leipzig, 1844.
Dibelius, M., *Die Pastoralbriefe,* second edition, Tübingen, 1931.
Easton, B. S., *The Pastoral Epistles,* London, 1948.
Ellicott, C. J., *Commentary on the Pastoral Epistles,* London, 1864.
Erdman, Charles R., *The Pastoral Epistles of Paul,* Philadelphia, 1923.
Everyday Life in Ancient Times, published by The National Geographic Society, Wash., D.C., 1953.
Falconer, R., *The Pastoral Epistles,* Oxford, 1937.
Goodspeed, E. J., *Paul,* Philadelphia and Toronto, 1947.
Greydanus, S., *Bizondere Canoniek,* Kampen, 1949.
Grosheide, F. W., *De Openbaring Gods In Het Nieuwe Testament,* Kampen, 1953.
Harrison, P. N., *The Problem of the Pastoral Epistles,* Oxford, 1921.
Hawkins, R. M., *The Recovery of the Historical Paul,* Nashville, Tenn., 1943.
Hendriksen, W., *The Meaning of the Preposition ANTI in the New Testament* (unpublished doctoral dissertation submitted to Princeton Seminary), 1948.
Hendriksen, W., *Bible Survey,* Grand Rapids, Mich., fourth edition, 1953.
Hendriksen, W., *More Than Conquerors, An Interpretation of the Book of Revelation,* Grand Rapids, Mich., eighth edition, 1957.

I-II TIMOTHY AND TITUS

Holtzmann, H. J., *Die Pastoralbriefe*, Leipzig, 1880.
James, J. D., *The Genuineness and Authorship of the Pastoral Epistles*, London, 1906.
Jeremias, Joachim, *Die Briefe an Timotheus und Titus*, Göttingen, 1934.
Keller, Werner, *The Bible as History*, New York, 1956.
Knox, John, *Chapters in a Life of Paul*, New York and Nashville, 1946.
Koole, J. L., *I en II Timotheus en Titus* (in *De Bijbel In Nieuwe Vertaling*), Kampen (no date).
Kraeling, Emil G., *Rand McNally Bible Atlas*, New York, 1956.
Lock, W., *The Pastoral Epistles* (in *International Critical Commentary*), Edinburgh, 1924.
Loeb Classical Library, New York (various dates). The volumes of this set have been consulted for the writings of Homer, Josephus, Menander, Philo, Plato, Plutarch, Thucydides, Xenophon, etc.
Michaelis, W., "Pastoralbriefe und Wortstatistik," *ZNTW* 28 (1929).
Michaelis, W., *Pastoralbriefe und Gefangenschaftbriefe. Zur Echtheitsfrage der Pastoralbriefe*, 1930.
Moffatt, J., *Introduction to the Literature of the New Testament*, New York, 3rd ed., 1918.
Moulton, W. F., and Geden, A. S., *A Concordance to the Greek New Testament*, Edinburgh, third edition, 1950.
Moulton, J. H., and Milligan, G., *The Vocabulary of the Greek Testament*, Edinburgh, 1930.
Nageli, Th., *Der Wortschatz des Apostels Paulus*, Göttingen, 1905.
National Geographic Map, *Lands of the Bible Today*, December, 1956.
Parry, John, *The Pastoral Epistles*, 1920.
Pherigo, Lindsey P., "Paul's Life After the Close of Acts," *JBL* 70 (December, 1951).
Plummer, Alfred, *The Pastoral Epistles* (in *The Expositor's Bible*), reprint Grand Rapids, Mich., 1943, Vol. 6.
Riddle, W., and Hutson, H. H., *New Testament Life and Literature*, Chicago, 1946.
Robertson, A. T., *Word Pictures in the New Testament*, New York and London, 1931, Vol. IV.
Robertson, A. T., *The Minister and his Greek New Testament*, New York, 1923.
Robertson, A. T., *Grammar of the Greek New Testament in the Light of Historical Research*, New York, 1923.
Sauer, E., *In the Arena of Faith*, Grand Rapids, 1955.
Schlatter, A., *Die Kirche der Griechen im Urteil des Paulus*, Stuttgart, 1936.
Schleiermacher, F., *Ueber den Sogenannten Brief von Paulus an den Timotheus*, 1807.
Schweitzer, A., *The Mysticism of Paul the Apostle*, New York, 1931.
Scott, E. F., *The Literature of the New Testament*, 6th ed., New York, 1940.
Simpson, E. K., "The Authenticity and Authorship of the Pastoral Epistles," *EQ* 12 (October, 1940).
Simpson, E. K., *The Pastoral Epistles*, London, 1954.
Sizoo, A., *De Antieke Wereld en het Nieuwe Testament*, Kampen, 1946.
Sizoo, A., *Uit de Wereld van het Nieuwe Testament*, Kampen, 1948.
Spicq, P. C., *Saint Paul, Les Épîtres Pastorales*, Paris, 1947.
Tenney, Merrill C., *The New Testament, A Survey*, Grand Rapids, 1953.
The Good News, The New Testament with over 500 Illustrations and Maps, published by the American Bible Society, New York, 1955.
Torm, F., "Ueber die Sprache in den Pastoralbriefen," *ZNTW* 18 (1918).

I-II TIMOTHY AND TITUS

Trench, R. C., *Synonyms of the New Testament*, edition Grand Rapids, 1948.
Tucker, T. C., *Life in the Roman World of Nero and St. Paul*, New York, 1922.
Van Andel, J., *Paulus' Brieven Aan Timotheus*, Leiden, 1904.
Van Dijk, *Paraphrase van de Eerste Brief aan Timotheus*, Franeker (no date).
Veldhoen, N. G., *Het Proces van den Apostel Paulus* (unpublished doctoral dissertation submitted to the university of Leiden), 1924.
Warfield, B. B., *The Inspiration and Authority of the Bible*, Philadelphia, Pa., 1948.
Westminster Dictionary of the Bible, by J. D. Davis (revised and rewritten by H. S. Gehman), Philadelphia, 1944.
Westminster Historical Atlas to the Bible, Philadelphia, 1945.
White, N. J. D., *The First and Second Epistles to Timothy and the Epistle to Titus* (in *The Expositor's Greek Testament*), reprint Grand Rapids, Mich., vol. 4 (no date).
Wohlenberg, G., *Die Pastoralbriefe*, Leipsig, 1906.
Wuest, Kenneth S., *The Pastoral Epistles in the Greek New Testament* (Twelfth in the Series of *Word Studies*), Grand Rapids, 1954.
Wuest, Kenneth S., *Golden Nuggets from the Greek New Testament*, Grand Rapids, 1939.
Zahn, Th., *Einleitung in das Neue Testament*, 1897-1900, Vol. II.

MICHIGAN
CHRISTIAN
COLLEGE
LIBRARY
ROCHESTER, MICH.

ENNIS AND NANCY HAM LIBRARY
ROCHESTER COLLEGE
800 WEST AVON ROAD
ROCHESTER HILLS, MI 48307